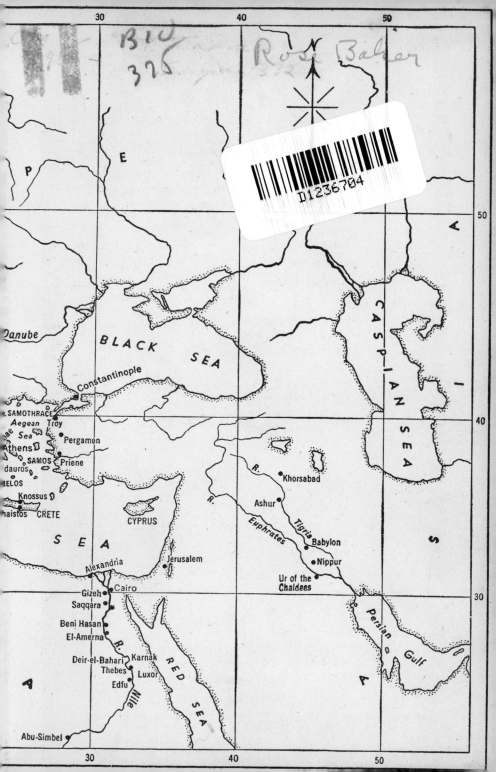

# Art in the Western World~~~~~~~~~~~~~~~

EL GRECO. View of Toledo

# ART IN THE WESTERN WORLD

## REVISED EDITION

By DAVID M. ROBB, Ph.D.

*Associate Professor of Art History*
*University of Pennsylvania*

AND

J. J. GARRISON, M.A.

*Associate Professor of Fine Arts*
*Michigan State College*

ILLUSTRATED

HARPER & BROTHERS PUBLISHERS
NEW YORK ~~~~~~~~~~~~~~~~ LONDON

# Contents .............................................

# CONTENTS *vii*

Pazzi Chapel, plan and design—Brunellesco's classicism—The
Renaissance Palace—Medici-Riccardi Palace in Florence—Alberti
and the Rucellai Palace—Applied orders and theoretical classicism
—San Francesco at Rimini; a pagan temple—15th-century architecture in northern Italy; at Venice—Bramante in Milan.

B. The High Renaissance—A Roman phenomenon—Bramante
and the new monumentality—The Farnese Palace—Peruzzi and
High Renaissance idealism—St. Peter's at Rome—Michelangelo
and the giant order—The Campidoglio—Palladio and Vitruvian
theory—Palladianism and its influence.

C. Baroque Architecture in Italy—Definition of the term—
The Counter-Reformation—Intimations of baroque in Michel-
angelo, and its climax in Bernini and others—The Gesù—Santa
Maria della Pace—San Carlo alle Quattro Fontane—Space in
baroque architectural design, an important factor in large-scale
planning—The Piazza di Spagna—Movement of form and surface
—Baroque landscape architecture—Decline and significance of the
Renaissance tradition.

Importation of Renaissance ideas by French nobility in early 16th
century—Mediaeval construction combined with Renaissance ornament in the Loire Valley—Growing classicism in the Louvre by
Lescot and Goujon, and Écouen by Bullant—The Luxembourg and
incipient baroque, but diverted into Palladian formalism through
the growth of academicism—Orléans wing at Blois—Colonnade of
the Louvre—Versailles; château and gardens; a planned community of far-reaching influence, and a symbol of the principle of
absolutism.

Persistent mediaevalism in Compton Winyates—Infiltration of
classicism in early 16th century, and development in Italianate and
Netherlandish idioms at Longleat and Wollaton Hall—Introduc-
tion of the Palladian academic point of view with Inigo Jones—
Wren and the baroque—St. Paul's; the plan for the rebuilding of
London along absolutist lines rejected—The Wren parish churches
—Baroque-Palladian compromise in Vanbrugh, and the early 18th
century.

The rococo in France—A style of intimate interiors and graceful
exteriors—Development of a science of history, and its influence in
creating an archaeological concept of classic architectural form—
Gabriel in the Place de la Concorde; and the Petit Trianon—
Classicism in Soufflot's Panthéon and in English town houses—
The Classic Revival—The cult of Nature and Gothicism—The

Formal and expressive limitations—Its character as an art of composed massive volumes—Magic, symbolic and religious function of sculpture in prehistoric times and in Egypt—Monumental sculpture in Egypt—Its purpose and conventions—Concepts of form in relief and free-standing figures of the Old Kingdom, and as an architectural adjunct—Consistency of Egyptian sculpture in the Middle Kingdom, and the New Empire, after the naturalistic interlude of Akhenaten—Decorative character and gigantism of New Empire sculpture—The Saïtic aftermath—Mesopotamian sculpture—Conceptual and formal parallels with Egypt—Difference in subject matter—Glorification of the king and his savage and war-like character—Protective symbolism—Aegean sculpture—Its limited resources—The Snake Goddess and the Lion Gate—Effectiveness of sculpture as a medium for expression of primitive experimental concepts.

Sculpture an ideal vehicle for Greek thought—Its religious character among the Greeks—Virtual limitation to treatment of the human form.

A. Archaic sculpture—Creation of types that continue later—Characteristics of archaic style—Primary concern with pattern rather than representation—Increasing naturalism at close of archaic period—Two-dimensional quality of archaic sculpture.

B. Transitional sculpture—Still conventional though conventions are based on more extensive observation of nature—Structural problems in representing human form less prominent—Attempts to suggest personality and to achieve unity of time and space.

C. Sculpture of the Golden Age—Attainment of still greater naturalism in the Polykleitan Canon—Difficulty imposed upon study of Greek sculpture by necessity of using Roman copies—Poised self-sufficiency of Golden Age ideal—Sculptures of the Parthenon—Emphasis on ideal and abstract—Modification of Greek thought and style toward the end of the fifth century.

D. Fourth-century sculpture—Development of an ideal of physical beauty—The Hermes of Praxiteles—Its increased naturalism and gracefulness when compared with fifth-century types—Skopas and emotionalism—Lysippos and his new canon of proportions—Three-dimensionalism and implications of space—Interpretation of fourth-century sculpture.

Expansiveness of Hellenistic thought and enlargement of the artist's world—Extension and diffusion of Hellenism through Alexander's conquests—Old types interpreted in new ways, and new types—Influence of painting, and heightened illusionism and emotionalism—Brilliance of Hellenistic technical achievements, and expressive emptiness.

figured styles—Figure concepts develop in parallel to sculpture in Greece—Monumental Greek painting reflected in the Alexander Mosaic—Hellenistic painting—Dominance of light and shade—Visual point of view—Primarily pictorial rather than sculptural—Illusionism continued in Roman painting.

B. Painting in the Middle Ages—In the service of the Church—in mosaic—and manuscript illustration—Importance of illumination in providing continuity of development—Celtic and Carolingian examples—and later—providing, with stained glass, the unique mediaeval forms in the art of painting.

B. The Romantic School—A renewal of Renaissance individualism—Emphasis on feeling—Goya—His directness and expressive violence in paintings and prints—Constable—A pioneer in the romantic cult of nature—His study of light and color—Géricault—Influence of Rubens on his style—Delacroix—His dramatic form and color—The exotic element in his art—The renewal of landscape in the Barbizon school—Corot and Millet.

C. The Realists—Courbet's materialism—Daumier; satirist—His humanity and monumentality.

D. Impressionism—A specialized branch of realism—Manet—Influenced by Dutch and Spanish painting and Japanese prints—"Moral" opposition—Monet's painting of sunlight with color—Scientific basis of his observations—Degas—Decorative color and pattern—Renoir—His creative colorism and sense of structural pattern.

E. The Post-Impressionists—Concerned with restoring the structural solidness lost by the Impressionists without sacrificing color—Cézanne—"Remake Poussin after nature"—His method—The primitive of his way, in finding a new pictorial architecture—Seurat—A builder of classic patterns—Van Gogh—Color as emotion—Gauguin—A decorative expressionist.

## THE MINOR ARTS

# Preface to the First Edition~~~~~~~~~~~~~~~

IN WRITING THIS BOOK, THE AUTHORS HAVE HOPED TO fill in some measure the need that exists for a discussion in relatively non-technical terms of the artistic tradition of the Occident. It is intended for those with an interest in art and who seek an adequate discussion of it, expressed in terms intelligible to the general as well as the professional reader. In trying to meet this need to some extent, the authors have dealt with the art of the western world alone, not only for the better result that might come from limitation but also because non-European styles are better understood with a field of reference in the art of the West, at least in so far as Occidental readers are concerned.

For the most part, an historical approach to the material involved has been maintained, for without understanding of the continuity of the Occidental artistic tradition, much of its significance is incomprehensible. At the same time, it has been considered advisable to present the material under the general categories of architecture, sculpture and painting instead of considering the entire artistic style of a given period as a unit. The latter approach, it seems to the authors, very frequently results in failure to grasp the essential characteristics of the individual arts, not only as regards the material points of difference, in mediums, forms, etc., but also the manner in which their development has been affected by virtue of distinctions which have appealed in varying degrees to the succeding civilizations of the western world. While believing that the foregoing method of approach is one whose value has not yet been fully appreciated, the authors have also tried to provide the means of using the book in the more traditional manner, as an exposition of the chronological development of entire periods, in the topical table of contents wherein the material pertaining to a given period can be found.

In a book of such extended scope, it may seem at first glance that an unduly large amount of space has been given over to discussion of art since 1800. If art is to be studied only in terms of abstract formal qualities, such criticism would be valid. When, however, it is approached as corollary to the development of thought and civilization, as a commentary upon experience, as a reflection of life itself and a statement of those things and ideas which are held to be true and significant, then it cannot be denied that from the point of view of the man of today, modern art must be given a prominent place in such discussion as that here attempted. To state that opinions concerning contemporary art must be tentative is a truism, but it is the feeling of the authors that the very complexity of modern art demands that it should receive proportionately ample treatment, and, though they are conscious of the transitory value of much of it, they have attempted to extract from the contemporary scene those things which apparently represent it in most characteristic fashion. In trying to apply to modern art the same methods as those followed in considering the art of past civilizations, namely by pointing out those qualities which seem best to reflect contemporary experience, the authors are merely maintaining that art is no less vital today than in the past.

# Preface to the Second Edition~~~~~~~~~~

*THE MATERIAL OF THE FIRST EDITION HAS BEEN* rewritten, amplified, and brought up to date by inclusion of later monuments. In addition to this, a section on the Minor Arts has been added. As is pointed out in the discussion thereof, the varied character of the Minor Arts is such that any presentation of ideas concerning them is of necessity lacking in the assurance of homogeneity of medium that gives physical continuity to the major arts, and the problem of selection is correspondingly more involved. The basis of selection has been made as consistent as possible, however, by choosing those representatives of the Minor Arts that seem most characteristically to embody the fundamental formal concepts of the periods involved. At the same time, it is hoped that the reflection therein of the same expressive values to be perceived in the more monumental mediums has not been overlooked.

Many helpful criticisms and suggestions received by the authors have been of value in this revision, and grateful acknowledgment is hereby made. Particular thanks are due the members of the staff of the Art Department of Pennsylvania State College, and to Dr. Eleanor Spencer of Goucher College for such suggestions. Professor James C. House of the School of Fine Arts of the University of Pennsylvania has given the benefit of his experience as a sculptor to the clarification of technical and expressive problems dealt with in that section of the book, his ability as a draftsman in the execution of the drawing used in Fig. 83, and his friendly and constructive criticism of many ideas in general; these are all acknowledged with gratitude. Whatever of clarity there may be in the chapter on Architectural Origins and Early Forms is in consequence of criticism and suggestions made by Professor E. Baldwin Smith of Princeton University whose generosity is hereby recorded with thanks.

The effectiveness of a book such as this is dependent in large measure upon the illustrations it contains; the authors wish to express their gratitude for the photographs used in the following illustrations and permission to reproduce them as indicated:

The Addison Gallery, Andover, Mass., Fig. 531; Professor Walter R. Agard, University of Wisconsin, Fig. 39; The *Architectural*

*Record,* Fig. 203; Mr. W. Pope Barney, Architect, Fig. 226; The *Chicago Tribune,* Figs. 210, 211; Mr. Kenneth Day, Architect, Fig. 220; The Detroit Institute of Arts, Figs. 451, 524; The Department of Egyptian Art, Metropolitan Museum, N.Y., Figs. 10, 13, 14, 15, 17, 19; The Essex Institute, Salem, Mass., Fig. 181; The Fogg Museum, Harvard University, Cambridge, Mass., Fig. 530; Mr. A. E. Gallatin, Fig. 518; Dr. A. I. Hallowell, Fig. 5; Dr. L. B. Holland, Fig. 33; Dr. Clarence Kennedy, Figs. 263, 319; Dr. Fiske Kimball, Fig. 185, from *Thomas Jefferson, Architect*; The Metropolitan Life Insurance Co., N.Y., Fig. 202; The Metropolitan Museum, N.Y., Figs. 8, 29, 40, 182, 250, 282, 337, 450, 456, 468, 469, 470, 488, 510, 546, 547, 549, 550, 553, 555, 560, 565, 566, 567, 571, 581, 584, 590, 592, 596, 603, 607, 610, 613, 614, 617, 620, 622, 623, 626, 627, 628, 629, 630, 631, 633, 634, 636, Frontispiece; Mr. Willard D. Morgan, *The Complete Photographer,* Color Plate III; The Morgan Library, N.Y., Fig. 588, Color Plate II; Professor Hugh Morrison, Fig. 199; The Museum of Modern Art, N.Y., Figs. 194, 198, 200, 204, 205, 206, 209, 213, 214, 215, 216, 217, 218, 221, 222, 347, 354, 503, 643, 644, 645, 646, Color Plate III; The National Gallery, Washington, D.C., Figs. 427, 481, 484, 498; The Philadelphia Museum of Art, Figs. 533, 534, 598, 599, 601, 612, 615, 616, 621, 625, 632, 635, 638; Mr. Lessing J. Rosenwald, Figs. 406, 467, 491, 492, 501, 536, 604; Dr. Paul Sachs, Fig. 473; The Smith College Museum of Art, Fig. 499; Dr. Hans Swarzenski, Fig. 576; The Topsfield, Mass., Historical Society, Fig. 180; The University Museum, Philadelphia, Figs. 242, 359, 360, 551, 552, 556, 557, 564, 569; Voorhees, Gmelin and Walker, Architects, N.Y., Fig. 212; The Wadsworth Athenaeum, Hartford, Conn., Fig. 528; The Walters Gallery, Baltimore, Figs. 494, 496; Dr. Clarence Ward, Figs. 86, 89, 93, 100, 101; The Wellesley College Museum of Art, Fig. 497; The Hon. Joseph E. Widener, Fig. 575; Miss Katherine Winckler, Figs. 223, 224. Acknowledgments other than these will be found in connection with the appropriate illustrations.

Thanks are also due to the Frick Art Reference Library in New York City, the Department of Photographs of the Metropolitan Museum in New York, the University Museum in Philadelphia, and the Department of Art and Archaeology of Princeton University for making available photographic material which would otherwise have been difficult if not impossible to obtain. To Mr. Frank Lloyd Wright of Taliesin, Spring Green, Wis., the authors are grateful for permission to illustrate those of his buildings which appear in the book.

To Anne Garrison, the authors are grateful for her cheerful assistance in matters of editing and stenography. Jane H. Robb has provided generously of time and energy in preparing the chronological table and the index, and Martha E. Robb has been of service in assisting with illustrative material; to them the authors hereby acknowledge their indebtedness. Finally, to the editorial and manufacturing departments of Harper & Brothers, the authors are grateful for the care taken to insure the maximum literal and pictorial effectiveness of the content of the book.

The sections on Architecture, Sculpture and the Minor Arts were written by Mr. Robb; that on Painting is by Mr. Garrison with the exception of the chapter on Painting before 1300 which was written by Mr. Robb and that on Principles and Techniques which is collaborative.

D. M. R.
J. J. G.

Art in the Western World~~~~~~~~~~~~~~~~

# Introduction

WHAT IS ART? WHAT IS ITS VALUE IN THE LIVES OF
men? If the first of these two questions has had the attention of thinkers
at least since the time that Plato wrote in *The Republic* of the place
of the artist in society, the second is one of peculiarly modern implications, for it has been only in the past few hundred years that any need
has been felt for justification or an explanation of art as a significant
aspect of human experience. The purpose of this chapter is to suggest
possible answers to these questions, and it is hoped that it will make
clear the attitude taken by the authors toward the material presented
in following sections of the book.

As a preliminary to answering the first question—What is Art?—
let us consider some of its more generally accepted definitions. One
which is so widely encountered that it has become a platitude is expressed in the familiar words, "I don't know anything about art, but
I know what I like." Now to the extent that this *cliché* emphasizes the
necessity of participation by the observer, hearer or reader in the experience of a work of art, whether it be a painting, a book or a
symphony, it presents one factor in the act of critical understanding
that makes a work of art significant, for it is obvious that music that is
not heard or paintings that are not seen can have no meaning save
for the artists creating them. But in assuming, as this *cliché* does, that
individual likes and dislikes are the sole grounds for judging a work of
art, there is the implication that amusement or entertainment is its
major function. While this is undoubtedly true of many works of art,
it is such a limited conception that it can hardly be felt to account for
those forms which past and present have come to feel as important and
significant.

Another definition of art which has somewhat more profound implications than the preceding one is that it is the representation of
beauty in such a way that it becomes comprehensible and capable of
being perceived through the medium of the senses. This definition too
contains an idea which must be considered in a broad characterization
of the nature of an art work, for it is a part of the artist's purpose to
reveal beauty that is often unseen by others. But it, too, raises a difficult

point, for it assumes the existence of an absolute Beauty which does not and cannot ever exist. A Greek living in the fifth century B.C., for example, considers the beauty of the human form to consist in proportions of a mathematical character that give the figure qualities of balance and symmetry (Fig. 260), while a sculptor of the 20th century A.D. finds his ideal in relationships producing an entirely different effect (Fig. 353). The *beautiful* varies so much from person to person, from time to time and from race to race that it becomes a term without exact meaning.

Yet a third definition of art would make it the form taken by expressing ideas in such a way that they are addressed most directly to the emotions of the observer. In this definition too there is an element that must be taken into account, for the quality of stimulating emotional response is one of the most important that an art work can possess. But the character and intensity of emotional reaction are again of such illimitable variety that, taken alone, this definition leaves much out of consideration. Poetry, music and the drama, for instance, affect the emotions of the participant far more directly than do painting, architecture or sculpture. Few if any pictures, statues or buildings thrill us so immediately as the performance of a play or symphony, yet it would be erroneous to conclude that an engraving by Dürer or a painting by Delacroix must be considered less effective as works of art than a fugue by Bach or a symphony by Beethoven. We can only say that emotional appeal as such cannot constitute the ultimate and final basis for judgment of a work of art.

The three definitions of art that have been discussed have all raised points to be taken into consideration, but none are sufficiently comprehensive. In trying to formulate a more inclusive one, let us attempt to follow in a general way the procedure of an artist painting a landscape. We have all had the experience of seeing a painting of a view with which we were familiar and of realizing in its presence, possibly for the first time, that the forms of nature in that particular landscape were arranged in a way very pleasing to the eye. Upon examining the painting more carefully, we note that some details of the actual scene have been left out while others have been made more prominent than we remembered them to be. This would seem to imply that the artist has considered some details of his subject more important than others for one reason or another, that he has not taken everything at its face value but that he has analyzed and evaluated the forms he sees and his painting embodies the evidence of that analysis and evaluation. This is the first step in the creation of a work of art, the analysis by the artist of his experience of the subject. Now, returning to the painting, we may next observe that the artist has sought to relate the various objects he has selected from the landscape to each other. There is space continuity, for instance, so that the observer can travel in imagination from foreground into middle distance and background through carefully planned passages. Or the form of a tree that is nearby may be repeated in another that is farther away, or the color of a figure in one place is employed again elsewhere in such a way that the eye relates them to each other. By this process, the artist takes the forms which his initial analysis has shown to be the significant ones and, by emphasizing or creating relationships between them, he gives them a new identity with a reality of existence that can be appreciated and understood entirely in its own terms. In analyzing his subject, he has taken it apart, so to speak, and determined the value of its various elements for his purpose; he has then put those parts together by a process of synthesis, and achieved a reality which is based upon that of his initial experience, it is true, but ordered and arranged and emphasized as it was not, and therefore a work of art.

The experience which is the point of departure for the artist does not necessarily have to be one of sight or vision; it may have been something that he read or imagined. But it must be an experience of such a nature that he is able to perceive in it qualities that require and justify the interpretation that he gives. It must, in other words, be a perception of a truth only partially or dimly realized before which his interpretation makes clear and inevitable. For a work of art is the record in comprehensible form of the essential truth which the artist has perceived in analyzing his experience. If truth is there, no matter whether it is great or small, and if the interpreter is able to make its sense clear, the resultant form is a work of art. The greatness of the artist depends upon the quality and perception of his analysis of experience, the greatness of the work of art upon the completeness of the synthesis which produces the tangible evidence of the artist's reaction to his experience. This holds true regardless of the nature of the experience or the medium in which the artist interprets it. In the "Ode to a Skylark" Shelley has created a symbol of the liberating impulse that carries the spirit far above thoughts of earthly things; Praxiteles' Hermes is a symbol of the ideal human form that was divinity for its creator and his time; in the Prelude to *Tristan and Isolde*, Wagner has wrought a musical symbol of the yearning passion that to him was love. Considered as intellectual analyses of experience, such forms as these have no meaning at all; if such be desired, they must be sought in scientific treatises in the fields of psychology, religion and morals. They are rather persuasive and immediately recognizable concepts embodying our most intimate experiences of nature, godhood and love.

Closely allied to this definition of the character of an art work is the determination of the elements in it by which the observer is enabled to participate in the experience that the artist has interpreted. Let us return again to the painter. If he is working on a portrait, our probable first reaction is that it does or does not resemble the person he is painting. Or if it is a landscape, we may feel that we are seeing the actual scene, if it is one with which we are familiar, or that this tree does not look right or that house is out of place. Our reaction is determined, in other words, by the extent to which the artist has succeeded in representing the appearance of the thing he is painting. Representation is one of the important elements in art, particularly in painting and sculpture. From it we derive much of the pleasure that the visual arts can give; for recognition of the thing portrayed is one means by which we may identify ourselves with the experience interpreted by the artist, since by representing the objective characteristics of things, certain aspects of the truth they symbolize for the artist are transmitted to us. But even though representation may be a very vital factor in a work of art, it is far from being the only one. Were this the case, the camera would be the greatest of artists because its lens can record the facts of appearance with a fidelity and accuracy that the most painstaking painter cannot approach. Other considerations than naturalistic appearance are involved in determining the quality of a work of art.

In speaking of the artist's treatment of the forms that go to make up his painting, it was suggested that one of the things he did was to create or emphasize relationships between them by his manner of arrangement. Such arrangement is called the design—a quality that is an absolute essential in any art form. The rules of rhetoric are the basis of literary design and the laws of harmony are fundamental to musical order. In the visual arts, balance, rhythm and contrast are employed to establish a perceptible pattern of forms that constitute the design; they are among the formal characteristics that make clear the idea which the artist wishes to express in just the same way that the design of a sentence or its grammatical structure makes clear the writer's idea. A building, a statue or a painting must have the qualities of unity, coherence and emphasis just as much as a poem, a story or a sonata. These are the qualities which a photograph almost invariably lacks; if it possesses them in any degree, the man who made it is to that extent an artist; when it lacks them, the detail in it is no more than a record of the accidents of appearance rather than a presentation of facts of inherent or relative significance.

The elements of design and representation are the foundation of every work of art. In the synthesis of ideas which the artist achieves, they are present in proportions that differ in some degree in each thing that he creates, depending upon the innumerable factors that go to make up his temperament; for at neither the extreme of pure design nor its opposite, naturalistic representation, is the greatest art to be found. If the emphasis be entirely on formal arrangement or abstract design as it appears to be in an Oriental rug, for instance, the result is a highly decorative arrangement of lines and colors that may be very pleasing in effect; but since such an arrangement provides no readily grasped symbols that correspond to our own knowledge of things, it possesses nothing by which it can be related to our own experience. Everyone has attempted to trace images of trees and animals in wall-paper designs. This is a natural reaction to purely abstract patterns which we of the western world, at least, instinctively try to vitalize by connecting them in some way with things that are familiar to us, since we more or less instinctively feel that such things are not complete in themselves. "Pure" abstract design is incapable of the universal significance that is essential in truly great art. A statue by Brancusi (Fig. 346) or a painting by Picasso (Color Plate III) is the tangible expression of significant experience, it is true, but of a personal rather than a general nature—significant in terms of texture and surface to a sculptor or in terms of color and line to a painter. For one whose processes of comprehension are not exactly the same as those of the artist—an obvious impossibility—they must stand or fall by the appeal of their purely formal elements, color, line, mass, etc. They lack the means of establishing that contact with our own experience which is essential if a work of art is to have significance for us, and their undeniably distinctive formal qualities do not seem capable of conveying the complete truth which we demand.

At the other end of the scale from the Oriental rug is the photograph. In its record of the facts of appearance, we perceive nothing of the timeless and characteristic quality that is necessary if those facts are to be invested with human significance. Let us assume that two photographs of a landscape are made from the same point of view but at different times and under differing conditions of light. Each will record what was factually true of the scene during the infinitesimal fraction of a second in which it was made, but obviously the two "true" representations will be quite different from each other. It is the artist's business in interpreting his experience of the landscape to correlate facts such as are objectively presented by the photographs, or better, to correlate his own observations of those facts. This correlation is the basis of his design in which he emphasizes the elements that he feels to be basic and important and omits those that are not. The chosen elements will not be the same for two artists; they may not be the same for the same artist at different times. But just so far as the artist achieves a penetrating analysis of his experience of the subject and a complete and unified synthesis in the record of that analysis which is the painting, just so far has he succeeded in creating a work of art. It is to achieve this end that he strives to find a consistent, ordered and logical pattern in the facts of appearance, or imposes such a pattern upon them, by the design. If he is a truly great artist, the design will seem to be inherent in the subject and inevitable in any comprehensive interpretation thereof. His painting will in consequence have a reality of its own which is even more impressive than that of the original subject, for it will possess in its own character the balanced proportions and unity which life itself appears to us to have in those rare moments of penetration when we are able to coordinate and relate the fragments of our experience and render them into a coherent whole, coming thereby to a realization of its potential profundity of meaning and the part which we ourselves may have in it.

The two factors of objective facts of the subject which are the object of the artist's analysis and the synthesis which he creates from the results of that analysis must be basic in any work of art, but a third one which is frequently important in determining its expressive significance is that of subject matter. The objective facts in a painting like the one illustrated in Fig. 446 are two pieces of wood fastened together to form a cross upon which a dead male figure is hung, while a second man stands on one side pointing his finger at the central one and on the other side a third man supports a fainting woman; all this is placed against a darkened sky; in the foreground are a kneeling woman and a lamb with its right front foot holding a small cross. These are the objective facts of the picture; yet no Occidental Christian can see them without realizing that in such an arrangement they have a meaning transcending their objective character for they represent the death of Christ on the cross for the salvation of mankind. This is the subject matter of the picture and, in such a case as this, it is probably of more immediate impressiveness to the observer than the pattern of form and color in determining its expressive character since it immediately calls up a response rendered significant by centuries of tradition in the Christian world. Conversely, an example of Oriental art which has quite as moving associations for a Buddhist might appeal to an Occidental only to the extent that he was sensitive to representational characteristics and formal design, for its conscious meaning or subject matter could have little or no significance for him. It is easy, however, for an artist to depend upon the traditional associations of subject matter to conceal his lack of creative imagination and for this reason it is difficult to depend upon it as a basis of sound critical judgment; an artist of the 20th century may paint a vase of flowers with the same intensity of feeling that his ancestor of seven hundred years ago reveals in portraying the Crucifixion. In the final analysis, the greatness of a work of art must be determined by its inherent artistic character rather than by its references to external or associative values.

If we are now prepared to accept the definition of art as the presentation in comprehensible form of the truth perceived by the artist in his experience of life, we can proceed to the second question posed at the beginning of this chapter—What is its value in the lives of men? In trying to answer this question, let us assume that we are standing before the portrait of a great man like the one of Voltaire by Houdon (Fig. 338). As we look at it, we observe the realistic manner in which the sculptor has portrayed the appearance of the man, the shrewd and penetrating eyes, thin nostrils and shaggy brows, and the smile on the lips that is at once cynical and benevolent. We may then become conscious of the way in which the details of the hair and costume are subordinated so that they do not distract attention from the face, even though they too are represented with great fidelity. We have thus observed the representational elements in the figure and also the design by which they are integrated; together, they result in an embodiment of the essential idea of Voltaire as a man. Representation and design cannot exist as separate things in the experience of the observer but are fused into an identity which means Voltaire; for through Houdon's perceptive analysis of the nature of his subject and the tangible symbol he has created in consequence thereof, we are enabled to know for ourselves the character of the great French writer. A different kind of reaction will of necessity characterize our experience of an art work such as a painting by Picasso (Color Plate III), in which it is clear that representational values are relatively unimportant and psychological ones, in the sense of interpreting a specific personality, are non-existent. Even here, however, there are certain objective characteristics to be discerned—contrasting textures of different areas of paint laid on thickly or thinly brushed, or the flatness of the canvas plane on which they are spread. And if it appears that the artist has been concerned solely with problems of arrangement and design and not at all with interpretation of psychological or physical experience, even in turning away from the picture we cannot but be conscious of a heightened awareness of brilliant reds or somber greens and the swinging rhythm of a curved line. If such experience as this may justifiably be considered as very limited, it is none the less couched in the terms of the painter's art and cannot be excluded from critical judgment.

Such analyses as these of the infinitely complex relationship that comes into being between the art work and the observer are obviously open to criticism. Such relationships are wholly intangible and undemonstrable, varying with each observer. One will react particularly to the objective facts of appearance in the forms portrayed; the elements of formal design may seem of greater importance to another. But even though the exact nature of the relationship between observer and work of art defies definition, it is no less real for that. Representation of the objective qualities of things strikes a responding chord in our recollections and we relive the experiences of those things. The artist goes further, for his design serves to relate representative characteristics in an ordered and logical pattern that gives to the whole a greater significance than can be found in any of the parts. By availing ourselves of his analysis of experience through the synthesis that is the work of art, we are led to the observation of new truths or to reaffirmation of the validity of known ones in the light shed upon them by genius. For it is as a *human* experience, giving direction and meaning to life, that a work of art attains significance. The experience of beauty that results from complete understanding of an art work arises from the sense of enrichment, of greater breadth and depth in his own life that the participant comes to realize as its lasting and vital contribution.

# ARCHITECTURE

# Chapter I. Architecture. Principles of Design and Construction

*ARCHITECTURE IS THE ONLY ONE OF THE THREE MAJOR* visual arts that can be called practical in the generally accepted sense of the word. Sculpture and painting can be put to some practical use, it is true; much very effective advertising is made possible by them. But one of the primary purposes of architecture is to satisfy the fundamental human need for shelter, a need which is next only to that for food among the human instincts that are spurs to the preservation of life. It follows from this that an example of architecture must be judged in part by the extent to which it fills the need that led to its creation. This same reason provides an explanation for the many existing architectural styles, for since the needs of different periods in history and different places in the world have never been the same, it follows that architectural forms designed to meet those needs and conditions must differ as well.

The purpose for which a building is to be used is one factor, therefore, in determining its form. Another is the way in which it is constructed. This aspect of architecture is closely related to the science of engineering; it is possible to trace the entire history of the art through changes in form resulting from the various methods of construction employed at different times. An obvious illustration is the skyscraper, for without the use of steel which did not become general until the latter part of the 19th century, the lofty towers of a modern American city could never have been erected. Construction is therefore an important element in determining architectural form, but it is none the less subordinate to function or purpose. The skyscraper would not have had to develop, for instance, had it not been made necessary by rising land values resulting from urban congestion; even the use of steel in constructing them is more a matter of greater financial return than considerations of formal character, for some of the first and most distinctive tall buildings were built entirely of masonry.

In applying to architecture the general theory of art developed in the Introduction, function and construction correspond to the element of representation in painting and sculpture. The purpose served by a building is generally quite clear, and if the structural method employed in building it is not always obvious, it can usually be determined from brief examination. These, in other words, are the facts of the idea that the building is to symbolize and they correspond to the facts of appearance in the representative arts. Now if the theory developed in the Introduction is to hold true for architecture, it should follow that great architecture is not the result of good construction and utilitarian efficiency alone. A garage well adapted to its purpose and built solidly to be capable of standing for centuries if need be is not necessarily good architecture; a railroad station that provides all in the way of accommodation that is needed and is of such a nature that its usefulness can be extended indefinitely may still fall short of architectural distinction. This is true of any building which lacks the significant element of design. This is as important in architecture as in the representative arts and for a similar reason, since it is through the design that order is imposed upon or made clear in the functional and structural facts with which the architect has to deal, relating them in a perceptible pattern of form. It is in the quality of the design of a building that lies the difference between great architecture and structures that are only tools for living.

The extent to which a building may be considered architecture is thus dependent upon the degree to which the three basic elements of function, construction and design have individually and collectively contributed to its form. It has been pointed out in the Introduction that great art is formed not of design or representation alone but in an integration of the two. This is as true of architecture as of sculpture and painting. The function of a building and its mode of construction should both be clearly expressed in the design, but in addition it should possess such formal character that it will appeal to the observer in its own right. This arises in buildings possessing true architectural distinction from a relationship of the parts that though dictated by useful purpose seems to be inherently and inevitably right; the result is beauty, for the forms are also expressions of the function of the building and its construction.

Architecture, like sculpture and painting, may go to either the extreme of literal factualness in the treatment of form or the opposite one of being intended solely for the sake of attractive appearance. The first extreme produces what is called "functional" style by its adherents and they justify their attitude by a limited interpretation of a phrase employed by Louis Sullivan, one of the greatest of American architects, that "form follows function." As they understand this phrase, utilitarian considerations alone should be taken into account in designing a building, for if it is well constructed and serves its intended purpose efficiently, its form will be inherently, almost automatically, beautiful. At the other end are the architects who hold that the appearance of a building is the thing of greatest importance in determining its form, design being something quite unrelated to its purpose and the way that it is built, for all that matters is the establishment of pleasant patterns of windows, columns and the like. From this point of view, beauty is a thing that can be put on a building like a coat instead of being inherent in the elements of purpose and structural methods employed in building it. Each theory fails to take some fundamental of architectural experience into account. Functionalism in the sense here defined is over-intellectual. No matter how sure the observer may be that a filling station is well built and efficient in the discharge of its duties, if it is no more than that he is certain to be aware of the lack of visual coordination between its various parts—the coordination that results from good design. On the other hand, the skyscraper surmounted by a Greek temple is equally meaningless regardless of the perfection of its various elements in design, because they are not created with the purpose and structural methods involved in building a skyscraper taken into account but simply for the supposed beauty of the resultant form.

Great architecture is produced only when the elements of function and construction are integrated by creative design and in that process acquire a significance that transcends their objective characters. To the observer of a building that owes its form to such a process, the experience of understanding it comes through comprehension of the synthesis of those three basic elements achieved by the architect, a comprehension that is intellectual in so far as the facts of purpose and construction are concerned but which is transmuted by the design into the emotion connoting beauty. To undergo this experience in the presence of the Parthenon or the cathedral at Amiens and thus to grasp their expressive meaning as well as the facts of their existence is to become aware of certain profoundly significant aspects of human thought and emotion.

It has been pointed out before that the materials used in building and the methods employed in assembling them are among the factors contributing to architectural style. Stone and wood are among the materials that have been longest in use, with the former employed by preference in structures of importance for the obvious reason that it is more durable; brick, however, has also been in use from very early times, either baked in the sun or fired in kilns to become almost as hard as stone. Concrete, too, was known and extensively employed at least as early as the Roman period, although many of its potentialities were not realized until iron and steel came into use on a large scale in the latter part of the 19th century. Glass and plastic materials synthetically created are other contributions that date from modern times to the list of substances which the architect may employ for building. Availability of materials is often an important factor in determining architectural ways of thinking, as will be seen; but it should also be borne in mind that in some cases the need of the architect seems to have resulted in the discovery or adaptation of materials to his purpose rather than the other way around.

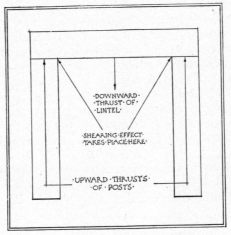

·DOWNWARD·
·THRUST·OF·
·LINTEL·

·SHEARING·EFFECT·
·TAKES·PLACE·HERE·

·UPWARD·THRUSTS·
·OF·POSTS·

FIG. 1.—THE POST AND LINTEL.

Three structural principles are of paramount importance in the history of building, and in various forms and variants account for almost any type of construction to be imagined. They are the post and lintel, the arch, and the cantilever. Of the three, the post and lintel is probably the earliest, although some very ancient examples of the arch have been found; the cantilever, on the other hand, has been extensively employed only with the advent of steel in building, although it does occur in some mediaeval wooden roofs.

The nature of the post and lintel system is implied by its name (Fig. 1). It consists in essence of two vertical members that support a horizontal one and is the simplest of the three basic structural principles in application, for the vertical members need only be sufficiently strong to support the weight of the lintel. Even if some additional weight is placed on the lintel—as in the case of the wall over a door, for instance—there is no threat to the stability of the system if the distance between the vertical members is not too great. This suggests, however, one of the inherent disadvantages of the post and lintel system that is particularly apparent if stone is the material being used; a stone beam of more than a certain length in proportion to its thickness will snap of its own weight if it is supported only at the ends, a disaster whose probability is heightened if there is additional pressure from above. Another disadvantage of the post and lintel system is the possibility that shearing may occur. This, too, is likely to happen if the lintel is subjected to pressure from above, in which case the end of the horizontal beam may be pinched off at the point indicated in the diagram (Fig. 1). These are relatively minor disadvantages, however, and this is the most frequently employed of the three structural principles, occurring even in modern steel-framed buildings which are composed largely of beams fastened together to form post and lintel units. In addition to being the simplest of the three principles in application, its structural effect is easily observed and it can be used to great advantage in a style that does not involve large openings or extensive unobstructed spaces.

The second structural principle is the arch (Fig. 2). In its simplest form, the arch consists of a semicircle of wedge-shaped blocks called

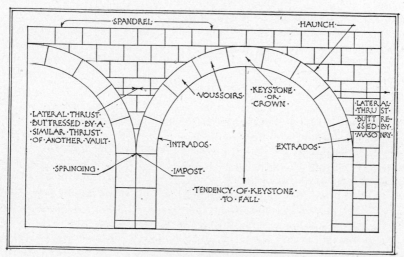

Fig. 2.—The Arch.

voussoirs, with the topmost one further distinguished as the keystone. The bottom face of the lowest voussoir on each side is called an impost and the top face of the uppermost stone of whatever member supports

it is called the springing. In an arch of this type, the inner and outer
faces are concentric semicircles, the outer one being the extrados and
the inner one the intrados or soffit. Midway between the keystone
or crown of the arch and the springing is the haunch. Like the post
and lintel system, the arch is not without some mechanical weaknesses.
It must, for instance, be supported on a scaffold while it is being built.
Such a scaffold is called centering and it is usually in the form and
size of the opening to be spanned by the completed arch. The voussoirs
are laid upon it and then locked in place by putting in the keystone.
If the centering were then removed, the arch would not stand, for
the most serious drawback of the arch as a structural principle would
then become apparent. The keystone, subjected to the action of the
law of gravitation, would have a constant tendency to fall which by
virtue of its wedge-shaped profile it could not do without first pushing
aside the voussoirs next to it. They are also unsupported, however, and
reveal the same tendency. This ever-present thrust exercised by the
central members of an arch against those on the outer sides is a phenomenon of arch construction that its employer must at all times take
into account for if it is not properly compensated the collapse of the
whole structure will be immediate. Such compensation is called buttressing. It may be accomplished in several ways, the basic principle of
all being the opposition to the lateral thrust of the arch of another force
of equal strength, thus neutralizing it and establishing an equilibrium.
One method of achieving this end is illustrated at the right side of
the arch in the diagram (Fig. 2) where the compensating force is the
dead weight of a massive wall that smothers the thrust by sheer inertia;
on the left side the thrust of the main arch is offset by that of another
one. In each case, the compensating force is applied at the haunch of
the arch, which is the point where the accumulated lateral thrusts of the
central members of the arch are strongest; at the left end, the two opposed lateral thrusts are brought together by filling the triangular space
between the arches with masonry forming a spandrel. A series of arches
so related is called an arcade.

An Arabic proverb to the effect that an arch never sleeps is a vivid
characterization of the nature of this structural form which contains
in its proper substance a force that can destroy it, for the stability of
an arch is entirely dependent upon the external buttressing force. This
disadvantage is of minor importance, however, in view of its many advantages. For one thing, an arch can be built of stones too small in
size to be used as lintels since it is a composite form in principle.
Moreover, if the necessary centering is at hand, an arch can be built
with relative ease over spaces that could be spanned by a straight lintel
of stone or wood only with the greatest difficulty. And even if an
arch is required to support weight other than its own, it is necessary

only to provide additional buttressing for the increased horizontal thrust.

The cantilever, which is the third basic structural principle, is utilized today largely in connection with steel (Fig. 3) as a medium since its mechanical operation involves forces that subject the structural parts to many different strains—twisting, bowing, tension, compression and the like. In the illustration, the horizontal projecting arms serve as brackets, supported at one end, upon which loads may be placed or from the end of which they may be hung, thanks to the toughness of the steel which is capable of resistance to the various strains involved. One of the most general applications of the cantilever in modern construction is its use in skyscrapers which depend for their support upon a steel frame or skeleton (Fig. 213); from the vertical members there are projecting horizontal arms upon which the floors are laid and from the ends of which the outer walls of the building are literally hung, a fact which makes possible the continuous horizontal bands of windows in the Philadelphia Saving Fund Society Building that are at the same time striking features in its appearance and highly efficient means of illuminating the interior. Another instance of its use is seen in the Robic House in Chicago (Fig. 204) where the porch roof is a cantilever arm permitting a free and unobstructed view in all directions.

FIG. 3.— THE CANTILEVER.

The materials used in a building and the structural principle involved in assembling them are both means to an end—the disposition of the materials in such a way that they will enclose a given volume of space whose size and arrangement will be determined by the use to which the building is to be put. Such disposition involves as well the arrangement of the different forms that go to make up the building—walls and columns and doors and windows—in such a way that it will be possible to use it most effectively for that purpose. These are determined by the plan of the structure (cf. Figs. 30, 98), which indicates the arrangement of the various supporting members and openings in a horizontal sense, and by the elevation (Fig. 64), which does the same thing vertically. The construction of a building need take no more than this into account since it is concerned only with assuring stability and adequacy for intended utilitarian purpose. The architect must go beyond this, however, if the building is to have character, to be a work of art as well as merely useful. To do this, his fundamental purpose is to *define* the volume of space involved in his structure by the forms that enclose it, establishing by his design a positive relationship between the solids of his building and the space involved, and going beyond the passive enclosure that is the result of construction alone. The nature of his definition of space will depend on many things— the purpose of the building, the materials at his disposal, the basic ways of thinking of the time in which he lives—but the character of his building will be ultimately determined by that consideration. The Greek's attitude toward space, for example, was negative, for the objective philosophy of the fifth century B.C. was concerned only with concrete values in experience; his architecture reflects this, for his temples (Fig. 39) are designed to be seen from the outside like sculptured figures and their interiors are almost entirely lacking in spatial character. In the 13th century, on the other hand, the philosophy of the mediaeval Christian was essentially abstract and concerned with spiritual rather than material values; space was a symbol of an all-pervading God, and its presence as a positive element in the interior of a Gothic cathedral (Fig. 101) is the basic factor in its expressive character. In contrast with both these attitudes, that of the modern world is analytical, seeking to isolate the essentials in abstract conception and concrete form alike. In architecture this results in an attempt to maintain the character of both form and space as individual things, clearly interacting yet always separate; and if there appears to be no great modern architectural style as yet, it is because there is still to be attained the integration of these concepts which must be achieved if they are to acquire genuine expressive meaning.

Of all the arts, architecture is that in which social values are of most immediate importance. Bad pictures can be painted but they do not have to be seen; bad poetry can be written but no one is required to read it; bad music can be composed but it does not have to be performed or heard. Bad architecture cannot be rejected in the same way, for in the absence of well-planned and comfortable houses, ill-designed and inefficient ones must be used; once an ugly office building is erected, it is there and cannot be overlooked. The obligation to society thus implied is of far greater importance than the architect's possible desire to embody an individual ideal of beauty in his building or his patron's insistence upon the satisfying of personal whims. Until this obligation is recognized and acknowledged, architecture must forswear the character and distinction that have been attained by the great styles of the past in those few periods when man's thought and expression were collectively unified and consistent.

# Chapter II. Architectural Origins and Early Forms

THE SHELTER PROVIDED BY NATURAL CAVES FOR EARLY man has little architectural significance because there is lacking that disposition of form in accordance with some creative instinct which is essential if sheltering forms are to be anything but utilitarian. The first structures that might have been so characterized were crude huts, no doubt, of woven tree branches plastered with mud or tents of skins and of matting such as are found in use today among primitive peoples (Fig. 4). Laid out in curvilinear plans for the most part since the small and flexible materials the builder had at his disposal were more easily woven in curves than angular planes, the result was a conical object with a pointed or rounded top. These were the crude beginnings of what might be called architectural thinking; the purpose of such structures was extremely simple and strictly utilitarian at the outset, but they came in time to acquire a meaning other than that of usefulness alone which is a powerful factor in the formative stages of all architectural styles of the early periods of western culture. The way in which such simple structures as these began to mean more than physical protection to those who built and owned them can hardly be more than surmised, but that in time they were valued for more than this is clear. The concept of a life after death, for example, must have come soon in the imaginative experience of early man—from dreaming of his departed ancestors whose forms he thought could not have appeared to him unless they had an existence other than mortal, and which he interpreted in terms of his own material existence. Protection from the forces of nature was the primal motivation of his own way of living and the desirability of a similar protection for the spirit of the dead seemed to him but natural. Hence, that he himself might be assured of that protection, he provided that he should be buried in or near the house that had sheltered his mortal body so that it might perform the same duty for his spiritual being. The house was then sealed up so that its spiritual occupant might not be disturbed and the structure then took on a symbolic value as the house of the dead.

An illustration of the tomb as an extension of the house concept is seen in the dolmens consisting of two upright slabs of stone supporting a third horizontal one (Fig. 5), of which considerable numbers have been found in various parts of Europe, particularly in Brittany in western France. Within the chamber thus formed, the body was placed and the whole was covered with a mound of earth, the purpose being to create a house for the dead that would be more lasting than the reed or skin shelters in which mortals lived. For from fear that the spirit would be unhappy if deprived of shelter and would return to

*Seligman*

FIG. 4.—PRIMITIVE REED HUTS IN THE SUDAN.

trouble the minds of those still on earth, it was believed to be of utmost importance that it should be provided with a permanent resting place. The dolmens are not particularly early in date—most of them appear to have been built later than the temples in Egypt, for instance —but they are none the less products of an environment and culture that were in a rudimentary stage of development and they illustrate one of the primary phases of architectural thinking.

Belief in the aid which could be rendered by supernatural forces to humans in prolonging life on earth was another factor that contributed to the acquisition of more than protective meaning by the house forms of early man. The development of a religious instinct from fetishism in which rocks and trees and mountains were believed to have magic powers through zoomorphism or the worship of animals to anthropomorphism when the gods are imagined in the likeness of men is a common pattern in the history of social evolution. Symbols of personal significance, the god of an individual, may come in time to have meaning for a group or family and even a tribe, and to it the fortunes of the community are ascribed. The protection and propitiation of this god were usually the task of the chieftain, who was thus priest at the same time; and the house which he shared with the god became a sanctuary. At such time as the chieftain-priest became the incarnation of the deity he served, the place in which he lived became the house of the god and thus acquired a new significance. This, in brief,

FIG. 5.—Carnac, Brittany. A DOLMEN.

is the way in which the concept of the temple was evolved; and as the house of the all-powerful it was only fitting that it should be greater and more lasting than those of mortals but still conceived in similar terms.

The concentric circles—some partial and some complete—of upright stones connected by horizontal lintels at *Stonehenge* near Salisbury in England (Fig. 6) appear to be a primitive temple form. It is called a cromlech and is built in such a way that a stone within the innermost circle was directly in the shadow cast by another at some distance outside called the "Friar's Heel" when illuminated by the rays of the rising sun on the morning of the summer solstice at the time it was built. The inference that it was a place of sun worship is inescapable; the fact that its form was determined by the house designs of those who built it is clearly indicated too, for at nearby Wiltshire are the remains of a large circular enclosure that was evidently some form of habitation made of wooden posts thrust vertically into the ground. The actual date of Stonehenge has been determined with some accuracy at about 1500 B.C. by calculating astronomically the time when the phenomenon of the sun's rays described took place on the day indicated. Like the dolmens, however, the architectural concept involved

*Hartmann*

FIG. 6.—STONEHENGE. Near Salisbury, England.

is a primitive one as is the fact that it was devoted to the worship of a natural force. Only in the fact that it is oriented, i.e., laid out with reference to the points of the compass, is there any suggestion of more than the most elementary architectural procedure.

The earliest architecture of history developed in the area of the eastern Mediterranean where fertile river valleys made possible the evolution of agricultural civilizations that replaced in time the more primitive hunting cultures of earliest man. In Egypt, for example, the stabilizing effect of a fixed and permanent society is to be seen architecturally in the continuity of tradition and the monumental character of the buildings there erected, to which material and social conditions contributed. The fertile fields that lie on either side of the river Nile, upon which the crops were raised and the herds grazed that made life possible, are bordered by desolate and mountainous regions in which were inexhaustible resources of stone for building. The annual flooding of these fields by the river renewed their fertility and by this phenomenon there was created a symbol of the life that comes from destruction and death, personified in the god Osiris. No less essential to the existence of the Egyptian was the warmth of the sun's rays that brought renewed life to the seemingly dead vegetation, whence it too became a force to be ingratiated and propitiated in the person of Re the sun god. These were the most powerful gods of the Egyptian hierarchy; in the manner suggested above, they were believed to be incarnate in the person of the Pharaoh, who was worshiped as divine during his life as well as after his death. So were formed the motives underlying the major architectural forms of Egypt during its long recorded history as an autonomous state. For the purposes of this discussion, that history may be considered as divided into three major periods, the Old Kingdom from *ca.* 3200 B.C. until 2160 B.C., the Middle Kingdom from 2160 B.C. until 1580 B.C. and the New Kingdom from 1580 B.C. until 1100 B.C. Egyptian chronology was actually

*Perrot & Chipiez*

Fig. 7.—Egyptian Mastabas. Restored.

recorded in terms of ruling dynasties, and equivalents of modern numerical chronology in such terms are frequently encountered; the Old Kingdom was most important, for example, during the first to

fifth dynasties, from *ca.* 3200 B.C. to *ca.* 2540 B.C., while the eleventh
and twelfth dynasties were of greatest importance in the Middle Kingdom, from 2160 B.C. until 1785 B.C. There were some periods during
these larger ones in which foreign influences prevailed in the country
but they did little, by and large, to alter the fundamental character of
Egyptian thinking.

Tombs of various types depending upon the importance of the person
buried therein constitute the largest class of Old Kingdom architectural

FIG. 8.—MASTABA OF PERNEB SHOWING PLAN. From a model.
*Metropolitan Museum, N. Y.*

examples. At all times, common people were simply buried in holes in
the ground or in their houses, but a nobleman's final resting place was
a low massive structure of stone called a *mastaba* (Fig. 7) from its
sloping or battered walls that make it resemble the Arabic benches
from which the name is derived. Rectangular in shape and usually laid
out with its four sides facing the cardinal points of the compass, it
has two entrances as a rule, one of which is an actual door and the
other a false one; these are for the most part on the north or east sides.
The internal arrangement of the mastaba varies with different examples, but certain elements are always to be found (Fig. 8); these are

a chapel or offering room in which presents were made to the spirit of the deceased, a separate chamber—the *serdab*—where a statue of the dead man was placed and which was often accessible only through very small apertures, and a shaft that runs vertically through the mass of the mastaba down into the ground where the actual burial chamber was located. This shaft, the opening of which can be seen in the flat top of the mastaba (Fig. 7), was filled with stones after carefully contrived barriers or portcullises were lowered following the final installation of the sarcophagus, the purpose being to prevent as far as possible the rifling of the grave for the riches buried with the deceased. Another false door was an invariable feature of the chapel or offering chamber (Fig. 9); through it the spirit of the dead man came to partake of the food that was first actually brought to him but later was carved and painted on the walls of the chamber along with the innumerable details of the daily activity involved in producing it. The statue in the *serdab* was placed there for comparable reasons—to provide the spirit with a body if the dreaded possibility of damage to the mummy in its sarcophagus should materialize. The whole character of the mastaba is thus seen to be a consequence of material and magical efforts to insure the personal immortality for which the Egyptian passionately hoped and prepared during his life on earth.

A mastaba such as the one described might have been built in the fourth or fifth dynasties of the Old Kingdom. Previous to that time, certain of its elements may have been present in tomb structures but built in brick or clay rather than stone. The way in which the form of the developed mastaba was determined by the more elemental concepts and structural practices of earlier periods is one of its significant characteristics from the point of view of the evolution of architectural thinking. The tomb was the house of the soul so it follows in its general character the house of the man who built it. This was very likely made of sun-dried mud brick laid in walls that were thick and heavy and sloped backward since they had to be thicker at the base than at the top to be stable, and it was in this same form that the mastaba was built with cut stone walls encasing a rubble fill even though they would have lost no structural strength by being vertical instead. Similarly traditional in their elements are the "false doors" of the chapels in a mastaba (Fig. 9) which show in conventionalized forms the front of a house; here, symbolically, the actual house of the dead where are carved in stone the various elements that went to make up a façade—the screens of matting that formed the walls or the panels made up of small pieces of wood, the bound reeds used for mouldings on the angles and the tips of others projecting above and bending forward to form a concave cornice. In some cases, there is a cylinder

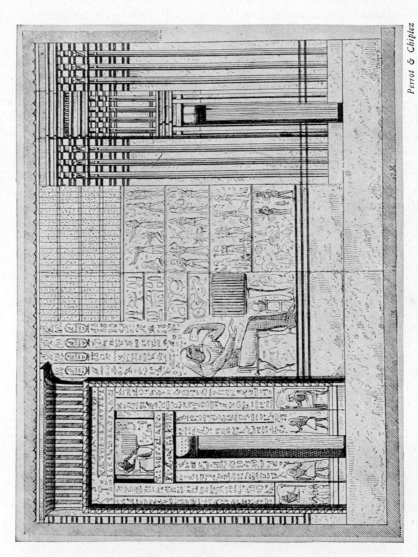

Fig. 9.—Saqqara. Mastaba of Ptahotep. "False doors" in chapel.

at the top of the false door itself on which a rope and matting pattern indicates it to be a representation of a rolled-up screen of reeds that served as curtain in the house door. The plan, too, of the mastaba is to be referred directly to that of the Egyptian house; the chapel or offering chamber is the courtyard or vestibule, the *serdab* the private room of the house and the underground burial chamber a direct continuation of the primitive practice of interment beneath the floor of the dwelling.

FIG. 10.—Saqqara. THE STEPPED PYRAMID OF ZOSER.

Like the house of mortals, those of the dead were grouped together in cities or *necropoli* (Fig. 11). In the Old Kingdom, these necropoli were usually on the west bank of the Nile—the "land of death"—two very important ones being at Saqqara and Gizeh where long rows of mastabas form regular patterns of streets. The social and religious hierarchy of Egypt demanded even in death an adequate symbol of rank and importance and the tomb of the king was of necessity more important than those befitting men of lesser degree, a circumstance which undoubtedly suggested the building of a second mastaba on top of the lower one and the continuation of this process until a suitable form was created. This, thanks to the inclined walls of the mastaba form, was a pyramidal mass with stepped sides (Fig. 10) such as was built at Saqqara by the architect Imhotep for King Zoser, who reigned in the early part of the third dynasty in the Old Kingdom. The Stepped Pyramid is the central element in a vast complex of buildings erected with the intention of reproducing in stone as the permanent resting

place of Zoser's soul the structures of wood, brick and reeds of his
fortified palace at Memphis; the ensemble as a whole is important as
the earliest known instance of translating the forms of earlier architecture from less durable materials into stone, and in supplying an illustration of the way in which the pyramid as a type of funereal architecture was developed from the mastaba.

The *Great Pyramids* at Gizeh (Fig. 11) were among the wonders of
the ancient world and retain that distinction in modern times. Built in
the fourth dynasty of the Old Kingdom—roughly between 2700 and
2600 B.C.—they were intended as the tombs of the Pharaohs Khufu,
Khafra and Menkaura and were built in that order, the Great Pyramid
of Khufu being the northernmost of the three and the largest. That
of Menkaura, the latest and smallest of the three, is not shown in the
illustration, which is a restoration of part of the necropolis at Gizeh.
The huge bulk of Khufu's pyramid—767 feet at the base and 479
feet in height when its original casing was in place—makes it the
largest mass of stone in the world created by human hands, which it
was in a literal sense since the elemental mechanical equipment of the
Egyptian builder could have been of but little use in handling the
limestone blocks averaging two and a half tons in weight that make
up the core. A system of corridors and passages within its mass provided carefully concealed means of access to the burial chambers of
the king and queen which were ingeniously built with triangular
roofs so constructed as to divert the pressure of the enormously heavy
masses of stone above away from the openings. The passages referred
to were lined with slabs of finely cut limestone of very precise dimensions which have been romantically interpreted as prophecies of future
history but are of more significance in revealing the extraordinary
technical skill of the Old Kingdom stone masons. The at present
rough exterior of the Great Pyramid was once covered by a casing of
highly polished slabs of stone similar to that of which a part can yet
be seen on the adjoining Pyramid of Khafra; the glittering effect of
this casing under the sun's rays was undoubtedly planned to make it
a symbol of Re, the sun god, who was worshiped in Lower Egypt in
the region of the delta during the Old Kingdom period in the form
of a gleaming obelisk with a tip of the same pyramidal form as Khufu's
tomb.

The Old Kingdom pyramid made provision only for the function of
interment in the burial concepts of ancient Egypt and left those of
the *serdab* with its statue and the offering chamber of the mastaba to
be discharged in other ways. Lying close to the second pyramid—that
of Khafra—on its east side is a structure that served as its chapel, of
considerable size and provided in various rooms with *serdabs* and false

Hölscher

Fig. 11.—Gizeh. The Pyramids of Khufu and Khafra, and the "Portico." Restored.

doors presumably similar in purpose to the comparable forms in a mastaba but on a larger and more elaborate scale. It is now in such a ruinous state that little but its plan can be made out, but it is connected by a covered causeway with a somewhat smaller and better-preserved structure about a quarter of a mile distant which apparently resembled it somewhat in plan and appearance. This structure lies near the famous

*Hölscher*

FIG. 12.—Gizeh. THE "PORTICO." Interior, restored.

statue of the Sphinx (Fig. 11) and is sometimes called its temple; it was probably intended as a portico or monumental approach to the ruined shrine-temple nearer the pyramid itself (Fig. 12). Inside are two halls so arranged as to form a T in plan in which square monolithic piers of granite support the roof; these are impressive alike in their massive proportions and the simplicity of their forms which are unobscured by any carved or painted ornament. As the earliest known examples of isolated stone supports, these piers are historically important; the fact that small pegs or dowels are carved at their tops and that cramps were used to bind the architrave blocks together shows that the conception underlying their form is one still based on the practice of wood joining. The façade, which was nearly forty feet in height, must have resembled a large mastaba in appearance; its battered walls with rounded corners and the flat roof are in the tradition of construction in mud and brick rather than stone.

There is reason to believe that temples were built during the eleventh and twelfth dynasties of the Middle Kingdom (2160-1785 B.C.), but

FIG. 13.—Beni-Hasan. THE ROCK-CUT TOMBS.

as they were of brick for the most part, they have not survived in a state permitting more than archaeological discussion. In the *Rock-cut Tombs* at Beni-Hasan about 125 miles up the river from Gizeh, there are, however, examples of a Middle Kingdom architectural type of great distinction and impressiveness (Fig. 13). Hewn literally from the live rock of the eastern bank of the river, these were the final resting places of the chieftains of the Oryx nome, one of the most powerful tribes in the feudal society that replaced in the Middle Kingdom the monarchic system of the Old Kingdom. Provided originally with external courtyards, partly built and partly cut from the rock, these tombs preserve in their general plan the traditional elements of the Egyptian sacred structure with its origins in the house-court, vestibule or portico, hall with pillars and a private or sacred chamber. In the rock-cut tombs, the latter are the main interior room and the smaller one at the rear which originally contained the statue of the deceased (Fig. 14), the mummies being placed in a pit on the floor of the main hall. Many details in the design of these tombs reflect

FIG. 14.—Beni-Hasan. THE ROCK-CUT TOMB OF AMENEMHAT. Interior.

the influence of forms originally created in materials other than the stone in which they appear. Both external and internal columns are polygonal in section with eight or sixteen sides—a form which might appear to have originated in cutting the corners from a square beam but which seems rather to have been originally a composite one resulting from binding a number of reeds together and filling the interstices between them with mud for plaster which was then smoothed off to a plane surface. The little blocks below the upper horizontal member of the façade would likewise appear to have originated in wooden construction, in the projecting ends of small roof beams. Within, the flattened arches of the ceilings in the main hall are painted with diaper and checkered patterns reproducing those of woven matting roofs such as actually covered the houses of the Oryx chieftains. Other than this, the painted decoration in the interiors of these rock-cut tombs continues the older tradition of detailed and lively portrayal of the life of the time for the sake of the spirit of those buried in them.

The mastabas and pyramids of the Old Kingdom and the rock-cut tombs of the Middle Kingdom were imposing and impressive monuments to the greatness of their builders and inhabitants, but massiveness and inaccessibility proved insufficient in making certain the preservation and permanent repose so deeply desired. Thus in spite of centuries-old traditions that tended to enforce the practices and crystallize the forms that had been hallowed by unquestioning usage over a long period of time, a change in the character of the Egyptian tomb was brought about in the New Kingdom that made more adequate provision for protection of the mummy but took the form as a whole entirely out of the category of architecture. It became the practice of the rulers of Egypt to make their tombs in the form of long underground corridors, frequently of great complexity of plan, which were cut in the cliffs of the Valley of the Kings lying in the Libyan desert west of Deir el-bahari on the west bank of the Nile not far from Thebes, which was then the political capital of the country. That concealment was the chief motive in dictating the form taken by these underground tombs is indicated by an inscription in the tomb of an architect responsible for one of the earliest of them—"I attended the excavation of the cliff-tomb of His Majesty alone, no one seeing, no one hearing"; and the occasional success of the designers in this respect is witnessed by the discovery in 1923 of the shaft tomb of Tutankhamen, a minor ruler of the eighteenth dynasty, which had been but slightly disturbed and provided one of the richest treasures in the history of Egyptology. It should also be noted, however, that the ingenuity of the designers in concealment has been equaled by that of many would-be looters in discovery; the majority of the graves now known have long since been despoiled.

With the place of actual burial in the New Kingdom tomb purposely deprived of its monumental and memorial character in the interests of more effective concealment there went a considerable augmentation of the temple or shrine in which the name and divinity of the deceased ruler could be properly venerated. As early as the eighteenth dynasty, it was the practice of the Theban rulers to erect their mortuary temples on the plains of the west bank of the Nile at Deir el-bahari

Fig. 15.—Deir el-bahari. The Temple of Hatshepsut. From the east.

before the cliffs at the edge of the Valley of the Kings and at some considerable distance from the tombs themselves. One of the most notable of these was that erected by Queen Hatshepsut (d. 1479 B.C.) of which the existent remains constitute one of the outstanding monuments of Egyptian architecture (Fig. 15). The temple was designed by the architect Senmut as a series of terraces with columnar porticoes combined with rock-cut chambers in the cliff against which the temple is set that are chapels to the gods Hathor, Anubis and Amon as well as Hatshepsut herself. Of monumental proportions—the upper terrace is more than 300 feet in width—the structure as a whole is none the less a repetition of the basic architectural elements previously noted, the portico, columnar hall and private chamber. Important details in design are the columns of the terrace porticoes—square or sixteen-sided—the use of statues as supports, and the carved and painted accounts on the wall of the upper terrace of the birth of Hatshepsut and the expedition to the land of Punt which—like the temple itself —was supervised by her architect Senmut.

Other than the mortuary temples which it was the duty as well as the privilege of Egyptian rulers to erect in their capacity as incarnations of divinity, there were buildings, consecrated to the gods themselves— a type both great in number and impressive in form by the time of the New Kingdom. Chief among Egyptian deities was the sun god, Amon-Re, and his temples, administered by a powerful priesthood ever increasingly jealous of prerogative and confirmed in privilege, were the largest and most important in the country. This was but natural in accordance with the belief that the temple was the house of the god and that its glory should be proportionate to his greatness, a fact which also permits the conceptual identity of mortal and divine houses to be recognized. One of the smaller Egyptian temples but one that illustrates the basic elements with more than usual clarity is the one erected to *Khons* at Karnak near Thebes, by Rameses III in the twentieth dynasty *ca.* 1100 B.C. (Fig. 16).

The temple was approached by an avenue of sphinxes leading up to a massive gate-wall called a pylon; this was characteristically a structure with sloping or battered walls heavier at the base than at the top which terminated in a cornice of concave profile. Through this pylon a portal opens into a court with colonnades forming covered galleries on the sides; steps in the gallery on the side opposite the portal lead to a chamber equal in length to the width of the temple in which the roof is supported by numerous columns, which is called the hypostyle hall. At the rear of this hall is a door leading into the sanctuary proper which was generally a room of rather small dimensions but surrounded by many others that were storage and treasure rooms in

*Perrot & Chipiez*

FIG. 16.—Karnak. THE TEMPLE OF KHONS. Restored perspective view.

which the often considerable possessions of the temple were kept. Deviations from this basic type are common—in fact, there is no other temple of such typical character as that of Khons; but modifications are almost invariably in the nature of duplications of one or more of the essential elements—two courts instead of one, or a hypostyle hall that is so large as to overshadow the rest of the structure—and the fundamental character of the plan is hardly ever changed except in buildings otherwise motivated. The organization of the plan on a longitudinal axis, for example, is a prevalent characteristic of the Egyptian temple and when any variation from this is found, it is because of particular physical circumstances that could not be modified.

The construction of an Egyptian temple involved the post and lintel principle exclusively; there is evidence to the effect that the arch was known to Egyptian builders, but its use was limited to certain types of tomb and to utilitarian structures for the most part and its monumental potentialities were realized hardly at all. By contrast, the possibilities of the column for impressive effect were extensively developed by the New Kingdom builders as those in the colonnade and forecourt of the temple of Amon-Re at Luxor (Fig. 17) make quite clear. This temple, one of the largest built in Egypt, was begun by Amenhotep III (1412-1376 B.C.) of the eighteenth dynasty. The colonnade that led to the original entrance pylon, which is now in ruins, is a later addition by the same monarch; its columns are surmounted by bell-shaped capitals which resemble the open flower of the papyrus plant in shape while those of the forecourt beyond are in the form of the buds of the same plant. These were not the only foliate forms used by the Egyptian to decorate his columns, for lotus blossoms and palm leaves were often employed in similar fashion. The effect of the capital as an element in the design of the building is to provide a transition from the vertical accent of the column shaft to the horizontal one of the lintel resting on it; the same visual function is performed in the simpler columns of the rock-cut tomb at Beni-Hasan (Figs. 13 and 14) by the rectangular blocks interposed between lintels and columns. It is doubtful, however, if such considerations as these were consciously observed by the Egyptian builder, for the column and capital as he used them were simply traditional structural elements whose forms had been determined by primitive practice in other materials than stone. What these were is indicated by certain details of the columns themselves; at the top of the shafts immediately beneath the swelling of expanded and bud capitals alike is a series of horizontal bands and the shafts of the bud columns are not simple cylinders but are carved in vertical stem-like members which cut in perceptibly at the base. If a cluster of long-stemmed papyrus buds growing from a single root be imagined as bound around just below the buds themselves, the source of the form executed in stone by the eighteenth-dynasty builder will at once be suggested.

FIG. 17.—Luxor. THE TEMPLE OF AMON-RE. From the north.

The architectural piety of the Egyptian is further indicated by an-other major element in the temple form—the pylon (Fig. 18). This example is from a *Temple* erected at *Edfu* in honor of the god Horus

Fig. 18.—Edfu. The Temple of Horus. Main pylon.

and although it is much later in date than the New Kingdom temples hitherto discussed—it was begun in 237 B.C. and finished by 212 B.C. —it repeats the basic pattern of the earlier structures without change. The vertical slots at the base of the pylon were sockets to hold the staves of banners on festal days. Both inner and outer faces are liberally decorated with figures in the characteristic sunken relief used by the Egyptian for wall ornament; these deal with the achievements of the ruler who built the temple which are here ascribed to the power given him by Horus, who is represented as a human figure with a hawk's head. The pylon itself consists of two towers with a doorway between them, a form which apparently had a traditionally symbolic value as the "Horizon of Heaven" which it is sometimes called in inscriptions; its sloping walls are likewise traditional, repeating the characteristics of construction in woven matting with a strengthening core of mud such as might well have been used in earlier times. Around the edges of the pylon runs a cylindrical moulding which at close view is seen to have a recurrent pattern of horizontal bands connected in groups by others that slant across the principal moulding. This, too, is a stone translation of a form originally of less permanent materials, it being a bundle of reeds placed on the edges of the original matting and mud wall to protect them from damage. The Egyptian pylon was usually crowned with a projecting cornice of pronounced concave section (cf. Fig. 16) although it has been broken off at Edfu; the preferred decoration for this cavetto cornice, as it is called, was a pattern of leaves, a characteristic that points to its ultimate derivation from the reed parapets upon the primitive houses.

By perpetuating in durable stone the forms that his ancestors had created and used in less permanent materials, the Egyptian architect provides an illuminating example of the unquestioning acceptance of conventions rendered significant by tradition which constitutes the primary characteristic of all Egyptian art forms. This is no less true of the temple plan as a whole; this was thought of as that of the god's house which in principle is simply a larger and more permanent dwelling composed in the manner of the house in which the Egyptian lived himself. The forecourt, the porticoed vestibule opening into the great hall, and the private chamber of the god all had their counterparts in the smaller and less distinguished house of the mortal. As has been pointed out before, these are the fundamental elements in the plan of every Egyptian temple regardless of apparent variations or added complexities that are invariably the consequence of repeating one or more of the basic forms without altering either function or traditional symbolic value.

The addition of ornament to utilitarian forms appears to have been practiced from earliest times and the decoration which is an element in Egyptian architectural style is one of its outstanding characteristics. It is to be seen in the figures carved in raised or sunken relief on façades (Fig. 18) and columns where they are often accentuated in effect by the use of color, and in the mouldings on the angles of pylons and the cavetto cornices surmounting them as well as the foliate forms used for column capitals. The symbolic origin of Egyptian decoration cannot be doubted. The lotus and papyrus blossoms that adorn the columns are conventionalized references to ancestral worship of growing stalks of bound reeds, the fetishes of fertility that were later symbolized by hanging bundles of flowers from the supporting posts of the priest's house in the annual celebration of the resurgence of life

FIG. 19.—Abu Simbel. THE TEMPLE OF RAMESES II. Façade.

brought by sun and river to the apparently lifeless vegetation of the Nile valley. The reliefs carved on walls and columns originated in the practice of scratching in the mud of the house wall or plastered reed column pictographic symbols that recorded the attainments and good deeds of the owner; these on tomb or temple are simply by way of being more permanent records in stone, but their purpose is nonetheless the same. Such is the motivation of the great seated figures in front of the temple that Rameses II caused to be carved from the solid rock of the west bank of the Nile at *Abu Simbel* (Fig. 19) in 1257 B.C. The façade was cut in the stone as well as the inner chambers of the temple and is conceived as a pylon complete with bound-reed and cavetto mouldings, surmounted by a row of dog-headed apes. These animals were sacred to the worship of the rising sun in whose honor the structure was ostensibly created and whose statue stands in a niche in the center of the façade. It is far overshadowed, however, by the four colossal statues of Rameses himself—sixty-five feet in height—representing the monarch in the royal enthroned pose while smaller figures representing the members of his family appear around the legs of the colossi. Other figures in relief on the façade and bands of hieroglyphic inscriptions indicate the nominal homage of the Pharaoh to the god, but the walls of the inner rock-cut chambers are crowded with pictorial and inscribed praises of the ruler himself once more.

In the magnitude of its dimensions—the façade is 119 feet wide and 100 feet high—the execution of which by a laborious process of cutting away the stone of the cliff was made possible only by almost unlimited amounts of slave labor, the temple at Abu Simbel is a characteristic instance of the preoccupation with size and bulk that existed from the very beginning in Egyptian art in consequence of primitive desire for certainty and permanence in a world of transient values. If this size is not at first apparent either in illustrations of the monuments or in their actual presence, it is to be accounted for by lack of scale in both individual forms and ensembles. Scale is the quality in the design of a building that allows its size to be sensed and creates the visual impression of bigness or smallness. A building may be enormous in bulk yet appear to be very small, or—as is usually the case with Egyptian forms—be devoid of any inherent character of proportion so that it may seem either large or small. Giving scale to architectural design is one of the most important functions of ornament as a rule, but it was one to which the Egyptian architect was oblivious, for the function of his ornament, like that of the building of which it was a part, was symbolic and not aesthetic.

It remains, finally, to examine the effect of the architectural forms of ancient Egypt as an indication of the way in which they reflect the communal beliefs of those who built them. From the exterior, the temple was an extended, low-lying mass of masonry set inside high walls through which the ordinary man might never pass. Unrelieved by openings save for that in the pylon, its massive proportions and forbidding aspect must have impressed the beholder with the extraordinary power of the inhabitant, an impression which was enhanced, were he privileged to pass into the courtyard, by the mysterious gloom of the hypostyle hall with gigantic carven forms dimly outlined on wall and column where the all-powerful dweller in this divine palace could reveal himself on occasion to his court, and which led in turn to the even more profound darkness of the sacred shrine wherein the god had his actual abode. Yet surrounded as the Egyptian was by symbols rendered significant by the weight of centuries-old tradition, symbols that he unconsciously employed in his own humble dwelling but here of a size that he could not hope to emulate and created in a medium whose permanence far transcended that of the mud bricks and reeds to which he was limited, he must have felt too that here was the house of one who would long continue after he had vanished from earth and to whom he would therefore willingly acknowledge the allegiance that made possible the rigidly conventional way of thinking that was at once the strength and weakness of Egyptian culture.

The second of the great pre-classical cultures whose architectural style reveals the change from construction of temporary and primarily utilitarian buildings to monumental and more lasting ones with the shift from a nomadic and hunting life to an agricultural one is that which developed in Mesopotamia. Here as in Egypt the fertile valleys of rivers—the Tigris and Euphrates—provided both sustenance for mortals and pliable materials in the form of reeds which, used in bundles or woven into matting and plastered with mud, were the substance of the builder in earliest times. Sun-dried brick was developed at a relatively early date and became the most prevalent building medium, but the influence of the early forms always persisted. Another

*Newton & Walcot*

Fig. 20.—Ur in Chaldaea. The Ziggurat. Restored.

element in the early house form that persisted as a salient characteristic of monumental Mesopotamian building was the courtyard; originally formed by walls surrounding the house for protective purposes, it came in time to be a controlling factor in the large city-palaces and temples. Fetishism with its deification of natural objects is also a factor to be taken into account in the origins of Mesopotamian architectural forms, for the staged towers called ziggurats, of which an early example dating from the fourth millennium B.C. has been sufficiently excavated at *Ur in Chaldaea* (Fig. 20) to permit reconstruction of its original form, appear to be the work of people investing mountains with religious meaning. This concept becomes modified in time to make the ziggurat the house of the god, in which capacity it is associated with that of the king-priest.

The "Land of the Two Rivers" was much fought over in ancient times and the culture that flourished there was a composite one of varied character in which the influences of different races and tribes prevailed at one time or another. Certain traditional forms persisted in the architecture, however, and when the great palace at *Khorsabad* (Fig. 21) was built by Sargon II in 722 B.C., it embodied many features of the older styles of the region which is Assyria, the northern part of Mesopotamia. The palace was part of a fortified city and was built on an artificial mound some fifty feet in height that straddled the walls of the city enclosure. Generally rectangular in plan, it is oriented by angles since the corners are directed toward the cardinal points of the compass. Otherwise the plan is notable for its asymmetry. The 209 rooms that go to make it up are grouped or agglomerated around open courtyards instead of being laid out with reference to a central axis, and the arrangement is determined in general by the use to which the different groups were put. At the left of the illustration, in the south angle, are the women's quarters or harem, somewhat apart from the main bulk of the palace as might be expected in a building of semi-Oriental character. Directly across the principal court from the harem and in the east angle of the palace are storerooms and offices, the administrative section; the men's quarters are on the northwest side of the same court. Continuing in this same direction are the private apartments of the monarch which lead to the chambers of state where the reception rooms used on great ceremonial occasions were located. These latter are grouped around the rather long and narrow court which is reached through a portal flanked by towers opening from the upper level of the mound at the left of the long ramp by which chariots and horsemen could ascend from the ground below. In this general layout, the traditional relationship of enclosed room to surrounding courtyard is maintained. Also included in the palace form, however, is the ziggurat which is located at Khorsabad in the angle between the harem and the men's quarters on the southwest side of the palace; the form in which it appears here—a rectangular tower

*Andrae*

FIG. 21.—Khorsabad. THE PALACE OF SARGON II. Restored.

ascended by ramps that spiral up its sloping sides—is no more than a conventionalized erected mound such as had been built centuries before at Ur (Fig. 20) in a somewhat less rigidly organized form. Its specific use was as an observation platform from which the astrologer-priests could make the observations of stars that guided the policies of the ruler.

The rooms of the palace were not very large for the most part, and were usually long and narrow in shape, with heavy walls ranging

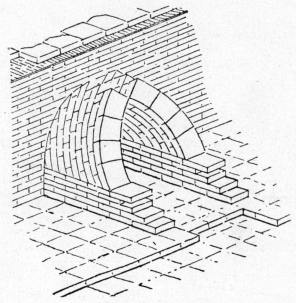

FIG. 22.—THE LAMINATED VAULT.

from twelve to twenty-eight feet in thickness built of mud brick and faced with stone. They were covered with flat roofs as a rule, made of mud and supported by beams of such wood as was locally available or could be imported. Certain rooms were probably vaulted, however, notably the royal chamber in which the curving profile of the vaulted ceiling appears to have been the result of attempting to reproduce the rounded matting coverings of the mud and reed huts of earlier times. The true vault with voussoirs and keystone (cf. Fig. 2) was used in some instances and the corbeled type in others where the courses are laid in such fashion that each one projects slightly beyond the one beneath and so diminishes the span until it is closed in at the top. Yet another type of vault, the laminated vault (Fig. 22), appears to have been extensively developed for utilitarian purposes in Mesopotamia—for covering underground chambers, drains and the like. Built of mud bricks laid at an angle so that the courses lean on each other and are supported at the end by a wall, this type of vault had the great advantage of requiring no centering or wooden scaffold for support while in process of erection; the bricks, which were sun-dried, were moistened slightly to make the faces sticky and cement them to those on which they rested until the next course anchored them in place by its weight.

*Koldewey*

Fig. 23.—Babylon. The Ishtar Gate. As restored in Berlin.

Clay in the form of glazed and enameled brick supplied the decoration as well as the substance for the walls of Mesopotamian buildings (Fig. 23). The *Ishtar Gate* in the northwest wall of the city of Babylon owed the form in which it appeared when excavated to Nebuchadnezzar, dating from about 570 B.C. The walls are of crude brick but faced with others that were modeled with the forms of lions and bulls in relief and then painted with an enamel that became hard and glassy upon being fired in an oven. This process involved taking the brick facing down after it was modeled, firing it and putting it back in place, but the striking color effects obtained seem to have been much desired. The background is blue, the animals are brown and yellow, and accents of red and white are employed in the margins. Such enameled and colored bricks were used in facing the ziggurat walls as well—a different color for each level identifying it with a certain god in the Mesopotamian hierarchy. Other than the decoration thus provided, carved reliefs of stone were often employed on Mesopotamian buildings for ornament. Largely concerned with glorification of the ruler by citation of his great accomplishments, these reliefs indicate by their details the character of the Mesopotamian monarchs— savage and warlike on the one hand and passionately fond of the battle and hunt (Fig. 246) yet at the same time given over to a degree of Oriental luxury that led to creating in this same city of Babylon the fabulous Hanging Gardens that were one of the wonders of the ancient world.

The absence of the tomb as a monumental type in Mesopotamian architecture is a point of direct contrast with the Egyptian tradition. The extraordinarily developed cult of the dead which explains so much in the Egyptian way of thinking had no counterpart in Mesopotamia where the practice of house burial was maintained with few exceptions. At the same time, however, the association of the ruler with the god was very close and his rôle as the chief priest of deity as well as monarch was one that invested his dwelling with significance and religious meaning, as the incorporation of the ziggurat—the sort of thing that the Biblical writer had in mind beyond any doubt in describing the Tower of Babel—with the king's palace makes quite clear (Fig. 21). The controlling concept was therefore the house, enlarged and rendered more permanent for the use of ruler and god and taking its larger meaning from the religious values with which it then became invested. It is thus clearly to be recognized that the attitudes of the Egyptian and the Mesopotamian were similar in principle however much they may have differed in the forms in which they were embodied.

The third great cultural area of the pre-classical Mediterranean world is the Aegean, the chief centers being the island of Crete, the southern part of the mainland peninsula of Greece and the western shores of Asia Minor, although the many islands in the Aegean Sea itself are also to be included. Certain features are common in the culture of the area as a whole. The religion of this general region, for instance, involved the worship of primeval forces such as the Earth Goddess, symbolized by snakes and by a curious object resembling a double-headed axe, and also the bull, which appears to have been the symbol of a fertility cult. Similar too are certain architectural forms that appear over the entire area while others seem to be more regional in character. In general, however, it may be noted that the inhabitants of Crete were less given to warlike pursuits than those of the mainland who were in constant danger of attack from which the islanders were

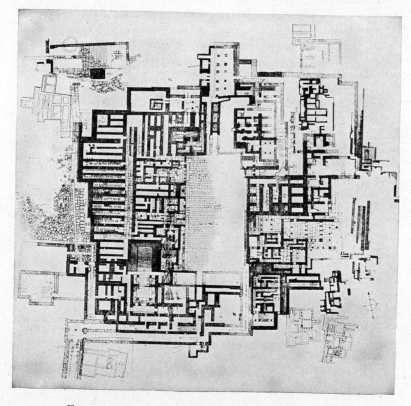

FIG. 24.—KNOSSOS. THE PALACE OF MINOS. Plan.

protected by the sea, a fact which explains some of the differences between the buildings of the island and those on the mainland.

At Knossos on the north coast of Crete the palace attributed by legend to King Minos was built; a vast conglomerate of building known in antiquity as "The Labyrinth," meaning the House of the Double-Axe, it was the fabled lair of the Minotaur whose slaying brought fame to Theseus, one of the great legendary heroes of Athens, in whose time the Minoan palace was already old. The structure revealed by exhaustive excavations in the early 20th century shows evidence of many rebuildings, of which that contributing chiefly to its present form took place in all likelihood between about 1800 and 1600 B.C. The catastrophe which reduced it to ruins—an earthquake, possibly, of which the building had experienced many, or an invasion—appears to have occurred about 1400 B.C. The plan (Fig. 24) is agglomerative in character, with groups of rooms disposed around a central area or plaza which is roughly rectangular in shape and whose long axis is oriented in a general north-south direction. This plaza is actually the top of a mound formed by the many rebuildings on the site which have raised the level of habitation quite perceptibly. The variation in levels of the site as a whole makes possible the different stories in height on the east and west sides of the central space—three on the east side where the slope was aided by a considerable excavation and through which a monumental staircase provided means of access to the plaza level, and two at least on the west side; the illustrated plan gives the ground level throughout.

The part of the palace lying immediately to the east of the central plaza constitutes the domestic quarter. It was provided with quite elaborate facilities including lavatories, running water and a very efficient drainage system; porticoes and terraces formed by the flat roofs supplied pleasantly open areas throughout. Here as elsewhere in the palace, rooms on lower levels were lighted and ventilated by shafts or wells rising through the entire structure. North of this area but still on the east side were service quarters. One of the main approaches to the palace was on the north side of the plaza where the principal approach from the sea was located, while to the west were the ceremonial rooms of the palace. The lower story which is shown in the plan is divided by a north-south corridor with a series of long narrow storage chambers on the west side, and various cult rooms on the east including the *Room of the Throne* (Fig. 25) which has been restored. The upper level of this part of the palace has also been restored in part on the basis of details carefully observed during the process of excavation in which the accumulated layers of material deposited in the original collapse of the structure were identified according to their original use. Many of the most ancient portions of the structure are found here, and the purpose of the various rooms indicated by their decoration leads to the conclusion that this whole wing of the palace was the ceremonial house of the Priest-King Minos, the hereditary name of the ruler of Crete. The clearly defined functions of the various

Evans

FIG. 25.—Knossos. The Palace of Minos. Room of the Throne, partially restored.

parts of the palace and the archaeological evidence of different periods of construction for them are grounds for concluding that the ensemble once existed as a series of separate and unrelated groups of buildings which were later made into a single structure of rather casual unity.

The Cretan builders utilized columns as supporting members quite extensively, making them of both stone and wood. Walls were of mixed materials—sun-dried brick and rubble or conglomerate for the most part, with wooden beams introduced to stiffen the mass. Stucco, brick and stone were employed to face the walls as a rule and in many cases were painted as well, as appears in the partially restored Room of the Throne (Fig. 25) in which one wall has been left undecorated to expose the materials used in forming it. Wood was also used for door frames while stone was employed for parts subjected to wear, like door jambs and sills, and also for column bases. The columns restored in the Room of the Throne stand near a low balustrade separating the room proper from a small enclosed basin probably used for ritual purposes; they are of wood and taper from top to bottom, a reversal of the usual procedure that is based on the evidence of some charred remains of the original shafts and on columns portrayed in some of the decorative frescoes. They are surmounted by heavy circular capitals of rather awkward profile and by rectangular abacus blocks. Not all Minoan columns were thus formed, and the origin of this particular type is not certain; but it would appear to be in consequence of feeling that the butt ends of tree trunks which were the first such supports were stronger in supporting horizontal loads than the smaller top ends.

Much of the effect of Minoan building was a consequence of its decoration. This was predominantly painting for which the stuccoed or plastered walls supplied many areas, an example in point being the Room of the Throne in which the royal seat was originally flanked by two griffons lying in a landscape of plant forms with a background of brightly colored undulating bands. These were probably of symbolic importance as are other paintings in the palace that have been found —stately processions of figures participating in some ceremonial rite or bull-baiting, which seems to have formed a part of Minoan religious practices. Elsewhere are flowers and marine and animal forms wrought into effectively stylized patterns (Fig. 359). The color scheme of these paintings is simple as a rule but the tones are brilliant and a note of gayety was added thereby to rooms which were usually lighted only indirectly through the light-wells.

The various elements of the palace at Knossos that have been mentioned are sufficient to indicate certain characteristics of the culture that produced it—materialistic in the concern for physical comfort and well-being evident in the plan and details of the domestic area, gay and pleasure-loving from the engaging frescoes that decorate the walls, yet conforming to the same fundamental principles of worship and religious belief that characterized its Egyptian and Mesopotamian contemporaries. Fetishism is apparent in the stone pillars inscribed with the sacred double-axe symbol in certain small and dark rooms that were probably shrines; the cult of the Earth Goddess with her snakes is a manifestly elemental form of belief. The character of the west wing of the palace is an architectural suggestion of the same idea for its complex plan and the ritualistic function apparently performed by many of its rooms are the consequence of pious traditionalism that preserved the character of sites used by countless generations for such purposes, incorporating them in only the most nominal fashion in the final ensemble when judged by purely aesthetic standards, but justified by the symbolic significance of the regions involved. This was made possible in considerable degree by the consistency of Minoan culture from earliest to latest times, itself the consequence of the geographic isolation enjoyed by the islanders and their relative freedom from attack.

The Aegean culture of the mainland is known as Mycenaean from the finding of many of its monuments at Mycenae and is roughly contemporary with that of Crete but reached its climax somewhat later than was the case there—between 1300 and 1200 B.C., after the catastrophe that reduced the island palaces to ruins. It was not, moreover, as consistent in character as the civilization of the Minoans for the region in which it developed was subjected to many invasions by neighboring tribes. These seem to have occurred with relative frequency from the earliest time in which it is known to have been inhabited beginning after the palaeolithic period. They brought to the peninsula of Greece the changing forms and practices of peoples from the regions to the north and northeast as well as from the Mediterranean, and the Mycenaean culture that existed from the closing years of the fourth millennium B.C. until the end of the second reveals not only many traits also seen in Crete but others that have no counterparts there. Thus although there are many decorative motives common to both mainland and island styles of painting, and the downward tapering column is found in structures in Mycenae and Tiryns as well as at Knossos, there are notable differences as well.

Necessity for protection from military attack was responsible for some features of mainland Aegean architecture that have no counterpart in Crete. Thus the city of Mycenae, the home of Agamemnon, the famous Greek hero of the Trojan War, was a fortified citadel surrounded by enormous walls of massive, boulder-like stones roughly shaped in what is called cyclopean masonry from the legend in classic

Greece that such walls were built by the race of giants called the Cyclops. The *Lion Gate* (Fig. 26) was the main entrance—an impressive portal over ten feet in height made of three enormous blocks of stone that serve as posts and lintel. Above, the side walls are corbeled over the lintel to frame a triangular slab of stone carved with two rampant lions heraldically opposed on either side of a column. This

FIG. 26.—Mycenae. THE LION GATE.

gate is placed at the end of a deep approaching passage between walls in such fashion that attackers would be subjected to fire from both sides, an indication of the constant need for protection that was a major consideration in planning the fortress palaces that are the mainland counterparts of the relatively undefended structures in Crete.

Near Mycenae are to be seen a series of tombs of a type that was not unknown in Crete and is not the only kind of funereal structure used on the mainland but is none the less of great intrinsic importance and supplies some of the most spectacular examples of pre-classical architecture still existing in Greece. These are the so-called "beehive tombs," of which the one called the *Treasury of Atreus* by its discoverer,

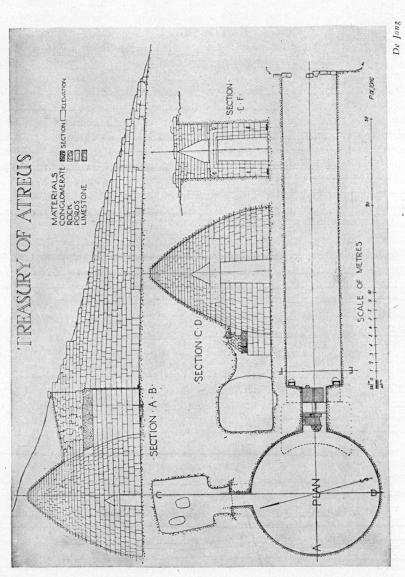

TREASURY OF ATREUS

MATERIALS
CONGLOMERATE
ROCK
POROS
LIMESTONE

SECTION ☐ ELEVATION

SECTION·A·B·

SECTION·C·D·

SECTION· E·F·

PLAN

SCALE OF METRES

De Jong

FIG. 27.—Mycenae. THE TREASURY OF ATREUS. Plan and sections.

the archaeologist Schliemann, is characteristic (Fig. 27). The principal chamber is circular in plan and has corbeled walls built of finely cut stone blocks laid in circular courses of successively smaller diameter, the elliptical section in elevation shown in the drawing being responsible for the popular name applied to the type. Within, these walls were dressed to a smooth surface which was presumably ornamented with bronze medallions fastened with pins in holes still to be seen. At one side, a small door led to an irregularly shaped room that may have been the place of actual burial. On the outside, this constructed chamber was partially covered by a mound of earth in which a long passage led to the entrance portal, whose decoration has been sufficiently re-covered in excavations to permit some knowledge of its original appearance. The lintel—a huge block of stone some twenty-five feet in depth and weighing over a hundred tons—was relieved of weight from above by a triangular corbeled opening which was filled by a slab of red porphyry carved with an all-over spiral pattern; the opening was flanked by applied half-columns of gray alabaster with spirals and chevrons on the downward tapering shafts and cushion-like capitals of semicircular profile. No other example of Aegean architecture has masonry equal in quality to that of the "beehive tombs"; it is not to be thought that its employment in them was motivated by any desire other than to create in the most permanent medium possible a house of the dead that was traditionally in the form of the primitive circular huts of past generations. As such, it is one of the mainland architectural types most clearly distinguished from any extensively represented forms of building of Minoan origin.

Another mainland architectural type of the Aegean period that is not only without Cretan parallel but is of great significance as an element in the background of the later classic Greek temple is illustrated by the *megaron* or chief hall of the fortified palace at Tiryns (Fig. 28), here illustrated in restored form. A more or less isolated structure, rectangular in plan, it was entered through a portico of two columns between projecting side walls that led to a vestibule through doors flanked by rectangular piers from which the megaron proper was reached through a single door. The principal room was over thirty feet in length with a fixed hearth in the center surrounded by four columns that supported the roof rafters. The walls were of sun-dried brick with wooden beams introduced for binding and wood was also used for the columns and as facing for the door jambs, but walls and columns alike rested on bases of stone that are still in place. The structure was probably covered by a gabled roof—a fact that distinguished it from the Cretan houses which were invariably flat-roofed, and also from the purely domestic structures at Tiryns itself, for the megaron was the ceremonial house, the symbol of the authority of the chief. As such, its form was traditionally determined and by its contrast with that of the other buildings of the palace from which it was isolated in plan, its particular significance was made clear. The probability that the "beehive tombs" and the gabled-roof megaron were both evolved from earlier conical house types first developed in flexible and impermanent materials is considerable. Their distinction from the flat-roofed houses of mud brick and rubble with wood bonding that

Fig. 28.—Tiryns. The Megaron. Restored.

appear to have been the prevalent type in Crete and for utilitarian or non-ceremonial structures on the mainland is clear indication of the mixture of traditions in the Mycenaean branch of Aegean culture.

The different names applied by the Homeric poet to the Greeks fighting the Trojans—Achaeans, Dorians, Danaans, and Argives—in the second book of the *Iliad* are likewise evidence of the varied origins of the peoples inhabiting the peninsula of Greece during the closing years of the Aegean period, for the generally accepted date of the Trojan War—the second decade of the twelfth century B.C.—would make it contemporary with the greater part of the structures discussed in the foregoing paragraphs. The picture there painted of a country divided among a number of feudal lords is significant too, for while the circumstances of the fall of the Mycenaean fortified palaces are far from clearly defined, the fact that they fell to foreign invaders is certain. This occurred in all likelihood about the close of the twelfth century, after which comes a period in Aegean history of which but the scantiest knowledge is to be had from any source. Such building as was done at that time could hardly have been other than most impermanent in character, the work of men still hunters and fighters who changed only slowly to agricultural ways. But the buildings of that earlier period still existed; and when the assimilation of the invaders to the soil had finally been consummated, they were not without influence in determining the character of later forms. Not the least significant thing about the achievements of the Mycenaean age is to be noted in this fact—that upon the foundations therein supplied the culture of Hellenic Greece was to rise.

# Chapter III. *The Architecture of Greece*

THE ARCHITECTURAL STYLE DEVELOPED IN GREECE
after the Dark Ages that followed the destruction of Aegean culture
has one characteristic at least in common with the way of building
that preceded it there and with the majority of pre-classical styles—
the employment of the post and lintel system of construction rather
than the arch. There is also, as in the greater part of earlier architecture, a predominant concern for the external effects of buildings and
relatively little for interiors. This may have been the result of the outdoor life that a mild climate encouraged the Greek to lead, but in any
event, the lack of interiors treated with a distinction that can be even
remotely compared with that of the exteriors is an outstanding trait
of Greek architecture. In this and in other characteristics to be noted
elsewhere, it is the product of an attitude that is still primitive but in
the refinement of structural forms and decoration and in the clarity
and logic that characterize their presentation, the outstanding contribution of Greek thought to western culture is symbolized and the
primary reason for considering it the culmination of the primitive point
of view is seen.

Clarity of effect, logical construction and refinement of detail are
qualities which characterize the Greek way of thinking in all its expressive forms, but many other values were sacrificed to attain them.
One of these was variety. Greek architecture expended its energy in
the creation of very few types of buildings, notably the temple and
the theatre; not more than a dozen subjects were considered worthy
of treatment in Greek tragedy, while Greek sculpture was limited
almost entirely to representation of the human body. These limitations were conscious, however, and self-imposed by the Greek temperament which sought to master the world by knowing it and which could
know it only through a process of simplification. A similar limitation
is apparent in the anthropocentric philosophy of the Greeks, according
to which man was the measure of all things, a factor which is combined with the emphasis on intellectual procedure and reasoned understanding implied by knowing as the final phase in evaluating experience

to establish the attitude that finds its architectural expression in the qualities of clarity, logic and refinement.

In making the temple the object of his best architectural efforts, the Greek was of the same mind as the Egyptian, and the procedure he followed in perfecting its form was very similar too (Fig. 29). Evidence for the early stages of the evolution that resulted in a building like the Parthenon is in the scope of archaeology rather than the history

Fig. 29.—Athens. The Parthenon. Restored model.
*Metropolitan Museum, N. Y.*

of art, but it is certain that the first temples in Greece were like thos of Egypt in being buildings like the houses of the time but larger in size and more permanent in construction. Some of the earliest of these date in the tenth century B.C. and were apparently little more than huts of round or elliptical shape from the testimony of their foundations. A subsequent stage is characterized by elongated walls on the sides but retains a curved or apsidal end which in time is also squared up to produce a rectangular form in plan. At this stage, the Greek house-temple must have been very similar in appearance to the Mycenaean megaron (Fig. 28), existing examples of which might indeed have influenced the conceptions of the eighth-century builders; it consisted of the walls enclosing the room that contained the image of the god, which was entered through a porch of columns enclosed between the projecting ends of the side walls and covered in all likelihood with a roof that curved up or may even have been gabled. The next step in the development of the monumental temple form in Greece appears to have been the surrounding of the building with a row of columns, a stage which was reached in all probability about the middle of the seventh century B.C., for it is found in the temple of Hera at Olympia, one of the oldest Greek temples of which there are more than the most fragmentary remains and which was erected about 640 B.C. This marks the final stage in the assembling of the various parts that went to make up the Greek temple; henceforth the efforts of Greek builders were directed toward refining these elements to achieve the most ideal and perfect effect.

The heart of the Greek temple plan was the sanctuary in which stood the statue of the deity to whom it was dedicated. Known in a Greek

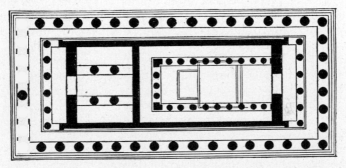

FIG. 30.—Athens. THE PARTHENON. Plan.

building as the *cella*, it may be the entire walled-in part of a small temple, but in such a structure as the Parthenon it is somewhat more developed (Fig. 30), being in two sections. The principal room is entered from the eastern end and is the shrine in which the statue of Athena to whom the temple was dedicated was placed; the smaller chamber at the western end was the treasure room. In a temple as large as the Parthenon, the cella and the treasure room are surrounded on the outside by a peristyle, the free-standing columns that provide a covered passage around the walled-in portion of the temple; smaller ones were usually provided only with columnar porticoes at one or both ends such as form the inner porches of the Parthenon. No fixed rule determined the number of columns so employed; there are eight on each end of the Parthenon, but six is more usual while larger structures had as many as ten or twelve.

The most distinctive external feature of the Greek temple, both structurally and decoratively, was the column, whether Doric (Fig. 31) or Ionic (Fig. 32) in style. These names are given in accordance with

the geographic area in which the two forms are most frequently found
—the Doric type having been used chiefly in the western part of the
Greek world that was settled by the Dorians while the Ionic predominated in the eastern or Ionian region. It was from the mingling of
these races that the Greek of the fifth century was descended and his
architecture indicates this fact in the use of Doric and Ionic forms side
by side and combined in the buildings on the Acropolis of Athens
(Fig. 36). Both types seem to have developed along somewhat similar
lines but without much interaction until the two general regions were
given temporary political unity by the founding of the Athenian Naval
Confederacy after the defeat of the Persians in the battle of Salamis in
480 B.C. and their final expulsion from Greece.

Before examining more closely the two basic types of Greek column,
it should be pointed out that both Doric and Ionic forms are determined
in accordance with rules which regulate not only the details of the
column but also its relationship to other parts of the building. This
relationship is known as the order—a term that implies the whole
organization of the building and is not limited to the column alone.
A third order in Greek architecture that makes its first appearance late
in the fifth century B.C. was the Corinthian; as the Greek used it, it
was a variation of the Ionic from which it differed only in the form of
the capital.

The Doric order is the more simple in appearance of the two principal
Greek types and is also the more straightforward in expression of function of the various elements that go to make it up (Fig. 31). The base
of the order is a series of steps—usually three—upon which the mass
of the temple rests. The shafts of the peristyle columns spring directly
from the topmost step which is usually called the stylobate although
this term is specifically applicable only to the portion immediately
under the column. These shafts are circular in section and taper slightly
toward the top with a very slight bulge or outward curve, called entasis,
in their profiles which reaches its greatest deviation from a straight line
about one-third of its height above the stylobate. The surface also
is grooved vertically with a series of hollows—usually twenty in number and elliptical in section—called flutes; the sharp edges at their
junctures are known as arrises. Near the top of the shaft, the arrises are
cut by a horizontal groove above which the shaft flares slightly in the
necking where the flutes die away. A series of horizontal grooves above
the necking separates it from the even more pronounced flare of the
echinus whose elliptical profile leads to a heavy square slab called the
abacus. Necking, echinus and abacus make up the capital, which
combines with the shaft to form the column. The space or inter-
columniation between two columns is called a bay.

Above the columns and resting directly on the abacus blocks in a

Doric building is a plain horizontal beam called the architrave. It is surmounted by the taenia, a continuous rectangular moulding, from

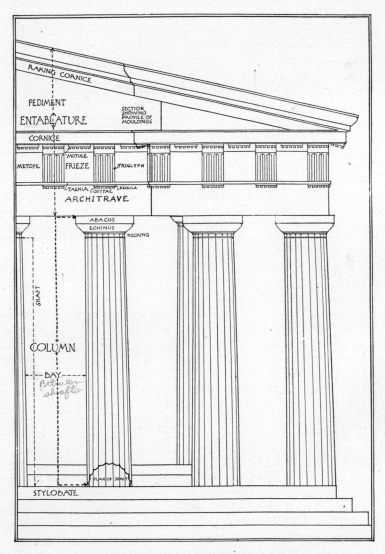

RAKING CORNICE

PEDIMENT

ENTABLATURE

SECTION
SHOWING
PROFILE OF
MOULDINGS

CORNICE

METOPE | MUTULE. FRIEZE | TRIGLYPH

TAENIA GUTTAE REGULA

ARCHITRAVE

ABACUS
ECHINUS
NECKING

SHAFT

COLUMN

BAY
Between
shafts

PLAN OF SHAFT

STYLOBATE.

FIG. 31.—THE GREEK DORIC ORDER.

whose lower edge a small block with six pegs depends over each column and each bay, the blocks being regulae and the pegs guttae.

Above the architrave comes the frieze of alternate triglyphs—the panels with flutes—and metopes; these latter may be plain or with forms

FIG. 32.—THE GREEK IONIC ORDER.

carved in relief (cf. Figs. 259, 264). The cornice projects immediately above the frieze, its soffit or lower face slanting to continue the line of the roof; it is provided with pegged slabs or mutules on the soffit, one for each triglyph and each metope. Above the cornice, a moulding is provided along the sides of the building with decorated openings for water spouts (Fig. 29); it slants upward on the ends to form the top of the gable. This slanting moulding is called the raking cornice; the flat triangle it forms with the horizontal cornice is the pediment, in which sculptured figures were often placed (cf. Fig. 256). All those parts of the order above the columns when taken together form the entablature.

Many details of the Doric order suggest—like those of Egyptian building—construction in material other than the stone in which they are best known, and there is ample justification for reaching the conclusion that they evolved in the process of reproducing in more durable materials traditional structural elements originally created in wood and brick. The capital, for instance, must have been originally a slab of wood placed between a supporting tree trunk and the architrave to keep it from splitting; a similar consideration produced the Minoan column (Fig. 25), of which the capital may well have suggested the form of the Doric echinus. The peg-like guttae on taeniae and mutules are also reminiscent of the practice of wood joiners in fastening one plank to another. Other details, notably the triglyph and metope frieze, seem to have developed out of using both brick and small pieces of wood for construction. The ingenious and plausible suggestion of L. B. Holland that provides the hypothetical origin of this feature of the Doric order (Fig. 33) is based on such an assumption from examination and correlation of many measurements from existing examples of the order in which elements like the regula, taenia, triglyph cap and mutule are all nearly equal in size, suggesting a basic unit of measurement or module such as would have been supplied originally by some small linear value like the thickness of a brick which is the mathematical root of all the larger dimensions of the building. In a brick wall surmounted by a roof, the openings near the top which may have been to let smoke out of the interior would have been ten bricks in height and separated by small piers upon which the roof rafters were supported and which were faced with blocks of wood with chamfered corners as protection from wind and rain. This supplies the triglyph of the frieze, the metopes being open spaces as, indeed, its name implies in Greek. Other than the suggestions inherent in the order itself, there is also literary evidence to the same effect of forms originally created in brick and wood used in Doric buildings. Pausanias, a Greek traveler of the 2nd century A.D., mentions in a guidebook of the ancient world which he wrote that a column at the entrance to the treasure room of the temple of Hera built at Olympia about 640 B.C. was still of wood when he visited the place, and the cella walls of the same temple are known to have been of sun-dried brick on a base course of stone. As was the case with the similar translation of forms that took place in Egypt, the motive was desire for greater impressiveness and permanence in the house of the god than was found in human habitations.

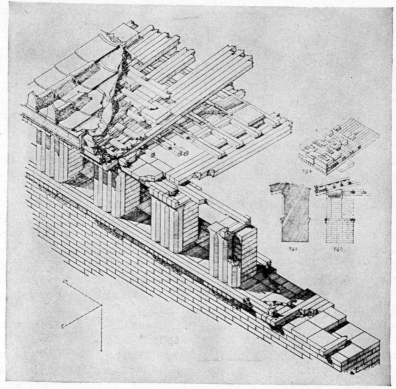

*Holland*

FIG. 33.—HYPOTHETICAL ORIGIN OF THE DORIC ENTABLATURE.

The proportions of the Ionic order (Fig. 32) are not as heavy as those of the Doric manner, the height of the shaft being from eight to ten times the greatest diameter which is at the bottom, while the Doric is about five or six times its greatest diameter as a rule. Another point of difference is the invariable use of a base between the Ionic shaft and the stylobate; this base is variously constituted, but the arrangement seen in the diagram of two convex mouldings separated by a concave one is the more usual type in Greece proper. Twenty-four flutes of semicircular section separated by flat fillets instead of the sharp Doric arrises are found on the shafts which taper, may have slight entasis, and are terminated at the top by a moulded necking. The capital of the Ionic order is its most strikingly individual feature; a band or echinus rests on the necking of the shaft and is usually carved with a pattern of alternately oval and pointed forms making an egg-and-tongue moulding. The cushion-like form resting on the echinus droops over its sides in two hanging spiral scrolls or volutes; upon it rests a square thin abacus of which the edge is moulded.

Like the Doric order, the Ionic entablature consists of architrave, frieze and cornice, but the nature of each of these parts is different. The architrave is in three horizontal bands of which the upper two are stepped slightly forward, and its upper edge is moulded, with the leaf and tongue in this case. The frieze above it may be either a continuous band of relief sculpture or a series of small blocks called dentils; the former was the case with the example here illustrated (Fig. 32) although the figures are not represented in the diagram; late examples, after the fourth century B.C., sometimes have both figured frieze and dentils in the same order. The cornice and raking cornice have the same general form as the comparable elements in the Doric order but differ in the character of their decorative mouldings. An origin in forms initially composed of brick and small pieces of wood may be assumed for the Ionic types as well as for the Doric, the voluted capital being originally a saddle block on top of a wooden shaft and the dentils of the frieze the projecting ends of roof beams.

The Corinthian order which the Greek employed as a variant of the Ionic in the latter part of the fifth century and during the fourth involves the use of all Ionic elements but the capital. For this was substituted a form composed of a core shaped like an inverted bell with rows of leaves around the bottom and volutes springing from them in the center of each side as well as at the angles where they support a rather heavy abacus block with concave sides (Fig. 34). The leaves are modeled after those of the acanthus plant, a perennial that still abounds in Greece and which also suggested the motives appearing in some Greek mouldings. Unlike the Doric and Ionic capitals, the Corinthian type was not developed from an originally structural form but appears to have been conceived from the outset as a decorative element. Its invention was attributed by classic tradition to a bronze-worker named Callimachus and the character of its details—both leaves and scrolls—suggests metal models. First used in interiors, its popularity in the Hellenistic period of the third century B.C. and afterwards, when it replaced the Doric and Ionic almost completely, was a consequence in part of its easy adaptation to certain problems in designing the angles of peristylar buildings that are presented by both Doric and Ionic styles. In the former, the problem is to achieve a satisfactory compromise between structural tradition and decorative perfection in establishing a relationship between the angle column of the peristyle and the end triglyph in the frieze above; in the latter, the basically two-sided volute pattern of the scrolls is not as effective in giving a sense of support to the top of the shaft when seen from the side as from the front. As long as the Greek was willing to strive for the visual perfection that characterizes the design of fifth-century buildings,

FIG. 34.—Epidauros. Museum. CORINTHIAN CAPITAL FROM THE THOLOS.

these problems were faced and disposed of, if not solved to perfection; with the relaxation of this idealism that came in later periods, the easier way of avoiding them altogether which the Corinthian capital made possible was preferred.

The history of Greek architectural thought which reaches its climax in the fifth century B.C. reveals an even and logical evolution that is one of the factors differentiating it most vividly from the static and unvarying forms of Egyptian building. An early temple like the *Basilica* at Paestum (Fig. 35) which was built about 550 B.C. in a Greek city a little to the south of Naples on the west coast of Italy is a good example of the archaic phase of the Doric style. One detail that so characterizes it is the odd number of columns in the façade colonnade, a direct reference to the elemental practice of having a row of columns running the length of the cella to aid in supporting the roof and carried out to the peristyle at each end where it results in placing a column in the center; the visual effect of placing a solid on the axis of the symmetrical design of the façade is seemingly to divide it in half and so impair its unity. The shape of these columns is another archaic characteristic; the taper and entasis are so pronounced that the shafts seem too weak to support the entablature in spite of their heavy proportions in which the height is but 4.4 times the greatest diameter.

Fig. 35.—Paestum. The Basilica.

The excessive flare of the echinus and the thickness of the abacus blocks are other details whose exaggeration is indicative of a style in its formative stages, reproducing as they do the descriptive characteristics of wooden forms but investing them with the ponderousness which the structural limitations of stone imposed. This is the point in the evolution of Greek architectural style that corresponds to the way of thinking revealed in the massive forms of Egyptian building, but beyond which the Egyptian never went.

The most complete and perfect statement of the ideals of Greek architecture corresponds in time with the highest achievements in all Greek thought, coming as it does in the Golden Age of the fifth century B.C. The political independence of the country had been made possible by the defeat of Persia at Marathon and Salamis in 490 and

480 B.C. and the sense of national individuality that began to develop in consequence found expression in the formation by the previously

FIG. 36.—Athens. THE ACROPOLIS.

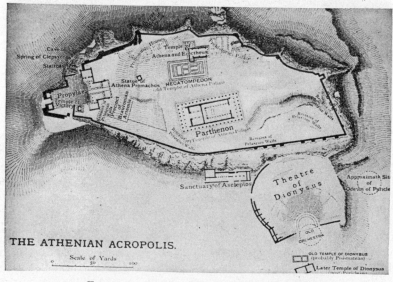

FIG. 37.—Athens. THE ACROPOLIS. Plan.

disunited city-states of a naval federation in which Athens played the dominant rôle from 461 to 430 B.C. Under the leadership of Pericles, funds raised by the federation to build a huge fleet were diverted to other ends, including the monumental embellishment of the *Acropolis of Athens* (Figs. 36, 37), the great hill of rock that is the heart of the city. A rough and irregular mass of stone that measures approximately 1000 feet in length in its longest dimension from west to east, it provided an unsurpassable site for the monuments erected upon it.

The main approach to the Acropolis from the city below was from the west through a monumental gate or entrance portico called the

FIG. 38.—Athens. THE PROPYLAEA. From the east.

*Propylaea* (Fig. 38). Begun in 437 by the architect Mnesicles, the work was forced to be abandoned in 432 before it had been completed and the unfinished building has suffered much damage, but the principle forms of the structure can be observed as a result of restorations that have given to the façade facing the Acropolis something of its original character. It was conceived as a gabled structure with Doric columns forming porches on west and east fronts, flanked by smaller buildings of which but one on the outer side was completed, the others being held up by previously existing structures that encroached upon the site required for the entire building, and left incomplete by cessation of the project. The central bay of each façade was wider than the others by the amount of one triglyph and metope to permit the passing of chariots in ceremonial procession; foot passengers used the openings on the side. This central passage was flanked by columns that sup-

FIG. 39.—Athens. THE PARTHENON. From the northwest.

ported the roof of the structure and were Ionic rather than Doric since the more slender proportions of that order made possible greater height for a given base diameter, one of the first instances known of the employment of both orders in one building. The general arrangement was traditional for entrance porticoes, but its perfection of structural and decorative detail was such that the Athenians took even greater pride in it than they did in the Parthenon.

Passing through the Propylaea, the observer beholds the *Parthenon* to his right on the south edge of the rocky plateau which is the summit of the Acropolis (Fig. 39). The most complete example of the Doric style in temple architecture ever built, it was begun by Iktinos and Kallikrates in 447 B.C. and completed fifteen years later. Approximately 100 feet wide on the stylobate and nearly 230 feet in length, it had eight columns on the front and seventeen on the sides, the angle columns being included in each figure. Inside the peristyle, a second row of columns at each end formed inner porticoes (cf. Fig. 30) from which wooden framed doors led into the cella at the eastern end and the treasure room at the western one. Above these inner portico columns, the usual Doric frieze of triglyphs and metopes was replaced by a continuous figured frieze in the Ionic manner which also encircled the entire cella; it represented the Panathenaic procession, a quadrennial celebration in honor of Athena to whom the temple was dedicated. Nothing remains today of the interior walls and columns of the cella, but descriptions make approximate restoration possible (Fig. 40) although some details such as the source of illumination arc points of controversy. The heroic statue of Athena made of ivory and gold by Pheidias stood near one end of the cella, which was surrounded on three sides by a double range of Doric columns that probably supported a flat timber ceiling under the gabled roof; four Ionic columns apparently performed the same function in the smaller treasure room at the other end.

Sculpture formed an integral part of the Parthenon design in the form of figures and carved mouldings. The frieze around the wall inside the peristyle has been mentioned, but in addition each metope in the building was carved—ninety-two in all—and there were groups of figures in the round in both east and west pediments, a body of sculpture superior in amount and quality to that of any other temple in the Greek world. The mouldings that are used in great profusion throughout the building are of a similar perfection. Color was used as an accessory to carving in all parts of the building as some remaining patches indicate, and the effect (cf. Fig. 29) must have been very different from the monotonous whiteness that is part of current notions of Greek architecture.

The construction of the Parthenon reveals a degree of technical skill that is astounding. Earlier temples like the Basilica at Paestum were usually built of some material like coarse limestone covered with a thin layer of marble stucco, but the Parthenon was of marble throughout with the exception of the wooden door frames, doors and the

FIG. 40.—Athens. THE PARTHENON. Interior. Restored model.
*Metropolitan Museum, N. Y.*

timbers of the roof. No mortar was used anywhere; the columns were built up in horizontal sections or drums fitted together with joints so tight they can hardly be seen; the blocks of marble forming the walls are laid with similar care, with adjacent faces highly polished and held together by iron cramps let into slots and fixed in place with melted lead. The marble used in its construction—and for all the fifth century buildings on the Acropolis—was quarried from nearby Mount Pentelicus; it contains a considerable amount of iron which has caused it to weather to a rich golden brown in color. It was also of very fine grain which made possible certain minute and delicate refinements of form that contribute greatly to the impression created by the building.

Some of these refinements have been mentioned previously such as the entasis of the columns, the subtle, almost imperceptible swelling of the shafts which makes them seem to yield slightly under the weight resting on them with the result that they appear to be alive and elastic instead of stiff and inert as would be the case if the profiles were mathematically straight. The same effect is secured in the building as a whole by making the surfaces of stylobate and entablature curve slightly upward in the center of façades and sides; the amounts of curvature are very slight—about two and three-quarter inches on the fronts and about four on the sides—but the part they play in the effect of the building is perceptible none the less, for they with other similar refinements are responsible for the impression of life and vitality in the structure. Other minute variations from mathematical regularity are seen in the columns, whose axes are not strictly vertical but tilt slightly inward, and the diminution in width of the space between the angle columns and those adjacent on each side. None of these variations are so large as to be obtrusive; a casual glance would lead an uninformed observer to conclude that everything in the design of the building was mathematically exact and regular and this was one impression which the architects wished to create. But they also wanted the structure to have a sense of life and organic unity which it would have lacked had it been no more than mathematically correct, and the manner in which they achieved this end was by these minute variations from mathematical exactitude. Nothing could illustrate better the pains which the fifth-century Greek would take to create plastic forms characterized alike by the semblance of mathematical perfection and of organic life than these meticulously calculated and executed effects.

Comparison of the Parthenon with the earlier Basilica at Paestum (Fig. 35) will make clear both the objective differences in detail of the two buildings and the ultimate formal purpose of the Doric architect. The exaggerations of mass and contour of the columns in the Basilica have disappeared, the shafts of the Parthenon examples being more slender, the tapering and entasis less pronounced and the bays of the peristyle somewhat wider. These qualities all contribute to an effect of organically articulated form rather than mere massiveness, of subtle refinement rather than power. That this was the ideal toward which the evolution of Doric style was directed and that its attainment was in the Parthenon is indicated by the fact that no changes of any importance in the order as it was embodied in that structure were made after it was completed. Whatever could be said with the vocabulary of the Doric order has been said once and for all in the Parthenon and any attempt to enlarge upon that involves a different ideal and a changed expressive idiom.

On the north side of the Athenian Acropolis almost directly across from the Parthenon stands the building which in many respects reveals the highest attainments of the Ionic way of thinking in architecture. The *Erechtheum* (Fig. 41) was begun about 421 B.C., but like the Propyla-a and unlike the Parthenon, it was never finished except in so far as the completion of the part now standing was concerned; this occurred about 406 B.C. The building occupies an extremely uneven site which slopes rather sharply toward the northwest with the result that the floor of the north porch—the one farthest away in the illustration—is about ten feet below the level of the eastern one. This was a circumstance which the architect had to accept, however, for the temple was erected to commemorate an event of great significance in the legendary history of Athens which occurred on that spot, the famous contest between Athena and Poseidon to determine which of the two should be the patron deity of the city. Poseidon struck the rock with his trident, causing a horse to spring out, his gift to mankind upon which he staked his claim to patronage of the city. Athena responded by making an olive tree grow nearby and was awarded the decision. The mementos of this contest—a spring of salt water marking the spot where the horse emerged, and an olive tree—had to be taken into account in laying out the building.

The cella of the Erechtheum was a rectangle about sixty feet in length and something over thirty feet wide, the longer dimension running in a general east-west direction. Like the Parthenon, its internal division is no longer visible and there are no remaining indications of its exact nature though it must have been subdivided since at least three deities were there worshiped—Athena, Poseidon, and Erechtheus in whose honor it was named, a legendary semi-divine being who had been reared by Athena and who established her worship in Athens. There are three porches, on the east, north and south sides; the east and north ones are provided with Ionic columns but these are replaced by statues of maidens called caryatides in the one on the south. It is possible that the complete original plan called for another chamber to the west which would have been equal in size to the one that was built. Had it been constructed, the entire plan would have been symmetrical with respect to the short north-south axis, with the north porch and that of the caryatides in the center of the long sides. This was not accomplished, however, for the area to the west of the existing portion of the building was consecrated to another deity whose priests

Photo Kidder Smith

Fig. 41.—Athens. The Erechtheum. From the southwest.

would not yield their rights and the Erechtheum was perforce left in a fragmentary state.

So great were the difficulties of general planning involved in the site of the Erechtheum that its architect apparently gave up all hope of achieving a harmonious and unified design such as that of the

FIG. 42.—Athens. THE ERECHTHEUM. DOOR OF THE NORTH PORCH.

Parthenon and lavished his best efforts instead upon the decorative details. The south wall of the cella for all its simplicity of character is beautifully proportioned and the texture of the fine-grained Pentelic marble of which it is formed lends itself admirably to the execution of the minute detail that characterizes the base and cornice mouldings. A notable feature of the building is the door opening into the cella from the north porch (Fig. 42), historically important as the first example of a portal in Athens framed in stone instead of wood, and luxuriously decorated with mouldings and rosettes. The Ionic capitals

of the six columns that support this porch are among the most elaborate
and beautifully executed in Greek building (Fig. 32), with the triple
spiral of the volutes and the delicate lotus and palmette moulding
on the necking of the shafts. Other decorative details of the building
include a palmette frieze along the top of the walls and a continuous
band of white marble figures against a background of black Eleusinian
limestone in the entablature.

FIG. 43.—Athens. THE ERECHTHEUM. THE PORCH OF THE MAIDENS.

The small porch on the south side of the Erechtheum (Fig. 43)
differs from those on the north and east fronts in having the figures
of maidens instead of columns to support the architrave. This practice
of substituting human forms for architectonic ones is not without
precedent in earlier Greek buildings in the Ionic style, but it was not
a general one, possibly because of a temperamental reticence in imposing mechanical functions upon an organic form which would have

been distasteful in general to the Greek. The Maidens of the Erechtheum are in no wise crushed beneath their burden, however, for the
straight drapery folds of the robes over the legs supporting the weight—
the outer one in each case—and the relaxed inner legs create an abstract rhythm of upward movement that successfully effects the impression of adequate support for the entablature. The bulk of the
entablature is reduced in actuality, furthermore, as well as in its effect
of weight in the design by omission of the figured frieze that surrounds
the rest of the building, a row of dentils being used instead.

FIG. 44.—Athens. THE CHORAGIC MONUMENT OF LYSIKRATES.

Like the Parthenon that is its counterpart in perfection in the Doric
style, the Erechtheum marked the end of a certain way of thinking since
no further progress along those lines seemed possible. That way of
thinking was one which preferred an opulence of effect not inherent
in the more severe Doric forms, and subsequent ventures in this direction found even the Ionic mode somewhat over-restrained. These are
the general circumstances that supply the background for the later
popularity of the *Corinthian* order which was first used in the late fifth
century B.C. and of which one of the finest examples of Greek times—

that in the Tholos at Epidauros (Fig. 34)—was executed about 350
B.C. The order was first used exclusively in the interiors of buildings,
however, the earliest instance of its employment as part of the external
design of a structure being supplied by the *Choragic Monument of
Lysikrates* (Fig. 44) erected in 334 B.C. as the monumental support of
a bronze tripod awarded the winner of a choral contest in Athens in
that year. Upon a square base or podium is a circular cella surrounded
by six columns recessed in the wall though free from it. The bases
and shafts are identical in design with those of the north porch of the
Erechtheum, but the capitals are composed of acanthus leaves and
spiral volutes that form an even more complex pattern than those in
the example from Epidauros. They support an entablature which is
also made up of Ionic elements but combines friezes of dentils and
figures in a way that has no precedent in fifth-century design. A single
slab of marble carved in imitation of tiles covers the monument and
is surmounted by an elaborate finial of acanthus leaves which supported
the bronze tripod for which the structure as a whole was planned to
serve as base. Although the monument is Greek in origin and the details
follow fifth-century models for the most part, the general effect is one
of more ostentation than characterizes earlier designs and indicates a
tendency that is even more pronounced in later architecture of the Hellenistic and Roman periods.

Among the most precious inheritances of western civilization from
the culture of Greece are the tragedies and comedies written by her
great playwrights such as Aeschylus, Sophocles and Aristophanes. The
origins of the drama in Greece are obscure and controversial and no
less so are those of the structures in which it was performed, save for
the fact that both were related to the worship of Dionysos. A theatre
with permanent seats built on the south slope of the Acropolis in the
fifth century B.C. seems to have been the first example of what was to
be one of the most characteristic Greek architectural forms. Its present
state is largely the result of modifications and rebuildings, but part at
least of the *Theatre at Epidauros* (Fig. 45) is as originally designed.
It was built about 330 B.C. after the designs of Polykleitos the Younger,
who was also the architect of the Tholos at the same place whence
came one of the finest of fourth-century Corinthian capitals (Fig. 34).
In plan it is characteristic of all Greek theatres in being built around
a circular orchestra with an altar dedicated to Dionysos in the center
about which the action of the play took place. The seats rise in circular curves from this orchestra and are supported on the sides of a
hill which naturally or as a result of excavation slope inward to form
concentric banks that are a little more than semicircles. On the other
side of the orchestra from this auditorium was a rectangular building

of which the foundations are still visible; this was not a stage as might
be thought from modern theatrical usage but the background of the
action in the orchestra, taking the place in all likelihood of the temple
façade that performed a similar function in the earliest dramatic per-
formances; it also served in all probability as a sounding board to enhance the acoustic properties of the structure which were always very
carefully considered. This background building was given character

FIG. 45.—Epidauros. THE THEATRE.

by the use of orders—usually Doric but sometimes Ionic; otherwise
the attention of the architect was directed chiefly toward laying out
the auditorium seats in such a way that hearing and seeing were
facilitated. Like the temple, the function of the Greek theatre was
primarily one of the loftiest character; it would be a mistake to consider
it solely as a place of entertainment and amusement as it is today.

   In selecting a site naturally adapted to the particular requirements of
his structure, the Greek theatre designer was following the usual procedure of his time. It would be difficult to imagine the buildings on
the Athenian Acropolis, for example, in any locations other than those
on which they stand that would reveal them to better advantage (Fig.
36); the identity of each is clearly established in its own and individual
terms like so many sculptured forms distinctly against the sky. This
formal self-sufficiency is, indeed, one of the outstanding characteristics
of Greek buildings of the Golden Age and of other Greek art forms
of that time too, as will be shown elsewhere; it is a direct consequence

of the enjoyment felt by the Greek in organically conceived plastic form controlled and directed by the same unerring sense of proportion that made the solution of a problem in geometry a source of genuine pleasure to him. There is another aspect of this self-sufficient perfection of the Greek building to be considered, however, and one that reveals both its limitations as an attitude and those of the period which accepted it as an ideal. A glance at the plan of the Acropolis (Fig. 37) will establish the fact that there was no attempt on the part of the architects to lay out their buildings with any concern whatsoever for their communal effect. Propylaea, Parthenon and Erechtheum each have a different axis of their own and exist as forms which not only can be understood as isolated entities but cannot be understood in any other way, for if a relationship to some other object be needed to establish the significance of the one in question, it follows that that significance is not inherently complete.

The conception of a building as something isolated from its surroundings and uninfluenced by them is an elemental one, and to the extent that Greek architecture illustrates this, it is a primitive way of architectural thinking. At the same time, it is also the most highly developed phase of primitive architectural style, for it represents an ideal of form that is organically integrated and organized—a whole that is the sum of its parts instead of being only a statement of them like the Egyptian temple (Fig. 16) which is as objective as the Greek in its presentation of detail but in which there is no controlling relationship between the various parts save for the simple order of the axis. If the Greek did not wish to perceive the possibility of an organic relationship between his building and its surroundings comparable to that which is realized with such perfection within the mass of the building itself, this is only characteristic of his attitude which accepted the facts of nature as fixed and permanent values that had to be recognized and understood, and that could be controlled and directed but not modified or changed. A later generation than that of the fifth-century Athens of Pericles and Iktinos was to question the attitude embodied in their works, however. When the Hellenistic city of *Priene* in Asia Minor was laid out in the late fourth century B.C. it was done not by seeking to develop a pattern from nature as the earlier Greek planners would have done but by imposing a pattern upon the natural elements of the site (Fig. 46). The fortification walls are irregular in following the conformations of the terrain, but the city within is laid out in regular blocks divided by streets which run due east and west the length of the city and north and south across. The latter are so steeply slanted up the side of the hill that the majority are negotiable only by steps, yet no trace of the differences in level appears in the relationship of the buildings to the plot plan as a whole or to each other. The most important single element in the plan is not a building but the open market square or agora which is surrounded by colonnades on three sides; the temple and precinct of Athena are given places of importance but without in any way modifying the basic compositional

Zippelius

FIG. 46.—Priene. THE CITY. Restored.

plan of rectangular blocks separated by the streets. The plan of Priene is important as one of the first attempts to lay out an entire city in accordance with a preconceived scheme instead of following the accidents of natural conformation; the gridiron that resulted is a type that has also been developed in many more modern cities.

Two outstanding characteristics appear in reviewing the architectural style of the Greeks. The first is its objectiveness. Nothing has to be added to the statement of function visibly implicit in the various forms in order to understand the part they play as details or as a whole, a factor which is involved, for example, in the almost exclusive pre-occupation of the Greek builder with post and lintel construction instead of the arch whose manner of operation cannot be so clearly grasped visually since comprehension of the objectively intangible lateral thrusts is essential if its form is to be understood. This makes for simplicity of form as well, but within that simplicity of the design as whole is great complexity of detail. This is the second outstanding quality of the Greek way of thinking in architecture, that from complex and involved detail it is able to distill a fundamental simplicity and unity of effect. It thus becomes a manifestation of a high order of the purpose of all Greek creative activity—to attain infinite variety and refinement within a consciously restricted expressive scope. The limitations that were self-imposed in the attainment of this goal make the Greek way of thinking seem far removed from application to modern problems, for the complexity of contemporary life is such that the conscious simplification which seemed justified to the Greek by the harmonious character of the results is impossible of reattainment. But the beauty of clear and logical thought continues as a constant element in the forms of Greek architecture and an imperishable reminder of the enrichment of experience that is now as then a possible consequence thereof.

# Chapter IV. Roman Architecture.~~~~

THE GREEK OF THE FIFTH CENTURY B.C. LIVED IN A
world characterized by infinite refinement of thought within a precisely delimited scope, hoping to master and control that world by purposely restricting his experience of it and by exploring its objective
characteristics to the greatest possible extent. As has been seen, this
world was one of short duration and the perfectionism that characterized it was modified almost in the very moment of its achievement.
The diffusion of Greek culture that followed the conquests of Alexander
the Great (356-323 B.C.) is the outstanding cultural phenomenon during
the Hellenistic period of the third and second centuries B.C. in which the
ways of thinking apparent in architecture might be characterized as
Greek at basis but colored by regional distinctions that result in forms
of quite different expressive content than those in which the original
types were created. Destined to become the foremost of these regional
architectural styles was that of Rome which, after a period of internal
consolidation and external expansion in which high points were the
destruction of Carthage and the conquest of Greece in 146 B.C., became
the dominant political and cultural force in the Mediterranean world
and so remained for the better part of six centuries. Architecturally this
dominance is symbolized by a remarkable consistency of style over almost the entire western part of Europe in the north and the lands
bordering on the Mediterranean from Spain in the west to Syria in
the east as well as a considerable portion of northern Africa. The
contrast between the vast area of Roman architectural style and the
geographically limited Greek manner is but one of the significant points
of difference between them.

Standing in relationship to the culture of Rome in somewhat the
same place as that of the Aegean period to Hellenic Greece was the
civilization of the Etruscans, the most powerful of the varied peoples
in the Italian peninsula before the Romans themselves. The remains
of their architecture are relatively scant but they are known to have
made effective use of the arch in stone construction, particularly in
walls, and also to have employed post and lintel forms. Among the most
impressive preserved examples of their buildings are tombs—some rock-

cut and others built of stone—in whose painted decoration points of contact with the archaic phases of Greek art are to be noted but whose architectural character is directly determined by a process of translating wood idioms into stone, the basic type being that of the house. The *Etruscan temple*, on the other hand, appears never to have been carried to that point; it was almost always preponderantly of wood (Fig. 47) with some portions, notably the entablature, protected by a casing

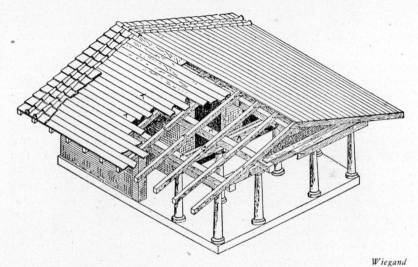

*Wiegand*

FIG. 47.—ETRUSCAN TEMPLE. After Vitruvius.

of terra cotta. The preservation of such buildings being manifestly impossible, the appearance of the temple is a matter of conjecture but with reasonably dependable evidence from two sources—small votive models made of terra cotta and the description of an Etruscan temple by Vitruvius, who wrote a book on Greek and Roman architectural theory in the 1st century A.D. The temple is almost square in plan with a porch of free-standing columns at one end and sanctuaries at the other, the whole raised above the ground on a rather high platform ascended by steps. The roof structure was of wooden beams and rafters covered with tiles. Such a superstructure being relatively light in weight, wooden columns were used quite extensively especially in the earlier period, and even when stone supports came into use the retention of the wooden entablature permitted a wide spacing of the columns that is a salient characteristic of the style. The most common form of column in Etruscan building was a variant of the Doric

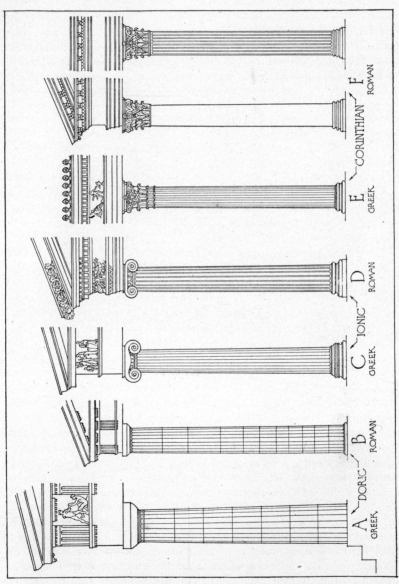

FIG. 48.—THE GREEK AND ROMAN ORDERS COMPARED.

A DORIC GREEK. B DORIC ROMAN. C IONIC GREEK. D IONIC ROMAN. E CORINTHIAN GREEK. F CORINTHIAN ROMAN.

from which it was possibly derived; the chief differences as indicated by Vitruvius' "Tuscan" column are the absence of fluting and entasis in the shaft and the presence of a compound moulded base equal in height to half the diameter of the shaft. As will shortly be apparent, certain characteristics of the Etruscan temple type reappear in Roman forms, supplying, indeed, a number of features that distinguish them from Greek examples.

The orders were used quite extensively in Roman building and the same types occur that are found in Greece, but with characteristic changes (Fig. 48). The Doric and Ionic were used only rarely by Roman architects and then in forms of somewhat lighter proportion than in Greek examples. The Roman Doric shaft is provided with a base, the echinus is a simple quarter-round moulding, and the entablature is relatively thin. Figured and dentil friezes were regularly employed together in the Roman Ionic, and the flutes of the shaft, when they occur, are grooves of semicircular rather than elliptical section. The flutes were commonly omitted in Roman columns in fact, a consequence of preference for colored and veined marbles over the more uniformly toned varieties found in most Greek buildings in which the flutes were a necessity in visually defining the column form itself. Most popular of the Greek orders in Rome was the Corinthian, a fact which is not surprising in view of the growing preference for its forms that has already been noted in later Greek and Hellenistic design. Its intrinsic richness of appearance was often augmented by various additions to the basic forms of acanthus leaves and volutes, one that was quite extensively employed being the so-called "Composite" capital in which Ionic scrolls are placed over the rows of leaves. The first appearance of this order was on the *Arch of Titus* in Rome (Fig. 49), which was built about 82 A.D. to celebrate the conquest of Jerusalem in 70. Another Roman addition to the orders was the console or modillion—a bracket in scroll form appearing under the horizontal and raking cornices (Fig. 48, E-F)—also for the purpose of enriching the decorative effect of the order as a whole.

No less important than the changes made by the Romans in the details of the orders is the way in which they were used. In any Greek building of the fifth century (Figs. 38, 39, 41) the column is a structural fact. It is used as a supporting member and its physical function is defined by its form; for, standing free as it does, it is at once apparent that what rests upon it is sustained by the column and by the column alone. This is true even of a Greek structure like the Monument of Lysikrates (Fig. 44) in which the columns are recessed in the wall of the circular cella but are none the less clearly distinguished from it. By contrast, the composite columns of the Arch of

Titus (Fig. 49) are applied to the mass of the rectangular piers. They are not completely in the round but are partially attached to the wall behind them, and are clearly far from being the supports of the super-structure, that physical function being performed by the piers and the barrel vault spanning the opening. The function of the columns in such a case as this is primarily descriptive—the column being a decorative symbol which, when applied to the pier, indicates its sup-porting function in a way that the basic form of the pier itself could not achieve.

FIG. 49.—ROME. THE ARCH OF TITUS.

The *Maison Carrée* at Nîmes in southern France (Fig. 50) was com-pleted in 16 B.C. Being the best-preserved Roman temple extant, it illustrates the typical characteristics of the form. It stands on a podium or base ascended at one end by a flight of steps in the manner of the Etruscan temple (Fig. 47) which it also resembles in having a porch of free-standing columns. The order is continued on the outside of the cella which is the entire width of the structure for two-thirds its length of about eighty-six feet; in the form of applied Corinthian half-columns, the order has the same descriptive purpose here that has been pointed out in discussing the Arch of Titus, though it is possibly even more appropriate in interpreting the function of the temple wall which

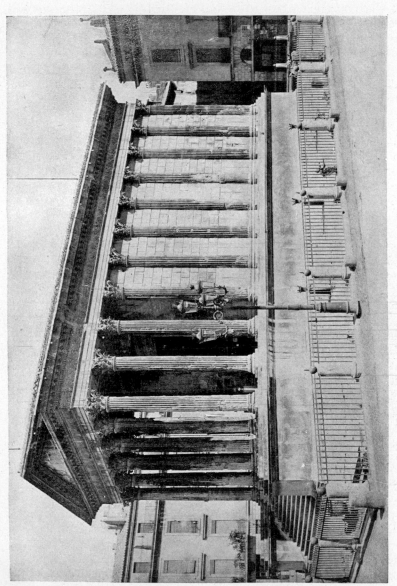

Fig. 50.—Nimes. The Maison Carrée.

supports the entablature as well as performing its more basic duty of enclosing the internal space of the sanctuary. The proportions of the entablature are more like those of Greek buildings than is usually the case in Roman structures, but the use of a rich *rinceau* or band of foliage for the frieze is different from the Greek figured type and the cornices are provided with modillions. The column shafts are monolithic instead of being built up in drums, another feature distinguishing usual Roman practice from that of the Greeks. The Maison Carrée is one of the few Roman buildings in which linear refinements like those of the Parthenon can be noted; there are convex curves in plan on the long sides and variations in the intercolumniations are visible on all four fronts. The fact that the temple was built under Augustus Caesar, who is known to have had great enthusiasm for Greek ideas, may explain the presence of refinements in this case at least.

No less significant as an indication of Roman character and temperament than the ways in which their temples differ in details of design from those of the Greeks is the different conception of the part to be played by the temple in designs involving not one but a series of buildings. Note has been taken elsewhere of the limited character of Greek ideas in this category which resulted in the casual relationships of buildings to each other illustrated by the plan of the Athenian Acropolis (Fig. 37). If this plan be compared with that of a characteristic Roman forum (Fig. 51), the contrast is immediately apparent. The forum in a Roman city was the principal place of public gathering. There is good reason to believe that it developed from the open space always found in the center of Roman military camps which were laid out in rectangular walled areas with two principal streets intersecting at right angles; this basic scheme seems to have been the point of departure for many Roman city plans as well, although the possibility of its employment in the latter for religious reasons cannot be overlooked. In the military camp, this space was dominated by the headquarters; in the city forum, the temple was the central element in a scheme that was as symmetrical with respect to it as circumstances of site permitted. In the case of *Trajan's Forum*, which was designed and laid out in the early 2nd century A.D. (Fig. 51), nothing was permitted to interfere with carrying through this formal idea; the result was one of the most grandiose large-scale architectural compositions of Roman times. A monumental gate led into an open court with columnar porticoes on three sides behind which to right and left of the central axis were buildings laid out in semicircular plan; this court was the forum in the specific sense. Beyond it lay the Basilica Ulpia, a structure whose main axis was at right angles to that of the forum, roofed over and surrounded within by colonnaded aisles; at each end were large apses where legal court was held. Continuing on the principal axis of the ensemble beyond the Basilica Ulpia was a smaller open court in the center of which rose the memorial column erected by Trajan to celebrate his victory over the Dacians; two buildings entered through porches at the sides of this court were libraries. At the rear of this court, Hadrian, Trajan's successor, erected a temple to his memory which like all the other principal buildings in the ensemble is placed

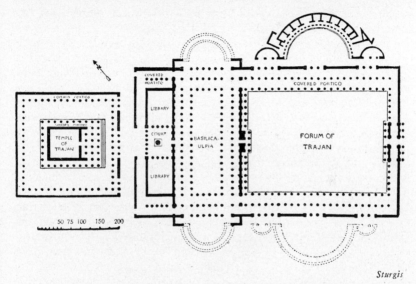

*Sturgis*

FIG. 51.—ROME. THE FORUM OF TRAJAN. Plan.

symmetrically on the principal axis; it is similar in general type to the Maison Carrée in being placed on a high podium with steps at one end and a porch of free-standing columns.

The scheme of the Forum of Trajan reveals an attitude basically different in principle from anything comparable with it in either the Greek or the Hellenistic phases of classic architecture. The Greek in planning his building sought only the site which would enable it to appear to best advantage as an isolated form; he tried to develop a pattern from nature, and the axis of his structure was a controlling element only in its individual design (Fig. 37). The Hellenistic designer attempted to impose a pattern upon nature (Fig. 46) by laying out his buildings in a preconceived scheme but without any pronounced accent upon any one. The Roman builder makes everything subordinate to the principle of the axis in planning, taking even less account of

Fig. 52.—Rome. The Colosseum.

natural conformation than his Hellenistic predecessor, creating the complex and abstract symmetrical perfection that was his ideal with no concern for anything but its realization as a means of attaining an overwhelming effect. It is the part played in such centralized ensembles by the temple that determines its form in large measure; the subordination of all elements in its design to the façade that results from making it accessible only from the front is a characteristic of the Etruscan temple too (Fig. 47), but it remained for the Roman to carry to their logical conclusion the implications of the form with respect to large-scale planning.

In developing the forum with its varied architectural forms and its grandiose effects, the Roman reveals an attitude quite different from that which produced the limited perfectionism of the Greek, and this contrast becomes even more apparent when the variety of types of building in the Roman style is observed. One of these types is the amphitheatre, a huge bowl-like structure in which great public spectacles like the gladiatorial combats were held. Of those which have been preserved in whole or in part, the largest is the *Colosseum* in Rome (Fig. 52), which was built between 75 and 82 A.D. From the outside, it consisted originally of an elliptical three-storied wall of arches and piers surmounted by a fourth without openings. All are decorated with orders—Doric on the ground level, Ionic for the second story and Corinthian for the third and fourth; the three lower orders are of columns with the shafts three-quarters free of the pier while the fourth is of flat pilasters which are rectangular in section. Like the columns applied to the cella of the Maison Carrée (Fig. 50), those of the Colosseum are descriptive rather than structural in function; their relationship to the piers behind them is such as to indicate the supporting purpose of those piers for it is clear from the fact that the arches still stand even in those places where the applied columns have been removed that they are the essential structural elements in the building.

The arches in the outer wall of the Colosseum are not the only ones to be noted in its construction. Behind them are vaults—long, uninterrupted semicircular ceilings of masonry which cover the corridors and passageways within the structure itself—the ends of some of which have been exposed by the removal of the outer shell of piers and orders. The vaults of the outer corridors that go around the Colosseum are of two types—barrel and groined (Fig. 53, A-B). The barrel vault is the simpler of the two, resembling nothing so much as a series of arches set face to face; the groined vault is formed by causing two barrel vaults of equal span and height to intersect at right angles, the resulting diagonal lines being the groins. The groined

vault is sometimes called a cross vault. In both cases, since the arch
is the basic structural principle, buttressing is essential to the stability
of the vault. That of the barrel type must be continuous because its
thrusts are uniform throughout its entire length; in the groined or
cross type of vault, buttressing is needed only at the angles since the
thrusts of the two barrel elements that make it up are mutually de-
flected along the groin. In the ground story of the Colosseum there are
two elliptical corridors which are both barrel vaulted, the lateral
thrusts of the outer one being absorbed by the heavy wall over the
arcade on the outside and by those of the inner vault on the inside.
This is buttressed in turn on the inside by the ends of other vaults
perpendicular to it which covered the passages leading into the interior of the amphitheatre and also supported the marble seats in the
two lower sections.

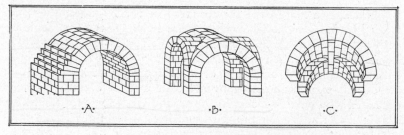

·A·                    ·B·                    ·C·

FIG. 53.—BARREL AND GROINED VAULTS.

The value of the vault in a structure like the Colosseum is considerable. It made possible, for example, relatively unobstructed passageways for circulation that would have been out of the question if the
heavy mass of the upper stories had been supported by lintels on posts.
Another advantage of a practical nature lay in the fact that it could
be built of concrete instead of stone at great saving in cost. Roman
concrete was a mixture of small stones or broken bricks combined with
a cement made up of volcanic dust mixed with water; this was poured
in moulds—first a layer of brick and stone and then the dust and
water mixture until the form was complete—where it hardened into
a homogeneous mass of surprising strength and durability. Reinforce-
ments of brick or of cut stone were often introduced into the moulds
before pouring. As an inexpensive medium lending itself to vast structural projects, concrete was admirably suited to the Roman architectural
temperament which found satisfaction in the large and grandiose and
had but little interest in refinement and perfection. The great public
buildings of the Empire, which could not possibly have been built

in any other medium known at the time, have no equal for sheer massiveness before the structures of the late 19th and 20th centuries constructed with the aid of steel. They were cheap to build, moreover, since material otherwise useless could be employed in the mixture; many buildings in the city of Rome erected after the famous fire of 64 A.D. in the time of Nero are of concrete in which the stones show signs of having been burned and hence were useless as structural material in their own right. In buildings of monumental character, the

Fig. 54.—Rome. The Basilica of Maxentius.

concrete of walls and vaults was concealed by a facing of cut stone or of brick laid to form a pattern—a type of ornament that parallels in principle the applied order.

Characteristically Roman in function, size, structural character and material is the *Basilica of Maxentius* (Figs. 54, 55), which was begun in 310 A.D. by the emperor for whom it is named although it is also associated with his successor, Constantine, who finished it about 320. Even in ruins, the structure is impressive as it stands between the Roman Forum and the Colosseum. The basilica as the Romans used it was a building designed to accommodate gatherings for various purposes—as places of business, law courts as in the case of the Basilica Ulpia in Trajan's Forum (Fig. 51) and the like—and the problem of providing unobstructed shelter on the scale involved made the vault an effective means of covering it, although some earlier examples—again like the Ulpia—were roofed with timber ceilings supported on columns. The size of the building was also a direct cause of the employment of concrete in its construction for it is 265 feet in length and 195 feet in width and the height to the top of the groined vault over the central aisle is 120 feet. The choice of a groined vault to cover the central aisle was dictated by the necessity of providing light in the interior. A barrel vault requires buttressing for its entire length and

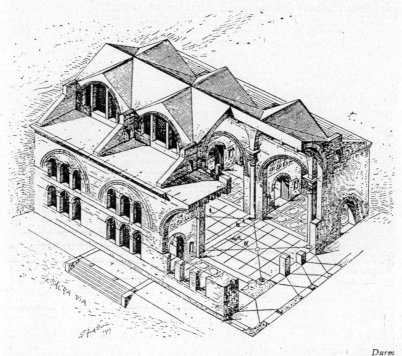

*Durm*

Fig. 55.—Rome. The Basilica of Maxentius. Restored perspective.

openings in the sides above the level of the vault spring weaken it for that purpose; but the groined vault permits openings in the sides as large as the entire arch if desired, since the thrusts are concentrated at the angles. In the Basilica of Maxentius, the large semicircular windows in the upper level are in the sides of the groined vaults over the central aisle which were covered on the outside with gabled roofs of tile to protect the masonry of the vaults. The thrusts of the vaults are buttressed by the sloping walls above the side-aisle roofs between the windows referred to, those being the points where they are concentrated. The side aisles were covered with barrel vaults whose axes were perpendicular to the principal one of the building; those over the north aisle still exist (Fig. 54), an impressive tribute to the durable concrete of which they are made, for they are still intact after centuries of neglect.

FIG. 56.—Rome. THE BATHS OF CARACALLA. Restored.

A problem in planning and construction similar to that of the Basilica of Maxentius was posed in another characteristically Roman type of building—the public baths which were the centers of Roman social life as the basilicas were their places of business. The necessity of accommodating large crowds of people in an enclosed space was present in them too, and the groined vault was extensively employed in the covering of the principal rooms (Fig. 56), as can be seen in the illustration of the changing room in the *Baths of Caracalla* built chiefly between the years 211 and 217 A.D. Here, as was generally the case with Roman buildings of purposely impressive character, the concrete walls and piers and vaults were faced with thin slabs of marble or covered with moulded stucco, and the huge Composite columns surmounted by partial entablatures which appear to support the vaults are likewise no more than decorative in function.

Concrete as the basic material and the arch principle of construction in yet another form—the dome—are the outstanding structural char-

FIG. 57.—ROME. THE PANTHEON. Exterior.

acteristics of another Roman building of great importance, the *Pantheon* (Figs. 57, 58). Historically it is of interest in being the oldest roofed building of monumental character in the world that is still intact, the major portion—the rotunda and its dome—having been erected by Hadrian about 120 A.D. It is built of brick and concrete with a stone facing. The exterior (Fig. 57) is impressive chiefly by virtue of its great bulk for the dome is so low that it can hardly be seen from the narrow side streets and is almost entirely cut off from view in front by the porch of sixteen columns surmounted by a broad pediment. The

interior (Fig. 58) is as high as it is wide at the greatest diameter—
141 feet—the dome being something less than a hemisphere as the circular wall supporting it rises vertically to a height of about 75 feet.
This wall is in two levels, separated by a full entablature resting on
Corinthian columns and pilasters which stand in and frame respectively a series of deep recesses in the thickness of the wall itself. Above
the columns framing the entrance portal and the niche immediately
opposite, the entablature breaks out from the wall in a characteristically
Roman way. The upper level of this wall is decorated with pilasters
that frame niches and panels and support a cornice from which the
dome springs. The inner surface of the dome is faced with concrete
and is decorated with a pattern of rectangular recessed panels known
as coffers, a motive also to be observed in the vaults of the Basilica of
Maxentius (Fig. 54) and the Baths of Caracalla (Fig. 56). The reduction in mass of vault or dome effected by this device is its structural
function; in the Pantheon, the coffers play a decorative part as well in
emphasizing the upward over-arching lines of the cupola and focusing
attention upon the circular opening at the top. This opening, known
as an oculus, is about twenty-nine feet in diameter and is the only
source of light in the interior.

The construction of the Pantheon is very ingenious. The recesses
in the circular wall supporting the dome are so deep that it is converted into what is actually a series of eight heavy piers. Upon these
piers, the weight of the wall above and that of the dome are concentrated by a system of arches built into the thickness of the wall itself
—arches which are both radial and tangent to the circumference of the
dome and wall. When used in this way, they are called discharging
arches since they serve to carry the crushing weight resting upon them
away from the space they span to the members by which they themselves are supported. The Pantheon is thus not an inarticulate mass of
brick, stone and concrete but a highly organized system of arches
clothed in a skin of facing material. Although the concrete is a hard
and homogeneous mass and became so as soon as it had dried out in
the forms, the lateral thrusts of the dome are carefully buttressed by
the stepped masses visible at its springing on the exterior (Fig. 57),
an indication of the care with which the purely structural problems
of the building were studied.

Interesting though these technical considerations are in explaining
how the Pantheon was built, they are subordinate in importance to
the effect created by the form to which they contribute. The Pantheon
was one of the first buildings to be consciously composed as an interior
—as a volume of space that is given character by the solids enclosing
it. In its case, this character is one of balanced geometrical unity,

created by equality of dimensions in height and diameter and isolated
by the cupping and defining effect of the dome which is emphasized
by the coffered pattern of its surface and is given scale by the precisely

*Isabelle*

FIG. 58.—ROME. THE PANTHEON. Interior, restored.

limited indication of external space that is provided by the oculus at
the top. So powerful is the sense of enclosed space created by the
interior design of the Pantheon that it seems almost a tangible substance to be isolated and handled as objectively as any Greek architect

treated column or architrave. In his endeavor to compose architecturally with elements that are specific and comprehensible through the senses, the Roman reveals himself of the same classic stock as the Greek; in his extension of that conception to include imponderable space as well as tangible and plastic forms the difference between his broadened point of view and the purposely limited one apparent in Greek design is equally apparent.

The impression created by the grandiose and ostentatious public buildings of Rome of a people quite materialistic in temperament is

FIG. 59.—TYPICAL POMPEIIAN HOUSE. Restored.

reinforced by observation of the houses in which they lived. The Greek of Pericles' time in Athens was privileged to gaze every day at temples of surpassing beauty, but he lived in a house that was little more than a place in which to eat and sleep and so lacking in qualities of monumentality or even of permanence that its form is indicated by but the scantiest remains. By contrast, Roman houses, though based on Greek prototypes, were relatively pretentious. The type of house found in excavating the city of Pompeii from the lava that swept over it when Mount Vesuvius erupted in 79 A.D. is not the only kind the Romans built, but the remains thus discovered permit a quite accurate restoration of the original forms (Fig. 59). The outside was unimpressive because the narrow streets in the residential district of the city did not permit any but the necessary features of enclosing walls and entrances to be developed. Within, the average house was divided into two main parts. The first is focused about an open court, entered from the street through a passageway and surrounded by columnar porticoes, which is called the atrium; it was usually provided with a fountain in the center, and was the semi-public portion of the building where the owner might carry on his business. At the back of the atrium was another passage, usually with a recessed niche or small room at one side in which the household gods were enshrined, which led to the second principal division of the house. This was also a porticoed court but it was called the peristyle (Fig. 60) and was often treated as a

FIG. 60.—Pompeii. THE HOUSE OF THE VETII. THE PERISTYLE.

garden with shrubs and plants and decorated with sculpture. This was the center of the domestic quarters of the building, with dining rooms, reception rooms and retiring rooms on the first floor; the bedrooms and the like were on the second floor. At the rear of the peristyle court, a large reception room was located which frequently overlooked another garden back of the house proper. The walls of this court and of the rooms opening from it were often painted very elaborately (Fig. 364) with episodes from myth and legend or with landscapes. The whole was well designed for ease in living with considerable regard for privacy and comfort.

Some of the most impressive examples of Roman building were of an entirely utilitarian nature and made no pretense to architectural distinction. Such are the aqueducts by which water was brought, frequently from points at some distance, to the cities of the Roman empire. They consisted in general of water channels, open or enclosed and lined with concrete or finely jointed stone, which were carried on arches where they appeared above ground or through tunnels in the mountainous regions in which the water supplies were usually found. The flow of water was insured by giving a slight slope to the level of the channel from its source to its termination. The *Pont du*

FIG. 61.—NÎMES. THE PONT DU GARD.

*Gard* near Nîmes in southern France which was an important Roman provincial city is part of one of these aqueducts (Fig. 61). Built in the 1st century A.D., it was a part of a system totaling more than twenty-five miles in length which was underground for the most part but crossed the river Gard on a system of arches some 900 feet in length and about 180 feet high. These arches were built of stone, laid in vertical slices, with wooden centering used only in the head where it was supported by the projecting courses still visible, a procedure that in its economy is characteristic of Roman structural practice. No attempt was made to give the Pont du Gard formal architectural character in the usual Roman manner by means of applied ornament, but in its fine proportions, the skillfully varied dimensions of the two lower ranges of arches and the strong rhythm set up in the heavy piers topped off by the smaller arches above, there are features which give it great distinction none the less. Comparison with a modern bridge (Fig. 196) reveals the parallel in method and effect of similar structures built with other materials and utilizing different principles but motivated in much the same way.

Roman architecture is nearest to general modern taste of all the historical styles. In its utilitarianism, its striving for effects of grandiose and overwhelming character and its frank divorcing of structural and ornamental facts, there are many parallels to average contemporary building. But it also produced many different types of building of which some have proved capable of adaptation to the needs of other and later civilizations. The football stadium of today is only a variation of the Roman amphitheatre (Fig. 52), and the vaulted walls of the public baths have served as models for the concourses of innumerable railroad stations, a notable instance being that of the Pennsylvania Station in New York whose design is based directly on that of the Baths of Caracalla in Rome (Fig. 56). Such parallels as these suffice to show the eminently practical point of view of the Roman architect to whom the form of a building was something to be established primarily by material considerations of usefulness and stability as determined by its plan and the materials of which it was constructed. His conscious conception of architectural character in a formal sense is indicated by the striving for effects of size and ostentation that appear in his monumental structures and that are achieved primarily in terms of sheer bulk and by lavish use of applied decoration. Both of these qualities are overshadowed in ultimate significance, however, by the space concepts that represent in the final analysis the most important contribution of the Roman to the art of building. Whether it is a question of relating the exterior design of a building to its environment or of giving character to its internal physical room, the value of space as an architectural element was first sensed by the Roman and has been a factor in the history of the art ever since.

# Chapter V. Architecture of the Early Middle Ages

THE GRANDEUR OF ROMAN BUILDINGS WAS A reflection of Roman military and economic power, and as long as those were maintained, the character of Roman architecture was consistent. Even at the moment when such a characteristic example of this style and attitude as the Basilica of Maxentius (Fig. 54) was in process of construction, however, there were positive indications of change in the life and thought of the Roman Empire, for in the year 313 A.D. a royal edict issued at Milan in northern Italy gave official recognition to a religious cult that had existed in Rome for many years but had never attained the status of such recognition before—Christianity. Ten years later, in 323 A.D., the emperor Constantine himself professed Christianity, which became thenceforth the religion of the state, a position of eminence that was to be maintained for many centuries to come. If recognition of Christianity was not in itself an indication of the undermined power of the Roman state—as might be inferred from the legend of Constantine's conversion on the field of battle when he renounced the pagan gods of Rome to avail himself of the help of God—the fact that it was followed seven years later by the establishment of Constantinople as a second capital of the Empire, located in the Near East at the juncture of the Bosporus and the Sea of Marmora, is a clear revelation that the rigid political and social discipline that was the core of Roman civilization no longer existed. The subsequent history of the Western or Latin Empire bears this out. Rome itself fell before the attack of Alaric, a German chieftain, in 410, and the once vast empire north of Italy was almost completely dismembered by Vandals, Goths and Franks during the 5th century. In 476, another German leader, Odoacer, ascended the throne of the Western Empire and although the relations he established with the Eastern Empire were maintained by Theodoric the Goth and were even strengthened briefly during the 6th century when Justinian reigned in Constantinople (527-565), there was no effective opposition to the incursions of yet another barbarian tribe—the Lombards—in

568 which may be considered as marking the end of even the smallest
pretense at maintenance of the political autonomy of the Western Empire. By contrast with this history of progressive decadence, the fortunes
of the Church mounted almost from the very beginning of its recognized existence. The appeal of its doctrines to those who were revolted
by the spiritual and moral laxity of the times was great and the integrity
of its leaders won many converts to the faith with the result that it
was upon the bishops who stayed in their churches to meet the invaders when officers of the Empire fled their posts that the ruling
authority fell. The relationship thus suggested is symbolic of the culture
of the Middle Ages; for the secular power of the Roman Empire the
spiritual power of the Church was substituted, and for the better part
of a thousand years such continuity and consistency of thought as is
to be found in western Europe is that which existed within the walls
of churches and monasteries.

In the Western or Latin Empire, the architecture of Christianity
differed but little at first from that of Rome in so far as comparable
types of buildings are concerned. The problem confronting the Christian architect was not without certain parallels in Roman building for
it was essentially the provision of an enclosed space wherein the faithful
might gather to partake of the sacraments and to hear the preaching
of the Word of God. The type of building developed to meet these
requirements is known as a basilica (Figs. 62-64), and its form appears
to have been based upon elements drawn from a number of sources,
notably the Roman house and basilica. It may seem strange that the
Church fathers did not hesitate to avail themselves of pagan ideas in
creating the earthly shrines of their faith, but it is to be noted that
this is a direct parallel of the forms of the faith itself, for many Christian practices were taken over almost directly from the numerous pagan
cults that flourished in Rome during the first centuries of the Christian
era. Furthermore, at the time that the first Christian edifices were being
built in the west, practical considerations weighed more heavily than
spiritual scruples. The Church was urgently in need of its own buildings in which the cult might be properly housed and it drew upon all
available sources for ideas of design and also for structural materials
—a fact responsible not only for the form and general character of the
buildings but also for much of the undeniably poor construction to be
noted in them.

The *Old Basilica of St. Peter* at Rome (Figs. 62-64) was built on
the site of the Circus of Nero in which the saint for whom it was
named met his death and near which he was buried. Erected at the
order of the emperor Constantine, it was begun in 324 and consecrated
in 326. The Constantinian basilica was demolished in the early 16th

century to make way for the Renaissance basilica of the same name, but its form is well known from drawings and descriptions, and the various restored plans and other views give a possibly more informative

FIG. 62.—Rome. OLD ST. PETER'S. Restored perspective view.

impression of the appearance of a typical Early Christian or Latin basilica than any single existing structure. It consisted in general of

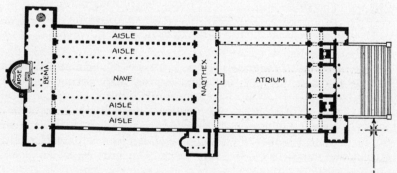

FIG. 63.—Rome. OLD ST. PETER'S. Plan.

two parts which are clearly seen in the perspective view and the plan —the atrium and the church proper.

The atrium is the open court surrounded by columnar porticoes with

a fountain in the center that stands before the church building. Its
general architectural character resembles that of the similarly named
part of the Roman house (Fig. 59) from which it was derived in all
likelihood since the form doubtless provided for certain features of the
rites celebrated in the church which had been developed earlier when
such celebrations were held in the houses of the faithful. In the Christian basilica, the atrium was a place where persons could assemble
who were not qualified to participate in the actual ritual inside the
church, such as the penitent or the unbaptized. Architecturally, it
served to seclude the building from the turmoil of the street. The

FIG. 64.—Rome. OLD ST. PETER'S. Restored elevation.

portico of the atrium through which access was had to the church proper
is known as the narthex; it sometimes appears alone as an entrance
porch in churches that do not have complete atriums.

The church of St. Peter's was divided internally into five aisles
(Fig. 64) extending almost its entire length and separated from each
other by rows of columns; the central and largest of these is called
the nave, the others being the side aisles. The number is not fixed,
for only the largest churches had five; as a rule the nave was flanked
by one aisle on each side but some very small churches had the nave
alone. At the opposite end of nave and side aisles from the entrance
is another aisle or space of which the longitudinal axis is at right angles
to that of the main body of the church; it may be seen in the exterior
view where it is covered by the gabled roof perpendicular to that of the

principal part of the building. This is called the transept and is a feature found as a rule only in the largest of the Latin basilicas where it usually projected beyond the side-aisle walls, giving the entire plan the shape of a capital letter T. Opposite the end of the nave on the other side of the transept, a semicircular space called the apse is seen. In it or directly in front stood the altar with the throne of the bishop placed at the end and flanked by the seats of the lesser clergy forming a semicircle.

The elevation or vertical design of the interior of an Early Christian basilica like the Old Church of St. Peter (Fig. 64) consists of the rows of columns defining the nave and side aisles, those on either side of the former being called the nave arcade and supporting a wall with a row of windows at its top. This row of windows supplies direct illumination for the nave and is called the clearstory. Light for the side aisles comes from windows in the outer walls which also support the slanting roofs by which they are covered. These roofs as well as the gabled ones over nave and transepts are supported by wooden beams assembled in triangular trusses which rest directly upon the walls.

Simple as the basic elements of the basilican church are, the importance of the type is very great for it is the fundamental scheme that is found in by far the majority of all Christian places of worship. The building is invariably oriented unless unavoidable conditions make it impossible. The usual Christian practice is to place the entrance at the west with the altar and apse at the eastern end—a procedure which was definitely established during the 4th century, although some of the first Christian basilicas like Old St. Peter's are oriented in the opposite direction. In either case, the practice of axial orientation is one of the points that distinguish the Christian basilica from the pagan buildings called by the same name (Figs. 51, 54, 55) and from which certain features of the churches appear to have been drawn. As has been pointed out before, the law and business basilicas of the Romans were primarily places for the accommodation of large crowds and in this they were the logical models for the Christian places of meeting. Some of the Roman basilicas were vaulted (Fig. 55), but most of them appear to have had wooden roofs resting on clearstoried walls which were supported by columns (Fig. 51); the division of the interior into spaces corresponding to nave and side aisles with apses at the ends is also quite clear. The changes made in the type by the Christian builders are of great importance, however, as indications of the differing significance of the forms involved. The entrance to the pagan basilica was usually in the center of one of the long sides and the effect of the interior from that point was one of static symmetry with the columnar arcades carried around the ends and the apses behind them completing an effect of balance and equilibrium, as can clearly be seen in the plan of the Basilica Ulpia in Trajan's Forum (Fig. 51). The entrance to the Christian basilica, on the other hand, is in one of the short sides with a single apse opposite that is made clearly visible by omitting the returned colonnades and thus becomes the focus of the interior design—the goal toward which the movement created by the rhythmic succession of the rows of side columns inevitably tends. Stated in strictly formal terms, the distinction between the Roman basilica interior and the Christian type is that between a design unified by symmetrical balance of plastic forms and one unified by an axis of movement; expressively, the distinction is between emphasis on visible and objective elements on the one hand and abstract and intangible sensation on the other. The significance of these distinctions lies in the intimation therein present of a new orientation of thought in the western world—an orientation that reaches its clearest exposition in the Gothic cathedral of the 13th century.

From a structural point of view, the Early Christian basilica was quite simple. In the first ones to be built, the nave arcade columns supported straight lintels (Fig. 64) which were often taken from pagan buildings and used without any concern for the continuity, or lack of it, in the consecutive carved patterns on them. Later on, semicircular arches were substituted for the architraves as in the church of Santa Sabina (Fig. 65) which was begun in 425. Apses were covered with half-domes of masonry, but a wooden roof over nave and side aisles was invariable. This was structurally the least satisfactory part of the building, for the liability of a roof of this type to destruction by fire was very great and constantly present if the numerous contemporary records of such buildings being struck by lightning and completely destroyed can be trusted. It may seem strange that the fireproof masonry vaults used with such skill by Roman architects were not employed over Christian buildings as well for there is evidence that such structural methods were practiced even later than the time when the first churches were built, but the explanation is not far to seek. The Roman buildings from which the Christian basilica was derived were usually roofed with timber, as has been pointed out, and the type was thus one with which coverings of this character were generally associated. Furthermore, wood was relatively plentiful and a trussed roof could be constructed more easily, rapidly and cheaply than even the simplest vault—considerations that weighed more heavily than both the relatively impermanent character of the wooden roof and the incoherent character of its relationship to the rest of the interior which is obvious in the view of Santa Sabina. The walls were usually of rubble faced with coarse stone or brick in the Roman manner and not very heavy as a rule.

Fig. 65.—Rome. Santa Sabina. Nave, looking toward the apse.

The exterior of the Latin basilica is rarely impressive. The principal façade was sometimes decorated with mosaic (Fig. 62), but the sides were seldom treated by anything more than a series of wall arcades framing the clearstory and side-aisle windows (Fig. 71). The interior, on the other hand, was made the object of extensive decoration designed to amplify and accentuate the focusing movement of the columnar arcades in rendering clear the significance of the altar as the heart of the design. This was preferably in the form of mosaics on the walls below and around the clearstory windows; and if those once at Santa Sabina (Fig. 65) have disappeared, other examples still remain to permit recognition of their effect. These consisted of scenes and figures portrayed by means of small cubes of colored glass held fast in the plaster of the wall (Fig. 365) and they are found in the apse as well (Fig. 72). The glow of shimmering and luminous color that they seemed to shed over the interior did much to assist in creating the abstract and immaterial atmosphere felt to be appropriate to Christian thought. It is hardly likely that this was a conscious factor in determining the character of the basilica for the procedure was a common one in Roman buildings as well; it is known, furthermore, that the ostensible purpose of such decorations was to inform those of the faithful who could not read. But the introduction of color and light in the basilican interior provided elements of an intangible character in the design that are complementary as expressive factors to the axis of movement created by the columns of the nave arcade. The history of European architecture for the better part of a millennium was to lie in attempts to create an adequate synthesis of these elements in the interests of a more comprehensive interpretation of the Christian ideal of emotional belief.

At the same time that the western or Latin portion of the Roman Empire was witnessing the parallel phenomena of political decline and the growth of the Christian Church, the Eastern Empire with its capital at Byzantium—renamed Constantinople—was enabled to pursue a course that was at least spared the physical disruption consequent upon constantly recurring attacks of invaders that so effectively undermined the power of Rome since it enjoyed a measure of protection from the wandering Teutonic and Slavic tribes by virtue of its geographic location. There were still social and economic factors to contend with, however, and the rulers following Constantine (272-337) were weak in authority for the most part; it was not until the reign of Justinian I (483-565) which began in 527 that a consistent architectural expression is found of the mingled classic, Oriental and Christian elements that constituted Byzantine culture.

Christian architecture of the eastern or Byzantine style was developed to meet requirements not unlike those of the Latin phase hitherto considered, in so far as the use to which the buildings were put was concerned. The basilican type of plan with its longitudinal axis lent itself best to provision for these requirements, as has been noted. There are a few structures of this type in the Byzantine area such as the church of St. Demetrius at Salonica in Greece and that of St. John of the Studion in Constantinople, both dating from the 5th century, which are similar in general character to the west Christian buildings of the 4th and 5th centuries in Rome in having naves and side aisles with columnar arcades and wooden roofs. The Byzantine architect was confronted with one very serious problem, however, that his western counterparts did not have to face in building their basilicas —a great scarcity of wood. This imposed the necessity of devising means of covering his structure in some other way and the method that was developed involved the use of the dome. This was a more or less traditional roofing device in the comparatively woodless regions of Anatolia which is now eastern Turkey and of Persia whence it appears the ideas of the Byzantine dome builders were largely drawn. The particular character of the Byzantine domed buildings lies in the method by which the basically circular form is adapted to rectangular shape imposed by the basilican type of plan.

As the Romans used the dome in covering the Pantheon, the problem of relationship between it and its supporting walls was a simple one since the plan of the structure as a whole was circular (Fig. 57); as the Byzantine builders employed it in connection with the basilica, it was a very difficult problem since the most that could be done in laying out the plan was to create a series of square areas over which the dome had to be placed as effectively as possible. The nature of the problem is evident in the first diagram (Fig. 66) where such a square is indicated by the letters ABCD, the sides being four arches as indicated in the fourth diagram; the circle E inscribed in this square is the base of a dome whose diameter is equal to the sides of the area, while the one outside the square has a diameter equal to its diagonal. It is obvious that a dome built in either of these ways cannot be fitted directly to the supporting arches. One method of solving the difficulty was by building a squinch at each angle of the area enclosed by the arches; this is done by laying a lintel across the corners, reducing the square to an octagon and repeating this process, which results in building up the supporting base above the level of the arch tops and at the same time increasing the number of angles in the polygon of the base until it approximates a circle. This method of transforming a square base to a circular one is good enough as a utilitarian measure but is not particularly effective in appearance; it was a makeshift at best and is found as a rule only in buildings of rather elemental character.

The most satisfactory method of fitting a circular dome to a square base is by means of spherical pendentives. In geometrical terms, a

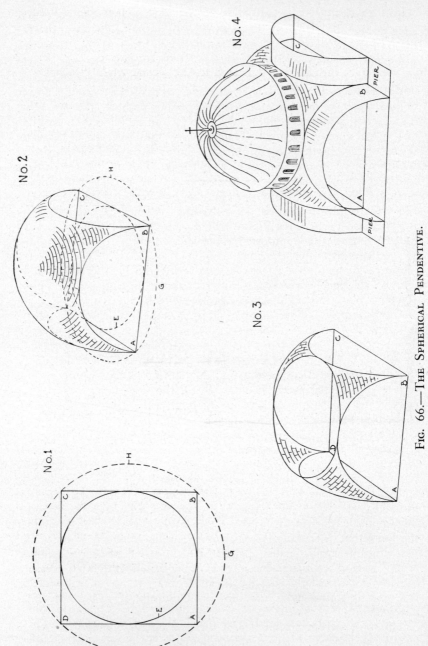

FIG. 66.—THE SPHERICAL PENDENTIVE.

spherical pendentive is a triangular section of a hollow hemisphere whose diameter is equal to the diagonal of a square inscribed in its largest section. The way a series of pendentives looks when arranged to form the support of a dome is seen in the third diagram (Fig. 66); their theoretical formation is indicated in the second where a dome of diameter equal to the diagonal of the square to be covered is shown with four segments cut from it on lines corresponding to the sides of the square base, i.e., *AB, BC, CD* and *DA*. The form shown in the second diagram is a sufficient solution of the problem mechanically because it is a domical covering fitted to a square area. Some *pendentive domes* are known in which the curve from one angle to the one diagonally opposite is a complete and unbroken semicircle. The more usual and more impressive treatment, since it permits greater height to any desired limit, is indicated by the third and fourth diagrams. In the

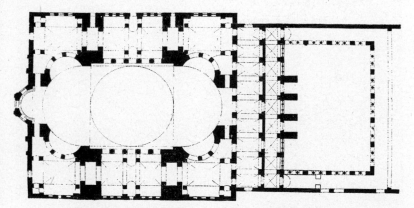

FIG. 67.—Constantinople. HAGIA SOPHIA. Plan.

third, the top of the pendentive dome shown in the second diagram has been removed leaving a circular base supported by the triangular sections that are the pendentives at the four angles; upon this base a cylinder called a drum can be built to any height and finished off with a hemispherical dome as seen in the fourth diagram. Like all arches, those that frame the area to be covered must be adequately buttressed and so must the dome since it functions mechanically like a number of arches intersecting at a common center.

The most impressive example of a dome on pendentives is that in the church of *Hagia Sophia* or Divine Wisdom in Constantinople (Figs. 67-69). Begun by order of Justinian I in 532 to replace an earlier structure on the same site that had been destroyed by fire, it was dedi-

Fig. 68.—Constantinople. Hagia Sophia. Interior.

cated with impressive ceremonies five years later on December 27, 537. The architects were Anthemius of Tralles and Isidorus of Miletus, both coming from regions in which the tradition of erecting buildings with vaults or domes was strong. The building is oriented on a north-west-southeast axis with the apse pointing in the latter direction and is almost a square in plan measuring about 240 by 250 feet exclusive of the narthex and apse. This area is reduced by a series of groined vaulted aisles on the sides in such fashion that the main spatial volume of the interior or nave is about 240 feet in length and 107 in width. This is covered, with the exception of the spaces immediately inside the portal and in front of the apse, by a dome on pendentives, whose diameter is equal to the width of the nave, and by two half-domes flanking it on the principal axis of the structure (Fig. 67). These half-domes are also buttresses for they oppose their masses against the thrusts exerted by the principal dome along the main axis of the building. In this function they are aided by smaller half-domes of which those at the east end may be seen in the view of the interior. The side thrusts of the central dome are not so effectively handled for they are opposed only by the heavy arches connecting the piers at the angles of the space covered by the dome and the massive piers at these same points on the exterior (Fig. 69). It was possibly this inadequate buttressing of the dome's side thrusts that was responsible for the collapse of the original one in 558, although it is probable that the dome itself was somewhat more shallow than the one now over the building and that the supporting arches were of catenary rather than semicircular shape and hence more difficult to buttress. The dome was rebuilt by Isidorus the Younger, a nephew of one of the original architects, who gave it a somewhat steeper pitch and also increased the size of the buttressing piers on the minor axes of the structure, precautions that enabled his dome to stand until the present time in spite of some further small displacements.

The exterior of Hagia Sophia falls short of the interior in distinction (Fig. 69). The four slender spires are minarets built when the church was turned into a mosque after the fall of Constantinople before the Turks in 1453 and must be left out of account. The dome as seen from the outside gives little impression of its actual height of 180 feet above the floor level. This is in part a consequence of its shape which is less than a complete hemisphere to begin with and is further dwarfed externally by the huge pier buttresses on the cross axes of the building. These latter are impressive enough as sheer bulk but are inconsistent in their effective relationship to the dome which is the crowning feature of the structure. This it would have been on the outside as it is within if it could have been higher—either from

resting on a drum or by having a steeper pitch—but the magnitude
of the dimensions involved seems to have precluded either of these
treatments.

The illustrated interior of Hagia Sophia (Fig. 68) reveals its appearance before it was secularized in 1934 when the medallions with
inscriptions from the Koran were removed with beneficial results as
far as its scale is concerned. Color is an important element in the
effect as a whole—from the marble and porphyry columns of dark
green and red, from the veneer on walls and piers of similar materials
sliced in thin slabs and applied to form regular patterns by the vein-

FIG. 69.—Constantinople. HAGIA SOPHIA. Exterior.

ing, and from the mosaics on the pendentives and domes. In the illustration only two of the great archangels in the pendentives can be
seen, for most of the figured ornament of Hagia Sophia was covered
with plaster or otherwise obscured when the structure was converted
to a Mohammedan mosque, a process that has been reversed in connection with its transformation beginning in 1934 from a place of
worship to a museum of Byzantine art.

The initial impression created by the design of the interior is of a
single vast domed space—an impression which yields to one of complexity as the relationship of the minor domes and the colonnaded
aisles and galleries to the central cupola is perceived, but without sac

rificing the effect of great size. This is a consequence of the fine scale of the interior—created by the interacting rhythms of forms and volumes of space in the columns and piers and in the domes and windows. In the effect of space enclosed by form that is thus seen to be the basic concept of the interior of Hagia Sophia, there is a parallel to the Roman Pantheon (Fig. 58) created some 400 years earlier. The pattern of space volumes in the Byzantine church is more complex and subtle than that of the Roman temple, and the definition of the forms enclosing them is blurred and softened by the gleam and color of the patterned marble and mosaic covering them, as if it had been the architects' intention to emphasize the emptiness of the space as the significant element of the interior. To this effect the row of windows at the springing of the dome contributes very powerfully, seeming by its diffusion of light almost to separate the cupola from its supports and suggesting to Procopius, a writer who described the building shortly after its completion, that the dome appeared "as if suspended by a chain from heaven." But the forms enclosing and articulating the space volumes remain definite and comprehensible in spite of the ambiguousness of line and surface induced by the color and gleam of mosaic and veneer, for with his classic heritage of rationalism the Byzantine could never forswear the significance of the tangible and concrete as his western co-believers had done. Classic too is the static balance of volumes created by raising the Oriental dome on pendentives over the Latin basilica in Hagia Sophia, for the vitalizing axis of movement which the western Christian architect introduced in the classic basilican plan is overwhelmed in the domed structure by its centralized and vertical axis. If the marvelous unity of the Byzantine structure seems infinitely more impressive than the inchoate and fragmentary patterns of the western churches, it is none the less the final statement of an attitude that long persisted but never surpassed its first comprehensive statement, whereas the humble Latin basilica was but the first step toward the realization of the most expressive religious architectural form the Occidental world has seen—the Gothic cathedral.

Justinian's reign over the Roman Empire was centralized in the eastern portion, but during his incumbency a measure of control was reestablished over some parts of the western kingdom that had been taken by the Goths from the north in the 5th century. At this time the western capital was Ravenna, a city to the north of Rome, lying on the east coast of Italy on the Adriatic Sea. There a number of buildings erected in the first half of the 6th century reveal the mingling of Latin and Byzantine elements of design. One of these was the church of *San Vitale* (Fig. 70), a structure of octagonal plan which is covered by a dome adjusted to the eight-sided base by warping the walls above the arches to a circle. It was begun in 526 and dedicated in 547. Being octagonal, it follows that it is composed upon a vertical rather than a horizontal axis and is thus of the central rather than the basilican type—a kind of building that was used in the west for some rather specialized purposes such as baptisteries but seldom for a church in the general sense. Much of the interior has been redecorated in a

FIG. 70.—Ravenna. SAN VITALE. Interior.

debased Renaissance style but the original mosaics of the sanctuary are still to be seen (Fig. 365), including representations of Justinian and his queen Theodora accompanied by members of the Byzantine court. Other Byzantine characteristics of the building include the capitals of the columns between the central domed space and the aisle that surrounds it. These are shaped like inverted truncated pyramids whose rectangular faces have been rounded to a circular base fitting the shaft; they are decorated with various patterns cut into the surface of the basket-shaped block which are emphasized by painting the backgrounds black. Above these capitals are other inverted truncated pyramids upon which the arches rest; these are known as stilt-blocks or pulvins and are instrumental in concentrating the weight of the superstructure upon the column shafts in order that the capitals would not be crushed under the varied thrusts to which they would have been subjected if the arches sprang directly from them. There is some precedent for the idea of the stilt-block in the partial entablatures used by

Fig. 71.—Ravenna. Sant' Apollinare in Classe.
Exterior from the northeast.

the Romans over columns from which arches were sprung, but the form in which it appears at San Vitale is characteristically Byzantine.

The church of *Sant' Apollinare in Classe* near Ravenna (Figs. 71, 72) illustrates even more clearly than San Vitale the mingling of Latin and Byzantine elements that took place in the architecture of Justinian's western capital. Built between 534 and 539 and dedicated in 549, it is basilican in plan and is covered with wooden roofs as are the churches of the 4th and 5th centuries in Rome. It lacks transepts, however, and has three apses instead of one (Fig. 71); this is an eastern characteristic as is also the fact that they are polygonal on the exterior and semicircular within. The tower that stands a short distance away from the north side of the building is a later addition. Inside (Fig. 72), the Corinthianesque capitals of the nave arcades are surmounted by

Byzantine stilt-blocks while the soffits or lower surfaces of the arches
are coffered in the Roman manner. Above the arcades, in a band on
the lower clearstory wall on each side, are portraits in mosaic of the
bishops of Ravenna; the half-dome of the apse and the arch opening into
it are adorned with representations in the same medium of Christ and
the apostles—the latter symbolized by lambs—and the saint to whom
the church was dedicated. The interior is otherwise quite similar to

FIG. 72.—Ravenna. SANT' APOLLINARE IN CLASSE. The Nave.

that of the early 5th-century Roman church of Santa Sabina (Fig. 65)
and creates a comparable effect.

Sant' Apollinare in Classe is a symbol in architectural terms of the
fusing elements of Latin and Byzantine cultures that Justinian was
able to bring about in his western capital, and it is also the ultimate
statement of the basically classical-Christian concepts underlying those
cultures. For in 568, within less than twenty-five years after its dedication, an invading horde of Lombards overrunning the Italian peninsula
from the north as far as Tuscany left only isolated regions under the
control of the Empire. These included Rome and Ravenna and Venice
where a late flowering of Byzantine architectural ideas in the west was
to produce one of the best-known examples of the style, the church
of San Marco, which was begun in 1063 after the model of the Church
of the Holy Apostles in Constantinople but which in spite of its
structural and decorative impressiveness was not destined to have any

very extensive influence upon later mediaeval architecture in western Europe. For the rest, Italy entered into a period that was truly a dark age in which the only ray of light came from the efforts of the Church to preserve a measure of culture. In this it was aided by the organized monasticism that was one of the outstanding phenomena of the early Middle Ages. This was a direct outgrowth of the impact of Christianity upon the declining world of classic antiquity which had its origins in the 4th century in the eastern Mediterranean area and spread rapidly in the west during the 5th and 6th centuries. The codification of monastic practice established by St. Benedict at Monte Cassino in southern Italy in 526 was the first attempt at regulating the procedure to be followed by those who wished to withdraw from a confused and chaotic world in seeking their own spiritual regeneration. Its aptness to the times is indicated by the great numbers of monasteries following the Benedictine rule that were founded in northern Europe as well as in Italy in the latter part of the first Christian millennium. If it is exaggeration to suggest that only in them was to be found any perception of the significance of spiritual experience during the Dark Ages, it cannot be denied that theirs was an important part in the preservation of such little of ancient culture as was kept alive at that time.

Under such circumstances as prevailed during the Dark Ages, it is not surprising that the practice of architecture came almost to a standstill. In the few buildings that were erected then, however, certain features which are of some importance make their appearance. The church of *Santa Maria in Cosmedin* in Rome (Fig. 73) was begun in 772 and finished in 795. Basilican in plan and with the tri-apsidal eastern end also noted at Sant' Apollinare in Classe (Fig. 71), the interior is notable for two details. The first is the enclosure by a parapet of marble slabs of a space at the end of the nave immediately in front of the altar; this is the choir in which the participants in the service took their places. The second is the substitution of rectangular masonry piers for some of the columns in the nave arcade. This may have been a consequence of failure to find sufficient Roman columns to complete the arcades which are made up for the most part of pilfered material, and of inability to create satisfactory ones to complement them, or the piers may have been introduced for needed additional strength in the supports of the clearstory walls. In any event, the effect of the pier in the design of the nave was fortunate from the point of view of its expressive character, for it significantly altered the character of the rhythmic procession toward the altar and apse which has been noted as the characteristic feature of the Christian basilican interior. This it did by introducing pauses in the swift and unvaried movement of the earlier interiors (Figs. 65, 72)—points upon which the eye rests momentarily—and the slowing up of the progression thus brought about resulted in a more profound sense of awe and reverence in the ultimate apprehension of the nature of its goal. To say that this effect is completely attained in the rather unprepossessing interior of Santa Maria in Cosmedin is not justified, but the incipient vertical motive there introduced in what had previously been an unequivocally

FIG. 73.—Rome. SANTA MARIA IN COSMEDIN. Interior.

horizontal type of architectural composition is an important innovation. On the outside, the Latin basilica underwent changes of similar formal character for it was during this same period of the 8th and 9th centuries that the practice of erecting bell towers or campaniles was initiated, that of Sant' Apollinare in Classe at Ravenna (Fig. 71) being an example. While the campanile there is not an integral structural element in the exterior design of the building, the fact that a vigorous vertical accent was felt necessary in what was otherwise a strictly horizontal composition is significant.

The modifications of the simple basilica that are seen in the campanile of Sant' Apollinare in Classe and the nave system of Santa Maria in Cosmedin are important as indications of perception by their builders of the unsatisfactory character of the basic type as an expressive

form. It was not in that part of Italy which maintained its relationship
with the existing political remnants of the Roman Empire that the
full possibilities of the modified and developed basilica were to be
realized, however, but rather in the region to the north of the Alps
and in those parts of Italy itself that were culturally allied to it that
the evolution leading to that realization was to occur. Spain, France
and England all preserve structures dating from the 7th and 8th centuries that reveal attempts to adapt regional building methods to
basilican forms; but while these are very interesting as archaeological
monuments, they have but little distinction as works of art, being
simple edifices of brick and rubble and timber for the greater part,
with the ornament consisting of little but rudely carved slabs and capitals and some polychrome materials for the walls. Not until the time
of Charlemagne (742-814) are any buildings to be found that are
comparable in character to the Christian structures thus far considered
when his attempt to rebuild the political structure of the Western
Empire of which he was crowned the ruler in 800 brought about a
brief revival of all the arts. The *Chapel* built at his command in
Aachen, his capital city in the Rhineland, was intended to serve as
the church of his palace and his mausoleum as well (Fig. 74). It is a
structure of the central type for it is a sixteen-sided polygon in plan
on the ground level with two-storied annular aisles, of which the lower
is covered with alternate rectangular and triangular groined vaults,
above which there rises an octagonal dome that is four stories in total
height. Although the building has been much altered since it was
erected between 790 and 804, enough of the central portion remains
to show the general similarity of its design to that of San Vitale in
Ravenna (Fig. 70) upon which it was modeled. The variants from
the prototype are no less important than the resemblances. Structurally
the Carolingian building is much simpler than the church in Ravenna
and in its general proportions it is somewhat heavier although the
Byzantine building must have been known to the Germans for some
of the materials they used came from Ravenna itself. That they chose
a building of central type with a vertical axis of composition as their
model may have been dictated by the somewhat specialized purpose
of the chapel, but the increase in height from three stories in San
Vitale to four at Aachen was hardly a matter of chance since it was
in accordance with what has already been noted as a definite tendency
toward stressing vertical elements in the basilican buildings of the
time.

Charlemagne's Chapel was the finest building of its period in northern Europe and evidently much impressed the men of its own and
subsequent times, for many copies in simplified form were built in

later years. As an architectural symbol of Charlemagne's attempt to recreate the political structure of the Roman Empire, its lack of distinction is evidence of the unintegrated thought of the time which sought its expression in forms that were incapable of embodying it, either political or artistic. For the Latin and Byzantine elements that entered into the amalgam of mediaeval thought supplied at least a

Fig. 74.—Aachen. The Chapel of Charlemagne. Interior.

classic common denominator to the Christian of Rome or Ravenna or Constantinople whereas they offered little if anything to the Teuton whose whole manner of thinking was couched in different terms. The time had not yet come, moreover, in which these various dialects of antique, Christian and northern origins should be fused into a new language. Charlemagne's "renaissance" produced many works of art; but in so far as the motivating impulses were limited in means of expression to the modified classic forms and idioms then current, they were to fail in finding adequate vehicles through which they might become comprehensible.

In the architecture of the early Middle Ages, the shifting emphasis from static and sculptural mass composed for the sake of its external effect that found its most convincing exposition in the Greek temple to a conception of interior space given character by scale and proportion that was the Roman contribution to the art of monumental architectural design is carried still further. But in becoming the instrument of a mode of thought that was intuitive and emotional rather than logical and intellectual, the static perfection of classic architecture underwent perforce certain modifications of which the establishment of an axis of movement in the basilican interior was the most significant. If the resultant forms are inchoate in design and confused in effect, there is in them none the less the germ of an architecture which was to become in time the only one to rival in its expressive unity and comprehensiveness the mode evolved by the Greeks of the fifth century B.C—the Gothic.

# Chapter VI. Romanesque Architecture

THE ARCHITECTURAL STYLES OF CHRISTIAN ROME
and Byzantium resulted from the first attempts to adapt the building
idioms of antiquity to the new functions created by the needs of the
Christian Church. They are manifestations of the same point of view
that framed the theology of the early Church by striving to clothe
the spiritual ideals of the new faith in the garb of classic thought; and
in theology and architecture alike, the antagonism between the antique
spirit that had created the forms and the Christian beliefs for which
expression was sought in them was too fundamental to be overcome.
So long as Christian architecture had to be cast in classic mould, so
long was it inevitable that perfect integration of design and function
should be lacking in the same way that the dialectic of ancient philosophers was incapable of supplying an adequate vehicle for the expression of Christian ideas. Thus because the varied elements of European
thought from the fall of Rome until about the year 1000 were not
integrated in any sense of the word, there was a notable lack of monumental achievement during those years in every field of human activity.
Then was the period of blackest night in the history of European culture in which the only ray of light, feeble as it was, came from Charlemagne's short-lived "renaissance" in the early 9th century. The in-
stability of the culture which he attempted to create artificially has
already been suggested in commenting upon the isolation of his chapel-
mausoleum at Aachen (Fig. 74); it is further indicated by the fate
which befell his kingdom after his death when the coalescing force
of his individual personality no longer existed and the political unity
he had been able to maintain during his lifetime was shattered. During the century after his death, the political picture of Europe was
one of feudal anarchy with no central and recognized authority. By
contrast, the power of the Church was stable and extensive. The
reorientation of European thought from the objective and material
values of classic antiquity to the intangible and spiritual ones of the
Middle Ages is illustrated by no political event more forcefully than
the humbling of Henry IV of Germany before Pope Gregory VII at
Canossa in 1077 as the culmination of a bitter disagreement over the

investiture of churchmen by temporal authorities. Under such conditions, when even the world's mightiest rulers could not but abase themselves before the power of the Church, it is easy to realize its domination of all forms of human activity and to understand how surcease could be found within its walls from the trials of life in a society in a state of ceaseless flux. In the monasteries which continued to flourish, the soul that longed for peace and permanence could find refuge, and it was in them that was cherished all that remained of the once vigorous and creative intellectual life of the ancient world. From that carefully nurtured seed there was to grow the new life of the Middle Ages, formed from a synthesis of the various contributing cultural elements, of which the effects first become evident about the year 1000.

Architecturally, the consequence of this synthesis is suggested by a striking passage in a chronicle of the times written by a monk of the 11th century named Raoul Glaber, in which the effect of the new churches built after the year 1000 is likened to a white blanket spread over all Europe. This apparition has been somewhat superficially explained as resulting from the reaction that took place when the popular belief current in the 10th century that Christ's second coming was to occur in 1000 was disproved by its uneventful passage. It is more reasonable to conclude that the previously lacking integration of thought so essential to the creation of distinctive architectural style was at last taking place. Charlemagne had attempted to bring about such an integration by political fiat and had failed. Now it was occurring in a natural way and with it came the need for expression always felt when there is prevailing consciousness of deep and profound significance in human experience.

The period in which the forms created from this need began to assume a definite character conditioned by it is called the Romanesque. In general, the Romanesque period may be considered to have lasted from about 1000 until 1200, although in some parts of western Europe the succeeding Gothic style is apparent as early as 1150 while in others the Romanesque remains until far into the 13th century. The name Romanesque is applied to the forms created during this time because the influence of Roman thought was an important factor in determining their style. This was but natural in view of the fact that western Europe was largely peopled at this time by races of mingled Roman and barbarian stock. The common language was Latin, varied in different regions by local northern idioms, a point which provides in the various Romance languages the closest analogy to the numerous local schools or types of Romanesque architecture. All based on Latin, they are distinguished from one another by regional distinctions that make them the modern Latin dialects of French, Italian or Spanish, corresponding to modern political divisions that are themselves often based upon the Romanesque feudal districts of the 11th and 12th centuries. In the same way, Romanesque architecture, while based on that of Rome, has many different aspects resulting from modifications of the basic Roman style by local traditions. Thus there is not one Romanesque style but many, all related to each other in some degree through the parent style; in nothing is the Romanesque so sharply distinguished from its classic source as in its abundant variety. In the Roman period, an arch of triumph in France might be almost exactly the same as one in Africa and a Spanish aqueduct differs in no essential from one in Italy. In the 11th and 12th centuries, there were no less than eight clearly defined regional schools of building in France alone; Italy had three and yet others are capable of being distinguished in Spain, Germany and England, to mention only the most important.

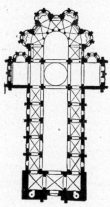

FIG. 75. — Clermont - Ferrand. Nôtre-Dame du Port. Plan.

A typical Romanesque church plan (Fig. 75) is of the basilican type in being composed primarily in length rather than height, and has some features in common with the earlier variety of the 4th and 5th centuries (cf. Fig. 63). There is a nave flanked by side aisles making up the principal part of the structure and the greater number have transepts though this is not always the case (cf. Fig. 85). A point of contrast with the Early Christian basilicas appears in the part of the church that lies beyond the transepts, however, where what seems to be an extension of the nave forms the choir; the side aisles are also carried across the transepts and around the choir to provide an ambulatory. Both of these features appear to have originated in consequence of expanding liturgical necessities in the monastic churches of the time. The practice of creating a special enclosure for those participating in the service had begun in earlier periods for there is one in the late 8th-century interior of Santa Maria in Cosmedin at Rome (Fig. 73) but in a tentative form only. The ambulatory and its accessory small apses or absidioles (also called radiating chapels) seem to have been contrived as a result of the extraordinary cult of relics that is one aspect of mediaeval monasticism whereby some part of a holy man's body was revered for its supposed power to perform miracles or confer grace upon those who visited it in the appropriate state of mind. These were kept in the altar or altars of the church and the necessity of permitting crowds of pilgrims to circulate without disturbing the services carried on at all times may have been one factor contributing to the development of the ambulatory passage from which the radiating chapels containing still further relics in altars opened out. The fact that a group of churches, including that of Saint-Sernin at Toulouse (Fig. 81), all located on one of the most famous of pilgrimage roads in the Middle Ages—that leading to the putative tomb of Saint James the Greater at Compostela in northwestern Spain—are provided with the most elaborate of these developed chevets, as the choir with its ambulatory and radiating chapels are called, is but one architectural indication of the importance as cultural factors in the Romanesque period of the pilgrimages and the cult of relics that gave rise to them.

In the elevation of Romanesque churches, the most evident point of contrast with that of an Early Christian building is the appearance of a third story in height consisting of a second row of arches on columns or piers between the nave arcade and the clearstory (Figs. 76, 77, 89). This is called a triforium gallery. Such galleries are not unknown in the Christian basilicas in Rome but they occur only in those churches where the Oriental practice of segregating the women of the congregation made it necessary to have separate places for them; as a rule the wall was unbroken between the nave arcade and the clearstory windows (Figs. 64, 65, 72, 73) and was covered with mosaics or paintings in fresco. In Romanesque building, the open triforium may have been introduced to lighten as much as possible the weight supported by the nave piers as at Vignory (Fig. 76) where there is no practical gallery at that level but where the walls are of considerable thickness. It is not an invariable feature of all Romanesque churches for it does not appear at all in some regional styles while in others it may take the place of the clearstory (Figs. 79, 80), but its value in establishing the expressive character of the interior was considerable, as will be noted elsewhere.

The church at *Vignory* in France (Fig. 76), which was built about 1050, reveals the characteristics in plan and elevation that have been noted as Romanesque—the three-part elevation of the nave, the developed choir and the ambulatory which is separated from it by the columns supporting the semi-dome of the apse; beyond it but not visible in the illustration are radiating chapels. The nave is covered with a trussed wooden roof and the side aisles are similarly treated. The nave system is distinguished from that of the older basilicas in consisting of piers instead of columns, an element that appeared in the nave of Santa Maria in Cosmedin (Fig. 73) but which is here used exclusively instead of with columns. In this feature appears another of the characteristics of Romanesque architectural style that distinguishes it most clearly from preceding ones, for the pier is the preferred isolated support in the majority of the northern schools of building during the later 11th and 12th centuries. A direct consequence of using piers in the nave system and the repetition of them in the triforium is the rather pronounced vertical element thereby introduced in the interior elevation of the building. This too was suggested in a tentative fashion in Santa Maria in Cosmedin, but it is much more apparent here, as will be made clear if it be compared with any Early Christian basilican nave (Figs. 65, 72) wherein the whole effect is one of horizontal movement, as has been pointed out elsewhere. Here at Vignory, the relationship of the openings in the nave elevation to each other is a rhythmic one ascending from the wide arches in the nave arcade through the smaller ones of the triforium to the clearstory. Each such vertical group makes up a bay and the composition is one conceived in terms of a series of these bays instead of a single and continuous form as it appears to be in the earlier basilicas in consequence of the more rapid rhythm created by the quickly repeated accents of the slender columns.

FIG. 76.—Vignory. CHURCH. Nave.

The *Cathedral at Pisa* (Figs. 77, 78) is an example of Tuscan Romanesque, one of the three regional styles of Italy. Begun in 1063 and finished in 1121 though somewhat modified in the 13th and 14th centuries, the nave elevation is in three levels with a triforium arcade of columns and piers like that at Vignory although the supports in the nave system are columns. In this respect, the Cathedral of Pisa resembles the Christian basilicas of the 4th and 5th centuries (Figs. 65, 72) and it is like them too in that the nave is covered by a wooden roof. The effect is one of greater height, however, and the decoration of the greater part of the interior consists of alternate bands of light and dark marble, a material which is found in large quantities in central Italy where Pisa is located and which has been extensively used for architectural ornament in the region at all times. The same use of marble facing gives the exterior of the building its character (Fig. 78), whether in the form of polychrome inlay or in the extensive use of decorative colonnades which is an individual characteristic of the Tuscan school. The campanile which is another characteristic Italian feature of the building is in this case the famous Leaning Tower. Like the Cathedral itself, its external decoration consists of colonnette arcades and the ensemble is one of the most striking in mediaeval architecture.

Fig. 77.—Pisa. The Cathedral. Nave.

In both the church at Vignory and the Cathedral of Pisa, the tendency in the direction of greater height, both actual and apparent, that made its appearance in a tentative form in certain churches of the later Dark Ages is carried further by increasing the number of levels in the nave elevation and by stressing the vertical elements in its design. There remained, however, the problem which the Christian basilican type of building always raised, namely, the working out of a roofing method that would contribute in some degree to the expressive effect of the church interior which the wooden ones of Vignory and Pisa do not do any more than those of Santa Sabina and Santa Maria in Cosmedin in Rome and Sant' Apollinare in Classe in

Ravenna (Figs. 65, 72, 73). There was also a practical problem presented by wooden roofs of this type that was probably of more immediate and conscious concern to Romanesque builders than their lack of expressive character—their relative impermanence and liability to destruction by fire. The task confronting the architects of the 11th and 12th centuries was to find some roofing method that would settle these difficulties; the ultimate solution lay in the use of masonry vaults. The character of Romanesque architectural style is determined in the

FIG. 78.—Pisa. THE CATHEDRAL AND THE LEANING TOWER.

final analysis by combination of the developed basilican plan with the stone vault in one form or another.

Vaulting had been extensively developed and applied by Roman architects, and in those parts of northern Europe in which Roman colonies had been maintained, their traditions of building had never been entirely forgotten. In southern France and in eastern Spain, for example, there are many small churches of the late 10th and early 11th centuries which have crude masonry vaults that are simplified and provincial versions of the monumental ones of ancient Rome. These were not of such a nature, however, that they could have served over the larger and higher naves such as the one at Vignory, and Romanesque vaulting has many characteristics of its own that distinguish it quite sharply from Roman practice and that were developed independently by the builders of the late 11th and 12th centuries. The church of *Notre-Dame du Port* at Clermont-Ferrand (Figs. 75, 79, 80),

which was begun about 1100, shows the simplest type of vault that can
be used for covering the nave. The plan is the developed basilican
type and the vault of the nave is the semi-cylindrical form called a
barrel vault (cf. Fig. 53, A); similar ones appear over the straight portion of the choir and over the transepts. The elevation, however, is
in but two levels, a fact which is explained by the mechanical necessity

Fig. 79.—Clermont-Ferrand. Notre-Dame du Port. Nave.

for buttressing the thrusts of the nave vault. This must be continuous
for the entire length of the vault and it must be applied at or near the
point where the lateral thrusts are strongest; this is the haunch. At
Notre-Dame du Port, the half-barrel vaults over the galleries above the
side aisles perform this buttressing function as well as covering the
triforium galleries which are here the upper story of the interior elevation. The way in which this buttressing effect is obtained can be
understood if the triforium vaults are thought of as leaning against

that over the nave and also as transmitting its thrust to the heavy outer wall which is sufficiently heavy to absorb it and render the whole system stable.

A barrel vault such as that over the nave of Notre-Dame du Port was a satisfactory solution mechanically of avoiding the fire hazard of a wooden roof, but its construction was rather costly. The side walls supporting it had to be very thick to absorb the lateral thrusts. Furthermore, until a barrel vault is completely built, it must be maintained by centering, the wood scaffold on which the fabric or web of the vault is laid. In a building of any size, the centering for a barrel vault requires almost as much if not more timber than a roof would, and this was a source of considerable expense in regions where wood was scarce. It was in such regions that means were sought to erect vaults with a minimum of preparatory centering as well as to evolve vault types which would not require the excessively heavy side walls of Notre-Dame du Port.

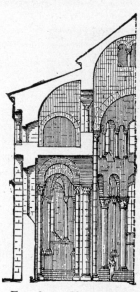

FIG. 80.—Clermont-Ferrand. NOTRE-DAME DU PORT. Section.

*Saint-Sernin* at Toulouse (Fig. 81) is vaulted in such a way as to avoid the drawbacks of the simple barrel vault that have been mentioned. Begun about 1080 and finished in the 12th century, its nave is spanned by a series of arches, connecting the piers directly opposite each other, that form a permanent support for the web of the barrel vault which rests directly upon them. With these transverse arches or ribs it became possible to reduce somewhat the thickness of the side walls and also to lighten the vault itself. Furthermore, since the transverse arches divide the nave vault into sections corresponding to the bays, each bay could be built individually with one set of centering serving for each in turn. As in Notre-Dame du Port, the lateral thrusts of the vault are buttressed directly by half-barrel vaults over the triforium gallery, and since these thrusts are slightly greater at the points where the transverse arches occur, the outer walls are strengthened at those points by strips of masonry called salient buttresses which rise the entire height of the wall on the outside.

The use of transverse arches provided a means by which the weight and costliness of construction of barrel vaulting could be reduced, but another great disadvantage remained—the difficulty of providing adequate illumination in the interior of a building so covered. In both Notre-Dame du Port and Saint-Sernin, the nave is very dark. There can be no windows in the vault itself for its stability would be seriously impaired by any openings; the only light in the nave comes from the door at the end or indirectly through the side-aisle and triforium

Fig. 81.—Toulouse. Saint-Sernin. Nave.

windows. Neither of these latter can be very large because the walls must be thick to sustain the thrusts of the nave and triforium vaults above; their effective opening can be somewhat enlarged by splaying or cutting the sides and bottoms away at an angle (cf. Fig. 80), but even this does not permit them to admit much light. A row of windows opening from the outside directly into the top of the nave—a clearstory—would have met this lighting difficulty, but this was impossible in either Notre-Dame du Port or Saint-Sernin since the nave vaults would have had to be raised considerably above the level of the triforium to permit its introduction and the buttressing function of the vaults over the galleries would have been lost. It is thus clear that while the barrel vault in either its simple form or with transverse arches is an adequate solution of the mechanical problems of the church roofed with masonry, the difficulties presented with respect

Fig. 82.—Morienval. Church. Interior, north side aisle.

to illumination are such that the expressive character of churches so covered is decidedly limited.

In the groined or cross vault, Romanesque builders found the form which permitted them to solve the problem of lighting their masonry-covered churches (Fig. 53, B-C), a form that was inherently applicable to the rectangular bays into which the nave was divided by the piers of nave and triforium galleries and by transverse arches. Providing windows in the side walls of a building covered with a groined vault is not difficult, for the thrusts in any given bay are concentrated at the angles and the whole of the space between may be left open if desired (cf. Fig. 55). Furthermore, the groined vault is even more economical in construction than the barrel vault with transverse arches since it requires buttressing only at the angles and the massive walls essential to the stability of barrel-vaulted structures can be considerably lightened.

Groined vaults had been used by the Romans over their great public baths and basilicas (Fig. 56) and they are found quite early in Romanesque building too, but on a smaller scale than their employment for vaulting a nave would have involved. At Notre-Dame du Port, the side aisles are covered with such vaults (Fig. 80), as indicated in the plan (Fig. 75) by the diagonal dotted lines in each bay; another example is to be seen in the north side aisle of the parish church at Morienval (Fig. 82) where the transverse arches separating the adjacent bays of the side aisle are also visible. In this form, the groined vault was widely used in Romanesque building from the beginning of the formation of the style, often appearing over the side aisles of churches whose naves still had wooden roofs, an example in point being the Cathedral at Pisa. Why it was not enlarged and employed over naves as well is not altogether clear; possibly the understanding of its potentialities was not sufficiently developed and fear of its physical limitations was such that the greater dimensions involved in so covering the wider spaces of naves seemed too much for it. In any event, it was not until a developed form of the groined vault had been evolved that the Romanesque builder dared to use it over the nave of a church— the ribbed groined vault.

A ribbed groined vault operates mechanically in much the same way as a simple groined vault to which it stands in a relationship like that of a barrel vault with transverse arches to a plain one in being supported by a system of arches or ribs constructed beforehand upon which the vault web is laid (Fig. 83). There are six of these arches in a ribbed groined vault; two are parallel to the principal axis of the nave and are called the longitudinal ribs, two more run transversely across the nave and are the transverse ribs, and the remaining two cross the bay to be vaulted diagonally on the groins and are called the diagonal ribs. If the bay is square and the arches are all semicircular in shape, as is usually the case in Romanesque buildings, the diagonal arches must rise to a higher level above the common springing than those on the sides since their radius is longer. As a result, the vault is domical in shape (Fig. 84).

Among the earliest extant buildings provided with ribbed groined vaults over the nave is the church of Sant' Ambrogio at Milan, a characteristic example of the North Italian or Lombard Romanesque style (Figs. 85-87). Its vaults were almost certainly first built in the last quarter of the 11th century and though the present ones are the result of a rebuilding that took place toward the end of the 12th, the plan of the structure shows that vaults of like character were provided for from the moment it was begun. The plan itself is of a modified

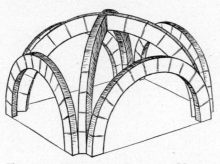

FIG. 83.—RIBS OF A GROINED VAULT WITH SEMICIRCULAR ARCHES.

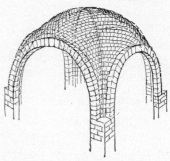

FIG. 84.—FOUR-PART RIBBED GROINED VAULT WITH SEMI-CIRCULAR ARCHES.

basilican type (Fig. 85). There is the usual nave with two side aisles and a crossing covered by an octagonal dome on squinches though there are no transepts. A short choir is flanked by a square bay on each side and ends in a rather large semicircular apse with a smaller one at the end of each aisle as well. The elevation is in two parts—

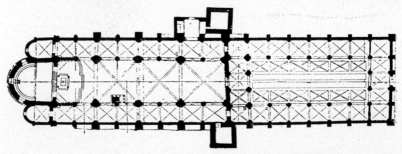

FIG. 85.—Milan. SANT' AMBROGIO. Plan.

the nave arcade and the triforium gallery (Fig. 86). The nave vaults are of the ribbed groined type and are domical in shape and the piers supporting them are compound forms made up of a rectangular core or nucleus to which columns and pilasters are applied. These applied members are the ostensible supports of the vault ribs above, there being one for each of the arches forming the armature upon which the vault web is laid. It is because the foundations of these piers have the characteristic compound section even in their lowest courses that the probability of ribbed vaults having been planned from the outset can be assumed, and it is in the organic conception thus implied wherein the structure as a whole is indicated by the elements in the plan that the most significant characteristic of the building is to be seen.

The nave vaults of Sant' Ambrogio are buttressed by the groined ones over the triforium galleries. They are aided in this function by heavy walls of masonry built over the transverse arches separating the triforium bays which thus assist in carrying the thrusts concentrated at the nave vault angles to the outer walls where salient buttresses are placed, as can be seen in the plan. Such walls as these are called dia- phragm walls. The nave vaults are domical since the bays they cover are square, and the semicircular diagonal ribs are consequently greater in height than those framing the bays on the sides. The effect of a sequence of domical vaults such as these is not particularly pleasing because the curving crown lines tend to stress the separate identity of each unit rather than contribute to a feeling of coherence in the nave as a whole. This effect could have been avoided by depressing the crowns of the diagonal arches to the same height as the transverse and longitudinal ones, but the resulting shape would then be elliptical which would have been both harder to build and harder to buttress since flatter arches always exert more lateral thrust than steeper ones. It was this consideration, no doubt, that led to sacrificing appearance to facility of construction and stability in these early ribbed groined vaults.

Another detail of the nave system at Sant' Ambrogio to be noted is the alternately large and small piers making up the arcade. The large ones support the ribs of the nave vaults as is obvious, but the smaller ones have no apparent relationship to them. They are necessary, how- ever, to the vaulting of the side aisles and the triforium galleries of which the bays would be oblong in plan without such divisions (cf. Fig. 85) since they would then be as long as each nave bay but only half as wide. Over a bay of such shape, it is exceedingly difficult to erect a groined vault with semicircular arches for in this case it is ob- vious that three pairs of different-sized arches would be required and the vault web would have to be adjusted to three different levels. It is such a vault that appears in the view of the north side aisle at Morienval (Fig. 82); although only a simple groined vault, its lower surfaces are warped and twisted in spite of efforts to make it level by springing the arches from different heights—as indicated by the vary- ing levels of the capitals—and by stilting the transverse arches. Instead of attempting to solve the problem of vaulting an oblong bay, the builders of Sant' Ambrogio preferred to divide the awkward space into easier square units by placing small piers between the large ones supporting the nave vaults and springing transverse arches across aisles and triforium galleries which were thus divided into small square bays

FIG. 86.—Milan. SANT' AMBROGIO. The Nave.

half as long on a side as those of the nave. These it was a comparatively easy matter to cover with simple groined vaults. The resultant arrangement of large and small piers is called an alternate system; its effect in Sant' Ambrogio is not entirely satisfactory since the relationship of the small piers to the large ones and to the main vaults of the structure is not at all clear when they are seen from the nave.

Lack of integration in the design of the nave is not the only evidence that the builders of Sant' Ambrogio were having to grope their way in using ribbed groined vaults, for the darkness of the interior is the result of omitting a clearstory which in principle is entirely feasible with such construction. Once more it was a question of sacrificing effect to structural considerations, for the buttressing of the nave vaults by means of those over the triforium galleries and their supplementary

Fig. 87.—Milan. SANT' AMBROGIO. Atrium and façade.

diaphragm walls was not any more than sufficient in any case. The builders doubtless were aware of this and were understandably timid about raising the heavy arches of the nave vault above those of the triforium galleries as would have had to be done to provide a clearstory, particularly in view of the fact that the first ribbed groined vaults of the building had collapsed. The importance of the construction at Sant' Ambrogio is great in spite of its tentative and hesitating character and it should not be under-estimated for the two basically Romanesque problems are definitely faced in it—the ribbed groined vault and the proper illumination of the structure covered with it.

Externally, Sant' Ambrogio is of interest in possessing an atrium (Fig. 87), one of the few Romanesque examples of what had been a typical feature of the earlier basilicas (cf. Figs. 63, 67). The porticoes are covered with groined vaults separated by transverse arches as in the side aisles within and are buttressed by strips of masonry applied to the outer walls. The narthex and the open gallery above it make up the façade of the building whose decoration is limited to rows of small stone brackets called corbels which are connected by arches; these appear on the cornice separating the two levels of the façade, its raking cornice, and also at the various stages of the north tower which is the later of the two, the south one dating from the 9th century when an earlier building had been erected on the same site. There is a certain amount of carving on the principal portal of the church and the capitals of nave and atrium, but by and large there is not as much ornament on it as on some Romanesque buildings.

Not all the schools of Romanesque building were equally advanced in treating the problem of a vaulted church that would be at the same time adequately illuminated within. The church of Notre-Dame la Grande at Poitiers (Fig. 88) was built for the most part in the 12th century, but its nave is covered with a heavy barrel vault that springs

FIG. 88.—Poitiers. NOTRE-DAME LA GRANDE. From the southwest.

directly from the level of the arcade in such fashion that even the triforium gallery is omitted. It is notable, however, for the lavish sculptural decoration of the façade, which is one of the most richly ornamented of all Romanesque examples. In the gable is a statue of Christ as the judge of the world on the day of Resurrection, the arcades in the middle levels enclose figures of the twelve apostles and of Saints

Martin and Hilary, and the spandrels between the arches on the ground level are filled with reliefs pertaining to the life of the Virgin to whom the church is dedicated. The immediate purpose of such decoration as this is to instruct those who could not read, but its value as an element in the architectural effect was also a factor. Here it serves to emphasize the flatness of the façade wall and its massiveness, for the portal and its flanking arches are recessed in the thickness of the wall itself. If the façade seems to lack organic relationship with the rest of the building, it none the less contains the elements of the basic mediaeval church front as it was developed in France, with its triple arch motive on the ground level, the figured arcades above and the two flanking towers. It is thus an example of the initial decorative phase of mediaeval architecture as Sant' Ambrogio illustrates the inception of its final structural character.

The importance of Sant' Ambrogio in the history of mediaeval building is considerable for it is one of the first structures in which the solution of the basic structural problems of the Romanesque style is suggested. It is only suggested, however, for three features of the nave design are open to criticism—the domical vaults with the halting and ineffective rhythm resulting from the uneven crown line, lack of coherent relationship between the vaults and the alternate system of the nave supports, and the darkness of the interior consequent upon omission of the clearstory. All of these limitations were avoided in the construction of *Saint-Étienne* at Caen (Figs. 89, 90) in northwestern France, which is an example of the Norman Romanesque style. It was begun in the latter part of the 11th century by order of William the Conqueror in expiation of a vow he had made and was first dedicated in 1077 as part of a monastery from which it has received the name of *Abbaye-aux-Hommes* in addition to its dedicatory title. The church of William's time was roofed with timber but it was rebuilt with the present vaults of the nave about 1135 (Fig. 89). The most obvious point of difference between its interior and that of Sant' Ambrogio (Fig. 86) is its better illumination. There is a clearstory above the triforium gallery which opens directly outside through the sides of a sexpartite ribbed groined vault. These were formed, as can be seen in the plan (Fig. 90), by springing a transverse arch across the nave in the middle of what would otherwise be a four-part vault like the one at Sant' Ambrogio, the extra arch being supported by the smaller intermediate pier in each bay of the alternating system.

Addition of the intermediate transverse arch which makes a six-part vault of the four-part ribbed groined type had the immediate effect of tying the otherwise unrelated small piers of the nave system into the design of the principal vaults. It also supplied additional support for the vault web and made possible the depressed diagonal ribs which appear in each bay at Saint-Étienne and which allow the laying of the web on a uniform level, thus avoiding the domical effect which is so

Fig. 89.—Caen. Saint-Étienne. The Nave.

obtrusive at Sant' Ambrogio. It was probably the knowledge of the added support provided by the additional transverse rib that led the builders of the Abbaye-aux-Hommes to venture a clearstory in their vaulted structure as well and thus gain a valuable adjunct to the expressive effect of the interior.

The use of sexpartite vaults did not eliminate the problem of buttressing, however, and at Saint-Étienne this function is performed for those of the nave by half-barrel vaults over the rather tall triforium galleries as in Notre-Dame du Port (Fig. 80). Since the counterthrusts of these half-barrel vaults are continuous for their total length and since the lateral thrusts of the ribbed groined vaults are not continuous but concentrated at the angles, it follows that there is actually more buttressing than is needed in the Abbaye-aux-Hommes. This fact

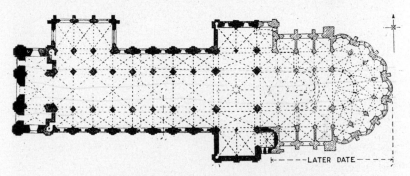

Fig. 90.—Caen. Saint-Étienne. Plan.

was observed by the builders of another church in Caen, *La Trinité* or the *Abbaye-aux-Dames*, which was erected by order of Matilda, wife of William the Conqueror (Fig. 91). It is generally similar in plan and elevation to the brother church and has a parallel history, having been first roofed with wood and then rebuilt in the fourth decade of the 12th century with sexpartite ribbed groined vaults. But when the problem of buttressing the nave vaults arose, the builders observed that the portion of a half-barrel vault over the triforium gallery between the piers was unnecessary as far as its buttressing function was concerned because the thrusts of the nave vault were exerted only at the piers. Therefore instead of building such a continuous half-barrel vault, they constructed a series of half-arches connecting the nave piers with the external salient buttresses (Fig. 92) and covered them with a slanting wooden roof; at the same time, the height of the triforium gallery was reduced since it was not to be used for purposes of accommodation as in the Abbaye-aux-Hommes. The economy resulting from the elimination of the greater part of the half-barrel vault was an immediate advantage gained by its use. More important than this, however, was the establishment of an hitherto unexploited structural form—the free buttress—which was to reach a high point of development as one of the essential features of Gothic style in the flying buttress.

Fig. 91.—Caen. La Trinité. The Nave.

The *façade* of the *Abbaye-aux-Hommes* (Fig. 93), of which the lower part at least was built in the later 11th century, is one of the first in which an attempt was made to indicate in the design the interior arrangement of the building. The four heavy vertical buttresses divide the façade into three parts corresponding to the nave and side aisles within, and the doors and windows express in similar fashion the three-part elevation of the interior. Comparison with the façade of Notre-Dame la Grande at Poitiers (Fig. 88) which is little more than a screen placed at the end of the building and which has no very direct relationship to it in design will show the relatively greater organic character of the Norman façade. The octagonal spires crowning the flanking towers are of a later period than the rest of the façade, but the effective termination they supply to the pronounced vertical effect of the design must have been a quality that was hoped for from the beginning of construction of the building.

It was in the Romanesque period that the various traditions of thought and feeling contributing to the culture of the Middle Ages first began to fuse and amalgamate into new conceptual patterns, when,

FIG. 92.—Caen. LA TRINITÉ. Buttressing arches in the triforium.

as it were, the traditional dialects of Greek and Latin and Teuton tend to become integrated in a new language. Architecturally, this is apparent in the progressive changes that take place in the basilican interior from the time when the orientation of the structure toward the apse introduced the idea of movement in the balanced and static classic form, and in the increasingly greater emphasis upon vertical character that results from the substitution of piers for columns and the use of masonry vaults instead of timber roofs. From the even spacing of the piers in the developed Romanesque interior (Fig. 89), there still results a sense of horizontal movement toward the altar, but it is slower than in the Latin basilica (Fig. 72) and hence charged with a deeper and more profound significance. It is evident, moreover, that the expressive importance of the vertical elements in the nave design is growing. No longer are simple piers supporting the triforium galleries and the clearstories sufficient (cf. Fig. 76); they are compounded and the applied shafts are carried up from the ground level into the vaults themselves. This feature of emphatic verticality has been introduced in the exterior as well, in bell towers (Fig. 87), angle turrets (Fig. 88) and spires (Fig. 93); and, indeed, its effect has been realized with somewhat more consistency than within the nave where the vertical movement of the piers and their shafts is turned back by the

Fig. 93.—Caen. Saint-Étienne. The Façade.

over-arching semicircles of the vaults. There is thus created in the interior an active opposition between the aspiring character of some elements in the design and the oppressive weighing down of others, between the vertical movement of the shafts and piers on the one hand and the crushing weight of the semicircular sexpartite vault with its rhythmically awkward pattern of ribs on the other. To return to an earlier analogy, the Frenchman is still speaking with a Latin accent in Romanesque style. His northern temperament leads him to find the deepest significance in Christian experiences of ecstatic piety and the architectural symbol thereof is the aspiration of his building upward toward the infinite space that connotes God to his emotional soul. But this aspiration is thwarted architecturally by precisely those elements which he has taken over from his Latin teachers—the rounded arches of his vaults and openings and the square sections into which he divides his nave in consequence. The modifications of Romanesque architectural vocabulary that make it into something northern affect these elements directly and lead to the formation and perfection of the Gothic style.

# Chapter VII. Gothic Architecture

DURING THE 12TH AND 13TH CENTURIES, THE CHURCH maintained its dominance over all human activity in Europe and continued to be the great unifying element in the culture of the time. It was at the behest of Pope Urban II in 1095, for example, that the first of the crusades to recapture the Holy Land from the infidel Turks was organized, possibly the most spectacular expression of Christian faith in the history of the Church; and if later crusades were not animated in every case by the highest motives, their ostensible purpose was none the less spiritual. The revival of intercourse with the East thus brought about was to have significant consequences of a different character, however. In Italy, for example, the flowing stream of crusaders to and from Palestine brought much industry and commerce that lifted many of its cities to heights of commercial power that were not threatened until the discovery of the New World in the late 15th century and its exploitation in following years. Elsewhere in Europe, the beginning of a secular and civic spirit is also to be noted in the gradual change from the feudal and agricultural world of the 10th and 11th centuries to one in which the man of business and commerce was the dominant figure. Politically, too, there were changes, in kind; if the barons and dukes of France and England seem to have owed no more than nominal allegiance to their kings, the fact remains that the right of a single ruler to their loyalty was recognized; and in the shifting and confused history of the time, the formation of modern European states is at least foreshadowed. All of these factors are involved in direct fashion in the formation of the Gothic cathedral which is no longer the church of a monastery, as were the majority of Romanesque buildings, but is built in a town or city under the patronage of secular rulers and commercial guilds rather than the abbots of religious orders.

It was in the Gothic period that mediaeval Europe came of age culturally speaking, when in the merging of the confluent streams of classic, Oriental and northern thought there was formed the second of the great and comprehensive human attitudes in the history of the western world. For the man of the 13th century was sure of the world in which he lived as was the Athenian of the fifth century B.C. The difference between those worlds was great. For the Greek, the real was the objective and his experience of things lay in perception through the senses of the qualities that gave them existence. There is no less consciousness of things in the 13th century, but they are evaluated in a different way for then the reality of things was not in their objective characteristics but in the degree to which they were elements in a system which itself was a symbol of abstract and ultimate realities.

The architectural expression of such an attitude as this involved the establishment of a vital relationship between the physical fabric of the church building and the space that it at the same time occupied and was filled by, for space was to mediaeval man the symbol that, more than any other, connoted the all-pervasive principle of God who exists in and gives significance to all things. In an incipient form, this ideal is the motive behind the ever-increasing emphasis upon height and verticality in the progressive evolution of mediaeval architectural style. Its most complete and monumental expression is found in the Gothic architecture of France in the early 13th century.

Romanesque builders were unable to attain completely the effect of height deemed ideal by the northern temperament because they were hampered by the semicircular arches which their vaulting methods involved. One consequence of this type of arch already pointed out was the lid-like effect of the vault which simply turns back the upward movement created by the vertical elements in the compound piers and their shafts. Another was the wide spacing of the supports which such arches made unavoidable, for the length of a bay must be equal to its width if semicircular arches of equal height support its vault. Even the sexpartite vault with its alternating system does not provide a completely satisfactory solution to this problem (cf. Figs. 89, 91) and the considerable separation of the piers introduces an element of horizontal movement that cannot be avoided. In order to achieve an effect of greater height in his interior and to render it more unified, the Gothic builder made two important changes in the Romanesque structural system. He introduced the oblong bay and the pointed structural arch. By substituting oblong individually vaulted bays for square ones, the width of each one was quite considerably reduced in relation to the nave span and the horizontal movement created by the more widely separated piers of a square bay was suppressed. Then to cover these oblong bays, he employed ribbed groined vaults laid on pointed instead of semicircular arches (Figs. 94, 95), for semicircular arches can be used over such a bay only with the greatest difficulty (cf. Fig. 82). The greater adaptability of the pointed arch under such circumstances lies in the fact that within rather wide limits it can be made to rise to any height above the springing, regardless of the space it spans, while the semicircular arch cannot attain a height above the springing that is greater than its own radius. Thus where the Romanesque builder had to juggle with stilted arches springing from various heights to make his vault crowns level when he tried to use semicircular ones over oblong bays, or else weaken the longer arches by depressing their crowns to the height of the shorter ones, the pointed arches of the Gothic builder can be varied in pitch to rise to any point and the three sets in a given vault (Fig. 94) are all more or less the same height. The

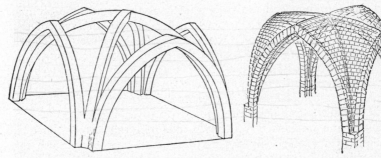

FIG. 94.—RIBS OF A GROINED VAULT WITH POINTED ARCHES.

FIG. 95.—FOUR-PART RIBBED GROINED VAULT WITH POINTED ARCHES.

attainment in this way of a level crowned vault without loss of structural strength was one of the triumphs of Gothic engineering (cf. Figs. 84, 95) for it was not only lighter and easier to build than the heavy Romanesque vaults but it could also be raised to much greater heights.

By substituting oblong nave bays for square ones, the Gothic builder was able to suppress the horizontal rhythm that still remained as an inheritance of the Latin basilica in the Romanesque interior, and by using pointed instead of semicircular arches, he was able to accentuate the effect of upward movement and to increase the actual height of his vaults. Full realization of the possibilities along these lines would still have been prevented, however, if adequate buttressing for the higher vaults had not been contrived. In the Romanesque styles of most developed organic character, the buttressing of the nave vaults was a function of those that covered the triforium gallery (Fig. 80); and even in the Abbaye-aux-Dames at Caen where the buttresses no longer have a roofing function, they are still associated structurally with the triforium gallery, which means that the height of the nave

vault above the triforium level is strictly limited (Fig. 92) although
it is sufficient in this case to permit a clearstory, the nave vault crown
being a little over fifty feet above the floor (Fig. 91).

It was from the buttressing half-arch concealed under the triforium
gallery roof as in the Abbaye-aux-Dames that the characteristic Gothic
buttressing device was to evolve, once it was divorced both structurally
and formally from its traditional association with the triforium. When

FIG. 96.—Paris. SAINT-GERMAIN-DES-PRÈS. Flying buttresses.

it was realized that the half-arch could be brought out from under
the triforium gallery roof and placed at any desired height, the flying
buttress had been conceived, and only the inherent limits of stone as a
structural medium restricted the loftiness of buildings whose vaults
were kept stable by its means. At *Saint-Germain-des-Près* in Paris (Fig.
96), flying buttresses were built to sustain the chevet vaults shortly after
the middle of the 12th century, and though they are rather heavy and
awkward in appearance, this is but natural in the early employment of
a new structural device whose potentialities were as yet unrealized.
It was soon realized that the effectiveness of the flying buttress depended upon the rigidity of the masonry bar rather than its weight,
however, and when the nave buttresses of Amiens Cathedral were
built in the second quarter of the 13th century they were more slender
in proportion and more decorative in effect (Fig. 97), with the weight
necessary to absorb the nave vault thrusts concentrated in the pier

buttresses that rise from a point beyond the side aisle wall. The struts have been doubled in number as well, with one abutting the clearstory at the level of the vault spring and the other at that of the haunch giving further reinforcement to the vault system. The flying buttress is the only major structural innovation in Gothic architecture, for pointed arches and oblong vaults had both been used by Romanesque builders although without full realization of their structural or expressive possi-

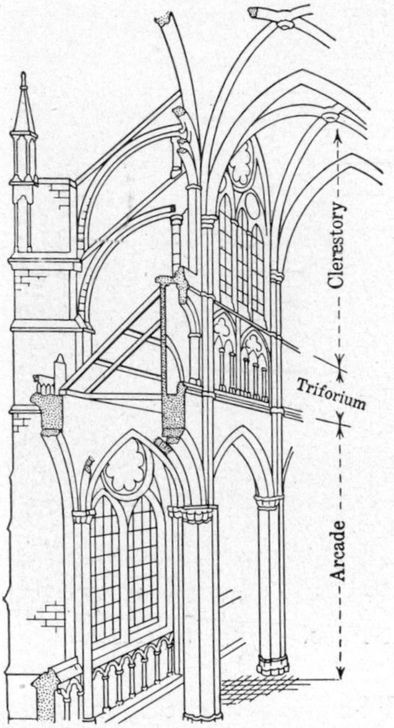

FIG. 97.—Amiens. THE CA-THEDRAL. Section in elevation.

bilities. It remained for all three to be used together before this could be achieved as it was in northern France during the first half of the 13th century.

From the very beginning of organic vaulted construction in the Middle Ages, the question of illumination had been one of almost equal importance with the engineering problems and the striving for greater apparent and actual height in the design of the interior. With the perfection of the Gothic structural system, this problem too was solved, for it is clear in the diagrammed section of the cathedral (Fig. 97) that there is almost no wall space to deal with in its general form. The supports of the structure are piers, whether the compound ones of the nave system or the heavy ones from which the flying buttresses are sprung, and they are so integrated with the covering vaults that they are mechanically quite independent of each other. In thus assuming the supporting function that is traditionally one purpose of a wall, the isolated piers need only sustain thin sheets of glass which discharge the second or screening function of a wall, and this is the case in the perfected Gothic building, which is no more than a cage or skeleton of organically articulated piers, vault ribs, and buttresses, with windows of glass between the stone supports. This was colored whenever possible and the jewel-like and brilliant patterns produced by it play an important part in establishing the expressive effect of the interior.

The fascination of Romanesque building lies in the variety of ways in which the various structural and expressive problems were approached; the beauty of Gothic is in the faultless logic apparent in the final solution of those problems. Save only for the flying buttress, the Gothic builder employs the same architectural elements that his Romanesque predecessor had used but he does so with greater knowledge and keener perception of what can be done with them structurally and a clearer understanding of the values to which he is attempting to give expression. In the completeness of its statement of all these things, there is no more characteristic or monumental example of Gothic design than the Cathedral of Notre-Dame at Amiens in northwestern France which was begun in 1220.

Amiens Cathedral is laid out according to a plan (Fig. 98) which contains many of the elements noted in the Romanesque type (Fig. 75) but which in general is more elaborate. This is most apparent in the chevet where there are doubled aisles flanking the choir, a vaulted ambulatory with numerous radiating chapels, and the choir with its semicircular end which is no longer covered by a simple half-dome but with a very complicated ribbed vault. Without the pointed arch, many of the vault forms used over the irregularly shaped bays of the Gothic chevet would have been impossible of construction, it being, indeed, over such bays that the arch may have first come into use in connection with a ribbed groined vault. For the rest, the plan of Amiens is char-

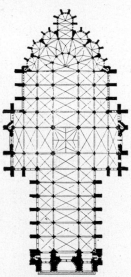

Fig. 98.—Amiens. The Cathedral. Plan.

acteristic in showing the elimination of the wall as a means of support, for between the heavy black bars representing the flying buttress piers there are only light lines indicating glass windows. The effect is almost that of sections of the wall turned at right angles to the plane which would enclose the inner space of the building, making them instead into the piers supporting the flying buttresses.

As an example of the High Gothic façade, that of Amiens (Fig. 100) stands as the culmination of an evolution to be traced from the Romanesque type as seen in Notre-Dame la Grande at Poitiers (Fig. 88) and the Abbaye-aux-Hommes at Caen (Fig. 93) through that of the Cathedral at Chartres (Fig. 99) which lies between the Romanesque and Gothic in point of both time and style. In the Abbaye-aux-Hommes and Chartres, the horizontal and vertical divisions into three parts corresponding in plan to nave and side aisles and in elevation to arcade, triforium and clearstory are to be noted. These are the basic features at Amiens as well but treated with greater refinement and integration of detail and with a more consistent vertical feeling throughout. At

FIG. 99.—Chartres. THE CATHEDRAL. The Façade.

Saint-Étienne, where the façade was largely completed by 1077, solid wall masses are still dominant in the design, for the windows and portals are small and not very important. The façade at Chartres is about seventy years later in date and is transitional between the Romanesque and Gothic types. There is a more vertical feeling resulting from emphasis on the angle towers and doubling the buttresses, and while something of Romanesque massiveness remains, the portals and windows are proportionately larger. The rose window which at Chartres replaces the upper row of three arched ones at Saint-Étienne is an example of one of the most popular and widely used decorative motives in Gothic architecture. The spires on the towers are of different periods; that to the south is contemporary with the lower part of the façade, but the northern one was not erected until the early years of the 16th century.

At Amiens, the climax of the development suggested by the Romanesque and transitional façades is seen (Fig. 100). It is not complete because the crowning spires of the towers were never erected; but even their absence cannot obscure the complete integration here achieved of structure and ornament, the goal of mediaeval architectural thought. The three-part division of the façade is prominent. Each part has its own portal that is no longer recessed in the wall as at Caen and Chartres but projects outward in a deep porch of which the sides are lined with statues representing personages of Biblical and Church history (Fig. 301). Two things stand out in the general impression created by this façade. The first is the complete disappearance of the wall as a structural member, its supporting function being taken over by the great isolated piers and its screening effect being achieved by the arcades and figures between the piers. The second quality of the façade as a whole is its pronounced verticality. No horizontal line is permitted to continue unbroken for more than a relatively small portion of its total width, for the carved stringcourses and the decorative arcades come out and around the buttresses in such a way that they seem from the normal point of view on the ground to be a succession of horizontal units rather than single and continuous ones. This effect is also contributed to by the cutting through of the peaked porch gables across the heavy carved moulding immediately beneath the open arcade under the row of figures about halfway up the façade.

The deep porches of the Amiens portals are one of the most characteristic forms in Gothic façade design and are effective elements in establishing a direct relationship between the exterior and interior of the building. At Saint-Étienne (Fig. 93), the portals are little more than holes cut in the massive façade wall and their effect is to emphasize its space-enclosing function. At Chartres (Fig. 99), the recession of the portals is almost as if to suggest that the wall is being pressed inward by the volume of space outside the building, but its heaviness is still a basic factor in the effect. At Amiens, on the other hand, the porches are a transition from exterior to interior space between which there is no sharply marked line of demarcation, a prime example of the integration of form with space that is inherent in the whole form and purpose of Gothic building.

Other details of the façade contribute to the same effect. By the pronounced verticality of the design as a whole, the eye is led upward from the tangibly heavy piers at the base to the intangible space that surrounds and pervades the towers. At the same time, as these forms

FIG. 100.—Amiens. THE CATHEDRAL. The Façade.

appear to grow lighter in their ascent, they also seem to merge with the space surrounding them. The transitional south tower at Chartres appears to be heavy and solid to the tip of the spire while the Gothic one that balances it seems to dissolve into the space around it, an impression resulting from the softening of its outlines by the small curling leaves called crockets growing out of them. At Amiens, every straight line of gable or pinnacle, stringcourse or capital, is broken by these foliate forms which are realistic to a degree in reproducing the forms of leaves and plants of the French countryside—all for the purpose of furthering the effect of the building as part of and one with the space in which it exists.

In the interior of Amiens (Fig. 101), the desire to achieve a fusion of form with space is equally apparent. The elements of the design are those inherited from the Romanesque style—nave arcade, triforium gallery and clearstory—but now even the vestigial remains of the horizontal rhythms that are an inconsistency in the Romanesque nave (Figs. 89, 91) have disappeared. Pointed arches and oblong bays have narrowed the spaces between the piers in such fashion that the eye perceives only a succession of vertical accents in the shafts. The proportionate height of the arcade is greater and its pointed arches contribute in no small degree to the upward movement that is carried further by the applied shafts whose vertical continuity is unbroken and by which the eye is led directly to the shadowed pointed vaults. Horizontal lines are subordinated throughout to vertical ones; stringcourses separating arcade from triforium and triforium from clearstory come out around the shafts and die away completely in the crossing piers whose vertical lines rise in unbroken sweeps from the ground to the spring of the vault where bands of foliage signify change in function to the supporting arches of the crossing vault.

The final effect of form merging with space which is achieved in the Gothic façade by crockets and pervasive penetration is established in the interior by color from the stained glass of the clearstory windows. This was the form in which painting entered into the decoration of the cathedral and its subject matter was chosen from the stories of Bible and Church to instruct the illiterate. Its importance as an adjunct to the architectural effect must have been recognized as greater than its dogmatic value, however, for many of the details are so far away as to be indistinguishable. The greatest value of the stained-glass windows was in diffusing and softening the light from the clearstory openings which would otherwise have made the structural details of the interior over-obtrusive. The original glass is no longer in the windows at Amiens and the effect of the nave is impaired by its absence for the bones of the structural skeleton stand out too clearly. But in a Gothic nave with its proper complement of colored light, such as that of Chartres Cathedral, the structural forms lose their material concreteness in the same way that the otherwise insistent lines of the spires and pinnacles of the façade are diffused by the crockets. All of these things contribute to a final experience which is of pure color unrelated to any suggestion of form. The eye of the observer is drawn upward by the massive piers which seem to become lighter the higher they go, as their vigorous outlines are diffused by the irregular patterns of

Fig. 101.—Amiens. The Cathedral. The Nave.

radiant color pouring from the windows. The lines of the pointed arches lead the eye and the spirit of the observer ever upward until they are enveloped in the luminous dusk that pervades the upper reaches of the nave and in which every tangible quality or objective characteristic is lost. It is thus that in the Gothic nave is realized the final achievement of the aspiration toward the infinite that first faintly stirred in the souls of the men building the Latin basilicas and was the guiding ideal of their successors throughout the Dark Ages and the Romanesque period. Only so could the hope of the human spirit to identify itself ultimately with God be expressed in architecture and never has it been more completely set forth in stone and glass wrought by the hands of man than in the Gothic cathedral.

In dominating the material forms of the mediaeval city as it did, the cathedral was an architectural symbol of the Church's authority over all aspects of human activity in the 13th century. It was by virtue of this fact that a truly communal spirit then prevailed, with the spiritual values of Christian faith giving significance and meaning to all aspects of western thought. In such a community of feeling, the importance of any one individual was very slight, a fact which is given point by the anonymity of the greater part of the artists of the Middle Ages. Occasionally a name is known such as that of Robert de Luzarches, but this an isolated fact in itself; of him as a personality there is no indication, and as an individual he has no existence because his achievement in designing the cathedral at Amiens was not for his personal glory but that of the Church. The subordination of the individual to the Church that this implies carriers over into the field of the arts as well where architecture is dominant and others are subservient to it. There is relatively little sculpture, for example, that was not intended as part of a building rather than for its own sake, and painting hardly existed except on the walls and in the windows of churches and the pages of religious books.

It is to be noted, moreover, that even the cathedral itself was not a self-sufficient entity. Its forms were evolved not as ends in themselves but as aids to an intuitive perception of the spiritual principle that gives them meaning, for their aspiring verticality involves a denial of certain objective architectonic values that is a direct parallel of the denial of significance in much human experience that was demanded of mediaeval man by his faith. The wall, for example, is a basic architectural element in the enclosure and definition of space by virtue of its various physical and aesthetic characteristics, yet space in the Gothic cathedral is defined by formless and weightless color. The massive stone of the vaults seems to hover in mid-air, so lightly do they rest upon the slender shafts that ostensibly support them, nor do the vaults themselves define and enclose the space over which they hover. It is impossible, moreover, to perceive the form of the cathedral as a whole as a rational unity; the flying buttress, for instance, has no inherent

structural meaning because the thrust of the interior vault which is
invisible from the outside must be supplied in imagination if its existence is to be explained. In other words, the identity and unity of
the cathedral are to be felt rather than understood, and if that feeling
is to be complete the reality of sensuous experience must be denied.
The observer is asked to *feel* that the gables and spires of the façade

Fig. 102.—Rouen. The Cathedral. Façade.

dissolve in the space around them and that the heavy stones of the
vaults hover over the nave without support even though this directly
contradicts the evidence of his senses by which he *knows* that such
things cannot be.

French architecture after the 13th century shows a reaction away
from the spiritual abstractions of High Gothic style. The façade of
*Rouen Cathedral* (Fig. 102) was added in the first quarter of the 16th
century to an earlier structure. In it, the 13th-century conception of
the Gothic façade in which an identity of structural and ornamental
forms is implicit has changed, for at Rouen decoration and construction are divorced and the separate character of the two elements is

clearly established. The ornament is now a lacy screen of stone standing clear of the wall behind, which has now recovered its basic function of space enclosure. No longer do the statues appear to grow from the portal embrasures as they do at Amiens (Fig. 100) but are free and complete in themselves, with a claim to existence in their own right rather than as subordinate forms in a prevailing architectural scheme.

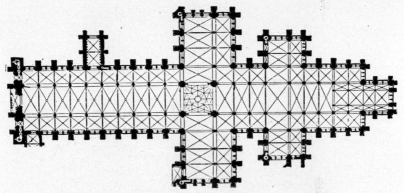

FIG. 103.—Salisbury. THE CATHEDRAL. Plan.

All this means that by the 16th century the arts had been freed from the expressive limitations imposed by the philosophy of the High Gothic period; sculpture and painting could pursue their inherent aims, as will be pointed out elsewhere, and architecture was no longer forced to deny the reality of its proper effects for the sake of abstract emotional sensation.

Earlier in this chapter it was stated that the most comprehensive and monumental expression of the architectural attitude called Gothic is to be found in buildings erected in France during the early part of the 13th century. Elsewhere in Europe at the same time, decorative and structural forms of similar character were used but never with the same overwhelming effect. In England, for example, Gothic buildings always retain something of the broad and low proportions of the Romanesque and lack the aspiring and vertical character of contemporary examples in France. *Salisbury Cathedral* (Figs. 103-105) was begun in 1220, the same year as Amiens Cathedral in France with which a comparison provides characteristic points of contrast. The plan seems much longer than that of Amiens (cf. Figs. 98 and 103) although both are actually the same length of 450 feet; the different impression of Salisbury is in consequence of its greater narrowness, for its width through nave and side aisles is 78 feet against 104 at Amiens.

The transepts are doubled in the English building too, and the chevet or eastern end is rectangular in plan instead of being rounded as it is in the French one. From the exterior (Fig. 104), the effect of Salisbury

FIG. 104.—Salisbury. THE CATHEDRAL. Façade.

is one of lowness and length and picturesqueness of silhouette instead of the vigorous masses and pronounced verticals of Amiens, the whole being dominated by the lofty spire of the crossing tower which reaches a height of 404 feet. The façade at Salisbury lacks the comprehensive integration of ornament and structure which characterizes that of the French Gothic building and is little but a screen wall concealing the building behind it, but the setting in a broad lawn or close permits the effect of the structure as a whole to be grasped to an extent rarely if ever possible in France, where the cathedrals are as a rule completely hemmed in by structures built up around them.

Fig. 105.—Salisbury. The Cathedral. The Nave.

Structurally an English Gothic cathedral such as Salisbury is not an organically contrived skeleton of piers, buttresses and ribs but is still dependent in large measure on heavy walls to support the vaults. The flying buttress in a form comparable in structural and decorative effectiveness to that which it attained in France is found only in a few buildings designed either by French architects or directly under the influence of French methods, and both actual and apparent height is not found in English buildings in any degree comparable to those in France. In the nave at Salisbury (Fig. 105), the horizontal division of the elevation into nave arcade, triforium and clearstory is quite pronounced and the vertical effect achieved by the vaulting shafts in French buildings (Fig. 101) is not even attempted. Lacking too is the diffusion of line that is effected by luxuriant and naturalistic floral mouldings in the French Gothic interior, the outstanding decorative effect being that of the polished black Purbeck marble shafts applied

FIG. 106.—Exeter. THE CATHEDRAL. The Nave.

to the lighter limestone of the piers. A specifically English Gothic feature that was developed in consequence of certain characteristics that are illustrated by the design of the Salisbury nave was the decorative vault rib. Here the vaults are simple four-part groined ones in which all the ribs are structural as they are at Amiens, but since the vault is much lower—it is 81 feet above the nave floor while that at Amiens is 140—the panels between the ribs are unpleasantly obtrusive in effect. It was to break up such plain surfaces as these that English builders introduced the practice of adding further ribs to the vault, springing them at first from the bay angles as in the nave vaults of *Exeter Cathedral* (Fig. 106) which date from the early 14th century. Later, still further ribs were added connecting the others in patterns of great complexity, as a result of which the vault appears to consist of great conical sheaves of ribs between the clearstory windows in which the sharp "plowshare" edges of the simple four-part ribbed groined vault are completely lost. The most developed examples of this elaborate ribbing in English vaults are the so-called fan vaults over

FIG. 107.—Gloucester. THE CATHEDRAL. Cloister.

the *Cloisters of Gloucester Cathedral* (Fig. 107) which were built between 1351 and 1412. An extraordinary revelation of the technical skill in design and in stonecutting developed by English Gothic architects which was not surpassed and hardly equaled by anything in France either before or after, these vaults are also a striking illustration of the lack of organic character in most English Gothic building that results from absence of integration of structure and ornament. In this, however, the style is typical of the majority of those in Europe outside of France in the 13th and 14th centuries, in which the formal characteristics of Gothic are present but without the sense of structural and expressive consistency that is the factor underlying the distinction attained by French builders in the style.

In discussing the character of late Gothic architecture in France as represented by the façade of Rouen Cathedral (Fig. 102), the difference was pointed out between the conception it embodies of self-sufficiency in the structural and decorative elements and the prevailingly architectonic character of all features of the 13th-century structures. This change was symbolic of a gradual shift from the predominantly spiritual and abstract values of High Gothic philosophy as summed up in the writings of Thomas Aquinas to more material and secular ways of thinking. Corresponding to this is the decreasing emphasis on religious architecture that is to be observed in the 14th and 15th cen-

Fig. 108.—Carcassonne. The City. From the air.

turies in France and a compensatingly greater interest in building of a secular character. Such structures had been built much earlier, it is true; the fortified city of *Carcassonne* (Fig. 108) occupies a site used for defensive purposes as early as the Roman period, but in its present form it is largely the result of construction in the late 13th and 14th centuries, and although much restored in the 19th century, the ensemble remains one of the most impressive secular monuments of the Gothic period. The heavy outer walls with their picturesque towers and bastions are irregular in plan to take the utmost military advantage of the site. In this respect, the mediaeval fortified city is like the Hellenistic one (Fig. 46), but within the walls of Carcassonne there is no such artificial order as in Priene for there too the controlling factor in the general scheme is conformity of the individual buildings to the peculiarities of level and orientation in the site as a whole. Designed primarily as protection, the inner and outer fortifications are clearly the principal elements in the ensemble, but it is characteristic that the church too should be a building of some importance. Individual

Fig. 109.—Cahors. The Pont Valentré.

forms in the category of mediaeval military architecture reveal a similar harmony with their setting that is at once picturesque and structurally sound. The *Pont Valentré* at Cahors in southwestern France (Fig. 109) was built in the 14th century across the river Lot; its six pointed arches are of unequal span determined by the conformation of the river bed, and the asymmetry thus created is also to be noted

in the two heavy towers which straddle the roadbed. Of utmost simplicity in design and with no ornament whatsoever, the effect of the
structure as a whole is none the less very impressive, arising from
the contrasting planes of the pier buttresses designed to deflect objects floating in the stream from direct blows against the supports, the
strong rhythm of the openings and the massive proportions. The fundamental soundness of Gothic architectural thinking is indicated by

FIG. 110.—Bourges. THE HOUSE OF JACQUES CŒUR.

the distinction with which a strictly utilitarian form like the bridge
can be designed in accordance with the same basic principles as the
cathedral with its immaterial and abstract expressive values.

It is but natural that the growing secular interests of the 14th and
15th centuries in Europe should have been reflected architecturally
in a more impressive type of domestic architecture in that period. One
of the best examples in this category of French building is the *House
of Jacques Cœur* in Bourges (Fig. 110), which was built in 1443.
Jacques Cœur was a prosperous banker and the leading citizen of
Bourges, and the ostentation of his dwelling is a striking indication of
the importance that a layman could attain in the 15th-century community. In plan, the house is an irregular pentagon built around an

open court that is reached through the large arched opening in the street façade which itself is bent to conform to the line of the street. Notable characteristics of the exterior otherwise are the steeply pitched roofs of irregular and asymmetrical grouping over the different rooms of the interior and the elaborate decorative detail of window tracery, crockets and pinnacles and sculptured figures. Within, the principal feature of the structure is the arrangement of the rooms for maximum ease and convenience of use and circulation. Staircases of characteristic spiral form covered by complicated ramping vaults are located in the small towers such as the octagonal one that appears in the street front and provides means of access to the chapel which lies behind the pointed window with flamboyant tracery in the main pavilion of the façade; other rooms of clearly defined purpose account for the remaining details of the external appearance of the building. Lavishly ornamented within, with richly carved doors and painted ceilings over walls hung with elaborate tapestries, such a house as that of Jacques Cœur provided a sumptuous setting for living on a scale well befitting the prominent position of its bourgeois owner, a scale to which only feudal lords or princes of the Church could have aspired in earlier times.

A further manifestation of the increasingly secular character of mediaeval culture in the Gothic period is the number of buildings then erected to serve as centers of civic life. The *Palazzo Vecchio* of Florence (Fig. 111) was built in 1298 after the designs of Arnolfo di Cambio as the town hall of the city, a function which it still performs. Mention was made at the beginning of this chapter of the early impulse to commerce and industry in Italy that was given by the crusades; the appearance of such a monumental structure as the Palazzo Vecchio at a relatively early date for a building of strictly secular character is an indication of this. In form it is an enlargement of the type of building used for residences by the Florentine burghers and it still retains much of the fortress-like character that was a necessary quality of domestic structures in a city that was periodically convulsed by internal strife; the bloody struggles of the Guelphs and Ghibellines who replaced each other in sanguinary alternation as the ruling factions in Florence during Dante's time are symbolized by the contrasting square and notched crenellations surmounting the main mass and the tower respectively. Otherwise, the chief characteristics of the structure externally are the rusticated walls of large roughcut blocks of stone, the windows with their double openings, the contrast between the graceful and slender tower in which hung the bell that called the Florentines together for defense of their city and the heavy mass of the building itself, and the characteristically Gothic asymmetry in the design as a whole.

The Norman city of Rouen in France is associated historically with Joan of Arc, who met her death there in 1431 while it was in the hands of English troops whose domination was not terminated until

FIG. 111.—Florence. THE PALAZZO VECCHIO.

1449. Its importance increased rapidly thereafter and some of the buildings erected or completed in the latter part of the 15th century are among the most impressive examples of late French Gothic or flamboyant style. The façade of the cathedral (Fig. 102) is one of these that has been discussed. Another is the *Palais de Justice* (Fig. 112), which was begun in 1493 as the place of meeting for the *Parlement* of Normandy and of which the central and left wings were finished by 1508; the architects were Jacques and Robert Leroux. Like the Palazzo Vecchio in Florence, the general scheme of the building is an enlargement of the current domestic type (cf. Fig. 110), for it is built around a large court of rather irregular plan with the main block of the structure at the back and two wings projecting forward from it, the entrance being no more than a screen wall to close in the court. Characteristic details of this late or flamboyant phase of Gothic style in France are the reversed curves of the pinnacle gables and the flattened arches framing the windows on the ground level and in the principal story. Like the ornament on the façade of Rouen Cathedral, that of the Palais de Justice is a screen of lace-like stonework relatively independent of the wall. If many of the forms appear to be used primarily for

FIG. 112.—Rouen. THE PALAIS DE JUSTICE.

decorative effect—such as the flying buttresses of the dormer gables in the roof—the richness of the resulting impression cannot be denied. As a whole, the relatively simple design of the side-wing façade is an effective foil to the more elaborate one of the main part of the structure.

Infinite variety is the keynote of Gothic style whether it be a matter of the details of a single structure or the different types of building in which it is found. In this is a clue to the fundamental purpose of all creative thinking of its time—to construct a system in which the multiplicity of nature should be resolved into order as a symbol of the pervading unity that was God. It is because of the Gothic architect's success in creating such a symbol that in the cathedral of the 13th century it is possible to realize, to an extent not approached before or since, the validity of religious experience. Whether Christian or unbeliever, the observer cannot but feel a powerful emotion created by the soaring lines and luminous color and the resultant sense of being enclosed in illimitable space. The nature of this emotion which can be called only one of religious character has never been more clearly stated than in the words of Suger, abbot of the monastery of Saint-Denis near Paris and one of the great personalities of the Middle Ages: "When the house of God, many colored as the radiance of precious jewels, called me from the cares of this world, then holy meditation led my mind to thoughts of piety, exalting my soul from the material to the immaterial, and I seemed to find myself, as it were, in some strange part of the universe which was neither wholly of the baseness of the earth, nor wholly of the serenity of heaven, but by the grace of God I seemed lifted in a mystic manner from this lower toward that upper sphere."

# Chapter VIII.  Architecture of the Renaissance in Italy~~~~~~~~~~~~~~

DURING THE MIDDLE AGES, WHATEVER THERE WAS of unity and coherence in European culture can be ascribed to the influence of the Church. As has been noted elsewhere, it was the sole institution of such comprehensive authority in Europe, from the time of Rome's decline as an autonomous political and economic entity, as to be able to give direction to the prevailing thought and feeling of the period; and in so doing, it was instrumental in creating the most abstract and spiritual philosophy in the western world. At the same time, the existence of secular elements in mediaeval culture must be realized; although these were always subordinate to the dominant spiritual ones, their importance in the later Middle Ages of the 14th and 15th centuries became increasingly greater, as has been observed in the architectural reflection thereof in the growing number and ostentation of buildings of non-religious character in northern Europe that were then built. The eventual outcome of this trend was inevitably the reversal of the relative importance of religious and secular elements in European culture. The place where this is first apparent was Italy, and the time when it began to be clear was in the early 15th century, in the period known in general as the Renaissance.

A partial explanation for the initial appearance of the way of thinking that is characteristic of the Renaissance in Italy is to be found in the economic history of that region. Throughout the entire mediaeval period, the most traveled routes of trade with the East had been through Italy and it was as trading posts on these routes that many of the cities in northern and central Italy grew up to become organized communities with unified civic governments. Venice and Milan, Florence and Pisa were among the leaders in this development—all owing their importance to success in contributing to the flourishing trade in goods from the Orient, in the manufacture of such commodities as wool and leather, and in the establishment of banking facilities and other institutions basic to commerce that brought to them ultimately the control of much of the business of the Occidental world. Paralleling these economic factors in the background of Renaissance Italy was the early establishment there of political institutions of somewhat different character from those which were to be found elsewhere in Europe. The feudal aristocracy that had developed in France and Germany and England in the wake of Charlemagne's dissolving empire had never been as numerous or powerful in Italy and the foundation of civil bodies called communes which are similar in some respects to the city-states of classic Greece is to be noted in Italy at a date appreciably earlier than any comparable development in northern Europe. Many of these communes came in time to be dominated by individuals or by families—the Sforzas of Milan, the Gonzagas of Mantua, the Malatestas of Rimini and the Medici of Florence—but these owed their authority nominally to the free choice of the communes themselves; and in the case of Florence, the simulation at least of democratic procedure in government was a basic factor in the firm grasp of the Medici upon the affairs of the city during the 15th century.

Important though economic and political factors are in contributing to the character of the Renaissance, they are not sufficient in themselves to explain it or its development. The literal meaning of the word Renaissance is "rebirth" and in using it to characterize the period in question as a whole, there is a direct reference to the reappearance at that time of a new interest in classicism. This has been accounted for as the consequence of suddenly discovering many examples of antique art, long-buried statues, or treasures of Greek and Roman literature that had been lying unread for centuries in monastery libraries. According to this theory, the Renaissance came about through attempts to emulate this beauty of past ages which had been revealed anew to the eyes of mediaeval man, and it was the result of striving to revitalize the forms which had been created originally in giving expression to the ideals of the classic world. Such a conception of Renaissance thinking is given a measure of support by the undeniably classic character of many elements in it, but as a complete explanation it is superficial and inadequate.

The character of Renaissance culture is an indication of the reorientation of European thought away from the abstract and spiritual values of mediaeval culture toward more material ones. In the Middle Ages, man was of no importance save as he was a part of the Church, and the physical earth was only a proving ground for the soul where it was prepared for the ultimate realities to be found in the next world. In the Renaissance, man's inherent dignity was once more perceived in a way comparable in some respects to that of classic antiquity, and in addition, the world in which he lived was no longer thought to be only a symbol but was considered as something of fundamental and intrinsic significance. The interest in nature that is apparent in Ren aissance thinking may seem at first to be a logical outcome of the realistic view of material forms in the Middle Ages. But mediaeval realism is an outgrowth of the conception then prevalent of nature as a manifestation of divine purpose while that of the Renaissance is scientific in the modern sense in being born of a searching inquisitiveness about things which are believed to have meaning in and of themselves rather than merely as symbols in a previously determined order of an abstract nature. It was in the Renaissance that an objectively analytical point of view toward nature is found for the first time; and as the most important institution therein, man once more became the focal point of human interest rather than being reduced to the status of a cog in a theological machine. In its basic humanism, Renaissance thought is distinguished from that of the Middle Ages in a much more significant way than by its classicism.

At the same time, it is because of Renaissance humanism that the art forms in which it is expressed have an undeniable affinity with those of classic antiquity. The essentially symbolic character of mediaeval art made it a poor vehicle at best for the expression of ideas in which an objective interest in man and nature is intrinsic, while classic art is conditioned in large measure by precisely similar interests. Instead, therefore, of saying that discovery of examples of classic art was instrumental in creating the Renaissance point of view, it would be more nearly correct to state that it was the formation of that point of view that made possible the rediscovery of the principles of classic art. This is borne out by the fact that during the Middle Ages there had been a fairly extensive knowledge of antique art in Europe and even some attempts to reproduce its forms, but without stimulating a renaissance like that which is found in the 15th and 16th centuries in Italy. Mere knowledge of the forms was not enough, for an attitude sympathetic to them and with capability of understanding them was first necessary. There is also in this consideration another explanation for the initial appearance of such appreciation and understanding in Italy instead of in other parts of Europe where economic and political conditions may have been quite as favorable. For the classic habit of thought was always strong in Italy, even in the Middle Ages. Romanesque and Gothic buildings in Italy often seem more like classic skeletons clothed in mediaeval details than anything else and some mediaeval sculptures there executed make this even more apparent (cf. Fig. 308). For Italy, the Renaissance was simply a reversion to the classic point of view that was her rightful heritage.

It should not be assumed from this that Renaissance architectural style was created by a process of copying Roman buildings. It was rather a matter of using classic decorative vocabularies primarily and structural ones to a lesser degree, but employing them in ways that, as will be seen, are basically different from those of Roman and Greek builders; for with his heritage of mediaeval structural technique, the Renaissance architect was unable to reproduce the forms of antique architecture as the literary humanists of the time, with the greater resources of verbal expression, were able to copy those of ancient literature. It should be observed, moreover, that the classic models available to the Renaissance designer were limited to Roman examples, for Greece was a part of the Orient culturally speaking at that time; three and a half centuries were to pass before Greek art became well enough known to western Europe to have any appreciable effect upon its creative efforts.

In the increasingly material culture of Europe in the 15th and 16th centuries, the dominance of the Church was progressively less apparent in a spiritual sense and the character of religious thought became quite different in those times than it had been during the Middle Ages. The great revolt against its spiritual authority that was the Reformation was directed, in fact, against the prevailingly profane principles guiding the Church in a time when it competed with temporal rulers for worldly power—a far cry from the state of affairs in 1077 when Henry IV of Germany had acknowledged his subordinacy to Pope Gregory VII in the snows at Canossa and thus provided a symbol of the Church's supreme control of human destiny. But the atmosphere was too rarefied in the world of the spirit in which man was forced to live in the Middle Ages when the value of the individual was determined solely by the part he was willing to play as an insignificant and anonymous unit in an intellectually perfect but abstract order maintained by inexorable principles. An unconscious revolt against the impersonal systematizing of mediaeval thought began even before the end of the Gothic period; its effect on architectural style has already been noted and will be seen elsewhere in the sculpture and painting of France in the 14th and 15th centuries. It is this same revolt that is the animating spirit of François Villon's poetry and, in a more genial form, infuses the doctrines of St. Francis of Assisi with a kindly spirit very different from the austere principles voiced by Bernard of Clairvaux. It is by such changes in sentiment as these that the place of the Church in Europe of the Renaissance is distinguished from that which it held in the Middle Ages; it is now a part of human experience but not all of it; spiritual values still have significance, but material ones must also be taken into account.

Renaissance humanism explains one final distinction between the arts embodying its principles and those of the Middle Ages which will be immediately apparent in considering the facts concerning the monuments themselves—the importance of the creators of those forms as individuals. In the mediaeval period, as has been pointed out, the individual was submerged in the community; in the Renaissance, he emerges from that impersonal social order and claims the right to express his ideas in his own way and thus creates in the arts the concept of the modern, self-conscious artist. Previously the arts had been the expression of communal rather than individual experience, a fact which is true of the classic as well as mediaeval styles. This does not minimize the importance of men like Iktinos and Kallikrates who built the Parthenon, or Isidorus of Miletus and Anthemius of Tralles, the designers of Hagia Sophia, or Robert de Luzarches who was the architect of the cathedral at Amiens; rather it emphasizes the fact that their names are bright spots in the anonymous gloom that obscures those of their equally brilliant contemporaries. All this is changed in the Renaissance. The architect no longer builds solely for the greater glory of the country or city in which he lives, or for the greater glory of God; he builds to win honor for himself in this world and in order that his name may live on in history after his death.

## A. THE EARLY RENAISSANCE

It is perhaps symbolic that the year 1401—first in the 15th century—should have witnessed an event which can well be taken as the beginning of Renaissance art, a competition established by the governing body of the city of Florence to determine the artist who should execute a pair of bronze doors for the Baptistery of the city. Two works were chosen for the final stage in the contest, one by Lorenzo Ghiberti and the other by Filippo Brunellesco di Brunelleschi (1377-1446), both men of good standing in the goldsmiths' guild of the city to which all sculptors had to belong in those days. The final award went to Ghiberti and such was Brunellesco's chagrin that he determined forthwith to seek success in a field where his supremacy would be unchallenged. With this as his motive, he went to Rome in 1403, taking with him a youth named Donatello who was destined for great distinction as a sculptor; here for a number of years he studied and measured the great examples of Roman architecture.

Brunellesco's researches in the methods and forms of Roman architecture came to fruition in 1420 when, after three years of argument, he was commissioned to build a dome over the crossing of the *Cathedral of Florence* (Fig. 113). This huge building, approximately 500 feet in length, had been begun in 1296 in the Tuscan Gothic style whose chief characteristic was a lavish use of colored marble for decoration similar in principle to that seen in Roman architecture; the designer was Arnolfo di Cambio, who had designed the Palazzo Vecchio in Florence (Fig. 111). Arnolfo died shortly after work started on the building and his place was taken by Giotto the painter in 1336, under whose direction the beautiful campanile at the western end of the structure was erected. Work continued under various supervisors during the 14th century and the structure was complete to the level of the dome springing when Brunellesco returned to Florence from Rome

Fig. 113.—Florence. The Cathedral. From the northwest.

in 1417, but the dome itself was lacking. Its construction presented considerable difficulties; the base from which it was to rise was 180 feet above the floor of the building and nearly 140 feet in diameter; the area to be covered was octagonal and the dome had to be built without centering to keep expense at a minimum. With his knowledge of Roman methods of construction, Brunellesco professed ability to erect the dome, but an obstacle to his being awarded the commission appeared in the refusal of the *Opera del Duomo*—a committee with the power of final and absolute decision regarding all matters pertaining to the physical fabric of the building as was commonly the case in mediaeval times—to permit him to proceed until his plans had been submitted and approved by its members. This Brunellesco refused to do, saying that if he did, credit for the accomplishment of the task that he felt should rightfully be his would go to the *Opera*. The three-year struggle that ensued between architect and committee was in many ways a symbol of the conflict between the old and the new orders, mediaeval impersonalism against Renaissance individualism. Symbolic too was the outcome, for Brunellesco won his way and his name has been associated with the dome of Florence Cathedral ever since.

In its final form, the dome of Florence Cathedral is the result of combining classic and mediaeval structural methods with the latter predominant. It is a skeleton of ribs—eight massive ones rising from the angles of the octagonal base and two in each space between making a total of twenty-four—supporting blocks of stone. The whole is pointed in profile to lighten the lateral thrusts which are offset by belts of stone and wooden beams bolted together that surround the dome near its base; these belts are buried in the masonry, but they are none the less essential to the stability of the structure for being invisible. The dome is thus not one at all in the sense that comparable forms in Roman or Byzantine building are, but is rather an eight-sided vault whose thrusts are compensated in the manner usual in Italian Gothic construction, by tying the ends of the arches together. The high pitch of the sides of the dome was also an aid in building it without center-ing, for the ribs and the filling could be raised without external support to a considerable height, after which the small amount of scaffolding necessary to close in the opening at the top was hung from the ribs themselves. It was completed by 1436 with the exception of the lantern tower at the apex; this was finished in 1461, fifteen years after Brunel-lesco's death.

In view of Brunellesco's long studies of Roman architecture, it might be thought that his dome in Florence would have been very much like that of the Pantheon in Rome (Figs. 57, 58) and some features of construction are similar in them. A considerable difference is appar-ent in the effects created, however, especially externally. The dome of the Pantheon is chiefly impressive when viewed from within, while the one at Florence is the dominant feature of the exterior design with its curvilinear form admirably set off by the lines of Giotto's slender campanile at the western end of the building. In order so to dominate the considerable bulk of the building supporting it, the dome of neces-sity had to be rather high and it rises more than 100 feet above its 180-foot-high base. In the interior, the actual height is so great that its effect would be somewhat impaired were there not an inner dome a little lower than the one visible on the outside but supported on the same set of ribs that sustain the outer one. Since the 15th century, nearly all monumental domes have been built in accordance with these principles.

The impression of size and loftiness created by the external design of the Florentine dome is one of the outstanding points of difference between it and earlier examples of the same architectural form such as those of the Roman Pantheon and Hagia Sophia at Constantinople (Fig. 69). In them, exterior effectiveness was sacrificed to structural necessity, for the crowning domes are hemmed in by the buttressing masses essential to their stability. This mechanical function is performed for Brunellesco's dome by the girdles of stone and timber buried in the masonry, its beauty of form thus being obtained at the expense of a complete statement of structural fact. Herein lies one of the most significant points of difference between architectural thinking of the Renaissance period and that which was responsible for the Greek and Gothic styles. In both of the latter, beauty of form is a concomitant of construction; the essential character of a building erected in accordance with the principles of either one can be grasped only if the structural factors involved are understood. In Renaissance architecture, problems of construction play little or no part in determining the form of buildings. The dome of the Cathedral of Florence is really a vault, but the buttressing essential to its stability contributes nothing to its visual effect, concealed as it is in the masonry. In thus subordinating structural facts to formal effects, Brunellesco's attitude is one that is to be typical of Renaissance architects in general who strove in their designs to realize preconceived ideals of beauty instead of thinking primarily in terms of construction which had to be integrated and unified in the final effect.

A chapel built by Brunellesco for the Pazzi family of Florence (Figs. 114, 115) illustrates the preoccupation of the Renaissance architect with problems of formal design rather than construction even more clearly than the dome of the Florentine Cathedral. Although it was built in the Gothic cloister of Santa Croce (the façade and tower of which can be seen above the roof of the Cathedral in the illustration in Fig. 113), it is completely in the Renaissance manner of which it was probably the first ecclesiastic example erected since it was begun about 1420 and completed by 1429. It is a rectangle in plan and is covered by a dome on pendentives within, flanked by barrel vaults on the cross axis. Another dome is in the center of the portico or loggia that forms the lower part of the façade; it too is flanked by barrel vaults which extend to the outer ends of the porch and are masked by the pilastered and paneled wall supported by the Corinthian columns of the portico. Here more than in the Cathedral dome are the results of Brunellesco's Roman studies apparent; the idea of a dome on pendentives is Byzantine, but the coffered ornament that covers it is in the best Roman tradition (cf. Figs. 56, 58) and the Corinthian order is likewise, in both general proportions and the detail of the capitals. Further direct references to Roman procedure appear in the band of strigils or wavy flutings at the top of the masking wall and in the triangular pediment of the portal.

FIG. 114.—Florence. THE PAZZI CHAPEL. Façade.

Other than the dome over the interior of which only an angle pendentive is shown in the illustration (Fig. 115), the most striking feature of the internal design is the decoration. Applied pilasters on the walls support an applied entablature from which moulding and framing arches rise on each of the principal walls and in the niche where the altar stands. Within the narrow rectangles thus formed are panels with arched heads and sculptured medallions, and the shallow barrel vaults flanking the central dome on the cross axis of the interior are ornamented with panels enclosing rosettes. The architectural elements in the decoration are in the classic tradition—Corinthian pilasters, the entablature above and the panels with rosettes. As ornament, their effectiveness is heightened by the contrast between the color of the stone from which they are carved which is gray-green, and the cream of the stucco walls. It is easy to see that the character of these principal features of the interior design is determined not by structural necessity of any kind but solely from desire to create with them a pattern of form and color that will be effective by virtue of pleasing tones and proportions. The latter are a consequence of employing simple geometrical shapes as the basis of the design and repeating them throughout; the half-circle of the panel heads, for instance, echoes the larger

Fig. 115.—Florence. The Pazzi Chapel. Interior.

ones of the barrel vaults and arches supporting the dome, and the rectangles framed by the pilasters are of the same dimensions and proportions as those formed by the exterior portico columns. In the façade design, a similar concern for mathematically coordinated forms is seen; the height of the applied order of pilasters on the upper masking wall with its architrave is one-half that of the columns beneath with their architrave, and the wall itself is divided into almost exact squares by the pilasters. Here, too, semicircular arches provide a curvilinear foil for the predominant rectangularity of the balanced and symmetrical whole.

Inasmuch as Brunellesco's intention was to produce a visually pleasing design by these various relationships, the result may be legitimately criticized if this end is not attained. For example, the mathematical relationship between the pilastered wall above the colonnade and the colonnade itself is overstudied and obvious, and contributes in some degree to the impression that the wall is too heavy for its supports, which it is in fact as well as appearance for some of the columns have split under the weight resting on them. Their equal spacing on either side of the central arch is another debatable characteristic of the design since this prevents any suggestion of framing the composition as a whole which can be done in such a pattern only by stressing the outer accents in one way or another; as was the case in classic peristylar compositions, the problem of the angle support, whether in loggias such as this or in courtyards surrounded by arcades, was one that challenged the skill in design of many Renaissance architects. Finally, the façade is open to criticism for its lack of scale; there is no indication of its actual size, which is not inconsiderable since the columns of the portico are nearly twenty-five feet in height, while its apparent size is if anything quite small.

Brunellesco is said to have been animated by a desire "to restore to light the good manner of architecture," meaning the classic, and it is thus important to perceive the differences in principle between his way of thinking architecturally and that of the Middle Ages with which he was consciously breaking in the Pazzi Chapel. Most obvious of these is his employment of classic decorative motives which have little or nothing to do with the structural features of the building. Different too is the balanced symmetry of the design as compared with the picturesque asymmetry of comparable mediaeval forms. Yet it should not be assumed that Brunellesco is thinking as a Greek or Roman would, for all the accuracy with which he has reproduced certain elements of their architectural styles. His building lacks the organic integration of structural and decorative elements that would be found in a Greek temple, for instance, and even in such a detail as the applied order which seems to parallel Roman usage, he employs it not as a form descriptive of structural function but for decorative reasons. His use of classic forms was motivated by an almost naïve delight in being able to reveal his knowledge of them, but his way of using them still has much of the mediaeval in it since the effect is one not of inherent and organic unity but of a piling up and multiplication of detail. The undeniable charm of the building lies in the freshness and novelty of his treatment of this detail which is eloquent of the new and vivacious interest of the Renaissance in both its classic past and its—for that time—modern present.

It was characteristic of the Renaissance attitude that secular architectural forms should have early attracted attention as worthy of monu-

*Michelozzo*

Fig. 116.—Florence. The Medici-Riccardi Palace. Façade.

mental treatment and the first half of the 15th century in Florence witnessed the erection of a number of palaces built for the wealthy burghers then becoming the most influential class in the city. Such was the *Medici-Riccardi Palace* (Figs. 116, 117), begun in 1444 by Michelozzo Michelozzi (*ca.* 1396-1472) for his patron Cosimo de' Medici, then the foremost citizen of Florence, and finished by 1459. The building passed into the ownership of the Riccardi family in the 16th century (hence the hyphenated name) and underwent modifications in design in 1517, when some of the original arched openings of the ground story were transformed into pedimented windows, and again in 1715, when the original length of ten bays was increased to the present seventeen. In plan it is a hollow rectangle, built around a court in the same fashion as the earlier Palazzo Vecchio (Fig. 111) and the later Farnese Palace in Rome (Fig. 124), with the façade rising directly from the street.

Externally, the chief features in design of the Medici-Riccardi Palace are the rustication of the wall surface, the treatment of the window openings in the second and third stories, the use of mouldings to distinguish the different levels in elevation and the crowning cornice (Fig. 116). Of these features, the first two are more or less traditional in Florentine architecture. The windows are divided by central mullions into two lights for each opening, and if the mullions themselves are in the form of Corinthian colonnettes, the divided window opening is found in earlier buildings like the Palazzo Vecchio (Fig. 111). The rough stone of the lowest story of the exterior is also a characteristic of the older structure where, however, it appears uniformly in all parts of the external elevation, whereas Michelozzo has distinguished the three levels of his elevation by varying the surfaces; they are massively irregular on the ground story, with smooth faces on the second but with the joints between the stones emphasized by beveling the angles, and the third smooth-faced throughout. In so treating the exterior of the building, Michelozzo has been able to create a sense of scale, for the different parts are at the same time related to and distinguished from each other. The horizontal emphasis created by the mouldings or stringcourses between the stories also aids in giving scale to the structure whose external bulk is dominated in effect by the bold and massive cornice surmounting it. These two features—the stringcourses and the cornice—have no counterparts in mediaeval Florentine building. The detail in them is classic in character, the dentils of the mouldings and the modillions of the cornice for example; and in their general function in the design there is a direct reference to Roman practice, for by their use Michelozzo has been able to invest his building with formal unity of a character quite different from that of the mediaeval palace from which he took some features. In its self-contained symmetry, the exterior of the Medici-Riccardi Palace represents a compositional ideal that is inherently classical in feeling just as does Brunellesco's Pazzi Chapel (Fig. 114), but with more character from its effective scale that is due in part at least to the retention of some traditional elements.

Many classic details are to be noted in the *Court* of the Medici-Riccardi Palace (Fig. 117) as well as on the exterior. Vaulted porticoes

FIG. 117.—Florence. THE MEDICI-RICCARDI PALACE. Court.

surround it, the colonnade arches springing from columns with modified Composite capitals in the manner of certain late Roman examples. The arches are moulded on their external faces and the same profile is repeated horizontally in the entablature resting upon them. As in the design of the Pazzi Chapel façade, structural considerations play no part in determining the form, for the groined vaults of the porticoes are built with tie-rods instead of buttresses to offset their thrusts. Also, as in the design by Brunellesco, the arcade is lacking in sense of adequate support at the angles in consequence of the uniform spacing of the columns and in seeming too light for the walls above. These are evidence of unfamiliarity with the basic principles of a structural vocabulary that is still appreciated more than it is understood; later architects are to improve upon these effects by virtue of greater understanding.

But here as in the sculpture and painting of the same period in the early 15th century in Florence, there is the charm of freshness and the appeal of a naïve vision that does much to offset all that may rightfully be said by way of academic criticism.

The Medici-Riccardi Palace is an important building in the history of architecture for it represents the first stage in transition from the concept of domestic architecture embodied in the mediaeval fortress to that of the city house. As one of the first buildings in Renaissance style to incorporate such ideas, it was influential in creating a type which was continued in Florence until far into the 16th century and was also a potent factor in determining the style of many important buildings in other parts of Italy as well. Significant too is its rôle as the home of the Medici family which probably contributed as much as any comparable social organism to the formation of Renaissance culture of the 15th century; within its walls occurred incidents that vitally affected not only the course of Florentine history but that of the entire western world. The treasures of art it once housed form the nucleus of one of the greatest extant collections of Renaissance sculpture and painting, and the picturesque Procession of the Magi painted on the walls of its chapel by Benozzo Gozzoli (Fig. 407), in which the members of the Medici family are represented as some of the Wise Men from the East, is a priceless source of knowledge regarding the costumes and customs of the time when it was executed.

Brunellesco and Michelozzo were of the first generation of Renaissance architects in that the classic style was a source of pleasure and inspiration to them. To Leon Battista Alberti (1404-1472) it was likewise a source of inspiration, but the use he made of it was of somewhat different character, as is seen in the façade of the Rucellai Palace in Florence (Fig. 118). Begun in 1446 and completed in 1455, it follows the general type of the Medici-Riccardi Palace in its three-storied elevation and in certain details like the windows which are openings whose frames are flush with the wall and divided by colonnette mullions. The effect is less massive and more ornate than that of Michelozzo's palace, however, and the primary decorative scheme is not rustication but a system of superimposed pilasters of modified Doric and Corinthian types which are used in the Roman manner (cf. Fig. 52) with one order, including a complete entablature, for each story. In so using the orders, Alberti developed a motive destined for great popularity in the later 15th century and for further elaboration in the 16th. A difficulty involved was the treatment of the main cornice which takes the place of the entablatures used for the two lower orders in the topmost one but which had to be made much more massive in proportion than they are in order to cap the building as a whole with any degree

*alberti*

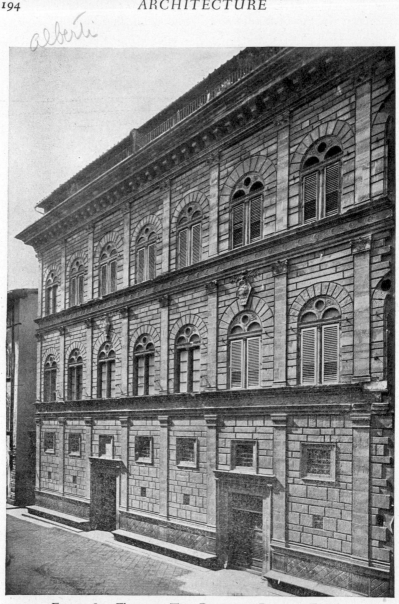

Fig. 118.—Florence. The Rucellai Palace. Façade.

of success and yet could not be entirely out of scale with the order of which it is theoretically a part. In trying to effect a compromise between these two formal functions, Alberti was forced to forego the bold and vigorous profile of Michelozzo's cornice of the Medici-Riccardi Palace and his structure is somewhat less forceful in character as a result.

Other than the innovation of the superimposed pilasters applied to the wall, the decoration of the Rucellai Palace façade consists of rustication of the surfaces enclosed by the orders which is similar to that of the second story of Medici-Riccardi Palace (Fig. 116), and continuous friezes of delicate arabesques in low relief that replace in the entablatures the stringcourses of Michelozzo's design. The rustication is only simulated in some places, notably the arched window heads, the pattern of the supposed joints being determined not by the size of the stone blocks employed but by desire to produce an even and uniform effect, a detail revealing the Renaissance tendency to divorce structure and ornament that has been noted elsewhere. As a study in formal relationships other than those mentioned, Alberti's design is notable for its fine balance of solids and voids and for the effective rhythm resulting from slight variations in the widths of the bays framed by the applied pilasters, those enclosing the doors being a little wider than the others. It is by this device that Alberti obtains variety and suggests scale in his façade which is as notable for its lyric delicacy as is Michelozzo's for its rugged boldness. In both the Medici-Riccardi and Rucellai Palaces, the original interior designs have been subsequently modified, but rooms of the period in other palaces (cf. Fig. 611) make it possible to complete in imagination the settings in which the Florentine burghers lived in the 15th century.

The greatest difference in principle between Alberti's use of classic architectural forms and that of Brunellesco and Michelozzo is the former's employment of them in accordance with Roman theory as contrasted with the compositions of the older men which might be said to be illiterate by comparison with his academically justifiable arrangements. This is borne out by what is known of the men themselves. Brunellesco and Michelozzo were craftsmen trained in the use of their hands and capable of demonstrating by example just how a stone should be cut and laid. Alberti was a scholar and humanist, versed in Latin and an accomplished author, mathematician, painter, sculptor and poet as well as architect. In the latter capacity, he was a designer and director in the sense that a modern architect is, rather than the master mason of mediaeval times to which Brunellesco and Michelozzo are more comparable. His scholarly interests led him to make a profound study of the writings of Vitruvius, the Roman architectural theorist of the 1st century A.D., a manuscript copy of which had been found and identified in the Swiss monastery of Saint Gall in 1414; Alberti's own theories of architectural design as set forth in the book he wrote, characteristically enough in Latin and called *De Re Aedificatoria* or *Concerning Building*, are deeply colored by the principles of the Roman writer. Alberti's book which was composed about 1450 and published in 1486, was instrumental in establishing his own somewhat academic theories as one of the fundamental factors in subsequent architectural practice in the Renaissance. In making classic usage as well as classic forms the basis of his creative thinking, Alberti was similar to many artists in other fields during the later 15th century in Italy; the principle implicit in his attitude of creation in accordance with a preconceived and consciously maintained ideal of beauty is in direct contrast to that of an intuitively felt and emotionally attained one in the Middle Ages.

The character of Renaissance conceptions of architectural beauty is clearly revealed in Alberti's remodeling between 1450 and 1468 of the

Fig. 119.—Rimini. San Francesco. Exterior.

13th-century church of *San Francesco* in Rimini (Fig. 119). The project was undertaken for Sigismondo Malatesta, the Tyrant of Rimini, and was one calculated to appeal to Alberti's classical and humanist tastes for the remodeled structure was to be a hall of fame in which

Sigismondo's mistress Isotta and the members of his "academy," founded to study the masterpieces of classic literature, were to be buried. Over the brick core of the earlier building, Alberti spread a marble veneer that would have transformed the façade into a veritable Roman arch of triumph had the projected upper story been completed, the design being a direct adaptation of a Roman gate that still stands in the walls of Rimini. It is probably the first Renaissance building in which an effort was made to reproduce the general form as well as the details of a classic architectural type, and the full entablature breaking out over the semi-detached columns of the façade creates an effect comparable in ostentation to that seen in many late Roman buildings, an impression intensified in the carving of the richly moulded and pedimented doorway. A great deal of the sculpture of the building is by Agostino di Duccio and its lightness and delicacy do much to relieve what would otherwise be a rather dry design. The niches along the side of the building were to receive the ashes of Sigismondo's associates in sarcophagi copied after those employed in classic Roman times.

Florentine artists were the first in Italy to develop consistent styles in accordance with Renaissance principles, and Florence is the city in which the character of the Early Renaissance phase of the arts is most clearly and comprehensively defined. Its commercial importance and economic power as one of the great centers of banking and of wool manufacture in the 15th century may have been partly responsible for this, but it can hardly be doubted that the free and democratic atmosphere of the city in which originality of thought and intellectual curiosity were encouraged did much to further the spirit of imaginative creativeness and a receptive attitude toward the results it achieved. Such an atmosphere did not exist in all parts of Italy at this time. In Venice, for instance, although the economic picture was highly favorable in consequence of the city's flourishing trade with the Near East, originality of thought was not encouraged by a government which was theoretically republican but actually an oligarchy exercising despotic control and possessing final judgment over all aspects of life in the city and its possessions. The restraining effect of such circumstances upon the architecture of Venice is evident in the continuation in it of many mediaeval forms even long after the innovations of Brunellesco and Michelozzo had given way to other and later ones in Florence. It should also be noted, however, that there were no classic remains in Venice, which had not been a Roman city but was founded in 568 by inhabitants of the northern inland region of Italy fleeing from invading Lombards. They thus lacked the direct classical heritage of which the Florentines were so proud. Renaissance motives are an importation there in a certain sense as compared with the way they were regarded in Florence and even elsewhere in northern Italy as for instance in Milan, where a rather important school of architecture had its center.

An example of the tardy appearance of Renaissance architectural style in Venice is the *Vendramini Palace* on the Grand Canal (Fig. 120) which was designed by Pietro Lombardo (1435-1515). It was begun in 1481, by which time the classical habit had been firmly established in Florence through the examples of Brunellesco and Alberti; but the Venetian palace still retains so characteristic a mediaeval motive as

Fig. 120.—Venice. The Vendramini Palace. Façade.

the traceried window with a dividing mullion though framed by superimposed orders of engaged columns on pedestals and with entablatures for the dividing courses between stories. A characteristically Venetian effect created by these orders is the triple division of the façade resulting from doubling the columns framing the outermost bays; this tripartite pattern appears in the earliest preserved examples of Venetian palace architecture and persisted until the 18th century. Otherwise the most characteristic feature of the Venetian palace as compared with the Florentine type (Figs. 116, 118) is the pronounced openness of the façade with its large and ample windows. These look out as a rule from spacious salons on the second and third floors, over the

Grand Canal which was the principal "street" of the city; the fact that they are a more or less invariable characteristic of Venetian domestic structures is a reflection architecturally of the civic peace of the city imposed by the arbitrary power of its Council of Ten as compared with the turbulence of Florence where a somewhat less open street façade was a wise precaution against flying stones and other missiles even in the 15th century.

The naïve pleasure with which Brunellesco and Michelozzo regarded the art of classic antiquity gave way to Alberti's scholarly enthusiasm

Fig. 121.—Milan. San Satiro. The Sacristy. Exterior.

in the mid-15th century and the closing years of this period brought further developments along this line in the work of Donato Bramante (1444-1514). Born in Umbria in central Italy, Bramante was a painter in his youth, possibly having studied this art under Piero della Francesca (cf. Fig. 398) and certainly being influenced by Mantegna (cf. Fig. 399), two of the most creative and classically-minded masters of painting in the 15th century. It was in Milan in northern Italy that Bramante began his career as an architect, however; here he designed

FIG. 122.—Milan. SAN SATIRO. The Sacristy. Interior.

the church of *San Satiro* (Figs. 121, 122) built between 1480 and 1488. Its sacristy is a structure of the central type in plan, with a circular lower level resolved into a Greek cross in the four gabled arms of equal length in the second stage, the whole terminating in an octagonal drum which is surmounted by a slender cylindrical tower and pinnacle. The central plan was a type that had great attraction for the architects of the later Renaissance since it provided an opportunity to develop monumental compositions of form and space to an extent which the basilican type of structure did not allow. This is quite apparent in the exterior of San Satiro (Fig. 121) which is quite imposing in effect although of rather modest dimensions, a consequence of the relationships between the various parts of the structure which were determined by giving its silhouette as a whole the form of an equilateral triangle. Within this basic geometrical form the applied pilasters, whose shafts are decorated with arabesques of vases and foliage on the lower level where they frame alternate wide panels and narrow niches, and are bent around the angles of the octagonal drum above, define and accent the plastic patterns formed by the different parts of the building. Internally (Fig. 122), the compositional problem was one of defining space and giving it adequate scale. The octagonal volume of the interior is emphasized by bending the pilasters at the angles and the problem of scale is solved by judicious adjustment of the proportions of the upper order to the lower one. Again the decoration of the orders is by arabesques—delicate patterns of lightly carved but crisply defined leaves—while the medallions flanked by groups of *putti* or nude infants in the panels between lower and upper stories are classic in type and strongly individualized in effect, suggesting the possibility that Bramante may well have known and admired the sculpture of Donatello (cf. Fig. 316) with its overtones of the antique, as well as the paintings of Mantegna and Piero della Francesca.

About 1500, Bramante was called from Milan to Rome in order that he might undertake certain architectural works for the pope, a circumstance that made him a transitional figure from the Early Renaissance style which is still apparent in his Milanese designs to the High Renaissance manner of which his Roman buildings are in many ways the initial statement. The differences between the two phases of Renaissance Italian style will be noted elsewhere. Here it will suffice to observe that the 15th-century architects of the Early Renaissance worked chiefly in Florence and northern Italy and only toward the close of that period do they reveal more than enthusiastic observation of the immediate and obvious qualities of classic architectural form. Brunellesco's Pazzi Chapel and Michelozzo's palace for the Medici family have many classic details of ornament, but the basic compositional schemes and the use of the ornament are dictated by the feeling of the designer rather than a comprehension of the larger plastic relationships that are as much a part of antique architectural procedure as the more immediately observable decoration. Alberti and Bramante reveal some perception of these more fundamental qualities

of architectural expression and although the ornament of their buildings has much of the lightness and exuberance that is typical of Early
Renaissance design in general, it is none the less used as an accessory
to well-designed and planned structures that are given character more
by effective relationships of mass and space than by surface decoration.
It is from their practice and theories that the Italian High Renaissance
style develops.

## B. The High Renaissance

With the turn of the 16th century, Rome became the chief center
of artistic activity in Italy, and the High Renaissance style whose
chronological span falls within the first half of the century is first and
foremost a Roman phenomenon. During the Middle Ages, Rome as a
city reflected but indifferently its spiritual importance as the seat of
the Church. Possibly the lowest point in its physical fortunes occurred
during the period of the so-called "Babylonian Captivity" from 1305
to 1377, when the papacy was moved to Avignon in France, but after
its return to Rome, a number of the popes who held office in the 15th
century took steps leading to the artistic regeneration of the city.
Nicholas V (1447-1455) called Fra Angelico from Florence to paint
the walls of his chapel with frescoes depicting the lives of Saints
Stephen and Laurence, and Sixtus IV (1471-1484) imported a Florentine architect to build the Sistine Chapel in the Vatican Palace between 1475 and 1481 and painters from Tuscany and Umbria to
decorate it. Other popes such as Pius II (1464-1471) and Alexander VI
(1492-1503) encouraged the development of humanistic and secular
interests in the papal court that frequently involved practices not at
all consistent with its spiritual character but which served to create
an atmosphere favorable to the growth of the attitude reflected in High
Renaissance style. The names of three popes are directly associated
with this by virtue of their patronage of the arts—Julius II (1503-1513),
Leo X (1513-1521) and Clement VII (1523-1534). The rise of Rome
as the chief artistic center of Italy in the 16th century and of the popes
as the chief patrons of the arts is paralleled by the decline of Florence
and the Medici family from the position of eminence artistically they
had attained in the 15th century; the death of Lorenzo the Magnificent
in 1492 and the ensuing unrest in the city well symbolized by Savonarola's abortive attempts at reform and the banishment of Piero de'
Medici are episodes in the history of Florence that indicate in some
measure the circumstances of this decline in worldly and creative
fortune. Although a number of outstanding artists of the early 16th
century are Florentine in background and training, and there are monu-

ments there of great importance in the High Renaissance style, the leadership is to be sought and found elsewhere, largely in Rome.

Bramante is the first name in the history of High Renaissance architectural style in Rome, and the first building there by him—the

FIG. 123.—Rome. S. PIETRO IN MONTORIO. The *Tempietto*.

*Tempietto* of *San Pietro in Montorio* (Fig. 123) which was finished in 1502—provides an outstanding instance of High Renaissance character in design. Like his earlier church of San Satiro in Milan (Fig. 121), it is a centrally planned structure and is of rather small dimensions, the outside diameter of the peristyle being only twenty-nine feet; but here resemblances between the two buildings stop. Where the earlier one is made up of varied plastic forms, circular, rectangular and octagonal, the Roman church is composed entirely in curvilinear patterns formed by the circular sanctuary and its surrounding peristyle surmounted by a dome resting on a tall drum. The order, too, is less ornate than in the Milanese structure where it consisted of arabesque paneled pilasters; here the sixteen columns of the peristyle are purest Roman Doric, complete with entablature and frieze of greatest accuracy in detail. The balustrade which crowns the lower level of the exterior elevation provides a visual transition to the drum with its recessed niches and the dome. As an example of architectural design intended primarily for monumental effect (it was erected on the spot where Saint Peter was thought to have met his death), the Tempietto is open to criticism for its lack of inherent scale because there is nothing to give an indication of its size when viewed as an isolated building. It was planned to be part of an ensemble, however, in a colonnaded court where its great dignity and impressiveness would have been more adequately accommodated than in its present surroundings.

Monumental formality has replaced picturesqueness as the chief characteristic of architectural design, and logic and reason are the basic expressive aim rather than charm and gayety. These are the fundamental points of difference between San Satiro (Fig. 121) and San Pietro in Montorio (Fig. 123). In thus revealing a new attitude, Bramante is an instance of a phenomenon that recurs over and over again in the Renaissance, among painters and sculptors as well as architects—the development of a more monumental, serious and significant style upon coming to Rome. The reason for this can hardly be specified; it may have been from intuitive perception on the part of the artists of the traditional significance of the Eternal City and a feeling of the necessity that their contributions thereto should contain implicit recognition of its venerable spiritual supremacy. However this may be, it is in the more monumental character of High Renaissance architecture that its most distinguishing characteristic is to be observed, and with it a growing appreciation of the need for designs well unified and consistent in formal qualities rather than superficially attractive. This involved among other things an extensive development of architectural theory as well as structural practice and the influence of writings such as those of Alberti becomes increasingly more apparent with the progress of the 16th century.

In the field of domestic architecture, the *Farnese Palace* in Rome (Figs. 124-126) illustrates certain features of the High Renaissance style. Built for Alessandro Farnese who was then a cardinal and was later to become Pope Paul III, it was begun in 1517 after the designs of Antonio da San Gallo the Younger (1485-1546), a Florentine who was nephew to two 15th-century architects of the same surname from whom he had gotten his early training which was completed by work with Bramante. His plans were followed only for the first and second stories, however; the third with its cornice was designed by Michelangelo Buonarroti (1475-1564). The building is a hollow rectangle in plan (Fig. 124) and symmetrically disposed in mass with respect to both major and minor axes. In this it is more or less traditional for, as has been noted, the 15th-century Florentine palaces have the same general arrangement (Fig. 117). Also reminiscent of Florentine prac-

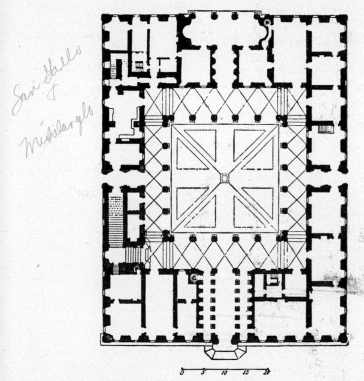

Fig. 124.—Rome. The Farnese Palace. Plan.

tice is the absence of superimposed orders in the façade design, although elsewhere in Italy and even in some earlier 16th-century palaces in Rome the use of the order after the examples of Alberti and Bramante was rather extensive. Florentine too is the heavy cornice, massive in proportions and bold in projection, which follows the general pattern of that on Michelozzo's Medici-Riccardi Palace (Fig. 116) which Michelangelo must have known well since it was he who had been engaged to modify the ground story of the Florentine structure in 1517, as has been noted elsewhere.

The devices of rustication and applied orders used on façades of

Fig. 116. Palace Ten Fellimeld Palace Façade.

Early Renaissance palaces (cf. Figs. 116, 118) make them largely studies in surfaces of contrasting tone and texture. These are omitted in the Farnese Palace façade, which is rather a study in proportion and mass, framed by the cornice and the alternately long and short projecting stones or quoins at the angles, unified horizontally by the carved and moulded stringcourses between the stories, and given interest by the plastic patterns of the window frames. These are treated in differing ways—with flat architraves and sills supported on consoles in the first story, with applied colonnettes on projecting bases and supporting alternately triangular and curved pediments in the second, and with round arched openings under broken triangular pediments in the third. In all cases, however, the window becomes a positive plastic motive by virtue of such treatment, as compared with the neutral effect of the openings in an Early Renaissance façade which are flush with the wall surface. In thus making a formal problem of fenestration or the handling of windows, instead of letting openings be determined by their practical function as transmitters of light and air to the interior, the concern of High Renaissance architects with perfection of appearance as the primary aim of building design is obvious. Somewhat weak in the façade ensemble is the entrance motive which is lacking in adequate scale, a limitation imposed by necessity for respecting the rhythmic pattern of the windows in the lower and second stories.

The court of the Farnese Palace (Fig. 126) is reached through an elaborately vaulted columnar vestibule whose Doric order and coffered covering appear to have been inspired by details of the ancient Roman Theatre of Marcellus from which much of the stone used in building the Renaissance palace was taken. The Colosseum (Fig. 52) was also looted for this purpose and the design of the court shows clearly the consequences of sympathetic study of the older structure. It is in three stories with vaulted arcades on the ground level and walls with windows above. Applied orders appear throughout—Doric and Ionic columns for the first and second floors and Corinthian pilasters for the third—in the same relationship that is to be seen on the exterior of the Colosseum, to which the treatment of the base courses and entablatures is also to be referred. Pediments are used over the windows as on the façade, but the framing colonnettes are omitted in the interests of scale which would have been impaired by too close juxtaposition of the small orders appropriate to the windows with the larger ones applied to the walls. The problem of the angle support which so taxed the ingenuity of 15th-century architects in designing arcaded courts (cf. Fig. 117) is solved here by using piers instead of columns, those at the corners being larger and angular in section so that they

enable the arcade to turn at right angles. The more massive and dignified effect of the Farnese court in comparison with that of the Medici-
Riccardi Palace and its more consistent classicism in detail are further
illustrations of fundamental distinctions between architectural ideals
of the Early and High Renaissance.

FIG. 126.—Rome. THE FARNESE PALACE. Court.

Symmetry of effect was a primary quality in the rational ideal of
architectural distinction sought by artists of the High Renaissance. In
the Farnese Palace this was not difficult to achieve, for the plan is
symmetrical in itself. In the double *Massimi Palace* in Rome (Figs.
127, 128), the problem confronting the architect Baldassare Peruzzi
(1481-1536) was much more difficult. The site on which it is erected
had been traditionally occupied by the palace of this family, one of
the oldest in Rome, and Peruzzi was called to build two houses on
it (to accommodate the households of Pietro and Angelo Massimi) in
replacement of an older structure destroyed in the sack of Rome in
1527. The street upon which the palaces fronted is narrow and curved,
a fact responsible for the striking treatment on a bowed plan of the
façade to Pietro's portion of the establishment (Fig. 128), which is the
one to the left in the plan. This façade extends beyond the structure of
which it is actually the front and which is much narrower, but in
the interests of symmetry such a solution was unavoidable. It is also
clear that the façade as a whole can hardly be said to have been com-

posed above the level of the first row of windows, for those in the third and fourth stories are little more than openings in the wall. The narrow width of the street explains this, for a tall façade of monumental proportions could not have been adequately perceived in the same way that the Farnese Palace is with a large piazza in front of it. It was for the same reason and Peruzzi's realization that the façade

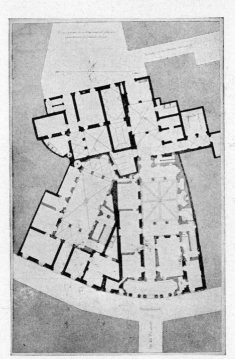

Fig. 127.—Rome. THE MASSIMI PALACE. Plan.

would have to be effective at close range that the decorative details of orders and mouldings are executed throughout with a delicacy and refinement that are beautifully in accord with the modest scale of the structure. At the same time, the entrance portico with its coupled freestanding Doric columns—possibly a reference to the full name of the family which was Massimi *alle Colonne*—is one of the most dignified and impressive of such motives in the domestic buildings of the High Renaissance in Rome, continuing as it does the rhythm of alternate wide and narrow bays established by the pilasters of the side walls in a motive similar to that used by Alberti in the façade of the Rucellai

Palace (Fig. 118) and also by Bramante in a number of his Roman buildings.

The High Renaissance palaces of Rome are effective symbols of the culture that produced them in their dignity and measured proportions —creations of the attitude set forth as ideal in Baldassare Castiglione's *Cortegiano* or "The Courtier." But there is another side to the High Renaissance temperament—that which found expression in the unscrupulous opportunism of Machiavelli's *The Prince* and the crafty

FIG. 128.—Rome. THE MASSIMI PALACE. Façade.

blackguardism of Aretino's polemics. This too was not without architectural expression, for it was the vaulting ambition and unfettered personal pride of Julius II that was responsible for one of the most characteristic examples of High Renaissance style, the present basilica of St. *Peter's* in Rome (Figs. 129-132) which stands on the site once occupied by the structure bearing the same name erected in 324-326 A.D. by Constantine (Figs. 62-64). This venerable building, which was one of the most important monuments of the early Church through its commemoration of the first bishop of Rome, had suffered much during the later Middle Ages and a project to reconstruct it had actually been initiated possibly by Alberti at the command of Pope Nicholas V in

1454. This had not been carried beyond the preliminary stages, however, and the old basilica was in a state of considerable disrepair by the end of the 15th century.

In 1505, Julius II commissioned Michelangelo to create a monumental tomb for him to stand in the Constantinian church. So huge in size was the projected mausoleum that the building in its existing form would not have been able to contain it and the ambitious pontiff characteristically ordered it to be demolished and replaced by a more ample one. A competition to determine the architect was won by Bramante and the first stone of the building was laid in 1506. It was to be a structure of the central type for which Bramante had a particular fondness, as has been noted in discussing his designs for San Satiro in Milan and San Pietro in Montorio in Rome—a Greek cross in plan with four equal arms and a dome over the crossing where the tomb was to stand. Three other men were associated with him on the project, Giuliano da San Gallo, Fra Giocondo of Verona, and Raphael, Bramante's nephew, who is better known as a painter (cf. Figs. 425-428) but also was active as an architect. The four piers to support the dome were completed according to Bramante's plans and the general proportions of the nave were established by 1514 when he died. The work was carried on by his associates but they all died by 1520 and construction was then halted for some time. Between 1520 and 1546, Baldassare Peruzzi and Antonio da San Gallo the Younger were successively in charge of the building and introduced considerable modifications of Bramante's plan, but actual work went little further than some reinforcement of the crossing piers and arches.

Michelangelo was appointed director of the construction in 1546 and the general character of the western end of the building (which faces east instead of west, as did the Constantinian basilica) is the consequence of his ideas. He reverted to a Greek cross plan, with the entrance through a portico of free-standing columns at the end of the eastern arm, so arranged that the tremendous dome which he planned to raise over the crossing would dominate the structure from every point of view. At the time of his death in 1564, the outer walls and the internal ordinance were completed; the small flanking domes around the principal one were built from his plans by Vignola between 1564 and 1585, and the large one by Giacomo della Porto between 1585 and 1590, with slight modifications of Michelangelo's original design, which is still preserved in the form of a large-scale wooden model. In 1605 it was thought necessary to lengthen the eastern arm of the structure to provide more adequate space for the great ceremonies celebrated in it and this was done by Carlo Maderna, who added three bays to Michelangelo's plan with a vestibule that carried the façade, also designed by him, much farther from the dome than Michelangelo's projected portico would have been (Fig. 130). Finally, in 1667, the Doric colonnades enclosing the vast piazza in front of the building were added by Gian Lorenzo Bernini (1589-1680). It is perhaps an appropriate comment on the futility of human ambition that the motive impelling Julius II to destroy the Constantinian basilica and to decree the erection of the present structure—the provision of an adequate

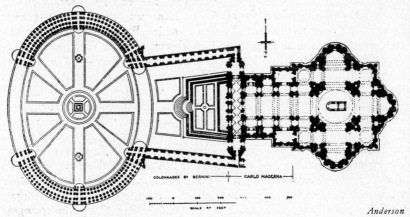

*Anderson*

FIG. 129.—Rome. ST. PETER'S. Plan.

setting for his stupendous mausoleum—was not consummated; the remains of the pontiff lie under an obscure and insignificant slab in the church. The magnificent tomb planned by Michelangelo was never completed and only an unhappy reduction of it is now to be seen in San Pietro in Vincoli.

Comparison of the views showing the façade and the apse of Saint Peter's as it now stands (Figs. 130, 131) will show the extent to which Maderna's façade impairs the effect planned by Michelangelo in which the dome would have been the dominant feature of the structure. From the Piazza di San Pietro, only a portion of the drum is visible and the dome appears in consequence to have no base, a proper transition from the horizontal lines of the façade cornice to the mounting arches of the cupola not having been achieved. From the west, however, the monumental grandeur of Michelangelo's design is immediately apparent (Fig. 131). The walls of apse and transepts are decorated with applied Corinthian pilasters 90 feet in height which rise from a basement course and are surmounted by an entablature with an attic story upon it, the total height from the ground to the

FIG. 130.—ROME. SAINT PETER'S. Façade and Piazza.

top of the attic story being nearly 170 feet. Over these towering cliffs
of masonry rise the small domes above the angle chapels which prepare
the eye for the bold curves of the principal one rising with its lantern
tower to a height of 450 feet. Like the dome designed by Brunellesco
for the cathedral of Florence (Fig. 113), that of Saint Peter's is in
two shells—the outer one of somewhat steeper pitch than that within
in order that its supremacy as the dominant element of the external

FIG. 131.—Rome. ST. PETER'S. Dome, from the west.

effect be assured. It is supported on sixteen ribs which are visible both
within and without and the lateral thrusts are buttressed by the coupled
columns on the level of the drum and by girdling iron chains embedded
in the masonry. No dome of such stupendous proportions had been
attempted before and the impressiveness of Michelangelo's solution of
the various structural and formal problems involved makes the cupola of
Saint Peter's at once the historical climax of the evolution of the dome
as an architectural element—led up to by those of the Roman Pantheon
(Fig. 57), Hagia Sophia (Fig. 69) and the cathedral of Florence (Fig.
113)—and the archetype of the form in succeeding periods (cf. Figs.
162, 172, 188).

No less grandiose than the dimensions of the exterior are those of the internal features of Saint Peter's (Fig. 132). The Corinthian pilasters applied to the nave piers are nearly 85 feet high and the entablature resting on them adds another 20 feet, the coffered barrel vault having its crown 150 feet above the floor level—higher than the vaults of Amiens Cathedral which were among the most lofty completed in the Middle Ages (Fig. 101). Such huge size in the supporting members of the structure was a necessity in view of the great physical forces

FIG. 132.—Rome. SAINT PETER'S. Nave.

involved in its construction, but it is size which is actual rather than apparent. The formal problem involved here is one of scale and this the interior lacks to a marked degree, the various elements being handled in such a way that their real size cannot be grasped directly. It is only after the original impression of the interior has been many times renewed that its immensity can be comprehended—that ten-foot-long decorative cherubs are realized to be that large and that orders of such height can be felt to be really so lofty. The interior dimensions as they stand were established by Bramante, whose plans were followed in building the crossing piers where the gigantic order was first used. Had Michelangelo's equal-armed Greek cross plan been left unmodified, the internal effect of the dome would have done much to create an adequate impression of the huge spatial volume of the interior, but

*michilangelo*

FIG. 133.—Rome. Capitoline Hill. THE CAMPIDOGLIO.

the increased length of the nave resulting from Maderna's added bays makes it impossible to be sensed from any but nearby points.

In striving for effects of largeness in scale, the architects of the High Renaissance frequently made use of the orders, as has already been seen; and when the building was on a basically human scale, the treatment the orders received could follow the practice of the classic builders as in, for example, the court of the Farnese Palace (Fig. 126). Orders of such dimensions as those could have been used on the craglike walls of the apse at Saint Peter's (Fig. 131) only by repetition and superposition with a resultant breaking up of the wall surfaces into many small units whose total effect would have been one of inherent smallness of scale. It was no doubt to emphasize the massive simplicity of the walls and the space volumes they enclose that Michelangelo used a single order instead, making it rise through both stories of the elevation below the attic story. When columns or pilasters are used in this way to include more than one story in height, they are called giant orders and this is one of the most individual architectural conceptions of the High Renaissance period. In Saint Peter's, the giant order of the exterior was doubtless dictated by the colossal pilasters planned for the interior by Bramate although these are limited to but one story in elevation. In the group of buildings called the *Campidoglio* on the *Capitoline Hill* in Rome (Fig. 133) which was begun by Michelangelo in 1546, the device was used with great success as the basic unifying motive tying the façades of the three buildings into a monumental and well-composed group. At the back of the piazza whose sides diverge from the steps by which the hill is ascended (Fig. 134) is the Palace of the Senate; its façade dominates the group by being raised on a high podium above which the giant order of Corinthian pilasters rises through two stories to support an entablature crowned with a balustrade. The end bays of this building project slightly beyond the wall plane to frame the façade as a whole, and the central axis is emphasized by the doorway approached by stairs from both sides. The proportions of the different parts of the façade are determined by a simple but effective system of compositional lines based on 90-degree-angle relationships, another factor contributing to the monumental homogeneity of the whole. To the right is the Palace of the Conservatory and to the left the Capitoline Museum; giant orders and crowning balustrades are prominent features in their designs too, as well as the pedimented windows. The group composition is aided by these reiterated devices and the whole constitutes a characteristic example of High Renaissance ensemble planning of great unity and impressiveness.

Michelangelo's activity as an architect came toward the end of his career and was largely in the second third of the 16th century. His free and individual treatment of classic elements represents one of the principal trends in the architecture of that period and stands in contrast to the more strict observance of antique procedure that characterizes the work of a number of contemporary designers, of whom one of the most notable was Andrea Palladio (1518-1580). Born in northern

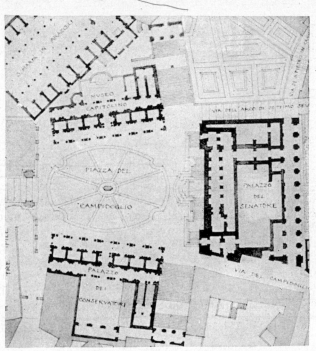

Fig. 134.—Rome. The Campidoglio. Plan.

Italy and chiefly active in his native city of Vicenza, Palladio was a devoted student of Vitruvius, the Roman theorist, and of Alberti whose *De Re Aedificatoria*, published in 1485, had become one of the recognized authorities in architectural design in the 16th century. His own writings, notably the *Quattro Libri dell' Architettura* or "Four Books on Architecture," published in 1570, in which he undertook a detailed and meticulous collation of Vitruvius' theories with existing monuments, were destined to become even more influential than the earlier works in subsequent periods and are one of the foundations of academic architectural procedure throughout Europe in the 17th and 18th centuries.

Palladio's practice reveals his veneration for classic procedure as clearly

as his writings. His first commission was to remodel the city hall of
Vicenza which had been built in Gothic style in 1444; Palladio's reconstruction was begun in 1549 and resulted in the structure known
today as the *Basilica* (Fig. 135) since it had been his purpose to reproduce in some degree the type of Roman building of that name. Little
was done to the interior, but the exterior was transformed into a series
of arcades with orders applied to the older façade, consisting of Doric
engaged columns on the first story and Ionic above, both supporting

FIG. 135.—Vicenza. THE BASILICA.

entablatures to frame the arched openings between. The orders are
adapted to the height and span of the existing Gothic framework by
arches springing from smaller intermediate columns within the arcade
openings, these columns being connected with those of the main order
by small entablatures. The resulting form of an arched opening
flanked by two smaller rectangular ones is called the "Palladian motive"; like the giant order, it is a characteristic High Renaissance
adaptation of classic elements that became very popular through the
wide dissemination of Palladio's theories and the effectiveness of his
designs and also because it provides a means of combining arch and
column in a single motive of considerable expressive value from a
structural point of view. As used by Palladio in the Basilica, it is successful in giving scale to the main order and richness of effect to the
façade as a whole which is well unified by the recurrence of the motive

FIG. 136.—Vicenza. THE VALMARANA PALACE. Façade.

in each bay, successfully composed in length from reducing the width of the end bays to give them a heavier accent, and prevented from a monotonous over-horizontality by carrying the vertical lines of the applied orders through the entablatures up into the sculptured figures on the crowning balustrade.

Profound and sincere as was Palladio's admiration for antique architectural procedure, it was inevitable that his style should reveal as well the formal ideals of his own period. The *Palazzo Valmarana* in Vicenza (Fig. 136) which was built between 1556 and 1566 is one of the town houses that make up a large part of his work. The order of pilasters is treated with restraint, rising above a basement and through two stories, surmounted by a broken entablature and an attic story; a smaller order frames each bay of the first story within the shafts of the giant one, enhancing the scale of the latter and contributing to a richness of effect that is further reinforced by the relief sculptures over the windows in the four central bays and the carving in the portal spandrels. A significant detail is to be noted in the treatment of the angles where only the first story order appears, surmounted by sculptured figures in the second story, instead of continuing the giant order to the façade ends. Palladio was led to this modification of the basic design by the fact that the building is not an isolated structure like some of the Florentine and Roman palaces considered previously (cf. Figs. 116, 125) but is connected directly with others on both sides; what might be considered a weakening of the plastic elements in the façade pattern at the angles is the result of conscious planning to relate it to its setting. Such an attitude as this foreshadows the concern of the 17th century with problems of composition in space as well as form and is a parallel manifestation to Michelangelo's plan of the Campidoglio (Fig. 134) in this respect.

A similar preoccupation with establishing a vital and positive relationship between structure and surroundings is apparent in many of the country houses designed by Palladio, of which the best known is the *Villa Rotonda* which he built near Vicenza for the Capra family between 1552 and 1591 (Fig. 137). Being more of a summer house than anything else, a functionally complicated plan was not necessary and the various rooms are laid out in a rigidly symmetrical and central scheme around the space covered by the dome. On the exterior, the dome, based in design on that of the Roman Pantheon (Fig. 57), rises above a square base from each side of which project porticoes with free-standing Ionic columns and pedimented fronts—one of the early examples of this most classic of architectural motives in Renaissance design. In ornament and proportions these porticoes are faithful embodiments of antique conceptions, but in their function with respect to the mass of the structure they are similar to the device noted in the angle orders of the Palazzo Valmarana (Fig. 136) since their projection creates a positive relationship between the building and its surroundings. As one of the most classically perfect buildings designed by Palladio, the Villa Rotonda was much admired by academically-minded architects of later generations and its design underlies those of many English and American buildings of the 18th century, Thomas Jefferson having used it almost verbatim—plan, porticoes and dome— for a projected house for the President of the United States in 1792.

FIG. 137.—THE VILLA ROTONDA. Near Vicenza.

The buildings of Michelangelo and Palladio fall outside the chronological limit of the mid-16th century set for High Renaissance style; and in the tendency toward more than passing emphasis on individualistically free use of classic elements in the one and likewise the academically pure handling of the same elements in the other, there is evidence of the modification that architectural thought in Italy had undergone since the reticent dignity of a Bramante or a Peruzzi was the prevailing ideal. This is a symbol in its way of the changing values in European thinking of the late 16th century when the economic and political fortunes of Europe were confused and disordered under the impact of new geographic and scientific discoveries, and when the Church under vacillating leadership and driven by the Reformation sentiment developing in northern Europe had renounced the major part of its claim to temporal power but had not as yet perfected a spiritual canon by which its policies could be determined. It is against this background that the baroque phase of Italian architecture must be placed to be seen in proper perspective.

## C. Baroque Architecture in Italy

The term "baroque" which is applied to the architectural style that prevailed in Italy between approximately 1580 and 1730 is one that, although used originally in a derogatory sense of effects considered contrary to good taste, has come to mean the quality of a work of art in which the artist has sought in the interests of more dramatic and spectacular effect to transcend the inherent limitations of his medium in the direction of a more fluent one. Thus baroque can be applied to sculpture that strives for effects more easily and completely attainable in painting, or to painting that seeks to explore the dynamic spatial  patterns that the dramatic stage handles with greater facility. As used with reference to architecture of the time and period in question, it is justified by the increasingly free use of classic elements therein seen, handled in such a way as to create patterns of plastic form and spatial depth that are suggestive of sculpture and painting in principle, although it is to be noted that not all buildings of this period have the exaggerated formal characteristics that arc usually associated with the term baroque. At its worst, the baroque style is bombastic and flatulent, and not undeserving of the criticism that it is no more than a degenerate phase of High Renaissance ideals. But at its best, baroque architectural style is at the same time varied and unified in its plastic and spatial elements and exciting in a way that is not found in any previous or subsequent style. At no other time in the history of architecture have designs been created with so much regard for their effect upon the observer as dramatic spectacle; it was with this end in mind that the baroque masters strove for and frequently attained a new synthesis of the arts by using painting and sculpture as integral features of their architectural designs. More than this, even the purely architectonic forms were employed in such a way as to attain effects closely akin to those of the representative arts. A column may be twisted or a pediment broken, denying inherent architectural functions to realize an effect comparable in its plasticity to that of a sculptured figure. Or a façade is designed in many planes that create a play of light and shade and thus suggest three-dimensional depth as in a painting.

To understand the change in architectural ideals from the static and dignified reticence of the High Renaissance to the dynamic and spectacular effects of the baroque, one must look to the history of the late 16th and 17th centuries. It was the time of the Counter-Reformation and the Church was marshaling all its resources to oppose the ascetic and intellectual Protestantism that was undermining its power in northern Europe. In the extended actions of the Council of Trent between 1545 and 1563, the naïve and childlike symbolism of the Middle Ages was formally banned. The simple faith of Franciscan and Dominican doctrines was subordinated in the spiritual order of the Church to the devices by which Ignatius Loyola (1493-1556) in his "Spiritual Exercises" sought to bring Christian belief to physical realization and to make it an aesthetic pleasure. It was but natural that the tremendous emotional resources of the arts should have made them a powerful instrument in achieving these ends. This was nothing new in itself for the Church had utilized the arts at all times as a means of addressing the faithful either for purposes of instruction or to create a proper attitude on the part of the worshiper. Thus the melody of Gregorian plain song and the color of stained glass aided in the Middle Ages in raising the spirits of the devout to that part of the universe not wholly of earth or of heaven of which Suger speaks, while in the 17th century the motet by Palestrina and the complex patterns of architecture with sculpture and painting that were the baroque church led to the same end. In both periods, the architectonic ideal was synthesis of the major visual arts, and it was in effective relationships between architectural, sculptural and pictorial elements that the most comprehensively expressive results were attained. But if the formal principles of the two periods seem to have something in common, the motivation thereof reveals a profound and significant contrast, for where the spiritual truth apprehended intuitively in the forms of the mediaeval building was itself the product of the intellectually created system of scholastic philosophy, the baroque structure is conditioned from the outset by intent to stimulate the emotions and to overwhelm by the suddenness and violence of its impact upon the physical senses.

Intimations of baroque character appear in certain phases of High Renaissance architectural style—more particularly in the buildings designed by Michelangelo which in some ways directly anticipate the methods of the 17th century. In the *Medici Chapel* designed by Michelangelo as a mausoleum for the famous Florentine family in the New Sacristy of the church of San Lorenzo (Fig. 138) and built between 1519 and 1534, nearly all the elements are ultimately classic in character but the way in which they are used is far from classic in effect. Thus the coupled pilasters flanking the central seated figure support nothing and their own supports are not visible since their bases are obscured by the heads of nude figures reclining on the sarcophagus. As an architectonic system, this arrangement of forms lacks stability; and this, combined with the physical magnitude of all the forms which are crowded into the relatively small room of the chapel, serves to create an effect of strain and discord that is augmented by the

Fig. 138.—Florence. The Medici Chapel. San Lorenzo.

angular lines and violent distortions of the gigantic sculptured forms on the sarcophagus. In a sense this is sculptural rather than architectonic design for the whole is conceived as a setting for the carved figures, but in pursuing the aim of design that should be emotively expressive through precisely the arbitrary and unstructural use of the elements involved, Michelangelo indicated possibilities in architecture as a vehicle for the expression of emotional values that were to be realized even more completely by the later baroque masters of the 17th century. Had the paintings originally planned for the niches flanking the central figure been executed, the baroque synthesis here seen in embryo would have been even more closely anticipated.

If baroque effects of form are forecast by Michelangelo in the Medici Chapel, his design for the buildings of the Roman Campidoglio (Figs. 133, 134) shows in an incipient form the baroque treatment of space. The façades of the Capitoline Museum and the Palazzo dei Conservatori on the sides are neither parallel with each other nor perpendicular to that of the Palazzo del Senatore at the rear but are divergent from the point of view of a spectator at the summit of the steps by which the top of the hill is reached. By this divergence there is created an impression of outward expansion—as if the space defined by the forms were not passive and static but an active force with an organic life of its own complementing the dynamic patterns of the architectural forms. Also contributing to the effect of space as a plastic and dynamic element in the architectural pattern of the Campidoglio group is the oval design in the pavement which centers about and radiates from a Roman equestrian statue of Marcus Aurelius.

The 17th century in Italy witnessed a more pronounced and emphatic treatment of form and space by baroque masters along the lines indicated by these works of Michelangelo. The arrangement of the great colonnades enclosing the Piazza di San Pietro in Rome (Figs. 129, 130), for instance, was dictated by a desire on the part of the designer, Gian Lorenzo Bernini (1589-1680), to achieve an effect of space as a living and pulsating force of which he apparently thought in terms of almost mystic symbolism, enclosed within the colonnades as the world is embraced by the arms of Christ. Built between 1656 and 1663, the columns are Doric and classic in detail, but the plan as a whole is essentially baroque (Fig. 129) in its combination of an ellipse with the obelisk in the center and fountains at the foci with the straight but diverging planes of the colonnades connecting it with the façade of the building. This choice of elements in plan that are complex rather than simple geometrical forms—the ellipse instead of the circle and the trapezoid instead of the rectangle—is characteristically baroque and again is motivated by a wish for vital and dynamic space effects. A pattern of radiating lines in the pavement similar to that of the Campidoglio is another feature introduced for like reasons; the central obelisk is the anchor for the whole composition, placed on the axis of building and piazza, and the point of departure into the space patterns defined by the colonnades, which do much by their dramatic and expansive effects to mitigate the ineptitude of Maderna's façade by giving scale to its formally inert bulk.

Bernini was one of the foremost sculptors of his time as well as being among the greatest of architects (cf. Figs. 334, 335) and some of his architectural work partakes of the quality of sculpture. Such is the canopy or *Baldacchino* which he designed for the high altar of San Pietro in Rome (Fig. 132) between 1624 and 1633. Measuring 100 feet in height or more than the façade of the Farnese Palace (Fig. 125), it would none the less be dwarfed by the gigantic proportions of the structure in which it stands were it not designed in a typically baroque manner to create an impression of size commensurate with its surroundings. This was done by making apparent movement an element in the design, created by the spiral columns which support an open crown and establish a silhouette that draws the eye up and through and past the curving scrolls at the top so that it ascends into the vast dome above. Such scale as is perceived in the crossing of the structure is a consequence of Bernini's achievement in designing the Baldacchino as an accessory to it, and his success in giving scale by movement is one of the most baroque qualities of his way of thinking in formal terms.

Light as well as movement played an important part in the dramatic and spectacular effects with which the baroque architect sought to induce the faithful to participate in the thrilling experience of Christian belief, a point which is well indicated by the nave of the first church built in Rome for the Jesuit Order—the *Gesù* (Fig. 139), which was begun by Giacomo Barozzi da Vignola (1507-1573) in 1568. The architectural project was completed after his death by his pupil, Giacomo della Porta, and the structure was consecrated in 1584 although the present decoration was not finished until 1683. The building was the parent church of the Jesuit Order and as such was very influential, for the type was employed with local modifications wherever the numerous missionaries of the Order went, a fact responsible for the appearance on an international scale of structures of this type during the 17th and 18th centuries and accounting for the baroque churches in such widely separated places as Mexico City in North America and Macao in southeastern Asia. The nave is broad with transepts of but the slightest projection—a disposition encouraged by the emphasis placed on the sermon in the Jesuit order of service—and is covered by a barrel vault with smaller penetrating ones from the clearstory windows. This

vault was originally plain—the present painted and stucco figures are
a later addition—and was a strongly directive force guiding the attention of the observer toward the central dome and the apse. This effect
of movement in depth is also contributed to by the bold cornice from
which the vault springs and to which both the applied pilasters of
the piers and the openings into the small side chapels are made subordinate in the design so that the dominance of the nave space might
not be weakened. This spatial volume is enlarged into the crossing

Fig. 139.—Rome. The Gesù. Interior.

with its dome, reduced to more narrow proportions by the arch of the
choir and finally closed in by the semi-dome and surrounding wall of
the apse. To the effect of movement created by the solid forms of the
interior, the light adds emphasis—ample but diffuse in the nave,
concentrated and intense in the crossing from which the eye escapes
with relief into the semi-gloom of the apse. The design of the nave
of the Gesù is thus seen to be primarily in terms of space, articulated
and unified by the plastic elements of vaults and mouldings and by the
lighting, its ultimate purpose being to focus attention upon the altar
which becomes in this way the heart of the building in fact as well
as symbolically in sheltering the sacred blood and body of Our Savior.

The dualism of High Renaissance architectural style that results from free adaptation and employment of classic forms on the one hand and more restrained use of similar elements on the other is continued in the baroque of the 17th century. The reticence and severity of detail in Bernini's colonnades for the Piazza di San Pietro (Fig. 130) are typical of the latter, as is also the façade of *Santa Maria della Pace* in Rome (Fig. 140), designed by Pietro da Cortona (1596-1669)

FIG. 140.—Rome. SANTA MARIA DELLA PACE. Façade.

and built in 1656. The semicircular portico has coupled Doric columns and an unbroken entablature which are quite pure in detail, but the upper story is composed somewhat more freely. Between the framing pilasters the wall seems to swell out, applied columns are directly juxtaposed with the pilasters, and the triangular gable that crowns the façade as a whole encloses a curvilinear one of which the horizontal moulding is broken to permit the insertion of an irregular cartouche. Both of these forms—the broken pediment and the cartouche —were favorite compositional devices of baroque designers. Two concave wings project from the sides of this central unit and serve as foils to its convexity, the whole being intended to create an effect of dynamic space which seems to force out the façade while the opposing curves of the side wings create a complementary effect of recession in the face of pressure from the outer space of the court in front of the building. Such formal and spatial complexity developing a number of points of view from which the structure must be seen for full comprehension is typically baroque. When compared with a High Renaissance façade like that of the Farnese Palace (Fig. 125) or of Peruzzi's palace for the Massimi families (Fig. 128), the contrasting formal purposes of the two styles are evident. Peruzzi's façade curves in plan like the baroque one, but the curve is a simple one and the effect is still that of an unbroken plane which controls and determines the character of the openings. There is nothing in either of the 16th-century façades, moreover, to imply the plastic bulk of the rest of the structure behind them for they are inherently two-dimensional and as such are complete and self-sufficient designs. At Santa Maria della Pace, oblique angles of view cannot be avoided and each carries with it implications of others in such a way that the observer must see the structure in its three-dimensional entirety before there is any sense of completeness. At the same time there is still in Pietro da Cortona's style a strong feeling for the substance of his forms which are clearly defined and plastically solid.

Francesco Borromini (1599-1667) was considered in his own time as the equal in importance of Bernini and Pietro da Cortona, and his designs for the church of *San Carlo alle Quattro Fontane* in Rome (Fig. 141) are among the most striking in the free category of baroque architecture. The façade was the last part of the structure to be built, it having been erected between 1662 and 1667 although the building had been started in 1638. The poverty of the mendicant order for which the church and its monastic adjuncts were built was responsible for the considerable length of time taken in erecting them and was also a factor in determining the site they occupy. This is on a narrow street near an intersection with four fountains, one on each angle, from which the name of the church—*alle Quattro Fontane*—was taken, and one of which is incorporated in the mass of the church building itself. The façade is no larger in bulk than one pier in the nave of Saint Peter's and within such physical limitations it would appear impossible to achieve an effect of such intensity as that of Borromini's design, nor could it have been done with the idioms of the High Renaissance or even of Bernini and Pietro da Cortona, whose effects can be realized only in large forms and ample spaces. Borromini's façade is built around the eight columns—four in each story—between which the wall and entablatures and cornices protrude and recede in wavy planes. The movement thus created in the design is brought to a focus by the placing of the sculptured figures in lower and upper levels, resulting in an effect of upward straining that comes to a climax in the oval medallion with its pointed frame formed by an upward projection of the top balustrade. In the same way that Bernini created the scale of the Baldacchino in Saint Peter's (Fig. 132), i.e., by movement, Borromini invested the façade of his building with an impressiveness of character that is obtained at the cost of such traditional qualities of

FIG. 141.—Rome. SAN CARLO ALLE QUATTRO FONTANE.

architectonic form as solidness and weight, for the wall seems more like a tenuous membrane rippling under the impulses of pulsating space than something made of stone, but it is undeniably very striking. The contrasting planes of the façade are also instrumental in creating varied and shifting effects of light and shade in the manner of a sculptural composition, and this along with the dependence on sculpture and painting in the design that has been noted makes the façade of San Carlo alle Quattro Fontane one of the most comprehensive examples of the baroque principle known in architectural thinking.

It was only natural that the feeling for space as a vital element in architectural design and the sense of the dramatic and grandiose that is a part of 17th-century thinking should have stimulated interest in large-scale planning—of the gardens and surroundings of individual buildings, and even of entire cities. In the latter category were the various modifications of Rome, from the unplanned and formless conglomeration of ancient and contemporary buildings that it still was at the close of the 16th century to the present arrangement of avenues commanding long vistas dominated by great buildings and accented by spacious plazas. The importance of Michelangelo's design for the three buildings of the Campidoglio (Figs. 133, 134) as an example of group planning has already been noted, and Bernini's colonnaded piazza of Saint Peter's (Fig. 130) is another instance in which a developed baroque concept of large-scale architectural relationships is apparent. In both of these cases, the planning was to emphasize the dominance of given buildings. In others it was the city as a whole that was considered the controlling form, with avenues laid out in such fashion as not only to facilitate circulation but also to create the expansive and exciting vistas demanded by the baroque temperament. Thus from the Piazza del Popolo which was the principal entrance to Rome from the north in the 17th century, three radiating streets led past two impressive baroque churches particularly designed to form a monumental approach to the city as part of a comprehensive scheme of avenues and piazzas connecting the important buildings that was drawn up about the middle of the century. Around 1700, the widely swinging steps rising from the *Piazza di Spagna* to the Pincian Hill (Fig. 142) were begun by Alessandro Specchi as a means of connecting that part of the city with the area then being built up. The result was also one of the most familiar views of modern Rome, with the façade of the church of SS. Trinità de' Monti in the background and an axis of movement in depth created by the obelisk on the upper level of the stairs which is in direct line with the fountain in the piazza below. This latter was designed by Bernini, who was as noted for his creations in this category as for his buildings (cf. Fig. 335); the use of fountains and obelisks as minor accents in the larger baroque elements of avenues and squares is one of the primary features of 17th-century large-scale planning. Undulations of surface and contour in steps and balustrades are similar in character to features of the buildings already noted (cf. Fig. 141) and contribute here as well to a sense of movement and organically vital space in the ensemble.

Landscape architecture as an art received strong stimulus from the the preoccupation of baroque architects with movement and space and light as elements in design, as the gardens of many country houses or villas laid out at that time make clear. These of the *Villa Torlonia* near Rome (Fig. 143) were designed by Carlo Rainaldi (1611-1691) in a series of ramps and terraces laid out along definite axes usually marked by cascading streams of water. The never-ending movement of flickering light thus produced as well as the flow of water over rocky surfaces or shooting up in plumes of spray was obviously congenial to baroque taste, and as in the urban squares discussed above, the gardens of the period were extensively accented by means of foun-

FIG. 142.—Rome. THE PIAZZA DI SPAGNA.

tains. Such effects as these are evidence in architecture of the same expansive interests that led to notable developments in landscape painting in the 17th century (cf. Figs. 473, 474, 475) which are discussed elsewhere.

The closing years of the 17th century and the first of the 18th saw Italy yielding up the architectural leadership of Europe which she had held since the beginning of the Renaissance in the 15th century. Weak and divided politically and with her one-time economic supremacy lost to the nations which had pioneered in exploring the new worlds to the west, her artistic vitality was also exhausted and her artists were capable of little more than acceptance of ideas emanating from France where the Academy ruled triumphant. Under this influence, Italian architecture of the 18th and 19th centuries subsided into sterile and ineffective classicism, the occasional building in which a trace of the old creative spirit is apparent emphasizing the uninspired character of the majority of designs then produced. But during the period when the Renaissance style was at its height in Italy, the influence of its ideas elsewhere in Europe had been great; seeds had been carried from the parent tree, as it were, to other soils where they

FIG. 143.—Frascati. THE VILLA TORLONIA. Gardens.

grew and flourished under conditions different from those in the home land but producing results of no less individual character and frequently of comparable distinction. Thus the Renaissance tradition of architectural thinking that had its origin in Italy has been continued elsewhere, in some cases long after the original stimulus to its formation has died out; but to the extent that a taste for the monumental and the grandiose in architecture persists in modern times, it may be said to represent a continuation of Renaissance conceptions of significant architectonic form.

# Chapter IX. Renaissance Architecture in France.

IN THE 14TH AND 15TH CENTURIES IN FRANCE, THE synthesis of all aspects of human experience that had been achieved by mediaeval theologians and is most comprehensively symbolized by the Gothic cathedral was breaking down. The progressive modifications of mediaeval style that appear in French art of the 15th century reveal a point of view not unlike that of the Early Renaissance period in Italy, although its forms of expression are not the classic ones current in the southern peninsula. Thus comparison of the façade of Rouen Cathedral (Fig. 102) with that of San Francesco at Rimini (Fig. 119) would hardly suggest that the Italian church was built fifty years earlier than the French one if both were judged by the classic elements in them, and Jacques Cœur's house in Bourges (Fig. 110) has little in common, formally speaking, with the contemporary Medici-Riccardi Palace in Florence (Fig. 116). French and Italian buildings are alike, however, in being expressions of a spirit of individualism different from communal principles prevailing in the 13th century, and they are alike too in that they represent modifications of the earlier styles of their respective countries along lines which were indigenous to the regions. In Italy, as has already been pointed out, the classicism of the Renaissance was in many respects a reversion of the country to its rightful formal heritage that was only natural when the dominance of Gothic style was broken in the late 14th and early 15th centuries. The only reason that Rouen Cathedral and Jacques Cœur's house show no such definite break with the immediate past in French style is that the inborn formal tradition there was mediaeval just as it was classic in Italy.

If French architecture had continued in the 16th century the trends apparent in the 15th without coming under the influence of Italian ideas, it is conceivable that a northern style characterized by the same individualism that is evident in Italy but evolving its own formal idioms might have resulted. The history of the times supplies one explanation of the fact that this did not occur. The growing spirit of nationalism following the expulsion of the English in 1453 by French troops inspired by the heroic patriotism of Joan of Arc soon found expression in ambitious projects for new conquests and territorial expansion. Various French rulers beginning with Charles VIII in 1495 attempted to establish claims by feudal rights to different regions in Italy; and under his successors, Louis XII, Francis I and Henry II, a series of military campaigns took thousands of Frenchmen across the Alps into the southern peninsula. There it was inevitable that they should have been much impressed by what must have been the vivid beauty of art forms the like of which their own country had never seen up to that time. The Renaissance ideal had been firmly established by then in all parts of Italy, and it was only natural that the forms embodying it should have appealed strongly to a temperament that itself was not without a strong classic element and was capable of reacting to the revitalized ideals of classic antiquity with an enthusiasm almost comparable to that of the Italians in achieving their rebirth. It was through the medium of Frenchmen so affected that Italian styles were brought back to France in the early years of the 16th century, where their novelty and grace soon won such following that the native modified Gothic tradition represented by the façade of Rouen and Jacques Cœur's house was abandoned. This was not equally true in all parts of France, to be sure, nor of all types of buildings. In the provinces the old tradition continued after it had died out in the cities, and the Gothic style was still used for churches long after secular design had gone over almost entirely to the new mode. But enthusiasm for the Italian forms was widespread among aristocracy and royalty; the great châteaux built in the Loire Valley during the first part of the 16th century that served Francis I and his nobles as lodges to accommodate the hunting expeditions of which he was so fond show without exception the taste for Renaissance style that developed first in court circles but soon became much more widespread and more popular.

The first examples of Renaissance style in French architecture are characterized chiefly by their combination of mediaeval structural principles with Italianate decorative forms. Attention has been directed elsewhere to the pronounced tendency in French design of the later Middle Ages toward separation of construction and ornament, and in substituting classic idoms for the previously employed mediaeval ones, there was no very violent break with prevailing concepts of architectural composition. Thus in decorating the façade of the château at *Azay-le-Rideau* (Fig. 144), which was built between 1518 and 1524 as one of these shooting lodges in the Loire Valley, acanthus leaves are used instead of the native flora of Gothic style, openings are framed by pilasters instead of the shafts that perform a similar function on the façade of

Jacques Cœur's house (Fig. 110) and classicizing pediments replace the gables with crockets and finials over the dormer windows. The character of this ornament is such as to suggest that the models used by the French craftsmen were the motives employed in North Italian Renaissance buildings (cf. Fig. 122), light and delicate arabesques of foliage being used quite extensively and often framing the salamander which was the heraldic device of Francis I. On the other hand, such features as the heavy round towers at the angles resemble the donjons of a fortified feudal castle, and the irregular silhouette of the steeply pitched roof with its conical towers of picturesque outline and the

FIG. 144.—Azay-le-Rideau. THE CHÂTEAU.

suggestion of battlements in the bracketed cornice are details in which the builders of Azay-le-Rideau adhered to earlier and French practice. Nor does the plan of the structure, which is L-shaped, partake of the symmetry characteristic of Italian models (cf. Fig. 124); rather it is an adaptation of the traditional French court arrangement with its screen entrance wall (cf. Fig. 112).

Azay-le-Rideau is an example of the Early Renaissance style in French architecture which is found in buildings erected for the most part between 1495, when the troops of Charles VIII returning from Italy brought with them the first inklings of Renaissance ideals, and about 1545. The succeeding High Renaissance lasted until approximately 1590, with its inception during the reign of Francis I who died in 1547, its climax in the time of Henry II who ruled France from 1547 until 1559, and a period of decline under Charles IX and Henry III between 1560 and 1589. As in the preceding Early Renaissance phase, the influence of Italian ideas is strong but of differing character since it derives from the Roman style of Bramante and his followers rather than the north Italian models to which Frenchmen were first attracted by force largely of military circumstances. It follows that French Renaissance design during the second half of the 16th century is distinguished from the earlier phase by greater formality and less picturesqueness, and by more complete understanding of classic architectural idioms. Two factors may be noted that were immediately responsible for these developments. The first was the importation of Italian architects who came to France in the service of Catherine de' Medici of the famous Florentine family, who was the queen of Henry II. Foremost among these were Primaticcio and Serlio—neither of whom could be considered equal in ability to men like Michelangelo or Palladio but were competent designers and well versed in the academic Italian High Renaissance tradition; the latter was influential as much through his theoretical treatises as the buildings actually constructed from his designs. The second factor contributing to the change from naïve picturesqueness to academic formality in French architecture of the later 16th century was the increasingly greater acquaintance of Frenchmen with Italian models through travel and study; Pierre Lescot, Jean Bullant, Philibert de l'Orme and Jacques Androuet du Cerceau all spent much time in Italy, where they observed and assimilated the principles of design there practiced and in the case of the three last named incorporated their ideas in handbooks that were as important in the dissemination of those principles as the similar works of their Italian contemporaries. In either case, it is significant to note that it was the restrained and academic Italian practice as exemplified by Palladio rather than the free and quasi-baroque manner of Michelangelo that formed the basis of the theories most generally applied and accepted in France at this time.

French High Renaissance style appears in one of its most distinguished examples in the *Court* of the *Louvre* in Paris (Fig. 145), designed by Pierre Lescot (*ca.* 1510-1578) in connection with the rebuilding carried on under his direction of the Gothic castle which was the royal palace in Paris. The nine bays of what is now the south part of the western façade of this court were built between 1541 and 1548 with the intention of making them the principal wing of a structure facing a court, with two subordinate side wings and a front screen wall, the traditional French domestic plan, as has been pointed out. Later enlargements increased the area of the court to its present size which is four times as great as that planned by Lescot; however, his designs were employed for the subsequent portions and the effect of

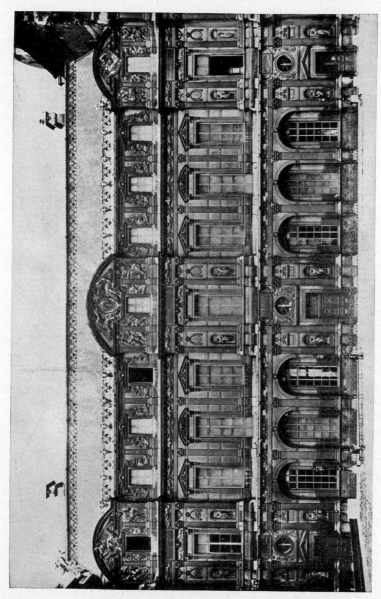

FIG. 145.—Paris. THE LOUVRE. Court, southwest front.

the whole is homogeneous although somewhat deficient in scale as it would not have been had the original dimensions been retained. In the nine bays designed by Lescot, the decoration consists of applied orders complete with entablatures and carved friezes on the two lower stories which are surmounted by a low attic and crowned by a balustrade. The end and center bays are accented by framing them with coupled columns instead of the single pilasters used between; they are thus transformed into projecting pavilions which should be compared as to effect with the circular angle towers at Azay-le-Rideau. The orders are also different in character from those of the older building and the pedimented windows they enclose are similar to those used by Italian architects in the 16th century (cf. Fig. 125). By emphasizing the end and central bays, however, Lescot has introduced a vertical element in the design, and in this he is French rather than Italian. French too are the relatively large windows and the introduction of much sculpture. This is largely the work of Jean Goujon (*ca.* 1510-*ca.* 1568), who was Lescot's collaborator in the project and an architect of some distinction in his own right as well as one of the leading French sculptors of the time (cf. Fig. 331). In the fine execution of the details and their relationship to the ensemble, in the well-calculated proportions and the decorative variety of a restrained and dignified scheme, the wing of the Louvre designed by Lescot takes rank with the best Italian masterpieces of the High Renaissance. As pure and scholarly in classical detail as Palladio's work, Lescot's design is still essentially French in spirit and not a mere aping of the mannerisms of other styles. This is particularly true of the introduction of engaged columns in the orders by which the end pavilions are distinguished from the pilastered bays between; in this way a characteristically French emphasis is imparted to the angles of façade, but it is achieved by means of well-understood classic forms.

Another example of High Renaissance style in France which illustrates the ready apprehension of new developments in Italy is the entrance portico in the court of the *Château* at *Ecouen* (Fig. 146). This was the work of Jean Bullant (*ca.* 1512-1578), who built it for Anne de Montmorency, High Constable of France and one of the most impassioned admirers of Italian art in his day; for this reason he was well pleased, no doubt, by the giant orders with which Bullant flanked the principle court entrance of his château near Paris. The first example of the motive in French building, this portico is dated probably between 1552 and 1564; it is obvious in any event that the inspiration for the order was Michelangelo's design for the Campidoglio buildings in Rome (Fig. 133) which were begun in 1546, although Bullant has used applied columns instead of pilasters. This detail reveals a more academic conception of classic form than appears in the Italian example and its use was obviously dictated by enthusiasm for the motive rather than desire to develop a formally integrated ensemble for there is no very effective relationship between the portico and the wall behind it. This does not reduce its significance as an in-

FIG. 146.—Ecouen. THE CHÂTEAU. Portico in the court.

dication of the increasingly Italianate taste of French patrons and architects alike which is also evident in the original emplacement in the arched niches between the columns of the two famous figures called the Bound Slaves by Michelangelo (Fig. 325) which the Constable had bought after being discarded by the sculptor when he was forced to reduce the great mausoleum for Julius II for which they had been intended.

Conditions were not favorable in France during the reigns of Charles IX (1560-1574) and Henry III (1574-1589) for building on a large scale, for the religious wars caused drains on financial resources and creative imagination alike. Possibly the most significant architectural products of this period were not buildings but books on architectural theory and principles. The difficult economic circumstances in which Henry IV found the kingdom on his accession to the throne in 1589 imposed limitations which that enlightened monarch could not do much to modify, although before his death in 1610 a beginning had been made on the plans for Paris that were to change it from a mediaeval town with dark and narrow streets to the city of broad vistas and great squares which it is today. Such building as was done usually involved the use of brick and stone, and designs were characterized by a tendency toward freer use of classic forms than the mid-16th-century architects had allowed themselves. The results are more nearly in the baroque style than at any other time in French architectural history, the chief example being the *Luxembourg Palace* in Paris (Fig. 147), which was built by Salomon de Brosse (1552-1626) between 1615 and 1624 for Marie de' Medici, who had been the queen of Henry IV. The building is of the usual French plan, with a court of honor entered by a pavilion and flanked by side wings of somewhat less height than the principal block of the structure which lies at the rear of the court. The outstanding feature of the design is the extensive use of rusticated walls and piers, a detail which may have been introduced to make the structure resemble as much as possible the Pitti Palace in Florence from which Marie had come to Paris. However this may have been, the more uniform roof line of the palace achieved by avoiding the pavilion and bay divisions employed in earlier buildings is evidence in itself of de Brosse's understanding of the monumental possibilities of simplified mass relationships that was undoubtedly derived from his study of the High Renaissance masters of Italy. Other than in its architectural character, the Luxembourg Palace is a notable example of baroque combining of the visual arts in a single ensemble, for the long galleries of the side wings were decorated with paintings brilliantly conceived and executed by Peter Paul Rubens, in which the nuptials of Marie and Henry IV were celebrated.

If the parallel between the evolution of architectural style in France and Italy that is perceptible through the early years of the 17th century had continued, an even more extensive development along baroque lines than is represented by the Luxembourg Palace might have ensued in the reign of Louis XIII (1610-1643). There was instead a very pronounced reaction toward formalism and academicism to which there were two outstanding contributing factors. The first was the traditionally systematic and logical mode of French thought that had found expression earlier in the inherently rational synthesis of form that is

Gothic style—the product of a temperament to which the unrestrained emotionalism upon which the more extreme forms of Italian baroque were based would have been intrinsically distasteful. It was this same indigenously French sentiment favoring rule and order that underlay the political structure there developed in the 17th century in which all power came more and more into the hands of fewer and fewer persons until Louis XIV could say in all truth—*"L'État, c'est moi"*—for in him as an individual was vested absolute power over every phase of human activity in the land. This was possible only by virtue of highly

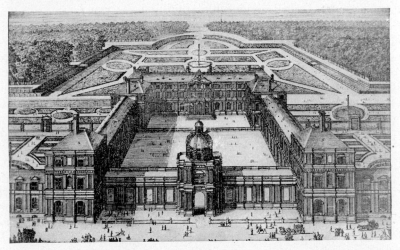

FIG. 147.—Paris. THE LUXEMBOURG PALACE. Court and Façade.

organized institutions exercising complete control by rigid regulation in their respective fields. The Academy of Letters was founded in 1635 with its object "to give certain rules to our language and to render it pure"; similar intention in the field of the visual arts led to the establishment of the Academy of Painting and Sculpture in 1648, and of Architecture in 1671. These, while they may be said to have come into existence in response to sentiments inherently French, gave expression to their ideas in forms which had little enough to do with French ways of thinking, as will shortly be apparent.

It was a more or less foregone conclusion that the style sanctioned by the Academy should have been classic. Over a century of close relationships artistically with Italy had served to confirm the classic habit in French minds, and it was but natural that it should be the academic phases of Italian design that would be most attractive to temperaments already disposed to value "reason" and "good sense" as evidence of logic. The writings of Palladio were translated into French in 1650 and became one of the foundation stones of French architectural theory. More and more it became the practice of Frenchmen to go to Italy whenever possible; there they still studied the buildings of classic antiquity, but also the interpretations of those forms which they found in the work of High Renaissance masters. It was to provide controlled instruction in understanding these models that the French Academy in Rome was founded in 1677 where students who had shown themselves capable were enabled by the state to continue their studies. The result was the domination of French architectural thinking for many years by the theory that only in classic usage and the interpretation thereof by the academic Italian and French theorists could there be an acceptable ideal of structural beauty.

The foundation of the Academies was a matter of considerably more than merely historical significance, for their establishment marked the final uprooting of artistic creative activity from its traditional place in the social fabric in the thoughts and emotions of the people. This separation had been begun in France when the Italian style was imported in the early 16th century; it was completed when the arts came under royal patronage through the intermediary of the Academies and artists thus became a class apart, owing allegiance only to the abstract ideal imposed upon them by academic regulations. This ideal was one of *a priori* perfection based on the art of classic antiquity as seen through the eyes of Italian and French theorists—a concept which of necessity takes account of nothing but preconceived formal and expressive values and makes little if any provision for the tradition and inspiration of individuals. It is from such a concept too that the notion of the art critic has developed; works of art are evaluated today by many criteria other than the classic of the French Academy in the 17th century, but the mere fact that there is still current the notion that only the select few to whom the mysteries of art have been disclosed are qualified to judge it is evidence of the persisting academic concept of art as something resulting from the application of rules of formal design. The reduction of artistic creation to compliance with reasoned and theoretical principles and rules instead of being developed by the inductive training of hand and eye was one of the most pernicious consequences of academic supervision of the arts. The consistent unity that has characterized French official art from the closing years of the 17th century to the present is another, a unity won by raising the quality of much work that would otherwise undoubtedly have been very poor but at the cost of circumscribing genius to the point of smothering it.

The ideals for which the French Academy of Architecture stood are evident in the wing added by François Mansart (1598-1666) to the *Château at Blois* (Fig. 148) at the request of Gaston d'Orléans its owner at that time (1635-1640). Earlier parts of the structure are of varied character, having been built in the styles of Louis XII and Francis I, but Mansart's wing takes no account of inconsistency with the older portions in its purity and sobriety of design. The order is used in a restrained form, with coupled pilasters and unbroken entablatures on each story arranged in the canonical relationship of Doric, Ionic and Corinthian on first, second and third stories respectively. The roof is

Fig. 148.—Blois. The Château. Orléans Wing. Façade.

still rather steeply pitched, but the dormer windows of the 16th and earlier 17th centuries have disappeared. The quietness and simplicity of the resultant effect contribute to the sense of repose that is created by the prevailing horizontality of the design and the impression is given monumentality by the well-studied proportions. Only in the sculptured figures on the pediment in the second story of the entrance bay and the curvilinear gable of its third story is there any suggestion at all of baroque exuberance in this well-nigh complete embodiment in architectural terms of the Gallic ideals of reason and logic.

The Gaston d'Orléans wing at Blois was built by Mansart late in the reign of Louis XIII before the complete centralization of power in the person of the king that was to develop later had been completed. That such an imposing structure could be erected for an individual other than royalty is one indication of this fact, for under Louis XIV, who reigned from 1643 to 1715, nearly all the great architectural creations in France were motivated more or less directly by his imperialistic ambition or by those of his immediate advisers. Among these were the enlargement of the royal palace of the Louvre in Paris and of the château at Versailles, which was to become one of the largest buildings in 17th-century Europe by virtue of Louis' interest in it. He was not so much concerned with the building in Paris, but his minister Colbert felt it essential to royal dignity that there should be a monumental residence for the king in his capital city. Lescot's building of the mid-16th century (Fig. 145) had already undergone a series of alterations and enlargements that quadrupled the area of the court of honor designed by him and connected it with the palace of the Tuileries nearly a third of a mile away, but it still lacked an appropriately imposing principal façade on the eastern front. Various plans for its completion were submitted in a competition in which nearly every important architect in France was represented, but none were felt to possess the necessary grandeur; hence in 1665, Gian Lorenzo Bernini was requested to come from Rome to Paris to undertake the project. He was received with the acclaim due the architect recognized as the greatest of his time, but his suggestion for the façade of the building was not acceptable because it could not have been built without destroying practically the whole of the existent structure. Its cornerstone was laid but the design was discarded as soon as Bernini returned to Rome, and the project was given into the care of Claude Perrault (1613-1688) with the assistance of Charles LeBrun the painter and Louis LeVau, who had been in charge of the last stages in the enlargement of the court begun by Lescot.

As it was finally built between 1667 and 1674, the *Colonnade of the Louvre* (Fig. 149), which is the eastern façade of the palace, shows a still further elimination of traditional French elements than was noted at Blois and an even more academic and monumental ideal. The high pointed roof which climatic considerations had imposed as a necessity in earlier buildings that were less rigidly controlled in design by formal considerations is no longer a factor and the flat roof is masked by a balustrade in the best Italian manner. This was a detail that Perrault might well have adapted from Bernini's rejected design, as was also the giant order, rising above the ground-story base, which is the chief feature of the façade. He retained the traditionally French five-part division of the façade, however, by making the end and center pavilions project slightly and using a pediment over the latter. Moreover, he enriched the classic vocabulary of his style by using coupled free-standing Corinthian columns in the order instead of engaged columns or pilasters.

The design is not uniformly effective in all details. The relationship of the central pediment to the cornice balustrade is unsatisfactory, and by springing the arch of the main entrance on the ground level from the stringcourse of the first story, it is made to break into the one above with rather ambiguous effect. But these are minor defects in a well-proportioned and unified design that is characterized by effective use of light and shade to create relief in the colonnades and thus realize a

FIG. 149.—Paris. THE LOUVRE. Colonnade.

just balance of voids against the solids of the projecting pavilions at the center and ends. A sense of great scale is also achieved by these means and the whole takes rank with the most impressive architectural embodiments of the spirit of the *Grand Siècle*, for the majestic dignity of the building is an eloquent testimonial to the absolute power of the monarch who caused it to be built. It is this quality that has made its design the basis of a formula for monumental buildings in France which has been almost standard from the closing years of the 17th century until very recent times.

In a sense, the completion of the Louvre was a matter of state that was consummated for political reasons. The enlargement of the château at *Versailles* (Figs. 150-153) was undertaken because of the personal preferences of Louis XIV for it over all his other residences. The scope of his purpose is indicated by his expressed desire to provide at Versailles for the accommodation of his entire court; the extent of its realization

FIG. 150.—Versailles. The Palace. From the air.

was so tremendous that the national treasury of France was almost entirely depleted by it, and if the building was on a scale unapproached before or unequaled since in structures of comparable type, this was achieved only at the cost of the national social and economic equilibrium. Size and effect are out of all proportion to function, and the total lack of relationship between the formal ideal embodied in the structure and the life of France when it was built in the 17th century makes it the most eloquent architectural symbol of the principle of absolutism the world has seen, for the unbelievable sacrifices its construction involved were decreed by the unquestionable whim of a single individual.

As it now exists, the *Palace of Versailles* (Fig. 150) is laid out along the basic lines of the traditional French country house with an open court flanked on the sides by projecting wings. It is at the rear of this court that there can still be seen the façade of the brick and stone hunting lodge built for Louis XIII in 1624 which was the nucleus of the present gigantic building. The initial phase of its remodeling took place between 1661 and 1671 under Louis LeVau (1612-1670), who was also then engaged in the completion of the court of the Louvre; he designed what amounted to an envelope enclosing the brick and stone château of Louis XIII on three sides, that toward the rear being developed as an element in the gardens which were also laid out at this time (cf. Fig. 153). After LeVau's death in 1670, little was done on the exterior of the palace for some time, but the appointment in 1678 of Jules Hardouin Mansart (1645-1708), nephew of François Mansart who designed the Gaston d'Orléans wing at Blois (Fig. 148), marked the beginning of an extraordinary amplification of the structure. After some modifications of LeVau's garden elevation and a readjustment of the rooms on that side of the building, Mansart undertook the extension of the south wing in 1682 and its northern counterpart in 1684. The Orangerie below the south end of the garden terrace was built between 1684 and 1687 and the chapel of which the roof can be seen from the garden above that of the palace itself (Fig. 151) was begun in 1699 though it had not been completed by Mansart's death in 1708.

The *Garden Front* of the Palace at Versailles (Fig. 151) is in three levels—a heavy rusticated basement, a somewhat taller second story with arched openings and an Ionic order of pilasters and columns, and a low attic with rectangular windows divided by paneled pilasters. A balustrade surmounts the whole, ornamented with urns and sculptured groups. Projecting pavilions—a large one in the center, smaller ones near the ends of the central block and three of equal size distributed symmetrically on the wing façades—give relief to the planes of the front as a whole. A rhythm of threes is carried through the entire design, beginning with the grouping of the openings by doubling the pilasters in the central block and extending to the disposition of the elements in the total length in such a way that the visual angles subtended by the three major elements are the same for an observer standing on the axis of the design at the top of the first terrace (Fig. 153). If the exterior of the garden front is characterized by purity of detail and sober if monumental effect, the interior is quite otherwise. Almost the total length of the central block is taken up on the second story by the *Galerie des Glaces* (Fig. 152), which was designed by Charles

FIG. 151.—Versailles. THE PALACE. Garden Front.

LeBrun and executed between 1680 and 1684. The measured rhythm of the windows opening on the garden is repeated on the opposite wall by the arched mirrors from which the name of the hall is taken; but where the effect created externally is one of monumental austerity, the painted and stucco ornament on wall panels and vault within are of an exuberance altogether baroque in character. Such is the nature of the compromise achieved in France between Palladian purity on the one hand and baroque extravagance on the other—by investing a mathematically unified basic pattern with movement through the medium of surface decoration.

Gigantic as the Palace at Versailles is—the garden façade is more than a quarter of a mile in length—its full effect is not to be understood without taking into account as well the *Gardens* designed to complement and to be complemented by it (Fig. 153). These were the creation of André LeNôtre (1613-1700), whose name is one of the most distinguished in the annals of landscape architecture. Begun in 1662 when LeVau undertook the remodeling of the château, they were not completed until 1684. LeNôtre's scheme involved the laying out of what are actually two gardens, a smaller one immediately next the palace proper and a larger one lying beyond. A system of terraces made the entire arrangement visible from the palace itself, of which the cen-

FIG. 152.—Versailles. THE PALACE. The *Galerie des Glaces.*

tral axis is continued to establish the median line of the grounds and to unify them as well as relate them to the building. Water effects play an important part in the composition; reflecting pools and spurting

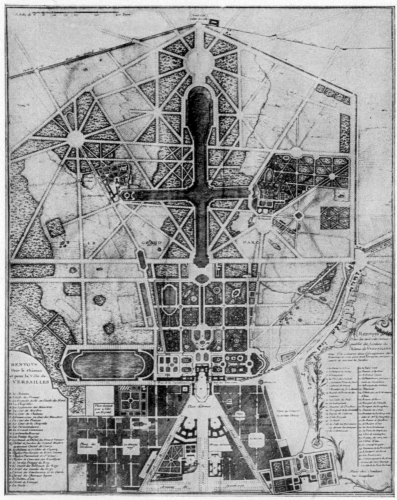

Fig. 153.—Versailles. Plan of the City and Gardens.

fountains are the nuclei in the smaller upper garden of carefully laid-out and clipped masses of shrubbery, growing from grassy lawns and accented by trees, which form varied geometrical patterns within a rigid framework of clearly indicated alleys. The shrubbery of the large garden is disposed in simpler forms, but two intersecting canals—the one on the principal axis of the composition and a smaller one at right angles —dominate this portion of the ensemble in which boldly indicated diagonal alleys radiate from focal points at each end. As in the Galerie des Glaces, the basic principle of the design is a logical and geometrical disciplined framework with unlimited variety in the details. Other than in their obvious enhancement of the effect of the palace, these gardens provided stimulus to artistic creation in the abundant opportunity offered for decorative sculpture (cf. Fig. 151), both as accents on the terraces and in connection with the innumerable fountains.

A glance at the plan of the gardens and also at the aerial view of the ensemble (Fig. 150) will make it clear that everything in the setting of the Palace at Versailles was considered in its relationship to the central structure. Up to the Place d'Armes, the great court in front of the building, three wide avenues lead in such fashion that no movement can be made that does not focus upon or radiate from it, and within the angles thus created the city of Versailles was built. There was thus upon one side of the Palace a completely architectural vista and upon the other a prospect of nature directed and controlled by human thought. Thus was completed the most overwhelming structural project of the 17th century in which form and space, the work of man and the symbol of nature are wrought into a single and unified scheme contrived for the sole purpose of creating by its focus upon the central structure a symbol of the unquestioned and absolute power of its builder. This scheme of radiating and focusing avenues controlled by a single building was destined to exercise a far-reaching influence in the 18th century; Mannheim and Karlsruhe in Germany were to be laid out along similar lines, and Pierre Charles de l'Enfant acknowledged his intention of planning the capital city of the newly created United States, Washington, D. C., after the pattern of Versailles.

But even more significant than its formal influence is the insight given by the plan of Versailles into the working of absolutism as a governing principle. The arbitrary creation of an entire city from the ground up in accordance with a preconceived notion of what it should be rather than as the result of organic growth is no more than the application in architectural thinking of the principle of absolutism on a scale seldom approached even remotely in earlier times. The design itself is based in similar fashion on rule and regulation of arbitrary character. Mathematical in principle—and it should not be forgotten that one of the most far-reaching systems of 17th-century philosophy was the creation of a mathematician and Frenchman, René Descartes —it is the most comprehensive example of the tyranny of the axis in the architectural thinking of the time. This is illustrated in graphic

fashion by the irresistible urge of every spectator considering the building from the gardens to place himself at the point where the symmetry
of the façade will be clearest, which is the center of the steps leading
from the upper terrace to the garden below (Fig. 153). When there,
he finds his angle of vision exactly filled by the palace as a whole, with
nothing else intruding to detract from its overwhelming dominance—
a symbol of the rigorous subjection of the individual to the impersonal
order of the state that is the unfailing consequence of absolutism as a
political and social principle.

The trend noted in French architectural evolution from the beginning of the 16th century to the close of the 17th is graphic evidence of
the altered function of art in European culture after the death of the
mediaeval point of view. Classic forms introduced there by kings and
nobles as exotic and decorative adjuncts to structural elements still
mediaeval in character were divorced from them to become the material
of a rigidly enforced canon of design from which there could be no
departure. The training of artists was taken from the trade guilds which
held that prerogative in the Middle Ages and given to the Academies,
and the artist was thus detached from his environment of communal
experience and his inspiration therein cut off from its rightful resources
of life and vitality. Art was no longer the literature of the people but
a source of entertainment for the elect, who forthwith imposed upon
it an ideal of formal unity and artificial perfection similar to the political
ideal forced upon a populace which had no part in its formulation.
The social order resulting from the arbitrarily created political institutions was made up of two classes—the aristocracy and the common
people—separated by a spiritual abyss that could not be spanned, and
in this order, art was the plaything of the former and had no function
for the latter. The Palace at Versailles is an overpowering monument
to this state of affairs in its swallowing up the taxes of decades for
initial construction and the exhaustive drain upon the state that its
subsequent maintenance has involved. Reaction was inevitable. The immediate one was away from the severe formality of 17th-century art
and social usage toward frivolity and license in both manners and
artistic style. The boudoir replaced the salon as the locale of social intercourse and the minutely scaled forms of the rococo appear instead of
the more massive baroque. But this reaction was superficial at best. It
only served to emphasize the social disparity created earlier and in some
measure to hasten the revolt which took place toward the close of the
18th century in the French Revolution. As the result of social and
economic upheavals attendant upon that, the problem of expressive style
in the 18th and 19th centuries involves different values than those that
have been discussed, as will be made apparent elsewhere.

# Chapter X. Renaissance Architecture in England.

IN THE DEVELOPMENT OF RENAISSANCE architectural style in England, there are many parallels to be noted with that of France although its inception was somewhat later in point of time and the two styles are quite distinct in character. An explanation of the tardy appearance of Renaissance style in more than isolated examples in England can be found in the fact that the continuity of building during the later Middle Ages had not been interrupted there by wars as it had across the English Channel, and the beginning of the 16th century came with no apparent wane in the vigor and originality of Gothic ways of architectural thinking in England. Some of the most distinguished examples of English Gothic style—the Chapel of Henry VII at Westminster in London, for example—were begun after the Italian High Renaissance was in full swing. The long-continued vitality of mediaeval style along with England's geographic isolation and her natural conservatism served to delay the appearance of Renaissance ideas there long after they were firmly established in nearly every other country in Europe.

During the 15th century, a characteristic type of country house well adapted to comfortable living had been evolved in England, and in this way the concept of worldly well-being inherent in the Renaissance ideal was an architectural factor there long before the style as such was introduced. An example is *Compton Winyates* (Figs. 154, 155), which dates from around 1520. As was usually the case with domestic buildings of the time, it is built around a court, and the general arrangement is irregular and picturesque to a degree with steeply pitched roofs and clustered chimneys, battlemented towers and ample windows which were a necessity in a northern latitude. A structural feature to be noted is the mixture of materials—stone, brick, wood and plaster—which results in attractive effects of contrasting color and texture. These are not consequences of any self-conscious desire for romantic charm, however, but result simply from use of material at hand in the most effective way. The same principle prevails in the plan, which is centered about the lofty, timber-roofed hall with a slightly raised platform at one end where the family table was placed, with provision for other members of the household in the longer portion of the room. The disposition of other rooms in the house was dictated by their relationship to the hall—kitchen and service quarters, chapel, drawing-room and bedrooms—the whole being characterized by a sense of having resulted from organic growth directed by practical necessities and not showing even as much of Italian Renaissance influence as would be found in a contemporary French building like Azay-le-Rideau (Fig. 144).

FIG. 154.—COMPTON WINYATES.

*Lord Leycester's Hospital* at Warwick (Fig. 156) is another case in point in which absence of Italian ideas in both design and construction is even more significant since its present form is the result of a rebuilding that occurred in 1571. Like Compton Winyates, the main façade is irregular in form and picturesque in outline, with steep roofs and clustered chimneys—the result of additions to the original structure required by the changing circumstances of its use. The construction is of the type known as half-timbered work, the structure consisting of a frame of heavy wooden posts joined by horizontal and diagonal beams, with the spaces between filled with brick or other material that was sometimes, as here, covered with stucco on the exterior. This was the favored method of erecting small buildings and domestic structures in mediaeval England and it was sometimes used in connection with masonry for larger ones as well, as at Compton Winyates where it appears in the gables (Fig. 154). It was continued for buildings of this type throughout the Elizabethan and subsequent periods in English history and is sometimes referred to as the Tudor style.

As in France, the first indication of Italian Renaissance influence is to be seen in decorative details, and also as in France, it occurs in buildings erected by royalty and the aristocracy. The tomb of Henry VII dates from 1516 and lies under the flamboyant Gothic vaults of the chapel he built at Westminster in London, but its detail is in the

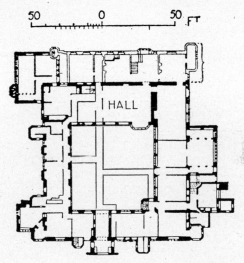

FIG. 155.—COMPTON WINYATES. Plan.

classicizing Italian Renaissance mode and probably the first example of it in England; it was the work of a certain Pietro Torrigiano, a Florentine sculptor who had been forced to flee from his native city after a brawl with Michelangelo. Other Italians were imported to meet the demands created by the fashion, and often worked side by side with native artisans on such buildings as Hampton Court Palace, which was built by Cardinal Wolsey and Henry VIII between 1513 and 1536. The character of English Renaissance architecture in this phase is very similar to that of contemporary France since it is a matter of Gothic construction overlaid with Italian detail. Probably the finest illustration of this type of work is the rood screen in King's College Chapel at Cambridge; the building in which it stands is in the late Gothic style throughout, but the screen, which probably dates between 1532 and 1536, shows hardly any trace of mediaeval detail.

Political conditions in England under Henry VIII and his immediate successors were not conducive to any further development of these beginnings of Renaissance style comparable to that which occurred in France under the patronage of Catherine de' Medici. For religious reasons, the Italian workmen responsible for the first Renaissance examples were unwilling to remain in the country, and even if they had, financial difficulties would have prevented any very extensive building activity. It was not until the reign of Elizabeth (1558-1603) that further

FIG. 156.—Warwick. LORD LEYCESTER'S HOSPITAL.

developments architecturally were made possible by greater economic and cultural stability—in the period of the beginning of England's greatness as a world power, and the time of Shakespeare and Marlowe.

The architectural picture of Elizabethan England has two outstanding features—the almost complete lack of ecclesiastic building, with domestic design in the form of country houses predominant, and a generally more extensive knowledge of continental Renaissance styles. In some buildings like *Longleat* (Fig. 157), which was built between 1567 and 1579, it is Italian precedent that has been followed quite closely, possibly because it was the design, supposedly, of a certain John of Padua. The plan is symmetrical and the chief exterior ornament consists of superposed classic pilasters that conform to academic principles of proportion and detail, the whole crowned by a balustrade in the best Italian High Renaissance manner (cf. Figs. 133, 135). Originally this latter feature may not have existed for apparently the house was first built with gables extending from front to back, but these were subsequently replaced by the present flat roof even though the gabled type was better adapted to prevailing climatic conditions. Certain features of earlier and indigenous character are still present; the projecting bays introduce a vertical note in the façade design and the clustered chimneys are a reminder of the fact that heating was a necessity in England for which provision had to be made even at the cost of academic formal character. But the main entrance is through a portico

FIG. 157.—LONGLEAT. The South Front.

with columns and a broken pediment and is approached by a broad flight of steps quite in the manner of the Italian 16th century.

The Italianism of Longleat is the exception rather than the rule, however, in late 16th-century English building. For the most part, the predominant Renaissance influence in English design of this period comes from the Low Countries—from Flanders and Holland—a circumstance for which the explanation is to be sought in the political picture of the times. The conflict with the Church begun by Henry VIII was continued by Elizabeth, and the rise of Protestantism in England was marked by increasing sympathy with similar movements in the Low Countries then fighting for their independence from Spain. Many refugees from those countries found their way to England, including many artisans who brought with them their own regional versions of Renaissance style which were thus transplanted to English soil. An example in point is *Wollaton Hall* in Nottinghamshire (Figs. 158, 159), which was built between 1580 and 1588. The plan (Fig. 159) is symmetrical with respect to both axes but is unusual even for houses of this period in making the great hall the nucleus around which the other rooms are grouped; this rises above the side wings with their symmetrically placed towers at the angles (Fig. 158). The gables of these towers are good examples of the Flemish influence on English design, made up as they are of pediments supported by scrolls and flanked by small obelisks and with the flat surfaces decorated by ribbon-like patterns known as strap-work. Orders are used in profusion for the external decoration—a separate one for each story in elevation with

Fig. 158.—Wollaton Hall. From the southeast.

entablatures that serve as stringcourses between the stories; the flat bands across the shafts are also Flemish in origin. The expansive windows with their mullions are specifically English, however, and the general picturesqueness of the sky-line with its chimneys, towers and pinnacles is likewise at variance with the Renaissance character of much of the detail.

One of the most individual features of country houses built in Elizabethan and Jacobean England is the *Long Gallery* (Fig. 160), a room that as its name implies was quite extended in length and was almost always on the topmost floor of the house. The long gallery of Hatfield House which was built between 1607 and 1611 is typical of these rooms in being paneled, or hung with tapestries, and in having the ceiling decorated with moulded plaster in elaborate designs. Very prominent, too, is the fireplace with its elaborately decorated over-mantel. The origin of the long gallery in the Elizabethan and Jacobean country houses is not clear; it was possibly a place for displaying paintings, as most of them are now used, or for the staging of pageants on the occasion of royal visits, or even for providing a room for exercise since it was in a part of the house in which space was not at a premium. In any event, it is one of the chief elements in houses of the late 16th and early 17th centuries in England in which a measure of regard is

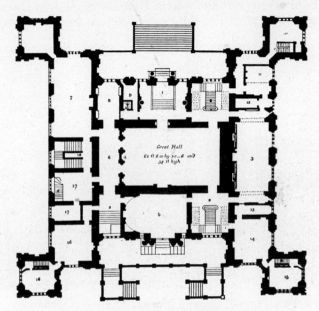

FIG. 159.—WOLLATON HALL. Plan.

still had for convenience and facility in planning and in which Renaissance ideals of a formal nature are still limited in application to details and to a general symmetry of mass.

During the 16th century and through the early years of the 17th, whatever of Renaissance character there is in English architecture is at best an indirect reflection of Italian usage. There were some Italian craftsmen brought to England as has been noted in the case of Longleat, and a few Englishmen like John Shute and John Thorpe had traveled to Italy and made some studies there of current practice, but the influence of these men counted for very little in the generally conservative trends of Elizabethan and Jacobean design. The almost phenomenal appearance of a puristic and academically rigid style in the third and fourth decades of 17th-century England is the more surprising in view of these facts; it was the achievement, almost single-handed, of Inigo

Jones (1573-1652). As a young man, Jones had been a designer of stage scenery, and in 1611 had been appointed surveyor to Henry, Prince of Wales. The years 1613 and 1614 were spent by him traveling in Italy, in the course of which he made the acquaintance of men like Maderna in Rome and Scamozzi, assistant and follower of Palladio, in Venice, and during which he also became acquainted with the buildings both of classic antiquity and of Palladio. So impressed was he by the latter that he purchased the *Four Books on Architecture* which he

FIG. 160.—HATFIELD HOUSE. The Long Gallery.

brought back to England; his study of it became almost immediately apparent in the buildings he designed in his capacity as the King's Surveyor, to which office he was appointed in 1615. In general, these buildings reveal almost none of the forms currently used in England but follow Italian and particularly Palladian precepts with almost literal exactitude. In this respect, Jones set a precedent for English architecture of the 17th century that makes it nearly unique in Europe, for even in France where there was a firmly entrenched academicism, the most puristic designs still are characterized by specifically French interpretations of Italian Renaissance idioms.

The *Banqueting Hall of Whitehall Palace* in London (Fig. 161) was designed by Jones for James I and was built between 1619 and 1622. The principal façade is more Italian in character than that of any contemporary building in Europe outside of Italy and might well have been designed by Palladio himself, so faithfully has Jones followed the precepts of the Italian master. The elevation is in three levels although the interior is but a single high room, with a rusticated basement, an Ionic order for the first story, and a Corinthian one above, the whole crowned by a balustrade. The orders consist of applied columns in the three central bays and those of the outer ones are pilasters which are doubled at the ends of the façade—a device by which a central axis is created and the framing ends subordinated in importance as Palladio himself had done in the Palazzo Valmarana at Vicenza (Fig. 136)

Fig. 161.—London. The Banqueting Hall.

though in a different way. Triangular and curvilinear pediments on brackets alternate over the windows of the first level, and swags of foliage form the frieze of the second, both following Italian High Renaissance precedents (cf. Figs. 125, 138). Other buildings by Jones, notably some of his country houses, show a similar respect for the precepts of the Italian High Renaissance theorists along with the considerable refinement that is his own outstanding quality and which did much to establish a taste for Palladianism that is one of the major elements in English architectural design in the later 17th and 18th centuries.

Once the habit of dependence on Italian precedent was established in England, it was inevitable that other than academic models should be studied, and the period of the Restoration with its incipient absolutism is marked architecturally by an infusion of baroque exuberance into the generally sober and restrained manner created by Jones and his immediate followers. The chief representative of the baroque in 17th-century English architecture is Sir Christopher Wren (1632-1723), whose preparation for a career as designer seems to have begun with his interests in science and mathematics of which he was an instructor at Oxford. He came to the attention of Charles II through his ingenious solution of a structural problem presented by the roofing of the Sheldonian Theatre in Oxford and was appointed Surveyor in

FIG. 162.—London. SAINT PAUL'S CATHEDRAL.

1662. In this capacity he traveled on the Continent, studying architectural activity there and being most particularly impressed by the ideas of Mansart and Bernini whom he met in Paris in 1665 when the Italian master was there in connection with the Louvre project. The Great Fire of London the following year brought Wren his great opportunity, and as architect in charge of the rebuilding, he drew up a plan for the restored city that would have surpassed even Versailles in magnitude had it been carried through. Typically baroque in character, it called for a radial distribution of buildings from certain key structures, notably the cathedral of Saint Paul, with the composition focused through the spires of the small parish churches of which a great number had also to be rebuilt and which would have led up to the principal points of the plan. The project failed of execution through the unwillingness of many landowners to wait for the rebuilding of their stores and houses in accordance with the new plans, and the disposition of the city as it grew up again in the late 17th and 18th centuries owed little or nothing to Wren's ideas.

*Saint Paul's Cathedral* was one of the major focal points of Wren's plan for the rebuilding of London and his original design called for a domed structure of the central type, that is, with a radial rather than a horizontal base. It was a genuinely baroque conception with a vast centralized space and many subordinate ones yielding a multitude of fine effects internally, but its realization was frustrated by the insistence of a conservative clergy upon a traditional plan with long nave and side aisles, transepts and a deep choir. It was along these general lines that the present structure was built (Fig. 162) between 1675 and 1710. Wren was able to retain the dome as the dominant element of the design externally at least, although the interior effect is one of rather confused spatial relationships. The cupola is supported by a drum surrounded by a free-standing peristyle which was apparently suggested to Wren by drawings of Bramante's unexecuted project for Saint Peter's at Rome, although the cupola itself is of quite different character from that designed by the Italian. Roman influence is apparent too in the treatment of the façade; the twin towers are not unlike those of a church by Borromini—Sant' Agnese in Piazza Navona—with corner colonnettes and entablatures placed at an angle to the plane of the façade as a whole (cf. Fig. 141). Here is revealed Wren's taste for the baroque; he combined it, however, with perception of the more monumental and restrained qualities of French contemporary design, for the superposed orders of coupled Corinthian columns in the two-storied portico are similar in conception to the single order of Perrault's eastern Colonnade of the Louvre (Fig. 149). The upper order is continued as a series of pilasters along the sides of the church, applied to a wall that masks flying buttresses which sustain the small domes covering the nave.

Throughout the entire building there is evidence of Wren's structural ingenuity, not the least striking example being the way in which the great dome is built. It is in two shells, like those of the cathedral at Florence (Fig. 113) and of Saint Peter's in Rome (Fig. 131), but the inner one is much lower relatively than is the case in either of the Italian buildings and supports the outer one by a heavy intermediate cone of brick and metal. This cone rests also upon the drum wall and functions actually as a point on which the outer dome of timber beams covered with lead is hung and which consequently exercises little or no lateral thrust. The effect thus attained is very striking, for the dome with its lantern tower rises over 350 feet from the ground and achieves almost alone the dominance of the city for which Wren had hoped. That this is done by suppressing expression of structural facts—for the actual means of its support cannot be seen from either within or without—in the interests of a more spectacular effect than could have been created if the design of the dome were more straightforward in its indication of supporting devices is only a typical illustration of Renaissance interest in formal qualities over structural problems. In point of fact, the margin of safety Wren allowed was so small that the vibrations of modern traffic in the city have developed more than a few fissures in the dome and its supports, keeping the building in a more or less constant state of repair in recent times.

The small parish churches designed by Wren as a part of the project for rebuilding London were completed to the number of fifty-eight and are effective accents in the city plan even though the comprehensive scheme failed of realization. Built for the most part on sites that are awkwardly shaped and limited in size, these structures are usually very ingenious in internal disposition to obtain maximum spatial effectiveness. Limitations of site usually restricted external effects to treatment of the bell tower in as impressive a way as possible, and some of Wren's most attractive designs are here seen. The church of *Saint Mary-le-Bow* (Fig. 163) was one of the first to be built, between 1671 and 1680, and the design of the spire with its reduction

Fig. 163.—London. St. Mary-le-Bow. Spire.

of the square base to the octagonal terminal was handled with such skillful application of classic forms that its influence was notable at once in buildings of comparable character. Many of the churches built in the English colonies in North America during the 18th century, such as Old North in Boston and Christ Church in Philadelphia (Fig. 184), can trace their formal ancestry back to the type created by Wren in these parish churches of London.

Baroque exuberance in some details and academic sobriety in others are the characteristics of buildings designed by Sir John Vanbrugh (1666-1726), which were among the last to reveal attempts at compromise between the two contrasting points of view in 17th-century English architecture. Vanbrugh is an interesting example of the amateur architect then beginning to appear in England for reasons to be noted elsewhere; he had a brilliant career as a writer of comedies before taking up architecture. *Blenheim Palace* (Fig. 164), built for the Duke of Marlborough, was completed about 1724. Baroque as to general

FIG. 164.—BLENHEIM PALACE.

effect, which is created by the contrasting masses of the central block with its outlying wings, and also in its great size—a quality of most of Vanbrugh's buildings that won for him the dubious distinction of being the butt of a satiric epigram by Pope—the ordinance of the principal portico, the character of the Doric colonnades used over a basement for the curving side wings and the balustrades surmounting them are details in the best academic style. The plan consists of a central mass preceded by a court that is flanked by wings which themselves are composed around smaller courts; symmetry is aimed at rather than convenience and the whole is an example of overemphasis that is not common in the general picture of restraint prevailing in late 17th- and early 18th-century English architecture.

The Palladian principles introduced in English design by Inigo Jones in the early 17th century continued without serious challenge from the baroque in one type of structure at least—that of the average town or small country house. *Swan House* at Chichester (Fig. 165), built in 1711, has been attributed to Sir Christopher Wren. The arrangement is typical of the middle-class houses of the later 17th century and the Georgian period of the 18th from which the characteristic term Georgian applied to the type is taken—a basement story for service quarters, with the rectangular block of the brick or stone-walled house rising

Fig. 165. Chichester. Swan House.

two or two and a half stories above. Character is attained externally by simple treatment of the symmetrically placed openings, the angles reinforced by quoins and the central axis emphasized by some such device as the projecting bay and an ordered entrance portico with its academically correct curvilinear pediment. Internally, the plans are relatively simple, a common arrangement being a central stair hall with rooms symmetrically placed on either side; these are given no small degree of charm by well-designed paneling and mouldings and by the furniture of the anonymous cabinet makers who paved the way for the great masters of the mid-18th century like Chippendale and Hepplewhite (cf. Figs. 623, 627). Like the parish churches by Wren, it was these houses, built for prosperous and quiet citizens, that served as models for the emigrants who left their Old World English homes for others in New World colonies (Fig. 181), rather than the more grandiloquent mansions like Blenheim Palace.

Even in its most Palladian aspects, English architecture of the late 17th and early 18th centuries was not sponsored by an official academy as it was in France but took form in response to a genuine and well-educated taste. This was in large measure created by the noble amateurs (such as Sir John Vanbrugh, though his personal preferences were for baroque effects), whose education invariably included the "grand tour" of Italy for which they were prepared by the most readily available documentation; architecturally, this was the writings of Palladio and other Italian theorists of academic persuasion. The many handbooks of architecture that were published in England in this period were both a consequence of this interest and a stimulus to its continuation, and the result was a well-grounded tradition of upper middle-class building in the Palladian manner of the type represented by Swan House and many others of the same period. It is interesting and significant to note that at the same time there was also a considerable amount of building going on in the yet older mediaeval fashion—modest houses of the half-timbered type (cf. Fig. 156) that represent architecturally the substratum of belief in the tradition of local self-determination still prevailing in England in spite of all efforts to raise upon it a superstructure of the forms of absolutism. This temper was indicated by other occurrences, both political and artistic. The attempt made by Charles I to erect a structure of government comparable in its absolutism to that of Louis XIV in France came to an end on the scaffold in 1649, and the replacement of James II by popular appeal to the democratic William of Orange in 1689 was a no less emphatic statement of England's insistence upon the retention of political forms that were the result of growth by accretion and adjustment to popular needs rather than those resulting from acts of arbitrary creation in accordance with a reasoned and symmetrical plan. Popular reaction against Wren's plan to rebuild London along lines that would admittedly have made it a more reasonable and effectively composed city but would have violated long-established rights is another indication of the same feeling. And if the modest Palladian town house or the unassuming half-timbered dwelling was preferred by those who built them because they had made a place for themselves in the English pattern of life and thought, it is because they won an echoing response in minds like those of Samuel Pepys and John Evelyn, whose instinctive reactions against the ostentatious and grandiloquent were more characteristic of the temper of their times than were the artificial glories preferred in a court inspired by alien values.

# Chapter XI. *European Architecture from 1700 to 1870.*

FRANCE AND ENGLAND HAD WITNESSED IN THE 17TH century the development of architectural styles that were essentially the result of compromise between baroque freedom on the one hand and puristic restraint on the other in the handling of classic forms. In France, baroque character is evident in the fondness for great size and lavish use of sculpture and painting as decorative accessories, but both used in conjunction with architectural elements composed with rigid regularity (cf. Figs. 151, 152). In England, apart from churches and a few exceptional country houses of large size, the sobriety of Palladian ideas is more apparent. The opening years of the 18th century brought certain modifications in both styles.

Life in France under Louis XIV was organized on a grand scale. The court at Versailles was the dominant factor in society and social usage was keyed to the great salons there—pompous and stately, with rules prescribing all aspects of human relationships. With the death of Louis XIV in 1715, the artificial social structure that had been held together by his dominating personality began to disintegrate and the first years of his successor, Louis XV, who reigned from 1715 until 1774, found many changes introduced that were duly reflected in the architecture of the time. Where, for example, in the latter part of the 17th century there had been an almost complete cessation of building by private individuals, the disestablishment of Versailles as the social center of the country in the early 18th century was followed by the building of numerous houses, many in Paris, of which the *Hôtel de Biron*, now the Musée Rodin (Fig. 166), is an example. It was designed by Jean Aubert and Jules Jacques Gabriel. Features of the exterior to be particularly noted are the omission of orders and the treatment of the walls by horizontal drafting or beveling of the joints, and the reversion from the flat roof with balustraded cornice of Versailles (cf. Fig. 151) to the indigenous pitched form. The scale too is relatively modest, and the internal arrangement while still generally symmetrical has been controlled by considerations of convenience and comfort rather than a desire for formal display.

It is in the interior decoration, in fact, that the architecture of the Louis XV style is most clearly distinguished from that of the preceding century. The *Oval Salon* of the *Hôtel de Soubise* in Paris (Fig. 167) was built about 1740 after the designs of Germain Boffrand and is one of the most comprehensive examples of rococo style, as this particular manner is called, the name being derived from the French *rocaille* and

Fig. 166.—Paris. The Hôtel de Biron. Garden Front.

*coquille* meaning rock work and shell respectively. The reference is to the fluid and irregular curves that predominate not only in the ornament but in the plan of the room, quite different from the formal rectangularity of Louis XIV interiors and with an entirely contrasting character as a result. Formalism has given way to intimacy and the setting is keyed to the *conversations à deux* that supply the motive for so much painting of the period (cf. Fig. 479) rather than to the solemn *tableaux* of the court at Versailles. A similar contrast is pointed out elsewhere between the furniture of the two styles (cf. Figs. 620, 621) that is dictated by similar considerations. A point of historic interest is raised by the appearance in the painted ornament of many rococo rooms like this one, of Oriental motives—*chinoiseries* and *singeries* they are called—an exotic element in the still prevailingly classical decorative repertory that is a direct reflection of newly established commercial relationships between Europe and the Far East in the early

18th century and also a symptom of tastes that were to have still more profound influences upon later 18th-century style.

At the same time that rococo architects were transforming the stately formality of the 17th-century salon into the intimate 18th-century boudoir, they were also engaged in giving new character to the concept

FIG. 167.—Paris. THE HÔTEL DE SOUBISE. The Oval Room.

of large-scale planning. At Nancy in northern France, Héré de Corny laid out a series of three interrelated squares between 1752 and 1755 that is one of the most effective compositions of this type in the period because of its fine coordination of the various elements of building, avenues, trees and the like. The *Place du Gouvernement*, one of these squares (Fig. 168), is given a characteristic rococo form in plan by the curving screens at each end which carry around the order of the first story in the Governor's Palace that dominates the ensemble on the left side of the illustration. The palace itself is illustrative of the Louis XV style in the fine scale obtained by well-proportioned orders for the three stories and in the character of the detail. At the same time there is a degree of formality in the complete ensemble of the three squares that derives from strict symmetry in disposition and refers directly to Palladian precedent.

Fig. 168.—Nancy. The Place du Gouvernement (hemicycle).

About the middle of the 18th century, the supremacy of Palladian ideas that was unquestioned in the architecture of the earlier decades was challenged by other concepts of style that were more or less direct reflections of certain changes in the prevailing thought of the time. These were, in general, along the lines of expanding still further the principles of free inquiry that had first been affirmed in the time of the Renaissance and the Reformation. Then these principles had been claimed in the fields of art and letters and religion; now it was in history, politics and science that the frontiers of human knowledge were being pushed back. The character of 18th-century thought was largely determined by the new outlook attained in the process. A period of seemingly great confusion and chaos, it was none the less from the spiritual turmoil of the 18th century that modern thought was born, for it was then that there developed conceptions of history, of nature and of ethics that have prevailed until comparatively recent times.

The evolution of a new concept of history is the factor of 18th-century thought most immediately evident in the architecture of the time, and it takes the form of attempts to revive more or less directly the practice and idioms of past periods in western civilization, notably the classic of ancient times and the mediaeval. The revival of classic forms is not hard to understand. The Italian Renaissance had been motivated in part by a desire to regenerate the beauties of classic art and the whole structure of academicism was raised on a foundation of respect for antique usage. But up to the middle of the 18th century, first-hand knowledge of classic buildings had been somewhat limited; the most general source of ideas employed by academic designers was not in the body of existing classic structures but the books of theorists like Palladio and Vignola. The ostensible ideal of the academicians was the classic; in actual practice, they varied greatly from the models by which in theory they were guided.

About 1750, however, a series of developments took place that were destined to change this theoretical concept of classic building and to open up different vistas for investigation. These were largely in the field of archaeology, the science of history, which was itself one of the most characteristic products of the new historical orientation of western thought in the 18th century. In 1738, for example, the Roman city of Herculaneum, which had been buried under the lava erupting from Mount Vesuvius near Naples in 79 A.D., was partially excavated, and a similar project was begun at Pompeii in 1763. In 1750-1751, the Greek temples at Paestum (cf. Fig. 35) were studied and measured by official representatives of the French Academy of Architecture. These scientific observations of certain aspects of classic art to which the academic theorists had been oblivious were made available in publications such as *The Antiquities of Athens* by Stuart and Revett in 1762, *Paestum* by Howard Major in 1768, and others by Cochin and Soufflot, to mention but a few. To eyes surfeited with the pompous and extravagant forms affected by the academicians, the clarity and logic of Greek design and the graceful delicacy of the previously unknown styles of Pompeii came as welcome relief. Furthermore, the spirit of the time was critical, rebelling against artificial and synthetic formulas, and the restraint and straightforwardness of the ancient styles were thoroughly congenial to temperaments that found in J. J. Winckelmann's exhortation to aspire for effects of "noble simplicity and quiet grandeur" (*History of Ancient Art*, 1764) the definition of ideal formal character.

The initial consequence of the more archaeological understanding of antique art that was developed by virtue of the circumstances indicated above was a reaction from the elaborate minutiae of the Louis XV style in the direction of greater simplicity and restraint in the Louis XVI manner. *The Place de la Concorde* in Paris (Fig. 169) was laid out by Jacques-Anges Gabriel (1698-1782) and created between 1753 and 1763; the two buildings flanking the rue Royale on the side of the Place opposite the river, also by Gabriel, were built between 1762 and 1770. Known originally as the Place Louis Quinze from the location of an equestrian statue of that monarch on the site now occupied by an Egyptian obelisk—it was also the place where the guillotine stood during the Revolution—it lies to the west of the gardens of the Tuileries, with its long axis extending to the east toward the Louvre and westward along the Champs Elysées to the Arc de Triomphe de l'Étoile. In its considerable size and the great formality of the plan, it is to be contrasted with the Place du Gouvernement at Nancy

FIG. 169.—Paris. THE PLACE DE LA CONCORDE.

(Fig. 168); in the careful relationship of architectural and natural elements, it is directly in the tradition of planned and monumental environment that was initiated in the great ensembles of the 17th century (cf. Fig. 150). A similar modification of Louis XIV concepts is to be noted in the façades of the buildings flanking the rue Royale; the motive of free-standing Corinthian columns over a rusticated basement story derives from Perrault's design for the East Colonnade of the Louvre (Fig. 149) but with a somewhat lighter effect from treating the lower story as an arcade.

On the smaller scale of the single building, the greater simplicity of the Louis XVI manner resulting from the archaeological concepts of later 18th-century classicism is apparent in the palace called the *Petit Trianon* (Figs. 170, 171) which was built at Versailles between 1762 and 1768 by Gabriel for the pleasure of Mme de Pompadour. The building is almost square in plan, and the façades are composed with notable reticence; the decoration is limited to an order of Corinthian columns or pilasters over a rusticated basement and mouldings of great delicacy around the openings, the character of the design residing for the most part in the well-studied proportions. The interior designs of the Petit Trianon are in both the rococo of Louis XV and the more pronounced classicism of Louis XVI, for the building was much favored by Marie Antoinette, who caused some parts of it to be redecorated. The dining salon (Fig. 171) with its ornament of notably restrained character in

Fig. 170.—Versailles. The Petit Trianon.

contrast with the vivacious rococo of the Hôtel de Soubise (Fig. 167) was executed in 1765 while Louis XV was still reigning, but the quality of the design relates it to the later style. Instead of the picturesquely irregular mouldings and panels and colorful paintings, there is geometrical regularity and simplicity in motives and details alike; the color is subdued and quiet in accordance with prevailing concepts of classicism.

At the same time that Gabriel was reacting to the archaeological spirit of the mid-18th century by restraining the decorative and pictorial exuberance of rococo style, some of his contemporaries were attempting even more scrupulous and exact applications of classic idioms. The church of *Sainte Geneviève* in Paris, also known as the *Panthéon* (Fig. 172), was the result of an attempt on the part of Jacques Germain Soufflot (1709-1780) to recreate in Paris the dome and portico of the famous Roman building whose name has been applied to the French one (Fig. 57), although the result is again more an illustration of what the period thought was classic than something actually so. The dome follows the pattern of that built by Wren for Saint Paul's in London (Fig. 162), both structurally and in the peristyle around the drum, much more closely than it does that of the Roman Pantheon, although the portico with its free-standing Corinthian columns and pediment is closer to the antique prototype. It was necessary to modify even this in application, for since the pitch of the gable is the same as in the orig-

FIG. 171.—Versailles. THE PETIT TRIANON. The Salon.

inal, the porch could not extend the entire width of the structure because that would have forced the gable peak up to a point where the dome would have been obscured. The porch is given the width necessary to span the façade by the device of adding supplementary columns at the ends and behind the central colonnade with which, however, they have no very effective relationship in design. Similarly lacking in coherent relationship with the rest of the building is the dome, which seems to have been merely placed on top of the lower part of the building instead of growing out of it as does that of Saint Peter's in Rome, for example (Fig. 131). Some details are more indicative of Soufflot's intention than the effect of the structure as a whole; the Corinthian order of the portico reproduces exactly that of the Roman building, and the suppression of all openings in the side walls, whose effect depends solely on proportions and contrast between plain surfaces and mouldings, was the result of mistaking mere simplicity for classic restraint.

An example of the revival of classicism in English architecture of the later 18th century that is similar in principle to the Parisian Panthéon is the façade of the house at *15 St. James Square* in London (Fig. 173), which dates from 1760. The architect was James Stuart (1713-1788)

FIG. 172.—Paris. THE PANTHÉON.

and the caliber of his ideas is suggested by the fact that he, like Soufflot in France who had studied and drawn the Greek temples at Paestum, was one of the pioneers in the archaeology of the time with his collaboration in the publication of *The Antiquities of Athens* and other books on previously little-known aspects of ancient art. Although there is still an element of Palladianism in the idea of an order raised above a rusticated basement story, the treatment of the upper stories in the form of a classic temple façade is an innovation and the accuracy with which the detail is studied toward this end is likewise new. The Ionic order reproduces that of the north porch of the Erechtheum in Athens (Fig. 32), and the proportions of entablature and pediment are archaeologically correct, producing an effect more like that of a true classic ensemble than can be noted in any building as yet considered.

From the introduction of classically correct details in buildings of academic character to the erection of structures that reproduced the forms of ancient examples was a step not long in taking. It is significant that it should have occurred first in Germany, where pioneering publications in classical archaeology by Winckelmann and Lessing had won great popular following. The *Brandenburg Gate* in Berlin (Fig. 174) was built between 1788 and 1791 after the designs of Karl Gottfried Langhans (1733-1808), who was clearly inspired by the Athenian Propylaea (Figs. 37, 38), the monumental approach to the Acropolis, with its central block and flanking wings in the form of small temples. There is some departure from the prototype in treatment of detail, but the intent to recreate the general form of the Greek structure is clear. The most complete realization of this ideal in Germany was the Walhalla or Hall of Fame at Regensburg, which was built in the form of the Parthenon between 1830 and 1842 by Leo von Klenze. A similar inspiration motivated the construction of the church of the Madeleine in Paris which stands at the head of the rue Royale leading northward from the Place de la Concorde (Fig. 169); a temple-like structure with a free-standing peristyle of Corinthian columns, it was begun in 1806

FIG. 173.—London. 15 St. JAMES SQUARE.

to comply with Napoleon's desire for a "Temple of Glory" that should be "a monument such as could be found at Athens and not in Paris" and the order does in fact reproduce that of the Athenian Temple of Olympian Zeus. Only the exterior is "Greek," however, for what should be the cella is covered with a series of domes. It is to be noted, moreover, that the unmodified temple type was rarely used in Europe for buildings of other than commemorative or decorative function even at the height of popular enthusiasm for classic forms, and the "temple house" which is one of the characteristic types in American architecture of the same period has no counterpart there.

At the same time that the Classic Revival was developing as one aspect, architecturally speaking, of the historical point of view being evolved in the thought of the 18th century, a parallel manifestation was also taking form in the Gothic Revival. This is most apparent in the architecture of England and Germany, where growing awareness of historical traditions had revived an interest in the mediaeval past, stimulated in no small degree by an increasingly self-conscious nationalism that saw in the art of the Middle Ages a heritage of northern culture as important as the classic one of Greece and Rome. Also to be taken into account as a contributory element in the background of the Gothic Revival was the romantic interest in far-off and exotic things that was responsible for the introduction of Chinese motives in some examples of

FIG. 174.—Berlin. THE BRANDENBURG GATE.

rococo art in the earlier 18th century, as has been noted above. In another form, but still fundamentally in response to emotional reactions, the same taste is apparent in the cult of mediaevalism, for if men like Horace Walpole in England and Goethe in Germany had no very sound intellectual comprehension of the nature of Gothic art, they none the less felt its expressiveness and saw in its forms an outlet for the feeling of their own age. This in turn was closely allied to the cult of nature that was developing in the writings of men like Richardson and Gray in England and Jean-Jacques Rousseau in France which was also romantic and sentimental at basis. It was for such reasons as these that in the realm of architecture, the picturesqueness of organic and therefore "natural" Gothic forms made them a symbol of all that was felt to be truly northern and emotively significant in the art, the religion and the philosophy of the 18th and early 19th centuries.

It is difficult if not impossible to speak of the first examples of the architectural Gothic Revival in terms other than critical, for the principles embodied in them are inherently non-artistic in the sense that other than plastic concepts dictated their forms. Thus one of the first buildings illustrating its principles was Strawberry Hill, which was built by Robert Morris between 1747 and 1776 for Horace Walpole the writer. Walpole's chief interest in the building was the provision it made for a background appropriate in mood to the writing of his novels, of which one called *The Castle of Otranto* appeared in 1764 with the significant subtitle, *A Gothic Tale*. This was the intention in the creation of the majority of Gothic Revival buildings of the later 18th century—to supply a setting of agreeable melancholy evoked by symbol and stimulated by associations that were primarily sentimental and literary. To achieve this end, it was not considered necessary to build soundly and well, for the symbol was more important than the fact; the most revealing illustration of the purely associative values expected of architectural design in this category is the imitation ruin or "fabrick," of which great numbers were built in the studiedly natural and romantic gardens of England in the 18th century.

The turn of the century brought with it a somewhat more substantial knowledge of mediaeval forms based on application of archaeological methods that had been developed earlier in the field of classic art. In such a building as the *Houses of Parliament* in London (Fig. 175), erected between 1840 and 1860, it is possible to discern a better understanding of the idioms. The general plan was the work of Sir Charles Barry (1795-1860), but the detail was created under the supervision of Augustus Welby Pugin (1813-1852), who was one of the first 19th-century students of mediaeval architecture to realize the essential unity of construction and design that gives true Gothic building its expressive character and to apply that idea. His workmen had been trained as completely as possible in the methods of mediaeval craftsmanship, but even this was an academic process at best, and the forms they created, while accurate enough as studies in the manner of Gothic, are stilted and lifeless in comparison with mediaeval work. Even in Pugin's work, the primary justification of the manner lay not so much in its plastic character as in associative values. These were no longer sentimental and literary but moral—a manifestation of Pugin's whole-hearted participation in the religious revivalism that was one of the significant phenomena in English 19th-century history; for it was his sincere and frequently expressed belief that only by returning to the ways of mediaeval thought and a deliberate and purposeful regeneration of the forms in which it found expression could a cure be found for the social and economic evils attendant upon the growth of industrialism. The same spirit animated others such as John Ruskin, whose fluent prose was largely responsible for the widespread popularity of the style called Victorian Gothic in England and the United States during the later 19th century. Of greater importance than either, however, was the work of William Morris which was motivated at the outset by a similar moralizing purpose but was based on a concept of creative craftsmanship that was destined to inspire some of the innovators of modern style in the closing years of the 19th century.

FIG. 175.—London. THE HOUSES OF PARLIAMENT.

In the revival tendencies that dominated European architecture in the first half of the 19th century, there was no perception of the basic principle that effective architectural style can be achieved only by taking into account the three fundamentals of plan, construction and design; for the purpose underlying the majority of buildings in either classic or mediaeval form then erected was primarily the creation of symbols that would be effective through association and sentimental identification rather than by virtue of formal qualities of mass and proportion and line and texture. This attitude was fostered by the prevailing historical point of view of the time and also, in a sense, by the increasingly more obvious consequences of industrial expansion as well which tended more and more to isolate the arts from the main stream of social expression by making them solely a means of escape from the tawdry and debasing circumstances of everyday existence. Not all the architects of the period accepted these standards, however, and some perceived the necessity of new architectural forms and methods to give appropriate expression to the new social scheme developing in the 19th century. As a group that had no conscious homogeneity and, indeed, consisted of men whose individual achievement is varied and uneven, these architects stood for a rational principle in building rather than a sentimental one, and de-developed forms that gave as direct expression to the fundamental structural elements of plan and material as the time was capable of producing.

Fig. 176.—Paris. The Bibliothèque Sainte-Geneviève. Exterior.

An example of this rational point of view in 19th-century architecture is seen in the *Bibliothèque Sainte-Geneviève* in Paris (Figs. 176, 177); it was designed by Henri Labrouste (1801-1875) and erected between 1843 and 1850. One of the first structures designed and built as a public library, in which it is a symbol of the new architectural demands created by the changing social fabric of the 19th century, the exterior gives reasonable expression to the internal division between stack space for storage below and the more open reading room above (Fig. 177), with its need for ample illumination that is served by the long unbroken row of arched windows. It is also an example of the inability of even the rational architect of the early 19th century to think of his problems in terms that were unaffected by historical considerations, for the proportions of the window arcade and its general spacing and rhythm were suggested by Alberti's treatment of the niches in the sides of the church

FIG. 177.—Paris. The Bibliothèque Sainte-Geneviève. Reading Room.

of San Francesco at Rimini (Fig. 119). The decorative mouldings that
enliven the somewhat severe masses and surfaces are profiled with a
delicacy that suggests Greek work and are a reminder of Labrouste's
study of the temples at Paestum (cf. Fig. 35) while a *pensionnaire* of
the French Academy at Rome. In the interior (Fig. 177), the same
dualism of structural rationalism and decorative revivalism is seen. The
internal supports are of cast iron; from them a series of transverse arched
girders of the same material are sprung to form the armature of two
barrel vaults running the length of the reading room. By using iron,
whose strength under compression is much greater than an equivalent
mass of masonry, maximum space and light were permitted and the
objective function of the structure was effectively realized. But the
supports are formed in the shape of slender Corinthian colonnettes
strangely attenuated in translation into metal, and the transverse girders
are pierced with a stylized foliate pattern derived from the classic
acanthus *rinceau*—neither motive being inherently suitable to the medium in which it is here used. Thus while Labrouste the builder and
engineer handled his material in such a way as to realize its structural
potentialities very effectively, Labrouste the architect had still to consider
the resultant forms in accordance with decorative principles entirely
alien to them, with the result that their expressive potentialities are
scarcely realized at all.

The conflict in the 19th century between the architect as a builder
and the architect as a designer of "pure form" was hardly perceived at
that time, and the importance of the few rationalistic buildings such as
the Bibliothèque Sainte-Geneviève in showing this dualism was un-
noticed. Instead, even the lesson of rationalism was not learned and the
revival principle was carried to even greater extremes in the later 19th
century than before 1850. Eclecticism was the guiding principle, with
the architect allowed complete freedom of choice in the historical styles,
the only criteria of judgment being the taste of the designer and the
supposed appropriateness of certain forms to particular purposes. Thus
religious structures were usually mediaeval, public buildings Renaissance, and monumental or commemorative edifices in the classic modes.
The *Opera House* in Paris (Fig. 178) is but one of literally thousands
of examples in point. Designed by Charles Garnier (1825-1898) and
finished in 1874, this structure has been a strong influence in theatre
design since it was built, a circumstance due in part to the prestige it
has enjoyed as the seat of the French National Academy of Music and
in part to the apparent appropriateness of baroque architectural forms
to opera, the most baroque of all the arts. In designing it, Garnier followed late Venetian Renaissance models for the most part, although the
applied order of doubled pilasters between projecting end bays with

pediments and over an arcaded basement story reverts directly to the French academic formula established by Perrault (Fig. 149) and continued by Gabriel (Fig. 169).

The state of affairs in European architecture of the late 19th century has been referred to as a "Battle of Styles," and the term is an eloquent indication of the chaos and confusion of architectural purpose that prevailed at that time. But this was no more than a reflection of the in-

FIG. 178.—Paris. THE OPERA HOUSE.

stability of thought in general in the period which saw the complete reorientation of western culture through the rise and spread of industrialism as a major economic and social phenomenon, with its consequent weakening and ultimate disruption of most of the traditional values of post-Renaissance civilization. Furthermore, as long as the western world was committed to an historical vocabulary of form in attempting to express its ideas, there was of necessity an emphasis upon purely formal considerations to compensate for the lack of genuine and vital inspiration in the ideas themselves. Thus in spite of the ever-increasing resources of historical vocabulary and the growing sophistication with which it was used, the sterility of eclecticism as a guiding principle of design is obvious and is the underlying explanation of the unmitigated dullness of the greater part of European architecture during the later 19th century.

# Chapter XII. American Architecture from Its Origins to 1870

ARCHITECTURE IN NORTH AMERICA DURING THE period in which that continent was colonized was based on the styles of the countries in which the settlers originated. The houses and churches of Colonial New England differ in no important respect from middle-class structures in England during the 17th and 18th centuries. In New York, Dutch types appear. The polyglot colonies in Pennsylvania and Delaware produced a mixture of Welsh, German and Swedish styles. To Florida, Mexico and California, the Jesuit missionaries carried the baroque of Italy and Spain though unavoidably modified by the conditions under which the buildings were erected. The dependence of the settlers upon the styles of their mother countries is obvious in descriptions of the first shelters they erected which have long since vanished. Captain John Smith wrote of the huts built by the first colonists in Virginia in terms indicating them to have been very similar to the rude shacks of the poorest laboring classes in England. By the end of the 17th century, more extensive settlement and greater security from attack gave the inhabitants of the New World more time to devote to architectural problems. Houses of some pretension and well adapted to their surroundings began to appear; and even though many of them were built of wood, so solidly were they constructed that a considerable number are still preserved.

Such was the *John Whipple House* at Ipswich, Mass. (Fig. 179), erected some time before 1669. It is very simple in plan, consisting of two rooms on each floor which occupy the entire width of the building. They are separated by a hall containing the main entrance and a staircase leading to the second floor. The house is of the wooden frame type which the English settlers in Massachusetts had known in their native land. Great corner posts support a rectangular framework of smaller beams on which the floors rest. The walls are a mixture of clay and straw filling the spaces between the wooden members of the frame and stiffened by studs or angle beams connecting the vertical posts and the horizontal joists. This is exactly the same construction employed in English mediaeval half-timbered houses (Fig. 156) from which the American type differs only in its exterior sheath of clapboards, which are overlapping pieces of wood. Clapboards were required in the severe New England climate where the unmodified English half-timber construction had proved insufficient to protect the inhabitants from the cold. If they were to be removed from the Whipple House, it would look like its English prototypes.

Protection from the bitter New England winters was the reason for many of the details of construction in such a building as the Whipple

FIG. 179.—Ipswich. THE JOHN WHIPPLE HOUSE.

House. The brick chimney rises through the center of the structure in order that the heat radiating from it might be retained inside. The central location of the chimney also made it possible to have one stack for all the fireplaces, of which there are four, one in each room. As the chimney is the most prominent feature of the exterior, so the fireplaces are focal points in the design of each room of the interior. An example is the parlor of the *Capen House* (Fig. 180) which was built at Topsfield in Essex County in Massachusetts in 1683. Notable and characteristic features otherwise are the use of wooden panels or wainscot on the fireplace wall, the plastering of the others—although this was apparently not a general practice in the earlier Colonial houses—and the straightforward acceptance of the structural beams and posts of the house frame as elements in the interior effect. Note should also be taken of the furniture, which is of the same general period as the house itself and, like it, follows the models currently used in England in houses of comparable character.

Frank revelation of structural facts and an almost total disregard for abstract formal beauty are the outstanding qualities of this first or

FIG. 180.—Topsfield. THE CAPEN HOUSE. The Parlor.

Colonial style of American architecture. A possible exception to this prevalent structuralism in the design might be made for the overhang, the slight projection of the attic of the Whipple House over the second story which in turn projects beyond the lowest level. But even this is a structural reminiscence, for in the houses of English tradesmen which also served them as stores, the overhang protected the wares exposed for sale on outdoor counters. Since the New England settlers were principally of the middle classes in England, this was the type of house with which they were most familiar and which they adapted to the different circumstances in which they found themselves in the New World. Although the use to which the overhang was put originally did not exist in the Massachusetts wilderness, the form remained as a decorative feature just as the guttae and triglyphs of the Greek Doric order persisted as ornamental details long after their original structural function was forgotten. The ends of the overhang were sometimes carved as they are in the Whipple House, but this is usually the only evidence of a conscious attempt to relieve the unpretentiousness of the exterior.

It is hardly necessary to point out that the Colonial builder was not primarily concerned with problems of formal design affecting the appearance of his structures. His main consideration was a practical and efficient arrangement of the interior for living purposes; and if, as frequently happened, the house became too small for a growing family, it was enlarged by a lean-to usually added to the rear in the form of another room with a slanting roof continuing the pitch of that on the earlier portion of the house. Such a lean-to appears as part of the Whipple House; the clapboards have been replaced to conceal the joint between the earlier and later parts. Though this made the ends of the house unsymmetrical in form, this was no more of a disadvantage in the eyes of the builder than is the irregular spacing of the windows which were placed in accordance with interior requirements rather than for external decorative effect.

It is for such reasons as these that the architecture of the Colonial period from 1620 to 1720 is often referred to as the mediaeval style in America. Like European mediaeval architecture, its character was determined by the constructive principles by which its forms were created. The parallel goes even further, for Colonial architecture is essentially organic in nature and distinguished by striking appropriateness to its setting and the conditions under which it was developed. In New England, the Colonial style is a wooden one since the inevitable preliminary to settlement was the clearing of the forests which made for a large supply of lumber. In New York and Pennsylvania, stone was easily obtained; the Colonial houses there are consequently of that material and different in character from the New England buildings. In the South, brick was commonly used and the less rigorous climate made possible a more open building than would have been possible in the North. A specific point of difference between the northern and southern types is the placing of the chimneys at the ends of the house in the latter since it was not so essential to conserve the radiated heat. Another contrast between the northern and southern Colonial houses arose from the differing antecedents of the settlers in the two regions. In the North, the colonists were of the middle class, whereas the southern settlers were usually of the aristocracy. Large numbers of servants were required to maintain the establishments and their housing was managed by outlying structures subordinate to the main one with which they might or might not be actually connected. Thus in all parts of the colonies regional styles were being developed, represented by buildings that were functional in character, comparatively unpretentious in appearance yet admirably adapted to their surroundings and the purposes for which they were intended.

By 1720, the unsettled political and social conditions of the Colonial period had become relatively stabilized. The colonists were able to turn their attention to matters which their earlier struggles to keep soul and body together had forced them to disregard. A more involved social order made its appearance, based on that of England and marked by very sharp distinctions between class levels. In architecture, a style was developed that is much more pretentious than the Colonial. It is known as the Georgian and it was employed largely from 1720 to about 1790, a period contemporary with the first representatives of the House of Hanover on the English throne, from whom the name of the style and period is derived. In general, the Georgian style in the colonies corresponds to that of the Renaissance in Europe, just as the Colonial style is essentially a mediaeval one. The points of contrast between the two reveal a growing preoccupation with problems of formal design similar to that which is evident in European Renaissance styles. The plan of the Georgian house is on a larger scale than the Colonial one. Usually there are four rooms on each floor; that is, the house is two rooms deep. The hall with its staircase is more prominent than in the earlier style and is more ornate in character. Methods of construction in the Georgian period were much the same as in the Colonial and also in the regional variations in materials employed. The greatest contrast between the two styles is in the appearance of the buildings.

The majority of Georgian house designs originated in the textbooks of architecture which were being written in ever-increasing numbers by English architects during the early years of the 18th century. At that time, English architecture was essentially classic and academic (cf. Fig. 165), and the theories elaborated in writings by such men as Colin Campbell, James Gibbs and Batty Langley were ultimately based on those of Palladio. Numerous books written by these men were brought to the colonies. In the hands of journeymen masons and carpenters, they gave rise to a flowering of classic details upon the buildings of the New World altogether comparable in spirit to that which occurred in 15th-century Italy even though differing from it in the character of the forms employed.

The academic quality of Georgian architecture is evident in the façade of the *Craigie* or *Longfellow House* in Cambridge, Mass. (Fig. 181), which was built about 1759. Details which reveal it are the giant order of Ionic pilasters on bases, the continuous frieze of dentils and the central pediment with horizontal and raking cornices both decorated with mouldings that follow closely the rules of academic design. The symmetry of the façade and the balustrade of the flat walk surmounting the hipped roof are other academic features. The hipped roof rises from all four sides of the house in an attempt to achieve a compromise between the flat roof dictated by academic formulas and the pointed one required by the rain and snow of a New England winter. That the builder of the house had no real understanding of the classic style is evident in his treatment of the Ionic pilasters. The base is not contin-

*Courtesy the Essex Institute*

Fig. 181.—Cambridge. The Longfellow House.

uous as in Roman and Renaissance examples (Figs. 50, 126) but appears only under the pilasters themselves. Similarly, above each pilaster is a small fragment of an entablature in addition to the complete one that circles the house. The architect was led into both these errors because he was copying a diagram of the order that consisted of a single column with partial base and entablature, the true functions of which he did not recognize.

The Georgian interior is no less academic than the exterior. A typical one is that from the *Charles Steadman* or *Powel House* in Philadelphia (Fig. 182), which was built about 1768. It is now in the American Wing of the Metropolitan Museum in New York. The bareness of the Colonial interior with its exposed ceiling beams and undecorated walls has given way to a more decorative effect. The fireplace wall is paneled in wood, with an elaborate mantel and over-mantel crowned by a typically academic broken pediment. The other walls are decorated with elaborately painted paper on which pagodas, trees, birds and mountains are represented. This type of wall paper was very popular in the Colonies during the third quarter of the 18th century when much of it was imported from China. Around the top of the walls is a classic moulding of the meander pattern, while the plaster ceiling is decorated with a delicate foliate design. The Chippendale furniture is of the same period

Fig. 182.—Metropolitan Museum, N. Y. Room from the Powel House, Philadelphia.

as the architecture and completes a design the equal in dignity and formality of anything contemporary with it in Europe.

In the South, different climatic conditions produced a type of house different from that in the North but no less academic in quality. *Mount Vernon* (Fig. 183) is typical of the southern Georgian style. It was given its present form by George Washington between 1758 and 1788, in several reconstructions of a previously existing building. The fact that he was his own architect is evidence that some architectural knowledge was then an indispensable adjunct to a gentleman's education. The square paneled columns of the portico are a variation of the usual round type. The balustrade of the portico roof had academic precedent, although the form in which it appears is not a traditional one but suggests the paneled latticework of a chair by Chippendale. Peculiarly southern qualities are the open portico and the outlying servants' quarters which are joined to the main building by arcaded passageways. The academic ideal is seen too in the Palladian window in the end of the house. The heavy pine boards of the sheathing are cut and painted to resemble jointed blocks of stone. This quite unjustifiable method of attempting to give a wooden structure the more monumental effect of stone was frequently employed in the Georgian period and furnishes an obvious point of contrast with the straightforward practices of the Colonial period.

FIG. 183.—MOUNT VERNON.

A glance at a middle-class Georgian house in England like the Swan House (Fig. 165) will show how similar in character were the results of working with comparable materials and for like purposes in both mother country and colony in the field of domestic architecture. There is also a resemblance between the churches of both countries. *Christ Church* in Philadelphia (Fig. 184) was designed by an amateur architect, John Kearsley, and completed in 1755. It follows the type of church erected by Sir Christopher Wren in London for the smaller parishes (cf. Fig. 163), although its immediate prototype was St. Martin's-in-the-Fields in London by James Gibbs. Various classic motives appear in the tower which is well designed to achieve a transition from the square base to the octagonal spire. The superposed orders of the side walls express the two-part elevation of the interior. The white sashes and divisions in the windows form an effective decorative contrast with the red brick walls which are given variety in themselves by slightly contrasting tones in adjacent courses. The balustrade with its urns is possibly too heavy in proportion to the rest of the building and the lack of agreement between the frieze of the side and that of the end wall reveals the hand of the amateur designer. The Palladian window of the end wall is a masterpiece, however, in its admirable proportions, its relationship to the wall and the restrained decorative quality of the details. It is deserving of admiration in its own right as well as being

FIG. 184.—Philadelphia. CHRIST CHURCH.

historically interesting as the first appearance of the Palladian motive in American Georgian architecture. Christ Church is closely associated with the pre-revolutionary history of Philadelphia by which it acquires an importance in addition to that of its excellent design. The latter has led many critics to pronounce it the finest example of Georgian church architecture in the United States.

The period following the Georgian in American architecture is that of the Classic Revival from about 1790 until approximately 1840. As in the European Classic Revival, structures of this period in America reveal efforts on the part of their designers to reproduce as exactly as they could the monuments of classic antiquity. However, the American Classic Revival differed from its European counterpart in this characteristic respect: to the interest in the past already noted was added the even more powerful stimulus to the use of classic forms of the growing spirit of nationalism that developed in the post-Revolutionary period in the United States. This was evident in the need expressed for an architectural style that would be particularly appropriate to America, owing nothing to any European country, particularly to England. A literary parallel is Webster's Dictionary which was an attempt to codify American as distinguished from English usage. At the same time, as compensation for the lack of background and tradition inevitable in a newly established country it seemed desirable that the style chosen as "American" should have something in common with those of the past. The one which seemed best to fulfill all these requirements was the classic.

Thomas Jefferson was the outstanding figure in the early Classic Revival in the United States. Today he is distinguished chiefly for his political accomplishments, but in his own time he was a leader in American architecture as well. His technical knowledge of architecture was equaled by his profound appreciation of its cultural value and philosophic implications. His approach to the problem of an American style was from the latter point of view, and it was that which finally led him to the conclusion that the forms of Roman architecture of the republican period were those best fitted for adaptation to the buildings of the new republic in the West. It was therefore the similarity in theory of government that was Jefferson's justification for believing that Roman architectural forms were the most appropriate for use in America whether they were really suitable to its needs or not. It was this fallacy that determined the architectural style of the young republic.

Jefferson was a practical as well as a theoretical architect, and he supported his thesis with actual designs. These he derived from direct observation of Roman buildings instead of seeing them "as through a glass darkly" in the writings of Palladio and the other theorists. In part this was due to his nationalistic opposition to the English academists whose works had exercised such a powerful influence on the American Georgian style. Thus when Jefferson was asked to draw up plans for the Virginia State Capitol in Richmond, he designed a modified form of the Maison Carrée in Nîmes (Fig. 50). This was one of the first actual examples of Roman architecture that he saw during a visit to Europe from 1784 to 1789 and its effect on him can be gathered from his statement that he gazed "whole hours at the *Maison Quarrée*, like a lover at his mistress." The model that he constructed as a part of his specifications for the *Virginia State Capitol* (Fig. 185) shows some variations from the original. One of these was the substitution of Ionic capitals for the original Corinthian to reduce the expense of carving.

The problem of doors and windows was one whose solution also required some deviation from classic models. In solving it, Jefferson followed the practice of the French classicists. Still further changes were unavoidable when the building was in the process of erection, but for all this, it marked an epoch in architectural history. For one thing, it was the first building designed specifically to meet the needs of modern republican government, not only in this country but in the world. It was also the first time that the unmodified temple form was employed in a building

*Courtesy Fiske Kimball*

Fig. 185.—Richmond. Virginia State Capitol. Original Model

that was intended for really practical use although it had been applied before to memorial and purely decorative structures. In this adaptation of exact classic forms to modern ends, the American Classic Revival anticipated that in Europe by many years.

As soon as the classic temple motive appeared in American architecture, enthusiasm for it swept all other forms aside. Jefferson himself employed it for many buildings, notably those of the University of Virginia in which he reproduced the Roman orders with great accuracy. In the professors' houses, the temple form was used for the first time in domestic structures. As the popularity of the style grew, Greek forms were employed as well as Roman. *The Bank of the United States* (Fig. 186) was designed by William Strickland (1787-1854) and built between 1819 and 1824. It reproduces the general proportions and order of the Parthenon although considerations of space made it necessary to limit the colonnades to the ends. In the Bank of the United States, Strickland gave expression to the ultra-classic principles which prevailed in American architecture in a form that won favor from many European commentators at the time. It antedates by at least ten years any foreign adaptation to modern needs of the Parthenon design, the employment of which in a commercial structure reflects a degree of classicism unparalleled in any other country.

The "Republican style," as it was currently known, soon spread over the entire United States. The geographical distinctions apparent in

FIG. 186.—Philadelphia. THE BANK OF THE UNITED STATES BUILDING.

the Colonial and Georgian period were wiped away and the pure classic style prevailed from Maine to Georgia and from New York to Michigan. Buildings of all kinds were designed in the form of Greek and Roman temples. In houses, a classic portico was the touchstone of social position even in regions which were then the backwoods. The *Spencer House* in Hamilton, N. Y. (Fig. 187), is an example of such a "temple," erected with its Doric porch some time after 1820. In all parts of the nation, the same phenomenon appears and classic porticoes were the order of the day.

It hardly needs to be repeated that the style of the Classic Revival was an artificial one. The pioneers in central New York and the wilds of Ohio and Michigan could not have been expected to express themselves naturally through the antique orders or to adapt the programs of their buildings to the restrictions of the temple form. Accordingly, the form itself was soon subjected to many changes. In the Spencer House, the Doric order is far from pure, with its crushed echinus and a base under the shaft. The doorway is set at one side to lead into the hall required by the severe winters, breaking the symmetry that is the chief characteristic of classic form. To gain additional interior space, a wing is added to one side of the main "temple," modifying even more the symmetry of the structure. Still further changes were made necessary in order that the upper rooms in the front of the house

Fig. 187.—Hamilton. The Spencer House.

might have some natural illumination. A full entablature would cut off almost all the light from those rooms. Sometimes this was remedied by inserting open grills in the frieze, while in other cases, as here, the entablature is practically eliminated. In either case, the purity of the classic form is destroyed. It is evident that the function of the classic temple house is actually hampered by its form instead of determining it. Attempts to arrive at a satisfactory compromise between them were never successful. It is patent that one basic form could not serve for private homes, banks, churches and statehouses. The classic builders themselves did not expect that the temple form could be used for every type of structure. The Classic Revival attempts to use it for all kinds of buildings only emphasize the impossibility of achieving effective results when exterior appearance is held to be the most important factor in architectural design.

With all the unfavorable characteristics of the Classic Revival style in mind, it cannot be denied that it contributed a much-needed element of dignity to American architecture. The best effects of the Georgian style are those of skillfully executed detail. In the hands of workmen possessing little taste or ability, it was often dry and monotonous. The Colonial style is that of a craftsman, attaining architectural effective-

*Copyright C. O. Buckingham, Washington, D. C.*

FIG. 188.—Washington. THE UNITED STATES CAPITOL.

ness by sound construction and an unconscious feeling for good proportions on the part of the builders. The buildings of the Classic Revival, on the other hand, possess an intrinsic solidity, sometimes in spite of the inexperienced designers. A few well-turned Doric or Ionic columns lend distinction to many a house of the early 19th century which would otherwise be only mediocre in effect. Furthermore, the style is an admirable indication of the growing sense of national importance which colored all American thought at that time.

The best-known example of the American Classic Revival is the *United States Capitol* in Washington, D. C. (Fig. 188). It is located on one of the focal points of a vast plan for the entire city, drawn up by Major Pierre Charles l'Enfant (1754-1825) after the model of Versailles (cf. Fig. 153). The plan of the original Capitol was by an amateur architect, Dr. William Thornton (1759-1828) of Philadelphia. As first constructed, a low central dome modeled after that of the Roman Pantheon rose from a base formed by the chambers of the Senate and of the House of Representatives. Various subsequent alterations gave the building its present form, the final and most extensive by Thomas U. Walter (1804-1888) in 1851. This involved the extension of the flanking wings by large blocks with pediments over the entrance fronts and free-standing colonnades along the side, and the construction of the present dome over the lower one by Thornton. It was completed in 1863 and is of cast iron painted to resemble stone. Its design is somewhat like that of the dome of Saint Paul's in London (Fig. 162) with a free-standing peristyle around the drum. The cupola dominates the masses of the wings that serve as a base to produce an effect which is not without impressiveness, a result that does something to justify the structural dishonesty by which it is attained. The building, like the greater part of those in the academic tradition, is quite dull, but this should not obscure its relative excellence in comparison with the majority of mid-19th-century examples of American architecture. Its widespread influence is attested by the many subsequently built state capitols that follow its general arrangement.

As in Europe, there was a Gothic Revival in American architecture of the 19th century. It was not without precedent in the American Colonial period, for the Gothic style had been used before the Revolution in the first building erected on the present site of Trinity Church in New York. This slender connection with the Middle Ages was reinforced in the early 19th century by the romantic novels of Sir Walter Scott and Washington Irving, the latter having gone so far in his mediaevalism as to rebuild his home, "Sunnyside," in a pseudo-Gothic style after Walpole's example in England. From 1835 until about 1860, the Gothic style was as popular as the classic one had been a few years before, an example being the so-called "Wedding-Cake" House at Kennebunkport, Me. (Fig. 189), which was built about 1850. The Gothic details here are obviously superficial. Underneath the pinnacles, pointed arches and other decorative incrustations, the house is little more than a box. Upon its rectangular form Gothic motives were festooned just as classic details would have been applied a hundred years earlier. The extensive use of mediaeval motives arose from the fact that they were fashionable, although their popularity was also due to a profound if unformulated and unconscious desire for beauty on the part of those who employed them which led them to seize upon anything to relieve the drab monotony of their structures. The ineptitude of the results can be attributed to lack of the background which imposed some restraint upon the use of revived historical forms in Europe. This fact too was unconsciously felt and the fumbling, almost pathetic attempts to acquire such background by arbitrarily creating its forms of expression without the capacity to understand them left its mark

*Photo Walker Evans*

Fig. 189.—Kennebunkport. The "Wedding-Cake" House.

on American architecture during the years immediately before the Civil War.

The closest approximations to mediaeval Gothic effects appear in examples of religious architecture in the American Gothic Revival. The use in churches of mediaeval forms as known to the 19th century did not require the fundamental alteration of their character that was involved when they were adapted to types with which they had never had any structural relationship. For this reason, such buildings as Trinity Church by Richard Upjohn, Grace Church and St. Patrick's Cathedral (Fig. 190) by James Renwick, all in New York, show less deviation from mediaeval models than do the Gothic houses that were being built at the same time. Without the possibility of immediate comparison with mediaeval originals, St. Patrick's (1850-1879) seems very convincing. Its Gothic characteristics are only superficial, however, the nave vaults, for example, being of papier-mâché painted to look like stone. Throughout, the effects were planned to conform to a preconceived idea of appearance instead of being attained by the logical integration of structural details.

The tendency toward superficial stylistic effects in American architecture before the Civil War appears in an aggravated form after it.

FIG. 190.—New York. SAINT PATRICK'S CATHEDRAL.

Three factors were chiefly instrumental in formulating the architectural style of the "Brown Decades," as the period from 1865 to about 1890 has been very aptly termed by Lewis Mumford. The first of these was the class of people who were responsible for most of the construction done, the *nouveau riche* created by economic conditions during and after the war. They had little or no taste for the most part and their idea of architectural effectiveness was in terms of the greatest number of gewgaws and knickknacks that could be crowded on a building. The second factor in determining the architectural style of this period was the invention of the jigsaw and the discovery of easier methods of casting iron. Both of these mechanical methods were employed to turn out yards of wooden fretwork, thousands of spindles and tons of metal grills and screens for use as architectural decoration. Most of these were in the Gothic style, owing to the third factor that influenced the architecture of the Brown Decades, the tremendous influence of John Ruskin and his fellow litterateurs who were preaching a return to mediaeval forms and ideals as a cure for the moral evils of an industrial world.

FIG. 191.—St. Paul. VICTORIAN HOUSE.

All three of these factors were important in the formation of the style popularly known as Victorian Gothic. Its chief characteristic is enormous pretentiousness whether the buildings are of wood or the brownstone so favored by the age. In either case, the buildings have very little genuine architectural quality, as can be seen in the edifices along the streets of the American cities and towns that grew up during the Brown Decades (Fig. 191). To secure what was fondly believed to be a picturesque effect, the building masses were broken up into irregular and unrelated forms. An ill-digested eclecticism was responsible for the incrustation of these forms with a profusion of Gothic, Renaissance and baroque details. Throughout, the dominant consideration was that of expressing the social position of the owner by the only means that would achieve that end, namely, by outdoing every building around in the amount of decoration. The heavy walnut and black oak furniture which infested the gloomy interiors served to complete an effect of unrelieved drabness. All of these qualities appear in the buildings of the Centennial Exposition of 1876 in Philadelphia which have been appropriately termed the nadir of American architecture.

The uniformly low level of American architectural achievement during the post-Civil War period apparently held no promise for its future. It must not be forgotten, however, that the hopeless ineptitude that characterizes it was due not to a deliberate preference for the forms employed but to ignorance. Lack of background made impossible any general appreciation of the beauty of past ages, a fact to which Mark Twain's remarks concerning the art he saw in Europe bear significant testimony. But even in the unfavorable atmosphere of parvenu taste and arrogant nationalism, the capacity to see beyond the insistent requirements of mere physical existence or the goal of financial affluence was present. To a few people, the exhibits sent by European countries to the Exposition of 1876 came as a marvelous revelation. Their eyes once opened, they were able to recognize the talent of the first great American architect of modern times, Henry Hobson Richardson (1838-1886). Richardson was one of the increasing number of Americans in the 19th century who had gone abroad for artistic training. He had studied in the École des Beaux-Arts in Paris, but his genius had not suffered from the stultifying atmosphere created by the academic principles for which that school is noted. His first buildings in this country were in the current Victorian Gothic mode, but the structure which brought him general recognition was not one of these. *Trinity Church* in Boston (Fig. 192), which was built between 1872 and 1877, is one of the first buildings in which appears the quality that was to distinguish Richardson's architectural thinking from that of the great majority of his contemporaries.

At first glance, Trinity Church may seem to be simply an example of the same historical revivalism that had produced St. Patrick's in New York a few years earlier, but in Romanesque instead of Gothic style; and it is true that the most prominent part of the structure—the great square tower—was admittedly copied after that of the 12th-century cathedral at Salamanca in Spain. But it must also be noted that the tower is not the individual work of Richardson but was the idea of one of his assistant draftsmen, Stanford White, to whom Richardson entrusted the problem of developing a suitable design for that part of the building when earlier plans proved incapable of construction. In the lower portion, which was designed by Richardson, it is possible to see a resemblance in character to Romanesque structures too, but a distinction must be drawn between Romanesque character in construction, which involves the use of material, and Romanesque ornament, which is only a matter of decorative detail. In the tower which was drawn up by Stanford White, it is the ornament that is Romanesque—in actual form as well as in general feeling since it follows closely that of the Spanish original; in the lower part of the structure, in the walls of the apse and transepts, there is no such copying, for the forms there are the result of Richardson's inspiration by Romanesque buildings to work in the same way as did the Romanesque builders—in heavy blocks of stone of vigorous rustication and massive proportions (cf. Fig. 88) that are eloquent of the architect's knowledge of his material and sense of the way it should be used. In

FIG. 192.—Boston. TRINITY CHURCH.

thus working as a builder in terms of material instead of as a decorator who works in terms of ornament, Richardson restored to architecture the fundamental quality of structural integrity that is so sadly lacking in the greater part of earlier 19th-century work in America, as has been noted. That the period in which he worked was incapable of realizing the importance of this and chose instead to see only superficial details that were identified by historical association as the consequence of attempting to revive Romanesque idioms as the Gothic had been by an earlier generation is no fault of Richardson's; the so-called Romanesque Revival in American architecture was not his achievement but that of men who thought to see in his work precisely what he had not taken from the forms that inspired him, namely, another system of historical ornament.

Sense of material and a corollary insistence upon sound construction were the qualities of Richardson's architectural thinking that more than anything else were invaluable potential antidotes to the superficial concepts prevalent in building styles of his time. They are present to a notable degree in the *Stoughton House* in Cambridge, Mass. (Fig. 193), which was built in 1882. The plan is an intelligent one in pro-

*Photo Berenice Abbott*

FIG. 193.—Cambridge. THE STOUGHTON HOUSE.

viding for the accommodation of a family of the period, with problems of orientation and circulation well solved. This is the basis for the L shape formed by the two wings which are joined by the circular stair tower; the mass of the house as a whole is held together visually by the long and even roof line. Coherence is given the wall which defines and encloses the spatial volume of the structure by its uniform surface of wood—beautiful in texture and a soft, silvery gray in color—a building material indigenous to New England which Richardson might well be said to have rediscovered following the long lapse from the straightforward and craftsmanlike use made of it by the Colonial builders of the 17th century (cf. Fig. 179). The clarity and realism with which Richardson approached the problem of domestic architectural style are readily apparent if the simple but beautifully proportioned form of the

Stoughton House is compared with the pseudo-monumental façade of the Victorian house with its meaningless confusion of applied ornament and would-be picturesque irregularity of outline.

Other than in reforms of a technical and structural nature in the use of material and emphasis on sound construction that Richardson contributed to American architecture in the late 19th century, the breadth of his imagination is seen in the great variety of building

FIG. 194.—Chicago. THE MARSHALL FIELD WHOLESALE BUILDING.

types to which he gave forms of character and distinction. One is to be observed in the stations he designed for the Boston and Albany Railroad in the suburban towns around Boston and another is the series of small libraries which were erected in many of the same towns; both appealed to him as forms characteristically of the time in providing for needs growing out of the social and economic conditions created by increasing industrialism and concentration of population around large manufacturing centers. Related to these in principle since it too was designed to meet a characteristic and contemporary need was the *Marshall Field Wholesale Building* in Chicago (Fig. 194), built in 1885-1887 but now, unhappily, destroyed. Seven stories in height and built around a central court covered by a skylight, the internal piers and floor beams were of metal while the outer walls, which were the major weight-bearing elements of the building, were of stone. The nature of the structure was such that maximum illumination of the interior was desirable; hence the relative proportion of window space to solid wall is considerable. It was from these features of the design alone that Richardson developed its character, for there is no applied ornament and very little carving, the contrasting texture of smooth and rusticated stone giving character to the surfaces and the rhythmic pattern of the openings providing the basic formal unity. The result is an example of masonry construction raised to its highest degree of architectural distinction by virtue of realistic but inspired employment in a timely and significantly contemporary structural problem. The greatness of Richardson's achievement is testified by the statement concerning the building made by one of the few men of the later 19th century who really comprehended it—Louis Sullivan: "Four-square and brown it stands, in physical fact a monument to trade, to the organized commercial spirit, to the power and progress of the age, to the strength and resource of individuality and force of character; spiritually it stands as the index of a mind large enough to cope with these things, taste them, absorb them and give them forth impressed with the stamp of a large and forceful personality, artistically it stands as the creation of one who knows well how to choose his words, who has somewhat to say and says it as the outpouring of a copious, direct, large and simple mind."

Objectively, Richardson's importance in the history of American architecture lies in the fact that he realized the necessity of judging building by standards of structural integrity and formal character rather than by picturesqueness. He perceived—as did none of his immediate predecessors and very few of his contemporaries and followers—that great architecture is not created by copying or even adapting the styles of the past. It results only when a profound understanding of the function of the building and its relationship in the broadest possible social sense to the period in which it is produced is given expression in a design that possesses the qualities of formal organization which make for distinction and character. That Richardson realized this is indicated by the hope he once expressed, that he might some time be able to design a grain elevator and the interior of a river steamboat—both characteristically American and both characteristically of the 19th century in America. Thus in theory as in practice, Richardson is a shining example of the theorem that an architectural style of force and individuality can be produced only by a race or nation strongly entrenched in its traditions and in such times as it feels through firm establishment therein the assurance and confidence essential to comprehensive and vital expression. Richardson's death in 1886, at the age of forty-eight, deprived the United States of its first modern architect at the moment when the influence of his example could have been of great significance and value. For it was at about this time that metal as a structural material of first rank in importance came into general usage in this country.

# Chapter XIII. Architecture of the Late 19th and Early 20th Centuries

*RICHARDSON'S ARCHITECTURE ILLUSTRATES IN THE* 19th-century tradition of the United States the same principle of rationalism that is embodied in Henri Labrouste's Bibliothèque Sainte-Geneviève in Paris (Fig. 176), in that it is an attempt to give expression to structural functions by means of design, and like the work of the Frenchman, that of the American was fundamentally misunderstood in its own time by being willfully classified as no more than another historical revival. So long as architecture as an art was evaluated in terms of sentimental and literary associative ideas and was conceived in historical patterns, there could be no understanding of architecture as an art involving perception of formal values. This fact was realized by one of the few sound critics of architecture in the early 19th century, the German Karl Friedrich Schinkel (1781-1841), when he wrote in 1824: "It would be a sorry thing for architecture, and it would not deserve its rank in the circle of the other arts, if all the individual parts developed in ancient times—such as the orders of columns and the kinds of mouldings—were filed away, and nothing were left to imagination but to make some new combination of these ready-made forms. A scanty matter for reason!" And he continues further to state that only by making use of the tremendously expanding resources of "new technical inventions" that were coming in ever-increasing numbers in the wake of the Industrial Revolution which was reorienting the whole trend of western culture could the architect gain for himself a place as the interpreter of that culture by creating a style appropriate to it. Not the least significant implication of this statement is the recognition it reveals of the principle that style must grow from structural rather than aesthetic procedure. The soundness of Schinkel's reasoning is proved by the fact that when a new and modern mode of architectural thinking ultimately made its appearance, it came after glass and metal, the typical contributions of industrialism to construction, were finally understood and mastered by architects.

In many ways, the development of effective processes of producing iron was the foundation of modern industrial manufacturing methods, and from the early years of the 19th century the employment of iron as a structural medium was attempted in various ways. Labrouste had covered the reading room of the Bibliothèque Sainte-Geneviève with barrel vaults supported in columns and arched girders of cast iron (Fig. 177) between 1843 and 1850, and had used domes built in the same way over the reading room of the Bibliothèque Nationale, also in Paris, a few years later. In the United States, the dome designed by Thomas U. Walter to be erected over the enlarged National Capitol in Washington, D. C. (Fig. 188), was built of the same material. In 1848 James Bogardus developed a method of prefabricating cast-iron columns and arches to be used as an adjunct to or instead of masonry outer walls for buildings that was extensively employed in commercial structures between 1850 and 1880, particularly important examples being the A. T. Stewart Store, now Wanamaker's, and Harper & Brothers' Building, both in New York. In all of these cases, however, iron was used simply as a substitute for masonry and with no realization of its inherent formal characteristics and potentialities; Labrouste's structural columns are in the form of Corinthian shafts and capitals, the front of the Harper Building was in the "Venetian Renaissance" style, and the Capitol dome was given artificially the texture and color of stone.

In contrast to the inability of architects to think of the forms they designed to be executed in iron in other than historical patterns, men in other fields arrived quite early at a more straightforward conception of the way in which it could be used, and thus to some degree the way that architecture was to follow later was prepared by engineers and builders who made no pretense to the attainment of conscious formal character in their work. An example was the *Crystal Palace* built in London for the Great Exhibition of 1851 (Fig. 195) by Joseph Paxton (1801-1865); originally in Hyde Park, it was taken down after the Exhibition closed and rebuilt at Sydenham in 1854, where it stood until destroyed by fire in 1936. Paxton was a greenhouse designer who had had some considerable experience in using iron and glass for such structures before he built the Crystal Palace; it resembled a gigantic nursery more than anything else. A framework of cast-iron beams and columns in the form of a long barrel-vaulted rectangle with smaller transverse vaults at one end and in the center furnished the support for an enclosing membrane of glass constituting the side walls and the fabric of the vaults above. No applied decoration marred the simple clarity of the external surfaces, and even though the iron beams of the interior were moulded and decked out with classical decorative motives, the scale of the structure was such that these counted for but little in the effect. This was essentially that of a great volume of space, defined by flat and curving planes of glass that were effectively weightless in character and whose sole function was the delimitation of the space they enclosed—an ideal which was to become conscious in the architectural thinking of the period following the First World War but which in the Crystal Palace was no more than incidental to an inexpensive yet spectacular way of using materials whose resources were unperceived by the architects of the time.

Fig. 195.—London. The Crystal Palace.

The bridge-building engineers of the 19th century were others who investigated the qualities of iron as a medium of construction and made effective use of it before it was taken up in a creative way by architects. A bridge of cast iron with a span of 100 feet was built across the Severn River at Coalbrookdale in Wales in 1779, and suspension bridges of even greater length were built in the United States and Europe in the early 19th century with the use of iron chains and cables. The perfection of cheap processes of producing steel—the Bessemer in 1855, and the Siemens open-hearth method in 1862—was particularly important in this field, for the greater structural flexibility of steel over iron of comparable cost in manufacture was a valuable asset in the construction of such a masterpiece of engineering as the *Brooklyn Bridge* (Fig. 196), which was designed by Washington Roebling (1837-1926), whose father John had been a pioneer in the field earlier in the 19th century. Built between 1871 and 1883, the Brooklyn Bridge is an outstanding example of an edifice with considerable character as a formal design yet which was built for inherently practical reasons and in such a way that those motives would be most effectively realized. The roadway is supported by great steel cables which hang from the granite piers in curves that are planned to realize completely the resources of tensile strength in the metal. Upon this the stability of

Fig. 196.—Brooklyn Bridge.

the bridge depends and from this its character as a design is derived; the form of the bridge is a consequence of solving with maximum efficiency the functional and structural problems it presented, the only concession to contemporary "Gothic" ideals of architectural beauty being the pointed arches of the granite piers. These are necessarily massive and the contrast between their solid bulk and the delicate tracery of the steel webs they support is another factor contributing to the formal distinction of the structure. The steel work itself is devoid of ornament; nothing detracts from the straightforward and simple effect of its logical and rational forms. This is the quality that distinguishes most sharply the products of late 19th-century engineering from the architecture contemporary with it (cf. Figs. 178, 191).

It is the direct simplicity of the Brooklyn Bridge that makes it a somewhat more effective example of the formal distinction capable of being achieved through an understanding of structural materials than another of the great monuments of steel construction in the late 19th century, the *Eiffel Tower* in Paris (Fig. 197). It was designed by Gustave Eiffel, one of the foremost engineers in France, for the International Exposition of 1889, and as is often the case in exhibition buildings, some concession had to be made to popular taste. Here it is to be noted in the treatment of the base, which is festooned with "artistic" ornament that is obviously applied and not organic and obscures the structural lines and pattern of the great piers. But this is not so insistent from a distance or in the unbroken upward sweep of the converging forms above. There can be noted the same unadorned, logical and simple patterns that appear in the Brooklyn Bridge and that make the Eiffel Tower like it in being an example of the realization of formal distinction through structural imaginativeness and integrity in the use of material.

FIG. 197.—Paris. THE EIFFEL TOWER.

Practical necessity and the flexibility of iron and steel as structural materials were the basic factors in the rapid adoption and successful use of these new mediums by 19th-century engineers which their architectural contemporaries were long in realizing. There came at last a time, however, when preoccupation with matters of formal design alone and obliviousness to structural considerations were no longer possible for architects and when under pressure of practical needs they had to make more than superficial use of the new structural materials. This was one of the consequences of the great demand for commercial buildings in the United States that resulted from the expansion of business after the Civil War. The labora-

Fig. 198.—Models Illustrating Masonry and Steel Skyscraper

tory for the architectural experiments that eventually produced the first use of steel as a medium of formally creative structural design was the city of Chicago, where the fire of 1871 destroyed practically the entire commercial district and created a situation in which the general trend toward expansion noted above was given a particular character by immediate necessity for new buildings for which the need was not only present but extremely urgent. Practical necessity and supposedly greater convenience in communication were factors also present in the concentration of these new buildings in a relatively limited area, the Loop in Chicago, and—although the immediate necessity was not so great—also in New York, in the financial district developed in the lower part of Manhattan. One consequence of this concentration of building in rather limited areas in the two cities in question—and in others too—was an immediate and considerable increase in land costs in those regions which made it highly desirable from a commercial point of view that buildings there erected should possess a maximum amount of profitable volume of space. It was from such circumstances that the tall commercial building or skyscraper came into being, for lateral expansion of low buildings to gain the needed space was of course prevented by the cost of the land on which they would have had to be extended. These circumstances were peculiarly American; and it was in solving the problems, both structural and formal, that arose in connection with the skyscraper as a building type that steel played its first important rôle in architecture, and gave to American developments in the art a character quite different from that of contemporary work in Europe where none of the conditions existed that led to the evolution of the skyscraper.

Some of the first tall commercial buildings in the United States were of masonry, but stone and brick could not be used as efficiently as steel in the skyscraper for reasons that are indicated graphically in the comparative models (Fig. 198). In a masonry building such as is shown in the model at the right of the illustration, the walls support the internal structure of floors and their own weight as well. Now if it were desirable to raise the height of the building, the walls would have to be made thicker at the base, for the increase in their weight attendant upon their augmented height would place the lower parts under greater compression in consequence of which they would tend to buckle outward unless made thicker. This thickening gives the walls the shape of a rather tall and thin pyramid in section; it also reduces the amount of useful space on the ground floors quite considerably and raises as well the problem of natural illumination, because windows in such walls, which are very deep, cannot admit as much light as openings of the same size in a wall of less thickness. A combination of masonry and metal supporting members such as is shown in the center model relieves these disadvantages to some extent and allows a somewhat greater height, but many of the drawbacks of all-masonry construction are still present.

The model to the left represents a building supported entirely by a steel framework. In such a building, the total area covered in plan is available for use from the ground floor to the top, save for the negligible space taken up by the relatively slight supporting members. These are vertical steel beams which sustain the entire weight of the structure, including that of the walls which are not required to be even self-supporting since they are suspended from the outer ends of the horizontal floor beams (cf. Fig. 3). In principle, the only purpose the walls serve in the building is as a screen or membrane to separate the enclosed volume of space that is the building from the space surrounding it on the outside. The advantages of this method of construction in a commercial building are many. There is practically no limit to the height it may attain. There is uniform floor area from bottom to top. Interior illumination by natural light is much facilitated because the entire space between the supporting members can be opened out if desired, whereas in a masonry building the size of the windows must depend upon the relative importance of the wall as a means of support at a given place.

Steel was not used only in the structural beams of the skyscraper. In the form of long cables, it was employed in connection with the elevators so essential to the skyscraper. Obviously even a ten-story building would require some means of vertical locomotion other than that of human legs and flights of steps. The first commercial building with an elevator in the United States was built in 1874; from that time on, the development of the elevator coincided with that of the skyscraper. Another problem of skyscraper construction that had to be solved was the protection of the metal skeleton from deterioration by the elements and destruction by fire. Such early skyscrapers as the Home Life Insurance Building in Chicago, built by William LeBaron Jenney in 1884, and the Tacoma Building in 1887 by Holabird and Roche, also in Chicago, had steel skeletons sheathed with masonry in forms reminiscent of Richardson's Romanesque. Later, terra cotta and concrete were used for this purpose, the latter medium also being employed for floors when reinforced with steel beams. These and similar materials are the structural elements in modern architecture, to which should also be added plate glass which like steel first came into commercial production in the last half of the 19th century.

New constructive principles and materials required a style appropriate to them. The importance of this factor in architectural design will be made clear by reference to some of the 19th-century buildings already considered. The Marshall Field Building (Fig. 194) is obviously a stone structure. Everything in the design points to that fact—proportions, wall and window membering, relation of solids to voids. The Brooklyn Bridge (Fig. 196), on the other hand, would be impossible in any medium other than one with the tensile strength of steel, for the outstanding element in its design is the great catenary curve of the cables. In each case, the design is functional as expressing the medium of construction. This is not true of a building like the Bibliothèque Sainte-Geneviève, whose exterior (Fig. 176) gives no inkling of the iron and glass vaults of the interior (Fig. 177). It stands to reason that the historical styles are fundamentally inappropriate to buildings of steel, for their forms are those of stone, wood, plaster or simple concrete, to distinguish the latter from modern ferro-concrete. This fact was apparently not realized by most of the architects of the period under discussion.

The name of one man stands out in the history of late 19th-century American architecture as an exception to the last statement in the foregoing paragraph. Louis Henry Sullivan (1856-1925) was the first American architect to undertake consciously the development of an architectural style based on modern methods and materials of construction. His aims are summed up in the phrase "Form follows Function." The principle thus embodied was the result of Sullivan's observation that the great styles of the past had been developed by giving expression to the purpose for which a building was intended, the constructive method involved and the material of which it was built. Sullivan thought to apply the same principle to the design of the tall, steel-framed modern office building. It was obvious that a prototype for such a building did not exist in the past. Its style had therefore to be developed according to a rule which would be, in the words of Sullivan's teacher, "so broad as to admit of no exceptions."

The realization of Sullivan's ideal was the *Wainwright Building* in St. Louis (Fig. 199), built in 1891. As a modern building, it has no relationship to the past, either in function or in form; hence the suggestion of any historical style is carefully avoided. The stability of the structure is derived from its steel skeleton, which is indicated by the protective terra-cotta sheath in strips so slender they are obviously incapable of supporting anything. The walls are reduced to mere panels underneath the windows; they bear no weight, for they are only screens separating interior from exterior space. Their non-structural function is indicated by delicate ornament of a type individual to Sullivan and bearing no resemblance to that of any other architect or style. The terra-cotta piers serve not only the practical function of pro-

tecting the steel frame of the building but the visual one of supplying
a vertical accent to the exterior by which the loftiness of the structure
is accentuated. This is the embodiment of another element of Sulli-

Fig. 199.—St. Louis. The Wainwright Building.

van's architectural creed. Since the modern office building is necessarily
tall, everything in the design should further the impression of tallness.
According to Sullivan, the basic idea of masonry construction, the super-
imposition of masses, is replaced in steel construction by the principle

of vertical continuity in consequence of which the building becomes "a proud and soaring thing."

The application of Sullivan's formula was not limited to tall office buildings. In the *Schlesinger-Mayer Building* in Chicago, now the store of Carson, Pirie & Scott (Fig. 200), he anticipated European methods of department store design by at least twenty years, the first unit of the Chicago structure having been built in 1899. Instead of being

FIG. 200.—Chicago. THE SCHLESINGER-MAYER BUILDING.
(NOW CARSON, PIRIE & SCOTT.)

vertical like the Wainwright Building, the Schlesinger-Mayer Building is predominantly horizontal in effect, more in keeping with the function of a department store, which requires large flat areas rather than the cubical volumes of an office building. The wide windows separated by narrow terra-cotta strips are admirably expressive of the open steel framework and also directly contributory to the efficiency of the building. Only in the lower stories is the clean-cut simplicity of the design somewhat obscured by the florid ornament that was at once Sullivan's personal delight and architectural weakness. In many of his buildings, particularly the later ones, the applied decoration is over-insistent. Although undeniably beautiful in itself, it tends to detract from the architectonic character of the designs. In this respect, Sullivan yielded to the idea so dear to the romantic mind, the expression of individuality, even though by so doing he violated the principles of an art which should be abstractly impersonal above all else.                                    .

It was this characteristic of Sullivan's temperament that prevented him from having the influence on American architecture that his genius would otherwise have made possible. He did not give a full account of the social stewardship which is part of the architect's duty. He realized this obligation and its importance; that is obvious in his writings. But his romantic background made him believe the right to express his own individuality to be even more important, and as a result, it was impossible for him to elicit from the forces of the society in which he lived a comprehensive architectural expression of the realities of modern life. In this respect he differed fundamentally from Richardson who, had he lived longer, would undoubtedly have succeeded in making his style intelligible to the country at large. Sullivan, on the other hand, attempted to break, finally and conclusively, with all that had gone before. In refusing to accept anything of the past he deprived his own artistic creed of foundation. The conflict in Sullivan's nature that this involved is reflected in his realization that the spirit which produced the tall office building was a profoundly anti-social one by virtue of the resultant congestion and chaos, a realization which he attempted to rationalize in his statement that a skyscraper should be a "proud and soaring thing." This was a romantic moral concept which even his own broad formula could not justify. The purpose of height in a skyscraper is not spiritual as is that of a Gothic cathedral. Rather it is to increase commercial value, as an advertisement in structures like the Woolworth and Empire State Buildings, by providing more rentable space, or in the augmented efficiency resulting from centralization of many diverse activities under a single roof. In Sullivan's own buildings, the vertical idea which he championed is not carried through consistently; witness the cornice of the Wainwright Building and the contradiction between the horizontal lines of the first two stories and the vertical ones above.

Sullivan's greatness is not to be found entirely in his buildings or in his expressed theories. Rather it lies in the example he gave of the architect's obligation to consider his art as a social manifestation, expressing the forces at work in society with the same clarity that characterized the work of Roebling and his fellow engineers. Sullivan stated that the architect should approach his work with the directness, simplicity and singleness of purpose that unconsciously made contemporary engineering projects a source of aesthetic delight. To achieve this end, the whole meaningless panoply of the forms of older cultures must be discarded, since they were the creation of social and religious complexes wholly unlike existent ones; the problem of architectural style must be worked out anew. Sullivan's relative failure to attain this goal himself detracts nothing either from its significance or from his own. His temperamental incapacity to give convincing form to his lofty conceptions was responsible for the personal tragedy that overtook him when he saw the very principles which he condemned exalted in the buildings of the eclectic movement, but the ideals for which he strove were destined to live in the works of his student and one-time assistant, Frank Lloyd Wright.

Before considering Wright's contribution to American architecture, the fate of Sullivan's idea must be observed. His kinship with Richardson has already been pointed out. The greatness of both lies in their recognition that architecture is an art of ideas, not of formulas. Its forms must be not mere symbols of past cultures but expressive of the civilization that creates them. In the last decade of the 19th century, the truth of this statement which had been proclaimed by both Richardson and Sullivan was completely obscured by the wave of eclecticism that swept over the United States following upon the renown achieved by the buildings of the Columbian Exposition of 1893 in Chicago. These buildings had been designed, with one exception, by architects who had been trained in the École des Beaux-Arts in Paris; the structures themselves were in the classic tradition as interpreted by the academic French school.

The effect of the gleaming white façades that embodied the classic formulas was immediate and powerful. In their plaster columns and arches, there was a directly perceptible attractiveness not apparent in the somber pile of the Marshall Field Building and the early steel buildings in Chicago. That this beauty was merely superficial in contrast to the sturdy honesty of Richardson's work and the other functional buildings was not appreciated. The one exception to the spurious stucco and plaster façades with their semblance of stone was Louis Sullivan's Transportation Building. Its design was a frank statement of the impermanent materials of which it was constructed, in contrast with the seemingly permanent classic and Renaissance façades on all sides. The immediate and popular reaction to these architectural falsehoods is further evidence of the lack of artistic tradition in the background of America in the '90's. Although many European critics perceived at once the strength and vitality of Sullivan's building at the Exposition and of many commercial buildings erected in Chicago and elsewhere in the preceding decade, and were disappointed in the majority of the structures at the Exposition which they rightly observed were the sort of thing being done better in Europe, popular American judgment was then incapable of following them. The architects who were chiefly influential in moulding public taste during the early decades of the 20th century in this country overlooked entirely the creative reintegration of construction and design that Richardson and Sullivan had achieved and continued the sterile tradition of historical eclecticism with its emphasis on superficial formal values at the cost of sound architectonic quality.

In the eclectic movement of the late 19th and early 20th centuries in the United States, all the historical styles were considered available to the architect in designing a cloak for the steel frames that were in common use by that time. Two general categories are to be noted, the classic which included Renaissance styles, and the mediaeval. The former is best represented by the work of McKim, Mead and White. McKim and White had both been trained at the Beaux-Arts and in Richardson's office in Boston. Their first works, dating from about 1880, have something of Richardson's sturdy ruggedness, but a break with this style appeared in the design for the Boston Public Library in 1888. It was based on Labrouste's Bibliothèque Sainte-Geneviève (Fig. 176), with some modifications suggested by Early Renaissance Italian types. Largely because of the influence of this firm, the Roman style was chosen for the buildings of the Columbian Exposition. The fame achieved by their own designs brought them commissions for many important buildings in the East during the first decade of the 20th century. These include the New York Municipal Building, many of the Columbia University buildings and the Pennsylvania Railroad Station in New York City, whose Grand Concourse, an almost verbatim transcription of the great hall of the Baths of Caracalla in Rome (cf. Fig. 56), is considered their finest work.

Foremost among the adherents of the mediaeval style in the eclectic movement was the firm of Cram, Goodhue and Ferguson. The output of this firm consisted principally of churches and college buildings, representative examples of the former being St. Thomas in New York and the First Baptist Church in Pittsburgh, while the buildings at West Point and a number at Princeton are characteristic of the latter category. The firm was dissolved in 1914, Cram and Ferguson continuing to produce mediaeval designs. Goodhue, on the other hand, developed a much more individual style that reached its climax in the magnificent State Capitol in Lincoln, Neb. (Fig. 201), which, finished in 1926, broke completely with the classic form that had been used for such structures ever since the erection of the National Capitol. Goodhue's death in 1924 was a serious blow to American architecture, for he was nearing the achievement of a modern style incorporating much that could profitably be learned from past styles without being thereby inhibited.

The lack of connection between form and function that is an inevitable corollary of eclecticism appears in its most exaggerated form in the skyscraper. When the classic eclectics attempted to adapt their chosen forms to the tall building, they apparently overlooked the fact that the classic styles are essentially horizontal in effect. To solve this paradox,

FIG. 201.—Lincoln. THE NEBRASKA STATE CAPITOL.

they generally regarded the skyscraper as a form comparable to a column with base, shaft and capital. The chief objection to such a solution is the unsatisfactory proportions that usually result. Thus in the New York Municipal Building by McKim, Mead and White, for all the undeniable beauty of the details, the final effect is that of superimposed masonry forms with little or no expression of the steel skeleton. The eclectic skyscraper is more successful when it is based on prototypes that involve some treatment of vertical elements. The *Metropolitan Life Insurance Co. Building* in New York (Fig. 202), by N. LeBrun & Sons, is derived from the campanile of St. Mark's in Venice. As in the New York Municipal Building, there is no expression of the steel framework but rather a suppression of it to produce the effect of solid masonry walls. As a study in abstract form, it weakly reflects the virtues of the original. As an organic expression of the function of a modern office building, it leaves much to be desired.

For an obvious reason, the Gothic style was better adapted to the sky-scraper form than the classic. Vertical accents predominate in both. This coincidence was responsible for the immediate success of the *Woolworth Building* in New York (Fig. 203) by Cass Gilbert (1859-1934), erected between 1910 and 1913. From a distance it is not un-impressive. The mass is imposing and the relationship of tower and base well conceived. Furthermore, the steel framework is clearly ex-pressed by the long, unbroken lines of the terra-cotta sheath, particu-larly from the rear. But even in the Gothic skyscraper such as the Wool-worth Building, there is a paradox in the blossoming-out of the hard metallic vertical lines of the build-ing into a frosting of pinnacles, pointed arches and flying buttresses. These are all intrinsically stone forms, employed by the Gothic builder to emphasize the vertical elements in his design and for struc-tural reasons. In the Woolworth Building, they do not occur for struc-tural reasons at all, for the strains in the steel framework are not lateral thrusts but forces of tension and compression. Furthermore, the Gothic quality of the Woolworth Building, in addition to being a matter of superficial ornament without structural justification, not only does not express the function of the structure but interferes with it, because the arched cornices cut off practically all the exterior illumination of the offices immediately behind them.

Fig. 202.—New York. The Metropolitan Life Insurance Co. Building.

The sterility of eclecticism as a guiding principle in architecture lies in the fact that its exponents failed to realize that their art should be one of ideas and not merely of forms. The methods they employed were a confession of their inability to give adequate expression to the many-sided character of modern life. Their concept of life was a funda-mentally static one, for there can be no organic growth in an art which

Fig. 203.—New York. The Woolworth Building.

deliberately turns to the dead symbols of past cultures instead of creating its own forms of expression. Eclecticism was merely another aspect of the romantic desire to escape from the reality of the living present into a world clothed with moribund beauty by minds overwhelmed by the complexity of contemporary thought. Its amazing popularity in the early years of the 20th century serves to emphasize the lack of tradition in the American background. Eclectic forms were stamped with academic approval and thereby gained a certain authority which was reinforced by their undeniably sensational qualities. To minds uneducated as yet to the more abstract elements of articulated mass, beauty of material and the like by which Richardson and Sullivan gave expression to their ideas, these forms passed muster as those of great architecture. The Renaissance ideal of art as pure form which separated it from the life of the people has had no more disastrous result than this, that it made the man in the street willing to accept as beautiful what was thrust upon him by the academic eclectics of the late 19th and early 20th centuries.

The Roman temples, Italian campaniles and Gothic cathedrals with which eclecticism clothed the American scene are only one aspect of architecture in the United States during the period under discussion. The reverse of these polished façades was the incredibly vile slums in which the poor classes were forced to live. So preoccupied were the Beaux-Arts architects with their formal problems that they were oblivious to the tenement regions which sprang up in direct consequence of the urban concentration of population. Only within the last few years has any attempt been made to relieve the shocking conditions that prevailed in these regions. The majority of the flats were of the "dumb-bell" type, so called by virtue of its shape which made no provision for the privacy, light and air essential to living, but was highly successful in producing maximum income from the smallest possible amount of real estate. It is a devastating commentary on the lack of interest in low-cost housing in the United States that "old law" tenements of this type were still permitted to operate until very recently. Like the congestion in the commercial districts of modern American cities which they rivaled and often surpassed, the conditions in the residential slums were a direct outcome of approaching the problem of human shelter solely from the point of view of maximum financial return on investment. It is to be said to Sullivan's credit that he was conscious in some measure of what the consequences of such a point of view would be; it is the everlasting disgrace of the eclectic designers of the late 19th and early 20th centuries in the United States that they were not even aware that such a state of affairs did or could exist.

Other than in the tenements, there was still little of distinction in the domestic architecture of the United States, for the carefully polished façades of eclectically designed houses with their interiors calculated to make the most impressive display of furniture and accessories differ from the tall and spiky exteriors of the earlier Victorian style (cf. Fig. 191) and its badly planned and gloomy rooms only in their somewhat greater sophistication. A significant exception to this concept of the house must be noted, however, in the designs of Frank Lloyd Wright (b. 1868), by whom, as has been mentioned before, the fundamental ideas and principles of Louis Sullivan were continued. It was in Sullivan's office, in fact, that Wright was prepared to achieve what he did in arriving at a new understanding of the problem of domestic design, for his training otherwise consisted of little but two years in the engineering school of the University of Wisconsin. But it was the example of Sullivan's logical and reasoned understanding of the commercial building as an architectural symbol of one aspect of modern life, combined with an inherently romantic antagonism to the lack of organic relationship between the Victorian house, with its artificially contrived and false monumentality, and the low-lying landscape of the mid-western prairies, that was the underlying factor determining the forms of Wright's style in which was embodied his expressive aim. This was to achieve a fusion of house and setting, to weld architecture and landscape into an organically integrated whole that should symbolize man's inherent oneness with nature. The "Prairie House" was the result.

The *Robie House* on Woodlawn Avenue in Chicago (Figs. 204, 205) was built in 1907-1908 and represents the highest development of the "Prairie House." It is long and low, the horizontal lines merging into the level surroundings while judiciously placed vertical accents in the chimney and window frames give the necessary sense of support in the design. The eaves and porches are wide, the roofs of the latter being hung by cantilevers from the framework of the house to afford the openness so essential to comfort in the summer months with the minimum of obstruction. The windows are grouped together in long rows instead of being treated as isolated units, resulting in a sense of organic relationship between exterior and interior space. The plan (Fig. 205) reveals the most original treatment of enclosed space in any style since the Gothic. Instead of considering the interior as a series of blocks cut off from each other by walls, Wright has handled it as a single elastic volume. One space flows into another, unobstructed by walls or doors and focused around deep fireplaces, thus establishing the oneness of the interior with the exterior, where the design centers around the chimney stack. The living room and dining room merge into each other, separated only by the chimney stack and the staircase. The service quarters are isolated and the privacy of the

FIG. 204.—Chicago. THE ROBIE HOUSE.

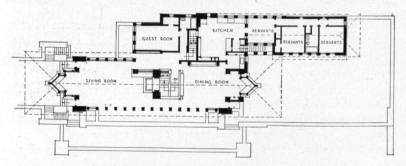

UPPER FLOOR

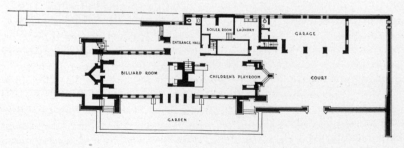

LOWER FLOOR

FIG. 205.—Chicago. THE ROBIE HOUSE. Plan.

bedrooms is assured by walls separating them from the rest of the house. The banded windows and broad openings leading to the courts and terraces emphasize the integral unity of interior and exterior. Decorative effects are obtained in the contrasted structural materials and by the fine proportions of the building, there being practically no applied ornament. In designing the "Prairie House," Wright faced squarely the problem of modern living and solved it in the most efficient way that he could. The result is another demonstration of the basic sound-

FIG. 206.—Oak Park. UNITY TEMPLE.

ness of Sullivan's creed that Form follows Function. Without concession to previous styles, Wright developed a style of his own that was capable of application to many different types of buildings. Incidentally, although Wright's approach to the problem of the modern house was primarily an artistic one, his solution of it revealed a thorough appreciation of the social significance of good architecture. In making provision for the necessities of modern life by insisting upon adequate light and air and free movement from interior to exterior, Wright simply incorporated in his designs the things which are the right of every human being.

In these early years of his career, Wright designed other types of buildings than houses. In the Administration Building of the Larkin Soap Factory in Buffalo, built in 1904, he created an architectural embodiment of the modern commercial spirit utterly different from any previous structure. *Unity Temple* in Oak Park, Ill. (Fig. 206), built in 1905-1906, was an innovation in construction as well as in design. It is of concrete poured in moulds and the structure is thus a huge articulated monolith. The flat roof is supported by four hollow piers which also serve as heating ducts. As befits a modern sect, the form of the church is unrelated to any past style, yet its provision for the needs of the spirit is manifest in the solid outside walls which cut off all disturbance from the exterior. Entirely different in purpose and form were Wright's designs for the Midway Gardens, an enormous recreation center in Chicago, and for the Imperial Hotel in Tokyo. The latter was a triumph of modern methods of construction. It is supported by huge expanding piles of reinforced concrete resting on the soft mud that underlies the entire city. These piles were so designed as to give the building a flexible and elastic foundation. It was because of this that the Imperial Hotel was able to survive the earthquake of 1923 in Tokyo, when practically all other buildings by foreign architects in the city were destroyed.

In Europe, architecture of the late 19th and early 20th centuries reveals much the same development that has been observed in the United States. The sharp clash of ideals that is evident in the American scene is not found in Europe, however. There no architect stands out by virtue of an attempt to break with the past as do Sullivan and Wright in America. The rationalism of certain architects, notably Karl Friedrich Schinkel and Henri Labrouste, in the early 19th century has already been pointed out. This rationalism, based on traditional forms, continued through the century as a latent and more or less unproductive force, destined, however, to produce significant results toward its close. Iron and steel were employed in engineering projects as in America, a notable example being the buildings of the Paris Exposition in 1889 (cf. Fig. 197). Between the use of iron and steel in these works and the more consciously aesthetic manner of such men as Labrouste, a sharp line was drawn. The purely architectural examples of iron and steel construction reveal a persistence of eclectic methods on the one hand and, on the other, occasional efforts to establish new styles by developing new ornamental motives, such as the short-lived *Art Nouveau* movement (cf. Fig. 642). In the early years of the 20th century, a more essentially modern and functional style begins to develop, based on the use of steel and reinforced concrete. The most significant examples of this style appear in Holland, France, Germany and the Scandinavian countries.

*The Wertheim Store* in Berlin (Fig. 207) by Alfred Messel is an early example of functional design in Europe, since it was completed in 1904. It is a large, irregularly rectangular structure, consisting of blocks around a number of courts. Some of these courts are open to furnish illumination for the interior while others are roofed over with

FIG. 207.—Berlin. THE WERTHEIM STORE.

several levels of galleries opening on them. There are many Gothic reminiscences in the exterior design, the natural consequence of a strong regional tradition. The mediaeval forms are used as a decorative sheath for the steel framework, which they express rather effectively in the long vistas of the unbroken street façades. In their compliance with mediaeval usage as regards detail, proportion and effect, they contrast with the more arbitrary methods seen in the Woolworth Building. Within, the steel construction is frankly exposed and unobscured by decoration as in the somewhat earlier Bon Marché and Printemps stores in Paris.

The similarity in purpose of Messel's store and Sullivan's Schlesinger-Mayer Building in Chicago (Fig. 200) suggests a comparison between them. Of the two, that by the American is more direct in its statement of function and construction. Even today it is an essentially modern design, whereas the Wertheim Store is a typical example of a past style. This does not detract from its importance. Had Sullivan revealed more sympathy for tradition, his design would doubtless have had a greater influence. As it is, it stood alone in the American development and its significance has only recently been fully appreciated. In contrast with this, Messel's building became a model for such structures almost at once; its influence can be noted during the entire decade following its construction. The Tietz Store by Olbrich, built in Düsseldorf in 1908, is an example.

FIG. 208.—Berlin. TURBINE FACTORY OF THE A. E. G.

In contrast to Messel, who employed traditional forms in the Wertheim Store as decorative adjuncts to modern construction, Peter Behrens (1868-1940) evolved a style which was based entirely on the use of steel, glass and concrete as building materials. In 1907 he was appointed architect of the A. E. G., the General Electric Company in Germany, and the many buildings in Berlin that he designed for that company constitute the most important single body of modern construction in Europe before the First World War. Almost all the buildings are factories and power plants, and practical efficiency was invariably the main consideration (Fig. 208). Since they were essentially utilitarian in character, applied decoration would have been not only costly but inappropriate. The materials are steel, glass and the brick used in the region as a medium of construction ever since the Middle

Ages. Color contrasts play an important part in the effect, the warm red of the brick against the grayish-green of the slate roofs and windows, with purplish accents in the stone trim of the doors. The construction is frankly expressed throughout and is as modern as the purpose of the building, which attains monumentality through its proportions and vigorous outlines. Perhaps the most modern feature is the way in which the texture and color of the materials employed are utilized for decoration. Not only the expense of applied ornament is thus avoided but also the diluting effect which such ornament would have upon the clean-cut lines and masses. It is not without significance that in Europe such strictly utilitarian buildings as these were designed by architects. In America, the nearest approach to them are the great grain elevators of the Middle West, whose anonymous designers created better than they knew. Prosaic as they are in function and appearance, the elevators contain an element of honesty that is all too often lacking in the more pretentious houses and offices of their owners.

If Behrens' work is open to criticism, it is on the grounds that his grasp of the nature of modern building materials was not complete. The legitimate effect of glass and steel used as constructive materials is one of openness, suggesting volumes of space that are defined by a weightless membrane. In Behrens' designs, however, these materials are often employed to secure traditional effects of mass through the treatment of surface and outline. In this type of effect, none of Behrens' buildings can compete with the *Stuttgart Railway Station* (Fig. 209) by Paul Bonatz (b. 1877), built between 1913 and 1927. There is a Romanesque air about it, but one due entirely to the material employed and the method of employing it rather than to any specifically Romanesque ornament. In this respect, it is not unlike Richardson's Marshall Field Building in Chicago (Fig. 194). The use of stone throughout is a traditional characteristic and, in regions where it is abundant, more rational than the use of steel and concrete. Because the building is of stone, the predominant effect is one of masses, well proportioned to each other in form and outline and with a fine sense of surface texture. For these qualities, the Stuttgart Station is beyond question one of the finest single examples of traditionalistic European architectural style in the early 20th century. Its effects are perfectly logical ones for the material employed and owe nothing to past styles, in which it stands in noticeable contrast to the Wertheim Store. At the same time, it reveals, as does the Marshall Field Building, the possibility of applying traditional methods to modern problems without subsidizing into sterile eclecticism.

The late 19th and early 20th centuries constitute the period in which modern architecture was born. New manners of living, new building programs, new methods and materials of construction, all made their appearance at this time. Their combined effect was to stimulate the development of a new architectural style. The nature of that style is first suggested by the steel-framed skyscrapers of the '80's in Chicago from which it might be concluded that the most fundamental developments in modern building are to be looked for in architecture in the United States. Actually, the style developed in Europe during this period of gestation produced more significant immediate results. There

FIG. 209.—Stuttgart. THE RAILWAY STATION.

the weight of tradition exercised a certain restraint, and while European architects were not so quick to seize upon the new methods and materials as the unencumbered Americans, by virtue of that tradition they were also able to avoid the difficulties that beset the path followed by Sullivan and Wright. For the same reason, the eclecticism that predominated in American architecture of the early 20th century is present to a lesser degree in Europe. As pioneers, Sullivan and Wright paid the penalty of all innovators; only within the last decades has American architecture in general caught up to them. Thus it is that while in the period under consideration there were no finer buildings erected in Europe than Sullivan's Schlesinger-Mayer Building, the number of distinguished modern buildings in America was far less than in Germany, Holland and France.

# Chapter XIV. Contemporary Architecture

IN THE PREDOMINANTLY ECLECTIC ARCHITECTURE OF the early 20th century in the United States, the skyscraper was treated according to one of two formulas. The classic method was to consider it as a column with base, shaft and capital. The Gothic skyscraper was a study in sheer unbroken vertical lines with a sheath of stylistic ornament. Whatever the superficial style of the individual buildings, the result when many of them were concentrated in a restricted area was the same. The streets became deep canyons whose bottoms were hardly ever reached by the sunlight, detracting considerably from the commercial value of the buildings involved, particularly the lower ones which were completely overshadowed by their loftier neighbors. The situation thus created was rapidly becoming worse, for there seemed to be no limit to which the height of the skyscraper might be pushed. To remedy it, ordinances that affected the basic form of the skyscraper were passed in many of the larger cities, the first being that of New York in 1916. In general, they stipulate that a building may not rise from the street in an unbroken vertical plane beyond a certain height which depends upon the width of the street. Any further vertical construction must begin at a point set back from the original vertical plane. Thus instead of being a tower or column whose unity depended upon its vertical continuity, the skyscraper prescribed by the setback ordinance was a series of superimposed blocks or masses. This posed an entirely new problem in skyscraper design, different from that which had engaged the attention of architects up to the time of the setback ordinances.

In the first buildings erected under its provisions, little attempt was made to do more than meet them. Cubical masses were set one upon the other, with nothing in the designs to clarify or unify their functional relationships. The eclectic habit was still strong. In such a structure as the Shelton Hotel in New York by Arthur Loomis Harmon, erected in 1923, the slight projection of the vertical strips only barely suggests the steel frame. The applied ornament of the entrance portico and the pseudo-gargoyles at the top are fundamentally eclectic. The same can be said of the suggestion of mass given by the design as a

FIG. 210.—Chicago. THE TRI-
BUNE TOWER.

FIG. 211.—SAARINEN'S PROJECT
FOR THE TRIBUNE TOWER.

whole, appropriate enough in masonry construction but directly opposed to the open lightness that is a legitimate effect of steel construction.

In 1922, a definite challenge was offered to American architects in their chosen field. The *Chicago Tribune* inaugurated a competition, open to any and all who wished to enter, to obtain a design for the new quarters of the newspaper which were to be "the most distinctive and beautiful office building in the world." Scores of projects were submitted ranging in quality from the depths of eclectic ineptitude to a height never reached before in a modern skyscraper design. First prize went to the firm of Raymond Hood (1881-1934) and John Mead Howells (b. 1869) and from their designs the *Chicago Tribune Tower* was erected (Fig. 210). It is Gothic, correct in detail, admirably studied in its abstract decorative effect and almost totally devoid of any meaning from a modern point of view. Above the base with its incrustation of Gothic ornament, the unvarying verticals of the Indiana limestone sheath give a direct impression of the steel framework of the tower. But at the top is a series of flying buttresses springing from the slender vertical shafts to form a transition to the central crown which resembles a Gothic shrine. Viewed as masonry, the entire upper part of the building is much too heavy for the delicate piers below. Viewed as steel, there is no justification for the undeniably stone forms of the buttresses and the shrine that seem to blossom out of the vertical shafts beneath. A setback appears in the small addition to the right. It has no definite connection with the main block of the building but seems rather like a separate and individual tower in its own right.

The second prize *Design in the Tribune Competition* (Fig. 211) was by Eliel Saarinen (b. 1873), a Finn. When all the projects submitted were published, there was a wave of protest against the decision that put Saarinen's design below that of Hood and Howells. Here was a skyscraper that was really original. It was as if the ideals of Louis Sullivan had come to life again, as indeed they had, for Saarinen willingly acknowledged his indebtedness to the older man. The design is perfectly straightforward in its statement of the steel frame, with nothing like Hood's stony buttresses to belie it. It is that of a tall building and height is the outstanding element in its effect. But the greatness of the design does not lie in objective details. Rather it is to be found in the revelation of Saarinen's ability to face squarely the problem of the skyscraper and to solve it with the straightforwardness and logic that constitute the ideal of modern efficiency. Formal beauty is attained through observance of functional requirements, rather than by superficial attractiveness as in the static eclectic forms of Hood's tower. Saarinen's design was for a building as modern in function and appearance as the great printing presses it was planned to house.

For all the fact that Saarinen's project was never erected, the ideas he incorporated in it exercised a profound influence on American architecture, whereas Hood's structure has been correctly classified since being erected as simply another eclectic building. The *New York Telephone Building* (Fig. 212) by the firm of Voorhees, Gmelin and Walker, which was erected in 1926, is an example. There are no reminiscences of historical styles with the possible exception of the arched openings at the top of the crowning central tower. The mass of the building is broken up by the setbacks but the resultant forms are

*Photo Sigurd Fischer*

Fig. 212.—New York. The New York Telephone Co. Building.

well related to each other. This is achieved by having them all build up to the central tower and by the pronounced vertical accents that reveal the steel framework. The sparing ornament consists of geometrical motives repeated unvaryingly in a design appropriate to the mechanical methods by which it was executed. In effect, the building is admirably expressive of the unlimited mechanical power of the Machine Age in its stark simplicity and the brutality of its massive forms. The same characteristics can be seen in other buildings by the same firm such as the Bell Telephone Building in Newark, N. J., and the Irving Trust Co. Building at No. 1 Wall Street in New York City. The influence of Saarinen's Chicago Tribune design is apparent even in later buildings by Hood and Howells such as the New York Daily News Building of 1930.

The tendency in skyscraper design revealed by the buildings discussed in the foregoing paragraph would have been encouraging were it not for the fact that every attempt to solve the problem of the tall building in an honest way was matched by at least one in which the eclectic method was continued. In the New York Life Insurance Building (1929) Cass Gilbert attempted to ring the changes on the Gothic style that had brought him such renown in the Woolworth Building. The New York Central Building occupies a site which might easily have made it the dominating accent in central Manhattan, and the problem of providing complete traffic facilities through the structure itself would have presented a stimulating challenge to a modern-minded architect. Yet Warren and Wetmore who executed the designs did nothing more than turn out another structure in the Renaissance manner. Even the skyscrapers which have been hailed as milestones of progress—the Chrysler Building by William Van Alen and the Empire State Building by Shreve, Harmon and Lamb—are not sincerely modern. At best, they are adaptations of a style made classic by pioneering designers of quite different temperament from these architects who have learned a few superficial "modernistic" mannerisms which they spread over their façades in much the same way that their predecessors of twenty-five or thirty years ago were spreading Renaissance and Gothic details. Time will reveal the results to have no more importance in one case than in the other.

Such structures as the Chrysler, Empire State and R.C.A. Buildings represent the climax of Sullivan's concept of the skyscraper as a "proud and soaring thing." They demonstrate well the basic unsoundness of that idea for there is little justification for their height beyond its advertising value. Furthermore, they are proof that emphasis on the tall building in its present form has had the results that Sullivan himself foresaw. As an element in city-planning, the skyscraper contributes directly to congestion in the financial districts of the larger cities, a congestion which has already strained available means of transportation beyond their capacity. In addition to this, even as financially profitable ventures, skyscrapers have not come up to expectations. Unrestrained competition has resulted in a vast over-production to which the untenanted floors of the Empire State and R.C.A. Buildings bear silent testimony. The problem of vertical transportation still presents many difficulties. The speed of an elevator is limited to not more than twelve or fifteen miles an hour by purely physiological considerations; the many shafts required in a modern skyscraper consume valuable space to the extent that the legitimate income of the building must be augmented by charging fees to ascend to the observation towers that are usually found at their summits. The proportion of returns to original investment is much higher in the first skyscrapers to be built, the fifteen- and twenty-story buildings of the '80's in Chicago.

The vertical height of the American skyscraper is open to criticism on the foregoing purely objective grounds. Equally questionable is its unity as a work of art. A skyscraper like the New York Telephone Building (Fig. 212) is vertical only on the outside. Its interior consists not of a multitude of thin shafts as might be deduced from the external appearance but of horizontal volumes of space. This is quite apparent when the superficial verticality of the exterior is not visible, as at night when lighted windows indicate the actual arrangement of the interior space. In other words, while the greater part of contemporary sky-scraper design may be partially functional in that it indicates the verti-cal steel supports, it is not completely so for it does not express the arrangement of interior space. In possessing this latter characteristic, the design of the *Philadelphia Saving Fund Society Building* (Fig. 213) is one of the outstanding developments in recent commercial architec-ture in America. The architects were George Howe (b. 1886) and William Lescaze (b. 1896) and the building was completed in 1932. The idea of verticality as an aesthetic end in itself is dispensed with. The vertical supports are expressed in the aluminum strips at the sides and the elevator shaft also provides a vertical accent that is func-tionally justified. But the floors are cantilevered throughout, making pos-sible the continuous banded windows which are not only more efficient but more justifiable aesthetically than the type seen in the New York Telephone Building (Fig. 212). In the latter, for all the verticality of the design, there is still the effect of a solid bearing wall, created by emphasizing the strips separating the windows. In the Philadelphia building, the openness of the framework is given full expression on the exterior which becomes thereby the outer surface of a plane defin-ing a volume of space rather than a mass whose apparent bulk belies its actual function as a mere dividing screen. Furthermore, it indicates the division of that volume of space into horizontal layers correspond-ing to the stories instead of denying it by a superficial verticality. Con-trasted materials play an important part in the exterior design of the building; the base is faced with granite slabs, the two stories immedi-ately above with limestone and the horizontal strips between the win-dows are of gray brick.

In comparison with the average American skyscraper, the structure by Howe and Lescaze is an example of architecture as an art rather than mere building. By this is meant acceptance of functional requirements as the raw material from which the architect evolves a design

Fig. 213.—Philadelphia. The Philadelphia Saving Fund Society Building.

possessing in its own right a beauty of form and material at the same time that it gives complete expression to the function of the building. In contrast with this, the form of the traditional American skyscraper either has little to do with its function or goes to the opposite extreme in being determined entirely by function with no regard for aesthetic quality. In either case, the result is something less than architecture.

The Philadelphia Saving Fund Society Building is an example of the architectural style that was developed in Europe in the decade of the '20's and that is currently termed the International Style by virtue of its diffusion during that period without regard for national boundaries. The inception of this style may be traced back ultimately to the conscious attempts of men like Behrens to develop an architectural vocabulary in terms of the new structural materials and in connection with the new building types of the 20th century. Among the earliest examples of the style, if not actually the first, is the factory designed by Walter Gropius for the Fagus Shoe Company at Alfeld a.d. Leine in Germany and built in 1909-1910, in which the character of the building is a direct consequence of using steel and glass and concrete to build it. But it was in the years following the First World War that the formal potentialities of these materials came to be generally realized in the characteristic qualities of the International Style, which are three-fold. The first of these is emphasis upon volume of space rather than volume of mass as a basic principle of design. The second is regularity in spacing the elements of the design rather than disposing them symmetrically on either side of a principal axis as in most of the historical styles. The third is dependence upon good proportion and the intrinsic qualities of the materials employed for decorative effect rather than on applied ornament. Each of these characteristics is a direct result of the new methods and mediums of construction made available by scientific progress in the late 19th century. The first is a logical corollary of the steel framework supporting sheets of glass or curtain walls of some opaque substance whose primary function is the delimitation of space. An effect of mass or solidness would hardly be appropriate in a form discharging such a function. The second characteristic is also a result of the steel frame as a basis of construction. The vertical supports and the horizontal girders that connect them are spaced at equal distances in order to achieve equal distribution of the strains. In consequence of this, the skeleton has a basic and regular rhythm which should find expression in the design of its protecting sheath. The legitimacy of these two characteristics admitted, the avoidance of applied ornament in the traditional sense is mandatory, for its use would result in an impression of mass as well as an obscuring of the regular rhythm of the design. From this it follows that decoration in the modern style must necessarily be intrinsic in the building itself, its general proportions, the elegance of the materials employed in its construction and the technical perfection of the construction.

In the *Bauhaus* at Dessau in Germany (Fig. 214) Walter Gropius (b. 1883), one of the foremost exponents of the International Style, demonstrated the possibilities of a style based on modern constructive methods and materials. The building illustrated was erected in 1926 as the workshop of the Grand Ducal Art School previously at Weimar, the purpose of which was to develop forms of architecture and interior furnishings appropriate to the Machine Age (cf. Fig. 645). The work-

FIG. 214.—Dessau. THE BAUHAUS. Machine Shop.

shop was one of a group of buildings which also included a studio, a school and an administrative office. In the design of the group as a whole, Gropius achieved an effective integration of the various units through fine proportions and appropriate treatment of constructive materials. His thorough grasp of the nature of those materials made the design one of volumes of space rather than mass, for if the screening function of a wall is performed by a sheet of glass, an effect of mass would be not only inappropriate but a denial of the supporting function of the steel frame. The regularity characteristic of modern design is created by a rhythmic recurrence of accents indicating the piers of the long side, a regularity broken on the short side by functional adjustment to the entrance. As a form determined by functional requirement and attaining an aesthetic effect in terms that are a logical consequence of the materials employed, the Bauhaus is as much an example of architectural style as the Parthenon or the Cathedral of Amiens. Furthermore, in its avowed purpose of applying Machine Age principles of efficiency to household furniture and appliances, the obligation of the creative artist to society is acknowledged. The Bauhaus is not the only proof of Gropius' understanding of the sociological problems of modern architecture. In various projects in the field of low-cost housing, he has applied his genius for organization to the achievement of results aesthetically fine as well as functionally efficient.

Another point of view than that of Gropius but still within the principles of the International Style is that of the Franco-Swiss architect, Charles Edouard Jeanneret-Gris (b. 1888), who is known professionally as Le Corbusier. To him, the formal element must be dominant in the attainment of character in architectural design, taking precedence even over matters of construction although he has made many contributions in that field as well. His most important work has been in the designing of houses and domestic architecture in general, and his concept of the house as a "machine for living" has been very influential in establishing an ideological relationship between the idioms of the International Style and the machine culture of the 20th century. But even in his own work this concept has been subordinated to aesthetic considerations, and in regarding the structure as a work of art before it is anything else, Le Corbusier opens the way for disregard of practical considerations that may have undesirable consequences. The *Savoye House* (Fig. 215) at Poissy-sur-Seine near Paris was built in 1929-1930. It is of steel and concrete with the principal level in elevation cantilevered out beyond the substructure and partially supported on unsheathed metal posts. Externally, this part of the house is quite symmetrical in effect though without doing violence to the regular spacing of the supporting members which establishes the rhythm of the window openings. These are treated as continuous bands which stop short of the corners to permit statement of the function of the screen walls as planes defining the volume of inner space which they limit as well. Contrasting with the symmetrical and rectilinear form of this part of the house is the curvilinear pattern of the windshelter on its flat roof, a contrast which is heightened by the color scheme of the exterior. The substructure, beneath the cantilevered projection, is dark green, the principal story is cream colored, and the windshelter is rose and blue. This color composition emphasizes functional distinctions between various parts of the structure, for the difference in practical purpose of the main portion of the building and the accessory pleasantry of the windshelter on the terrace roof is clearly stated thereby, but it must also be noted that the patterns of form and color thus created are very similar in effect to those in much of the painting contemporary with the building (cf. Plate III). And in this connection, it is significant that Le Corbusier is active as a painter as well as in architecture, a fact which explains much of the character of his designs and his preoccupation with formal over structural matters in creating them.

Organization of interior space is as much an interest of the architect seeking character in building as is the treatment of external features, and the conception of plan and furnishing that was developed in the International Style of the '20's is closely allied to that observed hitherto

Fig. 215.—Poissy-sur-Seine. The Savoye House.

in the exteriors by Gropius and Le Corbusier. It is concern for this aspect of architectural design that is paramount in the works of Miës van der Rohe (b. 1886), who began his career in the office of Bruno Paul in Germany where he was a furniture designer, an experience that gave him a respect for fine craftsmanship and carefully wrought detail that he later carried over into his treatment of the house as a whole. The view of the living room and library of the *Tugendhat House* at Brno in Czechoslovakia (Fig. 216), built in 1931, illustrates his concept of the interior. The two rooms are considered parts of a single space volume which is articulated but not divided by a great slab of polished onyx rising from floor to ceiling. This latter is supported by gleaming chromium steel beams, arranged in a regular pattern, which are also elements in a decorative scheme of contrasting colors

Fig. 216.—Brno. The Tugendhat House. Living Room and Library.

and textures. What would ordinarily be walls are great sheets of plate glass which can be lowered below the floor level thus permitting completely unobstructed passage from the room to the terrace outside overlooking the garden. This striking and effective relating of interior and exterior space is reached in consequence of Miës' feeling that the outside of a building is really part of the interior since its design should be determined by internal arrangement rather than for the sake of external effect. It follows from this that he is quite aware of the necessity of defining and giving character to the inner space of the house, which he does by emphasizing the quality and texture of the luxurious materials used in the building. The great windows can be screened, for example, by curtains of velvet woven in single pieces extending the entire length of the openings. Polished surfaces of glass, metal and rare woods contribute as well to an ensemble of great decorative distinction and character, in both the structural elements and the furniture. The chairs and tables were also designed by Miës after long and careful experiments to determine maximum comfort combined with the finest aesthetic effect in accordance with his conviction that the artistic ideas essential as a basis of successful creative activity must be developed while the artist is learning good building.

"Without succumbing to an arid rationalism, the new architecture will be essentially utilitarian; but utilitarian without excluding aspirations of a superior order." These are the words in which J. J. P. Oud (b. 1890), the outstanding figure in Dutch architecture during the years following the First World War, has expressed his concept of modern architectural aims. It is a concept that has peculiar validity coming from him, for it grows out of his extensive experience and success in one of the most important and challenging fields of contemporary architectural activity—that of large-scale and low-cost housing. Appointed in 1918 as architect to the city of Rotterdam, Oud has done little since in any other field, an outstanding example being the *Workers' Houses* at the *Hook of Holland* (Fig. 217), which were built in 1926-1927. They are of concrete and steel, and the design, of great distinction, is one that would have been possible only in those materials. Regularity of accent from the treatment of the windows is a basic quality in the long blocks in which balconies and flat roofs assist in creating an effect of horizontality in the ensemble. Round pavilions at the ends of the principal blocks are of functionally justified difference in effect since they are stores for the use of the inhabitants; through their plate-glass sides may be seen the structural steel members supporting the heavier upper floor. Color is skillfully used as a decorative adjunct to the well-proportioned planes and solids of the exterior.

Oud's design does not attain distinction by virtue of the accomplished organization in plan to be seen in Gropius' work of the same period (Fig. 214) or yet by virtue of the formal and decorative refinements of Corbusier and Miës van der Rohe (Figs. 215, 216). Rather it is by submission to the aesthetic discipline imposed by the requirements of a program which allowed little opportunity for anything but the essentials of plan and construction, and by working successfully with them to realize the "aspirations of a superior order" of which Oud speaks in the above-cited passage, that the Workers' Houses are at the same time

FIG. 217.—Hook of Holland. WORKERS' HOUSES.

so apparently simple yet satisfactory in effect. What this meant from the point of view of architecture as a matter of practical purpose is clearly shown by the fact that Oud's building in the exhibition of low-cost houses held at Stuttgart in 1928 was one of the two among those submitted by sixteen architects, including Gropius and Le Corbusier and Miës van der Rohe, that fulfilled the technical requirements within stipulated cost limits without sacrifice of formal character. What it meant from the point of view of architecture as an art is seen in the fact that in the entire body of low-cost housing created to meet the difficult conditions in Europe during the '20's there is no work superior to Oud's best, little to approach it in quality, and nothing to illustrate better the contribution that can be made by the architect in bringing together and integrating the disparate and often conflicting forces of modern society.

It is in the work of the four architects just discussed that the International Style as a coherent architectural idiom is first apparent and this is found largely in France, Germany and Holland in the '20's. Its geographic diffusion was rapid, however, and the close of the decade witnessed the construction of buildings in that style in the Scandinavian countries and Russia and in even more distant regions—the Orient and the United States. The Philadelphia Saving Fund Society Building (Fig. 213), for instance, was one of the earliest International Style structures in the latter country, and remains its most successful venture in skyscraper design. But it is to England that one must look for the most important developments in the International Style in the decade of the '30's. A few isolated examples of somewhat indifferent character in the late '20's were hardly even preparation for the solid and constructive developments in the period since the formation of the MARS Group (the initials stand for Modern Architectural Research) in 1931 by some of the younger architects of the country for the purpose of collective study and exchange of ideas. To such good effect was the work of this organization done that the acceptance of the new formal idioms of contemporary methods in design and construction has been quite general in England—to such an extent, indeed, that a critic writing in 1939 just before the outbreak of the Second World War could say in all truthfulness, "England may be said to be the headquarters of modern architecture."

Two examples of the International Style in English architecture in the '30's will indicate both the extent to which the principles developed by the continental pioneers of the preceding decade have been mastered and the variations that have been made by the English protagonists of the style. The *Penguin Pool in Regent's Park Zoo* in London (Fig. 218) was designed by a group of architects practicing under the name of Tecton; it was built in 1933. Frankly intended as a contribution to greater enjoyment of the movements of the comical birds, the pool is an elongated oval in plan, with curving ramps in the center up which the denizens parade in solemn fashion. Of relatively simple function, therefore, it has been treated more in the fashion of a piece of abstract sculpture than anything else, a concept to which the concrete of which it is built is admirably suited. Other buildings in the same zoo and also the Dudley Zoo in London, the latter built in 1938, reveal a similar comprehension on the part of the Tecton group of the possibilities to be realized of making the buildings not only fitting but expressive of the character of the exhibits in them, and have been instrumental in creating a new tradition for this type of design and exhibition installation. Mention should also be made of the middle-class suburban apartment building called Highpoint on Highgate Hill, London, built by

Tecton in 1935, using concrete as a medium and supplying a constructive solution of a difficult problem in urban accommodation as well as a structure of formal distinction.

It is by enlarging the repertory of materials used in the International Style idioms that English architects have made their most constructive contribution, however. As developed on the Continent in the '20's, con-

Fig. 218.—London. Regent's Park. The Penguin Pool.

crete and glass and steel were the substances most extensively employed. These, while admirably suited to the abstract patterns of plane and surface and texture upon which the designs of the buildings are in large part dependent for effect, also present a problem of maintenance. The precise and machine-like forms of a design by Le Corbusier, for instance, are seriously disfigured by ordinary and inevitable weathering and such a structure as the Savoye House (Fig. 215) must be kept in immaculate condition if its effect is not to be impaired. This is a disadvantage under which the more traditional materials of stone and brick and wood do not labor; in fact, their character is in general enhanced by the warmth and mellowness that time brings to them. By no means the least fruitful modification of the initial concepts of the Interna-

tional Style made by English practitioners of the manner is their employment of these traditional materials in structures which retain the flexibility of plan and simplicity of form that originally resulted from thinking in terms of these substances. An example in point is a *House at
Welwyn* designed by Eugen C. Kauffmann (Fig. 219) in 1939. The
material is brick, and the plan is admirable both in flexibility and in
the well-related forms resulting from it, both contributing to a struc-

FIG. 219.—Welwyn. HOUSE.

ture that will readily find its place in the well-ordered English scene
in the best tradition of the country that has treasured more than any
other, perhaps, the concept of the house as the shelter and symbol of
essentially human values in living.

In the United States as in England, the decade of the '30's witnessed
a considerable volume of creative building in the International Style
from the opening years when its protagonists were principally Europeans practicing in the New World or native architects adapting the
more easily borrowed characteristics of the manner to buildings that
were essentially traditional in form. These were found for the most part
in the Atlantic and Pacific seaboard regions, but the style has been diffused to such an extent that by 1940 there were few considerable areas
without some representative example. There have been certain obstacles
in the way of general acceptance of its principles, however, that have
prevented the attainment of even such a general level of distinction as
is to be noted in England. Urban building codes have restricted its

application in many cities, one result being that many of the most striking and successful examples are in rather limited types of structure—
week-end country houses, seaside summer homes and the like—which
supply no general solution to the problem of the individual house for
general year-round use. Exploitation of the spectacular effects of ever-
increasing material resources, notably the extraordinarily developing
category of synthetic plastics, for commercial or advertising purposes has

Fig. 220.—Miquon. THE KENNETH DAY HOUSE.

brought some discredit to the style on grounds of taste. Costs of building in ways with which the average artisan is not familiar or which he
is deterred from mastering by regulations imposed and enforced by
organizations whose vested interests might suffer from changes in
traditional procedures are another factor involved. But more than any
of these considerations are the great area and widely varying climatic
conditions of the United States an effective preventive of uniform acceptance of any single style however flexible its principles as abstract
ideas. The result has been the development of regional adaptations of
the manner in accordance with prevalent local conditions, producing in
some instances buildings of considerable individuality and distinction.
An example is the *Kenneth Day House* at Miquon, Pa. (Fig. 220), the

home of the architect, which was built in 1938. Like the house at Welwyn in England (Fig. 219), it conforms to regional tradition with respect to the structural materials employed, and is planned to make the utmost of an effective site. It is one of a group of three houses designed by Day that form an ensemble of structures in the International Style rather unusual for this country, and provide a convincing illustration

FIG. 221.—Pasadena. THE MILLARD HOUSE.

of the formal distinction that can be achieved with intelligent and perceptive employment of its idioms in community groups.

No less striking than the diffusion of the International Style in the architectural scene of the United States from 1930 on, and possibly of even more significance as an artistic phenomenon, is the work of Frank Lloyd Wright during that period. In the "Prairie House" of the early 20th century (cf. Figs. 204, 205), he had been a pioneer in the restatement of basic principles of architectural thinking that was widely influential, particularly in the matter of planning, as is immediately apparent in the precepts of the International Style, which owes much to him in this respect. Unaccepted for the most part in his own country,

Wright did little actual building in the years after the First World War, but such as was done reveals the same creative imagination and sound thinking that characterize the earlier work. The *Millard House* in Pasadena, Calif. (Fig. 221), was built in 1921, and is of a form quite different from that of the earlier houses since it meets other circumstances of climate and environment. The terrace roof and relatively small windows are as appropriate in California as the low gables and large openings of the Robie House to its mid-western setting. There is still the same effective relationship between house and site, however, and the same forthright treatment of structural material, concrete in this case. It is used in precast blocks with surface patterns formed by the moulds, the resulting ornament being integral in the material and creating a fine sense of texture from the play of light and shade. Although the medium is the same as that used in the majority of the European International Style buildings of the same period (cf. Fig. 215), the basic concept of the forms is quite different. To Le Corbusier, concrete is a flexible substance used simply to form a plane whose sole function is the definition and delimitation of the space volume of the house; to Wright it is a material of inherent weight and bulk to be handled in an almost sculptural way in forming walls that support as well as enclose. Different too is the sense of the structure in relationship to its surroundings. Le Corbusier's is inorganic in this respect—an artfully contrived entity isolated from its environment, existing for itself and to be understood only in its own terms; Wright's is organic in being one with its surroundings—the result of moulding nature to human purpose without sacrificing the character of either.

The caliber of Wright's architectural imagination and creativeness is shown by nothing more clearly than the great variety of types of building designed by him from 1934 on in a period when his greatness appears at last to have received recognition and the soundness of his ideas to have been perceived. Factories and offices, houses and apartments, churches and school buildings—all have been designed by Wright with an understanding of their nature and purpose that is of the greatest discernment and ability to translate that understanding into forms of the most individual and distinguished character. The *Administration Building of the Johnson Wax Co.* at Racine, Wisc. (Fig. 222), was completed in 1939. Built with the use of such widely varying materials as glass neon tubes which supply artificial illumination when needed and permit the infiltration of discreetly diffused natural light otherwise, concrete cast in ingeniously designed tapering columns with widely flaring "capitals" that support the glazed ceiling, and brick whose warm red color is the most striking external characteristic, the building is a summation of Wright's sense of material as an element in archi-

FIG. 222.—Racine. THE JOHNSON CO. BUILDING.

tectural character. To the right of the covered passage which is at once entrance and carport for automobiles is a single large room where the routine office work is carried on, with smaller individual offices of the administrative staff on balconies at one side. Elsewhere in the building are private offices, as well as facilities for sports and entertainment in accordance with the best and most enlightened social concept of the commercial community. It is in direct expression of this plan that the organization of planes and cylindrical forms which constitute the external design is achieved. And as a work of architectural art whose fundamental character is a volume of space that is defined and given formal distinction by the surfaces of walls and columns and the areas between them, the building is rivaled in originality only by another such creatively conceived structure by Wright himself, the house called Falling Water built for the Kaufman family at Bear Run, Pa., in 1938.

At the same time that Wright was engaged in creating the freely imaginative forms of the Johnson Co. Building and Falling Water which he was permitted to design without regard for cost and expense, he was also at work on other buildings of a much less spectacular and economically more restricted type. It is a question if time will not prove the modest houses built within the limits of average budgets to have been a more significant contribution to contemporary architectural thinking than the poetically beautiful yet extravagantly luxurious buildings that have been mentioned. Even in this more limited category there is great variety. The Suntop Houses built in Ardmore, Pa. in 1939 were an attempt to solve the problem of effective housing for middle-class families of modest means; highly ingenious as to plan, with a group of four homes organized in a single building unit, the structural realization of the idea fell short of the distinction of the space organization and the treatment of the materials. Less revolutionary is the plan and form of such a typical small home of Wright's in this period as the *Goetsch-Winckler House* (Figs. 223, 224) built near East Lansing, Mich., in 1940. The outstanding quality of the exterior is, like that of the Robie House of more than thirty years before (Fig. 204), its remarkably organic relationship to the landscape. This effect is created in a fashion very similar to that noted in the older building—by stressing the horizontal lines of roof and eaves, by the projection of walls and slabs to the end that space seems to pervade the solid forms, and by the warm earth colors of brick and wood that are at the same time clearly defined and blended with the surrounding greenery. There is, however, a less rugged quality in the effect of the building than is the case with the Robie House, as is fitting in a structure of relatively small size; externally this is a consequence of the relative openness of the design in which the proportion of void to solid is quite high. This bears, too, upon

FIG. 223.—Okemos, near E. Lansing. THE GOETSCH-WINCKLER HOUSE. Exterior.

the character of the interior (Fig. 224), which is organized around a large spatial volume that is the living room, with subordinate alcoves for kitchen and a small studio, the private rooms of the house being reached by a corridor opening from another side. A characteristic device is the row of small rectangular windows set at the top of the side walls, providing a softly diffused yet abundant illumination which was some-

FIG. 224.—Okemos, near E. Lansing. THE GOETSCH-WINCKLER HOUSE.
Interior.

times lacking in the interiors of the earlier "Prairie Houses," and also contributing to a sense of space that is at the same time enclosed and yet correlated with that surrounding the house externally. The materials used are inexpensive and homely, yet the decorative effect of color and texture they create is eminently satisfying—a proof both of the possibility of achieving distinction without the use of applied superficial ornament and of the fact that such an effect can be obtained without having to resort to costly and luxurious textiles and woods and metals (cf. Fig. 216).

An important factor in the contemporary architectural scene is the large-scale plan in which entire communities are designed and controlled by a unity of purpose of whatever character. Ever since the 17th century when the expanding horizons of man's intellectual and emotional experience sought an adequate symbol in the planned city (cf. Figs. 142, 150, 153), the formal problem of achieving a coherent pattern in such symbols has confronted the architect and in the solutions supplied to it the character of the time when it was done is reflected. Intimate in scale and refined in effect is the Hemicycle at Nancy of 1755 (Fig. 168) as befits the rococo 18th century, whereas the monumental pattern imposed by Georges-Eugène Haussmann upon the city of Paris between 1853 and 1869 in the most ambitious project of such a nature in the 19th century was the outcome of a paradoxical desire both to keep under control such uprisings of the populace as had wrought great damage in 1848 and 1852 when narrow crooked streets had complicated the task of the military in putting them down, and also to make the city conform to the ideals of splendid regularity characteristic of the industrial age against whose abuses the Parisians had revolted. It is also in the late 19th century, however, that a renewed appreciation of the landscape is to be noted in community planning; parks and boulevards lined with trees are a part of Haussmann's plan for Paris; Central Park in New York City was laid out by the foremost landscape architect in the United States, Frederick Law Olmsted, between 1857 and 1861, and Fairmount Park in Philadelphia acquired much of its present size and character in the period in question. Inherently romantic in purpose, these bits of "controlled nature" within urbanized communities might be considered attempts to compensate for the denial of human values that characterized the uncontrolled industrialism of the age but without being able to do more than mitigate its consequences. Of greater significance were the "Garden Cities" of Letchworth and Welwyn, built in England in 1904 after the plans of Sir Ebenezer Howard, in which for the first time there appeared a positive attempt to create a community in accordance with the need and function of modern industrial life on a human scale rather than from considerations of financial profit. But more than the enterprise of individuals was necessary for the successful accomplishment of the planned community and it was not until after the First World War that a combination of political and economic circumstances brought about the first attempts at the solution of the problem on a scale of such size as to have more than individual significance.

The character of a planned community is dependent, of course, upon the purpose for which it is intended, and its effectiveness as an example of design must take this into account as it does in the individual building. The problem is more than architectural, however, for legal and financial and sociological considerations are of paramount importance. One of the most important categories of the planned community in contemporary times is that of low-cost housing groups to provide other-wise poorly or inefficiently accommodated classes with an environment in which they can become effective and useful factors in society. The development of such groups constituted a large share of architectural activity in Holland and Germany and the Scandinavian countries in the decade of the '20's, and enlisted the services of the leading architects in those countries. The Houses at the Hook of Holland by Oud (Fig. 217) were designed as part of such a group. The Bauhaus at Dessau (Fig. 214) is part of a planned community; while it was not primarily in the low-cost housing category, the architect, Gropius, did some of his most distinguished work in Germany as director of housing for the city of Berlin following his tenure as director of the Bauhaus School. Le Corbusier, too, has designed a number of such communities, al-though his interests in large-scale planning lie rather in the direction of complete urban developments and the modernization of entire cities which he has brilliantly presented in his theoretical treatises on urban-ism, of which the most significant—*La Ville Radieuse*—was published in 1934. In all the cases cited and in many of the literally hundreds of such projects that were made necessary by post-war economic and socio-logical conditions in Europe, the obligation of the architect to create forms that are at the same time distinguished in character and effective in function has been realized.

In the United States, the most spectacular and best-known com-munity plan is not in the category of low-cost housing but is a direct development and enlargement of the idea of the tall commercial struc-ture—the complex of buildings between Forty-eighth and Fifty-first Streets and Fifth and Sixth Avenues in New York City known as *Radio City* (Fig. 225) or Rockefeller Center. Designed by three archi-tectural firms in collaboration—Hood and Fouilloux, Reinhard and Hofmeister, and Corbett, Harrison and MacMurray—it was built be-tween 1931 and 1939. The plan of the ensemble follows the rectangular grid pattern of the city blocks, with buildings of varying heights and sizes grouped around and dominated by the 850-foot high, slab-like mass of the R.C.A. Building. This form was determined by the technical and economic considerations of circulation and illumination. The grouping of the considerable number of elevators necessary in such a building, along with service rooms, in the center creates a core around which is composed a space volume whose proportions are determined by the maximum area capable of being effectively lighted from the windows. This same consideration dictates the rhythm of the ribbon-like vertical piers of the exterior curtain walls which are also cut back at levels in height corresponding to the terminations of the lower elevator shafts. It is thus seen that the R.C.A. Building represents the logical culmina-

*Photo Berenice Abbott*

FIG. 225.—New York. RADIO CITY.

tion on an unprecedentedly large scale of the principles set forth for the tall office building by Louis Sullivan, for its form is determined in the broadest sense by the mechanical and commercial functions of the structure. But it is also apparent that the fears which Sullivan himself felt for the consequences of the skyscraper as a social phenomenon are realized here on an inordinate scale. A recent critic writes of Radio City that "it introduces for the first time into a contemporary city the large scale that is to be found in the parkways and the great engineering works. Its buildings . . . introduce correspondingly new and original plastic elements" (S. Giedion, *Space, Time and Architecture*, 1941). But where the inhuman scale of the parkways and the great engineering works is a direct concomitant of the adequacy of their contribution to an enriched human experience in providing facilities for free movement and direct communion with nature, in Radio City it grows from no more significant a motive than desire for the spectacular and the overpowering—a symbol of the absolutism of the commercial spirit that dominates and crushes its surroundings in a manner comparable only with the parallel symbols of similar values, the Pyramids of Egypt (Fig. 11) and the Palace and Gardens at Versailles (Fig. 150).

The history of low-cost housing in the United States was limited to occasional planned communities such as Radburn in New Jersey and Sunnyside Gardens on Long Island in New York until 1932-1933. They were individually sponsored and financed and in this they differed in principle from the organized government sponsorship of such projects that from 1933 on has resulted in the creation of planned communities of low-cost housing groups in various parts of the country. These were carried on by the Public Works Administration and the Resettlement Administration concurrently until the consolidation of their separate but parallel activities in the United States Housing Authority in 1937, under which a policy making for less overlapping of effort and duplication of administrative function has been put into effect.

One of the first large projects undertaken by the Public Works Administration in the field of low-cost housing was the *Carl Mackley Houses* in Juniata Park in Philadelphia (Fig. 226), with W. Pope Barney, Kastner & Stonorov, Associated Architects, as designers, and built for a cooperative organization of workers in a hosiery mill. The group illustrates well the possibility of attaining architectural distinction even when bearing in mind the inexorable limitations of minimum-cost construction that is basic in all such projects. It is built of concrete stone with facing of terra cotta of which the warm color of variegated buff-brown with blue trim is utilized for a pleasing effect and the texture for a surface treatment in the absence of any type of applied ornament. Within the rigid rectangular framework of the Philadelphia street system, the buildings are well disposed to obtain maximum sunlight and air—also basic problems in community plans of this type. Adequate room space is provided within and community facilities for sports and entertainments are also made available. The design is sober and restrained, with the simply treated walls broken by well-proportioned ample windows and balconies that provide sufficient variety in the horizontal mass defined by their surfaces. On an even larger scale

Fig. 226.—Philadelphia. Juniata Park. THE CARL MACKLEY HOUSES.

are the *Williamsburg Houses* in Brooklyn (Fig. 227), also sponsored by the Public Works Administration and built in 1937. The chief architect was R. H. Shreve with whom were associated a number of other men including William Lescaze, who was one of the co-designers of the Philadelphia Saving Fund Society Building (Fig. 213). He was responsible for the orientation by angles of the housing blocks, determined from observation of prevailing directions of wind and sunlight in both summer and winter, to provide the maximum benefits of these natural commodities. This involved breaking with the gridiron pattern of the streets by closing off unnecessary cross streets and thus forming super-blocks in which the individual housing units are grouped around open spaces utilized as large lawns and playgrounds. The effectiveness

Photo Fairchild

Fig. 227.—Brooklyn. The Williamsburg Houses.

with which the idioms of terrace roofs, horizontal distribution of mass and consistent relationships in the scheme as a whole creates a clearly organized formal unit is well shown in the contrast between the pattern of the housing group and the confused chaos of the surrounding blocks. It is emphasized, moreover, by the awkwardly traditional bulk and conventionally four-square placing of the school building which was not designed by the architects responsible for the rest of the community.

The Carl Mackley and Williamsburg housing groups are examples of the steps to be taken in the regeneration of the modern city by undoing the evils of a period when the only guiding principles in domestic architectural design were uncontrolled individualism on the part of private owners and unrestrained commercialism on the part of the builder for purposes of investment. Such urban rehabilitation as a necessary preliminary to the planned community on the larger scale of the city must of necessity labor under the disadvantage of preexistent high land values, poorly planned and often superfluous streets and utilities and the like, all of which contribute to higher initial costs. In the even larger sense of the planned region comprising the community, the city and the peripheral area around it, some steps have been taken in the United States that though tentative hold promise for the future. The "garden city" as a development of areas previously unused but planned to anticipate future expansion is an attempt to foresee and solve ahead the problems of adequate and constructive housing in such fashion that the economic and social evils resulting from the slums of the contemporary city can be avoided. Three such "garden cities" have been created since 1937—Greendale, near Milwaukee in Wisconsin, Greenhills, near Cincinnati in Ohio, and *Greenbelt* in Maryland (Fig. 228), of which Hale Walker was the town planner and Ellington and Wadsworth the architects. The site plan was determined by a horseshoe-shaped plateau, upon which the houses of brick and cinder-block are arranged in super-blocks connected by a few major avenues but with much open space for gardens and playgrounds. The schools and community stores are placed in the hollow of the horseshoe. Such a community as this can exist only with adequate transportation facilities and it is reached through a convergence of major highway systems, but these are by-passed around the community itself in such fashion that it is spared the debilitating movement of through traffic and is traversed only by automobiles going to the town. The individual buildings are designed to keep the project costs within reasonable limits; without the superficial "style" of the houses in the average American suburb, they are colorful and attractive, well planned and open to take maximum advantage of the park-like setting. With all the considerable size

FIG. 228.—Berwyn, Md. GREENBELT.

of the project—it can accommodate 885 families—the scale is kept within human limits, an admirable illustration of the patterned order that intelligent planning can bring to the modern community, to the enrichment of the experience of all partaking in it.

Diversity is the outstanding impression in any comprehensive viewing of the contemporary architectural scene—diversity of form, style, material and purpose. In whatever limited phase it be observed the same is true—with houses as contrasting in type as those by Wright and Le Corbusier (Figs. 215, 223), commercial buildings like the Bauhaus and the Johnson Wax Co. Building (Figs. 214, 222), or large-scale building schemes like Radio City and Greenbelt (Figs. 225, 228). The basically formalistic purpose of a structure in the International Style (Fig. 216) which is intended to stimulate an emotion of primarily aesthetic character is at the opposite end of the expressive scale from the inherently romantic motivation of one by Wright (Fig. 224). The abstract and inhuman symbolism of Radio City (Fig. 225) is diametrically opposed to the human scale and unpretentious sobriety of the Carl Mackley Houses (Fig. 226). Yet even in this diversity there is a quality that makes these various buildings characteristic of their time in history—a quality that grows from a sense, whether conscious or otherwise on the part of their designers, of the obligation that is theirs to evolve from the material substance and the functional program of their structures a comprehensive and formally consistent symbol of that time. And if there is no one style that seems to do this—if there is no architectural idiom that may claim universal acceptance as that by which the builders of today can give expression to values which are universally held to be significant as did the Doric and the Ionic for the ancient world and Gothic for the Middle Ages, the explanation is to be sought not in the architects or in the work they do but in the intellectual, moral and spiritual caliber of the generation in which they live. When there is a perceptive and vital sense of significance in human experience as there was in those times in history when coherent and great architecture was created, it will be created again.

# SCULPTURE

# Chapter XV. Sculpture: Methods, Terminology, and Early Styles.———.

TO THE AVERAGE PERSON, THE TERM SCULPTURE evokes an image of a human figure in stone or metal. Sculpture is not limited to these materials, however, for any substance may be used which has sufficient density to retain the form given it by the artist. Some of the earliest sculpture is in bone or wood, while modern sculptors have been much interested in rare stones of the less expensive varieties as the materials of their art. There is, in fact, no limit to the substances available for sculpture, ranging all the way from soap and butter to solid silver. It is obvious that similar methods cannot be used in handling all materials. A medium that is soft, such as clay, will lend itself to a modeling technique that consists of squeezing and shaping the material and adding to it as the artist's conception of the figure grows. In contrast with this, a hard medium such as stone or wood requires a process of taking away from the original block. The sculptor cuts the figure out of the substance, shaping it with a chisel or file.

A metal statue is produced by a method that differs from both of those mentioned and is in general as follows. The desired figure is first modeled in clay or wax and then a mould is made from this figure by surrounding it, after it is well covered with some lubricant, with liquid plaster of Paris, gelatine or any fluid substance that becomes solid after exposure to the air. After the mould has hardened, it is removed in pieces and reassembled; the hollow formed by the original figure is filled with melted metal which flows into the cracks and crevices on the inside. When the metal cools and hardens, the mould is removed and a metal replica of the original clay or plaster figure is found. Two disadvantages result from this method of casting a metal figure. If it is a large one, its weight is very considerable. Moreover, the metal in the center cools much less rapidly than that near the outer surface, setting up strains in the statue which might cause it to crack. Both of these disadvantages can be avoided by making the metal figure hollow. A core is inserted in the hollow mould which follows the general form of the original clay or plaster figure but is somewhat smaller. This core is usually covered with soft wax which takes the exact shape of the original figure when the mould is squeezed around the core. The hot, liquefied metal is then poured into the space occupied by the wax, which melts and runs out of small openings or vents provided for the purpose. When the metal hardens, the outer mould is removed and the inner core raked out. The result is a metal shell reproducing exactly the configuration of the original clay or plaster figure. This is the essence of the *cire perdue* process of casting which has been employed in one form or another for metal statues from the earliest times to the present. In recent years, metal statues have been made by an electrolytic process which deposits the metal on a plaster core covered with plumbago or black lead, but this method has not replaced the *cire perdue* process in general favor.

A metal statue is usually of the modeled type since it reproduces a clay original, rather than the chiseled type of the stone or wooden figure cut out of a block. Until the Renaissance, stone figures were nearly always carved directly (cf. Fig. 294, B) with the sculptor using, at the most, only a small model as a guide. Since the beginning of the 16th century, a mechanical method known as pointing has been in general use. A full-size clay or plaster figure is made on which a number of points are marked. These are transferred mechanically to a block of stone by drills which bore into it to depths determined by the locations of the points on the original figure. When all the points have been transferred, the stone is cut away to the extent indicated by the depths of the holes. The result is a reasonably exact reproduction of the general form of the model, and the sculptor then finishes it off with chisels and rasps. The pointing method is practically the only one in general use today. It has largely supplanted the practice of cutting directly in the stone block for by indicating the depths beyond which the sculptor must not carve, the possibilities of ruining an expensive piece of material are considerably lessened.

Sculpture in general may be divided into types according to whether the figures are in relief or free-standing. The first term refers to figures which are attached to a background, while a free-standing figure can be seen from all sides. In the general category of relief, there are the subdivisions of high and low. High relief is that in which the objects represented project very definitely from the background (cf. Fig. 264) and appear to be almost in the round, while in low relief, the forms have relatively little projection (cf. Fig. 246). The difference between them is one of proportion, of course, for a large figure in low relief may actually project farther from its background than one a quarter of its size in high relief.

A still further general distinction in sculpture is that of decorative and free figures. Decorative sculpture is planned as part of a larger whole. This means that it is not independent and self-sufficient but depends for its effect upon relationship to something else, usually to a building. The greater part of relief sculpture is in this category. A form of decorative free-standing sculpture can be seen in the illustration of the Gardens of Versailles (Fig. 151) where the figures are accents in a planned landscape. Free sculpture, which is not to be confused with free-standing sculpture, is that which has not been planned with some definite relationship to a comprehensive scheme, such as the well-known Aphrodite of Melos (Fig. 276). It is usually in the round, although free relief is not unknown, a common example being the design on coins.

In many ways, the appreciation of sculpture is more difficult than that of either architecture or painting. It lacks the obvious practicality of the first nor does it lend itself as a medium to the complex arrangements whose cumulative force invests the second with a more immediate appeal than the restrained effects to which the sculptor is limited. Possibly because the earliest sculpture had a practical purpose, it appears to be more consistent in quality than that of today. In prehistoric times, the caveman carved his weapons with images of animals (cf. Fig. 543) and thus supposedly made them more effective in killing the prey upon which he depended for food. In Egypt and Greece, one of the chief duties of the sculptor was to create statues of the gods in human form, for the early religions of the world held the reverse of Christian belief to be true and made their gods in the image of man. The religious function of sculpture is almost non-existent today in the Occidental world, but in its place is an instinctive feeling that forms portrayed in indestructible stone or metal should be intrinsically worthy of the permanence thus acquired. The result of this feeling is that complete sculptural satisfaction can rarely be found except in representations of the human form. Some sculptors have attained distinction by their animal figures, but even the best of their works lack the significance of the greatest sculptural interpretations of the human figure. This fact also gives a clue to the inappropriateness in sculpture of many things that are quite justified in painting. Thus a picture of a man walking through a forest is perfectly legitimate whereas it would be ridiculous in sculpture, as the displays in a waxworks museum so painfully reveal. This is less true of relief than of free-standing sculpture. None the less, the sculptor who strives for the varied naturalistic details, even in relief, that a painter can use without question, usually sacrifices some quality which is appropriate to his art.

There is a fundamental reason for this. It is the necessity, which will be explained shortly, of keeping sculpture or painting from being merely an illusion of reality. In painting, this is partly accomplished by reducing the three dimensions of length, height and depth to the two of length and height, the third dimension being suggested but never actually present. Thus no painting can ever be so realistic that the observer feels he can see the back of a man's head by going around a portrait, or the other side of a house from the rear of a landscape. On the other hand, if these same subjects are represented in sculpture, and for the moment relief sculpture which approximates painting in effect is not considered, the observer *can* see the other side and the figure tends to approach the illusion of reality that must be avoided. It must always be the *sculptured* figure that is seen, not a facsimile in metal or stone of the flesh and blood figure.

What qualities, then, must sculpture possess if it must not be merely naturalistic? The answer is the same as that which was given to the question "What constitutes great architecture?" The human figure is the raw material with which the sculptor works, just as the immediate function of the building is the point of departure for the architect. This raw material the sculptor treats in such a way that the statue becomes expressive of the things that he feels or thinks about his subject, adding order and arrangement to it in such a fashion that the resultant form becomes harmonious with the spirit of his age. The greatness of the artist depends upon his ability to evolve in his statue the ideal form in which harmony of line, mass and surface reveals the true significance of his subject matter. The ideal of the sculptor is a formal order, based upon natural forms but with all accidental and temporal qualities eliminated so that in the end, the order of the sculptor is more perfect than that of nature. For the observer, the value of a work of art lies in its clarification of his own experience of those forms and the heightened sense he derives from it of their fundamental meaning as forms, resulting from their being placed in a logical and coherent pattern. This furnishes another reason why naturalism is not enough to make a painting or a piece of sculpture a great work of art. The inclusion of all the accidental details only obscures the characteristic pattern of which they are a part. This is well illustrated by the soldiers on the average Civil War monument. The most prominent features are the buttons and insignia, the wrinkles of the coat, the saber straps and the boot laces. The statue as a whole has no meaning other than a purely symbolic one, for the sculptor has been so concerned with superficial details that he has not attempted to give them any formal meaning by establishing them as essential parts of a well-ordered pattern. The beauty of representational sculpture does not lie in its record of observation. It is rather in the organization which the sculptor imposes upon that record. Where such organization does not exist, as in the soldier of the Civil War monument, there is no beauty and no work of art.

Thus to the sculptor, the form of his model is not as significant or real as the form which he evolves in his statue. Just as merely fulfilling the immediate function in architecture is not enough to produce a great building, so mere representation of form in sculpture is insufficient to result in a great statue. It is the organization of the figure that is significant, a pattern of volumes indicated by planes and outlines, a pattern by means of which the interrelationship of those volumes is emphasized and the ideal of the sculptor made tangible and apparent. For sculpture is primarily an art of form and mass, just as architecture is primarily an art of space. To the element of related forms, all others in sculpture are subservient and contributory.

Fig. 229.—Nude Woman. *Museum, Saint-Germain.*

Sculpture was among the earliest of the arts practiced by man. Excavation of the sites known to have been occupied in prehistoric periods has revealed small figures such as the *Nude Woman* of the late palaeolithic age (Fig. 229) found near Menton in France, which was probably a charm or fetish formed to symbolize the elemental belief of its creator in the power of his deity to bestow the gift of fertility. The motivation of all early sculpture was religious or magical—to create a tangible symbol of an abstract idea or emotional concept. The nature of the concept leading to the creation of the figure from Menton is clear, for the large breasts and thighs are so made as to emphasize those parts of the feminine form involved in the bearing and rearing of children. Other than these characteristics, the element of representation has been of no great importance for the primitive sculptor; the legs are shown only to the knees, the arms are included in the mass of the torso and the head is an oval bulk without any indication of the features. For the sculptor has selected from the facts of appearance of the female form only those that are pertinent to the embodiment of his basic idea and has subordinated all those which have no bearing upon it. He has thus arrived at an organized pattern of sculptured masses which can be identified as to symbolic function in consequence of the organization that emphasizes the significant elements of the form as a whole. The stone is a yellowish steatite that is slightly translucent, and the figure is hardly two inches high, but so effectively is the material handled and so thoroughly are the volumes of the form integrated in an organized pattern that its meaning could be no clearer if it were as many feet tall instead of inches.

Religious belief is the motivation and convention is the predominant formal characteristic of the first great monumental style to develop in historic times in the western world—that of Egypt. In figures that are sometimes as much as sixty-five feet high (cf. Fig. 19) and that embody the fundamental and memorable qualities of the things portrayed in conventions, i.e., forms that are traditionally significant through established usage, the Egyptian reveals the same passionate desire for immortality that is evident in his tombs and temples. It was in the house of the god or the house of the dead, in fact, that the greater part of Egyptian sculpture was to be placed—in the *serdab* of the mastaba (Fig. 8) where it provided the spirit of the dead with an acceptable substitute if the original mummified body were destroyed, or in the temple where it embodied in visible symbol the concept of king or god (Fig. 12).

Among the earliest examples of Egyptian sculpture for which a date can be suggested is a ceremonial tablet of slate called the *Palette of Narmer* (Fig. 230), which was made for one of the earliest dynastic rulers of Egypt between 3200 and 3000 B.C. A little over two feet in its greatest dimension, it is simply a decorated slab of stone upon which was placed the pigment with which the king's face was painted before participation in religious rituals, the circular hollow enclosed by the intertwined necks of the two animals in the middle register of the side illustrated on the left being the receptacle. The motivation of the ornament is consistent with this ceremonial purpose. Above the intertwined animals is a scene in which the king—much larger than his companions and wearing the crown of Lower Egypt—views the headless bodies of enemies slain in battle, while in the lower end of the same side he is shown symbolically as a bull destroying the wall of a hostile city. On the other side—the one on the right in the illustration

—he wears the crown of Upper Egypt and grasps the hair of his kneeling foe before a hawk symbolizing the god Horus; two defeated enemies lie in the lower end on this side. In the topmost register on both sides are representations of the goddess Hathor with the ears and horns of a cow, flanking hieroglyphs of the king's name enclosed in a symbol of his royal palace. Early though the Palette of Narmer is in the definable chronology of Egyptian sculpture, many of the conventions of Egyptian formal expression that appear in it are completely established. Thus the monarch is always shown as much larger than anyone else, an interpretation of a fact that was obvious to any Egyptian—namely, that

FIG. 230.—THE PALETTE OF NARMER. *Museum, Cairo.*

the king was more important than any other person of his time— and that could not be obscured representationally by portraying him in any fashion however naturalistic that would suggest a different idea. For a similar reason the ten headless bodies of his slain enemies are placed in two rows with one seemingly on top of the other in order that each will be clearly visible as an unmistakable symbol of a stated number of victims, for the sculptor is concerned not with representing things as they may have appeared to him but with objective and immutable facts.

The same concept is apparent in the portrayal of the individual figures. The king about to strike his helpless foe with the scepter is shown with his head in profile although the eye appears as if seen from directly in front. Equally inconsistent as naturalistic representation is the way the body is shown with the shoulders and torso in full-face while the striding legs are shown in profile again. But as a description in formal terms of the various parts of the human body that make up a figure it is completely adequate to the sculptor's purpose,

*Courtesy the Museum of Fine Arts, Boston*

FIG. 231.—MENKAURA AND HIS QUEEN.

*Museum of Fine Arts, Boston.*

for he was concerned with the embodiment of ideas that were objective and unchanging; to show them in that light, the forms must be presented in their most characteristic and memorable aspects. The experience to which the Egyptian gives expression is not, therefore, one resulting from direct and immediate physical participation on his part, but one of communal value rendered significant by traditional acceptance through the memory of generations. It is this memory concept or picture which the Egyptian artist represents, and every element contained therein must be a formal as well as conceptual whole contributing to a unity that is ideographic rather than organic. It is for this reason that the various symbols on the Palette are organized in the manner they are—in clearly defined registers and spaced in a pattern that impresses the spectator with its decorative coherence. Yet it is doubtful if this was a conscious intention on the part of the sculptor whose sole purpose was an arrangement that would make the concepts he was dealing with clear and unmistakable in import.

Early Egyptian statuary in the round contributes still further conventions in the portrayal of the human figure, an example being the double statue of *Menkaura and His Queen* (Fig. 231) in the Museum of Fine Arts in Boston. Menkaura was the builder of the third and latest of the Pyramids at Gizeh and this statue was probably carved about 2600 B.C. The material is a gray-green slate of great hardness,

.elected for its durability as a suitable medium in which to symbolize the eternal greatness of the Pharaoh. Corresponding to the memory picture which is the basic convention in two-dimensional representation in Egyptian art is the law of frontality in the figure in the round by which the body stands rigidly in such fashion that an axial plane cutting the figure vertically would pass through the nose, mouth, chin, torso and the juncture of the legs dividing it into two symmetrical portions. Whatever movement there is is kept parallel to this plane; it is limited in general to the forward stride of the left leg, although in the example under consideration the queen places her right arm around the king's waist and touches his left arm with her own left hand in gestures symbolic of her relationship to him. These again are descriptive conventions and do not affect the general impression of immobility resulting from the frontal poses which is contributed to by the clenched fists of the king and the arms held tightly to his sides. Another technical detail to be noted is the web of stone between the two figures (there is a similar joining between the legs of the king) and connecting the arms and sides; this was a mechanical device to stiffen the figures and prevent as far as possible the breaking off of essential parts.

Unfinished Egyptian statues have been found that reveal the process by which such forms as these were created. On the faces of the block of stone from which the figure was to be cut were drawn frontal and profile views of the traditional memory-picture type. These outlines were then cut into the block until they intersected to define the general form, which was then rounded off and modeled and the essential details were carved. The result of this process is a solid bulk organized in three dimensions that complies in every respect with the basic definition of sculpture as a pattern of formally related masses to which can be added in many instances the strong appeal of the medium in which the object is created. But again it must be pointed out that for the Egyptian such values were incidental and indeed unnecessary since it is a visual description of a traditional concept that he is striving to create, and the motivation of pattern and surface treatment and the other purely aesthetic qualities of the form are of importance only in so far as they may contribute to the completeness and clarity of that statement.

Menkaura and his Queen are shown as royal types provided with the symbols of their rank that were among the ideographic conventions of regal portraits, such as the Pharaoh's beard and his headdress. But as individuals they are not characterized beyond the most cursory personal traits for it was not consistent with the divine conception of royalty that any accidental peculiarities of appearance should be preserved to suggest the mortal flesh rather than the divine principle. In statues of persons of lesser rank, however, it is not uncommon to find remarkably individualized portraits, an example being the wooden figure in the Cairo Museum known as the *Sheikh el-Beled* (Fig. 232), which received the name when workmen excavating it from a tomb near Saqqara saw in the figure a great resemblance to the ruler of their village, which is what the term means. It is of the Fifth Dynasty in

Egyptian chronology, approximately 2550 B.C. Made up of a single block of wood for the legs, torso and head, with the arms in separate pieces, it was originally covered with stucco which was painted; this stucco has disappeared along with the wig that presumably once covered the head. These undoubtedly amplified but could hardly have rendered more striking the great realism of the head with its thick lips, flattened nose and heavy jowls and chin in an effect of vividly rendered individual traits that may still be perceived in the eyes, which are formed by inserts of colored paste in a metal frame. These are details essential to a complete statement of the identity and social rank of the man and thus can rightfully figure in the form by which those objective facts are recorded and preserved. Yet with all the individuality of the figure, there is the same immobility and lack of expression that characterize the royal

FIG. 232.—THE SHEIKH EL-BELED. *Museum, Cairo.*

statues, for its function as a potential body for the spirit in case the mummy were destroyed was also a social fact that had to be taken into account; hence the rigidly frontal stance with left leg advanced and right arm held tightly to the side as well as the mask-like and imperturbable expression on the face.

Naturalism is a term used to imply a complete and objective definition in visual terms of a form or idea, and to the extent that the Sheikh el-Beled is such a definition it might be said that Egyptian sculpture is a naturalistic art in intention. But it is a primitive naturalism that is

FIG. 233.—HUNTING THE HIPPOPOTAMUS. *Mastaba of Ti, Saqqara.*

here observed and, as one of the most perceptive critics of Egyptian art has pointed out, it "is not an affair of the eyes but of the whole man and his spiritual attitude towards his experience of nature" (Wilhelm Worringer, *Egyptian Art* [1928], English translation). It was to define the whole man, for example, that the Egyptian sought by elaborate pictographs on the walls of his tomb (cf. Fig. 9) to record the riches that were his in this life and assist in the nourishment of his soul in the next. These, apart from their immediate symbolic purpose, are a source of invaluable information concerning the everyday life of the Egyptian. Thus in a relief of *Hunting the Hippopotamus in the Papyrus* (Fig. 233) carved on the walls of the Fifth Dynasty

FIG. 234.—SPHINX OF AMENEMHET III. *Museum, Cairo.*

mastaba of Ti at Saqqara, the lord himself is seen standing in a small boat directing his servants in their activities. He is considerably larger than they in accordance with the same convention that makes King Narmer of greater size than his companions, and stands in the same pose as does the Sheikh el-Beled, with the combination of frontal and profile aspects of the two-dimensional convention of the memory picture. The water of the Nile is indicated by a well-defined register of minute wavy lines at the bottom, with fishes and the hippopotami outlined against it. Above this a regular ribbed pattern, representing the stems of the papyrus plants, forms a background for the human figures, topped by papyrus buds and flowers and thronged with birds of various kinds, some of which are being stalked by foxes. The flattening out of the forms and the clear separation into registers that strike the modern eye as effective decorative patterns are actually the consequence of the Egyptian's conventionalized descriptive vocabulary which sought to define all the objects in their most characteristic aspect and obtained an effect that is well in accordance with the flatness of the wall with no intention other than to fill every available square inch of surface.

Fig. 235.—Amenemhet III. *Ny Carlsberg Museum, Copenhagen.*

Once the methods of the Egyptian sculptor were developed and the types to be created by them were defined, there was relatively little change in the conceptions and forms throughout the history of the country as an autonomous cultural entity—a direct parallel to the persistence of basic forms to be noted in the architecture, as has been pointed out earlier. Thus the Sphinx of the Old Kingdom period (Fig. 11) was a type created to symbolize the power of the king by association of his head with the body of a lion; the same type recurs in the *Sphinx of Amenemhet III* (Fig. 234) of the Twelfth Dynasty in the Middle Kingdom period which was *ca.* 1800 B.C., the only difference of any importance being the framing of the ruler's features by the mane of the animal instead of the royal headdress (cf. Fig. 231). The Middle Kingdom example is also of more modest dimensions than the Sphinx at Gizeh, being only a little over three feet high, but it is carved from granite and has the same qualities of formal conventionalism noted in the earlier sculptures. In the face, however, there is an individualistic quality to be noted in the rather round general forms, the broad nose and thick lips that are unlike the more impersonal features of Menkaura and, indeed, are apparently of a different racial type. A head that is possibly also of *Amenemhet III* (Fig. 235) in the Ny-Carlsberg Museum of Sculpture in Copenhagen is even more clearly individualized. The material is a black-green slate of great hardness which no doubt imposed limitations in the rendering of minute detail in addition to the accepted conventions of form that led to generalization such as the mask-like expression; but in spite of these, there is a specific character in the rendering of such details as the shape of the lips, the lines slanting down from the nose and the bulges underneath the eyes that create the impression of a definite personality. As in the Old Kingdom examples, the quality of the execution is very high with the most scrupulous attention to the handling of minutest details.

Egypt's greatest power as a nation was reached in the period of the Empire or New Kingdom between 1580 and 1100 B.C., and it is but natural that the glory of her Pharaohs should have been reflected in the great amount of sculpture then executed and in the great size of many of the figures as well. A life-size statue of *Thutmose III* (Fig. 236) carved from basalt in the museum at Cairo is in the centuries-old tradition as far as the type is concerned—rigidly frontal in pose with individualistic details generalized in accordance with the concept of royalty as above the specific qualities of ordinary human beings. Thutmose III was the half-brother and the husband of Hatshepsut, the famous queen of the Eighteenth Dynasty who built the temple at Deir el-bahari (Fig. 15), with whom he first shared the throne of Egypt that later he occupied alone from about 1480 B.C. until his death in 1447 B.C. During that time he extended the power of Egypt as far as Syria in the north and Nubia in the south and established himself as one of the most capable rulers the country ever had. The basalt statue came from Karnak where he had built a great festival hall as part of the complex of structures dedicated to Amon, the sun god. He is shown wearing the crown of upper Egypt with the uraeus, the snake symbol of royalty, resting upon his brow. The details of the face are stylized in accordance with traditional formulas seen in the rendering of the eyebrows as flat, ribbon-like bands and the impassive expression, but the vigor and energy of the powerful ruler are also

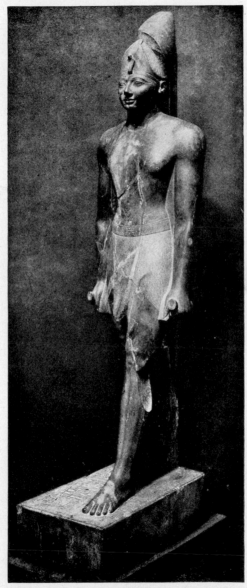

FIG. 236.—THUTMOSE III. *Museum, Cairo.*

apparent, and the statue is an excellent example of that primitive naturalism earlier referred to in which traditional symbols define not merely the appearance and individuality of the man but his spiritual attitude toward his experience of nature as well.

The conventions of Egyptian representative art were evolved to state with the greatest clarity the ideas composing the attitude toward experience that centuries had conceived as valid, and the unquestioning

FIG. 237.—AKHENATEN AND NOFRETETE. *Ägyptisches Museum, Berlin.*

assurance with which succeeding generations employed those conventions is a reflection of comparable spiritual certainty. Only for a brief period in the Eighteenth Dynasty, between 1375 and 1358 B.C., was there any departure from traditional modes of Egyptian thought and formal expression thereof, when Amenhotep IV, otherwise Akhenaten, attempted to bring about a reform of long-standing abuses in the religion of the country. Replacing the traditional sun god Amon-Re in the Egyptian religious hierarchy with Aten, whose name forms part of the cognomen he took for himself instead of the one he inherited, he moved the government of Egypt from Thebes to a newly

PL. 1. PORTRAIT BUST OF QUEEN NOFRETETE, WIFE OF IKHNATON AND
MOTHER-IN-LAW OF TUTENKHAMON

built capital on the site of modern Tell el-Amarna. The statues of himself and his queen Nofretete that stood in the buildings he caused to be erected there, and the relief carvings with which their walls were decorated reveal an intention no less revolutionary in character than his religious reforms. In a relief now in the Ägyptisches Museum in Berlin, *Akhenaten and Nofretete* (Fig. 237) confront each other in casual and easy poses, the king with crossed legs leaning on a staff while the queen extends a bouquet toward him. Both are lightly garbed as was the custom, and the bodies are represented with a degree of naturalism found at no other time in dynastic Egyptian art; the necks are long and thin, the abdomens swollen and misshapen and the hips of the queen are inordinately large. Her head, too, is enlarged to the point of deformity, in contrast with the delicately chiseled facial features that are also a characteristic of Akhenaten. That these are no conventions but conscious attempts to produce likenesses of the subjects is indicated by the recurrence of the same characteristics in a number of plaster masks made in all likelihood from the models that were found in a building at Tell el-Amarna which had been a sculptor's studio and where the well-known painted limestone bust of Nofretete now in the museum at Berlin (Color Plate I) was discovered at the same time. No less distinctive than these incisively individualized forms and faces in comparison with the traditionally generalized forms of royalty in Egyptian art is the difference between their negligent poses and the hieratic rigidity of King Narmer on his Old Kingdom slate palette (Fig. 230) or of Seti I on the walls of the temple he built at Abydos (Fig. 239), a rigidity as much of an interpretive convention as the memory picture was a formal one. This latter, it is significant to notice, was something that even the obviously naturalistic intention of the Tell el-Amarna sculptor could not transcend; the eyes are shown full-face in the profile heads and the torsos are formed of frontal shoulders related to abdomens and hips seen from the side.

The reforms initiated by Akhenaten and the modifications of traditional concepts of representation that were a parallel artistic development died with their creator, and the remaining years of the Eighteenth Dynasty period in Egyptian history witnessed a return to the old forms in religion and art alike. Under Tutankhamen, the son-in-law of Akhenaten, and Haremhab, who was one of his successors, the worship of Amon-Re was restored, and with the reorganization of the Empire which took place after about 1350 B.C. one of the most prolific periods in Egyptian art began. *A Relief from the Tomb of Haremhab* (Fig. 238) shows four Egyptians in charge of a group of Negro captives taken in one of Haremhab's many and successful military campaigns, an indication of the source of the labor by which the great

temples of the Empire period (cf. Figs. 17, 19) were built. It is interesting to observe the typical character of the Egyptians in the relief
as compared with the clearly defined negroid features and expressions
of the captives—another indication of the expressive value of the conventional formulas employed by the Egyptians. The accuracy of the
Egyptian artist's observation is unquestionable; elsewhere in the same
tomb are reliefs showing Syrians and Asiatics which are as sharply
characterized as the Negroes in this one, and the animals and fishes
in the Old Kingdom relief in the tomb of Ti (Fig. 233) are likewise
portrayed with considerable objective naturalism. From this it is to be
deduced that the formula of the figures representing Egyptians was a
thing of inherent significance, employed because its meaning was a
traditional one rather than from inability to see and portray accurately
the individual objective facts of appearance.  ·

FIG. 238.—NEGRO CAPTIVES. Relief from the Tomb of Haremhab.
*Museo Civico, Bologna.*

In the examples of relief sculpture that have been discussed, the
figures have been cut into the stone. This "sunken relief" is a characteristically Egyptian type of sculpture and is but seldom encountered in
other styles. Since such reliefs were almost invariably painted as well—
the background of the relief of Akhenaten and Nofretete from Tell
el-Amarna is yellow and the figures are gaily colored (Fig. 237)—it
seems probable that the sunken relief technique may have been employed to keep the pigment from being rubbed off. This type of relief
carving was utilized most extensively on the façades of buildings (cf.
Fig. 18) in figures glorifying the achievements of the Pharaohs and
on the shafts of columns as well as on the walls of tombs. The

Egyptians also employed the other variety of relief sculpture—with projecting forms—on their buildings, an example being *Seti I Offering an Image of Truth to Osiris* (Fig. 239) in the temple built by that ruler at Abydos in honor of seven deities including himself. Seti I, who ascended the throne of Egypt in 1313 B.C., was one of the first great rulers of the Nineteenth Dynasty in the Empire period, and was notable alike for the vigor with which he enforced Egyptian rule in

FIG. 239.—SETI I OFFERING. *Temple of Seti I, Abydos.*

conquered lands and the vast building program he undertook at home, which included the construction of the Hypostyle Hall in the great temple of Amon-Re at Karnak. The relief at Abydos is notable for the brilliance of its color and the fine execution of the delicately carved forms. Such refinement of line and surface would have been lost in the glaring sunlight illuminating it on an external wall but appears to excellent advantage in the more somber interior setting it occupies. The same formal conventions are to be noted that have been pointed out before, and if the vigor and austerity of Old Kingdom examples are lacking (cf. Figs. 230, 233), there is by compensation a grace of line and refinement of form of no small distinction. The accessory color is as conventionalized in effect as the drawing of the figures; a dark tone is invariably used for male figures and a light one for female ones, the purpose throughout being neither representative nor decorative but to render the forms clearer and more distinct in the ensemble effect.

FIG. 240.—RAMESES II.
*Museo di Antichità, Turin.*

Rameses II, who began his reign of sixty-seven years in 1292 B.C., was the son of Seti I and the longest-lived of the Nineteenth Dynasty rulers. Like his father, Rameses was a great warrior, and also like him he was indefatigable in erecting and decorating temples in honor of the gods and himself. The life-size seated figure of granite, carved about 1250 B.C. and now in the museum at Turin (Fig. 240) was intended for one of his many temples and shows another standard Egyptian type for the portrayal of royalty. Small figures carved on the sides of the statue, behind the legs and below the thighs, represent his queen and one of his sons. As in the majority of Egyptian statues, the difficulties of working in the intractable stone appear to have presented no problem whatsoever; a pattern of finely cut grooves represents the royal garment, the headdress is covered with minute medallions, and there is the same delicacy of line and contour, almost effeminate in character, that was noted in the relief of Seti I, the characteristic in which these examples of Empire or New Kingdom sculpture differ in most marked fashion from the rugged and powerful forms of the Old and Middle Kingdom statues of royalty (cf. Figs. 231, 235). It is interesting to observe that an antithesis to the graceful delicacy of such a figure as this is to be found in the same period in which this one was executed, for the colossal figures of more than sixty-five feet in height on the façade of the temple of Abu-Simbel (Fig. 19) are also of Rameses II and were begun at about the same time, in 1257 B.C. These enormous figures would be impressive through sheer bulk if for no other reason, the bulk which connoted the eternal for the Egyptian in that it provided a vehicle, supposedly impervious to any normal process of decay, in which could be recorded the communal belief in

*Courtesy the Museum of Fine Arts, Boston*

FIG. 241.—SAÏTIC DIGNITARY. *Museum of Fine Arts, Boston.*

regal power and divinity. It is possibly the grandiose proportions of the figures that led to the very considerable generalization of the features and expression—quite different in effect from the delicately rendered surfaces of the statue at Turin and with something of the imperturbable aloofness of the figures carved in earlier times.

Rameses II was the last of the great Egyptian rulers; his successors in the Twentieth Dynasty were unable to maintain a degree of power even remotely comparable to his. The Empire or New Kingdom period in Egyptian history comes to a close about 1100 B.C. after a succession of weak kings, many of whom bore the name of Rameses but had none of his power. There follow in the Twenty-first to Twenty-fifth Dynasties only a series of minor monarchs—Libyan, Ethiopian and Assyrian— between 1100 and 663 B.C., who show all too clearly the disintegration of the centralized power upon which rested the glory of the once mighty kingdom. Only in the Twenty-sixth Dynasty from 663 to 525 B.C. during the Saïtic Restoration does there appear even a vestige of the old power, and it is in this time that a few examples of sculpture comparable in quality if not in character to the older work can be found. A basalt *Head* (Fig. 241) in the Museum of Fine Arts at Boston is one of a number in this material that reveal craftsmanship the equal of anything to be noted in the great periods. It is employed, however, for different purposes than producing the conventionalized symbols of royal and divine power, for the Saïtic heads are individual in detail to the extent of portraying every blemish, like the wart under the left eye in the example illustrated, and specifically personal in character. The greater freedom allowed the sculptor in these matters results in forms more immediate in their appeal and in the best examples not lacking in impressiveness from perception of character and direct translation thereof into sculptural terms, but the grandeur of Menkaura (Fig. 231) and Amenemhet III (Fig. 235) is lacking and even the vital alertness of Rameses II (Fig. 240) has no counterpart here. It is in such forms as these that the centuries-old tradition of Egyptian sculpture comes to an end. Under the Persians, Greeks and Romans, it is increasingly diluted and modified by alien concepts and methods to the extent that whatever of truly Egyptian character remains is at most but one of numerous traits to be discerned.

Sculpture in Mesopotamia in the fourth and third millennia before the Christian era was similar in function to that of Egypt, and was of similar formal character as well, once allowance is made for the differences between the two regions in culture and material resources. The abundant supply of various kinds of stone available to the Egyptian sculptor had no counterpart in Mesopotamia, and as characteristic an example of early sculpture in the region as the *Sumerian Noble* (Fig. 242) is of very small dimensions compared with Egyptian figures of relative antiquity. The figure was executed about the year 3000 B.C. and was found at Khafaje in the course of excavations conducted by the University of Pennsylvania Museum, of whose collection it now forms a part. The material is a white limestone with inset eyes of shell and lapis lazuli. The figure is nude to the waist, the legs being covered by a ceremonial skirt that leaves the bare feet exposed. The pose is frontal and the left leg advanced as in Egyptian figures, and

*Photo Goldberg*

FIG. 242.—SUMERIAN NOBLE. *University Museum, Philadelphia.*

the hands were originally clasped over the breast. The torso is rendered by a few broadly modeled planes with only the nipples of the breast defined in detail. The head is round in shape with prominent ears; the eyebrows are indicated by incised curved lines over the widely staring eyes and the strongly protruding nose. These characteristics of the figure appear at first glance to be individual and personal and the initial impression created is that it is a rather summarily rendered portrait;

FIG. 243.—THE STELE OF NARAM-SIN. *Louvre, Paris.*

but the recurrence of the same shaven head, beak-like nose and staring eyes, along with the costume and stance described above, in many other statuettes of the same period makes it clear that this engaging little form is a conventional type evolved as a traditional symbol which is similar in basic character to the Old Kingdom figures of ancient Egypt.

Early relief sculpture in Mesopotamia likewise reveals conventions similar to those employed in Egypt. The *Stele of Naram-Sin* (Fig. 243), which is now in the Louvre in Paris, was erected originally at Susa in Babylonia about 2800 B.C. to commemorate a victory won by the son of Sargon I, and one of the most important of Mesopotamian rulers. Cuneiform inscriptions in wedge-shape characters describe the episode, which is represented in relief on a slab of stone a little over six feet in height and shows Naram-Sin leading his

troops in victorious battle through a mountainous country like that around Susa itself. As in comparable Egyptian reliefs (cf. Fig. 230), the figures are shown in profile with the king much larger than his followers, and the same memory-picture principle is to be noted in the organization of the bodies, which are described as a group of members shown in their most characteristic aspects rather than built up as organic and articulated entities. At the same time, it should be noted that an elemental rendering of space has been attempted; the king is not only above but also behind his troops and the mountain stronghold he approaches is outlined against the sky where two stars are represented, while the soldiers are obviously thought of as moving in several planes in depth by contrast with the completely flat pattern of those similarly engaged in the Egyptian commemorative relief of Narmer.

Among the most characteristic examples of early Mesopotamian sculpture are the numerous figures found at Tello, known in older times as Lagasch, in southern Babylonia. These refer by inscription to a certain *Gudea* who was a powerful lord in Asia Minor about the year

Fig. 244.—Gudea of Tello. *Louvre, Paris.*

2400 B.C., and the statuette of green diorite in the Louvre (Fig. 244) is believed to represent him. About a foot and a half in height, the figure is carved from a stone that is not indigenous in the region and must have been imported, a circumstance that accounts for its relatively small size although some others found at the same time are considerably larger. The pose is frontal and the traditional clasping of the hands noted also in the earlier figure from Khafaje (Fig. 242) suggests that its function was devotional. This may account as well for the rather heavy and squat proportions of the body which resembles

that of a dwarf, with its arbitrary rendering of the thighs and legs
in a rectangular block and the thick torso above. These characteristics
seem inconsistent with the accuracy in rendition of details like the
muscles and the modeling of lips and chin, but they confirm the conceptual and symbolic purpose of the form as a whole that is comparable
in its way to the Egyptian figures employed in like manner. The face

FIG. 245.—ASSURNASIRPAL II DRINKING. *Metropolitan Museum, N. Y.*

is blank and impassive in expression without even as much indication
of personal character as appears in the Sheikh el-Beled (Fig. 232), and
it is clear that the naturalism of the Mesopotamian sculptor is the
same in principle as that of the Egyptian, however different the details
in rendering the forms.

It is difficult to follow a line of development in Mesopotamian sculpture as can be done in that of Egypt, for the involved political and
military history of the region in the second millennium before Christ

was even less conducive to the consistent carrying-on of such activities than is to be noted in the interim between Middle and New Kingdom periods in Egypt. About the time of the tenth and ninth centuries B.C., however, a strong centralized power was developed in the northern or Assyrian region, and from this and subsequent periods until the destruction of this empire in 612 B.C., there are examples of later Mesopotamian sculpture in considerable numbers. An alabaster relief of *Assurnasirpal II Drinking* (Fig. 245) came from the palace built at Kalher by that ruler in the early ninth century B.C. and is now in the Metropolitan Museum in New York. The monarch stands with a bow in his left hand and a shallow drinking cup in his right, confronted by his attendant who extends another cup to him at the same time that he raises the ceremonial whisk that was his badge of office. All the conventions of primitive representation are present—the striding stance, profile head with full-front eye, shoulders distorted into both frontal and side views—and details like the fringes of garments and hair and beards are indicated by schematized patterns of wavy lines and ringlets. Specifically Mesopotamian are the heavy, massive proportions of the figures, the strongly emphasized muscles of the arms, and the cuneiform inscriptions incised in a continuous band that takes no account of the figures. This should be compared with the way in which the hieroglyphs of similar function are used in an Egyptian relief (Fig. 239) where the writing and the carved forms are organized in such a way as to complement each other in a clear definition of the idea embodied in them.

Typical too is the mundane character of the subject in the relief of Assurnasirpal. The Egyptian king-god showed himself doing honor to his fellow deities, while the Mesopotamian priest-king had carved on the stone sheathing of the mud-brick walls of his palace the record of his fondness for battle and the hunt. It has been pointed out elsewhere that the cult of the dead which was so enormously developed in Egypt and was responsible for nearly all Egyptian artistic concepts had no counterpart in Mesopotamia where the divine function of royalty was expressed rather in glorification of material achievement in worldly terms. It was this concept that underlay the ziggurat (Figs. 20, 21), which was a palace-temple, and it also explains the conventions emphasizing bodily strength and power in the Mesopotamian figures. And it is this which makes the *Wounded Lioness* (Fig. 246) the vigorous and forceful form that it is in portraying the futile rage of the crippled beast as she drags her paralyzed body over the ground in a final effort to attack her slayer. The relief is from a series depicting Assurbanipal hunting lions that originally decorated his palace at Nineveh which was built between 668 and 626 B.C. Much detail has been omitted, and there are obvious stylizations of more, as in the wavy lines representing blood flowing from the arrow holes and the long curving line formed by the profile of the outstretched front leg merging into the throat and the muzzle; but the accurately rendered snarl, the laid-back ears and the loosened tendons and muscles of the dragging hind legs are proof of the sculptor's ability to see clearly and record the essentials of a motive in which he must have had more than casual interest.

Fig. 246.—Wounded Lioness. *British Museum, London.*

The relative scarcity of good building stone in Mesopotamia was a factor in determining the architectural style of the region, as has been noted elsewhere, and it was also an element in the sculptural forms there developed for there is little sculpture in the round as compared with Egypt. A form developed in the later period that has some characteristics of free-standing sculpture is the *Winged Man-headed Lion* (Fig. 247), an example now in the British Museum in London that was carved for the palace of Assurnasirpal III at Nimrud between 885 and 860 B.C. These monsters which are conceptually similar to the sphinxes of Egypt (cf. Fig. 234) were the guardian genii of the Mesopotamian palace, standing on the jambs of portals in such wise that they scrutinized all persons and things passing through. As expressive concepts they belong to a culture still symbolizing its gods in zoomorphic form; formally they illustrate yet another aspect of the inorganic and descriptive conventionalism that has been noted in the human figures, a detail in point being the representation of the monster with five legs in order that he may be seen to have four legs from the side and also to appear properly supported when viewed from in front. Otherwise there is the same stylizing of details of hair and feathers and the

FIG. 247.—WINGED MAN-HEADED LION. *British Museum, London.*

strongly emphasized muscles noted in the human figures, as well as a notable heaviness of proportion and massiveness of form in patterns of rectilinear severity and bulk.

Sculpture was one of the major arts in both Egypt and Mesopotamia in that it was a medium for expression of the most significant concepts developed by the cultures of those regions in pre-classical times. This is not true of the third cultural area of that period—the Aegean. In Crete, for example, no stone sculpture of either monumental size or content has been found, and the case is little different on the mainland. The plastered rubble walls of the palaces at Phaistos and Knossos (cf. Fig. 25) lent themselves well to painted decoration, and there are some traces of modeled stucco relief to be discerned in the house of Minos. Relief sculpture was also used as an accessory to some utilitarian ob-

*Courtesy the Museum of Fine Arts, Boston*

Fig. 248.—The Snake Goddess. *Museum of Fine Arts, Boston.*

jects such as vases, an example being the Vaphio Cups (cf. Fig. 557), but sculpture in the round is limited almost entirely to images of very small size. Of these, one of the most striking is the statuette in ivory and gold of the *Snake Goddess* (Fig. 248) in the Museum of Fine Arts at Boston. Executed in all likelihood about 1500 B.C. and standing only some six and a half inches in height, it represents a female figure wearing the flounced skirt and open bodice of the Cretan women, with a crown upon her head and two gold snakes coiled about her outstretched arms. The theme, which is encountered in other examples of

Minoan art, refers to the cult of the snake as a deity of the earth. The figure is poised in stance, the backward curve of the torso balancing the forward thrust of the arms, while the head rises with vigor from the shoulders. These are conventions found elsewhere in cult figures in Aegean art, and it is probable that the expression on the face which is now a rather personal one was originally as stylized as the other features of the body, notably the prominent breasts (cf. Fig. 229).

As distinguished in its way as the Snake Goddess and unique in being a reasonably well-preserved example of large-scale stone sculpture from Aegean times is the triangular slab of the Lion Gate (Fig. 27) in the walls of Mycenae on the mainland of Greece. These walls were built about 1400 B.C. in all probability, and the relief slab is the earliest known example of monumental carving on the mainland of Greece. The symbolism is much the same as that of the Mesopotamian guardian monsters (Fig. 247). The two lions stand with their forepaws on a stereobate from which rises a column that tapers very slightly downward and is surmounted by a bulbous capital of semicircular profile and a schematic portrayal of the entablature of horizontal members separated by four disks representing roof beams. This column is a symbol of the house and it is defended by the lions flanking it. They once had heads that were carved from separate blocks attached to the bodies by means of wooden dowels, the square holes in which these were placed being still visible. The relief slab is nine and one-half feet high, and the lions are thus of considerable size; the modeling is well adapted to the limestone in which the forms are executed and at the same time is of such a nature as to make them seem large and powerful. It is possible that there were comparable works elsewhere in the Aegean world that have been entirely destroyed, but it is hardly likely that any more distinguished examples of monumental relief sculpture in stone than the Lion Gate existed in that region.

The character of sculpture as an expressive medium is such that it was peculiarly suited to effective embodiment of the ways of thinking most widely prevalent in pre-classical times. It is first of all an art which speaks most impressively in generalized terms, for the physical limitations of the materials involved operate to the disadvantage of minute and subtle distinctions of meaning and significance. It is secondly, and in part because of these material considerations, an art which seeks to define its forms with clarity and distinctness that can come only when the experience interpreted by the artist is understood in clear and precise terms. These are the qualities of primitive thought in which humankind sought to comprehend, evaluate and master the objective phenomena of nature and bend them to creative use in symbolic forms of unmistakable meaning and import. These are as often as not most comprehensively translated into the modeled forms of statues and reliefs in the period in question; if the power of the Egyptian Pharaoh is more immediately perceptible in his carved portrait than in the temple he caused to be erected, it is surely in part at least because the stone figure expresses that idea more directly in its massive simplicity than does the unrelated sequence of courts and halls that make up the architectural form.

# Chapter XVI. Greek Sculpture

OF ALL THE VISUAL ARTS, SCULPTURE WAS THE ONE best adapted to the embodiment of Greek thought. There are two reasons for this. The first is that the most significant sculpture appears to be that which deals with the human form, a limitation which parallels the restriction of Greek thought to matters pertaining to man alone. The second reason for the intrinsic appropriateness of sculpture to the expression of Greek thought is that it is primarily an art of form. This, too, has a parallel in the anthropocentric philosophy of the Greek, whose attitude toward knowledge is summed up in the assertion that man is the measure of all things. This leads inevitably to the conclusion that to the Greek that which was significant in experience was that which could be grasped by the senses, the degree of its reality depending on the directness of its impact upon the human mind. From this it follows that to be convincingly real, an object must have convincing form. It is for this reason that Greek architecture, to digress for a moment, is almost totally devoid of any spatial implications. Space is intangible. It becomes real only as the result of an intuitive interpretation of immediate and direct sensory experience. The ideal quality of Greek architecture is a result of its objective and self-explanatory forms which actually represent a sculptural point of view, for Greek architecture, as has been pointed out before, is an art of pure form in which it partakes of the quality of sculpture. It was only when Greek thought broke its self-imposed restriction to human values and became conscious of other things that a change is found in Greek art from the self-contained non-spatial forms with which it was exclusively concerned through the fifth century B.C.

Greek sculpture was primarily religious in character. The deep-rooted human instinct that the gods can best be approached through an image representing them was responsible for this. In the Aegean civilization of Crete and Mycenae, there was very little monumental sculpture, for religion in those times was very primitive, and natural forms of trees and rocks, the Biblical "stocks and stones," were worshiped. In the whole vast labyrinth that was the palace of King Minos at Knossos in Crete (cf. Fig. 24), the only religious symbol other than the building itself was a block of stone bearing a mystic mono-gram. A change occurred with the invasions of northern tribes between 1000 and 700 B.C., infusing new blood into the native stock of the Mediterranean basin and bringing an anthropomorphic religion whose gods were represented in human form. With this background, Greek sculpture developed. It was not exclusively religious for many secular subjects were represented, particularly in later times, but the religious element was always the predominant one.

FIG. 249.—HERA OF SAMOS. *Louvre, Paris.*

## A. THE ARCHAIC PERIOD

During the archaic period, which extended from about 625 to 480 B.C., the foundation was laid for Greek art in every field, resulting, in sculpture, in the creation of a number of basic types which continue through the greater part of the development of the art in Greek times. Of these types, the two most important are the draped standing female figure and the nude standing male. An example of the first is the *Hera of Samos* (Fig. 249), so called by virtue of having been dedi-cated to that goddess in her temple in Samos, about 550 B.C. At first glance, the statue seems more like a stone tree-trunk than anything else, evidence of the still very primitive concept of the deity then prevailing in its resemblance to the earlier images of the "stocks and stones" type. But a feeling of the neces-sity for a more human ideal led to the representation of toes at the bottom of the skirt and the suggestion of a torso as well as the portrayal of the arms, one of which is missing. Naturalistic representation was not the artist's in-tention, however. It was rather to effect a formal pattern in the firm and sweeping curves of the silhouette and the edge of the overgarment. The draperies also are a part of this design. They are stylized; that is, the folds are represented not as they actually appeared but in a pattern of parallel lines which serve as a visual foil to the curves of the outline. At the same time, the sculptor was not unobservant of the more significant naturalistic details of the figure. This can be seen in the contrasted textures of the heavy overgarment and the lighter one underneath, the toes and the suggestion of breasts under the draperies.

The standing male nude type in Greek archaic sculpture is seen in an *Apollo* (Fig. 250), in the Metropolitan Museum in New York, which

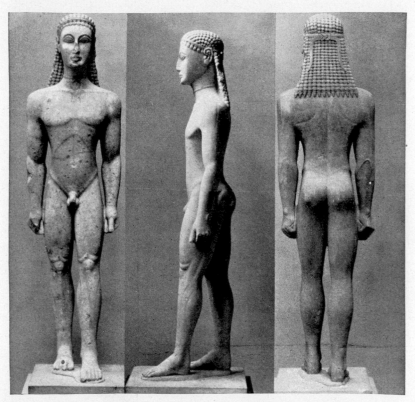

FIG. 250.—APOLLO. *Metropolitan Museum, N. Y.*

was carved about 600 B.C. This type of figure constitutes the largest single class in archaic sculpture. Its representatives are usually known as "Apollos" although the type was used for other gods as well as to represent human beings. The entire group reveals some characteristics that have been observed in Egyptian sculpture (Fig. 236), notably its rigid frontality with the left leg slightly advanced, the broad shoulders and narrow waist and the clenched fists. This similarity was probably due to an actual connection between the two styles, the Egyptian having influenced the Greek. The most obvious differences between them are the complete nudity of the Greek figure, and the absence of the supporting slab and the web of stone between the legs. Instead of the drapery pattern of parallel lines seen in the Hera of Samos (Fig. 249), the body itself is made into a pattern. The chest, abdomen and groin are indicated by stylized planes suggesting the rounded surfaces. The muscles of the lower abdomen are indicated by a projecting ridge from the hip to the genitals. The head is conventionalized, the

FIG. 251.—VICTORY OF DELOS. *National Museum, Athens.*

muscles of the cheeks and lips being reduced to smooth planes, while the eyes bulge from their shallow sockets and the lips form a straight line, though some other figures have them turned up at the corners in the curious "archaic smile." The hair is also treated in a conventional manner as a series of regular curls falling down the back, its bulk giving needed strength to the neck. The net result is a figure that has decorative unity arising from simplification of the large complex forms of the body. Its stiffness reveals quite clearly that the sculptor did not fully understand the complex mechanism of the human body. None the less, he did realize its organic unity, for he has indicated the joints of knees and ankles and wrists and elbows, as the Egyptian sculptor did not do, and has thus achieved an articulation of the various parts of the figure that gives it the spark of human life. He did not relate those parts in the statue just as they are in a living model, but he imposed a relationship upon them which is quite as tangible as that of the model. He thus created a reality analogous in general form to the human body but differing from it in elements of order and arrangement lacking in the other. From his knowledge of the human figure, limited though it was, he evolved a conception which has life and vigor in its own right.

The rapid development of Greek sculpture was due to a far-reaching and lively curiosity about the human figure which extended to all its aspects and attributes. A number of figures, for instance, reveal an attempt to suggest movement, an example being the *Victory of Delos* (Fig. 251), which was carved about 560 B.C. A conventionalized pose was evolved in which the kneeling legs are seen in profile while the upper part of the body and the outstretched arms are full-face. As in the Hera and the Apollo in New York, the form of the figure is deter-

FIG. 252.—PERSEUS SLAYING THE MEDUSA. Metope from Selinunte. *Museum, Palermo.*

mined by decorative considerations. It is an akroterion or figure to surmount the gable of a temple. The incised lines indicating the folds of the skirt are curved to suggest movement. The upper torso is stylized, reduced to the principal volumes of shoulders, breasts and upper abdomen. The face with its projecting cheek bones, bulging eyes and archaic smile is similarly stylized. As in the New York Apollo, the hair is treated as a mass of ringlets in long curls hanging down over the shoulders and reinforcing the neck.

Archaic sculpture was not limited to free-standing figures but also employed relief, chiefly as architectural decoration. About 550 B.C., the metopes of a temple at Selinunte in Sicily were carved with various mythological subjects, one of them being *Perseus Slaying the Medusa* while Athena looks on (Fig. 252). As in the Egyptian relief of Seti I (Fig. 239), the lower part of each figure appears in profile and the upper part in full-face. The figures themselves are rather heavy and squat, the dull faces lacking even the animation of the conventional archaic smile. Naturalistic details are stylized, notably the muscles of the calves and the hair. The problem in decorative sculpture of this type is to achieve an integration of its pattern with that of the architecture. With this end in view, the principal accents of the designs are vertical to agree with the flanking triglyphs. Crowding the figures into the available space resulted in Perseus' right arm and the Medusa's left leg both being shorter than their counterparts. The kneeling Medusa reproduces the type of the Delos Victory (Fig. 251).

The average observer of today who is accustomed to a naturalistic type of representation may find the beauty of archaic sculpture somewhat difficult to perceive. None the less, it is quite considerable. From an historic point of view, it is significant as the beginning of a sculptural tradition that is often considered, and not without some justification, as the greatest that ever existed. On the broadest aesthetic grounds, it reveals the most vital characteristic of artistic creation, the imposition of rhythm and order upon the chaotic material of human experience. Furthermore, it possesses to a high degree the essentially sculptural quality of form. It is impossible to see a good archaic statue without sensing this; its bulk and weight, the articulation of the forms of limbs and torso, the texture of the material are all impressed upon the observer. The statue stimulates a desire on his part to feel and handle it, to experience tactually the projection of the modeling and the planes of the surface. As an art of form, this is a test of sculptural quality in any style or period and one which proves the intrinsic greatness of much archaic art.

Toward the end of the archaic period, a more naturalistic style became possible by virtue of more extensive observation of the human body. The *Statue Dedicated by Euthydikos* (Fig. 253) was excavated from the debris used to level off some parts of the Athenian Acropolis (cf. Fig. 36) after the city had been sacked by the Persians in 480 B.C. Carved between 490 and 480 B.C., it was probably dedicated to Athena. It is evident in the figure that advances had been made in naturalistic observation since the time when the Delian Victory (Fig. 251) was carved. This is particularly true of the way the head is represented. The eye socket is deeper, the upper lid has definite thickness and seems to cover the eyeball instead of being just an incised line on its surface. The lips curve down at the ends instead of up and give the face an expression of sullen willfulness. Certain archaic conventions persist, however. The hair is stylized in waves which fall over the shoulders and the drapery is indicated by straight parallel lines. The upper arm is attached to the body in the same arbitrary way as in earlier work. Even in the head, which appears more naturalistic in the rendition of the planes of the face, the contours of mouth and eyes are unbroken and the sides of the nose are continued upward in a well-defined line and turned out to indicate the intersection of brow and eye-socket. All of these details are traditional conventions that were retained in spite of the close observation of natural appearance evident in the treatment of the lips and eyes. Doubtless they were less obtrusive when the figure had its original painting, for it was colored as were the majority of Greek statues. Traces of polychrome ornament are still visible on the Euthydikos figure and on the metope from Selinunte (Fig. 252).

FIG. 253.—STATUE DEDICATED BY
EUTHYDIKOS.
*Acropolis Museum, Athens.*

The climax of the archaic style in Greek sculpture appears in two groups of figures dating from about 480 B.C. which once occupied the pediments of the temple of Aphaia at Aegina. Each group represented a battle, and the two probably portrayed incidents in the Trojan War. A *Dying Warrior* from the eastern one (Fig. 254) reveals even more than the Euthydikos figure the considerable degree of knowledge concerning the structure of the human body amassed by the close of the archaic period. The law of frontality has been discarded and free movement on both sides of the main axis of the figure and in either direction is possible. The muscles are well represented though they appear rather hard, as they would be in the athletic type of figure upon which the sculptor based his ideal. The greatest degree of naturalism in the statue is seen in the accurately observed proportions of the body and the details of muscular and bony structure. In the head, a number of archaic conventions are still visible.

The rounded planes of the brow and nose are flattened out, intersecting in a sharp ridge. The beard is portrayed by a sharp angular projection on which wavy incisions indicate the hair. The archaic smile also persists, but it is modified by the shadow of the short mustache to become an appropriate grimace of pain. Naturalistic though many of the details of the figure are, it possesses great unity in design. The sweeping curves of the lower side of the body create this unity, establishing a rhythm that begins slowly in the slight curve of the leg, becomes more rapid in the body to culminate in the half circle of the helmet, and comes to a final close in the disk of the shield. The decorative rhythm of this

Fig. 254.—Dying Warrior. From the East Pediment, Temple at Aegina. *Glyptothek, Munich.*

progression of curves is accented by the straight lines and angular silhouette of the upper edge of the body.

The archaic statues that have been considered all demonstrate the tendency in Greek art to eliminate considerations of space. In the earliest statues such as the Victory of Delos (Fig. 251) the thickness of the figure is obviously controlled by that of the block from which it was carved. The sculptor was thus considerably hampered in the dimension of depth so he practically eliminated it and designed his figure to be seen only from the front. In later figures, such as the Apollo in New York (Fig. 250) and the Aegina Warrior (Fig. 254) the rounding off of the legs and arms in the interests of more naturalistic representation is utilized by the sculptor to create a sense of the third dimension but only in so far as it emphasizes the mass of the figures. Furthermore, this effect is apparent only if the figures are viewed directly from front or side; from an angle it is hardly perceptible. This goes to show how similar the methods of sculpture and architecture were in the

Greek world. Both were based on a conception of form that is two-dimensional, involving a simplification of space carried to the point of eliminating it. It was by this simplification that the Greek sculptor emphasized the mass and volume of his figures and thus invested them with the grandeur and impressiveness apparent from the time of the earliest works.

By the end of the archaic period, the ideal of Greek sculpture was one characterized by a considerable degree of naturalism, even though it was still expressed by means of many inflexible conventions. In subsequent periods, these conventions disappear to some extent, to be replaced by others based on closer observation of nature but none the less conventional for that. In the Aegina sculptures, the change has already begun to take place as far as the body is concerned even though the general impression is one of over-hardness. In the period subsequent to the archaic, known as the transitional, this change extends to the face and head as well as to the general proportions of the entire figure.

## B. The Transitional Period

The transitional period in Greek sculpture began about 480 B.C. and is generally considered to have lasted until 450 B.C. when the Golden Age of Greek art began. The term transitional can be used in reference to this period only with reservations against any implication that the art of that time is important only as a connecting link between the archaic style and that of the Golden Age. This is not the case, for transitional sculpture reveals an originality of conception and a quality of execution which are equal to those in the works of any other period in the history of Greek sculpture in forcefulness of expression.

A notable example of transitional style is the bronze *Delphi Charioteer* (Fig. 255), which dates from about 475 B.C. The statue is life size and was part of a group consisting of chariot, driver and horses which commemorated a chariot race victory. Although it was erected in honor of the accomplishment of one man, it is not a portrait in the exact sense of the term. Rather it embodies the type of aristocratic youth that took part in the athletic contests of the day. It is also typical rather than representative in not showing the figure in the rapid movement of the race but standing calmly in the chariot holding the reins. In the construction of the head, there is a closer approximation to actuality than has appeared hitherto, the realism being heightened by the colored eyeballs and the silver teeth seen between the slightly opened lips. The feet and the arm are also portrayed very naturalistically, as compared with archaic works. This naturalism does not detract, however, from the unified design of the figure as a whole that resides in the organically related volumes of the body and the decorative pattern of hair and draperies. At first glance, the latter seem to be in regular unvarying folds but they are actually very subtly distinguished from each other

to give interest to the pattern without destroying its simplicity. There is still no effort to reveal the body underneath the draperies. Both exist as separate entities, although the long robe seems to envelop the body in contrast to the tightly stretched sheaths that represent garments in the archaic style (Fig. 251).

The largest single body of transitional sculpture now existent is that which once decorated the temple of Zeus at Olympia, finished about 460 B.C.; it includes a number of figures from the pediments and several metopes. In the *Pediments* (Fig. 256) there was a problem in arrangement as well as in execution of the individual figures, namely, to relate them in such a way that the groups would fit naturally in the flat triangular space of the pediments as to both subject and the size of the figures. The Olympia sculptors solved this problem by making a god the central figure in each pediment, Zeus in the eastern one, which is above in the illustration, and Apollo in the western one. As divinities, they are larger than the mortals around them and are thus appropriately placed in the middle of the pediment from the

FIG. 255.—CHARIOTEER.
*Museum, Delphi.*

points of view both of design and of the subject matter. They appear as arbiters of the contests represented; the eastern pediment is the scene of preparation for the chariot race between Pelops and Oenomaus that was to decide the fate of the former as a suitor for Hippodamia, the latter's daughter; in the western one is the legendary battle between the Lapiths and the Centaurs. At the extreme ends of the pediments are reclining figures. In the eastern one they symbolize the two rivers Alpheios and Kladeos which bounded the area in which the chariot race was run. In the western pediment there are reclining feminine figures in the angles representing spectators. Between the two groups there is a contrast in

FIG. 256.—OLYMPIA. Temple of Zeus. Pediment Groups, restored.

action, one being quiet and the other violently animated, which is standard in subsequent examples of pedimental decoration. In both of those at Olympia, the design as a whole is rather obviously symmetrical, with a central figure and those on either side balancing each other in pose and action. None the less, the individual groups are well related to each other to form a unified whole, particularly in the western pediment where the calm figure of Apollo in the center and the passively reclining ones in the ends effectively stabilize the movement of the struggling groups.

The *Apollo from the Western Pediment* (Fig. 257) continues the standing nude male type of the archaic period (Fig. 250) but with certain changes. Where the pose of the archaic figure is mechanically exact, there is variety and elasticity in the transitional one, the weight resting on the right leg while the left one is partially relaxed, but without compromising its firmness. The Olympian Apollo also reveals a more extended observation of the muscular structure of the torso than was apparent even in the most advanced archaic work (Fig. 254). An athletic ideal is embodied in both the Aeginetan and Olympian figures, but the sculptor of the latter avoided the exaggerated hardness which makes the skin of the earlier figure resemble a tanned hide over strips of leather instead of firm flesh covering well-developed muscles. It is the latter effect which the sculptor of the Apollo succeeded in obtaining, particularly in the arms, the breast and the horizontal bands of muscle across the upper abdomen. It also appears in the head in spite of archaic formalisms in the ringlets of hair, the protruding eyeballs and the unbroken contour of the eyelids. The planes of the cheeks and mouth merge into each other and the hard intersection of the forehead and eye socket, characteristic of archaic work, has been softened. The draperies over the right shoulder and left forearm lie in naturalistic

Fig. 257.—Apollo. From the West Pediment, Temple of Zeus, Olympia. *Museum, Olympia.*

folds, although the broad planes and the sharp lines of the edges suggest the earlier, more stylized methods. There is still something of rigidness, but it is due here to the architectonic nature of the figure and is an important feature of the pattern that welds the details with their incidental naturalism into integral parts of a larger scheme. There are certain conventions that appear in addition to those mentioned above, notably the emphasis on the band that marks the lower edge of the abdomen and the continuation of the forehead line in the nose. The former is a characteristic that can be observed in well-developed athletic figures and is hence a naturalistic convention while the latter was adopted quite early by the Greeks as an arbitrary feature of beauty.

From the eastern pediment at Olympia, the figure symbolizing the river *Alpheios* (Fig. 258) also brings out the increasing naturalism evident in the transitional period. It is almost identical in pose with the Dying Warrior from Aegina (Fig. 254) but the details reveal many points of difference. The breast muscles are rendered as soft and pliant masses in the Olympia figure rather than as dry, hard lumps. There is also a suggestion that the muscles of the left side are more strained than those of the right, a characteristic not found in the earlier figure. In both, the long curves of the lower side of the body are contrasted with the straight lines forming angles of the upper side, but this contrast is not as obvious in the transitional work. The ideal of the sculptor was a more naturalistic one than in the earlier period, and formal abstraction is not so emphasized.

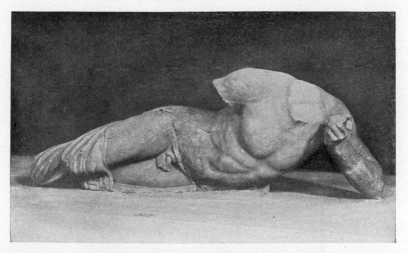

FIG. 258.—ALPHEIOS. From the East Pediment, Temple of Zeus, Olympia. *Museum, Olympia.*

The sculptural decoration of the temple of Zeus at Olympia included twelve carved metopes, six of which were placed over the entrance at either end of the cella. They represented the twelve labors of Heracles and were very similar in style to the pediment sculptures although probably a little earlier in date. One of those labors involved obtaining the golden apples of the Hesperides which could be done only with the aid of Atlas, the giant who supported the firmament on his shoulders according to Greek mythology. The metope sculpture represents *Heracles, Atlas and Athena* (Fig. 259); Heracles bows under the weight of the world symbolized by the architectural entablature above the frieze, taking the place of Atlas while the latter obtained the golden apples which he is shown holding out to the hero. Athena stands behind Heracles and relieves the weight on his shoulders. As in the pediment groups, the design is architectonic, the paramount consideration being its decorative relationship to the architecture. The three erect figures repeat the vertical accents of the colonnade below and of the flanking triglyphs. The modeling is direct and straightforward without many details, for most of these were painted on the figures instead of being carved. Again comparison with an archaic work such as the metope from Selinunte (Fig. 252) will reveal the more extensive observation of naturalistic details that characterizes transitional sculpture. The male figures are portrayed in full profile, even to the eyes which are no longer shown in the front view but are almost correctly foreshortened. Their

Fig. 259.—Heracles, Atlas and Athena. Metope from the Temple of Zeus, Olympia. *Museum, Olympia.*

heads are angular and somewhat archaic in form, but that of Athena has a rounded softness that anticipates the later style of the Golden Age. Very notable is the masterly design of the figures themselves in which broad planes and sharp contours articulate the masses of torso, limbs and head into a unified whole. The drapery of the female figure seems almost naturalistic yet its straight ordered folds are marvelously simple in arrangement, the realistic effect arising from subtle variations in the details.

The most immediately apparent difference between archaic and transitional sculpture is in the technique of representation, which is much more naturalistic in the later period although still highly conventionalized. Less obvious but of equal importance is the difference in content. In the archaic period, the sculptor was chiefly concerned with problems of bodily structure and appearance; the content of his figures is born of his effort to express his ideas by a relatively limited technique. In the transitional period, the technical difficulties that beset the earlier sculptor were no longer so numerous, many of them having disappeared with more extended and closer observation of the human figure. But with this increased knowledge there also came a need for more than a mere approximation of the appearance of the body. To satisfy this need, the transitional sculptor made a definite attempt to suggest personality. In the Olympian Apollo, the elevation of the god above the struggling groups around him conveys his superiority to mortal beings. The Delphi Charioteer likewise stands oblivious of the excitement and turmoil of the race just run. The ideal unity of personality thus suggested is reinforced by the ideal unity of environment which makes each figure complete in itself even though part of a group, and the ideal unity of time that is achieved by representing action at a moment immediately before or after the one of greatest activity. In the Charioteer, it is that just after the conclusion of the race; in the east pediment group at Olympia, it is the one just before the race begins. Even in subjects that are entirely in terms of movement such as the Discus Thrower, which is a well-known example of transitional sculpture, the instant portrayed is that in which opposing forces are balanced. In each case, the aim of the artist was to suggest both previous and subsequent action and thus attain an ideal unity of time.

With the attainment of an ideally unified time, environment and personality in transitional sculpture, there came a seriousness of expression and bearing. The Olympian Apollo is aloof and dignified, above the petty dissensions of humanity yet conscious of the importance of his position as arbiter. It is this realization of a profound inner meaning that is the most vital point of difference between archaic and transitional figures. The former (Fig. 250) are brisk and sprightly, their faces often animated by the archaic smile; the latter are heavier and almost somber in expression. In the prevailing tenseness of the archaic figure, there is an impression of an organism almost mechanical in function; in the transitional figure, the balance of contracted and relaxed muscles suggests an inner will that controls the mechanism. The more naturalistic details of the body thus acquire greater meaning in that they appear to be the instruments of personality. The whole statue thus embodies a conception which attains monumental effect in the large, simple, well-ordered pattern of volumes that makes the conception objective and tangible. It remained only for the Golden Age to give it even greater power by making it abstract.

### C. THE GOLDEN AGE

During the Golden Age of Greece from 450 to 400 B.C., the ideals that are outlined and suggested in the art and thought of the archaic and transitional periods were completely stated. The architectural ideal

FIG. 260.—THE DORYPHOROS.
After Polykleitos.
*Museum, Naples.*

is embodied in the Parthenon, the Erechtheum and the Propylaea (Figs. 38, 39, 41) all on the Acropolis of Athens. In literature, the great tragedies of Sophocles and Euripides were written then. In sculpture, Polykleitos and Pheidias produced their masterpieces. Architecture, drama and sculpture all reveal a matured concept of life, a philosophy that had been formed and tested. In the Golden Age, the Greek of Athens was sure of himself because the traditions of his race had been firmly established as valid and significant. The artistic expression of those traditions was thus completely integrated and in that integration lies the explanation of its greatness.

In the development from archaic through transitional sculpture, the changes that have been observed show the general trend to have been toward an ideal that was at once naturalistic and abstract. In the Golden Age that ideal was attained. In a copy of a statue carved by Polykleitos between 450 and 440 B.C. of an athlete carrying a spear (Fig. 260) which is known as the *Doryphoros* or Spearbearer, it is evident that the sculptor of the Golden Age had mastered the representation of the human figure. The pose, in which the weight rests entirely on the right leg while the left one is relaxed, is that of taking a forward step, an effect that results from emphasizing the slight variation between the two legs that is apparent in the Olympian Apollo (Fig. 257). The arms are also differentiated, the right one being inactive while the left holds the spear. The head is turned slightly to the right, the contour of the skull being revealed by the tight, closely adhering ringlets of hair. The deep eye sockets enclose the eyeballs and the upper lids overlap the lower ones at the outer end instead of forming an unbroken contour. These details together with others such as the indication of the muscles and veins show an extensive and rather accurate knowledge of human anatomy.

The muscles are well developed as would be expected in a statue of an athlete, although their prominence may be due to the fact that the Doryphoros as here represented is not the original but a Roman copy. It is from such copies that most of what is known today about the work of the great Greek sculptors is derived, the originals having long since disappeared. These copies vary in quality, depending upon the skill of the copyist, but at best they are only approximations of the originals. According to contemporary descriptions, this copy of the Doryphoros, which was found in the palaestra or athletic field at Pompeii and is now in the Naples Museum, reproduces the principal characteristics of Polykleitos' figure though some details, such as the muscles, bear traces of Roman style. The conventional heavy band below the abdomen is very prominent and also the breast muscles. Throughout, the form of the muscles is well observed and properly related to the movement of the body. To this relationship is due, in part at least, the impression of life in the statue, but even more does it come from the design as a whole. The right leg and arm are both straight, but the arm hangs limp while the leg plays a functional part in sustaining the weight of the body. On the left side, both arm and leg are bent, but there it is the arm that is functional. The rhythm of this balanced cross-relationship of tense and relaxed muscles is emphasized by the contrast between the lowered shoulder on the right side and the slightly raised left one. The result is to suggest that the figure has perfect freedom of movement. At the same time, its poise is assured, for the center of balance of the figure as a whole lies within its own mass, the vertical axis that indicates it passing along the inner side of the right leg.

In the Doryphoros it is evident that many of the problems of naturalistic representation of the human figure had been solved. The increased knowledge of bodily structure that made this possible brought with it not only greater realism but also an intensified awareness of the ideal

requirements of a work of art. This was set forth by Polykleitos in a
book called *The Canon*, meaning a rule, in which he gave the proportions of the Doryphoros as those of the ideal male figure. Characteristically enough, these proportions are based on mathematical relationship, just as in the Doric temple. Thus in addition to the organic
connection between the different parts of the body and the general
solidness and sense of weight, the bodily elements are commensurates
of a mathematical ratio. The head is one-seventh the height of the
whole body, a heavier proportion than in either archaic or transitional
figures where the ratio was one to ten and one to eight respectively.
Similarly, the sizes of all the details are determined by a fixed ratio,
the unit being one of those details, such as a finger or a hand.

The main characteristics of fifth-century sculpture of the Golden
Age appear in the Doryphoros; but as a Roman copy, it stands to reason
that its effect must vary to some extent from that of the original. One
thing which the copyist introduced, for example, is the tree stump beside the right leg. This he was forced to do for the sake of strengthening
the statue, which is of marble. Without it, the legs of brittle stone
would have broken under the weight of the body. This same consideration led to insertion of the bar between the right arm and the hip.
The heavy muscles have already been mentioned as a possible exaggeration by the copyist. It is manifestly impossible through such
examples to judge the full effect of the style of the Golden Age; for
this originals must be had.

The most impressive Greek originals of the Golden Age are the
sculptures which were once on the Parthenon in Athens (Figs. 39, 40).
There were groups in both pediments (Fig. 29), a continuous frieze
around the outside of the cella wall and figures in high relief on each
metope. The pediment figures were probably carved between 438 and
433 B.C., the others being a little earlier. The subjects of all the sculptures were related in some way to Athena, to whom the Parthenon
was dedicated. The east pediment represented her birth and the western
one her contest with Poseidon for the sponsorship of the city of Athens.
The frieze portrayed the Panathenaic Procession which ascended the
rocky slopes of the Acropolis once every four years as a part of the
ceremonies attendant upon the renewal of the sacred peplos or robe
which enshrouded the great ivory and gold statue of Athena in the
cella and was woven by the maidens of the city. The metopes were
devoted to various mythological subjects, combats between gods and
giants, Greeks and Amazons and Lapiths and Centaurs. Very little of
this sculpture remains on the Parthenon, much of it having been placed
in the British Museum by Lord Elgin. Many of the figures were badly
damaged by the explosion that nearly demolished the building in 1687

Fig. 261.—Mount Olympus. From the East Pediment of the Parthenon. British Museum, London.

and attempts previous to Lord Elgin's to lower the pediment sculptures resulted in irreparable damage to them.

The mind that conceived the decoration of the Parthenon was that of Pheidias, an artist whose genius was recognized by nearly all the writers of ancient times. Under his direction, the embellishment of Athens took place between 449 and 434 B.C., to which purpose the funds of the Athenian Naval Confederacy had been diverted by Pericles. His was the ruling spirit in the multitude of artists including Iktinos and Kallikrates, the architects of the Parthenon, and the numerous sculptors who actually carved the figures that decorated it. A noted sculptor himself, Pheidias' contribution to the sculptured ornament of the Parthenon was apparently only the ivory and gold statue of Athena that stood in the cella (cf. Fig. 40), but there can be no doubt that the conception of every figure on the building was his even if he did not execute them with his own hands.

In the eastern pediment was a group representing the birth of Athena. As in the Olympia group of the chariot race, setting and time were indicated by symbolic figures, the event taking place at dawn on Mount Olympus. At the left end of the pediment, the horses of the sun rise out of the ocean as those of the setting moon sink below the waves at the right end. Immediately beside the horses of the sun is a reclining male figure (Fig. 261) which is usually known as Theseus, the Athenian hero, but is more plausibly identified as a symbol of *Mount Olympus*, the dwelling place of the gods, lighted by the rays of the rising sun. In this figure is summed up all that had been achieved by earlier periods in the representation of the male body. The muscles are portrayed by the Polykleitan conventions as in the three horizontal bands across the breast, stomach and abdomen. However, the muscles of Polykleitos' figures are somewhat dry and exaggerated as is natural in an athletic type. In the Mount Olympus, the muscles are clearly indicated and their function is well understood, but the over-statement noticeable in the earlier styles is avoided. They are pliant and flexible; the skin and the firm, resilient flesh have definite thickness instead of being hard and thin like a tanned hide. The ideal portrayed is that of a perfectly developed man in contrast to the Polykleitan concept, which is that of a perfectly trained athlete. The figure is seated on a stone covered with a drapery that falls in highly naturalistic folds; its well-suggested texture forms a fine contrast with the smooth firm flesh of the man. The head, in spite of its damaged condition, reveals many of the same characteristics observed in the Doryphoros. Its proportion to the total height of the body is about one to seven. The hair clings closely to the skull, clearly revealing its contour and emphasizing its mass. The nose continues the line of the brow according to the Greek concept of beauty. The eye rests in its socket and the upper lid slightly overlaps the lower one at the outer end. As in the body, the modeling of the planes of the cheek and mouth is realistic without being merely representative. Again there is a carefully studied balance of movement resulting in a state of perfect poise. The facial expression is quiet and impersonal, for in fifth-century Greek art the face and head were not emphasized as expressive elements but were considered as contributory to an effect created by the entire body. The sense of serene repose in the Mount Olympus comes from the figure as a whole and would be as powerful even if the head were missing.

The three female figures on the right side of the east pediment of the Parthenon (Fig. 262) bear out the generalization concerning the

Fig. 262.—The Three Fates. From the East Pediment of the Parthenon. *British Museum, London.*

Mount Olympus. They represent the *Three Fates* who were believed by the Greeks to be present at every birth. All the heads are missing, yet it is doubtful if their presence would have made the figures any more impressive for, as in most Greek art, the concept of the whole is implied in the rhythms of the parts. There is a carefully studied contrast of movement in the group; the figure to the left is about to rise; the middle one has just turned toward her and the third is still in complete repose. This movement is a factor in the composition of the pediment group as a whole, a movement which related the outer figures to the central group of Zeus and Athena. It does not detract in the slightest from the compactness of the group itself or the unity of the individual figures. This last is due to two factors, the lofty conception of the figures themselves as physical entities and the complete harmony between that conception and the arrangement of the draperies. These are in many folds and at first glance seem very naturalistic, but examination will reveal them to have been disposed in a very subtle pattern. This is formed by the numerous folds and is of great interest in its own right but is none the less subordinated to the bodies underneath. This is seen in the way that the simplicity or complexity of the folds is determined by the functional importance of the part of the body covered. Over the legs the folds are broad, giving way to smooth planes over the knees and becoming quite involved over the thighs and abdomen. The breasts are indicated by plain surfaces in contrast to the swirls between them. The forms themselves are never obscured by the drapery but rather are made more clear through them, just as a subordinate theme played in counterpoint against a major one in a Bach fugue results in their mutual enrichment. In addition to their function of clarifying the structure of the figures, the draperies also serve to establish the three-dimensional volumes of the bodies, their curved lines leading inevitably to a sense of definite and solid mass beneath. The whole group is a masterpiece of effective detail, handled in such a way that it gives character and weight to a broad and comprehensive idea without losing its own individuality.

And what of the bodies themselves? A famous sculptor is reported to have said when he first saw the Three Fates, "They look as if they were modeled on human bodies, but where is one to find such bodies?" This was just the impression the sculptor wished to give, of beings in human form but without the individual and accidental imperfections that characterize mortal bodies. If the gods can be represented as humans, they must have forms of surpassing beauty, idealized. This the Parthenon sculptor realized and his statues of the gods represent an ideal of the human figure which could exist only in the minds of men, never in mortal flesh. It was for this reason that the writers of antiquity called Polykleitos the sculptor of men and Pheidias the sculptor of gods, for in the figures of the latter they beheld the embodiment of all the characteristics of the perfect physical beauty which they imagined the gods to possess.

Even in their present condition, the figures of the Three Fates convey the impression of sublime repose that characterizes all the great sculpture of the Golden Age. The heads doubtless contributed to this impression originally. While no original by Pheidias exists to prove this, a marble head, copied from that of a bronze statue by Pheidias known as the *Athena Lemnia* (Fig. 263), gives weight to such a supposition. The original figure was erected on the Athenian Acropolis as a memorial by the colony from Lemnos. That it was celebrated for its beauty in classic antiquity is indicated by a passage in Lucian praising it particularly for the outline of the head, the delicate modeling of the cheeks and the finely proportioned nose. All of these character-

FIG. 263.—HEAD OF THE ATHENA LEMNIA. After Pheidias.
*Museo Civico, Bologna.*

istics appear in the marble head, which is in the Municipal Museum at Bologna in Italy, even though it is a Roman copy. The details of construction are similar to those of the Mount Olympus from the east pediment of the Parthenon. The austere expression is an integral part of the classic ideal embodied in the figure. In its impersonality there is something of the same sense of powerful abstract force that is evident in the Parthenon and informs the lines of Sophocles' Oedipus Rex with such awful meaning.

To return now to the sculpture of the Parthenon itself, the style of the metopes is somewhat less advanced than that of the pediment figures. They were executed at an earlier date, probably having been begun at the same time as the building itself in 448 B.C. The example illustrated (Fig. 264) is from those on the south side and represents a

FIG. 264.—LAPITH BATTLING A CENTAUR. Metope from the Parthenon. *British Museum, London.*

*Lapith Battling a Centaur.* The figures are rather dry and hard, the style being one that would be expected of men trained in the manner of the transitional period. These characteristics are seen chiefly in the treatment of the muscles, for the head of the Lapith is not unlike that of the Mount Olympus (Fig. 261) in the east pediment. The designs of the best metopes represent a considerable advance over the somewhat inelastic formulas employed for similar purposes in earlier periods. The violent action of the figures is kept within the limits of the metope space by the vertical left arm of the Lapith and the emphatic curve of the Centaur's rump. The figures are so arranged as to make balanced geometrical forms which clarify the relationship between them. Such is the purpose of the parallel between the outstretched arms and the angle formed by the Lapith's right leg to support the Centaur's weight. The relief is high in order that the figures might not be overwhelmed by the massive architectural setting and that they might readily be seen from the ground.

Fig. 265.—Horsemen. Frieze. *Parthenon, Athens.*

The frieze that once surrounded the outside of the cella was probably carved between 442 and 438 B.C. The greater part of it was removed by Lord Elgin when the pediment figures were taken down and is now in the British Museum in London. It represented the Panathenaic Procession and began over the west end of the cella with a group of horsemen and charioteers, the victors in the Panathenaic Games that were a part of the ceremony. The procession moves eastward along the sides. The rulers of the city, priests and musicians, and the sacrificial animals appear in different groups, while over the east end of the cella are the maidens who wove the peplos, the magistrates and seated figures representing the gods.

The frieze is carved in low relief (Fig. 265), the figures projecting a little more from the background at the top of the band than at the bottom. This was necessary because they were illuminated from below by light which came between the columns of the peristyle, and the lower part of the frieze projected less than the upper part in order not to cast obscuring shadows on it. In the illustration, the lighting is incorrect because it is from above, thus creating an effect quite different from the one intended, for certain details are over-prominent, such as the veins of the horse's belly. The maximum projection of the objects represented is not more than about two and one-quarter inches, yet there is a pronounced effect of depth. It is sufficient, for example, to make the spatial relationship of the horse and the man behind it quite plausible. This was managed by carving the relief in a series of receding planes which are not parallel but are cut at very slight angles to each other. This refinement is so slight as to be hardly perceptible, yet combined with the extraordinarily delicate modeling of the figures it serves to establish them as three-dimensional forms which seem to have a depth much greater than their actual few inches.

Another characteristic of the frieze is the uniform level of the heads throughout, whether the figures are standing or seated. This principle of design is known as isocephalism and it is invoked here as an architecturally decorative requirement. The figures on horseback are thus smaller than the standing ones, but so well is the frieze as a whole composed and so convincing is each figure in itself that the disparities in size are not at all prominent. In the same way, the smallness of the horses in relationship to the human figures is hardly noticed in the effect of the frieze as a whole.

The date of the frieze midway between the metopes and the pediment figures explains the style which is somewhat more advanced than the former and less so than the latter. Nor is it uniform throughout, suggesting that a number of sculptors worked on it. They were probably men of lesser talent than those who executed the more prominent pediment figures and the style is definitely related to that of the preceding period. The figure to the left (Fig. 265) is reminiscent of the Polykleitan Canon in pose, but the modeling of the muscles is rather hard and the abdominal convention quite prominent. The somewhat exaggerated swing of the hips reveals the hand of an imitator of Polykleitos rather than a sculptor who was his equal in originality. The two figures to the right show an archaic persistence in the full-front view of the eye in a profile head. There are, however, some very naturalistic details such as the rough beard stubble on the older man's face, the veins on the stomach and legs of the horse and the leg muscles of the figure to the left.

The naturalistic details that occur in the figures of the frieze might lead to the conclusion that the aim of the entire work was to achieve a photographically realistic portrayal of the procession. But this could not have been the case, for there is no reference anywhere in it to the impressive setting in which it took place. The background is quite plain although it would seem to have been quite appropriate to represent the Acropolis itself and the various buildings on it in order to identify the event. This would have been directly contrary to the wish of the designer, however, whose intention was to create an ideal representation of the ceremony by which the city paid homage to its divine patroness rather than a concrete and specific illustration of it.

Even in portraiture which would logically be considered as one form of art in which specific and realistic elements should predominate, the Greek did not vary from the impersonal

idealism of the Parthenon sculptures. When Kresilas created a portrait of *Pericles* (Fig. 266), the result was not a record in bronze of the way the great Athenian statesman actually looked, even though certain personal traits are suggested such as the slight tilt of the head and the full sensuous lips. The statue is rather an ideal embodiment of the powerful personality that made Athens the foremost city of the Greek world for a few brief years in the fifth century. The original bronze figure no longer exists but there are several copies in stone such as the one illustrated, which is in the British Museum in London. Although Pericles was well past middle age when the portrait was made, about 440 B.C., the creases and wrinkles that would normally appear in the face are absent. Such individual accidents of

FIG. 266.—PERICLES. After Kresilas.
*British Museum, London.*

appearance were omitted by the artist in order to emphasize the ideal qualities he wished to suggest. It is not a portrait of Pericles the man as much as it is the representation of Pericles the statesman. The idea for which he stood was more important to the sculptor than the incidental facts of the way he looked.

The impersonal idealism seen in the Parthenon sculptures and the portrait of Pericles is the outstanding characteristic of sculpture during the Golden Age. The nature of the ideal embodied is suggested in the sixth book of Plato's *Republic*: "Painters must fix their eyes on perfect truth as a perpetual standard of reference, to be contemplated with the minutest care, before they proceed to deal with earthly canons about things beautiful." This conception of the artist's aims accounts for many characteristics of fifth-century art. The background is omitted from the Parthenon frieze to avoid suggesting the specific setting in time and space which would rob it of ideal unity. Similarly the free figures of the pediments, and such works as the Lemnian Athena, are impersonal and self-contained, for the establishment of any relationship between them and their surroundings or the observer would destroy the sense of integrated, self-sufficient personality that gives them ideal significance. The reason that the unity of frieze and free-standing figures alike would be destroyed by any reference to background and surroundings is that such reference would introduce an element of the specific which by its very presence would imply the existence of its opposite, namely, the indefinite. It has been pointed out before, in discussing Greek architecture and in the opening remarks concerning Greek sculpture, that one of the most fundamental characteristics of the Greek temperament was its abhorrence of the indefinite. Reality consisted only in what could be grasped by the senses, in the concrete and the tangible. But even what could be seen was not real if it implied something that could not be seen. Thus the neutral background of the Parthenon frieze, with its avoidance of any suggestion of background, also avoids suggesting the existence of space, for it exists as stone rather than as a portrayal of setting. The result is a unity which is ideal because it did not and could never have existed, but which is none the less expressed entirely in terms of concrete experience.

The value placed by the Greek upon concreteness as a proof of validity is exemplified by the concept of death revealed in the gravestones or funereal stelae of the fifth and fourth centuries. One of the finest is in the National Museum in Athens, the *Hegeso Stele* (Fig. 267), which is named from the woman in whose memory it was erected. She is represented as looking at her jewels in a box held by the maid who stands before her. The style is that of the fifth century though somewhat later than the Parthenon figures. The execution is less sophisticated than in the Parthenon sculptures for the artist was not one of the great figures of the Golden Age, as can be seen in the clumsily articulated wrists and the very summary modeling of the arms. The bodies have something of the maturity seen in the more monumental works of the period but the eyes are represented in the full-front view rather than in profile. The draperies are treated in a manner more characteristic of the later fifth century, being of some thin and clinging material that falls in minute folds and clearly indicates the bodies underneath. The design is in broad and sweeping curves, particularly fine details being the beautiful chair of the mistress and the subtle line of the robe hanging from the maid's shoulders. The figure

of Hegeso is not a portrait but an ideal type somewhat like that of the
Athena Lemnia.

There is no suggestion in the stele of the idea that death means the
end of mortal life. In fact, there is no suggestion of death at all. Hegeso

Fig. 267.—The Hegeso Stele. *National Museum, Athens.*

is represented in an act which was normal to her everyday life and
has no reference to the fact that it is ended. This conception is one
which makes objective the statement that the philosophy of the Greek
carried him to the mouth of the tomb and no farther. Reality for him
was that which could be grasped by the senses; before the great indefinite void of death, he was powerless. Thus in the eleventh book
of the *Odyssey* when Odysseus attempts to comfort the shade of Achilles

by telling him that he is a prince among the dead, the latter replies, "Nay, speak not comfortably to me of death, oh great Odysseus. Rather would I live on ground as the hireling of another, with a landless man who had no great livelihood, than bear sway among all the dead that be departed." Occasionally the idea of death is symbolized as the departure on a journey with friends saying farewell, but the subject is treated with great restraint. There is never the bitter grief or cloying sentimentality that appears so often in the funereal art of later periods.

In the Golden Age, the development that began in the archaic period and continued through the transitional one reached its climax. The stiff mechanical figures of the sixth century acquired greater weight and the ability to move in the early years of the fifth and then became the supple, quietly reposing ones of the Golden Age. With the changes in appearance of the figures, there went a corresponding change of mien and bearing. The rigid tension of the archaic figure in New York (Fig. 250) gives way to a sense of stern force in the Olympian Apollo (Fig. 257) which in turn is replaced in the Mount Olympus (Fig. 261) by a quiet repose that makes the strength of the figure seem the greater for not being explicit. Herein lies the greatness of sculpture in the Golden Age, that it gives final and definitive form to the ideals that are only. suggested in the previous periods. Where the archaic and transitional sculptors could portray only in part the beauty of which they dreamed, the sculptor of the Golden Age was able to reveal it in all its glory. Of the great ivory and gold statue of Zeus by Pheidias in the temple of Zeus at Olympia, Dio Chrysostom said, "No one, having seen it, will conceive him otherwise thereafter." This is true of all great art and is the secret of the consistent greatness of the sculpture of the Golden Age. The subjects therein represented are given ideal form, and they cannot be conceived in any other.

The lofty idealism of the Golden Age could not last indefinitely. Before the close of the fifth century, the spiritual fabric of Greek thought, which was based on belief in an established order revealed from time to time by the gods, was being weakened. Two factors were responsible for this, the materialistic thought of the Sophists on the one hand, and the abstraction of deity into moral order by Plato on the other. Coupled with these was the influence of naturalistic thought culminating in the scientific method of Aristotle. Moreover, the self-assurance of the Athenians, which had been such a vital factor in establishing the cultural and political supremacy of their city, had been badly shaken by the defeat of their armies at Syracuse in 411 B.C. and the destruction of the fleet in 407 B.C.; it was completely broken by the final victory of Sparta at the close of the Peloponnesian War in 404 B.C.

The net result of all these influences was the invasion of the isolated

Athenian civilization, which had reached its climax in the Golden Age, by new and previously unconsidered ideas. The old culture had been founded on belief in divine authority and that authority had been questioned. It was no longer valid in interpreting life and experience. Its place was taken by the mode of thought embodied in the philosophy

Fig. 268.—PAIONIOS. Victory. *Museum, Olympia.*

of Euripides, Plato and Aristotle, world-wide in scope rather than arbitrarily restricted to Athenians or even to Greeks, a mode of thought which shattered the complacent isolation in which the Golden Age had taken form. The basis of this mode of thought was not divine revelation but the study of man and nature. Obviously the art of the older culture could not give adequate expression to such ideas, and modifications of it appear even before the end of the fifth century. Instead of the austere impersonality of Sophocles, there is the pathos and sympathy for human suffering of Euripides, who interprets the myths of the old beliefs in the light of human nature as it is revealed by experience. A similar change occurs in sculpture. The marvelous descriptive technique of the Parthenon figures is utilized no longer to render objective a conception of ideal physical and moral beauty but as an end in itself. The figures are still ideal, it is true, but the ideal itself is on a less elevated plane.

An example of late fifth-century sculpture which indicates the beginning of many of these changes is the Nike or *Victory of Paionios* (Fig. 268), erected at Olympia about 425 B.C. It represents a winged feminine figure, borne down from the sky on the back of an eagle, the bird of Zeus, and about to come to rest upon a tall pedestal. The advances made in realistic representation during the century and a quarter that separates this figure in time from the archaic Victory of Delos (Fig. 251) are obvious. But the Victory of Paionios also represents a change from the methods of mid-fifth-century sculpture, particularly in the treatment of drapery. In the group of the Three Fates (Fig. 262), the robes are of a thick and heavy substance falling in carefully arranged folds and with an individuality independent of the bodies they cover even though contributory to their effect. In the later figure, the drapery is thin and transparent, hardly concealing the body at all. The covered right leg is as carefully modeled as the exposed left one, with only an occasional ridge to indicate the robe.

FIG. 269.—A VICTORY TYING HER SANDAL.
*Acropolis Museum, Athens.*

A little later than the Victory of Paionios are the reliefs which once formed a balustrade around the small Ionic temple of Wingless Victory on the Athenian Acropolis, carved about 410 B.C. The one illustrated shows an attendant *Victory* tying her sandal (Fig. 269). As in the free-standing figure by Paionios, the drapery is thin and transparent. It clings to the body, revealing it in every detail, but without the motivation of rapid movement which explains the similar effect in the other statue. This is not realistic art any more than that of the Parthenon pediments; the sheerest material will not reveal the form it covers as it does in this relief where the effect is as arbitrarily planned as that of the draperies of the Three Fates. The difference between the Nike relief and the Parthenon figures is in the ideal which the sculptor sought to express. In place of majestic repose, there is the simple act of tying the sandal. Such a subject is not appropriate to monumental treatment and the sculptor wisely refrained from attempting it. Instead, he gave full expression to his own delight in mastery of the technique by which solid stone is made more ephemeral than the finest silk, completely revealing the charming, gracefully poised figure. No longer does the observer breathe the rarefied atmosphere of Olympus for here is no goddess but a human being. The Victory tying her sandal represents not an ideal of divinity but rather a divinely beautiful mortal.

## D. THE FOURTH CENTURY

During the fourth century, the ideals expressed in Greek sculpture continue to change along the lines suggested by the Victory of Paionios and the relief of the Victory tying her sandal when they are compared with earlier works. To the ideal and abstract beauty of the fifth century, there succeeds a beauty which is nearer to that of physical reality. Gracefulness of form and the expression of emotion are the sculptor's aims. In achieving these aims, the human model is followed more closely and the figures become more naturalistic and less formalized. As one critic has remarked, "In the fourth century, the gods descend a little from Olympus and become more like human beings."

Two sculptors are outstanding in the first half of the fourth century, Praxiteles and Skopas. Both were celebrated in their own time for figures which, widely divergent in character as they are, exemplify the two tendencies in fourth-century art noted above. Of the work by the two men, it is easier to form a definite opinion of Praxiteles' from existing monuments, for a statue of *Hermes* (Figs. 270, 271) by him was found in the ruins of the temple of Hera at Olympia. It was carved about 350 B.C. The Hermes is unique as the only existent statue known to be by the hand of one of the great Greek sculptors, it having been surely identified as Praxiteles' work by a chance reference in the guidebook that Pausanias wrote about his travels in Greece during the 2nd century A.D. It is of marble and represents the god Hermes carrying the infant Dionysos on his left arm. The child is reaching for some object, probably a bunch of grapes which Hermes held in the missing right hand. The legs were both broken below the knee and have been restored, but the right foot is original.

The pose is like that of fifth-century standing figures (Fig. 260), but the right hip is thrown out, giving the body a broad S-curve sometimes referred to as the curve of Praxiteles. The body itself is not as heavy as in the fifth-century type, the proportions of limbs, torso and head being considerably lighter. With this change in the general proportions of the figure, there appears a method of modeling which is also different from fifth-century practice. In both styles the flesh is

Fig. 270.—PRAXITELES. Hermes. *Museum, Olympia.*

represented by planes that merge into each other to create an effect of roundness. In fifth-century figures (Fig. 261) these planes are relatively few in number and contrasted in direction. In the fourth century they are much more numerous and merge into each other almost imperceptibly. The result is an impression of real flesh translated into stone rather than an abstraction of that impression as in the earlier style. In other words, the sculptured figure is beginning to approximate the appearance of the model instead of attaining to a self-sufficient identity. Where the older sculptors caused flesh to become marble, Praxiteles caused marble to become flesh.

The head (Fig. 271) reveals other characteristics of Praxiteles' style.

Prominent among these is the oval skull with a strongly curved outline tapering toward the chin. The hair is represented by rough, irregular masses which simulate the effect of short curly locks, their texture
contrasting with that of the smooth lustrous skin. The eyes are narrow,
the upper lid projecting so that the glance seems to fall, although it
is clearly not directed toward any definite object. In the resulting effect
of dreamy contemplation, there is no specific emotion. The modeling
of the lips and cheeks is extraordinarily delicate and complex, creating
an arresting impression of physical reality. The nose continues the line

of the brow which is divided horizontally by a deep crease, both conventions
of the classic ideal of beauty. The sense
of texture which makes the figure so
convincingly real is also evident in the
drapery over the tree trunk which is
very carefully studied. It possesses an
individuality of its own yet does not
detract from the more important human
figure, the smooth flesh acquiring
greater effectiveness by contrast with its
involved folds.

All of these details combine to create
an impression of objective reality that
more nearly approximates that of the
living model than any figure which
has been hitherto considered. It is as if
a body of transcendent physical beauty
had been transmuted into an imperishable medium while retaining all its
proper qualities. In the serene detach-

FIG. 271.—PRAXITELES.
HERMES. Detail.
*Museum, Olympia.*

ment of the figure there is almost the majestic repose of the Parthenon
figures, but the lofty remoteness of the fifth century has gone. Austerity
has been replaced by a more immediately appealing bodily comeliness,
vigor by graceful languor. The Praxitelean ideal is not one of an inner
spirit that informs the body with meaning but one of physical gracefulness.

The Hermes was one of Praxiteles' minor works. It is not mentioned
by any of his contemporaries, although a number of his other statues
are highly praised. Of these, only the vaguest impression can be gained
through copies which convey little but the most general features of the
originals. One of these copies is a Satyr in the Capitoline Museum in
Rome, celebrated in literature by Hawthorne as the Marble Faun, and
a dim reflection of the work which Praxiteles himself considered his

best. His most famous statue was the Aphrodite of Knidos, its renown
being largely due to his success in suggesting the graceful softness of
the feminine body. The goddess was represented in the nude, the first
time that a female divinity had been so portrayed in monumental Greek
sculpture although such treatment was forecast by the lightly clothed
Nikes of the last years of the fifth century. The Aphrodite is known
today only through copies. The pose was similar to that of the Hermes,
the indolent posture creating the same languorous and dreamy air. Its
influence upon contemporary and subsequent sculpture was very great,
for in it Praxiteles created the ideal form of the Goddess of Love just
as Pheidias had made objective for all time the Greek conception of
Zeus. So true was this that for many years after the fourth century
Aphrodite was not represented in any form differing significantly from
that conceived by Praxiteles.

Writers of antiquity linked the name of Skopas with that of Praxiteles
as the greatest sculptors of their time. But instead of the graceful and

Fig. 272.—Head from Tegea. *National Museum, Athens.*

languid charm that characterizes Praxiteles' figures, those of Skopas
appear to be in the grip of powerful emotion. Unfortunately there are

no existing statues that can be positively identified as by Skopas and even those in which his style is certainly directly reflected are far from being well preserved. One of these is a male *Head from Tegea* (Fig. 272) where Skopas is said by Pausanias to have been in charge of rebuilding the temple of Athena Alea. From the same source, he is known to have executed some of the pediment sculpture, and although the head illustrated cannot be proved to have been actually carved by him, its style corresponds closely to that of figures by him described in contemporary writings. It prob-ably came from a group represent-ing a battle scene in the western pediment. Comparison with the Lapith's head in the Parthenon Metope (Fig. 264) will reveal the extent to which the fourth-century sculptor goes beyond the earlier one in the suggestion of emotion. The effect is obtained by a somewhat different treatment of details than has been seen hitherto. The entire head is turned to the left and tilted back. The eyes are opened wide, in contrast to the half-closed ones of the Hermes (Fig. 271) and are deeply sunken under oblique brows that cast a shadow over them. The glance is intent, focused upon some definite object. The mouth is open and the upper lip drawn back, rein-forcing the emotional effect created by the treatment of the eyes. The

FIG. 273.—RAVING MAENAD. After Skopas. *Museum, Dresden.*

head is almost square as compared with the ovoid type used by Praxi-teles, its massiveness lending strength to the suggestion of emotion in the general pose and the eyes and mouth.

These characteristics are encountered in copies of other works by Skopas, notably a statuette in Dresden which is a reduction of a *Raving Maenad* (Fig. 273) that stood originally in Byzantium. The Maenads were female followers of Dionysos and the statue by Skopas represented one of them rushing through the woods in an ecstatic frenzy generated by the orgiastic rites of the cult. The head is bent back and the body, revealed by the Doric chiton which is held in place only by a girdle, is strongly twisted on its axis. The details of the head correspond to those of the one from Tegea and the entire pose is expressive of the frantic ecstasy animating the figure. Other works by Skopas that were celebrated in antiquity include sculptures for the tomb of King Mausolos at Halikarnassos and the temple of Diana at Ephesos, but none of the existing fragments of sculpture from these buildings can be safely attributed to him.

The work of Praxiteles and Skopas falls in the first half of the fourth century. In the last half of the period, the outstanding sculptor was Lysippos, the last of the great original Greek sculptors. Although he was incredibly prolific, having made nearly fifteen hundred statues during his lifetime, there is not a single known original by him in existence and even the best available copies cannot be considered as entirely adequate reproductions. The most accurate impression of his style as described by classic writers is given by a statue in the Vatican Museum in Rome which is known as the *Apoxyomenos* (Fig. 274). This name means *The Scraper* and is derived from the sculptor's portrayal of an athlete scraping oil and dust from his body after exercising in the stadium. The figure is lighter and more agile than the fifth-century athletic type (Fig. 260), the head being about one-eighth the height of the total. The lithe body resembles the Praxitelean type in proportions but the muscles are dry and hard as compared with the softer form of the Hermes. Lysippos was known in his own time as a realist, for, according to his contemporaries, he made figures as they were rather than as they ideally ought to be. This may seem incompatible with the fact that like Polykleitos he developed an ideal canon of proportions, but if the Roman copy of the Apoxyomenos can be trusted, this canon was based on a series of conventions that were much more naturalistic than previous ones.

FIG. 274.—THE APOXYOMENOS.
After Lysippos.
*Vatican Museum, Rome.*

The greatest point of difference between Lysippos' statue and those considered hitherto lies in the conception of the figure as a whole. The Doryphoros by Polykleitos (Fig. 260) is represented in the act of taking a step; the contrasted tense and relaxed muscles suggest that it is capable of moving but the figure is rendered immovable by the functional balance of the arms and legs. In the Apoxyomenos (Fig. 274) the movement is actually represented for the figure is twisted in the act of shifting weight from one leg to the other, in contrast with the Polykleitan figure which is capable of moving but does not. There is thus introduced an element of time, an intangibility quite foreign to the ideal if arbitrarily unified concepts of the fifth century. The impression of actual movement is made even stronger by the tenseness of the body and the excited awareness of environment in the face. This latter characteristic implies a consciousness of setting that is also foreign to the fifth-century ideal and which is emphasized in the Apoxyomenos by the three-dimensional spatial concept of the figure. It has been pointed out that the prevailing conception of the statue in earlier styles was one of a two-dimensional unity which could be grasped from a single point of view and no other. Even in such a work as the Three Fates (Fig. 262), the impression of three-dimensional solidness essential to its unity can be felt only from a specific standpoint. The Apoxyomenos, on the other hand, is so designed that its full effect can be grasped only from several points of view successively assumed. From the angle at which the motion of the left arm and its relationship to the right arm is perfectly clear, the movement of the lower part of the body is much less intelligible. It is thus necessary for the observer to move *around* the statue to obtain the full effect of its action, an implicit acknowledgment that it is surrounded by space with which it is definitely related.

The significance of these characteristics of fourth-century style which appear in the sculpture of Praxiteles, Skopas and Lysippos does not consist only in changes in appearance from fifth-century types. These changes are indicative of a different philosophy of life. For the self-sufficient impersonality of the earlier figures, the fourth century substituted the languorous grace of Praxiteles, the passion of Skopas and the space-implying three-dimensional concepts of Lysippos. The presence of any or all of these qualities in a statue renders it incapable of being an isolated entity, for its full significance can be grasped only by assuming the existence of things other than the statue itself. In the Hermes, the suggestion of elements lying outside the figure is a negative one, implied by the air of dreamy reverie that results from lack of the comprehensive assurance that gives a fifth-century figure its impersonal poise. In Skopas' work, the suggestion becomes positive, for the fixed glance of the eyes carries the observer away from the figures. In

Lysippos' figure, the suggestion becomes objective in the three-dimensional conception which establishes a definite relationship between the statue and its environment as well as in the awareness of that environment apparent in the face. All these details reveal clearly that every artist is the child of his age, no matter how original he may be or how great his creative genius. It would have been impossible for the fourth-century artist to work in the style of the fifth because his background of thought was different. By the close of the fourth century, man was becoming increasingly aware of his surroundings and the earlier anthropocentric philosophy which was based on consciousness only of himself was inadequate to interpret experiences that had hitherto been disregarded. The sublime self-sufficiency of the Golden Age was born of a conscious simplification of life. The relative complexity of experience in the fourth century demanded a more elastic philosophical scheme as a basis of interpretation and a more naturalistic style in art to give expression to it. The Aristotelian code replaced the Socratic; the art of Praxiteles, Skopas and Lysippos succeeded to that of Polykleitos and Pheidias.

# Chapter XVII. *Hellenistic Sculpture*

FOR ALL THE GREATNESS OF ITS ACHIEVEMENTS, THE
culture of the Golden Age was a primitive one. Its philosophical method
was one of restriction, in that it was concerned with the interpretation
of human experience within an arbitrarily limited scope. In its most
comprehensive aspect, this culture was Hellenic, that is, it existed in
Hellas or the peninsula of Greece; in its narrowest aspect, it was
Athenian. Similar restrictions are apparent in art of the Golden Age
as well, as has been pointed out. The political dominance of Athens
in the Greek world came to a close at the end of the fifth century,
coincident with the appearance of new modes of thought that shattered the intellectual isolation established in the Golden Age. During
the fourth century, the expansion of artistic productivity in Greece
is marked, geographically as well as in the greater variety of expressive
effects. When the various Greek city-states were subjugated by Mace-
donia and incorporated in the empire of Alexander the Great between
336 and 323 B.C., it was possible to speak of a general Hellenic art.
The great military leader's appreciation of the intellectual and artistic
achievements of the race he had conquered is well known; it is illustrated by his patronage of Aristotle, whose pupil he was, and of
Lysippos, who was the only sculptor permitted to make portraits of
him. The encouragement which he gave to Greek artists and the
spreading of the principles of Greek art over the entire known world
by his military conquests were instrumental in finally destroying the
isolation in which fifth-century art had been born, and which was modified in the fourth century. The third century witnessed the establishment of a new style known as Hellenistic.

Hellenistic is the term applied to the art of the whole Mediterranean
world from the death of Alexander the Great in 323 B.C. to the conquest of Greece by Rome in 146 B.C. During that time, the productive
centers of art were no longer on the Greek mainland but in the new
states that grew up in the Alexandrian empire. The prosperity that
they attained drew the successors of the great fourth-century artists
away from Athens, which sank rapidly in power and prestige in the
subordinate political rôle which she then assumed. Pergamon, Rhodes

FIG. 275.—THE VICTORY OF SAMOTHRACE. *Louvre, Paris.*

and Alexandria were the chief centers of artistic activity, with minor ones in Antioch and Corinth. The sculpture produced in these centers represents a development of the tendencies noted in fourth-century art; the style they embody is Hellenistic because it represents a diffusion of Hellenic ideals both geographically and artistically as a result of influences from other traditions.

By a Rhodian was the famous Nike or *Victory of Samothrace* (Fig. 275) now in the Louvre in Paris. The exact date of its creation cannot be determined, suggestions of equal plausibility having been made for one as early as 325 B.C. and another as late as 258 B.C. It commemorates a naval victory and represents a winged female figure that has just descended from the sky upon the prow of a ship. In the Victory of Samothrace, the culmination of a long series of flying figures is seen, beginning with the Victory of Delos (Fig. 251) and continuing through that of Paionios at Olympia (Fig. 268). Both arms are missing and nothing in the figure gives a clue to their arrangement, but it is probable that the right hand held a trumpet on which a triumphal blast was being sounded. The strongly built body is twisted on its axis as in the figures of Skopas and Lysippos. The draperies are in contrasting light and heavy folds which reveal the body underneath and contribute to the sense of sweeping, forward movement. The achievement of a logical articulation of wings and body had always been a problem in representing flying figures; it is solved in the Nike of Samothrace by balancing the backward thrust of the wings against the forward one of the breasts and the powerful chest. In its successful embodiment of the violent emotions attendant upon battle and victory, the Nike of Samothrace is one of the finest achievements of Hellenistic sculpture.

No less effective than the Nike of Samothrace as the concrete portrayal of an ideal is the *Aphrodite of Melos* (Fig. 276) in the Louvre in Paris, more generally known as the Venus de Milo. It is probably the best-known classic statue in the world, its popularity being due in some measure at least to the enthusiasm created by its discovery in the early 19th century when the Classic Revival was at its height. Its place of origin and date are unknown but it was probably carved during the third or second centuries B.C. As in the case of the Nike of Samothrace, the action of the missing arms can only be surmised; it has been suggested that the right hand was represented holding the draperies while the left rested on a column that served to support the figure. The hair is in conventionalized strands not unlike those of the Lemnian Athena (Fig. 263), but the face is more expressive than in the Pheidian type, being closer in this respect to the Praxitelean. The head is small in relationship to the body, which has the slightness of the Lysippic canon and its twisted stance. The flesh is modeled in broad, simplified planes and has the softness seen in Praxiteles' work without the sensuality which appears in that of many of his followers. Its texture contrasts with that of the draperies which are naturalistically rendered and at the same time arbitrarily arranged to display the figure to its best advantage. This introduces an

FIG. 276.—THE APHRODITE OF MELOS. *Louvre, Paris.*

artificial note in the effect of the figure that is rather disquieting; the draperies could hardly remain in place if the figure were to take a step which it appears to be quite capable of doing. But the lack of complete unity in the effect of the statue does not obscure the fact that it represents a noble and dignified conception of humanity. In the fifth century the ideal of the sculptor was divine; in the fourth century it became semi-divine and in the Hellenistic period it became human. Such is the ideal embodied in the Aphrodite of Melos, an ideal of earthly rather than supernatural beauty as befitted a worldly age and civilization.

The Nike of Samothrace and the Aphrodite of Melos are examples of Hellenistic sculpture based more or less directly on forms developed in previous ages. In the *Dying Gaul* (Fig. 277), in the Capitoline Museum in Rome, a subject foreign to fifth- and fourth-century art is represented. The bronze original, here copied in marble, was one of a group of statues erected at Pergamon shortly after 241 B.C. to celebrate the military victory of Attalus I over the northern barbarians who had invaded Asia Minor. The wounded warrior is on the point of death, supporting himself on his right arm which is about to yield as his strength ebbs away. The details of the mustache, matted hair and twisted gold collar around the neck are represented very realistically and distinguish the figure as a barbarian by contrast with the ideal type used to portray Greeks. The realistic trend of Hellenistic art is further indicated by the hard dry skin and the heavy muscles, as well as the drops of blood oozing from the open wound. The proportions of the figure conform to the canon of Lysippos but the emphasis on emotional content is in the manner of Skopas. The use of naturalistic details in portraying a subject of the nature of the

Dying Gaul might easily have resulted in a highly disagreeable effect had not the sculptor introduced them with great restraint. They exist not as mere *tours de force* of technique but to give concreteness to the idea which the figure represents, the anguish of defeat that kills the spirit rather than the pain of physical violence that destroys the flesh.

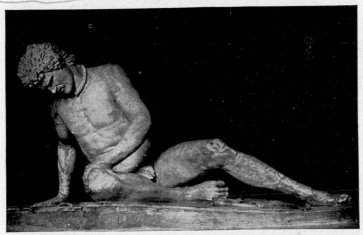

FIG. 277.—DYING GAUL. *Capitoline Museum, Rome.*

Still another aspect of Hellenistic art is seen in a relief of *Athena slaying a giant* (Fig. 278) that once decorated the Altar of Zeus at Pergamon, erected between 180 and 160 B.C. It forms part of a long frieze representing the mythical battle between the gods of Olympus and the giants of the earth, a favorite subject for architectural sculpture from the beginning of Greek art. The manner of treating it has little resemblance to that in previous examples, however, even though the theme was a traditional one. The struggling forms of serpent-legged giants and gods fill the entire frieze, the design being unified by the violent action that pervades the ensemble. This sense of action is conveyed by the knotted muscles and contorted faces and, more abstractly, in the diagonal accents of the composition as a whole. The animation of the figures is carried to the point of exaggeration, there being hardly a single body in repose in the entire frieze. The influence of Skopas' style is apparent in the heads, both in the shapes and in the emotional expressions. Throughout the entire frieze, the great technical skill of the sculptors is evident in the accurately rendered anatomical details, the texture of the draperies and flesh and the powerful wings of the gods, no less than in the masterful achievement of a unified design.

In striking contrast with the violence and unrestrained emotion of the Pergamon frieze is the gentle sentiment that pervades a series of reliefs such as the *Peasant driving a cow to market* (Fig. 279) in the Sculpture Museum at Munich. The term Alexandrian is applied to the entire category, for the first examples seem to have originated in Alexandria during the Hellenistic period. The one illustrated was probably carved about 50 A.D. The pastoral subject embodies the same idyllic

FIG. 278.—ATHENA SLAYING A GIANT. From the Frieze of the Altar of Zeus, Pergamon. *Pergamon Museum, Berlin.*

concept of rural life that underlies the poems of Theocritus. In contrast to fifth-century reliefs (Fig. 264), the background is very naturalistic. The figures themselves are different from those of fifth-century sculpture in that their forms are suggested by a play of light and shade rather than by modeling. This means that the various details are not actually carved to reproduce those of the model but that the stone is worked in such a way that hollows and projections create a pattern of shadows and highlights suggesting the form of the original. The result is an illusion of reality, from which the style is often called an illusionistic one. There is an illusion of space as well as of form in the relief. It results from the varying projections of the different objects, the peasant and cow standing almost free from the background while the temple and the statue base stand out only slightly. The tree growing out through the temple portal is an important factor in creating the illusion of depth in the relief, serving as it does to connect the foreground with the background. The illusionism of such a relief implies a point of view that is optical rather than tactile as in the earlier styles. A fifth-century relief would be reasonably intelligible to the touch without being seen; a Hellenistic relief such as this one is intended primarily to be seen and makes hardly any appeal to the sense of touch. Still another point differentiates the pastoral relief from that of the fifth century. It begins to take on the quality of a picture in

Fig. 279.—Peasant Driving a Cow to Market. *Glyptothek, Munich.*

stone, quite independent of its surroundings, whereas fifth-century relief is almost entirely architectonic, subordinate to the decorative scheme of the building it ornaments. To some extent, this new conception of relief may have been due to a similar tendency that made itself apparent in painting, easel pictures to be hung up as wall ornaments taking the place of the earlier architectural murals that were painted directly on the wall.

At the beginning of this chapter, the dates of the Hellenistic period were given as from 323 to 146 B.C. This might be somewhat amended, for in the broadest sense the Hellenistic period did not come to a close until several centuries after the beginning of the Christian era, the influence of Hellenistic ideas being perceptible in much of the art produced during the first millennium. None the less, after 146 B.C. the Greek strain in Hellenistic art becomes less prominent and the influence of other racial ideals correspondingly greater. Thus the sculpture produced from 146 until 27 B.C. is usually called Graeco-Roman. Much of it was created in Greece or by Greek artists but in response to the demands of Roman patrons. Many of the copies of fourth- and fifth-century statues that now constitute almost the only source of objective information about the sculpture of those periods were made at this time. But the influence of Roman taste is also evident in original works of the period, in the subject matter and the striving for ultrarealistic effects that is one of the main characteristics of certain types of Graeco-Roman sculpture.

One of the most famous statues of classic antiquity, the group of *Laocoön and His Sons* (Fig. 280), is an example of Hellenistic sculp-

FIG. 280.—LAOCOÖN AND HIS SONS. *Vatican Museum, Rome.*

ture produced during the Graeco-Roman period, having been executed about 50 B.C. It is now in the Vatican Museum in Rome. Its fame is due in part to the circumstances surrounding its discovery in 1506 when it was hailed as a masterpiece of the finest period of Greek sculpture. Another factor contributing to its popularity was the renown achieved by the book of the same name written by the German aesthetician Lessing embodying one of the most widely accepted theories of art in the 18th century. The arrangement of the group follows the account in the *Aeneid* of the punishment of Laocoön and his sons, though not in all details. It is pyramidal in form, the bodies united in a compact mass. The right arm of the father and that of the son to his right have been incorrectly restored; they should be lower, in which case the coherence of the group would be even more marked. The marvelously naturalistic modeling of the bodies is characteristic of the period. It is employed to establish effective contrasts in the group as a whole such as that between the adult body and the adolescent ones. Another contrast is seen in the muscles of the figures, the father's strained in an almost superhuman effort to free himself and his sons from the entwining snakes, those of the son to his left likewise being tense while the other youth has collapsed. The expression of agony on the father's face is created by the downward sloping brows, the drooping eyes, the contorted forehead and the parted lips, producing an effect that is very convincing. The group was the work of three sculptors of the Rhodian school and their skill in representation and design is obvious. It is difficult to find words of praise for the ideal upon which the technical skill is lavished, however. The extent to which the sculptors have gone in dwelling upon the details of physical pain and suffering is almost pathological. It should be compared with the Dying Gaul (Fig. 277), in which mental anguish is portrayed rather than bodily torture. The sympathy aroused in the spectator by the earlier work is not felt in the presence of the Laocoön group; rather there is a sense of repulsion.

The realism of the Laocoön is an outstanding characteristic of Graeco-Roman art in certain of its phases. In this particular case, it cannot be said to be the result of Roman taste, for the sculptors were Greeks and the entire concept might be rightly considered a continuation of the style observed in the relief from the Pergamon Altar (Fig. 278). A more direct Roman influence upon a Greek artist is seen in the statue of a *Boxer* (Fig. 281) in the Terme Museum in Rome, for it is signed by Apollonios, the son of Nestor, an Athenian who was active about 50 B.C. It is probably a free copy of a third-century Pergamene original modified in the direction of greater naturalism in accordance with Roman tastes. It is of bronze, the color of the metal suggesting the weather-beaten hide that is stretched taut by enormously developed muscles. The professional fighter is indicated by the gnarled fingers of the stubby, powerful hands, the cestus or gloves of metal knuckles joined by strips of leather, the broken nose and thick cauliflower ears. Other veracious details are the hairy chest and legs and the beetling brows. The realism of the face was originally even greater by virtue of colored paste eyeballs which have since disappeared. The sense of actuality which all these characteristics give to the figure is heightened by its momentary pose, the head being turned to one side as if in response to a question while the jolted brain seeks painfully for an answer.

Fig. 281.—Boxer. *Terme Museum, Rome.*

One of the outstanding features of Hellenistic sculpture is its great variety of methods, forms and subjects. The Nike of Samothrace and the Aphrodite of Melos are themes that were treated in earlier periods and the sculptural methods employed in them also have precedent in earlier styles. The Pergamon Frieze, on the other hand, is an old subject treated in a new way, and the Dying Gaul and the Peasant driving a Cow to Market are new subjects without prototypes in fifth- and fourth-century sculpture and involving, in the case of the latter at least, a new sculptural technique. But the lack of unity in Hellenistic sculpture as a whole and the resultant impression of confusion reflect truthfully enough a comparable state of fluidity in Hellenistic thought. In the fifth century, an integrated philosophical system had been evolved and the art of that century is correspondingly homogeneous though primitive still in that it was an attempt to interpret life only in terms of arbitrarily limited experience. In the Hellenistic period, the scope of experience had been tremendously enlarged. The complex life of this period was something that the old philosophical and artistic forms were no longer capable of interpreting. The varied aspects of Hellenistic sculpture are the result of attempts to meet this complexity by adaptation of old forms on the one hand and by the development of new forms on the other.

Hellenistic sculpture is often termed decadent, a judgment manifestly unfair to the high degree of technical skill apparent in it and its vitality. The qualities which are considered evidence of decadence are rather due to the lack of an ideal that could be effectively expressed in sculpture. As has been pointed out, fifth-century thought lent itself admirably to this end for it was one that involved isolation of the individual from his surroundings, an ideal which can be portrayed with relative ease in terms of concrete form. Even in the fourth century, which conceived the individual as aware of his surroundings, an art of form could be employed as a means of expression. But in the Hellenistic period the individual was considered no longer as isolated from his environment or merely conscious of it but as conditioned by it. To portray man as part of his surroundings, some means of suggesting space is essential, an effect which is intrinsically one of painting as far as the representative arts are concerned, and relatively difficult of attainment in sculpture. To the Hellenistic mind, the world was one of space, of light and shade, in contrast to the fifth- and fourth-century concept in terms of form and expressive outline. The Hellenistic world was that of the painter rather than the sculptor and Hellenistic art is most significant when it deals with space and *chiaroscuro* effects in easel paintings and frescoes (Fig. 363). The apparent decadence of Hellenistic sculpture is due to the fact that although its technique had been perfected in previous periods, the ideals to which that technique gave expression were no longer valid and the new ones still in the process of evolution did not lend themselves to sculptural treatment. The result was that which is inevitable when a means of expression exists with nothing to express. Without new problems to solve or new subjects to interpret, sculpture could only turn back upon itself or attempt to follow the path taken by painting. In either case, there was little to be gained. In the latter (Fig. 279), the results serve chiefly to point out the limitations of the art. In the former, a brilliant eclecticism only emphasizes the relative lack of content, as in the Aphrodite of Melos (Fig. 276), though an occasional new theme (Fig. 277) is invested with ideal meaning that acquires force through a superb technique.

# Chapter XVIII. Roman Sculpture

*Begin*

ITALY, THE LAND OF THE ROMANS, HAD BEEN
partially colonized by the Greeks as early as the seventh century B.C.,
and in some parts of the country there are still remains of Greek temples (cf. Fig. 35) and many relics of Greek origin have been discovered,
particularly in the southern regions of the peninsula. At the same time,
there was established in other parts of Italy, particularly in the central
area, a race known as the Etruscans who represented a culture even
more ancient than that of the Greeks in so far as the archaeological
evidence of its character can be discerned. Their temples were built
of wood more often than not (cf. Fig. 47), and lavish use was made
of terra cotta in the form of revetments and moulded figures in decorating them. It was in such a capacity, no doubt, that the great *Striding
Warrior* (Fig. 282) now in the Metropolitan Museum in New York
was intended when it was created about 500 B.C. Standing about eight
feet in height, it is made of terra cotta which was moulded and
painted before being fired to bake it to proper hardness, and the statue
is a triumph of ceramic skill in execution. There are certain conventions to be noticed similar to those of archaic Greek art. The skin is
dark brown in color as was usual for male figures, while the greaves,
corselet and helmet are red, signifying that they were supposedly
of leather. The spirals and palmettes painted in white that figure as
ornament are reminiscent of Greek decorative motives, and it has
been rightly observed that the pose and details such as the treatment
of beard and lips recall the ripe archaic Greek style as represented in
figures from the pediment groups of the temple of Aphaia at Aegina
(cf. Fig. 254). The massive proportions and dynamic movement of
the figure are unlike contemporary Greek work, however, and the
impression of a savage and war-like spirit resulting therefrom is consistent with what is known otherwise of the Etruscan temperament.
The figure illustrates, therefore, the native Latin sculptural style with
certain influences from Greek ways of thinking which became more
powerful in the Graeco-Roman period from about 150 until 27 B.C.,
during which time the sculpture that was produced in Italy could be

considered as forming one of the many regional Hellenistic styles (cf. Fig. 281).

With the establishment of the Roman Empire, a change appears in the character of Latin sculpture. The reason for this change is to be found in the need which then arose to give expression to ideas that were specifically Roman and as such, could not be effectively embodied in the forms used before that time. It is for this reason that in Roman sculpture the mannerism and artificiality that characterize much Hel-

Fig. 282.—Striding Warrior. *Metropolitan Museum, N. Y.*

lenistic sculpture are not so apparent. New subjects supplied the impulse to the creation of new forms, the lack of which had forced Hellenistic sculptors to meaningless displays of technical skill, for in the need to give expression to the grandeur of Rome and to glorify the deeds of the Emperor, there was a stimulus which led once more to the investment of figures with definite expressive character. The sculptures in which these ideas were embodied fall into two classes, each of which may be considered as specifically Roman contributions to the art of sculpture—portraits and historical reliefs. In both, the highly developed Roman taste for realistic portrayal is evident. Both have precedent in Hellenistic style, it is true, but in Roman hands both are treated in an individual manner that makes them genuinely original and quite different in character from any prototypes that may be found.

The fondness of the Romans for realistic portraiture may have had its origin in the Etruscan practice of preserving the features of the

dead by wax death masks which were later used as the basis for portrait statues. Needless to say, such a procedure involved no idealization of the face nor was it desired. Perfection was the "speaking likeness", and any variation from the exact appearance of the model was avoided. Thus in the green basalt bust of *Julius Caesar* (Fig. 283) in the Imperial Museum in Berlin, the sculptor omitted no detail essential to an exact likeness of the living man, in striking contrast to the idealization apparent in Kresilas' portrait of Pericles (Fig. 266). The taut muscles of the lean throat, the furrowed brow, the lines around the mouth and chin and the sparse hair of the head are specific and individual traits. At the same time, the bust is more than just a photograph in stone for it suggests the keen and incisive mind of the man. The fleck of light in the drilled pupil of the eye creates an impression of alert awareness. The sensuality for which Caesar was famous in a sensual age can be read in the thin lips, no less than the burning ambition whose implacable demands are evident in every line of the ravaged countenance. In contrast with the portrait of Pericles, this bust is an embodiment of the individual qualities of Caesar as a person rather than a symbol of the idea of Caesar as a statesman or general.

Fig. 283.—Julius Caesar. *Imperial Museum, Berlin.*

An attempt to combine traditional Roman realism with Greek idealism is seen in the statue of *Augustus from Prima Porta* (Fig. 284) in the Vatican Museum in Rome. Executed about 15 B.C., it represents the Emperor as a general addressing his troops. Individual traits are prominent in the head; the skull tapering sharply toward the chin, the high cheek bones, deeply recessed eyes and the arrangement of the hair are all details that can be observed in other portraits of Augustus. Realistic touches are seen in the elaborately carved breast-plate, the numerous folds of the drapery and the tunic fringe. The literal treatment of these details contrasts strangely with the idealizing tendency apparent in others. The feet are bare in the Greek tradition

Fig. 284.—Augustus from Prima Porta. *Vatican Museum, Rome.*

of the heroic figure and the expression of the face is calm and self-contained. The pose and proportions are based on the Polykleitan canon and furnish evidence of the renewed influence of Greek sculpture on that of Rome in the Augustan age. This was due in large measure to the taste of Augustus himself, whose appreciation of Greek art was quite genuine. The combination of naturalistic and generalized details in the Prima Porta statue that results from the more or less conscious efforts of the Roman sculptors to create a figure with ideal significance is not entirely successful. In an attempt to raise the concept to that level, the sculptor introduced Cupid astride a dolphin at the feet of the

Emperor, a symbolic reference to the divine ancestry of the Julian
family which claimed descent from Aeneas, the son of Venus and a
half-brother of Cupid. The relief on the breastplate also has symbolic
meaning, referring as it does to the peace and harmony that prevailed
throughout the Roman Empire under Augustus' wise and benevolent
reign. Such attempts as these to invest a concretely conceived figure
with ideal meaning by allegoric attributes are typical of the methods
employed by an art of naturalism to transcend its innate materialism.

A combination of naturalism and allegory somewhat similar in effect
to that of the Augustus from Prima Porta appears in the greatest sculptural monument of Augustus' reign, the *Ara Pacis Augustae* or the
Altar of Augustan Peace which once stood by the Via Flaminia. The

FIG. 285.—TELLUS. From the Ara Pacis, Rome. *Uffizi, Florence.*

altar was a rectangular building about thirty-five feet square, the
inner and outer walls of which were covered with relief sculptures
representing state officials and the Emperor with his family making a
sacrifice of thanksgiving to the Earth for peace and prosperity. Its
erection was ordered by the Senate in 13 B.C. to commemorate the
final pacification of Gaul and Spain by Augustus. The Earth or *Tellus*
(Fig. 285), happy and productive under Roman rule, is personified by
a feminine figure. On her lap are two children typifying Humanity
which thrives upon the Earth's bounty symbolized by animals and the
life-giving elements of Air and Water. This relief was the goal of
a procession formed by the royal family and a retinue of officials. The
ideal type of the Tellus figure is in strong contrast to the naturalism
of the animals and the garlands. The technique is not unlike that of the

Hellenistic pictorial reliefs (Fig. 279), the figures being built up in many planes of varying depths. The relative nearness of the seated figures is indicated by pronounced projection while the foliage is barely raised from the relief background. By this means, an identification of the neutral background with real space is achieved, an illusion that

FIG. 286.—Rome. THE ARCH OF TITUS. THE TRIUMPH OF TITUS.

is furthered by the extremely naturalistic rendering of the draperies and the modeling of the figures which seem to merge into the stone.

The illusionistic relief style exemplified by the *Ara Pacis* reaches the climax of its development in the *Reliefs on the Arch of Titus* (Fig. 286), which was erected near the Roman Forum to commemorate the conquest of Jerusalem in 70 A.D. (cf. Fig. 49). These reliefs portray the triumphal procession in which the spoils of the Temple in

Jerusalem were displayed to the Roman populace. In the upper panel the Emperor rides in his chariot, accompanied by a symbolic figure of Victory, while others personifying Rome and the Roman people appear elsewhere. In the lower panel a group of soldiers carrying the table of the showbread, the long trumpets that called the Jews to prayer or battle, and the seven-branched candlestick, are about to pass through a triumphal arch. In both panels the sculptor attempted to portray the scene as it would actually appear to a spectator looking through a window represented by the frame of the panel. To give the scenes reality, an illusion of space is created by subtle variations in the depth of the relief, the foreground figures standing out very clearly while objects in the background are almost imperceptible. In this way, an effect of light and shade is obtained that gives the impression of real air circulating between the figures. Only absence of a systematic rendering of the effect of perspective prevented the sculptor from attaining the complete illusion of concrete reality that was his ideal. It is because of this, for example, that the figures in the lower panel do not march through the arch, and that the chariot horses in the upper one are represented as if they were one in front of the other instead of abreast.

In the Arch of Titus reliefs, composition and arrangement do not exist. The figures are not subordinated either to an architectural scheme or to order that is formal in its own right. Instead, they are placed in the relief space with a casualness that is entirely naturalistic, moving about in real space as if seen through an opening in the side of the arch. They are therefore mainly descriptive in purpose, without the ideal unities of time, of space or of plastic form that a Greek sculptor would have maintained (Fig. 265). The lack of chronological unity in the reliefs is apparent in their arrangement parallel to each other across the central passage of the arch, although their actual relationship to each other was consecutive.

In the reliefs of the Arch of Titus, coherence is attained in the life and vitality that seem to animate each figure. This liveliness is produced by the play of light and shade over the whole panel, creating patterns that conform to the actual appearance of the objects represented. A considerable degree of technical skill was essential to the attainment of such an effect, for the artist had to have complete understanding of the modeling of the figures in order to create the effects of light and shade which such modeling would produce. When that understanding disappeared, as it did in the late years of the Roman Empire, the illusionistic style was no longer capable of producing intelligible results. This is clearly demonstrated by the *Reliefs on the Arch of Constantine* (Fig. 287), erected in Rome in 315 A.D. The particular reliefs under consideration are those in the long rectangular

band which are later in date than those in the round medallions. Instead
of being united in a common action, the figures are arranged in monotonous rows, each one carefully isolated from those around it. In them,
the descriptive tendency of the earlier reliefs has been carried to
excess; the sculptor felt it necessary to portray each figure and each
detail of each figure quite clearly, neglecting entirely the dramatic
and spatial relationships that unify the earlier works. It is as if one
of the animated scenes of the earlier style had been crystallized; the

FIG. 287.—Rome. THE ARCH OF CONSTANTINE. Commemorative Reliefs.

separate components are very carefully depicted but there is no element
to establish a connection between them, whether dramatic and spatial as
in the Arch of Titus reliefs or formal and rhythmic as in Greek relief.

The squat and unprepossessing figures that people the reliefs on
the Arch of Constantine represent the complete decay of the classic
tradition of sculpture in the west. Superficially they bear some resemblance to the archaic figures with which the tradition began (Fig.
252), for in them also each part of the body is represented in its
most characteristic aspect. In both styles, the figures are portrayed by
means of conventions, but between the conventions themselves there is
a very significant difference; those of the archaic method are conven-

tions of form whereas those of the decayed illusionistic style are conventions of light and shade. The result in either case is not naturalistic; in the archaic figure, this is a minor consideration for the source of its appeal is its strongly developed plasticity; in the late Latin figure, it is a very important consideration for without naturalism it is nothing, inasmuch as the entire illusionistic tradition was one which tended to disregard plastic values in favor of dramatic or spatial ones. When the ability to represent things in a naturalistic fashion no longer existed, there was no longer anything in the figure for it had never had formal plastic values but only an illusion of them.

Roman sculpture, and Roman art in general, represents a continuation of the Hellenistic tradition. In one sense, it may be considered as reflecting the first step toward an evaluation of the tremendously varied experiences which were inevitable in consequence of the universal and comprehensive nature of Hellenistic thought. The initial bewilderment of the Hellenistic mind in the face of such complexity can be read in the diffuse character of Hellenistic sculpture. In the Roman period, there is an effort to resolve this complexity into order in terms that are still classic in that they are factual and concrete. It has been pointed out before that the Roman architect sought to make space a plastic and objective thing in the interior of the Pantheon (Fig. 58). A similar motive animated the Roman sculptor when, as in the Arch of Titus reliefs, by portraying definite persons in a specific setting at a definite moment, he attempted to make both time and space objective. The difference between the Greek point of view and the Roman lies in the fact that the Greek sought to establish ideal unities of time and space by subordinating them to other things while the Roman sought the same end by making them specific and concrete. In architecture this attempt was successful; in sculpture it was only relatively so, for the Roman sculptor was able to attain spatial values only at the expense of formal ones by virtue of his illusionistic technique of light and shade.

At the beginning of this chapter it was pointed out that Roman sculpture attained the level of an individual and characteristic style by infusing Hellenistic forms with new meaning to give expression to ideals that were specifically Roman. The decadence of Roman art set in when there were no longer valid ideals to serve as a stimulus to creation. Furthermore, even in this respect there is a difference from the prevailing state of affairs in the Hellenistic period. For all the emptiness that characterizes many of the brilliant *tours de force* of the Hellenistic style, there still remained something of the old Greek tradition of expressive form, as well as the obvious delight taken by many Hellenistic sculptors in displaying their technical skill. A period thus characterized can hardly be termed decadent as is often done. By contrast, the Roman period from about 200 A.D. to 330 A.D. can hardly be termed anything else. There are neither abstract ideals nor technical skill apparent in the sculpture of that period in which the final stage of the direct classic tradition is reached. New ideals had to be evolved and a new technique developed before a new sculptural tradition could take form. These processes take place during the first millennium of the Christian era.

*STOP*

# Chapter XIX. Mediaeval Sculpture

## A. THE EARLY MIDDLE AGES

*DURING THE FIRST MILLENNIUM OF THE CHRISTIAN* era, sculpture, like the other arts, became a handmaiden of the Church in spite of the Biblical injunction against the creation of images that had been an essential feature of the Jewish faith as long as it was found only among Semitic peoples. When Christianity spread to western Europe, this interdiction was more or less disregarded as were many others. The whole fabric of Christianity in the Occident was erected on a foundation of compromises which involved the adaptation of many pagan beliefs and their incorporation in the new faith. One aspect of this adaptation appears in Early Christian sculpture, which consists almost entirely of forms derived from the current decadent Latin style to which new meaning was given by symbolic devices. One of the outstanding examples of this practice is the new significance in Christian art of a subject that had appeared in classic art from the earliest period of Greek sculpture, a shepherd carrying a lamb over his shoulders. It was not difficult for the Christian to see the Good Shepherd in statues of this subject and it was carried over into the iconography of Early Christian art almost unchanged.

As the Latin Church passed through the earliest stages of its development and its beliefs outgrew the primitive ones that had sufficed in the beginning, the comparatively simple way of expressing those beliefs in concrete form that is exemplified by the adaptation of the Good Shepherd type was no longer adequate. By the middle of the 4th century, a more complicated symbolism appeared in Early Christian art. Most of the sculptural examples are sarcophagi such as the one in the Lateran Museum in Rome known as the *Sarcophagus of the Two Brothers* (Fig. 288) from the portraits of the deceased in the conch shell. The friezes are made up of Old and New Testament scenes that expressed symbolically a belief in life after death, the element in the Christian faith that appealed the most strongly to the early adherents of the Church. The figures are in the same decadent illusionistic style that has been noted in the frieze on the Arch of Constantine (Fig. 287). In the nude figure representing Daniel in the den of lions below and to the left of the conch shell, there is a vague reminiscence of the Lysippic canon of the fourth century. There is some attempt to distinguish the heads of the two brothers, but the woefully inadequate technique of the sculptor falls far short of investing them with the life and vigor of the Roman portraits. The decay of the Hellenistic and Roman illusionistic style is even more evident in the dull formulas of the heads and draperies and the monotonous repetition of the figures. The scenes are neither separated from each other nor related in this art which can achieve neither decorative nor dramatic unity. The classic tradition in the west was worn out; even the powerful stimulus of new beliefs could no longer invest its decadent forms with significance or beauty.

While the sculptors in the service of the western Church were fruitlessly endeavoring to fill the old bottle of decadent and crystallized

FIG. 288.—THE SARCOPHAGUS OF THE TWO BROTHERS.
*Lateran Museum, Rome.*

illusionism with the new wine of Christian symbolism, a process also to be observed in the related art of ivory carving (cf. Fig. 577), their contemporaries in Byzantium and the Near East were developing a style which was similar in having its roots also in classic art. A *Fragment of a Sarcophagus* (Fig. 289) in the Kaiser Friedrich Museum in Berlin which dates from about 400 A.D. is carved with figures representing Christ standing between two apostles in an architectural setting of columns and a gable. As in the Latin sarcophagus (Fig. 288), the figures are direct adaptations of classic models in posture and movement, the apostles being a type that served the sculptors of Greek and Roman antiquity in representing philosophers to which a new and Christian meaning is given by symbols such as the cruciform nimbus behind the head of Christ. Changes also occurred in the formal character of the

figures and objects portrayed. The capitals of the colonnettes forming
the setting are similar to those in Byzantine architecture (cf. Fig. 70)
in being masses defined by planes in which the ornament is incised to
create a pattern in contrasting accents of light and shade instead of
being plastically modeled. A comparable effect is seen in the figures
which are flattened out by contrast with the antique prototypes and
tend to become two-dimensional areas of linear patterns created by incisions cut with a running drill.

In making use of light and dark accents as the major compositional
elements, the Byzantine sculptor followed Hellenistic precedent (cf. Fig.

FIG. 289.—FRAGMENT OF A SARCOPHAGUS.
*Kaiser Friedrich Museum, Berlin.*

279), but he departs from it in utilizing them in patterns that are not
plastic and three-dimensional in effect but are organized in a single
plane and unified by rhythmic accents. The figures are de-materialized
in the process, losing the organic articulation that made the prototypes effective embodiments of the objective evaluation of experience
for which the classic mind ever strove, but they become in consequence

of their very immateriality more suitable vehicles for giving expression to the transcendental content of Christianity. Thus is seen in sculpture the initial result of the impact of Oriental prepossession with the indefinite and the immaterial upon ways of thinking in which much of classic character persisted, comparable in its way to the architectural compromise between the same principles in the church of Hagia Sophia (Fig. 68). In varying degrees, depending upon the extent to which Hellenic or Oriental ideas predominate, the ivories of Byzantine origin such as the leaf of a diptych in the British Museum (Fig. 578) or the Throne of Maximianus at Ravenna (Fig. 579) illustrate the same transformation of classic forms when brought into the service of the Church.

It was the nature of Christian thought that it should express itself in symbolic terms rather than representative ones, and inasmuch as

Fig. 290.—The Sarcophagus of Theodorus.
*S. Apollinare in Classe, Ravenna.*

such forms lend themselves with particular aptness to decorative treatment, it is not surprising that Byzantine artists should have used them very often. The *Sarcophagus of Theodorus* (Fig. 290) was executed for a 6th century archbishop of the Byzantine city of Ravenna in Italy, and is in the church of Sant' Apollinare there (Figs. 71, 72). There are still classic elements in the decoration—the simplified pilasters at the ends of the long side and the mouldings across the top and on the lid—but symbols of Christian ideas are the most important features of the design. The cross occurs in two forms, one with the Greek letters Alpha and Omega hanging from the horizontal arm and a rounded end on the vertical one making it into the letter Rho, while the other is characterized by a superimposed X, the Greek letter Chi which taken with the Rho forms the initials of Christ's name. The Alpha and Omega are of similar meaning (Rev. i, 11), as is also the vine (John xv, 1-5) that figures in the decoration of the long side. The symbolism of wine as the blood of Christ, which was one of the most frequently employed symbols of the Savior in Christian art, is also referred to in this. The heraldic peacocks are another motive of great popularity in the religious art of the first millennium, being a symbol of eternal life of even greater antiquity. Clarity and simplicity are the outstanding characteristics of the pattern created of these forms which are defined in two planes against a neutral background. The arrangement is symmetrical, but it is the rhythmic recurrence of circular motives—in the branches of the vine and the medallion with the monogram of Christ—that is the major unifying element in this design, which is one of the most characteristic examples of Byzantine stone sculpture in both expressive and formal character.

The amount of large-scale Byzantine sculpture in stone was probably never very great, for the Oriental distaste for such images that is expressed in the admonition against graven images in the Second Commandment of the Decalogue was a constant element in Byzantine thought, conflicting with the inheritance of classic concepts indigenous in the Eastern Empire. It was this element coming to the fore in the iconoclast period in the 8th century that resulted in the extensive destruction of images from which the name of the movement was derived, and it is unlikely that the Moslem conquerors of Byzantine in the 15th century were more appreciative of the figures they saw than the earlier image-breakers. It is for this reason that the most comprehensive understanding of Byzantine plastic art from the 9th to the 14th centuries is to be obtained from ivories like the Harbaville Triptych in the Louvre (Fig. 580). There are still preserved some examples of late Byzantine stone sculpture, however, such as the *Madonna Orans* (Fig. 291), so called from the raising of the arms in prayer, in the church of Santa Maria in Porto in Ravenna, which was probably carved in the 11th century. The figure is carved in low relief and stands in a frontal pose with the right leg slightly relaxed. It is possible to discern in the schematized draperies a reflection of the antique formula but it is reduced to a system of flat planes and incised lines that reveals little enough of the form beneath. In this it resembles the figures in the Triptych, and if the resulting effect in both is far from that of the world of nature in which lived the forms carved by the sculptors of Greece and Rome, there is instead a sense of hieratic and supernatural beings standing immobile in the performance of a solemn and impressive rite. In this way the Byzantine artist sought to convey, in forms of classic self-sufficiency but Oriental in their unworldliness, his concept of the profound significance of Christian dogma.

At the same time that classic style was being transformed into Byzantine under the influence of the Oriental cultures impinging upon the east Mediterranean areas, it was also being modified in the west. There the weakening Empire was subjected to recurrent infiltrations of the non-Mediterranean Teutonic tribes which had never been assimilated into the Roman world and maintained a degree of independence from its political order. But as these barbarians overran the land, they were themselves subjected to the influences of the Hellenistic-Christian culture of the Empire, and the history of the period from the end of the 6th century on is as much that of the rise of the Church as of the decay and fall of Rome. Christian art in western Europe in the latter half of the first millennium was a product of these conditions, and its growth from the formal traditions of both the dissolving Empire and the Teutonic barbarians is comparable to that of Byzantine art from the fusion of Hellenistic style with that of the Oriental cultures of the Near East.

FIG. 291.—MADONNA ORANS.
*Sta. Maria in Porto, Ravenna.*

The art of the Teutonic tribes in its native purity can best be illustrated in such works as the manuscript illustrations which were executed for a Gospel book written in an Irish monastery at Kells toward the close of the 8th century (Fig. 367) and can be characterized essentially by two words—linear and dynamic. These are the qualities that are dominant in all the art forms of the northern races, and are those whose impact upon the already weakened Latin tradition in which the western Church gave form to its concepts (cf. Fig. 288)

resulted in its further disintegration, the nature of which can be
judged by the style of the Sigwald Relief (Fig. 292) in the Baptistery
of Cividale, a small town in northern Italy. It was carved between 762
and 776 as part of a canopy built over the baptismal font by the
Patriarch Sigwald, as is recorded in the inscription on the band below
the cross. This latter is flanked by stylized palmettes and rosettes and two
forms suggesting candelabra; below is a tree, of which some of the
branches end in animal heads; birds are sitting in it and it is flanked

Fig. 292.—The Sigwald Relief. *Baptistery, Cividale.*

by two grotesques, part animal and part bird. Four medallions complete the carved decoration of the panel, each enclosing a winged figure
that symbolizes one of the Four Evangelists, the compilers of the Four
Gospels; that in the upper left corner is an eagle representing John
and the one to the right above is the winged man of Matthew; below
to the left is a winged bull, which is the symbol of Luke, the winged
lion of Mark completing the quartet. It is in the symbolism of the
relief that the Christian component of its character is most clear. The
cross is an obvious detail of this nature, and the Four Evangelist
symbols are the interpretation of the Vision of Ezekiel (Ezekiel i,
5-11) in accordance with mediaeval theology; they constitute a motive
that was one of the most important in the art of the Middle Ages
since it occurs in almost all representations of the Last Judgment. The
style is the linear one of the Teutonic tribes—of some distinction in

the purely decorative motives such as the interlace on the cross and the tree in the lower center, but weak and unconvincing in the Evangelist symbols in which the form was dictated by Christian iconography; the model was in the plastic late antique style, no doubt, which the linear and two-dimensional prepossession of the barbarian sculptor did not permit him to understand. It was this way of seeing things solely in terms of line and movement which gives the purely ornamental elements in this style their vitality and unity, and which reduces the plastic and solid forms portrayed with some naturalism in the model to these weightless and clumsy ideographs. Certain of the motives in the Sigwald Relief are also primarily of northern origin—the interlace, the grotesque animals, and the animal-headed branches of the tree; of classic character, other than the assumed nature of the model presumptively copied by the sculptor, there is nothing unless the symmetrical arrangement of the motives can be considered a feeble reminder of the splendid order that had been achieved by the artists of the Hellenic world.

The Sigwald Relief can hardly be considered sculpture at all in the sense that this means organization of plastic elements, for it is executed in but two planes—the background and the face of the slab on which the forms appear to have been drawn as a preliminary to simply cutting them straight back to the desired level. Its ineptitude is due to the fact that neither the classic nor the northern component in its style is sufficiently forceful to give point and positiveness to the forms. These are characteristics that appear only with certainty of meaning and conviction of the significance of experience—creative factors that were supplied in some measure in mediaeval culture in the time of Charlemagne (742-814) and immediately thereafter in consequence of that monarch's attempt to recreate in his Holy Roman Empire something of the grandeur that had been Rome. Notice has been taken elsewhere of the limited success attending Carolingian efforts to contrive a monumental architectural style (cf. Fig. 74) and there is a similar sparseness in the field of large-scale sculpture. In the more limited category of ivory relief carving, the story is different, however (cf. Fig. 582), and in small panels, such as this, which were made to decorate the covers of manuscript books or to adorn reliquary caskets, there is the individuality and unity of style that is so sadly wanting in the Sigwald Relief.

On a larger scale than the ivory book-cover panel, the same quality is to be noted in the bronze reliefs of the doors made for the church of St. Michael in Hildesheim in Germany between 1007 and 1015 and later moved to the cathedral of the same city. They were executed for the Bishop of Hildesheim, Bernward by name, who was probably inspired by his admiration for the elaborately carved 5th century wooden doors of the church of Santa Sabina in Rome (cf. Fig. 65). There are two doors of eight panels each, those on the left relating the story of the book of Genesis from the Creation of Man through the Murder of Abel, and those on the right depicting the life of Christ. The most immediate impression of these panels (Fig. 293) is the amazing forcefulness and vitality of the figures with which they are decorated. Compared with the heavy and stolid ones of the Latin sarcophagus

Fig. 293.—Hildesheim. Cathedral. Bronze Doors. Detail, The Judgment of Adam and Eve.

(Fig. 288), the dignified Byzantine forms (Fig. 289) or the ugly and formless creatures on the Sigwald Relief (Fig. 292), those of the Hildesheim Doors are dynamically alive, instinct with a vigor that seems almost to tear them free of their relief backing. The *Judgment of Adam and Eve* is rendered with a naïve sense of the dramatic that makes the observer forget the crudely shaped bodies with their over-large heads and unarticulated limbs. The unknown sculptor's power of characterization transcends his lack of anatomical knowledge, for there is no mistaking the significance of the threatening head and denunciatory finger of the Deity whose accusation is promptly passed on by the apprehensive Adam to Eve who in her turn shifts the blame by a gesture to the Tempter in the form of a dragon on the ground. The sense of a powerful force which animates the figures is present even in the twisted tree and the wiry foliage of the panel border. It is this sense of an abstract, prevalent force that gives unity to the composition. There is obviously none of the formal or architectonic unity of Greek relief, or the spatial unity of Hellenistic or Roman relief, or the rhythmic, decorative unity of the Byzantine. Instead, the sense of movement arising from the sheer vitality of the figures themselves unites them in common submission to some unseen but irresistible power. Technically, this effect is brought about by the linear method employed by the sculptor to delineate the various objects in the relief, as compared with the classic tradition of modeling and the Hellenistic-Byzantine dependence on effects of light and shade. This linear method of portrayal is the barbarian contribution to the artistic synthesis which was born in the first millennium and attained its majority in the Romanesque period.

Of the three principal sculptural styles of the early Middle Ages, that of the Hildesheim Doors was the most vital. The decadence of the Latin or west Christian mode has been commented upon. In the last years of the Byzantine Empire, a falling off from the level attained in the earlier works is evident although a certain stiff and hieratic dignity, nearly always present even in the least accomplished examples of the Byzantine style, saves them from the ineptitude of late Latin sculpture. But it was the northern or barbarian style with its dramatic intensity and windy movement that galvanized these outworn modes into life and produced the monumental art of the Romanesque and Gothic periods, just as the fusion of the vigorous northern tribes with the exhausted Roman stock brought about the renewed spiritual and intellectual activity of the 12th and 13th centuries.

## B. Romanesque Sculpture

The renewed vitality of western thought in the 11th and 12th centuries is apparent in sculpture as it is in all fields of human activity. In general, it is evident in the search for a style that would be capable of giving full expression to the synthesis of thought which was then taking place. Throughout the entire period, however, and through the entire Middle Ages, sculpture did not develop as a free and independent art but was subordinated to architecture. From the beginning of the Romanesque period until the end of the Gothic, little sculpture was produced that was not related in some way to architecture. Even when freestanding figures were carved, they were conceived in terms that implied an architectural setting, a consideration that must always be borne in mind in arriving at an evaluation of the results. The period of Romanesque sculpture corresponds rather closely to that of Romanesque architecture save for the fact that it begins a little later, the first important

works coming about 1100. This was a natural consequence of its subordination to architecture, for the structural problems of building required solution before resultant forms could be decorated. It comes to a
close about 1200 when the Gothic style makes its appearance.

Romanesque sculptural forms have something in common with those
of the Greek archaic period, the similarity between them being explained by the fact that both result from attempts to give expression
to ideas through the medium of a limited technique. The lack of
extensive knowledge of the human body on the part of the archaic
sculptor has been pointed out elsewhere. The Romanesque sculptor was
hardly any better off at the beginning of the 12th century for in the
years that had intervened since the death of the classic tradition
of figure sculpture, none of comparable authority had taken its place.
Thus when he attempted to give expression to his ideas through the
medium of the human form, he had no formulas to guide him in representing it and was forced to develop them anew. To aid him, there was
his unconscious heritage from the past, comprising the triple influence
of the Roman, Byzantine and barbarian traditions embodied in the
illuminated illustrations of manuscripts (Figs. 368, 369) and carved
ivory panels (Figs. 582, 583), which mingled in various proportions to
determine the individual character of the various schools of Romanesque sculpture. These schools correspond in general to those of Romanesque architecture.

Limitation of technique is thus a characteristic common to both
Greek archaic sculpture and that of the Romanesque period. The thing
that makes them so different in effect is the difference between the
ideals expressed in them. The archaic sculptor, and all Greek sculptors
for that matter, conceived their gods in the image of man; divinity
for them became concrete and real in the human form and perfection
was attained in complete understanding of it. "Know thyself" was the
aim of the Greek, for in knowing himself he also knew all that his
world could mean to him. In the Middle Ages, on the other hand,
God was conceived as a completely abstract principle, as a spirit and
so incapable of representation. He could not be comprehended intellectually but only sensed intuitively since He existed only as a
supernatural principle, manifest in all things that have being and constituting the element that gives them reality. This furnishes an explanation for the naturalism of mediaeval art in its later phases, for since
all objects are in themselves a reflection to some extent of the all-
embracing divine principle, it follows that they are beautiful and so
worthy of portrayal. At the same time, the greatest value of the objects
portrayed is symbolic since they stand for the divine principle rather
than represent it. The difference that will be noted between Roman-

esque and Gothic sculpture lies in the fact that the figures of the former are emotional symbols of reality while those of the latter are intellectual in that they form part of an ordered system by which the spirit could begin its ascent from earthly things to heavenly ones. In both cases, the complete realization of the reality that lies behind the figures can result only from an intuitive perception of it. Herein lies the essential difference between the classic point of view and that of the Middle Ages; in the former, reality was understood by a process of knowing; in the latter, it could be understood only by a process of feeling.

The function of monumental sculpture in the Romanesque world of the late 11th and 12th centuries was twofold. On the one hand, it

A.                                    B.

FIG. 294.—VÉZELAY. La Madeleine. Capitals.

was a means of giving instruction to those who could not read, a dogmatic function, and on the other, it was an accessory to architectural form, i.e., it was decorative. Thus its subject matter deals almost entirely with Christian beliefs—stories from the Bible, the lives of the saints, etc.—and the forms in which this subject matter is interpreted are those which play a part in the architectural style of the period. Of these, two are preeminent—the historiated capital on which figures illustrate a story (Fig. 294, A-B), and the wall relief (Figs. 297, 298). The *Capitals* are in the church of the *Madeleine at Vézelay* in Burgundy in France, a monastic establishment that dates from the latter part of the 11th century although it is probable that the capitals were not carved until about 1110. One of them (Fig. 294, B) is of particular interest because it is unfinished; the roughly shaped block of stone was put in place to support the arch sprung from it and the carving was done later, a practice that may not have been invariable in Romanesque times but which was certainly general and which illustrates the primarily architectonic concept of the sculptured form of the capital. The same consideration applies to the way in which the subjects are treated. That of the unfinished capital has not been identified, but the other (Fig. 294, A) represents Moses breaking the tablets of the law while a demon escapes from the open mouth of the Golden Calf. The human figures are given over-large heads, if judged by a naturalistic standard, and there is only the most summary suggestion of bodies beneath the fluttering draperies. If, however, these various details are regarded not as parts of a physiologically articulated human figure but rather as making up a pattern of accents in an architectural scheme, they will be seen to stress those portions of the capital where a sense of support is needed and that these are united by the flow of line into a coherent whole. The capital form is basically that of the classic Corinthian, of which there is a reminiscence in the angle volutes, the foliate background and the moulded impost-block, but the style of the figures is based on that of the manuscript illuminations which served the sculptor as models.

There is considerable variety in the wall relief category of Romanesque sculpture ranging from examples that seem to have been carved directly on the wall as at Modena (Fig. 298) to the more complex relationships of the *Façade of St. Trophime* (Fig. 295) at Arles in southern France, where the wall appears to have been hollowed out to provide niches in which figures are placed. They are examples, considered from the point of view of style, of the Roman contribution to Romanesque art, a fact which is not surprising since Arles was the center of a flourishing school of sculpture in the Roman period and many Roman monuments are still preserved there. These undoubtedly served as models for the mediaeval sculptor at St. Trophime who attempted as best he could to reproduce their forms. The subject of the portal sculpture is the Last Judgment. Christ is seated in the tympanum of the main portal with the twelve apostles below him on the lintel which is just visible at the right of the illustration. On the same level as the lintel is a frieze of figures representing the souls of the saved in paradise; a corresponding one on the other side shows the damned on their way to hell. In the niches below are large figures of the apostles and one representing the saint who established Christianity at Arles. In carving these figures, the sculptor was very obviously influenced by

Roman models. The bodies are similar in pose and proportions to those on the Lateran sarcophagus (Fig. 288). Similar conventions for representing hair, eyes and drapery occur in both, and the garments worn by the Arlesian figures are not unlike the Roman toga. Another classic principle of design evident in this sculpture is isocephalism, as a result of which the heads of the standing figures of the saved and those of the seated apostles on the lintel are all on the same level. Other evidences of Roman influence are apparent in the foliage carved on the

FIG. 295.—Arles. SAINT-TROPHIME. Detail of the Façade.

pilasters separating the large figures and in the colonnette capitals, some of which are rather good approximations of a classic Corinthian type.

Byzantine influences, on the other hand, predominate in the sculpture on the *Main Portal of S. Niccola* at Bari (Fig. 296) in southern Italy. The Corinthianesque capitals, for example, are of the type employed in Byzantine architecture (Fig. 72) and sculpture (Fig. 289) of the 5th and 6th centuries in which the leaves are suggested by a play of light and shade resulting from incisions in the surface of the stone rather than being modeled to project outward. The foliate design in the arch is similarly carved to produce an effect of flat bright surfaces marked off by lines of shadow. The acanthus leaves on the stilt-block are the sharp-pointed, weedy type seen in Byzantine ornament although the egg-and-dart above it follows classic prototypes. To the left in the illustration is the figure of an angel whose draperies are suggested by the same illusionistic technique of incised lines that has been observed in the Byzantine Madonna Orans (Fig. 291). The influence of Byzantine models upon the style of the Bari sculpture was direct, for the whole southern region of Italy had been colonized by the Greeks and it had always been in close connection with the eastern Mediterranean countries. In other parts of Europe, the Byzantine mode seems to have affected Romanesque sculpture less directly, largely through the medium of illuminated manuscripts and ivory carvings imported from the Orient.

Fig. 296.—Bari. SAN NICCOLA. Detail of the Main Portal.

The third of the three basic elements that entered in the formation of the Romanesque style was the barbarian. Examples in which it predominates can be found chiefly in France (cf. Fig. 294), its influence being apparent in the tremendous linear movement of the figures, both in surface detail and in outline. Such is the figure of the prophet *Isaiah* (Fig. 297) on the west wall of the church at Souillac, carved during the first half of the 12th century. As in the figures on the Hildesheim Doors (Fig. 293), the linear patterns create the impression of a powerful force animating the swirling draperies and motivating the twisted posture. The immediate origin of this linear style which is seen at Hildesheim and Souillac seems to have been the pen-and-ink illustrations with which the Reims school of Carolingian manuscript illuminators decorated their books, such as those in a Psalter in the University Library at Utrecht (Fig. 368). It is easy to understand in looking at the illustration why the pen-and-ink technique was a medium of expression peculiarly appropriate to the emotional Teutonic barbarian temperament. It must have been a miniature like this that the Souillac Prophet sculptor had before him as a guide. The folds of drapery that were suggested in the drawing by heavy pen strokes are rendered here by meticulously cut parallel lines. The hollow under the sweeping curve of the skirt is a painful transcription into stone of an effect that was easily secured in the original drawing by shading. None the less, with a technique that is entirely linear, the sculptor has succeeded in achieving a very definite plasticity of form which gives even more strength to the general emotional effect generated by the ceaseless flow of the outlines and the sense of unrest in the flying draperies for which a supernatural motive must be imagined.

Fig. 297.—Souillac. Church. Isaiah.

The nervous, animated figures of the Utrecht Psalter and the Hildesheim Doors embody the ideal of effective force which was the specifically northern or barbarian contribution to the mediaeval synthesis of thought, an ideal which is given monumental form in the Souillac Prophet. The same ideal is also expressed in figures of such a considerably different type as those representing the *Sin of Adam and Eve* which were carved on the façade of Modena Cathedral (Fig. 298) about 1100 by a sculptor called Guglielmus. The immediate origin of this figure style is also to be found in manuscript illuminations of the pre-Romanesque period (Fig. 369) but illuminations of a type very different from those in the Utrecht Psalter. These solid figures have a static power quite different from the dynamic energy in those of the Utrecht Psalter, and exist as plastic forms rather than linear patterns. They represent a still further modification of classic concepts than that seen in the Arles sculpture, a modification of a type that had been developed originally to express physical or moral beauty toward one expressing the northern ideal of effective force by giving it a racial Teutonic appearance. The head and shoulders jut forward, the gestures

FIG. 298.—GUGLIELMUS. THE SIN OF ADAM AND EVE. Façade. *Cathedral, Modena.*

are clumsy and awkward but fraught with a certain power by that very awkwardness.

These characteristics appear in Guglielmus' figures of Adam and Eve at Modena. It is unnecessary to point out that the sculptor had little knowledge of human anatomy but this is of small importance in light of the fact that he has revived once more the ideal of plastic form which gave such impressiveness to the carved figures of classic antiquity. However awkward these great hulking bodies may be with their clumsy hands and peasant heads, they reveal the sculptor's awareness of the significance of the human body. And nowhere in Romanesque art is this idea conveyed more forcefully than in these reliefs, although there are other examples of comparable style and character such as the episcopal chair in San Niccola at Bari (Fig. 597) of about the same period. Handicapped though the sculptor was by his limited technique, and naïve and unsophisticated though these figures may be, they are instinct with a primitive power that fills them with life and gives significance to the sculptor's crudely embodied conception of the human form.

The method adopted by Guglielmus to attain this end is very similar to that of the classic sculptor although he did not copy classic originals in any sense. The figures appear against a neutral background with all but the essential features of the landscape eliminated, the story being told entirely by means of the figures. Classic precedent also exists for the subordination of the figures to an architectural setting, standing as they do under a series of pendant arches with an occasional colonnette and surmounted by a foliate cornice. The term classic is used advisedly with no suggestion that a direct classic influence is to be seen in these figures. It means rather that Guglielmus had discovered for himself the principles that governed classic sculpture, in that he gave expression to his ideals through the medium of the human form, creating a rhythmic pattern of its masses which in turn is subordinate to the larger pattern of the architecture.

A pause at this point in tracing the development of mediaeval sculpture to glance back over the various examples of Romanesque art that have been considered will bring two outstanding impressions. The first is the lack of homogeneity in the style itself. On the one hand are figures like those at Arles and Modena, heavy and solid, retaining something of classic sobriety in pose and restrained movement. On the other hand there is the nervous and agitated figure of the Souillac Prophet. The apparent lack of any similarity in the conception of these figures reveals the fact that a synthesis of content and expression has not yet been achieved in mediaeval art. In the Arles and Modena figures, there is an attempt to embody the emotionalism characteristic of the northern temperament in forms that still smack of the intellectually attained unity of the classic ideal. In the Souillac Prophet, on the contrary, the emotional content of the figure has overflowed, swamping the form with linear movement to such an extent that its plasticity is almost lost. In both, it is obvious that the effect is due to superficial characteristics, to the movement of the drapery, to the physical bulk of the bodies, and not to an inner, spiritual contemplation intrinsic in the figures themselves. In other words, the content or meaning of these figures is still symbolic rather than couched and interpreted in terms of human experience.

The synthesis of form and content lacking in the earlier phases of Romanesque sculpture is attained in the figures representing the

*Ancestors of Christ* (Fig. 299) on the west front of Chartres Cathedral (cf. Fig. 99). The part of the cathedral where they are found dates from about 1150, about fifty years earlier than the rest of the edifice. An important point of distinction from the earlier Romanesque figures is the closer relationship of the Chartres statues to the architecture, in

FIG. 299.—Chartres. Cathedral. ANCESTORS OF CHRIST. West Portal.

consequence of which they appear to be a part of the building itself and not just attached to its surface. Judged by a naturalistic standard, this involves "deformation" of the bodies, a quality that is often incorrectly interpreted as indicating lack of skill on the part of the sculptor. Actually, it is the result of a modification of superficial facts of appearance in the interests of a definite pattern by means of which the ideal embodied in the figures becomes tangible and intelligible. This has been the purpose of the sculptor in all times, as has already been pointed out in the discussion of Greek sculpture. The difference between the patterns evolved by the Greek sculptor and those of the mediaeval artist is accounted for by the different ideal they sought to express; that of the Greek is concrete and physical while that of the mediaeval sculptor is abstract and spiritual.

Along with the architectonic quality of the Chartres figures and the resultant abstraction of the forms, there appears another characteristic which at first sight would seem to be directly antithetical to it. This is a new interest in nature, evident in the treatment of the faces; the features are decidedly French and differentiated in a way that indicates an extraordinarily realistic point of view. Notice, for example, the distinction between the heads of the two Queens of Judah that occupy the outermost columns in the illustration (Fig. 299). Thus in spite of the fact that the bodies exist chiefly as abstract patterns in stone, the faces are so expressive that these figures have a real and individual existence by means of which they become symbols, not of an abstract theological idea but of a concept of life that is filled with a comprehension of human need. In this connection, it is interesting to compare the mediaeval sculptor's method of investing his figures with human significance with that of the Greek. The ideal of the latter is expressed in terms of the entire body; the head is considered only as a part of it and not emphasized in any way, as is clearly demonstrated in the Three Fates (Fig. 262) where the absence of the heads does not detract materially from the meaning of the group. Significance is attained in the logical and organic structure of the bodies and by emphasizing their existence as independent and self-sufficient entities. In contrast with this method, the Chartres sculptor treats the bodies as an abstract pattern, the embodiment of a spiritual concept which is rendered concrete by the remarkable expressiveness of the faces and which attains ideal significance through relationship to the architectural background.

The sculpture at Chartres represents the final harmonization of the various elements that went to make up the Romanesque style. Two characteristics stand out among those which distinguish it from the preceding examples. The first of these is the more ordered arrangement of the figures, not only with respect to the architectural setting but in themselves. In this, there appears one of the outstanding features of later mediaeval thought in which the significance of all things was determined in accordance with a preconceived system. The larger significance of this fact is its indication of a point of view that is intellectual rather than purely emotional, and since mediaeval thought was essentially and almost exclusively religious, it indicates a faith that is rational and analytical rather than intuitive. The effect of this change on the Romanesque art is shown by the difference between the Souillac Prophet and the figures at Chartres. As long as the basis of Christian thought was emotional fervor, its ideals could be embodied in an art of linear movement. When it became tinged with an intellectual leaven, a greater degree of form and static strength was essential.

The second characteristic that distinguishes the sculpture at Chartres from earlier examples is its intensely human quality. There is a world of difference between the ideally youthful Kings and Queens of Judah and the meager saints or brutal peasants that gave form to earlier ideals. Again the change in art reflects one that took place in the religious tenets of the Church. Up to the middle of the 12th century, mediaeval theology was to all intents and purposes the code of the Early Church fathers which was highly intellectualized and abstract. The literal and objective Middle Ages could interpret such a theology only with the aid of an emotional fervor that swept away all the obstacles placed in the way of its acceptance by naïve minds, an emotional fervor powerful to that point of fanaticism which inspired the incredible undertaking of the early Crusades. In the latter part of the Romanesque period, a more human spirit transforms the doctrines of the Church, a development contemporary with the decline of the monasteries and the rise of the communes. From this time on, however much the idea of art may have been determined by the Church, the forms by which they were expressed came from the minds of the people. In consequence of this, the figures themselves become more human, subject to the same laws of order as the people who carved them, and expressive of a point of view that finds significance in intellectually contrived systems rather than emotionally felt abstractions. It is this that brings about the more realistic art of Chartres as well as its higher degree of organization and formal discipline.

## C. GOTHIC SCULPTURE

The sculpture of the west front of Chartres occupies a pivotal position in French mediaeval art, for it is at once the culmination of the Romanesque style and the beginning of the Gothic. Characteristic features of the latter style are the cheerful gravity of the figures which replaces the ecstasy or stolid reserve of the earlier ones, a greater naturalism, and the heightened significance which results from physical as well as decorative integration with architectural setting. All of these changes are direct consequences of the shift from the emotional approach to spiritual reality of the Romanesque period to an intellectual one in the Gothic. In this respect, Gothic sculpture is one with the various other manifestations in Europe of the human creative instinct during the 13th century. In every field of activity, intellectual interpretations of experience as the preliminary to an intuitive perception of its ultimate significance took the form of complex systems in which every detail of every aspect of human experience was wrought into a comprehensive and well-articulated scheme. In philosophy, this produced the scholasticism of Thomas Aquinas; in literature, the *Divine Comedy* of Dante; in architecture, the cathedral, of which the sculptured ornament was an integral part. Even in the sculpture moreover, this passion for system and order is apparent in the complex iconography or scheme that governs its arrangement. The ornament is highly naturalistic, reflecting the Gothic conception of the universe as the revelation of God's will whence it is beautiful in every detail and each individual characteristic worthy of representation. In consequence of this, Gothic sculpture is organic and varied as nature itself in its seeming lack of coherence, but it is rendered significant by the iconography or arrangement and by its relationship to the architectural background with which it is indissolubly wedded.

Just as the transitional sculptures of the temple of Zeus at Olympia suggest the ideal that is fully attained in the Parthenon figures, so those of Chartres forecast the culmination of the Gothic style in sculpture of the early 13th century. In the decoration of the western portal of Amiens Cathedral (Fig. 100), which was executed in all probability between 1220 and 1230, the idea of a structural union of sculpture and architecture appears in its most developed form, the subject matter and the way in which it is represented being typical of Gothic iconography, the name given to the rule or tradition determining the portrayal of subjects and, in the design of the cathedral, the place that it occupies. Thus the north portal sculpture at Amiens is devoted principally to the story of Saint Firmin, the patron of the city of Amiens, and the south one relates the story of the Virgin to whom the building is dedicated (Fig. 301), while the *Central Portal* (Fig. 300) is given over to the Last Judgment. This is shown in detail in the tympanum, the arched relief above the doors, which is divided into three registers or levels, with the Resurrection and Judgment of the Souls in the lowest, the Separation of the Elect and the Damned in the middle, and Christ as Judge at the top. The theme is carried over into the voussoirs or arches of the splayed vaulted porch on which are carved, proceeding outward from the tympanum, various personages involved in or symbolizing it—angels with the Elect, Martyrs and Confessors, the Wise and Foolish Virgins, the Elders of the Apocalypse, the Tree of Jesse with the Genealogy of Christ, and the Patriarchs of the Old Law. In the embrasures below, on the level of the doors, are figures of over life-size representing the Apostles of the New Testament and some of the Prophets of the Old; they are identified by attributes of the instruments of their martyrdom or by other means. The Prophets, for example, stand above quatrefoil medallions in the wall beneath which

Fig. 300.—Amiens. Cathedral. The Last Judgment. West Façade. Central Portal.

are carved illustrations of their prophecies, those under the Apostles
having instead the Virtues and their opposite Vices which was one
of the most ancient Christian themes in dogmatic art. On the *trumeau*
or central pier is a standing figure of Christ (Fig. 302). The decoration of the other portals is arranged in similar fashion, differing only
in subject matter; the large figures in the north portal of Saint Firmin
represent the Church Fathers and Saints, while those in the southern

FIG. 301.—Amiens. Cathedral. ANNUNCIATION, VISITATION, AND PRESENTA-
TION. West Façade. South Portal.

one are of the Queen of Sheba, Solomon, Herod and the Three Magi
on one side, and the Annunciation, Visitation and Presentation in the
Temple on the other (Fig. 301), with *trumeau* figures of St. Firmin
and the Virgin respectively. The choice and arrangement of these
figures and their subjects were not left to chance or individual preference on the part of the sculptors, but were determined in accordance
with the most authoritative theological opinion of the time, the source
in this case being the encyclopaedia written by Vincent of Beauvais
called the *Four Mirrors of Human Knowledge*. The sculpture of Amiens
has been called "the Bible in stone," and its instructive function for
those who could not read is clearly indicated.

In considering the style of the sculpture, it must be noted first of

FIG. 302.—Amiens. Cathedral.
THE *Beau-Dieu*. West Façade.
Central Portal.

all that its architectonic purpose is
a paramount consideration. It is this,
for example, that dictates the relative size of the figures which is determined by the part they play in
the design of the building regardless of inconsistency with those adjoining them. Within these limits,
however, there are certain changes
from the similarly conceived figures
at Chartres (Fig. 299) which can
be noted in the *New Testament
Scenes* of the south portal at Amiens
(Fig. 301). There is still very little
movement in the bodies themselves.
The draperies are heavier than those
of the Chartres figures and fall in
more plastic folds, evidence of the
naturalistic trend of Gothic development. The same characteristic is apparent in the turning of the heads
by which the figures are related to
each other in three groups, the Annunciation, the Visitation and the
Presentation in the Temple, reading
from left to right. This turning of
the heads and the loosening of the
draperies represent a modification
of the rigidness seen in the Chartres
figures, but the canopies over the
heads serve to integrate them with
the architectural setting. The heads
are somewhat larger in proportion
to the bodies than at Chartres but,
curiously enough, they are much
less sharply differentiated than are
the earlier figures, being types
rather than portraits.

The *Beau-Dieu of Amiens* (Fig.
302) might well be considered the
complete embodiment of the 13th-
century ideal. It occupies the *trumeau* or central post in the Last

Judgment portal (Fig. 300) and represents Christ holding the Book of the Law in His left hand, the right being raised in benediction. Under His feet are the adder and the basilisk, symbolic of the forces of evil which He overcomes. The full draperies are arranged according to the High Gothic formula, vertical folds on one side and a cascade of horizontal ones on the other. The heavy band around the hips was a favorite device in Gothic sculpture to conceal the artist's inability to achieve correct articulation of the legs with the torso. The lack of anatomical knowledge this indicates is also evident in the absence of any suggestion of an actual body underneath the draperies. The face is modeled in large and simple planes whose broad surfaces create the effect of firm and youthful roundness which was an integral part of the robust High Gothic ideal. Gothic too is the calm, cheerful dignity of the figure, embodying a very different ideal than that seen in the Romanesque prophets (Fig. 297). Here is no fanatic threatening sinners with the tortures of Hell but a just and benevolent ruler who deals with each according to his deserts. No single figure could better reveal the emphasis placed on the joys of earth and heaven in Gothic theology in contrast to the preoccupation of Romanesque thought with the punishments waiting in the next life for him who sinned in this.

The fine balance between concrete naturalism and abstract decoration attained in the figures of the west front of Amiens Cathedral is characteristic of sculpture through the first half of the 13th century and is the outstanding trait of the French High Gothic style. During the second half of the century, the latent naturalism of the style becomes more prominent as in the *Vierge Dorée* of Amiens (Fig. 303), dating from about 1280, on the *trumeau* of the south transept portal. The name is derived from the fact that the figure was originally covered with gold leaf. In the hawthorn borders of the lintel, the sculptor's close observation of simpler natural forms has resulted in a quite realistic effect but one attained without sacrificing decorative unity. In the human figures, a disposition toward naturalism is also apparent, but the effect falls short of the admirable synthesis that creates an ordered whole out of infinite variety in the foliate borders. Two things are responsible for this. The first was the sculptor's ignorance of anatomical construction because of which it was impossible for him to make them convincing in themselves. The second is the less architectural character of the figures which was the result of attempting to make them more naturalistic. In an effort to give the bodies a realistic appearance, the sculptor resorted to mannerisms of gesture and conventions of form to compensate for their lack of convincing anatomical articulation. This is quite apparent in the Apostles on the lintel, a group of debonair figures very different from the sturdy burghers in the same rôle in

FIG. 303.—Amiens. Cathedral. THE *Vierge Dorée*. South Transept Portal.

the west portals (cf. Fig. 300). They stand rather casually under canopies which have lost architectural significance by being merged into a continuous border, the only motive that gives the figures any relation to each other being light-hearted conversation that only partially occupies their attention. The effect is not convincing, for the sculptor still conceives the forms in terms of architectural conventions, such as the fall and cascade of the draperies noted in the Beau-Dieu. But the significance which the earlier figure derived from its architectural setting is not so great in the later ones and the naturalism of the figures themselves is not sufficient in itself to make them convincing in another way.

The disintegration of the High Gothic architectonic style that came with a more naturalistic ideal and the attendant weakening of dogmatic content is also apparent in the Madonna. In contrast with the bourgeois ladies of the western portals (Fig. 301), the Vierge Dorée appears in the form imagined by humble minds as an aristocratic one. The noble gravity of the earlier figures is replaced by gracefulness; the concept of the Virgin as the Queen of Heaven to which a rigidly architectonic form added dignity is replaced by one of an altogether human mother. The youthful freshness of the faces in the High Gothic style is exaggerated and an attempt to attain greater expressiveness without adequate anatomical knowledge results in mannerisms such as the slanted eyes and the smile on the lips. In the body, an effort to attain gracefulness of posture produces the "hip-shot" pose with the weight of the swaying figure resting on one leg. The resultant contrast between the lines of the figure and the rigidly vertical ones of the pillar of which it is a part is the first step in the separation of sculpture from the architecture that had given it stability and significance in the High Gothic period.

In 14th-century French sculpture, the mannerisms that appear in the Vierge Dorée continue and are exaggerated. It has already been pointed out that the spiritual content of late 13th-century sculpture had been weakened by attempts to secure greater naturalism on the one hand and to evolve a standard of objective beauty intrinsic in the figures themselves on the other. In the *Virgin of Paris* (Fig. 304) in the Cathedral of Notre-Dame, the effect of substituting a purely aesthetic ideal for one of religious significance becomes apparent. No pretense is made of relating it to an architectural setting. The drapery folds, which formed a discreet contrast with the rigid lines of the architecture in the High Gothic figures, have become a major interest; the robes are designed as an end in themselves and form a unity quite independent of the body which is not even suggested underneath them. The human sentiment noted in the Vierge Dorée is here carried to the point of artificiality by the exaggeration of the pose and the childish head with its almond eyes and thin mouth whose immaturity is emphasized by the over-large crown. This affectation of pose and sentiment reveals an ideal that is devoid of any very profound meaning, but none the less the figure retains the saving grace of a certain distinction or elegance. However artificial the concept, the figure possesses style, a quality that has characterized French art ever since the Middle Ages even in its most uncreative and sterile phases. It was due to this distinction that French 14th-century sculpture exerted a powerful influence on late mediaeval sculpture in all parts of Europe, particularly in Italy.

FIG. 304.—THE VIRGIN OF PARIS. *Notre-Dame, Paris.*

The mannered grace and delicacy of the Virgin of Paris indicate one trend in French 14th-century sculpture. Another one, characterized by greater naturalism, is apparent in such statues as those of Charles V and Jeanne de Bourbon in the Louvre, which are fine examples of the best mediaeval portraiture. This tendency in 14th-century sculpture had its roots in the latent naturalism of the High Gothic style to which a stimulus was given by a desire for greater realism in sepulchral figures, a cause and effect analogous to the similar phenomena observed in Roman sculpture. The realism of 14th-century art indicates better than words the relaxation of High Gothic idealism. Although it was a definite factor in native French style, the immediate source of this realistic element was in the art of the Netherlands where it had dominated the High Gothic manner, in contrast to the pronounced idealism of contemporary French art. Transferred to France by a school of Flemish artists in Paris, this realistic mode soon became very popular. It appears in monumental form in the art produced in Dijon toward the end of the 14th century and during the early years of the 15th by Flemish artists attached to the court of the Dukes of Burgundy.

The outstanding example of this realistic Franco-Flemish style in sculpture is the *Well of Moses* (Fig. 305) in the erstwhile monastery of Champmol near Dijon. The illustration shows one of six figures representing prophets of the Old Testament that were carved as decorations for a well-head by the Netherlandish sculptor Claus Sluter (d. 1405) between 1395 and 1403. The motivation is interesting. The well-head was originally the base of a carved group representing the Crucifixion. The

FIG. 305.—Claus Sluter. MOSES. THE WELL OF MOSES.
*Chartreuse at Champmol, near Dijon.*

idea of relating the Old Testament prophets to this scene came from one of the mystery plays that were so popular during the Middle Ages. The source of this particular idea was the prologue to a passion play, such as that which is recurrently celebrated at Oberammergau, in which Christ is condemned to die for humanity by a tribunal of patriarchs and prophets who pass sentence upon Him. In the sculptured figures, the pronouncement of each judge was inscribed upon the long scroll which he holds. Moses (Fig. 305) speaks in words from the book of Exodus, "At eventide, he sacrificed a lamb before the multitude of the children of Israel." In creating this figure, from which the whole group derives its name, Sluter omitted no detail of appearance, yet it is no mere study in realism. The venerable patriarch seems to bear the weight of centuries upon his shoulders in the realistically draped folds of the robe. The ease with which he supports them is translated in the observer's mind into an indication of intellectual as well as physical power, an impression which is furthered by the sense of superhuman vision in the piercing eyes. The only suggestion of symbolism is the horns on the forehead. The architectural background is a reminiscence of the High Gothic method of investing the figures with authority, but the poses are not motivated by it. Originally, the realism of the figures was greatly intensified by color in accordance with Flemish tradition in which sculpture consisted of little more than painting in high relief. At the same time, the group is characteristically French in the powerful impression of definite form and bulk, for the figures are conceived as sculptural forms rather than as painted images.

In Sluter's works, objective realism is transfigured and ennobled by the epic poetry of lofty conceptions. His less gifted followers were seldom able to do more than record the facts of appearance, confounding the truth of his figures with mere ugliness. As a result, they were

Fig. 306.—The Holy Sepulcher. *Hospital, Tonnerre.*

only rarely capable of investing their own works with genuine expressiveness. In parts of France outside of Burgundy, as in the Loire region, the crude realism of Sluter's followers was never popular and the prevailing style was one which is only mildly naturalistic. A characteristic example is the *Holy Sepulcher* in the Hospital at Tonnerre (Fig. 306) in Burgundy, which dates from 1454. The Flemish realism that is forceful to the point of harshness in the Well of Moses is considerably tempered here. Again the idea is derived from the mysteries. The grouping of the figures around the tomb is naturalistic, based on a scene from a passion play. The carefully studied contemporary costumes, as well as the faces, reveal a similar dependence on actual models. This is particularly true of the Virgin, the figure in the center, in whom a type is seen that is frequently found in contemporary Flemish painting. The naturalism does not detract in any way from the emotional content of the group, however, but adds poignancy to it by making it individual and specific. The sense of bitter grief and depression in these figures is conveyed by the heavy draperies whose broad folds weigh down the wearers so oppressively. The emotion of each person is focused on the dead Christ Who thus unites the group spiritually, just as the various figures are wrought into a plastic unit by the strong horizontal accent of the corpse.

It is no exaggeration to say that the Tonnerre Holy Sepulcher represents the initial step in the final phase of French mediaeval art. The culmination of this phase, and in many ways the most captivating forms it produced, appear in the Champagne region. The inhabitants of that locality were of the bourgeoisie and a deep spirituality almost High Gothic in quality is apparent in their art for some time after the upper circles of French society had adopted the more fashionable and consciously aesthetic style imported from Italy by royal order. It was this sense of the reality of spiritual experience that animated the style known as the *détente,* meaning a relaxation of the unsparing naturalism of the 15th-century Franco-Flemish manner, which apparently had its center in the city of Troyes. The *détente* ideal is beautifully portrayed in a limestone statue of a *Feminine Saint* (Fig. 307) in the Museum of Historic Art of Princeton University. It was a realistic ideal, for the face is characteristically French and the drapery obviously studied from nature. At the same time, these realistic elements are generalized; they exist not as ends in themselves but to give point to the emotional content of the figure. This in turn is expressed in a quiet and restrained fashion, very different from the unfettered manifestations of grief that are seen in the Franco-Flemish style, and indicative of a profoundly felt inner experience. The figure originally formed part of an Entombment group similar to that at Tonnerre although it is later in date, probably coming from the first quarter of the 16th century. Since the group was intended to stand in a niche, the modeling

FIG. 307.—HEAD OF A FEMININE SAINT.
*Museum of Historic Art, Princeton University, Princeton, N. J.*

of the features is quite broad and summary, in sharply intersecting planes. Such treatment was essential to a proper effect in the relatively subdued light of a secluded interior, for over-refined details would escape observation under such conditions. The generalized effect that results from the summary modeling invests the figure with lofty idealism, a characteristic of all *détente* art. In this quality, it is not unlike the art of the 13th century but with this significant difference, that the idealism of the High Gothic period was an impersonal and abstract one based on a theological interpretation of experience while that of the 16th century is individual and concrete and has its roots in human emotion. In giving form to this ideal in the last years of the 16th century, sculpture became once more a self-sufficient art possessing inherent significance. It thus recovered the individuality it had been forced to yield in being subordinated to architecture in the all-embracing Gothic synthesis of the 13th century.

*Détente* art was the final manifestation of the French mediaeval spirit and in many ways it was the most complete and effective expression of the humanizing tendency that characterized Gothic art from the outset. The lyric grace of its forms was peculiarly appropriate to the pathos of its favorite subjects, but the style lacked intrinsic vigor. This vigor it might have developed but for the fact that it was overwhelmed by the powerful Italianizing style propagated by the school of art established by royal decree at Fontainebleau. The French *détente* was contemporary with the Italian High Renaissance and the winsome saints of the Troyes school gave way to athletic figures embodying the more virile but alien concepts of the southern country. Their supremacy in French art spelled the doom of the mediaeval tradition. Henceforward French artists were concerned no longer with giving form to spiritual ideals but to aesthetic ones. The mediaeval spirit was dead.

# Chapter XX. Renaissance Sculpture in Italy.

THE ORIGINAL FACTOR IN THE DISINTEGRATION OF the High Gothic system that occurred in the 14th century was a growing distrust of the leadership of the Church. In French sculpture, the effect of this disintegration is apparent in the separation of figures from the architectural setting which had given them significance in the High Gothic period and a lapse into mannered artificiality of pose, gesture and expression. At the same time, the naturalism that was an important element in mediaeval style continued with unabated vigor, forceful and masculine in Claus Sluter's Moses (Fig. 305), delicate and feminine and transfigured by profoundly felt emotion in the figures of the *détente* (Fig. 307). Both extremes reveal an interest in the individual which is diametrically opposed to 13th-century collectivism. In the 15th century, nature was no longer viewed as a symbolic manifestation of the mystic order conceived in the minds of theologians and interpreted by scholastic thought. Instead, it was considered as a revelation of the manifold aspects of life itself, experienced directly by the individual with a poignancy that is reflected in all the art of the 15th century, as has been seen in French *détente* figures and as will be observed in Italian ones as well. To give ideal meaning to the expression of this idea, the northern painters had recourse to the infinite vistas of landscape (Fig. 373). In Italy, where the classic tradition had always been strong, the same end was attained in the classic manner by giving the figures significant form, i.e., form which possesses inherent meaning and character.

At first glance, it would seem that such an approach to the problem of giving concrete form to ideas might have resulted in the reproduction of classic figures. Actually this was not the case. The goal of classic thought and art was the determination of universal types and any individual manifestation of those types was considered an accidental aberration. The 15th century began at the other end and conceived of the universal only in terms of the particular owing to its unavoidable heritage of mediaeval thought with its emphasis on specific and indi-

500

vidual qualities. As a result of this, Renaissance art contains an element of dynamic force, even in its most classic aspects, which is quite foreign to the self-sufficient repose that had been the ideal of classic antiquity. Thought in the 15th century was much more complex than in the fifth century, and its full expression could not be embodied in forms whose very existence depended upon a process of generalization and simplification.

This is clearly revealed by an attempt to employ classic forms that took place in Italy in the 13th century. When Niccolo Pisano (ca.1205?-

Fig. 308.—NICCOLO PISANO. The Nativity. Detail of the Pulpit.
*Baptistery, Pisa.*

1278?) constructed a monumental pulpit for the Baptistery of Pisa in 1260, he decorated it with a series of panels carved with the story of the New Testament. The pulpit was a hexagonal box supported by Corinthian colonnettes and reached by a flight of steps leading to one side which was left open. On the first of the five remaining sides, the *Nativity* is represented (Fig. 308). Niccolo employed classic types in the figures. The Virgin reclines on her couch in the guise of a dignified Roman matron. The angel of the Annunciation at the left is a youth clad in a Roman toga, reproducing a type often found on late

Latin sarcophagi. The formulas of hair and drapery came from the same source, notably the manner in which Joseph's beard is represented in tight curls with a drill hole in the center of each one, as well as the broad angular folds of the robes. The figures are generalized and the composition is simple with its quiet vertical and horizontal accents, both contributing to a classic sense of repose. At the same time, there is an intensity in the expression of the announcing angel that reveals Niccolo's discontent with his classicizing forms as a medium of conveying the emotional content of the subject. It is clear from this that he was no precursor of the Renaissance, as he has sometimes been called. The idea underlying his representation of the Nativity is still mediaeval and its forms are only incidentally cast in a classic mould.

How little the 13th century was prepared even in Italy to give expression to its thought in classic terms is shown by the work of Niccolo Pisano's son Giovanni (ca.1250-ca.1317). In a pulpit which he made

Fig. 309.—GIOVANNI PISANO. The Nativity. Detail of the Pulpit. Sant' Andrea, Pistoia.

for the church of Sant' Andrea at Pistoia between 1298 and 1301, he reproduced the general form and subject matter of the Pisa Baptistery pulpit, but the similarity between the two works goes no further than that. Giovanni's Nativity (Fig. 309) is a scene of tremendous agitation in contrast with the calm of Niccolo's. This effect is created by the predominantly diagonal accents of the composition as well as by the sense of movement in the figures themselves. The angel of the Annunciation rushes into the presence of the Virgin, who shrinks before him. The Madonna reaches out to lift the covering of the infant Jesus with a gesture eloquently expressive of a mother's concern for her firstborn. The midwives are almost painfully intent upon their duties, while Joseph, who sits stolidly at one side in Niccolo's version of the scene, is rendered in Giovanni's as a figure striving with moving intensity to comprehend the significance of the mystery that has taken place. The style of the figures shows the influence of late mediaeval sculpture in France in the contrasting broad simplified areas and the involved folds of the draperies. The robe of the annunciate Virgin is arranged according to the mediaeval method of fall and cascade, but it is motivated by the action of the shrinking body and the left hand which grasps the skirt. Comparison of this figure with the Virgin of Paris (Fig. 304) will show how the Italian sculptor has filled the Gothic formula with meaning by giving a reason for the drapery effect. The French figure is artificial and mannered, its gestures merely quaint and ingenuous. The Italian figure, on the other hand, is informed with profound intent and tragic sensibility, and moves as a protagonist in a powerfully emotional drama. The gestures are somewhat over-emphatic, it is true, nor are they as convincing as more extensive anatomical knowledge would have made them. None the less, where the contortions of the Virgin of Paris are simply characteristics of an affected ideal of elegance and grace, the movement of Giovanni's Madonna is expressive of sincerely felt emotion.

Italian sculpture of the 14th century followed, in general, the path indicated by Giovanni's work. In Italian hands, the modish figures of the late Gothic style in France acquired ideal significance by virtue of the Italian heritage of the classic tradition of expressive form. The meaningless gestures of the French figures were invested with genuine meaning by making them indicative of deeply felt emotion. Thus in Italy of the 14th century as well as in France, sculpture was developing a style that would give adequate expression to the concepts of the personal and individual interpretation of experience that were developing in consequence of the breakdown of the High Gothic synthesis.

## A. THE EARLY RENAISSANCE

Toward the beginning of the 15th century, the hitherto basically mediaeval style of Italian sculpture begins to change in accordance with one or both of two concepts previously not found therein—a renewed interest in classic forms and a more positive realism. Both of these tendencies appear very extensively in Early Renaissance sculpture. The interest in classic art may be traced to the affinity between Renaissance humanism and antique thought with its exclusive preoccupation with human values. But at the same time, Renaissance humanism also led to the development of a spirit of genuine scientific curiosity which found much to intrigue it in the naturalism that characterized the closing phases of northern mediaeval art. However, the approach of the 15th century to nature was very different from that of the Middle Ages in that it was analytical rather than synthetic, leading to study of the existing facts of the world for their own sake, rather than as symbols of a divine order. Not the least important result of this attitude was the reappearance in sculpture of the nude human figure as a subject for monumental treatment. Its use had been limited in the theological art of the Middle Ages to a very few themes and it rarely if ever appeared in statues in the round.

In the work of Lorenzo Ghiberti (1378-1455), one of the three outstanding sculptors of the Early Renaissance in Italy, an interest in classic forms is quite evident. Ghiberti first won distinction as the victor in a competition held in his native city of Florence in 1401 for the honor of creating a pair of bronze doors for the Baptistery of San Giovanni. In this competition his chief opponent was Brunellesco, whose failure to win it was instrumental in causing him to turn his attention to architecture as a field of endeavor. All sculptors participating in the competition were required to interpret the same subject, Abraham's Sacrifice of Isaac, as a basis for judgment, and the panels by Brunellesco and Ghiberti are preserved today in the Cathedral Museum in Florence. Of the two, Brunellesco's is the more mediaeval in the diffusion of interest in the composition, the lack of spatial effects and the dramatic intensity of the protagonists. In contrast with Brunellesco's panel, there is unity of interest in Ghiberti's, the result of well-suggested space and a modification of dramatic content in the interest of greater decorativeness. The doors which Ghiberti designed relate the life of Christ and are felt by some critics to fall short of the competitive panel in achievement as they contain many mediaeval stylistic traits. Whatever the judgment of posterity, they were received with great acclaim when Ghiberti finished them in 1423 and they were placed in the eastern portal of the Baptistery.

The following year, Ghiberti was commissioned to execute another pair of doors for the same building which he fashioned between 1425 and 1447. Upon completion, they replaced the first set in the eastern portal of the Baptistery, the other doors being moved to the southern entrance. In the panels of the second doors, called worthy to be the

*Gates of Paradise* (Fig. 310) by Michelangelo, Ghiberti produced a masterpiece of relief sculpture which has never been surpassed for sheer technical skill and has served as a model for such projects ever

Fig. 310.—GHIBERTI. The Gates of Paradise. East Portal.
*Baptistery, Florence.*

since. The subject laid down for Ghiberti was a symbolic parallel of Old and New Testament subjects, a typically mediaeval concept. With characteristic Renaissance individualism, he rejected this scheme and executed one of his own instead. In ten large panels, the Old Testament story is told from the Creation of Man to the Meeting of Solomon and the Queen of Sheba, beginning in the upper left corner and reading across both valves of the portal, each relief being devoted to one character or group of characters although a number of them relate more than one incident. Thus there are two episodes in the *Story of Abraham* (Fig. 311) which appears in the second panel from the top on the right side—the visit of the three angels and the sacrifice of Isaac.

Fig. 311.—GHIBERTI. The Story of Abraham. Detail of Fig. 310.

To attain unity in the representation in one composition of two subjects unrelated in time, Ghiberti portrayed them against a magnificently wrought landscape background which brings the two incidents together by establishing a single volume of space in which they take place. This sense of space in the panel is the result of variations in the depth of the relief planes, ranging from great projection in the foreground figures which are almost free-standing to hardly perceptible lines in the distant ones. The result of this is an impression of air circulating around the figures themselves, an effect similar to that obtained by the same means in the Arch of Titus reliefs (Fig. 286). The greater realism of Ghiberti's relief as compared with the Roman ones is due to his knowledge of the laws of perspective that had been codified by his rival Brunellesco. His rather naïve pride in this knowledge is indicated by the way in which the donkey in the immediate foreground stands with his rump pointing toward the observer, providing the artist with an excuse to demonstrate his skill in foreshortening.

The style of the human figures reveals Ghiberti as standing between the mediaeval and the classic traditions. In the small niche to the left of the Abraham panel, there is a feminine figure representing one of the pagan sybils who foretold the coming of Christ. The pose is the "hip-shot" one of the 14th-century Gothic style (cf. Fig. 304), nor is there an effective correlation of the body and drapery. In the lovely group of the three angels, the anatomical construction is still far from being accurate, but this is overlooked in the stately rhythm of their progress toward the kneeling patriarch, a rhythm which is repeated in the row of trees in the middle distance. Such details reveal the extent to which Ghiberti had reacted to the decorative quality of classic art. In the nude male figure in the niche to the right of the panel, his dependence on classic prototypes is even more apparent. It represents Samson, whom Ghiberti portrays in the guise of a Hercules of Praxitelean pose and Roman muscularity. In spite of such classic elements, Ghiberti's mediaeval background is apparent in such things as the bushy hair and small skull of the Samson, traits which appear in 13th- and 14th-century Gothic figures. The mixture of floral and animal motives in the border surrounding the whole portal is also mediaeval rather than classic in that it is conceived in terms that are linear and not plastic.

In the final analysis, Ghiberti's classicism was more or less incidental to a style which was fundamentally mediaeval. In nothing is this shown more clearly than his employment of landscape and architectural backgrounds to give meaning to his reliefs, depending upon their heroic character to invest the representation of the Old Testament legends with the significance which he could not convey by the figures. How little Ghiberti was capable of informing the figures with character is apparent in the meaningless and rhetorical gestures in such dramatic scenes as the Expulsion of Adam and Eve from the Garden of Eden. Instead of attempting to make his figures other than decorative, he creates a sense of awe in the spectator by the epic grandeur of the deep backgrounds which his incomparable command of relief made so convincingly real. The panels are thus effective as ensembles rather than from the intrinsic character of the individual figures, a conception which is as mediaeval as the decorative scheme of a Gothic cathedral.

In the sculpture of Jacopo della Quercia (1371-1438), there is a very different concept of the human form than Ghiberti's decorative one. In creating the *Sin of Adam and Eve* (Fig. 312) on the main portal of S. Petronio at Bologna, which dates between 1425 and 1438, Jacopo reverted directly to classic methods by suppressing the background al-

most entirely, telling the story by the figures alone. As a result, they
acquire heroic importance, just as do the crudely powerful figures by
Guglielmus on the façade of Modena Cathedral (Fig. 298). The tragic
import of the scene is thus conveyed directly to the observer instead of

FIG. 312.—JACOPO DELLA QUERCIA. THE SIN OF ADAM AND EVE.
Main Portal. S. *Petronio, Bologna.*

indirectly and vaguely as in the case of Ghiberti's landscape backgrounds. The hip-shot pose is a mediaeval reminiscence but it is motivated by the sense of horror in Adam and Eve's seductive pleading. The
proportions of the figures and the treatment of the muscles show the
influence of antique models, but the personal and dramatic note is entirely Renaissance in spirit.

It cannot be denied that Jacopo's figures have certain faults. His knowledge of anatomy and sense of form were not sufficient to give them weight or convincing movement. In the technique of relief carving, he was not the equal of Ghiberti, as is apparent in his failure to suggest the space that exists between the near and distant legs, or to achieve a satisfactory spatial relationship between Adam's right arm, his body and the tree around which the snake is entwined. But the concept of life revealed by these figures is lofty and dignified, and Jacopo's limited technique does not obscure it any more than the restricted methods of the Romanesque sculptor could stifle the emotion he sought to express. In regarding backgrounds and accessories as so many hindrances to clear expression and in giving form to his ideas by the human figure alone, Jacopo is closer in spirit to Greek methods than to Roman ones. Whence he derived this manner, which is unique in the early 15th century, it is impossible to say. But his contemporaries and immediate successors failed to realize its potentialities and not until Michelangelo appeared in the early years of the 16th century was it developed to the fullest possible extent.

The influence of classic art upon Ghiberti and Jacopo della Quercia is quite evident, each reacting to it according to his own nature. Ghiberti, the decorator, saw the formal beauty of its rhythmic patterns, while Jacopo was chiefly impressed by its great expressiveness. Neither one was wholly successful, however, in developing forms possessing these qualities which were capable at the same time of giving full expression to the thought of their own age. This is explained by the fact that neither one was technically equipped to give his figures the concreteness that has ever been the ideal of scientifically-minded ages such as the Renaissance. We have seen that Ghiberti was unable to make his figures act convincingly and that Jacopo's do not give the impression of having weight commensurate with their physical size. In both cases, the sculptors lacked the knowledge of human anatomy necessary to a portrayal of the human body that would carry conviction to the observer. It was the acquisition of this scientific knowledge that made Donatello (1386-1466) one of the most important figures in Early Renaissance art. During his long career, he posed nearly every problem connected with the objective portrayal of the human body and solved a great many of them. He was enabled to do this by his study of the mechanics of the body and, on the basis of the knowledge thus acquired, he adapted the classic idiom to forms that were capable of giving adequate expression to the complicated involutions of modern Christian thought. In so doing, Donatello established himself as the outstanding sculptor of the early 15th century, his only equal as an artistic personality being the painter Masaccio, who was carrying on similar investigations in his field of endeavor (cf. Figs. 394, 395). These two men completely dominated the art of their time.

One of the earliest incidents in Donatello's career was his journey to Rome with the disgruntled Brunellesco in 1403. Although he must have come in contact with many examples of Roman art during the years he was there, his style seems to have been at first very little affected by them, for his earliest known works are two statues for the north portal of the Cathedral of Florence, executed between 1406 and 1408, in which the figures are still conceived in the Gothic manner. Around 1410, Donatello began a series of experiments with classic forms, again without producing any very important results; but about 1416, a number of works characterized by most intense realism appeared. The figure called *Lo Zuccone* or Pumpkin-head from its bald pate (Fig. 313) is one of these statues that were carved for the niches in the Cathedral Campanile in Florence (Fig. 113). The highly individualized features of the head and the draperies show the impatience which Donatello always felt for meaningless generalization and are characteristic examples of the ugliness that is almost invariably found in the early stages of a realistic art. Donatello did not hesitate to portray all details of the powerful figure however short they fell of an abstract standard of beauty. But the tensed muscles of the neck, the bent right wrist, the strong hands instinct with power and the crumpled folds of the drapery create an impression of vital force that transfigures the repellent face, while the shadow over the eyes introduces a note of abstraction. The effect created of a spirit within the figure is the quality distinguishing its Italian and Renaissance realism from that of the Franco-Flemish Moses by Sluter (Fig. 305), whose meaning is conveyed in the mediaeval way by the ac-

Fig. 313.—DONATELLO.
*Lo Zuccone. Campanile, Florence.*

cessory draperies. But with all its realism, the Zuccone shows Donatello's familiarity with classic formulas in the lowered shoulder above the leg supporting the weight of the body, a formula which he employs to heighten the sense of power in the figure itself by the *contrapposto* or twist that it creates.

During the latter part of the 1420's, Donatello executed commissions in various parts of Italy and it seems probable that his travels brought him once more in contact with examples of classic art. The effect of this renewed contact is apparent in a group representing *The Annunciation*

Fig. 314.—DONATELLO. The Annunciation. S. *Croce, Florence.*

(Fig. 314), made between 1426 and 1433 for the church of Santa Croce in Florence, in which the extravagant realism of the Zuccone has been tempered by a degree of antique idealism. The background and the architecture of the niche reveal many classic motives. The head of the Virgin is almost Greek in its purity of line and the modeling of the features, but invested, by virtue of Donatello's sense of the concrete, with a humanness of expression that is rarely absent even from his most

decorative works. Also classic is the drapery treatment, the robes revealing the bodies they cover, yet instinct with a vitality of their own. In
the nude cherubs or *putti* at the ends of the entablature, one of the
favorite subjects of the Renaissance artist appears, a theme which gave
ample opportunity for realistic treatment of the chubby childish bodies
and their abandoned movement.

In the two examples of Donatello's sculpture that have been considered, we can observe two of the outstanding traits of Italian Renaissance
humanistic thought, an interest in classic art and a realistic conception

FIG. 315.—DONATELLO. DAVID. *Bargello, Florence.*

of the human body. Progressing along these lines, it was inevitable that
Donatello should come to realize that the highest achievement in sculpture is the portrayal of the undraped human figure. One of his earliest
nude figures, a Crucified Christ in wood made about 1420, is notable
for the relentless realism that led the outspoken Brunellesco to characterize it as a peasant's conception of the Savior. As a figure to be seen
from only one point of view the Crucifixion is still in the mediaeval
tradition which almost invariably limited the nude to treatment in
relief. The bronze *David* (Fig. 315), which dates from about 1430,
breaks sharply with that tradition by being in the round; and in repre-

senting the youthful figure unclothed, Donatello created the first free-standing nude figure of monumental character since classic antiquity. His debt to antique concepts is apparent in the quietness of the figure and its lack of tension, as well as in the pose, the body being supported by one leg while the other one is relaxed. The modeling is generalized but there are some specific and individual details; the most apparent are

FIG. 316.—DONATELLO. GATTAMELATA. *Padua.*

the thin arms and the bony protuberance of the right hip which creates an awkward angle in the outline of the figure. Both of these are features of the undeveloped adolescent body observed by Donatello's realistic eye. The hat, similar to those worn by Tuscan shepherd lads, is another specific detail that is rather disquieting in the predominant generalization. It casts a shadow over the face which again is unclassic in effect, creating as it does a sense of thought that is personal and individual. The mixture of concreteness and generalization in the figure contributes directly to the extraordinary impression of nudity it creates.

Donatello's best-known work is the statue he created in 1444 of the Venetian general *Gattamelata* (Fig. 316) in Padua, in which he revived another sculptural type that had disappeared in the Middle Ages—the equestrian figure. It is based on classic prototypes, the most immediate one being the statue of Marcus Aurelius on the Capitoline Hill in Rome (Fig. 133), which Donatello had doubtless seen. The quietness and repose of the Renaissance group are a classic effect attained by the broad planes delineating the massive volumes and the balanced design of the group as a whole. The triangles formed by the horse's legs support the heavy body which is a horizontal accent in the arrangement, contrasted with the vertical of the rider and the one sharp diagonal in the line formed by the sword and the general's baton. The ball under the left front hoof is introduced to assure the stability of the group, decoratively as well as in actuality, for it prevents the horse from seeming to march off the pedestal in addition to maintaining its physical equilibrium. In attempting to solve the problem of the equestrian statue, which is one of the most difficult in sculpture, Donatello investigated the anatomy of the horse with the same scientific spirit that is evident in his realistic treatment of the human figure. The veins of the legs and the nose are portrayed very specifically, as well as the peculiar bony structure of the skull. Equally realistic is the contrast between the different textures of horse's hide, saddle blanket and armor. The horse itself is of a heavy draft type and seems somewhat over-large in proportion to the size of the rider, but this, too, is a realistic detail for a smaller horse could not support the weight of a grown man in full armor. The apparent disproportion in the group that results is a partial explanation of the rider's failure to dominate the composition as he should. Seeking to compensate for this to some extent, the sculptor has attempted to emphasize the importance of the rider by a wealth of minute detail on the armor and by the *putti* playing on the saddle behind him, details which attract the observer's attention away from the more broadly modeled charger. The *putti* are a classic motive as are also the winged genii on the relief decorating the pedestal.

As stated above, Donatello followed classic prototypes in the Gattamelata but, as we have seen in his other works, he used the classic form to give expression to concepts which are quite different from those of the antique. Thus in the Gattamelata, he has suggested in the face something of the mentality of the successful military strategist by introducing a concrete and personal note in the prevailing generalization in the fixed, steady glance of the eyes. The greatness of the figure lies in its transcendence of specific details; it is a type rather than an individual. The statue represents Erasmo da Narni, but it does more than represent him for it suggests his subtle and crafty mind as well.

Donatello towers head and shoulders above his contemporaries for the reason that his work is the complete embodiment of the Early

Renaissance spirit. His achievements cannot be summed up in a phrase, as can Ghiberti's by graceful decoration, or Jacopo della Quercia's by robust power; his genius was too great to be restricted to a single mode. He found sculpture still in the grip of mediaeval thought and restricted by mediaeval technique; he left it a powerful instrument, capable of expressing the widely varied ideals of the Renaissance, its apprehension of the antique, its realism which is so concrete and modern in its intellectuality, and above all, the enthusiasm with which it regarded the drama of life with its joy and pain, the drama which had been so long obscured by the veil of mediaeval theological symbolism.

During the second half of the 15th century, two trends can be distinguished in Florentine sculpture, both originating in Donatello's style. One is a search for lyric beauty, the other a tendency toward drastic realism that developed out of the scientific aspect of Donatello's art. An example of the latter is a portrait bust of the Florentine philosopher *Matteo Palmieri* (Fig. 317), modeled in 1468 by Antonio Rossellino (1427-1478). There was no attempt to idealize the homely features which were probably reproduced, as in Roman portraits, from a death mask. Moreover, there was no wish to modify specific qualities, for the naïve pleasure of the Early Renaissance in its newly realized ability to represent the actual appearance of things was still too keen to permit any generalization. It was not until the end of the century that an effort was made in Leonardo da Vinci's painting to determine an ideal aspect of the aged face; up to that time, in the hands of the realists, it was simply ugly.

Fig. 317.—A. ROSSELLINO. MATTEO PALMIERI. *Bargello, Florence.*

The other tendency in Florentine sculpture, toward an expression of lyric feeling, found its outlet in the creation of youthful or feminine forms that stand in sharp contrast to the aged male portraits preferred by the realists. One of the most ingratiating examples of this lyric style is a relief of the *Virgin and Child* (Fig. 318) by Desiderio da Settignano (1428-1464). A pupil of Donatello, Desiderio inherited from his master something of the honesty of observation that appears in the older man's style, and also the technical skill that makes his linear low relief such an expressive vehicle of tender sentiment. The aristocratic elegance of Desiderio's figures is a personal characteristic in which he differs from the best-known of the 15th-century lyric sculptors, Luca della Robbia (1400-1482). Luca's career fell chiefly in the early years of the century, but in the sturdy, almost rustic types he portrays, the gentle charm emphasized in the later period is anticipated. His favorite subject was the Madonna and Child which he never tired

Fig. 318.—DESIDERIO DA SETTIGNANO. Madonna and Child.
*Panciatichi Palace, Florence.*

of representing in plaques made of the glazed terra cotta with which his name is associated. The technique of these plaques was one that lent itself to broadly generalized effects rather than the specific and concrete ones obtainable in bronze or marble and was thus well adapted to embodiment of an ideal of tenderness and grace.

These characteristics appear even in portraits of the last half of the 15th century when they are of feminine rather than masculine subjects. Such is the marble bust of *Beatrice of Aragon* (Fig. 319), the fourth daughter of Ferdinand I, King of Naples, carved by Francesco Laurana (ca. 1425-ca. 1502) about 1471. It is realistic in so far as it portrays the fashionable lady of the time, with slender neck, sloping shoulders, plucked eyebrows and shaven forehead, the type immortalized by Leonardo da Vinci in the Mona Lisa. The realism of these details was accented by that of the originally colored hair and the gold inlay in the Cufic letters that form the garment borders. The classic taste of the period is reflected in the nymphs and volutes on the base. The features are generalized to the point of impersonality, but this may have been the result of an attempt to suggest the courtly and aristocratic

FIG. 319.—LAURANA. BEATRICE OF ARAGON.
*Kaiser Friedrich Museum, Berlin.*

bearing of the princess. The half-closed eyes are a trait that has been observed in the ultra-sophisticated Virgins of French 14th-century sculpture (Fig. 304) where it is also the hallmark of a fashionable type. But the subtle modeling of the marble to suggest the smooth luster of youthful flesh and the sly demureness of the expression invest the Laurana head with a concreteness that is very different in effect from the artificial mannerism of the earlier figure.

By contrast with the lyric beauty that appears in the work of Desiderio da Settignano and Laurana, the unsparing realism that characterizes the figures of their more scientific contemporaries is all the more striking. It represents a logical continuation of Donatello's tradition of scientific curiosity in that it led to searching investigations into the structure of the human body. Thus in the statuette of *Hercules and Antaeus* (Fig. 320), Antonio Pollaiuolo (1432-1498) attempted to solve the problem of representing muscular movement in a convincing fashion. Like most of the scientific realists, he preferred to work in bronze for the greater accuracy in detail it made possible, and in the statuette he has rendered the muscular organization of the struggling

FIG. 320.—A. POLLAIUOLO. HERCULES AND ANTAEUS.
*Bargello, Florence.*

giants with great faithfulness. In the hands of a lesser man, this might have resulted in the dryness of an academic study, but Pollaiuolo succeeded in giving the figures character by the tremendous energy with which he has endowed them and in which they should be compared with those in his equally vigorous engraving of the Ten Fighting Nudes (Fig. 406). Although the group stands only a few inches high, it radiates a dynamic force that raises it far above the level of a mere *tour de force* of representation.

Contemporary with Pollaiuolo and like him a representative of the scientific trend in Florentine sculpture of the late 15th century was Andrea Verrocchio (1435-1488). He is like Pollaiuolo also in the fact that his sculpture reveals an attempt to make the human form something more than simply an accurate portrayal of anatomical structure. His interest in anatomy is apparent in a bronze *David* (Fig. 321), modeled about 1465 for the Medici family, in which the bony structure of the spare adolescent figure is so strongly emphasized that the ribs show through the hard leather corselet the young hero wears. This results in a pattern of bumps and hollows in the torso that should be compared with

Fig. 321.—VERROCCHIO. DAVID. *Bargello, Florence.*

the smoothly rounded planes of Donatello's figure of the same name (Fig. 315), for it creates an effect of muscular tension that is quite different from the quiet relaxation of the earlier form. The staccato effect of such details is confirmed by the angularity of the body as a whole; the left arm, for instance, whose bending recalls that of the Donatello figure, adds a note of still further harshness instead of balancing in classic rhythm the movement of the right arm in supporting the sword. The head is uncovered, and the minutely rendered planes of the face, with its subtle and baffling expression that reminds us of the fact that Verrocchio was the master of Leonardo da Vinci, are clearly visible. The various details noted are anatomically accurate and are well composed in an organically structural pattern, but in addition to this they are also contributory to the impression of nervous vitality that keys the figure up and is the most significant point of difference between it and the earlier one by Donatello. For it reveals the realization on the part of the late 15th century artist of the limited expressive resources of unmodulated naturalism which had been in large measure the major interest of his predecessors, and shows him trying to use creatively, as it were, the vocabulary of form upon which the earlier

FIG. 322.—VERROCCHIO. COLLEONI. *Venice.*

men had exhausted their inspiration in doing no more than bringing it together.

Similar characteristics appear in Verrocchio's equestrian statue of Colleoni (Fig. 322) in Venice. A comparison with Donatello's Gattamelata (Fig. 316) will show even more clearly than that of the two Davids the changes that occurred in sculpture during the course of the 15th century. Donatello is under the spell of the classic, clothing his figure with the form of a Roman general and endowing it with a force that is potential and intellectual. Verrocchio, on the other hand, has all that the 15th century had learned of emotional expression at his command, and his figure seems to be alive with nervous energy, an impression arising from the sense of general movement created by the innumerable planes of the modeling. The pose of the rider also contributes to this effect. In contrast with the easy relaxation of Gattamelata, Colleoni stands erect in the stirrups, with his body turned to the right although he is glancing to the other side. The steed is high-spirited, quite different from the heavy animal bestridden by Donatello's general, yet he is effectively dominated by his rider. His forward movement is controlled by the backward pull on the mouth as indicated by the creases in the neck, thus attaining directly the balance of opposed forces essential to decorative stability that Donatello could bring about only indirectly by the ball under the horse's front hoof. Psychologically, Donatello's work is superior. It conveys the shrewd personality of the mercenary soldier more effectively than Verrocchio's figure. But as an embodiment of the fiery passion of the warrior, the theatrical pose and defiant expression of Verrocchio's statue undoubtedly surpass the more restrained Gattamelata. The savage spirit of Colleoni, very different from the cool passionless intellectualism of Donatello's general, is conveyed directly to the observer by the grim face with its features so strongly emphasized as to be almost caricatured, the absolute control of the rider over his mount and the suggestion of tremendous power in the twist of the body.

Verrocchio was the last great sculptor of the Early Renaissance in Italy, and in his work there is still much of the indiscriminate love of life that characterizes the entire period and explains the intense interest of its artists in natural forms. During the early years of the 15th century, the expression of this interest was somewhat tempered by the feeling, unconsciously inherited from the Middle Ages, of a need for universal significance. It was that feeling that led Ghiberti to place his Old Testament scenes in the midst of heroic landscapes from which the decorative figures might indirectly acquire an authority they did not have in themselves. It is apparent too in the lofty conception of the human figure that transcends the technical limitations of Jacopo della Quercia's style, and in the personal, intellectual note in Donatello's manner. But the deep undertones of mediaeval thought became fainter with the progress of time; even in Donatello's last works, the classic balance of the Annunciation and the Gattamelata gives way to unrestrained emotion. Furthermore, the example of Donatello stimulated a scientific interest in the exact portrayal of the human body which, combined with the fascination intrinsic in representing things as they appear to be, served to create in later sculptors an increasing fondness for natural forms for their own sake, seen most characteristically in the male portraits (Fig. 317). The implication of this attitude is that all that is natural is therefore good in its own right. This cult of the natural was not limited to 15th-century sculpture; it is evident in painting also, and underlies Lorenzo de' Medici's *Canzoni*. Its connotation of personal and individual values as criteria appears even in what political theory existed at the time, the only ideal being achievement of personal ambition without regard for the good of community or state. The consequence of such a mode of thought was that which inevitably follows in the train of a philosophy whose highest ideals are expressed in purely physical terms—moral decay. In Florence, this is manifest in the wanton festivals which alternated with periods of bitter armed strife, both of which so weakened the city that it fell an easy prey to Charles VIII of France when he invaded Italy in 1494 after the Medici had been exiled. The position of eminence in 15th-century European art that Florence had attained under their benevolent tyranny was lost, never to be recovered, for the increasing power of the papacy made Rome the center of the most important creative artistic activity in Italy during the early years of the 16th century or the High Renaissance.

## B. The High Renaissance

The second phase of the Renaissance in Italy falls in the first half of the 16th century. It is differentiated from the earlier one by the term High Renaissance and is distinguished by a reaction against the excesses to which the naturalistic thought of the 15th century had led. This reaction had already set in before the beginning of the 16th century. It appears in the temporary transformation of the libertine morals of Florence into a puritanically austere mode of conduct as a result of Savonarola's wrathful fulminations. In painting, it is evident in the discontent with 15th-century formulas that Botticelli expresses in the wistful sadness of his Virgins and pagan goddesses (cf. Fig. 412), and in the simplification of forms and compositions that characterizes Leonardo's work (cf. Fig. 414). In sculpture, it is apparent in the more pointedly expressive qualities of Verrocchio's Colleoni when compared with the earlier Gattamelata.

The significance of this reaction is its indication of a growing feeling that modes of conduct and forms of artistic expression should have greater authority than that of an entirely personal or individual point of view. It was this feeling that led the High Renaissance to search for ideals that would have universal meaning, and that led its artists to evolve forms that would be capable of giving concrete expression to those ideals. In some cases, they sought to solve this problem by close reproduction of antique forms which seemed to be adapted to the desired end by virtue of their generalized character, but this proved unfruitful, for their heritage of Early Renaissance individualism was inescapable. Because of it, the only available path to universal truth lay through the individual, whereas classic thought had attained that end by beginning with generalization. The artistic forms of the classic were thus fundamentally incapable of expressing Renaissance thought. As the Renaissance could understand the universal only in terms of the particular, it had to be attained by means that were intrinsic in the particular. This is the direct cause of the restlessness that characterizes all the great art of the period, for the straining away from life on an ordinary plane to the higher one where universal truths are realized left its mark on the style. In contrast to Greek art, with which that of the High Renaissance is often compared and which acts on the observer as a soothing anodyne descending from the heights of ethereal beauty, art of the 16th century seems to arrest him by its concreteness while transmuting the base material of his experience into golden beauty by the intense fire of sheer physical and intellectual force.

FIG. 323.—MICHELANGELO. DAVID. *Accademia, Florence.*

The dominant personality in High Renaissance sculpture is Michelangelo Buonarroti (1475-1564), in whose works the spirit of the time is completely embodied. He was a man of amazing versatility as architect, sculptor, painter, poet and engineer, but of all the fields in which he worked, sculpture was the most congenial to him. In his earliest figures, a relationship to 15th-century art is apparent. The *David* (Fig. 323) of 1504 shows unmistakable traces of Donatello's style—the hooked wrist of the right hand, to mention but one, that has been noted in the Zuccone (Fig. 313). The detailed anatomical rendering and the fixed glance of the eyes are also 15th-century characteristics. But the face, for all its concreteness of expression, is an idealized type, and one which reappears in later works. The great size of the figure (it stands eighteen feet in height) reveals another method employed by the High Renaissance to attain ideality, the magnification of physical proportions. Still a third High Renaissance characteristic is the sense of strain in the figure which is created by exaggerating the different levels of the shoulders and the tenseness of the neck muscles that results from turning the head toward the left or raised side of the body. The impression of unrest thus created is emphasized by the arrangement of the figure in two opposed structural axes, the torso and head against the legs. This should be compared with a classic statue (Fig. 270) which is constructed in three axes, head, torso and legs, achieving thereby a formal stability which the Renaissance sculptor

FIG. 324.—MICHELANGELO. MADONNA AND CHILD.
*Notre-Dame, Bruges.*

deliberately avoided. The generalizations of Michelangelo's figure make it seem almost classic in feeling when compared with Donatello's romantic shepherd lad or with the realistic one by Verrocchio. But at the same time, its concreteness is such that this David seems capable of performing the deeds attributed to the Biblical hero; this cannot be said for the 15th-century examples, for Michelangelo did not attempt to produce either a symphony of classic grace or a specific portrayal of an individual youth. His aim was to create a form that would typify the unbounded energy and confidence of youth in all its physical strength; the beauty of the statue lies in the completeness of his interpretation of that idea.

At about the same time that he was working on the David, Michelangelo carved a statue of the *Virgin and Child* (Fig. 324) which is in the church of Notre-Dame at Bruges in Flanders. His conception of the subject differs in several important characteristics from the 15th-century type employed by Desiderio (Fig. 318), particularly the treatment as a free-standing group. Different too is the relationship of the two figures to each other. In Desiderio's relief, the Child is seated on his Mother's lap, while in Michelangelo's group he stands between her knees, his figure outlined against the shadows of the drapery folds. The tender playfulness that is such a human element in the 15th-century relief gives way to grave solemnity. The Virgin's face is turned away from the Child, whose mien is as thoughtful as her own. The impersonal dignity of the expressions is given authority by the treatment of the bodies. In the twisting of the torso, the *contrapposto* which becomes an effective instrument of emotional expression in Michelangelo's later works makes its appearance. The body is perfectly expressed by the draperies, which are arranged to emphasize the important structural facts of the anatomy—for example, the heavy folds at the juncture of arm and shoulder. The whole group is marvelously compact in mass whereby it attains unity in spite of the variety of movement in the figures themselves. Made between 1501 and 1505, it reveals a trace of the sculptor's 15th-century background in the detailed treatment of the drapery, but at the same time, the subordination of the accessories to the body forecasts Michelangelo's later manner in which the human figure alone serves as the vehicle of expression. Another detail that also appears in later works is the ideal sexless mask of the face which is deliberately subordinated as an expressive factor.

Michelangelo's later style begins with the tomb that Julius II commissioned from him in 1513. It was partly to provide a suitable setting for this that the Old Basilica of St. Peter in Rome was destroyed, to be replaced by the half-Renaissance, half-baroque structure that now bears the name (cf. Figs. 130-132). Much of the bitterness that clouded the sculptor's last years can be traced to the many interruptions that constantly militated against the completion of this project. The tomb now stands in the church of S. Pietro in Vincoli in Rome, a sorry compromise between Michelangelo's ambition and the niggardliness of Julius' heirs, and gives but a meager impression of the original conception. Only the colossal Moses on the tomb itself is by Michelangelo, but a number of figures elsewhere are known to have been planned for it. Two of these are the so-called *Bound Slaves* in the Louvre in Paris,

Fig. 325.—MICHELANGELO. Bound Slave. *Louvre, Paris.*

one of which is illustrated (Fig. 325). It was probably intended as a symbol of one of the liberal arts, freed by the munificence of Julius but fettered once more after his death. Whatever the symbolic meaning, its larger significance lies in its embodiment of an idea of tremendous power, conveyed objectively by the great muscles and the body twisted in the *contrapposto* noted above in the Christ Child of the Bruges group. To this extent, the sculptor works in the same manner as in the David, but he goes further here than in the earlier work and gives the abstract power of poignancy to the physical potential of the figure in representing it as restricted by the bands around the chest against which it has struggled in vain. The motive thus given for the exhaustion of the figure may appear at first glance to be insufficient, just as the snakes in the Laocoön group (Fig. 280) do not seem to provide an adequate motive for the agony of the dying father and his sons. But by representing not the moment when the figure is exerting its strength to the utmost but the collapse of the body after its energy is spent, the whole concept is lifted from the realm of the physical into the abstract. The sense of tragedy comes from the futility of the magnificent physique in the face of a power that is the greater because it is not represented but suggested.

In the Bound Slave, Michelangelo approaches his ideal of the plastic expression of ideas solely by means of the human form. The progress of his style toward this goal can be observed by comparing the Madonna of Bruges (Fig. 324) with the *Virgin and Child* in the Medici Chapel in S. Lorenzo in Florence (Fig. 326), which was probably executed between 1525 and 1533. The comparatively simple movement of the figures in the earlier group has become more complex, with a consequent enhancement of expressive poignancy. Notice, for example, the torsion created in the upper part of the Virgin's body by forcing the right shoulder back while the head is turned to the left. The legs are crossed, resulting in more complex patterns of form in that part of the body also than in the Bruges group where the only movement is the raising of the left foot higher than the right one. The compactness of the earlier composition is retained, however, by placing the Child astride his Mother's knee, the body twisted around as the infant searches for the Mother's breast. The face of the Virgin is almost masculine in type and has become definitely a subordinate expressive element in Michelangelo's vocabulary of form, a fact explained by his ever-increasing intolerance of details that might detract from the major importance of the concept as a whole. The same thing is true of the manner in which the drapery is treated. Where in the earlier group it was represented in some detail and with a suggestion of its intrinsic texture, it has now become a neutral substance that is of value primarily in making clear the articulation of the powerful body underneath. Thus although there is hardly any contrast between the surface of the left foot and the drapery covering the leg, the three folds radiating from a point immediately underneath the knee are emphasized to make clear the organic function of the joint, thus accenting a detail that must be understood if the structural unity of the pattern of volumes making up the figure is to be grasped.

The *Medici Tombs* in the New Sacristy of S. Lorenzo in Florence

FIG. 326.—MICHELANGELO. Madonna and Child.
*Medici Chapel, S. Lorenzo, Florence.*

(Fig. 138) represent the climax of Michelangelo's plastic style. He designed both the architecture and the sculpture and although the chapel was never entirely completed, there is a consistency of effect throughout which forecasts the artistic synthesis that was to take place in the baroque period. Planned originally as a commemorative mausoleum for the Medici family, the sacristy would have contained four tombs, two single ones for Giuliano de' Medici and Lorenzo, the Duke of Urbino, and a double one for Lorenzo the Magnificent and his brother Giuliano, but only the two single tombs were completed after generally similar designs. A seated statue of the deceased occupies an architectural niche above the sarcophagus on which are two recumbent nude figures, one male and one female. These represent Night and Day on Giuliano's tomb (Fig. 327), while those on Lorenzo's sarcophagus are Morning and Evening (Fig. 138). No pretense is made to portraiture in the statues of the deceased, for the face of each is the same sexless mask that appears in the Madonna and Child in the same chapel (Fig. 326). Only in the postures is there any differentia-

FIG. 327.—MICHELANGELO. THE TOMB OF GIULIANO DE' MEDICI.
*Medici Chapel, S. Lorenzo, Florence.*

tion, Giuliano as the alert symbol of an active life balanced against the contemplative Lorenzo. The shadow over the face of the latter heightens the impression of an abstract and impersonal entity, an expressive device that anticipates baroque methods.

In the nude figures on the sarcophagi, Michelangelo attained his ideal of the human form as the sole means of giving expression to abstract ideas. Drapery is omitted for it would have been an impediment to the fullest realization of this ideal. Even the faces are relatively unimportant as individual expressive factors, drowned in shadow in the *Night* (Fig. 328) and left unfinished in the figure of *Day* (Fig. 327). In the bodies, stylistic characteristics that have been noted in Michelangelo's earlier figures are emphasized. In the *Night* (Fig. 328), a powerful *contrapposto* is created by forcing back the left leg against the forward twist of the right arm and shoulder, resulting in violently contrasted movements within the body. The pose is one that seems impossible of human attainment, yet Michelangelo renders it plausible by investing the figure with all the concreteness that Renaissance naturalism made possible. Another expressive contrast is that

Fig. 328.—MICHELANGELO. Night. Detail of Fig. 327.

between the face with its delicate profile and the heavy torso of brutally masculine proportions with hanging breasts and wrinkled abdomen. These physical discordancies are poignant details in the general impression created by the figure of superhuman bodily strength sapped by deadly weariness to which its precarious poise on the sarcophagus also contributes. The figure becomes thereby an element in the greater dissonance that exists in the whole design as a result of the conflict between the sculpture and its architectural setting.

In the spectator viewing these powerful bodies that are wracked and exhausted by forces of superhuman power, there arises an indescribably tragic emotion. He experiences in their presence the same sense of human futility that invests the Bound Slave with such pathetic meaning, but it is achieved more subtly than in the earlier work—by the languor and weariness of the figures instead of the bonds—and is consequently more powerful in effect. Michelangelo has thus evolved a method of expression comparable in character to that employed by the fifth-century Greek sculptor, namely, a formal arrangement of the human body; yet nothing could be less classic in effect than these tremendous figures. The difference between the beauty of the Mount Olympus of the Parthenon (Fig. 261) and that of Day on the tomb of Giuliano de' Medici (Fig. 327) is explained by the different ideals they embody, intellectual and impersonal in the Greek figure, individual and emotional in that of the Renaissance. In these figures, Michelangelo gave concrete form to the disillusionment and sense of frustration in his own soul. A sincere Christian, he lived in an age notable for its disbelief. A champion of municipal and national political freedom, he saw his beloved Florence crushed under the heel of anarchy and Italy enslaved by foreign powers. A consummate artist, he was prevented from completing every one of the projects that had been dearest to him. In the light of these facts, it is no wonder that below the personifications of the Active and Contemplative Lives over the sarcophagi of the Medici scions, he placed these gigantic beings, of superhuman power, but overcome by lassitude and exhaustion, a withering commentary upon the futility of all human endeavor before the forces of ignorance and evil. The superlative thing about them is the transmutation by the alchemy of genius of such personal feelings into universal symbols, providing an investiture of beauty for human suffering in all ages to come.

# Chapter XXI.   European Sculpture
# from 1550 to 1800

*MICHELANGELO'S INFLUENCE UPON SCULPTURE WAS* very great and not invariably beneficial. So authoritative were the gigantic forms that gave expression to his ideas that, by comparison, figures by his predecessors and the majority of his contemporaries who still employed 15th-century methods seemed pallid and feeble, and there was but little demand for such work after Michelangelo's time. Instead there is evidence of a taste for the extraordinary and the striking in the work of many of his successors, who employed forms similar to his but inevitably without their profound meaning. In this respect, Michelangelo stands in much the same relationship to sculpture of the late 16th century as Donatello to that of the 15th; the technical problems that he posed were observed, but the content that gave his figures significance was not perceived. This is apparent in the three main tendencies in Italian sculpture after 1550. The first was to reproduce the colossal size of Michelangelo's figures, trusting to their physical bulk to achieve a monumental effect. The second was to utilize his forms for decorative purposes. The third is seen in attempts to transform the effect of suppressed power implicit in his figures into explicit movement.

Of the first of these three tendencies, there is no necessity to speak in detail. The technical proficiency which is sometimes evident in the work of the exponents of the colossal is never sufficient to offset the magnificent ineptitude of their ideas. The best-known if not the most important exemplar of the second tendency is Benvenuto Cellini (1500-1571). His intriguing personality lives again in the lines of his *Autobiography*, whose rapid prose invests his sculpture with a literary and anecdotal interest greater than that of its plastic patterns. The fascinating account of casting the bronze *Perseus with Medusa's Head* (Fig. 329) in the Loggia dei Lanzi before the Palazzo Vecchio in Florence (Fig. 111) has much greater vitality than the figure itself, which was executed in 1548. The statue is an excellent example of the technique of bronze-casting. It is in two separate parts, one being the body of Medusa and the other the hero holding her severed head. The drama of the subject is entirely lost in the ostentation of the Michelangelesque form which combines emphasis on muscular structure with the over-minute rendering of detail that reveals Cellini's training as a goldsmith. In the contrasted horizontal and vertical accents of the two bodies, there was a possibility of diffusing the interest of the group, a danger which the sculptor sought to avoid by the somewhat ludicrous device of having Medusa's leg pulled around the base by her left arm. The same subordination of dramatic considerations to decorative ones is evident in the treatment of the blood spurting from the severed neck and head. The irrepressible egotism of the sculptor that is evident in every line of his *Autobiography* led him to inscribe his name in a prominent position on the diagonal strap across Perseus' shoulder and also to introduce a mask with his own features on the top of the helmet where its invisibility protected him from the jeers with which his contemporaries would certainly have greeted it.

Fig. 329.—CELLINI. Perseus.
*Loggia dei Lanzi, Florence.*

The third tendency in Italian sculpture of the late 16th century is seen in the work of Giovanni da Bologna (*ca.* 1524-1608), who attempted to give his figures something of the power latent in Michelangelo's by highly animated poses. The three bodies in the *Rape of the Sabine Woman* (Fig. 330), which was executed in 1583, resemble those created by the great Florentine in their *contrapposto*. But it is a decorative device rather than a means of emotional expression, the twist of one figure being opposed to that of the others to achieve an effect of balanced spiral upward movement in the contours. The same static movement appears in his best-known work, the bronze Flying Mercury. The effectiveness from all points of view thus attained anticipates the formal conceptions of the 17th-century baroque art.

It has been pointed out in discussing late 16th-century architecture in Italy that the taste of the time shows a decided tendency toward academic conceits. This is no less true in sculpture. In the Rape of the

Sabine Woman, for example, the faces of the three figures are ideal generalized types in the classic manner. The old man is clearly related to Laocoön (Fig. 280) in both expression and the gesture of the hand, and the body of the woman, for all its naturalism, was evidently modeled on that of the youth to the left in the same group. It should be noted in passing that the Hellenistic statue was discovered in 1506 and its immediate popularity was doubtless considerably increased by the taste

FIG. 330.—GIOVANNI DA BOLOGNA. THE RAPE OF THE SABINE WOMAN. *Loggia dei Lanzi, Florence.*

for violent movement created by Michelangelo's works, so it is not surprising that it should have exerted a notable influence upon the late 16th-century sculptors who were attempting similar effects. No less academic than the style was the formal problem that Giovanni set for himself in executing the group, to portray and contrast in a single statue three different nudes, the feminine, the youthful masculine and the aged masculine. He was interested only in the technicalities of the problem, but the humanist critics of the time promptly christened it with the classic title by which it has been known ever since. Under such circumstances, it could hardly be expected to have any profound meaning nor does it have. It is highly decorative, however, a fact which explains its considerable influence on later sculpture, not only in Italy but elsewhere in Europe.

Outside of Italy, the most important sculpture produced in Europe during the last half of the 16th century originated in France. As in architecture, the first Renaissance sculpture in France reveals more or less superficial Italianisms, evident chiefly in attempts to modify the concrete and realistic native style toward a more consciously aesthetic and decorative ideal. The Italian sculptural modes made their entrance into France in the same way as the architectural ones; both were introduced by the rulers whose eyes had been opened to the novel beauty of Italian art in the course of their military expeditions into the southern peninsula. As a result of the interest thus aroused, Italian artists were encouraged to come to France, among the sculptors being Benvenuto Cellini, whose accounts of his experiences in the French court constitute some of the most entertaining pages of his *Autobiography*. The decoration of the palace built at Fontainebleau by Francis I and his successors from about 1530 on was almost entirely by these Italians, and their *atelier* at Fontainebleau soon became a school to which many French artists went for training. It was the source, moreover, of an enthusiasm for classic ideas that led among other things to the importation from Rome of a number of bronze replicas of antique statues that had been discovered there. The ingredients of the late 16th-century style of French sculpture were thus threefold—the native, realistic mediaeval tradition, the classic, and the interpretation of the latter that appears in Italian High Renaissance art.

In the development that took place in French 16th-century sculpture, the classic and Italian manners soon became preeminent, thanks to the fashionable prestige lent them by aristocratic patronage. There is an important difference, however, between French 16th-century classicism and that of Italy in the 15th. The latter country turned naturally to the antique when the yoke of Gothic dominance was thrown off, for it was a rightful inheritance from the past. In France, on the other hand, the classic mode was no more than an imitation, based on an absolute ideal of *a priori* perfection. In consequence of this, it was incapable of such development as that which characterized Italian 15th-century art or the earlier French Gothic for that matter, both of which originated in an intuitively felt need for expression and which changed in form with the ideals of the civilizations that produced them. In contrast to this, the French classic ideal of the 16th century was realized not intuitively but by a purely intellectual process; once attained, there was no possibility of further development. The larger significance of this contrast is that it meant depriving art of the vitality derived from connection with the contemporary thought by making it entirely a matter of theory. Evidence of this latter is seen in the appearance during the 16th and 17th centuries of many theories of art and in the establishment in the 18th of the science of aesthetics. From them, it is only a step to the modern idea of art as a thing apart from life, capable of theoretical exposition, intelligible only to the favored few and similarly restricted as a medium of expression. The authority attained later by this conception of art was a result of the thoroughly logical and therefore typically French synthesis achieved in the style developed by the end of the 17th century which bore the stamp of formal approval by the Academies. It was thenceforward accepted as the basis of artistic judgment throughout the western world.

Attempts by French sculptors to work on preconceived principles derived from classic art can be found as early as 1549. In that year, Jean Goujon (*ca.* 1510-*ca.* 1568) produced his masterpiece, the *Water Nymphs* (Fig. 331) on the Fountain of the Innocents in Paris. The manner in which the bodies appear underneath the draperies suggests comparison with the Greek reliefs of the late fifth-century Nike Balustrade (Fig. 269). The technique is very similar in both, the upper surfaces of the drapery folds being kept quite narrow and the lower planes broadened. In the French example, the clinging effect is motivated by the action of the nymphs, who pour water from the jars they hold. It should not be inferred from this comparison that Goujon was actually inspired by the reliefs of the Nike Balustrade, but only that he was undoubtedly influenced by classic methods. With these he was well acquainted by virtue of the fact that he executed the drawings for the first French edition of Vitruvius. His style is saved from dryness by his lively sense of beauty and feeling for graceful design. That the mediaeval tradition was not completely dead is indicated by the fact that Goujon attained his most effective results in sculpture that was architectonic, as in the Nymphs on the Fountain of Innocents and the reliefs on the early 16th-century portion of the Louvre (Fig. 145). Mediaeval too is the sense of concreteness apparent in the differentiation of the faces of the nymphs and the modish coiffures, a persistence of late Gothic realism. Here it is combined with the alien Italian decorative ideal to produce a somewhat artificial type that is characterized as "aristocratic genre" for lack of a better term. To this same concreteness, which is never wholly absent from French art, is due the remarkable naturalism of the beautiful sinuous bodies revealed by the clinging draperies.

Even more striking than the realism of Goujon's Nymphs is that of the bronze portrait statue of *René Birague* (Fig. 332), made in 1584 as an adjunct to his tomb by Germain Pilon (1535-1590). So powerful is the characterization of this head that all the numerous and insistent details of the naturalistically portrayed draperies and other accessories

FIG. 331.—GOUJON. WATER NYMPHS.
*The Fountain of the Innocents, Paris.*

cannot draw attention away from it. This intrinsic realism was originally even more pronounced because the figure was painted. But even Pilon, confirmed realist that he was, succumbed to a force which made itself apparent in Catholic European countries during the last years of the 16th century, the reaction against the Protestant Reformation in the north. Evidences of this reaction are to be found in all phases of 16th-century life—the Jesuit movement and the bloody Massacre of

FIG. 332.—PILON. RENÉ BIRAGUE. *Louvre, Paris.*

St. Bartholomew's Day at Paris in 1572, to mention only two. In Pilon's sculpture it is apparent in the emotion that practically overwhelms the content of his figures, as in the case of a statue of St. Francis of Assisi which had to be removed from the Louvre and placed in a church because the great number of votary gifts heaped about it in the museum was a source of some inconvenience to the officials. But Pilon's figures are only minor examples of the emotional art in which the Catholic Reaction is made manifest. This is the baroque, and its greatest exponent was the Italian, Bernini.

It has been pointed out before that the outstanding characteristic of baroque art is its striving for intensely emotional effects. In sculpture, this was achieved by investing the animated but cold forms of the late 16th century (Fig. 330) with a new content that involved a definite modification of the style. Just how this was brought about can

be seen in the statue of *Saint Theresa in Ecstasy* (Fig. 333), executed by Gian Lorenzo Bernini (1598-1680) in 1646. The subject is
a typical illustration of the emotional fervor that characterized the
Counter-Reformation. The statue represents a dream, described by the
saint in her writings, in which an angel appeared before her holding
a dart, symbolic of divine love, with which he pierced her heart.
The static movement of Giovanni da Bologna's group has become
dynamic in Bernini's, an effect achieved by avoiding the closed con-

Fig. 333.—BERNINI. Saint Theresa in Ecstasy.
S. *Maria della Vittoria,* Rome.

tours that limit the action in the earlier work and employing broken,
indeterminate ones. By this means, the movement generated in the
animated draperies is not restrained by a firm silhouette but seems to
extend beyond the figure itself, an effect which is heightened by such
devices as the hanging foot and the inclination of the saint's head.
The resulting impression involves not only the carved group but also
the surrounding space with which it is related, a sculptural concept
of a piece with that of 17th-century architecture. The closed contours
that emphasize the bulk and weight of 16th-century figures (Figs. 328,
330) are abandoned. The definiteness of High Renaissance style gives

way to indefiniteness in the baroque and the method of portraying the figures, becoming suggestive rather than representative, is correspondingly more fluent as a medium of expression. Light and shade also play an important part. Michelangelo employed effects of *chiaroscuro* to affirm the static plastic values of his figures, whereas Bernini uses them to emphasize movement of surface and contour, and by creating a specific light source for the group he makes its relationship to space more positive.

In all of these characteristics, the baroque quality of Bernini's style is apparent. The term baroque is usually applied to any art in which an arbitrary handling of material to produce striking effects causes it to pass beyond its proper limits into those of another art whose medium lends itself to more fluent expression. Thus the fluid surfaces employed in baroque architecture produce effects that are intrinsically sculptural (Fig 141). The term might easily be applied to the Laocoön group (Fig. 280) or the Souillac Prophet (Fig. 297), so definitely do both transcend their medium to attain emotional effects. It might even be used to describe Ghiberti's Old Testament panels (Fig. 310) in their approximation of the effect of painting. But the meaning of the term can be most fully realized in Bernini's sculpture. In the sense of space around the figures and their relationship to it, in the play of light and shade created by a light source within the composition and existing as an end in itself, Bernini has employed visual effects appropriate to painting at the expense of primarily sculptural values of weight and volume. That this was his aim he admitted himself in stating that he was trying to "paint in marble." But more fundamental than this is the idea underlying all art of the baroque period, to astonish the observer and so arouse in him a positive emotional reaction. It is for this reason, rather than to demonstrate the skill of the artist, that tons of marble seem to float in the air in the Saint Theresa group, the very form of the material denying its essential weight.

The group of Saint Theresa is characteristic of the art inspired by the Counter-Reformation in its attempt to express spiritual emotion in terms of fleshly experience. The rapture in the saint's soul takes form in physical transports that come dangerously near the sensual, as, in fact, it was described in her own writings. In this respect, the statue makes objective the whole purpose of the Counter-Reformation in which the Church sought to reestablish its power by addressing itself to the emotions of its constituents through the medium of ideas that could be interpreted in terms of human experience. In the Middle Ages, this had been done by appealing to the spirit through the intellect, but that was no longer possible, for the 17th century was separated from the 13th by the Renaissance. Man had been awakened once more to the reality of physical experience, a reality that he was never to forget. As a result, the message of the Church had to be cast in a different form, which it attained abstractly in the doctrines of the Jesuit movement and concretely in baroque art.

The pervasive movement that contributes so materially to the emotional expressiveness of the Saint Theresa is a characteristic baroque feature. In Bernini's portraits, such as that of his mistress *Costanza Buonarelli* (Fig. 334), it is utilized to create an impression of mobile expressiveness that is highly realistic. The same irregularity of contour is seen here that appears in the religious group and is a vital factor in the impression that differentiates a baroque portrait from one of the 15th century (Fig. 319) with

its closed silhouette. Again as in the religious work, the restlessness that results from the broken contour appears in the details as well, in the flowing lines of the tossed hair and the play of light and shade on the crumpled folds of the garment. To this is added the momentary quality of the pose, the open bodice partially revealing the breast, the slight turn of the head, the flicker of light in the eye produced by drilling a hole for the pupil, and the partly opened mouth. The vivacity which all these details give to the portrait is undeniable, but the movement of outline and surface by which it is attained renders impossible the recording of the telling details of personality which are essential to great portraiture.

FIG. 334.—BERNINI. Costanza Buonarelli. *Bargello, Florence.*

The sense of movement that plays so important a part in the emotional effect of baroque religious sculpture and the naturalism of its portraiture is employed to achieve most ingratiating results in works of a decorative nature, such as the fountains with which many of the Roman piazzas or open squares, like the one in the Piazza de Spagna (Fig. 142), were ornamented in the 17th century. In them, the actual movement of water over the fluid surfaces of the figures considerably heightens their animation. One may also be seen before the Pantheon in Rome (Fig. 57), made up of writhing tritons spurting water from their mouths and grouped around a base surmounted by an Egyptian obelisk, of which a great number were brought to Rome in the Roman period. An obelisk is also the crowning motive of the *Fountain of the Four Rivers* (Fig. 335) in the Piazza Navona in Rome, which was executed between 1647 and 1651 by assistants of Bernini after the master's designs. The four figures represent the Rhine, Ganges, Nile and de la Plata Rivers which in turn are allegorical symbols of the four parts of the world, all of which acknowledge their allegiance to the spiritual rule of the Church which is symbolized by the papal tiara and keys. The symbolism is not over-prominent, however, as the sculptor's chief aim was to produce a decorative ensemble which should be unified by the flow of water over the irregular natural rock forms. The fountain was used as a decorative motif by baroque architects in other capacities than urban ornament, a particularly effec-

FIG. 335.—BERNINI AND OTHERS. THE FOUNTAIN OF THE FOUR RIVERS. *Piazza Navona, Rome.*

tive one being in conjunction with the extensive gardens that formed an essential part of the great country estates such as the Villa Torlonia at Frascati near Rome (Fig. 143).

Baroque style such as that of Bernini's figures is hardly apparent in French sculpture. It appears to some extent in the exaggerated gestures of the groups in which Pierre Puget (1622-1694) tried vainly to reconcile his own stormy nature to the classic taste of 17th-century

France, but his case is an isolated one, and baroque sculpture, in the Italian sense had little more currency in 17th-century France than did its parallel architectural style. This fact can be explained in some measure by the inability of the Church to acquire control of the French state, unified as it was under the absolute rule of Louis XIV. Baroque art, as has been seen, was primarily the instrument of the Counter-Reformation which had brought about a condition of religious absolutism in the Church under the pope that was comparable to the political one established by the French monarch. But since the royal style in France was esentially classic, no encouragement was given the baroque, with its emphasis upon certain qualities that were foreign to a classic point of view.

The foundation of the French Academy of Sculpture in 1648 and of the Academy at Rome in 1677 served to confirm the classic mode of thought initiated by the school of Fontainebleau. More than this, it extended to the field of sculpture the principle of absolutism that had already been established politically in the methods of government practiced by Louis XIV. The ideal which this absolutism imposed on French sculptors is stated concisely in a letter from Colbert, Louis XIV's Minister, to the director of the French Academy at Rome, "Take good care that the sculptors copy purely the antique, but without adding anything"; and again, "See that there is no change from the originals, i.e., that the copies which you have them make are of the same measurements." With such restrictions as these, in force, it is no cause for wonder that there is not a single French sculptor of first rank from the time of Louis XIV's accession to the throne until the close of the 18th century. That the same is not as true of 17th-century painters and architects is due only to the absence of classic models for the first and the persistence of an indigenous architectural tradition in the second.

Just as French classic sculpture was born and spent its childhood in the decoration of Fontainebleau, so its early maturity was reached in the ornament of the palace and gardens at Versailles (Fig. 151). A relief of *Bathing Nymphs* (Fig. 336) from the Fountain of Diana by François Girardon (1628-1715) is an example of its style. Girardon had traveled in Italy but he had not been influenced so much by the baroque expressions of Bernini's genius as by Giovanni da Bologna's more academic concepts. The latter influence is apparent in the more material quality of Girardon's Nymphs in comparison with Bernini's unsubstantial marble visions (Fig. 333). But their robustness is derived from the baroque canon rather than the more slender and muscular type employed by Giovanni (Fig. 330), and is suggestive of the fleshy ideal which Rubens had done much to popularize in the northern countries (Fig. 455). Other features of French 17th-century sculpture that appear in the relief are the elegance that never completely deserts the French artist, and the concreteness apparent in the careful delineation of the reeds as well as the disquietingly individual and personal note in the Nymphs themselves which makes them appear, for all the classic generalization of the faces, like a group of buxom French *demoiselles* in an unsuspecting moment of idle sport. The relief is an excellent example of all that is meant by the Louis XIV style, for even in the supposedly abandoned movement of the figures there is a correctness which becomes stiff pomposity in more formal subjects. This correctness is an element of the norm of perfection to which the academic sculptors were forced to conform, a fact that made all of their work good and none of it interesting. In the dull vistas of the Louvre sculp-

FIG. 336.—GIRARDON. BATHING NYMPHS.
*The Fountain of Diana, Versailles.*

ture galleries, it sometimes seems that it would be a pleasure to see an incorrectly drawn figure for the note of vitality it might sound in the soporific symphony of all-prevailing exactitude. Only in occasional portraits does the native French sense of the concrete thrust through the meaningless conventions forced upon the creative genius of the country by the Academy.

In the 18th century there is a reaction in France against the formality and correctness that prevailed in the 17th. At first this appears as a relaxation of the stately decorum maintained in society of the Louis XIV period, a relaxation that degenerated into licentiousness in the last part of the century during the reign of Louis XVI. In art, the change is more apparent in architecture and painting than in sculpture. The formal halls of Versailles (Fig. 152) give way to intimate boudoirs as in the Hôtel de Soubise (Fig. 167), ornamented with light and graceful forms that represent an application of baroque principles of design to surfaces rather than outlines, producing the style known as rococo. The movement and variety that characterize rococo architecture also appear in the painting of Watteau (Fig. 477), only to lapse into calculated voluptuousness in Boucher and Fragonard (Fig. 479).

It is usual to decry the 18th century in France as a period of unbounded licentiousness and to condemn it as decadent. That the latter criticism at least is not unqualifiedly merited is evident in the manifest vitality of such a group as the *Nymph and Satyr* (Fig. 337) by Claude Michel, who is usually known as Clodion (1738-1814). Here we see the old French sense of the actual welling up once more, to invest the academic 17th-century formulas with new life. That Clodion's conceptions were no more lofty is the fault of his time rather than his temperament. The greater part of his work consists of small statuettes such as the Nymph and Satyr, designed primarily for interior ornament and as appropriate to the boudoir as the heroic 17th-century figures were to the formal gardens in which they were placed. The brisk if artificial gaiety of the 18th century is well suggested in the animation of Clodion's figures, not only by the poses but also by the highly naturalistic modeling. His facility was due in part at least to his use of terra cotta as a medium, for it lent itself quite readily to rendition of the flowing surfaces of rounded limbs, mobile lips and expressive nostrils that embodied his sensual ideal.

Fig. 337.—CLODION. Nymph and Satyr. *Metropolitan Museum, N. Y.*

In many ways, Jean Antoine Houdon (1741-1828) is the most interesting of the French 18th-century sculptors. Judged by his work, he appears to have been particularly sensitive to the intellectual currents of his time, although his assimilation of their ideas must have been intuitive rather than conscious. The Bathing Nymph in the Altman Collection at the Metropolitan Museum in New York is rococo in technique but the sentiment is that of Rousseau's cult of nature. In other works, he follows the generally classic trend of contemporary taste but always with a measure of concrete and objective realism. It was this characteristic of his style that finally brought him to the sphere of activity in which he achieved his greatest success, that of portraiture. He executed busts of the most prominent personali-

ties of the day, among them *Voltaire* (Fig. 338), the example illustrated
being one of many that he made of the illustrious dramatist and poet.
The technique is still rococo in the curling line of the hair and in such
details as the deliberately roughened edge of the hole representing the
pupil of the eye to give it a glint. Houdon's naturalism is apparent in the
scrupulous exactness with which the features are represented, but the
bust is more than a translation of the model into marble. By emphasizing

FIG. 338.—HOUDON. VOLTAIRE. *Louvre, Paris.*

the essential traits and subordinating the irrelevant ones, the sculptor has
made his work not only a record of individual appearance but the embodiment of a type. The glint in the eye, for example, is the sparkle of half-
cynical, half-benevolent amusement, the same spirit that we feel in
reading Voltaire's poems and plays. By such means, Houdon tells not
only how Voltaire looked but also the way in which his personality
affected those who came in contact with him and has thus created a
telling and powerful portrait.

For Americans, more than usual interest is attached to Houdon by virtue of his association with the United States during the years immediately following the Revolution. He crossed the Atlantic to make a portrait statue of Washington, now in the Capitol at Richmond, Va., which is somewhat less flattering to the subject than many of his painted portraits. While in the United States he also executed busts of some of the most prominent citizens of the Republic, notably Franklin, Jefferson, John Paul Jones and Robert Fulton. Probably his best-known work is the full-length seated portrait of Voltaire in the Comédie Française at Paris, in which neo-classic draperies contrast most strangely with the characteristically realistic head. Apart from their intrinsic value as works of art, Houdon's sculptures are of great interest by virtue of their reflection of the changing thought during the late 18th and early 19th centuries. It is this quality of his work that makes it more or less independent of any school or movement and invests it with a peculiarly timeless character.

# Chapter XXII. *Sculpture Since 1800*

THE NEO-CLASSIC MOVEMENT IN ART WITH WHICH the 19th century opened was the first and intellectual phase of the revolt against the old absolutism, a revolt which had already taken place politically and socially in the American and French Revolutions. The academic and rococo styles of the old régime had been swept away with its political and religious paraphernalia, to be replaced by the neo-classic. The intellectual and social background of the neo-classic movement has been discussed in connection with its architectural examples, to which it might here be added that the conscious attempts to recreate the artistic forms of classic antiquity which gave birth to the movement are more apparent in sculpture than in either painting or architecture for a reason that is more or less self-evident. The antique mode in painting could not be recovered because no monumental examples of it existed. Similarly the practical nature of architecture placed an obstruction in the way of unvarying reproductions of classic buildings to be put to modern uses. Neither of these considerations applied to sculpture, for it had no preeminently practical purpose and genuine classic statues existed in great numbers to serve as models.

The neo-classic movement was partly a result of popular enthusiasm for antique art created in the 18th century by the discoveries at Pompeii and Herculaneum. It is this enthusiasm that underlies the writings of the German scholar Winckelmann, who has been termed the father of modern archaeology. The theory developed in his writings is that the purpose of all good art is the attainment of "pure beauty," i.e., beauty of form without consideration of its content. This "pure beauty," according to Winckelmann, had been realized only by the Greeks and by those moderns who approached nature as he imagined the Greeks had, by striving only for effects of "noble simplicity" and "quiet grandeur." These terms reveal the moral turn in his propaganda for art, a moral turn which was undoubtedly a reaction against the sensual mode of the time, for Winckelmann believed that his gospel of the beautiful was to regenerate Europe spiritually as well as artistically. His formal ideal was based on classic sculpture in which he clearly recognized the beauty of line and contour but failed entirely to observe the important function of modeling. It seems strange today that the most popular dissemination of Winckelmann's theories, through the writing of his pupil Lessing, should have centered around a discussion of the Laocoön group which is the very antithesis of his ideal in content as well as technique (Fig. 280).

The extent to which Winckelmann's aesthetic pervaded early 19th-century sculpture can be seen in the work of the Italian, Antonio

FIG. 339.—CANOVA. PAULINE BORGHESE. *Villa Borghese, Rome.*

Canova (1757-1822). His best-known piece, the group of Cupid and Psyche, reveals a scrupulous observance of the Winckelmann formula in its formal beauty and total lack of content. His portraits can be similarly characterized, an example being that of *Pauline Borghese* (Fig. 339), the sister of Napoleon, in which a compromise was attempted between the generalization that was considered the primary characteristic of classicism and the realism essential to a portrait. This compromise was achieved by placing the stamp of individuality upon the face alone, the body being treated according to classic models. As a result, the features of the Corsican princess surmount the half-nude body of a Roman goddess, the lower part of the figure having been modeled after a late Hellenistic Venus type. Even the effort to generalize the torso could not conceal the sculptor's contemporaneity with the rococo which is revealed by the rippling surfaces of the flesh. The drapery on the other hand is rendered in a strictly linear fashion and the hard contour lines throughout are typical of the neo-classic style.

The popularity of the neo-classic ideal is attested by its wide geographic diffusion. The Danish sculptor Thorwaldsen (1770-1844) was probably a better exponent of Winckelmann's theories than Canova, for he was less affected by the rococo than his Italian contemporary. As a result, his figures are even more frigid in effect. That he had no real understanding of classic sculpture is apparent from the fact that after Thorwaldsen had restored the sculptures from Aegina (cf. Fig. 254) his own style showed no effects of his knowledge of the Greek work. The neo-classic style also obtained a strong foothold in England, for its linear quality appealed strongly to a taste that is apparent in the art of that country from mediaeval times. Its outstanding English protagonist was John Flaxman (1755-1826), of whom no more need be said than that he considered the acquisition of the Parthenon sculptures by the British Museum to be of "doubtful value." Sculpture in France and Germany during the early 19th century was also dominated by neo-classic concepts.

The same thing is true of the first attempts at sculpture in the United States. Of all the visual arts, sculpture was the last to appear in the young republic, a fact which can be explained by the complete lack of any need for it. Even as late as 1820, the painter John Trumbull discouraged a young stone-cutter who came to him for advice by saying that "nothing in sculpture would be wanted in this country for yet a hundred years." To men who persisted in pursuing their interest in sculpture in the face of such an attitude, there was but one course to follow, namely, to go to Europe and study there. In the early 19th century, Europe meant Italy from an artist's point of view and there the neo-classic style was firmly entrenched. The effect of the training that was received by early American sculptors under such circumstances can be seen in the work of Hiram Powers (1805-1873). There is little to distinguish the *Greek Slave* (Fig. 340), which is his best-known piece, from the rank and file of neo-classic work save possibly the sense of fact evident in the emphasis on inanimate details, such as the chain and the shawl, which is characteristically American. The pose is derived from the so-called Medici Venus, a late Hellenistic statue based on the Aphrodite of Knidos. The over-generalized modeling of the figure makes it seem very lifeless and cold; but in spite of this, its nudity would hardly have been tolerated in puritan America had it not been for the title which appealed to sympathies already aroused by the Greek fight for freedom from Turkish rule. It was, for example, this sentimental and entirely unsculptural consideration which led a group of clergymen in Cincinnati to pronounce the statue unsubversive of public morals when they examined it prior to exhibition in that city. The same reason must account for the popularity that made a reproduction of it an indispensable adjunct to any American household with pretensions to culture in the mid-19th century.

The consequences attendant upon the birth of American sculpture at the time when neo-classic ideals were predominant are evident even today. The feeling that an ideal figure must be treated in the classic manner is one, as well as the dependence on frigidly abstract symbols to invest such figures with meaning. The persistence of these ideas in American sculpture long after they had disappeared in that of Europe may be traced directly to the lack of artistic background in the United States and the consequent absence of any but the most elementary critical sense. American sculptors clung to pseudo-classic Italianate ideals long after their inanities had been observed in Europe and artistic leadership had passed once more from Italy to France where the romantic movement was in full swing.

In the romantic movement, the revolt against 17th-century absolutism enters its second phase. It is distinguished from the earlier intellectual one expressed in the stale evocations of the neo-classic style by its emotionalism and insistence upon the complete freedom of the artist to

Fig. 340.—POWERS. The
Greek Slave.
*Corcoran Gallery, Washington,
D. C.*

express his emotions according to his own desires. Such a personal point of view naturally resulted in a subjective and individual criterion of taste; the test of a work of art is whether or not it "grips you," rather than the extent to which the rules of good composition are followed. According to such a point of view, feeling is the proper content of artistic expression, rather than thought; *vide* Wordsworth's definition of poetry as "the spontaneous overflow of overpowering feelings." Such a concept has been encountered before; it is the very essence of the baroque. But between baroque art and that of the romantic movement there is this significant difference: the feeling expressed in baroque forms is impersonal and abstract while that which animates those of the romantic period is individual and concrete too, at least so far as the artist is concerned. Here is the genesis of an attitude toward art that has not been invariably beneficial. The academic point of view was bad enough but at least it laid stress upon the need to learn the prin-

FIG. 341.—RUDE. THE MARSEILLAISE. *Arc de Triomphe, Paris.*

ciples of artistic expression and thus made possible some understanding on the part of observer and public. But the romanticist places the whole matter in the hands of the artist. The form taken by his creations depends entirely upon his own feeling; if the result is art for him, its meaning to anyone else is of no importance. Thus the effect of the separation of art from environment brought about by the Academies was intensified by the separation of the artist from his public produced by the romantic movement.

The art of sculpture is not the one best adapted to give full expression to a movement so lyric in character, for its material limitations

turn it toward general rather than personal expression. The effect of
romanticism can be more immediately discerned in literature and painting, but in so far as it appears in sculpture at all, it is seen first in a
preference for subjects of inherently emotional or dramatic character
and subsequently in the development of a style incorporating effects
of surface movement and of light by which emotive or dramatic values
are conveyed somewhat more abstractly. In the first category is the

Fig. 342.—CARPEAUX. Flora. *Pavillon de Flore, Louvre, Paris.*

group by François Rude (1784-1855) known as *Le Départ pour la
Guerre* or more popularly as *The Marseillaise* (Fig. 341), carved for
the Arc de Triomphe de l'Étoile in Paris between 1830 and 1835. The
theme is the spontaneous response of the men of France of all ages to
the call of their country voiced by the shouting figure flying above
them. Rude remains traditionalist in some respects; the costumes of
the volunteers are those of Roman warriors, and the modeling of the
figures has something of neo-classic hardness of surface, but the group
as a whole is instinct with movement to such an extent that the soldiers seem actually to be filing past, and the shrieking Bellona above
is a furiously animated personification of the violently clashing emotions attendant upon physical combat. The popular name bestowed
upon the group is sufficient proof of its effective interpretation of French
patriotism, for its forms arouse the same sentiment as the stirring lines
and music of the song whose title it shares. Its romanticism lies in the

fact that it is so directly addressed to the emotions rather than by symbol alone to reason and intellect.

Less profound in significance but equally romantic in character is the group of *Flora* (Fig. 342) crouching among rollicking *putti*, carved by Jean Baptiste Carpeaux (1827-1875) to decorate the Pavillon de Flore of the Louvre in Paris. The forms are almost baroque in effect, although it is a baroque closer to the pictorial style of the Fleming Rubens (cf. Fig. 455) than to Bernini's sculptural idioms. The impression created by the form of the kneeling woman, for example, is frankly carnal by virtue of the extraordinarily skillful rendering of the flesh in movement, an effect heightened by the contrast between its flickering highlights and the deep shadow of the background. In thus using a device which anticipates those of Rodin a little later in the century, Carpeaux reveals himself as a pictorial sculptor depending upon effects of *chiaroscuro* rather than form and mass as means of expression. It is these effects, however, that invest his figures with the *joie de vivre* that links his work to the romantic movement, although it appears as an abstract and general quality rather than as a significance inherent in individual figures.

The entire achievement of French 19th-century sculpture is summed up in the work of Auguste Rodin (1840-1917). This is tantamount to saying the achievement of all Occidental sculpture, for at no time, not even in the Middle Ages, was French art so universally dominant as in this period. Technically, Rodin's sculpture represents a continuation of Carpeaux' style in which expressive modeling gave the figures abstract vitality. He thus takes his place in the long line of French artists extending back through Clodion to the Flemish painter Rubens. But where his predecessors were content to achieve no more than a sense of movement in their figures, Rodin attempted to make that movement expressive of psychological activity and, in so doing, to give his figures character. In this respect, he is akin to Houdon and, going back again to 17th-century painting, to Rembrandt, both of whom were primarily interested in their subjects and bent their energies to the expression of character while more or less contemptuous of formal or absolute beauty in their figures. Thus Rodin's sculptures appear astonishingly real by virtue of the play of light and shade created by the expressive modeling of the surfaces which also bestows psychological validity upon the ideas they embody.

All of this is apparent in *The Kiss* (Fig. 343), in which Rodin set forth his conception of the ill-fated lovers Paolo and Francesca whose tragic story is told in the fifth canto of the Inferno in Dante's *Divine Comedy*. It illustrates admirably his frequently repeated statement that sculpture should consist only of successive hollows and projections; by means of them, the effect of actual warm flesh is strikingly simulated. This simulation was not an end in itself, however, for Rodin empha- sized many details to achieve a clearer expression of the inner meaning of the group. Notice, for example, the contrast between the tenseness of the man's hand and the lightness of its contact with the woman's thigh, and the convulsive contraction of the toes of his right foot. These and other similar contrasts in the group are eloquent of the passion animating the figures. But where the effect would be sensual and sug-

FIG. 343.—RODIN. THE KISS. *Musée Rodin, Paris.*

gestive in the hands of an artist who aimed at nothing more than rep- resentation of the entwined forms, Rodin deliberately made it abstract by veiling the heads in shadow and achieved thereby a more powerful expression.

In using light and shade to create an impression of actuality, Rodin was only availing himself of methods already employed by contemporary painters of the Impressionist school (cf. Fig. 505). The movement of surface that resulted from the play of light and shade on the figure is part of the general movement of the entire body which is real to an extent never approached by any of Rodin's predecessors. In The Kiss, for example, there is no sense at all of artificially posed figures, for the artist's analysis of their movements was so complete that he was able to give his representation of them every appearance of naturalness. Such a use of light and shade is pictorial rather than sculptural, yet with it Rodin employed a closed contour that gives sculptural mass and weight to the figures. Their energy and life come from the strain of form and muscle within the contour and pictorial *chiaroscuro* is employed only to the extent that it contributes to that effect, and to create the sense of environment demanded by modern taste.

In Rodin's later pieces, much of the spontaneity seen in The Kiss disappears and with it the beauty of the figures. To a large extent, this was due to his practice of theorizing concerning the function of sculpture and then creating his sculpture to illustrate the theories. Instead of embodying abstract ideas, as in The Kiss, his figures tend to become sculptural interpretations of his own temperament which was notably bizarre in a time when the unusual was deliberately sought out, a combination of bitter pessimism and extreme eroticism. Thus he created a female centaur with outstretched arms, seeking to objectify the soul's struggle to raise itself above the level to which it is restrained by mortal flesh. Rodin failed to give significant expression to this idea, and failed because he was unable to clothe it with formal beauty. Michelangelo, inspired by a similar concept, produced the symphony of volumes which is the Medici Tombs (cf. Fig. 328). It is this essential of sculptural beauty, form in arranged and related masses, that Rodin's later work lacks, or, to put it briefly, the organization that means style. In The Kiss, the emotional content of the group acquires ideal meaning by virtue of formal arrangement to which the naturalism of the figures gives power and intensity. It thus becomes a moving symbol of the tragedy inherent in modern life, the soul attempting to find surcease from its besetting fears and uncertainties in the purging emotion of love.

At first glance, the *Adams Memorial* (Fig. 344) by Augustus Saint-Gaudens (1848-1907) seems to have very little in common with The Kiss, yet both of them reveal the sense of doubt that is the tragedy of the modern mind. The figure was commissioned by Henry Adams in memory of his wife, the only specification being that it should convey a sense of the loss that he felt in her death; he left the form that it should take to the sculptor. This idea Saint-Gaudens interpreted by suggesting overwhelming depression in the figure, an effect attained by the broad and simplified folds of the ponderous draperies, made abstract by the simplicity of background and the sexless face of the bronze figure, and given poignancy by the single visible arm and the listless fold between the knees. The result is a sense of spiritual exhaustion, for its repose is that of weariness rather than quiet and serene faith.

The various names that have been applied to the statue—"Grief," "Death," "The Peace of God"—all show the breadth of the sculptor's concept which acquires universal meaning in the abstractions of figure and setting. To every observer it gives in measure according to his spiritual need, whether he be cynic or believer. It thus stands for all that modern man feels of life in the hereafter, just as the Hegeso Stele (Fig. 267) reveals the calm objectiveness of the Greek and the Saint of the French *détente* (Fig. 307) the serene and trusting faith that was the finest flower of the Middle Ages.

The position of Saint-Gaudens in American sculpture of the late 19th century is comparable to that of Rodin in France in that both represent a summing-up of the technical and interpretive traditions that preceded them. Saint-Gaudens was able to expand the technical

Fig. 344.—SAINT-GAUDENS. The Adams Memorial.
*Rock Creek Cemetery, Washington, D. C.*

resources of American sculpture by introducing the delicate low relief of Italian 15th-century work (cf. Fig. 318) and by bringing about a revived appreciation of the enhanced significance of sculpture when associated with architecture. At the same time, his figures are American

in the sense of fact apparent in them as well as their broad vague idealism, both characteristics of American thought from pioneer days. This
apparently irreconcilable dualism is evident in American sculpture of
the early 19th century which consists of vapid generalizations in the
Italian manner on the one hand, and mere translations of fact into

FIG. 345.—MAILLOL. THE MEDITERRANEAN. *Reinhart Coll., Winterthur.*

stone and bronze on the other. Saint-Gaudens' great contribution to
American sculpture was to unite fact and generalization in a rugged
and poetic harmony. Thus his sense of actuality gives poignance to
the figure of the Adams Memorial, just as his lofty idealism makes the
Lincoln in Lincoln Park, Chicago, the embodiment of all that the
martyred President means to the American people, much as the Pheidian

Zeus summed up all that could be thought of him by the fifth-century Greek.

Returning now to the European tradition, we witness in the closing years of the 19th century and the first decade of the 20th the tremendous popularity of Rodinesque methods, evident in the vast number of figures turned out by his pupils and followers in which Rodin's impressionistic technique was employed to give expression to vague metaphysical ideas. In America, the outstanding protagonist of this mode was George Gray Barnard (1863-1938), at least as regards his earlier figures. Rodin's example was a powerful stimulus that awoke European sculpture from the academic torpor into which it had sunk, but it also opened the way for all manner of technical and expressive exaggerations on the part of his less gifted followers and imitators. It was inevitable that such a stimulus should be followed by a reaction, and this is seen most strikingly in the emphasis on sculptural form in the work of Aristide Maillol (b. 1861). In *The Mediterranean* (Fig. 345), executed about 1902, Maillol conceives the sculptured human figure as a pattern of volumes, a manner which has led him to be characterized as the most Hellenic of living sculptors. It is not without significance, perhaps, that when he was in Greece he was most interested by the Olympia sculptures (cf. Fig. 257), although it should be pointed out that Maillol's Hellenism is in no way an archaistic reversion to older forms. It is rather a matter of figures that are powerful, rugged and self-contained. To the realization of this conception, which might be characterized as classic rather than classical, Maillol adds a fine sensibility of the nature of his mediums; if Rodin's ideal was to translate marble and bronze into flesh, Maillol's is to transform flesh into stone, terra cotta or bronze. More than this, he takes an obvious delight in the robustness and animal vigor of the body which is quite foreign to the classic point of view. But by avoiding the romantic interpretive attitude that is responsible for the sensuality of Rodin's figures and by emphasizing the relationship between the masses of the figure as a whole, he achieves the necessary balance between abstraction and realism. If there is ground for criticism in Maillol's figures, it is to be found in their relative lack of content. There is no suggestion of environment and the personal note that is essential to a complete expression of modern thought is also lacking.

The extent to which Rodin influenced his immediate followers appears in the literalness with which they interpreted one of the epigrams he was so fond of making, to the effect that mathematics is the basis of all good art. Rodin himself probably meant no more by this statement than to emphasize the necessity of formal arrangement in a work of art, but to his followers it meant that the greatest validity of a painting or statue lies in the possible mathematical relationship underlying such an arrangement. Out of this attitude there developed the movement popularly known as Cubism. The aim of Cubist sculptors and painters was to portray the quintessential character of their subjects which they believed could be done only by emphasizing the mathematical relationships existing in them. Thus Constantin Brancusi (b. 1879) strives in his portrait of *Mlle Pogany* (Fig. 346) to portray the mental and spiritual character of his subject freed from the obscuring accidents of naturalistic appearance. To do this, he has carried the

FIG. 346.—BRANCUSI. MLLE POGANY.

processes of selecting and defining experience which are essential to artistic creation to the point where they come dangerously near to defeating their ultimate purpose. There can be no denying the fact that the portrait of Mlle Pogany has many sculptural qualities. It possesses the formal organization essential in a work of art. There is a fine feeling for the nature of the medium and it incidentally illustrates the interest of modern sculptors in rare and costly materials, for the figure is of silver. But by forcing his conception of the subject completely into the realm of the abstract, Brancusi's interpretation of it has become a purely personal one. The content is so rarefied by lack of concreteness that it has no character. There is nothing intrinsic in the figure to relate it to the observer's experience save the formal organization and the sense of the material, both of which are abstract and impersonal qualities. By emphasizing them to the exclusion of the personal and the human, the sculptor deliberately deprived the figure of its most immediate appeal to the observer.

Brancusi's Mlle Pogany illustrates a type of abstraction that might be called organic since the individual features of the head are grouped together in such a way that for all their lack of naturalism as details, the concept of head resulting from their organization is still clearly indicated. Going beyond even this in search of ultimate sculptural values are such forms as the bronze *Figure* (Fig. 347) by Jacques Lipchitz (b. 1891), executed between 1926 and 1930, which is now in the collection of the Museum of Modern Art in New York, and the *Stone Woman* (Fig. 348) of 1930 by the English sculptor Frank Dobson (b. 1887). To understand the motivation of figures like these, the dictum of Maurice Denis concerning the nature of painting might be paraphrased: "A sculptured form before it is anything else is an organized pattern of solid masses of stone or metal or wood or whatever medium," which could be carried still further to exclude as non-sculptural anything not specified in the definition. That Lipchitz' figure is a

Fig. 347.—LIPCHITZ. Figure. *Museum of Modern Art, N. Y.*

pattern of masses is indisputable, ranging in variety of form from circular through elliptical to rectangular, with occasionally a void serving as foil to the solids. The sense of material is also prominent in the total effect for it is obvious even in the illustration that the masses are of metal that has been melted and flowed into the desired form. Dobson's Woman is likewise obviously of stone for the nature of which he has a particularly sensitive feeling that leads him to cut directly in the block rather than having his model transferred to it by pointing. The two examples under consideration illustrate the possibilities of considerable variety within the definition of basic sculpture given above; Lipchitz has chosen to stress pattern as the most fundamental element in the manner of certain painters of the early 20th century (cf. Fig. 518) while to Dobson it is massive bulk that counts for the most in the attainment of sculptural significance. Both concepts are entirely legitimate and both may lead to unsound conclusions; it is doubtful if the enrichment of experience through heightened awareness of geometrical pattern is of more than temporary significance, and simplification of mass to emphasize its three-dimensionality results all too often in effects that are simply bulky.

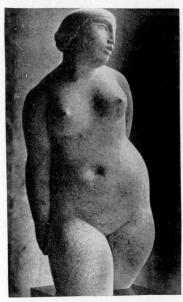

FIG. 348.—DOBSON. FIGURE IN
HOPTON WOOD STONE.
*Artist's Coll.*

In contrast to the foregoing sculptors in whose figures there is an attempt to interpret modern thought by emphasizing certain aspects of it, there is a group of sculptors who are seemingly so overwhelmed by its complexity that they have no hope, and possibly no power, to express it at all. In consequence of this, they take refuge in the pure design of other periods, untainted by contemporary thought or feeling. This 20th-century manifestation of the romantic point of view is represented in American sculpture by the work of Paul Manship (b. 1885). A decorator by temperament, Manship's training in the American Academy at Rome served to turn his attention to the classic styles. The repertory of forms he derived from them was later expanded by contact with art of the Far East. His development as an artist is the history of attempted assimilation of these various influences to which may be added the factual sense apparent in his portraits. The fusion of all these elements into what may be considered Manship's personal style has produced such figures as the *Prometheus* (Fig. 349) of 1934 on the Radio City Fountain in New York City. It is characterized by great technical skill in the handling of bronze, a notable feature in all Manship's work; it is decorative, and it is utterly devoid of meaning. The motive of the flying figure has been used by the sculptor in several other works and also the idea of the band with the signs of the Zodiac, objective proof of the sterility of such an eclectic conception of art. Unrooted in experience as such conceptions are, they leave the door open to all the current eccentric methods of conveying mere impressions, which reveal, disturbingly, the lack of that meditation upon experience and logical analysis thereof which is prerequisite to great artistic creation.

In striking contrast to the decorative emptiness of Manship's figures is the virile force that permeates those of Ivan Meštrović (b. 1883). A native of Yugoslavia, his sculpture is intensely nationalistic in spirit.

FIG. 349.—MANSHIP. PROMETHEUS. *Radio City, N. Y.*

The forms he employs often appear to be based on Balkan types and however incongruous this may be in his statues of equestrian Indians in Chicago, it is a source of tremendous power in his evocations of the ideals of his own country. Such is the bronze *Portrait of a Lady* (Fig. 350). Outstanding in its technical features is the simplification of the draperies, reduced to a pattern of broad folds which effectively suggest the massive volumes of the body they cover. This effect is obtained by a system of planes which he also employs in relief sculpture, a field in which none of his contemporaries have attained greater distinction. The head is fine portraiture, realistic in type yet formal in pattern and imbued with the calm serenity of profound assurance. In the objectiveness of the portrait, there is something of Hellenic impersonality, yet it is far from the calm impassiveness of Maillol's figures. The directness of its impact upon the observer is a consequence of its intense human-

From Vanity Fair. Copyright the Condé Nast Publications, Inc.

FIG. 350.—MEŠTROVIĆ. PORTRAIT OF A LADY.

ity, comparable to that which ennobles Rodin's best work, yet it speaks through means that are essentially sculptural. It results in an impression of profound emotion, but the emotion is in the spectator rather than the figure. To the command of form that Meštrović reveals in his treatment of plane and volume, there must be added an incomparable sensitiveness to materials that explains the feeling that the bronze of the figure has actually melted and flowed instead of being transformed by some mysterious alchemy from clay or plaster. Those

Fig. 351.—BARLACH. Sorrowing Woman.

works of Meštrović which are least effective are usually so because of a clumsy forcefulness that verges on the brutal, but in his best, there is a balance of realism, formal design and content that makes him one of the most individual and distinctive sculptors of the early 20th century.

Emotional content is implicit in Meštrović's Lady, to which extent the motivation is just that much more forceful than in the Hellenically placid Mediterranean of Maillol (Fig. 345), or in the abstractions of Brancusi, Lipchitz and Dobson whose emotive content is aesthetic only. It should not be assumed from this that 20th-century sculptors have been oblivious to the possibilities of deep emotion as an expressive quality in their figures; Ernst Barlach (1870-1938) a German sculptor who has done much of his work, like the *Sorrowing Woman* (Fig. 351), in wood, is notable for the vivid expression which he gives to his notably simplified figures. As a young man he was much impressed by the expressive fury of Van Gogh's painting (cf. Fig. 514), and it was the same quality of poignant expressionism that attracted him to the arts of primitive peoples and of the Middle Ages with their purposeful and significant distortions (cf. Fig. 297). His own work is characterized by strongly drawn silhouettes that function by virtue of an inimitable sense of the material as the definitions of planes enclosing solids. In the Sorrowing Woman, these planes are so organized as to suggest both the deep anguish of the figure and the unconscious rocking movement by which such emotion is often instinctively expressed, yet at the same time the simplified volumes of the statue are composed in a stable and three-dimensional pattern of great plastic forcefulness. Effective use is made also of the color of the wood and its texture, the substance becoming in Barlach's hands a sculptural medium of highly individual yet genuinely sculptural character.

It has been mentioned previously that the influence of Rodin, either interpretive or technical, is one of the basic factors in the evolution of 20th-century sculptural style, and that it is apparent either by way of direct emulation on the part of his followers or by contrary reaction, as in the case of Maillol. Carl Milles (b. 1875) is Swedish by birth but has been almost continuously in the United States since 1933. He studied in Paris as a youth, and learned much from the example of Rodin whose influence is to be noted in his early works. From the outset, however, the individuality of his sculptural conceptions is apparent —a character that derives from his craftsman's feeling for the medium in which he works, from his rhythmically abstract figure patterns, and from his clear realization of the need for expressive content in sculptured forms. Thus in his monuments dedicated to the great heroes of Swedish history, Folke Filbyter and Gustav Vasa, Milles gives form to a sentiment of patriotism in symbols of moving pathos. No less expressive but imbued with more abstract significance is the *Orpheus Fountain* (Figs. 352, 353), which was completed in 1936 and stands before the Hall of Music designed by Ragnar Ostberg in Stockholm. Orpheus, a figure of heroic proportions, rises from the center of the fountain from which other figures also emerge in response to the music sounding from his lyre. The play of water contributes in no small degree to the effect of surging upward movement in this lower group,

FIG. 352.—MILLES. THE ORPHEUS FOUNTAIN. *Stockholm.*

but this is also intrinsic in the individual forms (Fig. 353) by virtue
of the rhythmically drawn contours and stylized surface planes of the
abstractly rendered bodies. One figure of particularly moving force is
that with the mask of Beethoven visible at the extreme right in the
view of the ensemble, in which the upraised arms, the tensed muscles
and the general pose convey in unforgettable patterns the desperate
anguish of the great Titan doomed by his deafness to hear his own
music only in his mind. The figures are of bronze, which is the medium

Fig. 353.—MILLES. Figure. The Orpheus Fountain.
Detail. *Stockholm.*

most extensively employed by Milles, but the basin is of stone in
which he has also done very effective work. Milles' inherent decorative
sense is apparent in all his many fountains, a sculptural type he has
done much to restore to significance in his productive career, and his
appreciation of the possibility of effective relationship between plastic
and architectural forms is likewise a creative concept long lacking in
Occidental art.

The varied character of sculpture in the 20th century is considerable as the foregoing examples will have made clear, and if there is no dominant trend to be noted in it comparable to the clearly defined stylistic concepts in contemporary architecture or painting, it may be explained by the fact that sculpture as an art appears to lend itself best to the definition of broadly comprehensive ideas felt with such conviction that they require monumental treatment. Such ideas as these are as yet not sufficiently well established in 20th-century thought to make possible a sculptural canon of significance comparable to that of the classic and mediaeval periods. The examples considered are of moving character, it is true, and there can be no discounting the sincerity with which men like Maillol, Barlach, Meštrović and Milles have attempted to invest their figures with more than decorative charm; but the fact remains that the results are forceful in measure as the concepts of the sculptor are derived from poignant personal experience rather than for the power accruing from relating them to universally comprehensible values. Thus Barlach's Sorrowing Woman (Fig. 351) for all its pathos does not rise to the expressive heights of Michelangelo's Night (Fig. 328) in the formal beauty with which it invests human suffering, nor does Maillol's Mediterranean (Fig. 345) convey in the same universally comprehensive volumes the ideal of sentient humanity that gives such authority to the Mount Olympus of the Parthenon (Fig. 261). Milles' Orpheus (Fig. 352) attains a measure of significance from the association of its abstract rhythms of line and mass with the architecture of the building behind it in a manner comparable to that of the Kings and Queens of Judah in the western façade portal of Chartres Cathedral (Fig. 299), but even here the concept is an inherently personal and subjective one. These have ever been the values in human experience that lend themselves least effectively to the generalizing methods upon which sculpture as an art depends for effectiveness. It follows that sculpture must await the time when Occidental thought is again capable of conviction through awareness of more than individually significant values, whether formal or expressive, before it will be able to say something with its vocabulary of mass and volume.

# PAINTING

# Chapter XXIII. Painting: Principles and Techniques~~~~~~~~~~~~~~~~~~~~

TO THE AVERAGE PERSON, ART ALMOST INVARIABLY means painting. Architecture is popularly thought to be the science of construction rather than an art. Sculpture, as we have seen, plays a relatively small part in our lives today and so does not receive much consideration as an art. But painting in one or another of its various forms is an everyday experience, in advertisements, magazine illustrations and as wall decorations, to mention only a few. In the general mind, the term artist carries with it the connotation of *painter* and can mean something else only if it is specifically stated. What, it might well be asked, is the reason for this, and why is painting the most generally practiced of the visual arts today?

To begin with, painting is a more flexible medium of expression than either architecture or sculpture and hence capable of a greater variety of effects. In this respect, it can be compared with the piano which, as a medium of musical expression, can produce both harmony and melody, employing the extended polyphony that is a legitimate orchestral effect and also the melodic line appropriate to vocal music or that of the solo wind and string instruments. So in painting it is possible to convey effects of space, which we have seen to be an essential characteristic of architecture, and also of plastic form which lies in the province of sculpture. The painter, working in a medium more fluent than either architecture or sculpture, is able to incorporate effects in his paintings which are legitimate in both of the other art forms. His advantage over the architect or the sculptor is that he is not restricted as they are by the danger of sacrificing effects appropriate to their respective arts if they attempt to go beyond them. Iktinos, for example, in designing the Parthenon (Fig. 39), treated it as a sculptural form and space-implying effects were relegated to a secondary degree of importance. Bernini, on the other hand, in his Saint Theresa in Ecstasy (Fig. 333), employed every available means to suggest space, not only that in which the group exists but also that which extends far beyond. In consequence of this, the group lacks the sense of heavy plastic

volumes which we look for in sculpture. In contrast with these limitations of architecture and sculpture, painting can suggest both space and
plastic form and so is able to produce cumulative effects of realistic
appearance that are both more immediately and more powerfully appealing than the abstract ones to which the other visual arts are limited.
To this is due in great part the more general appreciation of painting
than of either architecture or sculpture in our own time.

In view of this greater fluency enjoyed by painting, it may seem a
paradox to state that in some ways it is also more limited than either
architecture or sculpture. To revert to the earlier simile, the piano,
capable of the massive harmonies of the orchestra as well as the melodic
line of vocal and solo instrumental music, is yet incapable of the contrasted tonal colors and textures possible in them. Instead of the shimmering tone created by flutes, harps and violins that pours from the
orchestra, the piano can produce only a cascade of notes all more or
less similar in quality. The continuous melodic line of the voice or
violin becomes a series of isolated tones to which even the greatest
pianist cannot give the organic flow that characterizes the products
of the others. On the piano, in other words, effects possible in other
forms of musical expression can be rendered only in an abstract form
which bears no more than a suggestive resemblance to them. In similar
fashion, the painter does not deal with actual space like the architect,
nor does he have to do with tangible three-dimensional form like the
sculptor. At best, those qualities can only be *suggested* in a painting,
for the painter seeking to create a synthesis of analyzed experience is
limited to two dimensions, those of length and width. He can no more
compose his picture in actual depth than the pianist can recreate the
variegated tonal color of a symphony orchestra. Nor can he paint a
figure, house or tree so that it is actually round to the touch any more
than Rachmaninoff can make his piano produce an unbroken line of
melody that sounds like the human voice or the violin. He can evolve
only abstractions in pictorial idioms of the qualities of form and space
and so suggest them to the observer.

The first step the painter must take, then, is to subject his three-
dimensional experience to a process of abstraction in order to express
it in terms that involve only two dimensions. The extent to which this
is true can be observed by turning for a moment to an example of
two-dimensional representation in which this principle is violated, the
Gates of Paradise by Lorenzo Ghiberti (Figs. 310, 311). In creating
the panels for these doors, Ghiberti was working two-dimensionally to
all intents and purposes. Space is suggested by skillfully varied planes
in the backgrounds so that we sense an almost endless vista behind
the figures. But the figures, at least those in the foreground, are so

contrived that they stand free of the relief and have an actual third dimension, as a result of which they often cast shadows on parts of the background that are supposed to be an infinite distance away. This incongruity is a consequence of attempting to combine effects that have no common ground. Ghiberti was working partly as a sculptor and partly as a painter, employing figures with an actual third dimension in a two-dimensional scheme. Idioms of both arts are mixed together and an unalloyed effect of realism is impossible. The effect is much the same as that often observed in the theatre when the shadow of an actor falls on the painted backdrop and seems to extend miles away. In both cases, failure to attain a consistently real effect is the result of attempting to be realistic in terms which have no basic relationship to each other.

Upon the two-dimensional plane of canvas, wall or paper, the painter organizes a pattern of forms that are defined by lines or by colors, or by a combination of the two. These are the basic elements in pictorial expression, whatever the period or style or subject of the picture may be, and the complex variety of effects which the painter can obtain are ultimately reduced in origin to these fundamental devices. In the work of some painters such as Ingres (cf. Fig. 488), the line may be the dominant factor to the almost total exclusion of color, while in others it is color that is used so extensively that lines as such hardly appear (cf. Frontispiece). By juxtaposition of lines to create areas of dark or light, the painter may suggest an effect of solid form, or by varying the tonal value of an area of color he may contrive the same result; but in either case, the effect is something attained in terms of the basic pictorial element. For line and color being essentially without inherent dimension except in a flat plane are of necessity the means by which the painter, limited as he is to two dimensions in the physical sense, must achieve the patterns of his picture. The relative importance of line and color as pictorial elements varies in different times and styles; in some of the earliest known pictures (cf. Fig. 354), the line is predominant, whereas the significant trends in painting since the late 19th century have tended to stress color as the important element; but whatever the character of an individual style or period may be in respect to these devices, it can always be identified in terms of one or the other or in combination of the two.

Painting in the western world has been directed during the greater part of its history toward the portrayal by means of line and color of effects of three-dimensional form in space. In seeking such effects, painters have made extensive use of two principles of visual representation—perspective and modeling. Two perspective methods are generally employed, linear and aerial. Linear perspective is based on the fact that parallel lines receding into space from the observer seem to converge on the horizon. This phenomenon can be readily observed on a long straight road or railroad track, the sides or rails and the telegraph wires all appearing to come together at a single point on the horizon. Another of the qualities of linear perspective is that objects of the same size seem smaller the farther away they are from the observer. This involves the idea of scale, that is, the measuring of objects by each cther, which is also an integral part of the two-dimensional portrayal of three-dimensional space. The second of the two perspective methods, aerial perspective, is based on the diffusing, softening effect which atmosphere has upon the forms and outlines of distant objects. This can be observed by looking at a tree that is close at hand and comparing it with one far away. The nearer one will be seen to consist of many individual leaves and branches, each quite clearly distinguished from the others in form and color. In the distant one, the individual parts merge, the brilliant green of the leaves becomes less intense and the whole outline is less sharp and clear. The representation of such an effect in a painting will suggest that the object portrayed is at some distance.

Both aerial and linear perspective were known to artists as early as the Hellenistic period (Figs. 279, 286, 363), although the former was more generally employed then than the latter. Before the Renaissance, linear perspective was intuitively felt rather than intellectually understood and it was not until Brunellesco evolved a system incorporating it to give an impression of reality to his architectural drawings that it was analyzed as in the method outlined above which depends upon relationships that can be mathematically determined. The absence of such system is responsible for the curious distortions that have been noted in the architectural background of the reliefs of the Arch of Titus in Rome (Fig. 286).

Perspective is the device by which pictorial depth is suggested. To produce an effect of plastic form in painting, the painter employs modeling, of which there are two types: modeling by contrasts of light and shade, or *chiaroscuro*, and by color. In either case, the result is an impression of objects possessing the roundness of form and solidness which our experience leads us to believe they have. *Chiaroscuro* modeling is based on the fact that an illuminated solid object will cast a shadow and that one side will be more brightly lighted than the other unless the observer happens to be directly in line with object and light source. The achievement of such an effect in painting often involves the use of color, as in pictures in which shadows are a darker hue of the intrinsic color of the object itself. However, it is possible to suggest it with no other means than varying values of black and white (Figs. 411, 478). Many of the monochrome reproductions of paintings in this book illustrate this point, for the photographic process reduces color modeling to values of gray. *Chiaroscuro* modeling has been employed by painters from comparatively early times (Fig. 363), but modeling in pure color was almost unknown before the end of the 19th century. It was Paul Cézanne, the great French Post-Impressionist painter, who first made systematic observations of the receding effect of some colors and the advancing one of others. These characteristics he employed not only to give roundness and solidity to the objects in his paintings but also to secure effects of depth. It is the absence of color values in photographic reproductions that makes Cézanne's pictures so hard to comprehend in that form (Figs. 510, 511), although in their actual presence, the sense of solid forms existing in space is very powerful.

The discussion up to this point has been directed by the belief (which is generally held) that painting is the art of portraying in two dimensions the appearance of objects that actually exist in three. This belief has been an important element in the ideals of painters since the Renaissance and is still a consideration of great potency. It must not be forgotten, however, that there have been times when it was not the purpose of painting to produce such realistic two-dimensional abstractions of a three-dimensional world. In the Middle Ages, for example, painting served ends that were didactic and expressive instead of striving to produce more or less realistic images of objects. Comparison of the stained-glass window of the Madonna and Child in Chalons Cathedral (Fig. 371) with Filippo Lippi's matter-of-fact representation of the same subject (Fig. 405) will show how greatly the aim of the mediaeval craftsman differed from that of the Renaissance painter. The latter considered his panel an area upon which to record the lineaments of his mistress in a reasonably realistic fashion; to the former, the glass of the window was the means by which, to quote C. R. Morey, "the light of day became the Light Divine." To the supernal glow of his image, the realism bestowed by perspective and modeling would have been not only superfluous but detrimental. For similar reasons, the spiritual ideal which Stephan Lochner sought to express in his Adoration of the Magi (Fig. 383) appears disembodied of the incidentally realistic qualities that are usually felt to be essential to the painter's art.

The extent to which problems of representing the actual appearance of things have been the particular preoccupation of the modern painter is still further revealed if the use of the line as a delineating mechanism in mediaeval art be compared with that in post-mediaeval examples. In the illustrations of the Utrecht Psalter (Fig. 368), it will be seen that the artist has created his figures entirely by means of lines. Similarly, in drawings by Signorelli (Fig. 411), Watteau (Fig. 478) and Van Gogh (Fig. 515), the figures are represented by combinations of lines. Between the mediaeval method of employing line and the modern one, there is this very important difference. In the former, the line exists as a thing in itself; the artist conceives his subject in terms of line and the line alone is real. Space and plastic form are disregarded, or suggested only in so far as the *idea* of those qualities seemed to the artist to be real. The opposite is true of the post-mediaeval examples. In them, the line has meaning only as it suggests the realistic qualities of form and space, as a two-dimensional convention for the suggestion of three-dimensional values. Thus in the Watteau, the roundness of the head is suggested by the curved line of its contour. The hatchings in the Signorelli result in a sense of solid flesh and muscle. In the Van Gogh, the line is thick here and thin there, a fluent instrument in the drama of trees outlined against the sky. In all three, the line has meaning primarily as a symbol of some realistic characteristic, not as an aesthetic end in itself as in the mediaeval psalter illustration.

Since the Renaissance, the primary purpose of painting has been the realistic portrayal of objects, an aim which is clear from the comparisons made in the two foregoing paragraphs. This is true even of paintings by ultra-modern artists, the Cubists, the Super-Realists, etc., who have sought to find in abstract formal patterns of line and color the "true" reality of things but have all too often expressed them in a manner so individual and personal that it fails to be convincing. It is this realistic quality of painting that has led to the frequent confusion of its aims with those of photography. The difference between them has already. been dwelt upon in the Introduction. Here it will be said in addition that in itself, the photograph is incapable of making that distinction between the transitory and the significant which is the essence of artistic creation. To take but one instance of this, we have often seen photographs of tall buildings in which all the vertical lines converge because the camera was tilted upward when the picture was made. This distortion is due to the operation of the laws of linear perspective which the camera applies to vertical as well as horizontal lines. But the human eye accepts the horizontal convergence and rejects the vertical one. Even though we actually do see vertical parallel lines as converging, they are always interpreted by the mind as parallel. It is for this reason that when we are confronted in the photograph with a mechanically accurate transcription of what we really see, we refuse to accept it as real, for the camera only records visual experience without interpreting it. More than this is necessary if a picture is to be a true work of art.

The foregoing paragraph should not be taken to mean that the camera cannot be used as an instrument of artistic expression. In the hands of some men, it becomes a powerful tool, searching out the most characteristic aspects of things and portraying them in pictures of astonishing vividness. But it is a far cry from such products to the casual snapshots displayed in drug-store windows, as far as from Michelangelo's Creation of Adam to the insensate scrawls and blots of color produced by a kindergarten pupil. In neither case do we have to deal with a work of art but with something unillumined by human personality and so devoid of significance.

The materials of the painter are pigments applied to wet plaster, canvas, wood panel or paper. The most familiar type of painting is done with oils on canvas, a method that has been employed since the Renaissance. Pigments mixed with oil provide a medium that gives richness in opacity of light and depth of shadow. Great precision and infinite *nuance* of color are possible to the painter in oils, since corrections and retouching are a relatively simple matter. On the other hand, oil paintings are subject to destruction by time. Unless the painter is highly skilled in the science of sizing the canvas, mixing his oils with pigments, varnishing the canvas, he cannot expect his pictures to last more than a few years.

Before oils were generally used, a type of painting called tempera was popular. Egg was mixed with dry pigment, and resin or wax added for transparency. This substance was applied to prepared wood panels. In appearance such painting sometimes resulted in flat dry effects like fresco and sometimes attained the richness of oil, depending upon the mixture. The most permanent type of painting is fresco. In this process colors are mixed with water and applied to fresh plaster which absorbs the color. Since the pigment has been incorporated with the plaster, it will last until the wall is destroyed. Fresco painting requires great skill and knowledge to be used effectively. Each day the painter must have prepared a small area of fresh plaster which has to be painted before it dries. Once dry, it cannot of course be altered or retouched, so the master must work with great speed and sureness of hand. Fresco painting flourished during the 15th and 16th centuries, when Masaccio, Michelangelo, Raphael, Tintoretto and many others covered the walls of Italian churches with their great masterpieces, but the 20th century has witnessed its revival in the work of the Mexican nationalist painters, and in that of some men in the United States.

Pastel is a process more recently invented than any of the foregoing. The pigment is bound so as to form a crayon which is applied directly to the surface, usually paper. Pastel is a delicate and seductive medium, but subject to damage. It is customary to spray it with a fixative lest the dry powdery color rub off. Water color is a process familiar to every school child. Here colored powder is formed into cakes with gum arabic, then mixed with water. The transparency of the medium allows the paper to show through, adding its own color and luminosity to the finished effect. Though most popular with the amateur and dilettante, water color is a difficult medium. It was much used by the Old Masters for studies and preparatory sketches.

With painting we may group the *graphic arts*, the art of the black and white print. The woodcut, the etching and the engraving were first developed in order that many copies might be made of a single work. But instead of continuing as a mere reproducing medium, these processes have become definitely established as techniques with laws of their own. In the case of the woodcut, a drawing is made upon the long grain of a block of wood. With a sharp instrument, the artist gouges out the parts that are to be white in the picture, leaving the parts that are to be black flush with the surface of the block. The block is then inked and pressed upon the paper which absorbs the ink. With etching and engraving the process is just the reverse. The engraver gouges out of his copper plate the parts that are to be black. His sharp graver digs out grooves in the copper plate, which is then sponged with thick black ink. When the surface is wiped clean the ink remains in the grooves, and under the pressure of the press the spongy paper is forced into these, where it absorbs the ink. The result is a crisp definite linear impression. In etching the metal is covered with a thin coat of gum. Then the artist draws a picture in the gum with his pointed etching instrument, laying bare the metal beneath. He then places the plate in an acid bath. The acid acts upon the exposed metal, the part under the gum being unaffected. When sufficiently bitten, the plate is taken from the bath, the gum removed. The plate is inked and wiped, the ink catching in the bitten places. Then it is pressed against the paper as in the case of the engraving. The plates and blocks may be used again and again, though of course they deteriorate after many impressions have been made.

# Chapter XXIV. *Painting Before 1300*

## A. Pre-classic and Classic Painting

*PAINTING IS AN ART THAT HAS BEEN PRACTICED FROM* the earliest periods of known human existence, and vies with sculpture as a medium in which primitive man embodied the concepts and ideas significant to his experience of life. These, as might readily be expected, were of the most elemental nature—concerned largely with preserving and continuing his mortal existence and assuring himself a future life beyond this one in accordance with his dimly realized feeling that another world existed beyond this one. Thus in the cave of Altamira in northern Spain which is covered with paintings on the rock walls that are of the palaeolithic period when much of Europe still lay under the glaciers of the Ice Age, there are pictures of *Bison* (Fig. 354) upon which the cave man depended in large measure for food. Made by combinations of lines incised in the rock and heightened by color, the basic pictorial elements, animals such as this one are portrayed with remarkable fidelity to facts of appearance in spite of the simplification of detail. This is due to two circumstances—the sharp eye of the hunter-artist whose life depended as often as not upon his ability to see his prey under the most difficult conditions, and his concern with the usefulness of the animal as food which leads to emphasis on those parts of the beast best suited to that purpose. Thus he has caught with sure strokes of sharp stick or crude brush the most characteristic features of form or movement (some of the animals are lying down) and in representing them has emphasized the salient visual facts.

It is unlikely that the palaeolithic painter was interested in the forms of beasts, as in this case, or of human beings such as appear in some other examples of prehistoric rock painting, for reasons other than magical. The forms are isolated unities, and in the *Ensemble* (Fig. 355) there is very little if anything in the way of decorative organization, since to modern eyes at least there is no perceivable relationship between the various animals shown. For the significance of these forms is not a fundamentally aesthetic one, created simply because of an urge to create something pleasing and attractive to the eye; they are a direct and realistic statement on the part of the artist concerning something that was of utmost importance to him, hence their credibility as an interpretation of experience from which arises the truthfulness of this art as an expression and the satisfaction taken by the observer who experiences it in turn.

In Egypt, painting hardly existed as an independent art; it generally appears as an accessory to statues and the relief carvings on the walls of

FIG. 354.—Altamira. Cave. A BISON COW.

tombs (cf. Figs. 9, 233) and temples (cf. Fig. 18), where it accents forms created in the more durable medium of stone. For permanence was an essential quality in the means by which the Egyptian sought to record for eternity those forms which embodied his experiential concepts, and the relatively fragile character of painting alone did not encourage its extensive development. There are certain periods, however, and there were presumably always some places in which this was not a critical weakness. On the walls of the Middle Kingdom rock-cut tomb of Khnumhotep at Beni-Hasan (cf. Figs. 13, 14), the *Slaves Feeding Oryxes* (Fig. 356) are painted directly without the preliminary relief carving of the other examples cited. The forms are indicated by outlines, and the contours of arms and legs inside the general silhouettes are shown in the same way. These outlines are then filled with color which is laid on flat, i.e., without modeling tones, terra-cotta red, yellow,

green, brown and white being used. It is hardly necessary to point out
the conventions of drawing in the figures; they parallel those of Egyp-

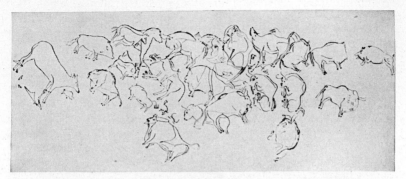

Fig. 355.—Altamira. Cave. Palaeolithic Paintings.

tian relief sculpture (Figs. 230, 233, 238), involving simultaneous presentation of frontal and profile views of the same form in order that the

Fig. 356.—Beni-Hasan. Tomb of Khnumhotep. Slaves Feeding Oryxes.

most characteristic aspect of any given portion may be comprehensively
described. This is an attitude well adapted to effective portrayal of the

animals—for the profile view represents them quite adequately—but does not lend itself so well to organic consistency in the human figures. Even in the latter, however, there is somewhat greater flexibility than in comparable relief sculptures because an attempt at least has been made to suggest the foreshortening of the shoulders and backs of the profiled forms. But there is no perspective, and the figures exist in depth

Fig. 357.—NOBLEMAN HUNTING. From an 18th-dynasty Theban Tomb. *British Museum, London.*

only descriptively for their forms are as flat as the wall on which they and the identifying hieroglyphs are painted.

A wall painting showing a *Nobleman Hunting* (Fig. 357) from an Eighteenth Dynasty tomb at Thebes is similar in theme to the Old Kingdom relief from the Tomb of Ti (Fig. 233) and many of the conventions are also the same, notably the proportionately greater size of the master and the familiar profile views. He is gesturing with considerable animation, however, as he holds three birds by their legs in one hand and a flexible wand in the other, in contrast with the static pose of Ti. A typical statement of the problem of representing perspective

depth inherent in such an art as this in conveying ideas descriptively
is seen in the birds, which are shown simply as a series of overlapping
profiles. There are, however, certain bits of naturalism of a high order;
the birds and fishes are shown with great accuracy, and the hunting
cat that sits in the bending lotus stems before its master with birds
clutched in teeth and claws is a small masterpiece of portrayal and char
acterization. Again it must be repeated that Egyptian art is basically
conceptual rather than sensuous in motivation, and that in the repre-

Fig. 358.—Girl Acrobat. *Museo di Antichità, Turin.*

sentation of the activities of the master upon the walls of his tomb, the
purpose is incorporation of typically comprehensive qualities rather than
momentarily naturalistic ones; this accounts for the clarity and order of
the arrangement which modern eyes may interpret as the consequence
of a desire for decorative beauty but which is simply the Egyptian's
way of defining his ideas with the greatest possible accuracy. The training of eye and hand that this involved was selective and intense; occasionally it was manifested in more informal themes like the *Girl Acrobat*
(Fig. 358) of the Twentieth Dynasty, about 1180 B.C., painted on a
flake of limestone and presumably the pastime of an artist in a moment
of idleness. Although conventions are still present, notably the portrayal
of the eye, and the feet are rather summarily indicated, the precisely
drawn lines of the arched body render the action with amazing vividness and accuracy.

Of the painting that decorated the walls of Aegean and Mesopotamian palaces in the pre-Hellenic period of Mediterranean culture, it is

possible to speak with assurance only concerning the former. Color in the form of enameled glazes was a decorative accessory to the Tower of Ishtar in Babylon (Fig. 23), but its employment here is in the category of ceramic rather than pictorial arts. In Crete, on the other hand, where the conglomerate walls of the Palace of Minos were ideal for treatment in the pictorial mural medium of fresco, a considerable number of fragments, some of rather large size, have been recovered and restored. The griffon on one of the flanking walls in the Room of the Throne at Knossos (Fig. 25) has been pieced together from fragments found on

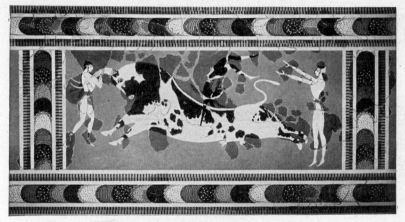

Fig. 359.—The Toreador Fresco. From Knossos. Restored. *Museum, Candia.*

the floor where they fell in the catastrophe that damaged the structure, in all probability about 1400 B.C.; the bare rubble of the other wall shows the necessity for the stucco finish upon which the decoration was painted. The colors are bright and varied, with yellow and red, blue and green used in vigorous and highly decorative patterns. The wavy bands and the foliate forms constitute a stylized landscape setting for the animal which was probably a guardian, with its presumed counterpart on the other wall, sacred to the earth goddess served by the priest-king, in the manner of the heraldic lions on the fortified gate of the mainland Aegean city of Mycenae (Fig. 27).

Also of religious significance in all probability is the *Toreador Fresco* (Fig. 359), which is one of the most striking examples of Cretan painting found in the Palace of Minos, as to both subject and formal character. Much of the picture has been restored, but a sufficient number of original fragments were recovered to indicate the principal features. Against a blue background, a male figure, nude save for a loin cloth, is about to spring from his hands off the back of a charging bull. A girl, equally lightly clothed, reaches out her arms to catch him, and another is about to leap through the bull's horns after her male companion. The youth is a dark red in color while the girls are white—a distinction of sex that is commonly found in the early representative arts. The

Fig. 360.—Departure for the Hunt. From Tiryns. Restored. *National Museum, Athens.*

flying gallop of the bull is another convention often employed to convey the idea of movement. The frame of variegated patterns and colors to suggest different kinds of stones is an element in the architectural function of the painting. The bull is a frequent motive in Aegean art, occurring also, for example, on the gold Vaphio Cups which were found in a pre-Hellenic mainland tomb (Fig. 557), and the figure style is likewise common to the Aegean area in general. The narrow-waisted girls with sharp noses, pointed chins and curling strands of hair are similar in type to the ivory and gold Snake Goddess (Fig. 248), and they appear as well in the two ladies in a chariot in *Departure for the Hunt* (Fig. 360) which has been restored from fragments found in the ruins of the citadel at Tiryns (cf. Fig. 28). Dating in all likelihood from between 1350 and 1200 B.C., this fresco is somewhat later than those of the palace at Knossos. The color is strongly conventionalized, the trees being blue, gray and terra cotta with yellow borders; the leaves are outlined in black against their fan-like silhouettes. The chariot is crimson and the horses are red and white. The figures, standing in stiff profile, are white, with a blue and a violet robe; they have the characteristic small pointed features noted in the Cretan girls. The decorative sense of the Aegean artist which makes these architectural paintings so effective is also to be noted in the naturalistic ornament of the vases and jars from both island and mainland sites in the pre-Hellenic world (cf. Figs. 553-555).

Writers of antiquity have described great paintings that adorned the walls of many Greek buildings of the Hellenic age, but no trace of them remains. What little can be surmised of them, other than from written descriptions, is on the basis of adaptations in the form of mosaic copies (cf. Fig. 362) or in the still further reductions that appear on vases. But the art of vase painting seems to have developed independently of monumental forms in Greece and to have followed its own line of evolution for some time. It is thus possible to speak with assurance of painting among the Greeks even though there is little that corresponds directly with popular concepts of the art today; the religious and mythological scenes from jars and cups of various shapes and sizes can be used as examples. The techniques employed are discussed in detail under the Minor Arts; here it will only be noted that three basic methods are found—one in which the figures are dark on a relatively light background (Fig. 563), another that reverses this relationship (Fig. 361), and the third wherein the figures are drawn in outline against a creamy white ground (Fig. 566). Areas that appear light in the majority of monochromatic illustrations such as those which will be found here are actually a reddish brown, the color taken by the clay of the vessel after it was hardened by being baked in an oven.

Greek vase painting, like Greek sculpture, was largely concerned with subjects involving representation of the human form, and the way in which this was treated by the vase painter develops along lines very similar to those noted in Greek sculpture. Thus the figures representing a funeral procession on the great Dipylon Vase in the Metropolitan Museum in New York (Fig. 560), which dates from between 1100 and 700 B.C., are portrayed as combinations of geometric forms. In the upper frieze the dead man lies on the bier, mourned by his family and women who tear their hair; the chariots and armed figures in the lower one represent the athletic games celebrated in his honor. The heads are circles with pointed beaks for nose and enclosing a dot, the torsos are triangles and the arms no more than straight lines. The descriptive intent of the artist is clear; each figure is defined as individually as possible within the conventions of form available to the painter, and the result, if child-like in its naïveté, is highly decorative. By the second quarter of the sixth century B.C. when the François Vase was painted by Klitias ca. 560 (Fig. 561), the intent of the artist has become more complex and it finds expression in a more flexible figure style. There are still archaisms such as profile legs joined to frontal torsos and the forms are usually shown viewed either from directly in front or from the side, but by incising the black silhouettes of the forms the painter has attempted to indicate surface modeling, drapery folds and even a certain amount of anatomical structure. One of the high points in this black-figured style of Greek vase painting is reached in the work of Exekias, whose kylix with Dionysos in a boat painted on its bottom (Fig. 562) and amphora with Achilles and Ajax playing draughts (Fig. 563) are among the most ingratiating examples of the art. Though still pervaded by conventions, the superb draftsmanship of the painter makes the physical limitations of the medium seem as nothing, and the figures are not only well realized in a decorative sense but also characterized by a spritely grace that is akin to that of the archaic sculptures with which they are contemporary (cf. Fig. 251).

The black-figured style of Greek vase painting reached its highest point of development in the third quarter of the sixth century B.C. Further progress in realistic portrayal of the human form required a new technique which made its appearance about 530 B.C. in the so-called red-figured style. A vase in the University of Pennsylvania Museum (Fig. 564) by the master called the Kleophrades Painter, executed about 500 B.C., shows the character of the style. The background is now dark, the figures having been "reserved" when the vase was painted and thus appearing lighter in tone; the details of anatomy and drapery are painted on with a fine brush instead of incised as in black-figured examples. With this greater ease of portrayal, the artist has ventured effects that would have been very difficult in the earlier manner, such as the foreshortening of the body of Heracles struggling with the lion and the torsion within the figure. Contributory to these effects is the construction of the forms in planes so that they appear to have a sculptural roundness instead of being entirely flat, as seems to be the case with the black-figured examples. The painting from the interior of a kylix showing an old man and a girl (Fig. 558) is possibly a little later than the Kleophrades Vase but shows many of the same qualities, and both represent a stage in the freeing of the vase painter from the limitations of archaic technique comparable to that seen in sculpture in the figure from the pediment of the temple at Aegina (Fig. 254) and that dedicated by Euthydikos with which it is contemporary (Fig. 253).

According to popular Greek tradition, Polygnotos, an artist active in the middle of the fifth century B.C., was the inventor of painting, by which recognition was given his achievement in perfecting a style of monumental mural decoration. Of these paintings only descriptions and reduced adaptations on vases are known, and whether or not it was the

*Courtesy the Museum of Fine Arts, Boston*

FIG. 361.—ODYSSEUS AND THE GHOST OF ELPENOR. Detail of an Amphora. *Museum of Fine Arts, Boston.*

taste for more complex and involved effects created by his achievement that contributed to the decline of vase painting as an art is a matter that can only be surmised. There continued to be vase painting of distinction in the late fifth century, to be sure; an example is the meeting of *Odysseus and the Ghost of Elpenor in the Underworld* (Fig. 361) of about 440 B.C. on an amphora in the Museum of Fine Arts in Boston. The figure to the right is Hermes, who does not appear in the Homeric account of this episode in the eleventh book of the *Odyssey* but is represented because it was among his duties to escort the souls of the dead to the underworld. Elpenor stands in a trench filled with blood from the slaughtered sheep that magically gives him temporary substantiality, while Odysseus sits with drawn sword to fend off other spirits desirous of drinking it. The style of the figures has certain characteristics also found in contemporary relief sculpture; the proportions and muscular conventions of Elpenor's torso are very similar to those of figures in the Parthenon frieze (Fig. 265), and Odysseus' head can be compared almost directly with that of the man standing behind the horse on the frieze slab. There is an even further attempt at foreshortening, however, and the painter has also ventured beyond the relief sculptor in representing some features of the setting. This may have been in part because the Homeric poem mentions some of them, but there can be no doubt that painters were beginning to be more and more interested in such things as the fifth century progressed. Thus in a scene of Thamyris and the Muses on an amphora in the Metropolitan Museum in New York (Fig. 565), which was executed in the last quarter of the fifth century in the manner of the Meidias Painter, the figures are represented in the freest attitudes with varied foreshortenings and relationships in perspective that reveal the greatest skill in drawing but are considerably less effective as decoration than in the earlier red-figured and black-figured examples. There is also more variety in color, and in this as well as in the greater complexity of effects there is indication of the attempts by the late fifth-century vase painters to vie with contemporary masters of monumental mural decoration such as Polygnotos.

The art of mural painting continued to develop in fourth-century Greece and one at least of its notable achievements has been preserved in a monumental copy—the *Battle of Alexander and Darius* (Fig. 362), the original of which was painted by Philoxenos in all probability about 310 B.C. and which is known today through the later version in mosaic of the Hellenistic period discovered in a house in Pompeii. It has been considerably damaged, but the upper part of the youthful conqueror's body is seen, and also the spear with which he slays the Persian general who sacrificed his life that Darius, seen at the right, might escape in his chariot. Although the technique was an awkward one, the forms being built up by placing hundreds of thousands of small marble and glass cubes of different colors together in the desired patterns, there are many devices by which the effect of three-dimensional forms in space is suggested. There are contrasted areas of light and dark and highlight accents to model the figures, and diminution of scale in those farther away to create an effect of depth in perspective; the horse in the foreground before the wheel of Darius' chariot is quite accurately foreshortened. The spears outlined against the sky contribute to the sense of air surrounding the figures, as well as to the decorative pattern of the composition. The colors are sober—white, yellow, red and black —but in a variety of tones. There is still a considerable dramatic quality in the picture too, in spite of its being a copy in a technique more

Fig. 362.—The Battle of Alexander and Darius. From Pompeii. *Museum, Naples.*

laborious than that of the original; the violent movement of battle is shown, and the clear characterization of the protagonists—Alexander's impetuous courage and the grief of Darius at the death of his friend—is a reminder of the heightened expressive values for which the sculptors of the fourth century also strove.

Painting in the Hellenistic period continued advancing in the portrayal of the visible world, as is clearly seen in a fresco taken from one

Fig. 363.—Theseus. From Pompeii. *Museum, Naples.*

of the excavated houses of Pompeii showing the hero *Theseus* emerging triumphant from the labyrinth after slaying the fabulous Minotaur (Fig. 363). It was probably copied from a Greek original, like the Alexander Mosaic, but the Hellenistic painter has put into his work the results of observing many phenomena of light and space to which his predecessor was oblivious. Thus in the Meeting of Odysseus and Elpenor (Fig. 361) neither light nor space is suggested. The modeling of the figures is achieved entirely by curving lines, the setting is created by similar devices and the whole scene is reduced to a flat decorative pattern. In the Hellenistic fresco, the background seems actually to be set back in space, owing to the contrasted areas of light and dark on the walls; and though the figure of Theseus may have been inspired by a statue such as Lysippos' Apoxyomenos (Fig. 274), it too is given the effect of three-dimensional form by the light and shade playing over its surfaces. The bystanders are grouped in such a way as to suggest the space even more, and are subordinated to the main figure by the grouping and the obscuring shadow. Throughout, with the exception of the sharply outlined figure of Theseus, the forms are blurred and hazy as if dimmed by atmosphere, again contrasting with the boldly delineated silhouettes of the figures on the vases (Fig. 361) but readily comparable with such contemporary sculptural works as the pastoral reliefs (Fig. 279).

In attempting to represent objects in a definite and comprehensible spatial environment, the Hellenistic painter was moving toward realization of certain concepts that are fundamentally and characteristically pictorial. In the vase paintings of the pre-Polygnotan period (Fig. 564), the figures partake more of the quality of sculptured than painted forms with their specific contours and planes; in the fresco, on the other hand, the effects of light and shade by which the illusion of form is created are specifically pictorial devices. Thus at a time when sculpture had more or less exhausted its limited repertory of effects and subjects and was evolving brilliant but meaningless and mannered technical show pieces, painting was only beginning to realize the extent of its still largely unexplored possibilities. The visual point of view developed in this exploration, whereby rendering of form and space is the result of patterns of light and shade, is in strong contrast to the formal one that dominated the earlier periods of Greek art and reached its climax in the architecture and sculpture of the Golden Age in effects characteristically stated in terms of plane, volume and mass.

The development that occurs in painting during the Hellenistic period is a manifestation of the changing point of view in thought of the Mediterranean world. The civilization of the fifth century was dominated by Athens, which was in actuality little more than a provincial town. Its philosophy had been developed to meet certain very restricted requirements and the art which gave it expression was similarly restricted in scope. It was an art of form, and little else was considered of significance in comparison with that. In contrast with Hellenic civilization, that of the Hellenistic world was extensive geographically and cosmopolitan in character. Its philosophy was broad and comprehensive, attempting to include the evaluation of man's experience in relationship to his environment as well as the human values to

which the earlier concepts had been consciously limited. It was a natural result of this mode of thought that the eyes of artists should have
been opened to the many aspects of nature which the purposely narrow vision of the fifth century had never observed. The effect is ap-

FIG. 364.—PARIS ON MT. IDA. From Pompeii. *Museum, Naples.*

parent in the sculpture of the period, as has been pointed out. But the
very nature of the widened comprehension of natural phenomena in
the Hellenistic world made painting the logical form of its expression.
Art moves from a world of form into one of space filled with depths of

shadow and gleaming light, from a world of sculpture into one of painting.

The enthusiasm with which this illusionistic art of light and shade and spatial effects was received is apparent in the important part played by such effects in Roman art. In the reliefs of the Arch of Titus (Fig. 286) in Rome, the whole purpose of the artist is to force the recalcitrant stone to the effects that contemporaneous painters were able to attain so easily. Even in architecture, a sense of space achieved by light and shade is an important element (Fig. 58). In painting, it lends surprising naturalism to the extensive landscapes which the Roman added to the repertory of the painter, well illustrated in the fresco of *Paris on Mount Ida* (Fig. 364) in the museum at Naples, thus posing the final problem of realistic representation, the convincing relationship of objects to infinite space. In the forms, blurred by atmosphere, of tree and shrine in the middle ground and of mountains in the distance, there is an effect anticipating the concepts of 19th-century Impressionism though the mood is lyric and Horatian, with a characteristic detail in the reclining figure in the background symbolizing the mountain with typical classic anthropomorphism. In the brief period of a few hundred years, classic painting thus passed from a stage in the sixth and fifth centuries B.C. which for all its distinction is still evidence of a primitive mode of thought, to these realistic Roman landscapes that at least forecast the comprehensive complexity of modern concepts. The trend thus revealed toward ever more detailed naturalism is a manifestation of the increasing awareness in western thought of the overwhelming extensiveness of human experience and its search for significance which finds expression in emphasis on the specific and the concrete.

## B. Painting in the Middle Ages

During the first millennium A.D. painting of the western world, like architecture and sculpture, was in the service of the Church, in which capacity it functioned in two major categories—the monumental one of decorating religious buildings, and the physically smaller but no less significant pictures or illuminations in religious books. Its immediate and ostensible purpose, at least as far as the monumental examples are concerned, was didactic, to give instruction in the dogma of the Christian faith to those who could not read. The walls of churches were decorated with fresco paintings and also with mosaic executed like the classic Alexander Mosaic (Fig. 362) of small cubes of colored glass or marble set in the plaster of the wall while it was still soft and held firmly in place after the hardening of the base. Being of relatively permanent materials, a number of these mosaics have been preserved in much their original state, an example being the *Story of*

*Abraham* (Fig. 365), which is on the walls of the choir in San Vitale at Ravenna (cf. Fig. 70). In the center of the semicircular lunette are the three angels who came to visit Abraham in the plains of Mamre (Genesis xviii, 1-8) and to whom he serves food while Sarah his wife stands in the door of their tent at the left; on the right side of the lunette is the Sacrifice of Isaac. In the upper left spandrel above the arch is the prophet Jeremiah, and at the right is Moses receiving the

FIG. 365.—Ravenna. San Vitale. THE STORY OF ABRAHAM.

Ten Commandments, with the murmuring children of Israel below. It is obvious that between the time of the Roman fresco of Paris (Fig. 364) and the middle of the 6th century, there has been a considerable decline in the interest of artists in representing the appearance of things. This is especially true of the spatial relationships which are suggested in the earlier work. The grouping in the central lunette is reduced to a single plane even though it is quite clear that the artist thought of the seated angels as being farther away than Abraham, and comparison of the group of Jews at the right with the crowd of people in the Hellenistic fresco (Fig. 363) reveals the same contrast. Averse as he was to creating a realistic representation of the subject, the artist has emphasized decorative elements. The whole work is an adjunct to the architecture of the building, and the absence of spatial implications thus preserves the integrity of the wall surface. The hills of the background are suggested by a rhythmic succession of cylindrical objects and the draperies are reduced to a formula of lines radiating fanwise from a single point.

The meaning of the entire composition other than as a pictorial story is a symbolic one. Dramatic and representative values are subordinated to symbolic ones. In themselves, the subjects represented have little dramatic significance, a fact readily demonstrable by the inclusion in one composition of two different incidents, but both together represent the idea of Abraham who stood in the mediaeval theology for the old order of Jewish faith which was transformed into the new one of Christian belief by the death of Christ on the cross, symbolized here by the Sacrifice of Isaac. This symbolic idea is carried out still further by the figures of Jeremiah and Moses who represent the Old Law just as Christ, symbolized by the Cross held by the flying angels, represents the New Law. The artist attempts no further interpretation as later ones might; he merely presents his subject for contemplation. The figures in the lunette could mean to a Christian only those of the story of Abraham. For the figures of the prophets where the identification might not be so easy, the artist has used inscriptions. But the effectiveness of mosaic ornament goes beyond its adaptation to the architectural setting or its exposition of a point of abstract theology. Its greater purpose was an emotional one, achieved by the gleaming gold backgrounds and the luminous colors which glow softly in the darkness of the interior and bestow upon it the effect of a living entity. Under such conditions, the figures take on a mystic significance that completely transcends their character as objective images.

An important example of the illustration of books in the early years of Christianity is provided by the miniatures of the *Rotulus of Joshua* (Fig. 366) in the Vatican Library in Rome. These are of interest, in addition to that of their style, in having once formed part of a long scroll, the form in which books were first made, which was read by rolling the illustrated text sheet from one spindle to another. The relative importance of the pictures is clear, for the text is written into the spaces left in the landscape background peopled by the protagonists in the epic of the Israelitish diaspora. Joshua is here represented twice— once standing as he salutes the angel of God and once kneeling before him to receive the command to attack the city of Jericho in the background. There is good reason to believe that the Joshua Rotulus originated in the Hellenistic city of Alexandria in Egypt, whence came also the style at least of another masterpiece of Early Christian art, the Episcopal Throne of Maximianus in Ravenna (Fig. 579), and that it was executed in the 7th or 8th centuries. A Hellenistic prototype is reflected, moreover, in the free movement of the figures and their somewhat casual placing in space, and in the rendering by accents of light and dark of the forms of humans, trees, buildings and mountains. The whole is a convincing illustration of the manner in which

FIG. 366.—JOSHUA AND THE ANGEL OF GOD. The Rotulus of Joshua.
*Vatican Library, Rome.*

Christian content was infused into the forms of classic antiquity in the initial phases of their assimilation by the new faith.

The pictures that were drawn or painted on the pages of the hand-written books used in the service of the Church are significant out of all proportion to their physical size for they are almost the sole evidence of pictorial creation in the western world between the 6th and 11th centuries. They served as well, moreover, in the revival of the monumental arts of painting and sculpture in the later Romanesque and Gothic periods, for, as has been pointed out elsewhere, it was often on the basis of manuscript illuminations that the artists worked in decorating the churches of the 11th and 12th centuries. The character of this early mediaeval art is the result, as has also been noted before, of fusing together the various concepts of style developed in or under the influence of the three great pre-Christian cultures or traditions in the western world. One of these was the classic tradition with its embodiment of an ideal of physical or moral beauty which was expanded in Hellenistic and Roman times to include landscape and setting as well as the human body. The second was the Byzantine tradition, whose outstanding characteristic is its decorative unity. These two elements are represented in our illustrations by the Hellenistic and Roman frescoes (Figs. 363, 364) and the Joshua miniature (Fig. 366), and the Ravenna mosaic (Fig. 365) respectively. The third element is that contributed by the barbarian tradition; it is best described as the idea of effective force made evident in powerful decorative abstract patterns wholly unlike those evolved by the classic tradition. It appears in its purest form in the illuminated initial letters of the *Book of Kells* (Fig. 367), an Irish manuscript of the late 8th century, in patterns of line that are utterly unreal and unsymmetrical but possessed of a unity which can be the result only of the sheer vitality and continuity of the line itself. In itself, this barbarian mode of expression did not develop a formula for the representation of the human figure for it gained its effects chiefly by means of abstract geometrical forms. But when it came in contact with the classic and Byzantine concepts through the medium of Christian art in the late antique tradition, it galvanized their forms with new life and produced a style that was the embryo from which the monumental sculptures and paintings of the Romanesque and Gothic periods were destined to grow. The manifold aspect of this style is best seen in the 9th and 10th century manuscript illuminations, the most significant artistic achievements of the short-lived Carolingian Renaissance initiated by Charlemagne's desire to recapture the glory that had been Rome and continued sporadically under his successors.

There were many different styles of Carolingian illumination developed in the various monasteries to which Charlemagne had entrusted the reestablishment of classic culture. They can be grouped together, however, in two main categories, the East Frankish and the West Frankish, according to their stylistic characteristics and the geographic distribution of the monasteries in which they originated. The East Frankish style included the output of a monastery at Reichenau which can be considered as typical of the whole, while the West Frankish manner is best observed in the manuscripts that form the Reims school, so called by virtue of the fact that most of them seem to have originated in monasteries near that city. Much though the

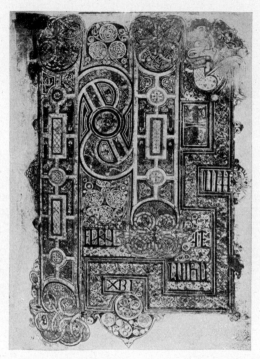

Fig. 367.—Initial IN. The Book of Kells. *Trinity College, Dublin.*

two styles differ in details and effect, the basic intent of both is the same, to give expression to the ideal of vital force which was the Teutonic contribution to the background out of which grew the culture of the later Middle Ages.

The outstanding example of the Reims style is the series of pen drawings in a psalter in the library of the University at Utrecht in Holland. These drawings are naïvely objective in their references to the accompanying text as in the *Illustration of the 74th Psalm* (Fig. 368) in the English version. At the extreme right is the figure of Christ on a high mountain representing Zion, described in the second verse, extending a wand toward the sun, moon and stars, and two figures symbolizing Summer and Winter, mentioned in the sixteenth and seventeenth verses. In the center are the enemies of the Lord breaking down the carved work of the temple with axes and hammers. At the right is the Nativity, a symbolic reference to the twelfth verse, "For God is my King of old, working salvation in the midst of the earth." In the left foreground a wingless angel smites the heads of the dragons in the waters as described in the thirteenth verse and at the right are

FIG. 368.—ILLUSTRATION OF THE 74TH PSALM. The Utrecht Psalter.
*University Library, Utrecht.*

the people of the wilderness cutting up leviathan to be meat, as in the fourteenth verse. The artist who made this drawing was evidently trying to copy with pen and ink a miniature in the illusionistic style (cf. Fig. 366) that prevailed in late classic painting. The personifications of Summer and Winter continue an anthropomorphic type of symbolism that had its origin in Hellenistic art. In the heads, the representation of the eye by a triangular dab that suggests the shadow in the eye socket carries over from an illusionistic original. But these are only details that indicate the source of the figure style seen in the Utrecht Psalter drawings, for the purpose of the artist was not the suggestion of form in space but the expression of dynamic force by the intrinsic vivacity of linear movement. It is probable that the

Carolingian artist was attracted to the illusionistic style of the late
Hellenistic original by its lively play of light and shade, but that
effect was translated in his own work into linear terms. The West
Frankish style that appears in the linear illuminations of the Reims
school acquired great prestige and spread over the better part of
western Europe, as far as England and Spain. Miniatures in this
style served as models for the scenes on the Hildesheim Doors (Fig.
293) and the Prophet Isaiah at Souillac (Fig. 297) in which linear
effects predominate in a style that is monumental rather than descriptive or narrative.

Fig. 369.—THE RESURRECTION OF LAZARUS. The Gospels of Otto III.
*Staatsbibliothek, Munich.*

The East Frankish style was also derived from Hellenistic art, but
instead of the vivacious illusionism that the Reims style translated into
linear terms, it took the solid and sculptural figures. Thus the figures
in the *Resurrection of Lazarus* (Fig. 369) from the *Gospels of Otto III*,
a manuscript in the State Library at Munich which dates from about
1000, retain something of the classic in their restrained gestures and

bulky forms, quite different in effect from the exaggerated movements and wispy, wind-swept figures in the West Frankish style. But the antique types are transformed into one that embodies a Teutonic ideal of effective force in the heads jutting forward on the shoulders, the staring eyes and the huge misshapen hands and feet. It is static force rather than dynamic as in the Utrecht Psalter miniature whence it was reticent of the emotional intensity of the linear style, but it is none the less a northern concept and one that owes but little in the form of its expression to classic models. Like the West Frankish style, the eastern one exercised a definite influence upon later art. It furnished the direct inspiration for the bulky, crudely powerful figures by Guglielmus on the façade of Modena Cathedral (Fig. 298). When the emotional fervor of the Romanesque which found expression in the contorted forms of the monumentalized Reims style (Fig. 297) had begun to yield to intellectual discipline in the Gothic period, the consequent need for static strength in its forms of expression was filled indirectly by the East Frankish style through the medium of north Italian Romanesque sculpture.

Manuscript illumination is one of the most characteristically mediaeval of arts, and as long as the Word of God was held to be implicit in literal symbols, the surface upon which it was inscribed was thought worthy of enhancement by line and color. Illuminations are also found in books other than of the Scriptures, however, an example being the *Flying Fish of Tyre* (Color Plate II) which is from a Bestiary in the Morgan Library in New York. The mediaeval Bestiary was a moralizing treatise on animals in which their traits were interpreted symbolically as allegories of Christian concepts; the particular example under consideration was written about 1170 at a monastery near Lincoln in England. The Flying Fish of Tyre was supposed in mediaeval times to be of huge size and to fly after ships until its wings tired, when it would turn back to the place from which it came, a symbol of those who willfully refused to abjure their sinful ways and believe in God. That such a monster actually existed was doubted by no one although none had ever been seen, for mediaeval man trusted the evidence of his imagination before that of his senses, and in any event, the reality of the concept symbolized by the fish was much more significant to him than any possible unreality of its physical substance. Words and picture are composed to form an ensemble, the wings of the fish breaking through the frame enclosing the greater part of the miniature to intrude into the text field. Both are also considered in relationship to the page on which they lie, the figures being as two-dimensional as the letters of the hand-written script; there is thus

iuitas syrie que nunc tyrus dicit̃. olim
serra uocabat̃ a pisce quodam qui illic
abundabat. quem sua lingua sar apellat̃
ex quo diriuatū est huī similitudinis pis
ciculos sardas. sardinas       q̃ uocari.

PL. II. FLYING FISH OF TYRE

achieved a decorative unity or aesthetic "reality" which is the formal equivalent of the conceptual reality with which mediaeval man invested these imagined creatures. The style of the figures is comparable to that of the Romanesque sculptures with which it is contemporary (cf. Figs. 294, 298); the gestures, naïvely expressive of fear and

FIG. 370.—THE ENTHRONED MADONNA. Psalter of Robert de Lisle. *British Museum, London.*

wonder at the baleful phenomenon in the sky, are conveyed in terms of a rhythmically swinging heavy line that also serves to define the color areas with emphasis. These are of quite simple character for the most part as is the scheme of the color composition in being limited to a few basic hues—red, yellow, blue and green—but the effect as a whole is one of great vivacity and charm.

It is possible to trace the complete evolution of mediaeval thought in the field of manuscript pictures alone, and one further example will show the attitude as it is revealed in work of the 13th century. The *Enthroned Madonna* (Fig. 370) is from a manuscript psalter now in the British Museum in London that was made for an Englishman named Robert de Lisle in the last years of the 13th century. It is thus contemporary with the Vierge Dorée at Amiens (Fig. 303) and is quite similar to it in its mannered gracefulness. More significant, however, is the way in which the various figures are related to each other in an arrangement dictated by architectural forms; the Virgin is seated under a pointed and cusped arch and the smaller figures at the sides representing angels above and saints below look like the statues in niches on the flying buttresses of a cathedral. Behind the Virgin the background is tooled and burnished gold, while above the central arch is an all-over diaper pattern of brightly colored small medallions. Note has been taken elsewhere of the way in which the arts of the Gothic period all reveal the formal dominance of architecture, and it is characteristic that even the decoration on the page of a book should be disposed in patterns originating in that art.

The importance of manuscript illumination lies in the fact that it gave expression to mediaeval concepts long before they were sufficiently defined to be embodied in sculpture and architecture. In the Romanesque and Gothic periods, the need for monumental expression led to a tremendous development of the latter arts, as has been seen, and painting was also involved in this, for in the form of stained glass it played an important part in the emotional effect for which the Gothic builder strove. It is obvious that the elimination of walls which was a part of the Gothic architectural development made it impossible to employ traditional methods of fresco or mosaic for painted decoration. But in the stained-glass window, the mediaeval painter made his contribution to the glory of God and the Church, developing a form which has never been used with comparable effectiveness since that time.

In the stained-glass window of the *Madonna and Child* (Fig. 371) made in the late twelfth century for the cathedral at Châlons in France, the technical methods employed can be observed. It consists of innumerable pieces of glass in which the color has been definitely fixed by firing. These are fitted together and held in place by strips of lead. In the finished design, the figure is made up of large patches of color, each of which consists of many small pieces held together, the details such as the eyes and nose being painted on the glass after its original firing and then baked on to it in the oven. The effect when the window is in place is one of pure and intense color. Curiously enough, this is the direct result of the black lines of the leading that separates the colors. Without them, the colors would blend in the eye, and instead of giving the impression of pure blue and red side by side, the effect would be a violet less intense in hue than either of the original colors.

Needless to say, the stained-glass maker of the Middle Ages did

FIG. 371.—MADONNA AND CHILD. *Cathedral, Châlons.*

not strive for naturalism in his figures. Like the mediaeval sculptor, he was primarily concerned with making his panels in such a way that they would fit the architectural scheme rather than as independent compositions. His ideal was a flat pattern of color, and representation as such was always subordinated to this consideration. This was essential not only for the decorative needs of the architecture itself but also as a part of the moving effect that the whole interior produces, the sense of luminous darkness with its suggestion of infinite space.

Stained glass was not the only form of late mediaeval painting, for the art of manuscript illumination continued to the end of the mediaeval period. In Gothic miniatures, as has been seen, the figures stand against architectural backgrounds, in accordance with the same architectonic conception that controlled mediaeval sculpture. These backgrounds are themselves framed by wreaths of foliage, particularly in the later examples of the art, which are portrayed very naturalistically. With the break-up of the Gothic synthesis in the 14th and 15th centuries, different conceptions of painting took the place of the miniature and the stained-glass window. The easel picture appears and the prestige which this form acquired as treated by the artists of the Low Countries and of Italy remains undiminished down to the present.

# Chapter XXV. Painting of the Late Middle Ages

## A. The Franco-Flemish Tradition

*EVERY ARTIST WHEN HE LIFTS HIS CHISEL, BRUSH, OR* pen, acts in accordance with patterns of thought evolved in past times. The artist's personality is formed by what he inherits from the past and his adjustment to his present; hence the record of art is the story of men interpreting their world. Every generation must reinterpret old legends and myths according to the view of a new age. So it will be seen that in a dynamic and intellectually restless culture, art forms never remain fixed. There are *styles* which live briefly during a few years only to give way to others as new conditions of mind and temper, of economy and religion come into being.

The history of western painting as a continuous major growth of popular expression has two main branches: the Italian and the Franco-Flemish tradition. In the late Middle Ages painting emerges vitalized with particularly strong popular appeal as a voice of the Church. Unlike the hidden art of earlier book illumination and the architectural formalism of stained-glass windows, the painting which emerges in the 15th century is basically sensuous and realistic. To a considerable degree the new painting comes to surpass the other arts, notably architecture and sculpture, since its realism offered wider scope for individualism than was presented by the other arts. Painting could serve the Church but it was also a ready agent for expressing the values of the new worldliness inherent in humanism.

Painting in the 14th and 15th centuries is commonly called primitive though there is nothing crude or barbaric about it. Flemish painting at the beginning of the 15th century is highly refined and often extremely sophisticated. Its richness and refinement are readily understood in the light of the great epoch of Gothic art of which painting is an integral part. When one is familiar with the transition from the stark and inert sculpture of the Romanesque period (cf. Fig. 298) to the freer, more naturalistic sculpture of the late Gothic (cf. Fig. 305), the parallel development in painting which accompanied it seems natural. The pathetic element in thought and expression introduced by the mysticism of St. Bernard had manifested itself in an emotional dramatization of the Christian legend. Having affirmed the reality of universals, men sought to represent them in objective visual terms by means of symbols and allegory. In trying to understand experience in the light of Christianity, all material things have symbolic meaning, relating them to the hierarchy of established Christian cosmology. This method of understanding the world is foreign to the modern way of thinking which has abandoned the systematic theology of the Middle Ages. Instead of finding connections between things by investigating the hidden paths of relationships based upon cause and effect, the mediaeval mind sought these relations in terms of finality in accord with established dogma of divinely revealed truth. Thus to the mediaeval mind everything had meaning and life in terms of God. "When we see all Things in God, and refer all things to Him, we read in common matters superior expressions of meaning."

The demand that abstract concepts of love, death, compassion or piety be externalized into tangible symbols and allegory led directly to naturalism in art. And further it was a manifestation of the decline of faith, since in the earlier mediaeval period the validity of these abstractions did not demand proof through demonstration but was taken on faith. The historian Huizinga says of the late mediaeval times, "All life was saturated with religion to such an extent that the people were in constant danger of losing sight of the distinction between things spiritual and things temporal. If, on the one hand, all details of ordinary life may be raised to a sacred level, on the other hand, all that is holy sinks to the commonplace, by the fact of being blended with everyday life. In the Middle Ages the demarcation of the sphere of religious thought and that of worldly concerns was nearly obliterated."

At the end of the mediaeval period in 15th-century France and Flanders, there was a tremendous passion for the creation of pictorial images. Gorgeous pageants were contrived, and elaborate costumes; realistic pictures and statues abounded. As if to assure meaning to life, all activities were formalized, love into a fantastic code, honor into a ritual. The idea of the Trinity was reduced to tangible form, to a mere plaything; it was common for people to have statuettes of the Virgin which opened up to reveal the Trinity inside. Jean Fouquet, one of the greatest French artists, even went so far as to paint the King's mistress as the Virgin, fashionably clothed and offering her bared breast to the Christ Child.

Though this symbol-making was a symptom of the decline of faith, it had positive results of great significance to art. At its best it produced the sculptures of Claus Sluter (cf. Fig. 305) and the paintings of the van Eycks. At its worst it produced tedious and vulgar literature, ingenious toys and empty rituals. While religion was becoming a travesty and public and private morals a scandal, the means had been found for the beginning of a realistic art. The painting of this period is called *primitive*, since it marks the beginning of realistic art in the northern countries, but it is primitive only in the respect that it is a beginning. It has been termed decadent, for it marks the end of the

Fig. 372.—POL DE LIMBOURG. February.
The *Très Riches Heures du Duc de Berry. Musée Condé, Chantilly.*

mediaeval epoch, but this is to ignore its amazing vigor in the hands of a few masters. Its significance lies in the fact that though the ages of faith were coming to an end, the culture of the north had the vitality to establish firmly a tradition of naturalism which, fused with the Renaissance tradition of Italy, was to create the modern world.

The impulse to seize the image of things and, by representation, to make them part of the mind that perceived them, came to a focus in the Burgundian court of the Duc de Berry. He surrounded himself in the early years of the 15th century with countless artists, among them the greatest book illuminators of his time and perhaps of all time. Among them was Pol de Limbourg, who with his brothers painted the illustrations for the *Très Riches Heures du Duc de Berry*. This Book of Hours is a collection of prayers, a calendar, psalms, and lessons for the layman's devotions. In Limbourg's *Book of Hours* are painted vividly realistic landscapes such as the world had never seen. Never before had men recorded so faithfully and vigorously the spectacle of common things. Freed from the highly abstract and traditionalized ecclesiastical subjects and rules, the artist pays abundant homage to the joy of sensual experience. The months are illustrated by scenes of common activity peculiar to the season. In June, men with scythes slash wide paths through the tall grass while two barefoot girls with rake and fork pile the dried grass into small stacks. The windows of the Duke's castle look out toward Paris; through the distance winds the river Seine, with the *Ile de la Cité* and its edifices, some of which may still be seen today after more than five hundred years.

With lively interest the painter represents *February* (Fig. 372) by a scene of a farmyard where deep snow covers the ground and the roof of the sheepfold full of huddling sheep. All creatures are cold: the animals seek the communal warmth of their own wool, the girl blows her frosty hands, the woman and the two little children within the shelter lift their wet garments and warm their bare bodies at the fireside. The artist has missed nothing; he sees the row of beehives, the crinkly branches of the barren tree, the woodsman, and the peasant plodding through the heavy snow driving a donkey laden with firewood. For all this great wealth of narrative detail, there is no crowding or confusion. And if there is a slight lack of proper perspective, it is scarcely noticed in the vivid rendering of the details. Though executed on a scale no larger than the page of this book, these landscapes are among the first truly modern ones in painting. The symbol of active man shaping the physical character of the world he dominates by the strength of his hand has been achieved and will be echoed again and again in later art. In earlier illuminations the landscape had been stylized (Fig. 369) or the figures were placed against a flat gold background. But with Pol de Limbourg that tradition was definitely abandoned in favor of greater naturalism.

The significance of Limbourg's innovation was far-reaching. In the school of book illumination to which it belongs were educated the greatest Flemish masters of the 15th century: Hubert van Eyck (*ca.* 1370-1426) and his brother Jan (*ca.* 1385-1440). It is reasonably certain that Hubert van Eyck was the painter of miniatures which for knowledge of the effect of atmosphere upon the appearance of distant

Fig. 373.—JAN and HUBERT VAN EYCK. The Adoration of the Lamb. The Ghent Altarpiece. St. Bavon, Ghent.

objects surpassed even those of Pol de Limbourg. Together the two van Eyck brothers painted the great Ghent Altarpiece, a framework of pictured panels that swing open like doors to reveal the central subject. Begun by Hubert, it was completed after his death by Jan in 1432.

It should be observed that the task of painting a large altarpiece for public display requires a method somewhat different from that of the tiny book pictures. The van Eycks could not simply enlarge the miniatures because tradition dictated an exacting formula for the painting of the altar pictures. The subject was of prescribed religious character and must be treated with appropriate dignity. The central part of the Ghent Altarpiece is the *Adoration of the Lamb* (Fig. 373). It is apparent that the van Eycks have departed from the usual manner of the book illuminators. The subject is taken from the Apocalypse, "I looked, and Lo, a Lamb stood on Mount Sion" (Rev. xiv, 1). In a deep landscape, the Lamb, a symbol of Christ's sacrifice and human salvation, stands upon an altar that is part of the Fountain of Life. Large groups of martyrs, prophets, sibyls, judges and knights have come to witness this proof of God's love. One will observe at once the richness of the painting, the great detail in the treatment of garments, individual faces, and even the flowers in the grass. But it is evident that the perspective is not arranged so that all things appear as if seen from a single point of view. It is rather as if van Eyck had placed several groups of spectators together and was not concerned that they be unified in atmosphere and perspective. This lack of unity results from the fact that the mediaeval painter is chiefly interested in his subject matter and less in how the subject is handled with regard to the atmosphere, the landscape and so on. As in the miniatures of Pol de Limbourg, here too the pictures are built up by the addition of thousands of details. Consequently the eye is somewhat bewildered by the profusion of objects, all of which are rendered with arresting distinctness in brilliant colors. The van Eycks had perfected the technique of oil painting and with it produced effects that have never been surpassed for luminous richness. It is the incredibly transparent greens, the lustrous reds and crystal whites which give authenticity and unity to the picture and compensate for the pinched uncorrelated space effects. To the mediaeval mind every object in the world had a peculiarly mystic significance by the very fact that it was a divine creation. For the artist to record its isolated qualities was to recognize that holy splendor which was its intrinsic virtue. There are about twenty separate panels comprising the altar, some of which are related to adjoining scenes, but the majority are treated in isolation. Later ages were to aim at a logically unified pictorial treatment, but the mediaeval painter was satisfied with an aggregate of kindred subjects symbolically held together by the enveloping landscape.

FIG. 374.—JAN VAN EYCK. Jan Arnolfini and His Wife.
*National Gallery, London.*

One of the new uses to which this realistic art could be put is demonstrated by Jan van Eyck's portraits. Jan was the younger of the brothers and the more modern in his point of view. With an unprecedented sense of realism, he illuminated the personality by rendering not only the outer appearance of his subject but also the relationship to its surroundings, thus making a profoundly important advance beyond the more symbolic manner of the Ghent Altarpiece. In *Jan Arnolfini and His Wife* (Fig. 374), painted in 1434, all the intimate details of the surrounding room are portrayed. Much as one marvels at the painter's skill in recording the texture of fur trimming, heavy brocade, the quality of the light shining from the brass chandelier, the very grain of the planked floor, what astonishes most is the way these details are subordinated to the personalities of the two people. In this subordination of unessentials, van Eyck proves himself one of the greatest masters of pictorial interpretation. A lesser man working in the same mediaeval technique would have presented merely a dull and pointless display of chairs, bed, mirror and, incidentally, the two occupants of the room. As it is, the eye is drawn unerringly to the faces and hands; all else, though sharply delineated, is blended into a background of atmosphere and adjuncts. We observe the rather self-conscious attitude of the pair, the shrewd and possessive Arnolfini and his meek wife. It is not an intimate scene; rather they seem conscious of their friend the painter whose unseen presence is felt as a third in the room. Few paintings are so charged with humanity. Not a little of its vitality is due to the rendering of space. The light that filters through the room seems to set the space vibrating. It strikes the chandelier; it touches a spot on the floor and plays against the wall where it sparkles from the convex mirror. In this mirror we catch a glimpse of the interior from another angle, and so the space is further enriched. The Gothic feeling for intangible space so powerfully exploited in the cathedrals is now finding a further expression in painting as an instrument to give significance to isolated objects, as the structure of the cathedral gave meaning to the carved images that adorned it. The landscape with its inexhaustible possibilities of space patterns replaces architecture as a setting for figures, and in pictorial art it became the dream of painters down to our own day to plumb the fathomless mysteries of abstract space.

The great development occurring within Jan van Eyck's art is apparent in comparing the harsh veracious *Adam and Eve* (Fig. 375) from the Ghent Altar with the Arnolfini portrait which is a later work. In the latter, following Pol de Limbourg, he has created a space pattern within which his figures come to life. Here we must observe that *space,* not in its sheer physical presence in art but as an element of design, becomes in both Italian and northern art a primary artistic problem. The Flemings were especially concerned with it since space had been a major consideration in architecture in the Middle Ages. In the 13th century, the architects gave in the lofty vaults and stained-glass windows a tangible symbol of the eternal Christian Heaven. In the 15th century, the painters transformed the panel of an altar into a remoter but none-the-less real vision of a self-sustaining, complete and inviolable world in microcosm. They perfected oil painting in order to effect not so much simple illusion as the compelling presence of space glowing with the fiery life of jewels. In the Adam and Eve, van Eyck painted in a singularly harsh and almost photographic method, an ecclesiastical symbol; in the Arnolfini portrait, while many mediaeval symbols are found in the marriage images (chandelier, the dog, carving of the furniture, etc.), they are largely unrecognized as symbols in our time, but the cohesion of objects in a quickening drama of space and color gives a more universal validity to the painting. Similarly one may be moved by the exhilarating drama of space in Gothic churches without reference to the symbolism of the crossing, the meaning of the sculptures or the stories related in the glass painting. Symbols which may originally have had specific but relatively local and limited significance assume universal value when shaped in color and space by the hand of an artist.

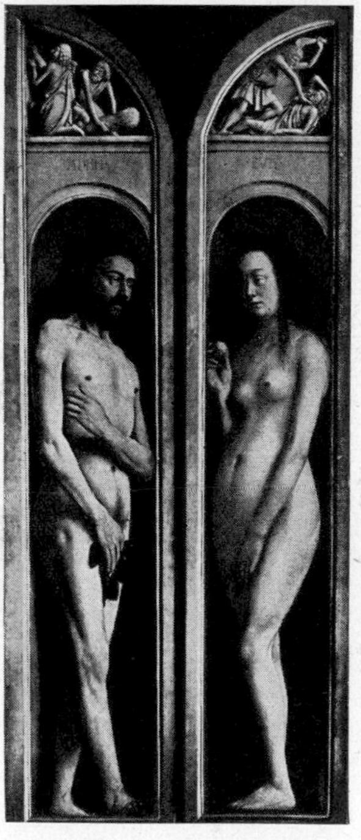

Among the many artists to follow the van Eycks was Rogier van der Weyden (1400-1464). About the middle of the 15th century he painted his great *Descent from the Cross* (Fig. 376). While Rogier employed the same technique of minute detail as Jan van Eyck, he did not obtain the same arrested objectivity. More literal than van Eyck, he seeks to sway by emotion through concrete expression of tearful and tortured faces. Rogier, trained in the tradition of Gothic woodcarving, gives only the tangible figures without the enveloping atmosphere and its vibrant space. In this respect he is archaic where Jan van Eyck is modern.

Though lacking the artistic stature of Jan van Eyck, Rogier was a master of great talent. His influence was felt by his student Memling

FIG. 375.—JAN VAN EYCK. ADAM AND EVE. The Ghent Altarpiece. *St. Bavon, Ghent.*

and by a whole generation of other Flemings. The vitality of late Gothic art was such that Rogier on visiting Italy in 1450 was in no way inclined to yield his Gothic idiom. He did observe certain types of composition in Italy that appear years later in his own work, perhaps most notably in the Portrait of a Woman and the Portrait of an Este, now in museums in New York and Washington.

The northern masters painted small pictures for the most part since

FIG. 376.—ROGIER VAN DER WEYDEN. THE DESCENT FROM THE CROSS. *Escorial, Madrid.*

the Gothic style of architecture provided no large wall surfaces like those found in Italy. It is interesting to observe the result when an Italian patron demanded of Hugo van der Goes (active 1465-1482) a large *Nativity* (Fig. 377) broad enough to fill the wall space of a good-sized living room. Judged by the standards of Italian painting, it appears lacking in unity and order. We seem to see the Madonna from one distance, the angels from another. The eye is first engaged by the angels and the still-life of irises and columbine in a vase. Then by virtue of putting two and two together it is seen that the people, the angels, the shepherds and the Virgin form an adoring circle about the Holy Child lying naked upon the rude pavement. The picture is in truth a series of brilliant fragments. When the donor Portinari presented it to a Florentine hospital in 1476, it was the despair of all the Italian masters who came flocking to see it, for they had never met with such vivid realism or delicacy in drawing combined with astonishingly brilliant colors. Their Madonnas had not been given such homely features alight with lyrical tenderness. And never had

Fig. 377.—HUGO VAN DER GOES. The Nativity. *Uffizi, Florence.*

they seen such uncouth, horny-handed fellows as the shepherds appearing in art—these genuine peasants that gaped with loutish adoration at the Babe.

The presence of a large and notable northern painting in Florence created one more of the many incidents of contact between northern Europe and Italy. The impact of Flemish art upon Italian and of Italian upon Flemish continued increasingly during the next two hundred years. The Italians profited no doubt from a demonstration of brilliant craftsmanship in color and drawing. In turn the Northerners were to benefit from the Italians' capacity to organize plastically and psychologically. A comparison of van der Goes' Nativity *ca.* 1476 with Leonardo's Adoration *ca.* 1480 (Fig. 414) will suggest the divergent

aims of the two schools as well as their common dedication to the concrete and specific.

Of all the early Flemish masters perhaps Hans Memling (*ca.* 1430-
1494) is the best loved. He was no investigator or pioneer but, coming
in the latter half of the 15th century, he sums up the achievements of the age. His style is poetic, urbane and sensitive. The portrait of Barbara and Willem Moreel in Brussels and the same couple

FIG. 378.—MEMLING. Madonna and Child.
*Kaiser Friedrich Museum, Berlin.*

with portraits of their numerous offspring in Bruges suggest the quality
of his painting. Unself-conscious sentiment delicately expressed gives
authenticity to his best work. The requirements of theological exposition called for elaborate and complex narrative which often taxed
the limited capacity of Memling, but in intimate portraiture and in
the treatment of the Madonna and saints he attains a lyrical expression
that has to a large degree become popularly identified with the whole
of early Flemish art. The charm of his *Madonna and Child* (Fig. 378)
of about 1470 is undeniable even when the idiom of simplified surfaces

and rhythmical movement of line is recognized as a popularization of the work of more originative masters like Rogier van der Weyden. In Memling's art is a rarefied poetry of childlike simplicity and faith. His vision is that of saints and holy ones like Fra Angelico's, though not so passionate and sustained as his.

The final phase of the waning Middle Ages in the Netherlands is scarcely suggested by Memling's deliberate narratives or his lyrical and sensitive portraits and Madonnas. There are depths of experiences yet to be recorded. Jerome Bosch (1450-1516) and Quentin Massys (1460-1540) did much to reveal the temper of their age and its culture. Both were of a peculiarly cosmopolitan vein, Massys being responsive to the art forms emanating from Italy while Bosch created pictorial and psychological types that are as valid today as when they were painted in the late 15th and early 16th centuries.

Unlike Memling, Bosch presents to the world spectacles of almost incredible horror. The Middle Ages produced minds of the most humane and balanced character but it also frequently inflicted upon the common run of humanity a terrorism unrivaled in history. Bosch lifts the veil from the shadowy nether world of creeping, writhing, tortured beings. No misshapen monstrosity is loathsome enough to convey his conception of the seven deadly sins. He invents a thousand diabolical creatures combining features of man, beast, and bird to illustrate the psychological hell of man's depravity. One must not suppose that Bosch was merely a cataloguer of mediaeval superstitions, an illustrator of neurotic and psychotic personalities of his day. While occasionally he masses vast amounts of material with studied disregard for continuity and cohesion, in most instances he proves himself a master of pictorial invention. Like that pioneer in the cinema, David W. Griffith, he employs the close-up as means of increasing the effectiveness of his psychological study. Before anyone else had discovered it, he learned how best to relate small dramatic figures with a dominant landscape. His peculiar genius is for observing human behavior, observing it without malice or condescension and with a searing lucidity. The *Christ Before Pilate* (Fig. 379) in the Museum of Historic Art at Princeton, painted in 1502, makes it clear that the horrors represented in Bosch's art are no inventions of a morbid mind but actualities based on man's ever-constant capacity for suffering torment and inflicting it. The greatest tortures are those of the mind and the most excruciating are those inflicted for reasons of official expediency. One finds in the terrible complacency of the Pharisees, the dour habitual gesture of Pilate, a manifestation of naked power more chilling than the overt brutality of the soldiers or the insane shrieks of the mob. Bosch makes no attempt to make Christ dominate; in fact, He cowers numbed before the torrent of malediction. What Bosch has given is the spectacle of a Gestapo court, a lynching party, in this demonstration of the warping and perversion possible to human nature. Sometimes these scalding revelations by their very shock bring into focus moral issues too often left untouched in the expression of the noble and heroic. As a superb master of irony, as an analyst of man's basest and noblest impulses, as a landscapist and recorder of the com-

FIG. 379.—BOSCH. CHRIST BEFORE PILATE.
*Museum of Historic Art, Princeton University, Princeton, N. J.*

mon man, Bosch had a wide influence. He became the spiritual guide to Bruegel in the Flanders of the next century.

In the person of Quentin Massys the turn of the century finds a more conventional artist. Yet working in the tradition of Hugo van der Goes and Rogier van der Weyden, he broadens and heightens their style, deepening his work with close-knit patterns enriched with color which becomes strong, singing and sustained with dramatic force. In pointing up the dramatic and integrating psychological elements of design, Massys parallels the mood of his Italian contemporaries, Leonardo and Botticelli. Comparison of his *Deposition* (Fig. 380) with a similar subject painted about the same time in Italy—Perugino's

Lamentation (Fig. 401)—will offer some clue as to the relation between these two dominant schools.

Regular harmonious patterns in Perugino's treatment of the seated Christ are opposed to Massys' painfully disposed figure. The poignance of the sufferers so deeply studied by Massys is more broadly handled by the Italian. The silhouette of landscape tellingly integrated with

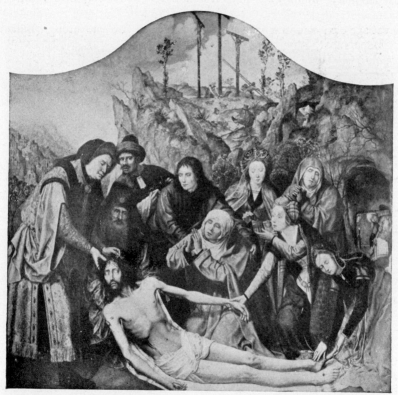

FIG. 380.—MASSYS. THE DEPOSITION. *Museum, Antwerp.*

the figures in both paintings is characteristic of each. For all of their differences it is apparent that both masters are approaching the sustained psychological and formal equilibrium that is called classic. Massys with his heightened feeling for psychological phrasing goes in dramatic vigor beyond his Italian contemporaries and foreshadows the tumultuous art of Rubens and psychological penetration of Rembrandt in the 17th century. But Massys' art is reticent even in the face of sensational themes like Salome's Dance and the Martyrdom of St.

John the Evangelist, two subjects treated in the wings of the altarpiece cited. His faces somehow stick in the memory, haunting and deeply human. Massys and Bosch together dominated artistic Flanders before that country was engulfed by the flood of Italian imitators. The authority and the vitality of the Middle Ages drew to a close in all artistic spheres. A new age called for a more cosmopolitan, more systematic art language. From Italy came the impulse to new forms in music, literature and the plastic arts. Engish poetry—Wyatt and Surrey—the great age of drama in Elizabeth's time, came to fruition through Italian

FIG. 381.—JEAN FOUQUET. CHARLES VII. *Louvre, Paris.*

influences. In painting, northern Gothic and classic Italian were not to become reconciled in a day and the period of reconciliation was often painfully affected and barren, but in the end Flemish art emerged revivified with Rubens in the 17th century, who was to make Flanders one of the most influential European art centers in that fertile age.

French art in the 15th century is so closely related to Flemish as to be at times almost indistinguishable from it. Jean Fouquet (*ca.* 1415-1482), one of the many gifted Frenchmen of this period, was a prolific illuminator of manuscripts in the Franco-Flemish tradition, and as a portraitist he was even more celebrated. The international trend of his style foreshadowed the interaction between north Europe and Italy which became the rule in the 16th century. More sober and abstract than the Flemings, Fouquet readily absorbed the Italian influences toward formalization and the subordination of details to large effects. The pinched and meager face of *Charles VII* (Fig. 381), finely modeled, emerges from the flat schematic drapery of the curtain and costume in an unforgettable pattern. He is Charles *Le Victorieux*, the unhappy weakling whom Joan of Arc made King of France.

The greatest single monument in French painting of the later 15th

FIG. 382.—THE AVIGNON PIETÀ. *Louvre, Paris.*

century is undoubtedly the *Avignon Pietà* (Fig. 382), painted by an anonymous master or masters about 1465. The often-repeated theme of the Virgin mourning her dead Son is here treated with sublime pathos. The large figures and monumental effect of their arrangement indicate the influence of the formal and abstract contemporary Italian style. The main figures are characterized by a noble and ascetic restraint in their mute expressions of grief. The very human donor who kneels at the left participates only in so far as he shares the grief of the sacred persons imaginatively in his devotion. That a layman should be represented so realistically and given great prominence in a sacred picture signifies the growing importance of the individual in the social and religious thought of the times; in late Gothic sculpture (cf. Figs. 306,

307) there is found the same combination of realism exquisitely blended with religious sentiment. The stage of the picture is set in a barren landscape, brown and austere, illuminated only by the burnished gold background against which loom the towers of Jerusalem. The use of this gold background (for it can scarcely be called a sky) at a time long after it had been displaced in other styles by realistic landscape is significant of the sophisticated and eclectic character of the painter, who used every device he knew to express a mood of deep spirituality. It is thus a product of the various artistic influences current in 15th

Fig. 383.—STEPHAN LOCHNER. The Adoration of the Magi. *Cathedral, Cologne.*

century France, and though stylistically a *tour de force* it is withal a creation of transcendent beauty.

In Germany, in the 15th century, the Gothic manner continued at first without modification by the naturalistic and classic ideas sweeping across Europe. Stephan Lochner (d. 1451) in the *Adoration of the Magi* (Fig. 383) shows no effect of the vigorous Flemish art with which he must have been acquainted. Lochner removes from his subject any concrete reference to specific place and sets it in an imaginative realm of pure meditation. With sweetness and absorption his Madonna and Magi dwell apart from the intense psychological dramas of Rogier van der Weyden and beyond the passionate world of love and anguish of the Avignon Pietà. The mystical experience of the individual speaks as it does so frequently in German art. In Lochner the mystical vision does not obtain a consummate expression but lingers in an engaging border land between myth and fairy tale. Other Germans of this age are bolder and more forthright in exploration of the physical—men like Moser, Pacher and Witz—and they, rather than Lochner, point the way to the emergence of a great school of art in Germany in the 16th century; the development of the graphic arts overshadows painting in Germany and one must look there for the main current leading to Dürer.

While the spiritual leadership of the Church was beginning to decline in the northern countries of France, the Netherlands and Germany, there was at the same time a political chaos marked by the disastrous Hundred Years' War in France, the conquest of the Netherlands by Spain, and the division of Germany into its many feudal states. The transition from feudalism to nationalism was characterized by bloody wars and unbelievable violence that laid waste whole kingdoms. The wonder is that, with comparative little stability of cultural tradition, art flourished at all. When it does appear it is confined to local schools, sometimes highly abstract in the German schools, and again surprisingly naturalistic as for instance in Flanders. The provincial isolation of schools was somewhat relieved by the sporadic movement of painters to and from Italy. With the unification of France and her subsequent invasions of Italy, the international trend became increasingly greater until, in the early 16th century, Francis I of France, a great patron of the arts, called to Fontainebleau a group of Italian painters, decorators and craftsmen who formed a school of art that was a potent factor in unifying the European tradition. The nature of that fusion will be considered in the discussion of Renaissance art.

## B. LATE MEDIAEVAL PAINTING IN ITALY

South of the Alps in Italy, the late Middle Ages witnessed a flowering of painting comparable to that found in the Franco-Flemish area. The northern countries had during the 12th and 13th centuries produced a striking synthesis of mediaeval thought, of which the Gothic cathedral is the most monumental and comprehensive statement in art. Italy witnessed no comparable dramatic climax. She always looked upon the Gothic forms with suspicion and, indeed, invented the name *Gothic* in the 16th century to suggest what was barbaric. When she borrowed the forms of Gothic architecture, she used them gingerly and without full understanding of their organic implications.

Italy inherited an older intellectual tradition than her northern neighbors, a heritage that went clear back into the pagan world of

Greece and Rome. In her own countryside were many fragments of Roman art, temples, aqueducts, sculptures. But for centuries Italian painters worked in a style handed down from Byzantium (Constantinople). Old forms of Byzantine times, frozen and apparently lifeless, had been endlessly copied, and a formalism reminiscent of Egypt prevailed until the late 13th and early 14th centuries. At the turn of the century, however, there occurred a quickening in religious thought, in literature and art, that culminated in what is known as the Renaissance. In this late mediaeval stirring, the influence of the art of Graeco-Roman antiquity was more strongly felt in Italy than in the north. Italian art, stimulated by classic models and by the vigorous Gothic sculptures and miniatures, underwent a revivification.

The intellectual ferment throughout Europe of the 14th century is perhaps most eloquently expressed by the emergence of Chaucer in England and Petrarch and Boccaccio in Italy. They wrote not in the international scholars' language, Latin, but in the vernacular. English and Italian, the languages of the people, were now adopted as the medium for robust, naturalistic narrative prose and lyric poetry. Something like this recognition of the vitality of common speech will be seen to occur in painting. In the 14th century painting became humanistic. It became with Giotto an art for the people, rich in narrative and dramatic force. The revival of art occurred chiefly in Siena and Florence, but though these cities were close neighbors each had its own very peculiar character. Siena clung to the Middle Ages while Florence explored new avenues of thought.

### I. PAINTING IN SIENA

From the 13th century through the 16th, the development of Italian art centered in Siena, Florence and Venice. Siena was the most isolated and the most thoroughly mediaeval; her art at the close of the 13th century and from the beginning of the 14th held close to the Romanesque-Byzantine tradition of abstraction, with just enough naturalism to be consistent with the effective narration of Biblical tales and the expression of delicate sentiment. A city characterized by mystic religious fervor and dedicated to the cult of the Virgin with its lofty sentiment, Siena was no pioneer in art or science; this rôle belonged to her neighbor Florence.

Duccio, active around 1300, felt no need to expand the boundaries of his art much beyond the scope established by tradition. In 1311 he completed his masterpiece, The Madonna in Majesty, a large altar painting. The Virgin sits holding the Child Jesus, flanked by monotonous rows of nimbed angels and martyrs. It is essentially Byzantine in character; there is no space represented and the figures have little bulk.

The forms fill the surface to the point of crowding. It differs from the older pictures, however, in its breadth and sweetness. The Mother holding the Child (no longer represented as a little old man) is sober and gracious, unlike the harsh and dour Madonnas of the old paintings. Sweetness and humility are the positive qualities that make Duccio such an effective interpreter of the religious sentiment of Siena. On the reverse of this altarpiece are forty small narrative panels, scenes from the Bible and the early Christian legends. Abstract symbols are no longer sufficient; in these panels fresh and sensitive interpretations

FIG. 384.—DUCCIO. CHRIST IN THE GARDEN.
The *Maestà. Opera del Duomo, Siena.*

are found in lively narrative. The Christian epic not only must be recited, it must be vivified with sympathetic images that appeal to the hearts of the beholders. One of the forty episodes, which were painted between 1310 and 1320, is *Christ in the Garden of Gethsemane* (Fig. 384) when He asks that the cup may pass from Him. Gethsemane is a barren hill-slope dotted with miniature trees. Christ addresses the saddened and attentive disciples who have accompanied Him; then, while they rest, He prays for the strength that the morrow will demand, stretching forth His hand to receive a chalice, the symbol of His destiny, from an angel. The sky is still a flat gold surface in the Byzantine manner, and the landscape is only sufficient to contain the figures and give them a general location. The figures are highly generalized and yet characteristic in their attitudes. Typical is the sharp gold band that forms the edges of Christ's robe and makes a lively linear pattern serving to set off the dominant person in the tableau. The decorative calligraphy of garment folds and contours is characteristic of the Sienese style.

Duccio was the greatest master of the school, but he was followed by other superb artists; notably the brothers Ambrogio and Pietro Lorenzetti, and Simone Martini. Pietro Lorenzetti, active 1320-1348, suggests the diversity of Sienese painting and its problems. The triptych of 1342 representing the *Birth of the Virgin* (Fig. 385) indicates the current predilection for narrative. In a Gothic house with the front walls removed, he presents the domestic drama of the birth chamber

Fig. 385.—PIETRO LORENZETTI. The Birth of the Virgin.
*Opera del Duomo, Siena.*

and the adjoining room where Joachim eagerly awaits information. Here the artist is seeking an interior space commensurate with the figures. This planning of pictorial space is the same problem the Flemish masters were to face and one which was to be a major consideration of painters for centuries to come. The way the Sienese master meets the problem is indicative of the aesthetic approach of the whole school. The perspective construction of the rooms is only approximated. Our eyes, accustomed to later naturalistic examples, are conscious of numerous discrepancies like the tilting floors and over-large proportions of the mother. A photograph suggests nothing of the exquisite patterns of color that make this work a supremely beautiful painting. To find a close parallel for the stimulating, self-sustained drama of small patterns alternating with broad surfaces all enriched with interlocking colors of rare and unexpected relationships, one would have to look to the work of Picasso and Matisse in our time, and then it must be said that these masters have themselves to some degree derived much in their own art directly or indirectly from Siena.

Because of the more modern naturalistic development in the school of Florence, the steps taken by these masters of Siena are sometimes overlooked. One finds the Sienese replacing the stern hieratic art of Byzantine masters with one of sensuous charm and pictorial drama. Their refinement in color, in sentiment, in sensitivity to composition reflects an aristocratic culture for which Siena was celebrated. In her exquisite and passionate devotion to the arts, Siena marks the widening avenue through which the rest of Europe was soon to pass. The elements of pathos, narration and rich decoration found in her art reveal an acute awareness of nature which is at the basis of modern art; but for a more comprehensive intellectual analysis of reality one must look elsewhere, notably to Florence.

Outside of art other new voices are heard in mediaeval Italy, voices that are symptoms of a revivified life and that will have the most significant bearing upon the temper of the modern world. In a small hill town near Siena, St. Francis of Assisi in the early 13th century established his brotherhood to be organized later as the order of Franciscan monks. This little monk preaching the brotherhood of man, his sympathies embracing all nature, even animals, trees and flowers, so vitalized and dramatized the dry scholastic doctrines of the Church that he embodies as no other man the truly living thought and feeling of the late Middle Ages. Many see in him the origins of the Renaissance itself. St. Francis is the exemplar of passionate Christian love in practice. Teaching a way of life through the denial of property and an affirmation of the kinship of all earthly things, he asserted a pantheistic harmony of worldly and spiritual experience. Through a love which was focused on this world as St. Bernard's love of God was not, he denied the primitive Christian dualism which separates body from soul. His love of birds and beasts, of men and fire, was for him the unifying and humanizing force in the world. The thought of St. Francis swayed the minds of the poet Dante and the painter Giotto, the two greatest artists of mediaeval Italy. The vitality of the experience he revealed compelled these masters to explore their own hearts and the world about them, and in so doing to produce a world of images which would be models for centuries to come.

## II. PAINTING IN FLORENCE

Siena, absorbed in her exquisite dream, played a relatively minor rôle in the development of the art that reflected a transformed mediaeval culture. She understood the sentiment which moved St. Francis to obedience, poverty and humility, but the Florentine mind as exem-

FIG. 386.—GIOTTO. THE MADONNA AND CHILD ENTHRONED.
*Uffizi, Florence.*

plified in Dante and Giotto was the most effective vehicle of Franciscan mysticism. Giotto, essentially worldly and intellectual in his outlook, accepted the thought of St. Francis and tested its authenticity in a rational exposition of ordered and understood naturalism.

When Giotto (1266-1336) painted a great image of the *Madonna* (Fig. 386), he did not show her amid an army of saints and martyrs as Duccio and other Sienese had done, as if to give visual proof of her divinity. Rather, he approached the idea from a new direction, seeking to dramatize the compassionate spirit of the Virgin, to make her moral qualities felt and understood by all who viewed his picture, and thereby to command their worship. To evoke in men's minds the reality of these qualities, it was necessary to create images which in themselves were persuasively real. Here, then, was the problem: to translate the abstract ideas of the Middle Ages into readily understandable images of people and situations. The great intellectual refinement to which scholasticism submitted the concepts of life had placed the essentials of Christian thought beyond the grasp of the mass of humanity in the 13th century. Formulas, fixed codes and systems had been imposed upon the simple faith of the people and made them spiritually destitute. Christian doctrine originally was largely a humanization and dramatization of the abstract ethical and metaphysical ideas of antiquity, but now had come a time when Christianity itself must undergo the same process of revivification. Simultaneously the process was occurring in the north and in Italy, in each case according to innate differences of temperament and cultural background.

FIG. 387.—CIMABUE. THE MADONNA AND CHILD ENTHRONED. *Uffizi, Florence.*

Giotto makes his images of angels, Mother and Child palpable and real by working out a scheme of light and shadow. He arranges the figures so that space is provided for each tangible form. The sides of the Gothic throne are shown in foreshortening; heads of prophets are seen through the side frames. The steps that lead to the throne project illusionistically into space. In all these details, Giotto departs radically from the Byzantine tradition of his teacher Cimabue (*ca.* 1240-1302), who, content with the old forms, had represented the *Virgin Enthroned* (Fig. 387) as an object of adoration but without any attempt to interpret what the Madonna means in terms of human mercy, love and compassion. He felt no need to create an illusion or to prove, since the faith in his symbol was unquestioned. Giotto felt the potential emptiness of such symbol painting—anyone who has seen the dreary monotony of the traditional paintings of this period knows with what dry rot they were infected. Cimabue could, however, inform his paintings with fervor and express in powerful linear patterns something of the passion that is felt in the Romanesque sculptures in the north, notably the Prophet at Souillac (Fig. 297). But his art is spatially flat and static. Observe the absence of any life-giving gesture or expression; the faces are almost exactly alike; the angels stare out fixedly at the beholder. In Giotto's picture there is a wide variety of types among the angels in regard to gesture and feature (Fig. 388). The congregation of

FIG. 388.—GIOTTO. An ANGEL. Detail of Fig. 386.

angels direct their attention toward the Mother and Babe as though they, like the spectators, were devotees. This device serves to augment the illusion of spaciousness and to heighten vastly the dramatic effect. While the traditional Byzantine masters present us with static universal concepts, Giotto does the opposite. He defines the time, the place and the circumstance, and thereby permits us to identify ourselves more completely with the figures he represents. It is this feeling of sympathetic identification that gives such overwhelming intensity to his painting of 1305, in the Arena chapel at Padua, the *Lamentation* (Fig. 389), one of the most affecting images of love and death ever painted. The forms move in a slow measured symphony of grief; they are borne down by the appalling spectacle of the dead Savior. Power-

ful as is this sense of death, the tragic reverberation of love among the mourners strikes a stronger note. Each responds according to his nature: the women with wailing and despair, the older men with quiet resignation. The face of the Virgin (Fig. 390) is distorted by excruciating anguish as she bends low over the still body of her Son.

The awful intensity of the tragic drama results largely from the plan of organization. The lower half of the space is packed with figures, yet there is no crowding or inclusion of irrelevant detail; only the barest necessities of the drama are shown. The mourners form two rectangular main groups which are linked by the figure of Christ and by the barren ledge of rock that slopes from the right. The body about which the figures are gathered forms a unit with the seated women and

links the groups left and right. One might well say that these group-
ings conform to the emotional and psychological attitudes of the people involved. They are units in a perfectly organized plan that gives
optical clarity to the composition and articulation to the dramatic content. Christ is not only the psychological motivation for the action,
drawing all eyes to Himself, but the plastic core of the formal organization as well. Even the landscape bends to this universal grief. It consists of a narrow ledge of rock that terminates at the head of Christ

Fig. 389.—GIOTTO. The Lamentation. *Arena Chapel, Padua.*

and serves to unify the group and direct attention to Him. Through
the large design with which the action is logically and dramatically
articulated, the story attains an expression of the deepest tragic pathos
befitting the language of the Scriptures. These bulky figures, these gestures and movements, have meaning only in so far as they are consciously organized and directed toward a definite end. The Gothic
painters in the north became far greater masters of nature than Giotto,
but they lacked his sense of the underlying rhythm of the emotions
and his sense for the unity of the theme as a whole. We miss in them

the human understanding that gives his figures intrinsic rather than symbolic value.

The impression which St. Francis made upon his world is reflected in Giotto's frequent painting of the St. Francis theme. He or his pupils portray the little monk preaching to the birds or receiving in his own hands and side the wounds suffered by Christ. One of the greatest of these paintings is a fresco of about 1320 depicting the *Death of St. Francis* (Fig. 391), which rivals the earlier Lamentation in dramatic intensity. The stage is more ample, the design more structurally law·

FIG. 390.—GIOTTO. THE VIRGIN AND THE DEAD CHRIST. Detail of Fig. 389.

ful and imposing. The architectual setting lends itself to a severer and more powerful schematic arrangement, with the two sides marked by small gables which enframe the solemn groups. The love by which the saint lived now seems to pervade his brothers whom he is leaving. The prevalent mood of restrained grief is interrupted and at the same time intensified by a single gesture of the monk beside the head of the saint, who alone sees the vision of his master's soul being borne to heaven. It is impossible to conceive of a more perfect realization of the theme.

To an eye accustomed to the infinite variety in form and space patterns and to the involved colorism of modern art, Giotto's frescoes may appear rigid and flat. But more likely the impression will be of freshness and unaffected directness of intention. His economy of means is the despair of any would-be emulator. The disarming simplicity with which he sets forth an involved narrative marks him as one of the few great masters of dramatic art. His position in the history of pictorial design is eloquently revealed when his painting of the *Raising of Lazarus* (Fig. 392) in the Arena Chapel at Padua is compared with a miniature in the Gospels of Otto III of about the year 1000 (Fig. 369). The latter, painted by an anonymous master before the age of naturalism, presents suggestive symbols of the narration. His interpretation of the legend places the emphasis upon the supernatural power of Christ, who as if by magic stuns all who witness his feat. As though

FIG. 391.—GIOTTO. THE DEATH OF ST. FRANCIS.
*Bardi Chapel. Santa Croce, Florence.*

to verify the authenticity of the magical act a spectator obtrusively holds his nose against the stench of the corpse.

To Giotto the miracle is nothing so simple and childish. His Christ is no performer of amazing feats but a teacher of the way of life. By a grave and authoritative gesture the Lord summons Lazarus back to life as He summons the world to a way of life through love. The folk myth so frequently misinterpreted has here passed through the mind of a great seer to return fresh and revitalized, rational and human. In the reshaping of elemental myths, in dealing with experience at its ethical core, Giotto occupies a lofty place in art along with Goethe, Michelangelo and the Greek tragedians. Ethical laws must be consistent with natural law and so Giotto, following the classic humanists, shapes an art that is earthy and familiar. Witchcraft and primitive obscurantism are banished from his thought, to be replaced by the light of reason and faith.

Though there is to be found in Italy no master of Giotto's stature in the later 14th century, he does not stand as an isolated pioneer in thought. The age witnessed parallel and comparable developments in philosophy, education, science and art. It is the period when Chaucer, Petrarch and Boccaccio appear as founders of a popular literature in English and Italian—in the common language of the people. They

Fig. 392.—GIOTTO. The Raising of Lazarus. *Arena Chapel, Padua.*

freed language from provincialism and obscurantism much as Giotto freed painting from formal cloistered and esoteric restrictions.

While the stream of Italian art flowed through the firm channels of humanism, it was augmented by floods of Gothic thought to make the full tide of the Renaissance. The fusion of the north with Italy is as difficult to graph as the mingling of the waters of two converging streams. The Italian sense for form and harmony and the Northerners' sense of space and variety in nature reinforce each other. As Europe became more culturally integrated these two sets of ideals merged to find their highest expression in Rembrandt, who will appear three hundred years later.

# Chapter XXVI. Renaissance Painting in Italy

## A. THE EARLY RENAISSANCE, THE 15TH CENTURY

*TO UNDERSTAND THE LUXURIANT FLOWERING OF ART* which occurred in the 15th and 16th centuries, the period known as the Renaissance, one must carefully gauge the force of Giotto's work. He effected a revolution in the modes of artistic thought that was to influence every major work of art for hundreds of years, for the sober naturalism of his great murals stimulated the imagination of all who saw them. But the sweet color, the flat schematic decoration of the older mediaeval art were not destined to disappear at once. Indeed, some of the most splendid paintings for two centuries after Giotto were created in the old manner. The immediate effects of this Florentine master were not revolutionary. For almost a century there was in Florence no painting comparable to his. His pupils and disciples repeated again and again the new words and phrases he had given them, embroidering his themes with small essays in realism and perilously complicating his space patterns. No one seemed able to use the new instrument of expression that Giotto had forged except to make hollow and novel narratives which at best were ingenious and charming. On the master's death his assistant Taddeo Gaddi (*ca.* 1300-1366) industriously borrowed everything of Giotto that was lively and picturesque and little that was central to the main thought. His *Presentation in the Temple* (Fig. 393) is as prolix, trivial and confusing as Giotto's version of the same subject is condensed, pointed and sober. Gaddi's bewilderment in attempting to create a complex space pattern is revealing in the light of the mastery attained in subsequent times (Fig. 425).

Nevertheless, the bold innovations in Giotto's work set a pattern for the centuries to come. Once and for all he broke the anonymous uniformity marking the work of artists in the Middle Ages and paved the way for the modern period of the Renaissance in which his individualism became a commonplace. With the opening of the 15th century there began a succession of masters who interpreted the world in concrete and individual terms. It is still to be noted, however, that in creating an art that was universally intelligible, one couched in the sensate realities of color and shape, the masters of the modern epoch were but continuing the impulses evident in every phase of life already active in the late Middle Ages. In the magnificent Gothic sculp-

FIG. 393.—TADDEO GADDI. THE PRESENTATION OF MARY.
*Baroncelli Chapel, Santa Croce, Florence.*

tures of the 13th and 14th centuries in the north one may read the signs of the times, for here as nowhere else is evidence of the path which was followed by the artists of the subsequent era.

As the authority of the Church declined, men as individuals eagerly accepted the task of interpreting the world according to their own light. We must now speak of artists who are strongly marked by their peculiar idiom or style, men who consciously or unconsciously strive for originality and fresh interpretation of old familiar themes and develop new ones. The portrait, for example, becomes fashionable and even an obsession as men become more conscious of themselves as distinguishable islands of their culture, and other secular subjects also begin to appear, side by side with traditional religious motives.

The first and perhaps greatest Italian painter of the 15th century is Masaccio (1401-1428). Like Giotto he was one of the Florentines who made that city celebrated as the fountainhead of European art. His painting may be seen in the Brancacci Chapel in the Church of the Carmine in Florence where he decorated the walls in fresco. At first glance these paintings are modest in appearance, and even in Masaccio's own time there were few who fully understood the force of these somber murals. Giotto had all but been forgotten as masters like Masolino (1383-1447), who was Masaccio's teacher, and Gentile da Fabriano (1370-1427) (Fig. 402) contented themselves with the refinements of Gothic idioms. Only after more than two further generations of 15th century painters had passed was the full force of Masaccio's originality realized.

In the *Expulsion from Paradise* (Fig. 394) the new spirit in painting is abundantly evident in the spontaneous action, the feeling for actuality and, above all the dramatic movement. Adam and Eve, thrust from Paradise by the angel with a flaming sword, are two common people with the emotions common to humanity. The tearful lamentation of Eve and Adam's withering shame are integral parts of the design of their bodies, which move rhythmically through well-defined space. To understand the harmonious organization of this painting, its broad handling in

Fig. 394.—MASACCIO. The Expulsion from Paradise.
*Brancacci Chapel, Church of the Carmine, Florence.*

*chiaroscuro*, one should contrast it with the Adam and Eve by Jan van Eyck of Flanders (Fig. 375) painted about the same time. The northerner amazes us by his explicit naturalism; he seems to thrust us

Fig. 395.—MASACCIO. The Tribute Money. Brancacci Chapel, Church of the Carmine, Florence.

into the very room where two stodgy Flemings have taken off their clothes in a bright light. The effect is startling but little else. The Italian master, on the other hand, shapes his figures in such a manner that the dramatic meaning becomes apparent without ambiguity. He expresses the feeling for the episode without striking an ingenious illusionism. Italian art is marked by a special talent for treating the human figure with philosophical depth in broad and rhythmically decorative patterns, an inheritance from the ancient figure art of the Graeco-Roman tradition which was a constant force in the evolution of Italian painting and sculpture. This peculiar background gave these arts a special rôle to play in the age of the Renaissance.

Masaccio demonstrates most compellingly the new outlook of his time in the *Tribute Money* (Fig. 395), the chief fresco in the Brancacci Chapel and the master's greatest single work. A Roman tax gatherer in a short tunic thrusts out his hand, demanding tribute for Caesar. The poor disciples turn in their dilemma to Christ, who directs Peter to go to the river's edge. At the extreme left Peter finds the money in the mouth of a fish, and at the right he gravely tenders it to the collector. One marvels at the simple ease with which the complex action is narrated. In contrast with Giotto's art, that of Masaccio reveals a new freedom. His men seem to stand upon their own feet, to move about freely of their own volition. With Giotto it appears that men are arranged and placed, acting less in accord with their impulses than in response to some external compulsion. Technically, painting by 1428 had advanced far along the path to a rationally understood naturalism. For the first time the action takes place in a deep landscape. The figures, hills, trees, architecture are bathed in atmosphere. *Aerial perspective* (the effect of atmosphere in blurring distant objects) is now understood as well as *linear perspective*, the conducting of the eye into space through converging lines as shown here in the foreshortening of the architecture. In such ways Masaccio creates the effect of space and bulk, and through the rounding of figures by alternating areas of light and shadow, forms are blended together so that they reveal structure and mass. The disciples radiate in a circle about Christ to produce an ample space pattern. Yet with all of these innovations, the artist retains Giotto's monumental effects, his gravity and his coherence. All of the great Florentine artists—Leonardo, Michelangelo and Raphael—will flock in the next century to this little chapel to learn from Masaccio how to gain dignity and simplicity for their own paintings and sculptures.

If Giotto is called the father of modern painting, then it may be said that the seed of his genius came to a rich harvest in Masaccio and others who followed in the 15th century—masters like him in having a rare sense for fixing the ever-fluid surface of nature. By simplification, condensation and coordination their figures were drawn in unforgettable patterns of fine amplitude and force. Some of these masters are Uccello, Castagno, Piero della Francesca, Perugino and Mantegna. Because of the clean force and simple grandeur of their work they may be called Monumentalists. While they were all students of the new realism, they were even more significant in being bold and original thinkers in the sphere of pictorial design. Their aim was not so much novelty or even accuracy as it was the life-giving disposition of mass, line and color.

Castagno (1423-1457) bears the imprint of two of the greatest minds

Fig. 396.—CASTAGNO. The Crucifixion. *Uffizi, Florence.*

of the century. He shares the austere temper of Masaccio and the searching scientific curiosity of the sculptor Donatello (cf. Figs. 313-316). His *Crucifixion* (Fig. 396) shows him lacking the native instincts of Masaccio for composition and the handling of light, but his very harshness becomes a virtue when, with peasant-like directness, he shapes the statuesque pillars of saints beneath the awful reality of the slain Christ. Castagno's Last Supper is one of the most powerful treatments of the theme ever painted before Leonardo's. In his concentration upon the somber intensity conveyed by the human figure he is of all the early Renaissance masters most like Michelangelo.

To render figures weighted and massive and deep-cut in space is a passion with the monumentalists. In contrast to this tradition another scarcely less-gifted group was more ingratiating in the decorative treatment of color and linear design. Chief among them is Domenico Veneziano (active *ca.* 1438-1461), whose *Madonna* (Fig. 397), from the Berenson collection, is one of the loveliest creations of the century. Baldovinetti (1425-1499) and Melozzo da Forlì (1438-1494) while minor masters are men whose works are justly celebrated for their indescribable charm. Although these men played a lesser rôle in the evolution of pictorial vision, they are of chief interest to the student of art for the exquisite sense for color, the flow of line, the *nuance* of human feeling. Domenico Veneziano gave currency to an extraordinarily sensitive type of portrait and to the panoramic landscape used as background for figures.

Fig. 397.—DOMENICO VENEZIANO. Madonna and Child. Detail. *Berenson Coll., Settignano.*

In Piero della Francesca (*ca.* 1416-1492) is found the painter with a more natural gift for art than any man in the century. His knowledge is profound and his taste unfaltering. The frescoes which he painted in the church of San Francesco in Arezzo are in their cool reserve and sustained energy among the finest in the world. Portraits, landscapes, battle scenes and Biblical subjects are handled with deliberation and the rarest feeling for cool articulate design. His pictures reveal a world of peculiarly arrested action breathless with suspense. Of contemporary painters Picasso, who has felt his strength, is most like him. Each is a *natural* painter in the sense that whatever he touches has some deliberate and arresting character.

The rarefied sphere of Piero's work is seen in *The Resurrection* (Fig. 398). The risen Christ stands bolt upright in the watery light of early dawn, the stark energy of the figure dramatically set forth

FIG. 398.—PIERO DELLA FRANCESCA. THE RESURRECTION.
*Palazzo Communale. Borgo San Sepolcro.*

by the weak light and the contrasting languor of slumbering guards. Mystery and passion illumine the face that seems to search a world beyond any known by man. Only in the rarest moments have artists so completely expressed the union of the physical and the spiritual. Piero was perhaps the most learned and articulate painter of his day. He was a searcher into the theories of space forms, an author of mathematical treatises on perspective. In the Dream of Constantine at Arezzo he portrays a night scene which for its mastery of mood and illumination can hardly be surpassed. In all of Italian painting there is no master whose work is so restrained, so deliberate and discriminating. And there is none so rewarding of study. He never makes dangerous concessions to the developing taste for lively illustration and picturesque fragments that is seen in the work of men like Ghirlandaio or Gozzoli, who made their art catchalls for random sentiments and graphic memoranda. Piero ennobled and clarified his art, lifting it to sublime levels of thought and passion.

Though Florence with her expanding industries and her world commerce was the brilliant capital of Italian culture, some of the foremost artists of the time were active outside her domain. Piero della Francesca, an Umbrian, was one and Mantegna (1431-1506) another. Padua, the city where Mantegna obtained his training in art, is an ancient university town near Venice. There Giotto had gone to decorate the Arena Chapel (cf. Figs. 389, 392), and Donatello the sculptor had worked there for years (cf. Fig. 316). To a marked degree, Mantegna shared the enthusiasm of his time for classical art. In his early works especially he dwells upon ancient themes, classical architectural ruins, statuesque figures. He was obsessed by precise definition of forms and introduced marvelously crisp intricate details. The tiniest shrub or figure in a deep landscape is defined as though he feared to obscure

FIG. 399.—MANTEGNA. THE CIRCUMCISION. *Uffizi, Florence.*

the least particle of essential structure. An altar painting of 1464, *The Circumcision* (Fig. 399) is alive with rich detail in the architectural background—veins of marble, sculptured relief, panels and scrolls. The figures are sharply drawn as to accessories of costume, yet the details are rigorously subordinated in the stable composition so that no confusion or over-richness results. The story or drama is indeed directed and articulated by the architectural setting. Few masters surpass him in the portrayal of character. Especially we notice the rare and exquisite tact in his understanding of children.

Mantegna's great learning enabled him to satisfy his impulse to experimentation. The boldness which marks his work from the beginning may be seen in the striking frog's-eye perspective of his murals in Padua, and later, in 1474, he was to create the novel decorations for the bridal chamber in the Gonzaga Palace at Mantua (Fig. 400) in which the wonderfully foreshortened dome painted on the ceiling

FIG. 400.—MANTEGNA. CEILING DECORATION.
*Bridal Chamber of the Gonzaga Palace, Mantua.*

anticipates the work of Correggio and the baroque masters of the 17th century. This ceiling and the great Lamentation in which the body of the dead Christ is drawn in radical foreshortening only suggest the range and depth of the man's genius. There is, with the exception of Piero della Francesca, scarcely a more penetrating intellect or surer hand in the 15th century. His landscapes, religious themes, portraits and decorations are works of consummate craft and imagination. He was one of the first and the greatest of Italian engravers, his prints circulating freely in Italy; even the great Dürer in Germany used them to inform himself of Italian art. The force of his work was such that he transformed the art of northern Italy from a school of local importance to one of world-wide fame. In his marriage to the daughter of the old Venetian painter, Jacopo Bellini, he became the brother-in-law, instructor and friend of Gentile and Giovanni Bellini, and contributed significantly through them to the development of the Venetian school.

If the profound intellect and probing experimentation of Mantegna suggest the emergence of Leonardo da Vinci then it may be said that

Fig. 401.—PERUGINO. Pietà. *Pitti, Florence.*

Perugino (*ca.* 1450-1523) anticipated the art of Raphael upon which, as teacher of the younger man, his influence was direct and enduring. In his *Pietà* of 1495 (Fig. 401) may be seen the qualities which characterize his murals and altar pictures. Taking his cue from Giotto whose arrangement he adopts (cf. Fig. 389), he goes further in expanding his pictorial setting to include the sweeping Umbrian hills. The mood of the landscape becomes an inseparable part of the brooding drama of contemplation and tenderness. The inclination of a head, the outline of a figure, conform to the slope of a hillside. Each figure is so placed in relation to the group that we witness a world in which all is lawful and harmonious. With economy and severity he strips his compositions of all the impedimenta of unessential detail. Like an architect he simplifies lines, combines masses, the better to balance and harmonize them with others. His native Umbrian landscape is transformed into symbols akin to the form language of architecture and music. It is no

FIG. 402.—GENTILE DA FABRIANO. THE ADORATION OF THE MAGI. *Uffizi, Florence.*

accident that Raphael in the next generation found in him his most abiding single guide. In such ways was the path to the harmonious forms of the High Renaissance prepared.

It would be a mistake to suppose that the 15th century as a whole followed closely the pattern set by the monumentalists. Mediaeval attitudes of thought and expression still persisted, and many painters were almost untouched by the imposing synthesis erected by Masaccio and other monumentalists. Gentile da Fabriano (*ca.* 1370-1427), for example, seems to belong to another world—to the age that produced the exquisite book illuminations of the north. His *Adoration of the Magi* (Fig. 402) of 1423 shows how profoundly his imagination had been fired by the Gothic artists and at the same time ennobled by Sienese piety. The Gothic frame of delicate carving encloses a panel crowded with kings, pilgrims, servants, birds and dogs, and the whole retinue of the Wise Men. A thousand small details claim attention. Tucked into a corner, the Virgin unobtrusively receives the homage of the magnificently arrayed kings. Heedless of any

FIG. 403.—FRA ANGELICO. THE LAMENTATION. *San Marco, Florence.*

need for logical spacing and rational motivation for the action, the painter tumbles a wealth of detail before our eyes, and endeavors to make evident the splendor of the homage that the Christ Child commands. It is like an endless mediaeval romance in which an inexhaustible enumeration of episodes takes the place of a carefully constructed plot. Gothic painting has its parallel in mediaeval romances and in Gothic architecture of the flamboyant period. The more modern painting of Masaccio finds its equivalent in the sculpture of Donatello and in the architecture of Brunellesco.

Of all the mediaevalists surviving in 15th-century Italy, none was so gentle and spiritual as Fra Angelico (1387-1455), nor was any so able to expound his religious mysticism on panel or wall. More modern than Gentile da Fabriano, this Dominican monk simplifies and clarifies his thought. His *Lamentation* (Fig. 403), which was painted about 1440, cannot be analyzed as exactly as can a composition of Giotto or Perugino. There is apparent no well-planned system of figure grouping although the extended wall of Jerusalem in the distance sets off the mourners in the foreground. The hushed mood of contemplation finds its counterpart in the landscape stretching forth in the wonderfully luminous green and gold of a late afternoon. The saints absorbed in meditation seem filled with rapture that suffuses the luminous landscape. Unlike the monumentalists, Fra Angelico did not construct sturdy substantial figures. They tend to flatness; their garments are treated rhythmically in flowing lines that do not emphasize the bodily structure. At a time when haloes were falling into disuse, Fra Angelico freely employs these gleaming symbols and they properly belong to his reverent visions. In style and expression he is often very close to the early Sienese masters.

For all his gentleness and sweetness, he is never soft or sentimental. His paintings are informed with passion and strength. Perhaps he may be considered the last of the mediaevalists, but this view of him must be conditioned by the fact that he was keenly aware of the reforming development in the arts, and a close student of the architect Michelozzo (cf. Fig. 117), whose structures are reflected in his paintings for a period of ten years. In some of the frescoes in his own monastery of San Marco in Florence where he decorated each cell with a sacred picture, he shows himself a thorough master of monumental decoration. And in his last years at Rome he painted episodes from the life of St. Stephen in the realistic modern style. But these later frescoes are not his best work; his genius was for the more lyrical religious sentiment couched in spiritually abstract terms.

The synthesis taking place in the early Renaissance was a very complex process. The revolution in thought, based upon the rational interpretation of experience as opposed to the intuitional mysticism of the Middle Ages, involved a wholly new way of approaching reality. It implies a systematic investigation of the world as we know it through our senses, and a correlation of sense impressions with the organized knowledge of science. The artist participated in this revolution. The mediaevalist might dispense with any profound analysis of the physical appearance of the external world, and, relying upon bright decorative colors and a lively sense of design, express his feelings and convictions without recourse to analysis of the visible world. When Fra Angelico painted the kneeling Virgin of the Annunciation, he felt obliged to paint only a credible symbol of the act of kneeling, whereas a more modern naturalistic master would ask himself what exact physical arrangement of legs and torso was involved in the simple act of balancing the body upon the knees. The physical phenomenon has its two coexistent and inseparable aspects, the act and the will. The artist fails to express the reality of the experience unless he reveals this dual truth without ambiguity. This attitude is implicit in the naturalism of the early Renaissance.

The Renaissance study of nature was motivated by a desire to understand and hence to control it, and to shape life in accordance with its laws. For the modern man this is the great meaning that naturalism holds. For a thousand years nature had been subordinated to the view that truth had been revealed once and for all in the body of ecclesiastical literature. In the Renaissance, man woke from his

FIG. 404.—UCCELLO. A BATTLE OF CAVALRY. *Uffizi, Florence.*

long dogmatic slumber to explore the physical and psychological realities, to discover himself and to accept the perilous way of a life based upon self-knowledge and science. We speak of the Renaissance as the modern world because we today are still interpreting the world in terms first articulated in 15th-century Italy.

The mastery of the physical world in realistic images was a long and difficult process. It was more than a process of learning to *draw* and *compose* realistically. The images had to be reshaped and reorganized in relation to the inner experience of the artist. To the creative artist there is no such thing as *correct* drawing; it is only correct when the picture becomes the means of externalizing some real experience. That means of externalizing was made possible in the 15th century through composition based upon nature. From the technical aspect, much had to be learned: how to render objects in motion, how to represent distance through proper diminution in perspective, how to create the illusion of depth on a flat surface through linear and aerial perspective. The interaction of atmosphere and local colors, the blending of colors in the light and air, were also problems of the first magnitude. Piero della Francesca wrote several books on scientific perspective, and Paolo Uccello spent his life investigating the mysteries of perspective drawing. Pollaiuolo was especially concerned with the rendering of the nude. Uccello (1397-1475), probing the abstract principles of perspective, undertook to represent the complex subjects presented by a series of battle pictures. In the *Battle of Cavalry*, 1435 (Fig. 404) he tried to capture the spectacle of charging fighters in violent movement against a deep landscape. A few clashing riders stand out in the foreground on a stage made spacious by foreshortened pikes and weapons pointing inward on the ground. The hedges of the fields converge in an apex at the top of the picture. It is a rich pageant of gorgeous knights and chargers, shining armor and weapons, but anyone can see that the artist has not been altogether successful in fusing the details in an integrated space design. While the dogs and rabbits in the field, the oranges in the trees and the details of the trappings are marvelously interesting, still they do not contribute materially to the central idea of the battle as such. Uccello had never seen factual pictures of horses in motion or fallen upon the ground; his attempts to paint them realistically are fanciful and grotesque. Those lying in the foreground look like horses stuffed with sawdust that have tipped over on his studio floor. The one kicking his heels in the air is a figment of purest imagination, for no horse ever looked like that. But despite these more or less mechanical shortcomings and the diffuse dramatic treatment, the composition is a triumph of lively fancy and invention, and one of the finest decorations produced during the entire century.

The uncovering of the external world went on apace in the sphere of scientific theoretical investigations. But another aspect of the process and one of equal importance is that of taste and feeling. The rich industrial and commercial life of Florence had bred a leisure class worldly and keen for the simple delights of charming faces and picturesque views. As the Florentine patrons of art became secure in their fortunes they wanted to enjoy the fruits of their toil. So the artist assumes a new rôle as he indulges that taste for worldly pleasure. Fra Filippo Lippi (1406-1469) took considerable pleasure in viewing a handsome face. A pretty girl was something intrinsically charming to cherish; she needn't suggest necessarily the exalted loveliness of the Mother of Sorrows. It is true that conventions still restricted his expression; that is to say, like other painters he was commissioned to paint altarpieces and wall decorations appropriate to their church settings. But in these conventional pictures he gave free reign to his spontaneous warm feelings. His *Madonna and Child* (Fig. 405) of about 1440 in the Uffizi Gallery is not a Saint and the Holy Child, not even an abstract symbol of maternity—none of these; merely a portrait group of a lovely girl, a robust bambino and a ragamuffin who pertly

FIG. 405.—LIPPI. MADONNA AND CHILD. *Uffizi, Florence*

masquerades as an angel. What we find there is not a religious painting but a naturalistic and mundane portrait group.

Such art reminds us that the Church itself was beginning to accept a more secular view as well as that there was a growing society rich enough to bid against it for the talents of artists. But more important still, it indicates the broad humanistic base upon which the thinking of the century was developing. The lively prosaic imagery of Filippo Lippi deeply colored the stream of Italian painting. He is almost the first master to make his religious figures wholly realistic, presenting

FIG. 406.—A. POLLAIUOLO. TEN FIGHTING NUDES. *Rosenwald Coll., Jenkintown.*

them in the current fashions of dress and coiffure. Common they may be but never shallowly conceived or carelessly drawn. The artist's wife is the model for his Madonna and their son is the Savior. The son, Filippino Lippi, lived to be a celebrated painter carrying on his father's work with an increasing amount of sentiment and over-embellishment of detail and dramatic expression. Indeed the floodgates of secular narration fly open after the middle of the century. The masters with a scientific interest continue studying the anatomy

Fig. 407.—GOZZOLI. The Journey of the Magi. Detail.
*Medici-Riccardi Palace, Florence.*

of nature, among them Antonio Pollaiuolo (1433-1498), a specialist in the dramatic nude in action (Fig. 406). Through sculpture (cf. Fig. 320), painting and engraving, he made his knowledge accessible to greater spirits than his own.

*The Ten Nudes,* which dates from around 1470, is characteristic of the vein of much 15th-century art. Half scientific or didactic, and half artistic in conception, it shows Pollaiuolo's interest in the systematic investigation of anatomy and at the same time his instinctive grasp of decorative design. These rather over-developed muscular figures provided scores of later painters, notably Albrecht Dürer, with

material for study in difficult anatomical problems, even though artists
of the next generation were able to surpass them both scientifically
and expressively.

But a good deal of the art at this time is popular, descriptive and
superficial. An elaborate parade is the theme of Benozzo Gozzoli
(1420-1497), a one-time pupil of Fra Angelico, in painting the *Journey
of the Magi* (Fig. 407) in fresco in the chapel of the Medici-Riccardi
Palace in Florence (cf. Figs. 116, 117). It is really a souvenir of a

FIG. 408.—GENTILE BELLINI. MIRACLE OF THE TRUE CROSS.
*Accademia, Venice.*

splendid procession in honor of a visiting Oriental potentate the master
had witnessed in his youth, and the religious subject is only a pretext
for celebrating the faces, the wealth and power of the ruling dynasty
and the artist's patrons—the Medici family. Obviously this mood of
the worldly new culture had little in common with the soul-searching
of the earlier masters. Content to reflect the knowledge gained by
more original minds, this art was charmingly illustrative, decorative
and popular.

In Venice Carpaccio painted in this same vein the most delightfully
convincing legends of long ago. But it is Gentile Bellini (1426-1507)
who outranks all Venetian painters in this group for knowledge of
his craft. Beside the fine firm structure of his pictures like the *Miracle
of the True Cross* (Fig. 408) most others seem tentative and superficial. His knowledge of perspective makes him a master of the most

complex architectural arrangements and his skill in painting vivid
out-of-door scenes that appear almost to glow with sunlight puts
him in the first rank of his age. Only his custom of arranging portrait
heads in a rather mechanical manner gives his work a somewhat archaic
cast.

In Florence the prolific muralist Domenico Ghirlandaio (1449-1497)
lavished his vigorous talents on a series of religious pictures representing ostensibly the episodes of the New Testament, but in reality

Fig. 409.—GHIRLANDAIO. The Last Supper. *San Marco, Florence.*

illustrating with gossipy elaboration the life and manners of his own
fifteenth-century Florence. In one, Mary and Elizabeth are seen in
the guise of two well-known Florentine women; they meet and em-
brace in a familiar spot overlooking the Arno River with the Palazzo
Vecchio (cf. Fig. 111) and church steeples in the background that
can be seen in Florence to this day. His familiarity with the lively
Flemish realism of Hugo van der Goes' altarpiece (Fig. 377) had given
impetus to his natural predilection for copious illustration. The current flair for enumeration of casual detail may be seen in his *Last
Supper* (Fig. 409). The theme does not inspire him to any unusual
design; taking the traditional plan of a long table with the disciples
and Christ on one side and Judas the betrayer isolated on the other,
he merely embroiders the composition with a wide variety of realistic
details. While he has a good deal to say about the trivialities—the cat
on the floor, vases of flowers on the wall, the garden outside the
monastery with birds sweeping through the air—the treatment of

the story is rather dull and pedestrian. The disciples sit gloomily like guests at a boring banquet, apparently unaware of the fateful words of the Savior.

Where Ghirlandaio is phlegmatic, deliberative and a little dull, Luca Signorelli (1441-1523) is the very opposite. Not content with the superficial appearance of things, he set himself the task of investi-

Fig. 410.—SIGNORELLI. Torments of the Damned. *Cathedral, Orvieto.*

gating their underlying physical construction the better to represent all their qualities of bulk and texture. His special concern was the nude. Through secret and patient dissection of cadavers, he studied the structure of the skeleton, the muscles interacting with it through tendons and ligaments; for he knew that only through accurate knowledge could he acquire the skill to render the organic movement of the body convincingly. As no painter before him he correlated emotion with physical action, a commonplace to us but novel in the Renaissance. The breadth of his vision and the fire with which he informs it appears in the *Torments of the Damned* (Fig. 410), where the writhing of men suffering intense agony is realistically portrayed. Compared with this caldron of torment, the images of Hell propounded in the Middle Ages seem unreal and fantastic. Whether his theme is a Madonna and Child or a study of an athletic nude (Fig. 411) he measures the psychological in terms of its physical manifestation. The compressed joints, the swelling line of muscle, the high lights of the skin—all these are observed and recorded with a powerful hand and a resolute mind. The result of his analysis is reflected in a tendency to compose

Fig. 411.—SIGNORELLI. Nude. Drawing. *Louvre, Paris.*

in details somewhat loosely organized rather than large units organically interacting. The nudes seem stripped of their skin, so intent is Signorelli upon obtaining the effect of powerful muscular action.

The images released in a flood in the 15th century are characterized by the utmost vividness and freshness. If the pictures sometimes seem crowded and too complex for the eye to grasp them readily as a unit, it is because of a healthy eagerness to master the spate of bewildering new material that for the first time now poured in upon the artistic consciousness. But obviously the mastery of nature could not be an end in itself; and with the close of the century there is noted a desire to impart to the forms something of the meaning that they held for Giotto and Masaccio. It was not sufficient any longer to represent the surface of things with faithful realism, to marvel at one's own facility to hold the mirror up to nature. Michelangelo in the next century was to give the nude a more articulate and intense interpretation than the earlier masters, but even so it was at the expense of the thrilling and intoxicating vitality and primitive sensualism that informs the work of Signorelli.

Sandro Botticelli (1447-1510) reveals the more reflective attitude characteristic of the end of the century. He courted not so much the

Fig. 412.—BOTTICELLI. The Birth of Venus. *Uffizi, Florence.*

glories of the fresh landscape or the physical vigor and beauty of the athletic nude as the expression of spiritual and intangible values. His eye turns from sensuous experience inward to the intellect, from tangible materials to thought and feeling about them. His style reflects this tendency to objectify abstract thought. There is something artificial about his *Birth of Venus* (Fig. 412), artificial in the sense that the subject and its arrangement are not derived spontaneously from a familiar experience. The figures are drawn up close to the edge of the frame to produce a continuous sequence in the foreground. The sea and the shore line are conventionalized, the waves reduced to a pattern of V-shaped lines, and the shore to a sharp zigzag that gives no real impression of depth. The Venus, in a pose of self-conscious modesty inspired by Hellenistic copies of the fourth-century statue by Praxiteles, is sharp in contour; her long coiling hair seems of spun metallic strands. She approaches the shore sadly as with reluctance to encounter the hostility of the modern world. The artist's mood is one of nostalgia for the happier times of long ago. This illustration of a myth from antiquity indicates the current enthusiasm

Fig. 413.—GIOVANNI BELLINI. Virgin and Child with Saints. *Accademia, Venice.*

for classical learning and is another evidence of the tendency on the part of the painter to search outside of Christian legend for subject matter. Though Botticelli was in his earlier years one of the foremost realists, he turned from the methods of realism and the current thought of his times to dream of the past. While he was an artist gifted with vast talents for poetic expression, his art was so thoroughly personal that his influence was inconsiderable. He developed a naturalistic style and then abruptly turned from nature to increasing idealism and abstractions. His later style, to which the Birth of Venus belongs, is one that made full use of animated linear patterns. Atmosphere is almost wholly excluded in his emphasis upon a lash-like line that is inexpressibly nervous and living.

The same tendency to formalism and lyric expression is found in Venetian art at the end of the century. If we compare Botticelli with his contemporary in Venice, Giovanni Bellini (1428-1516)—the brother of Gentile who painted the Miracle of the Cross—we note many similarities. In his *Virgin and Child with Saints* (Fig. 413) made about 1484, the grouping is as formally and harmoniously balanced as in the Birth of Venus. In both, the subject is no longer familiar or plebeian. The behavior of the saints is neither commonplace nor intimate, but urbane and dignified. Botticelli evokes a mood of melancholy, Bellini one of brooding religious revery embodied in vibrant colors. The Italians call such mute gatherings of saints "Sacred Conversations." Both masters exclude irrelevant details, subordinating and suppressing the trivial and accidental to the grand action of the main theme. The differences too are profound. Botticelli, typically Florentine, obtains his effects by precision of line and astringent colors, and the painted forms are often closely akin to sculptured ones. The work of the Venetian, on the other hand, is rich in softening atmospheric effects, and the figures are delicately modeled in warm sensuous flesh tones. Compare the nude St. Sebastian on the right in the Virgin and Child with Saints of Bellini with Botticelli's Venus and the difference is at once apparent.

With the turn of the century, elaborate detail and complicated narrative were abandoned for a style that is highly unified and formalized. There was a continuation of the process of consolidating and integrating the discoveries of the pioneers in naturalism that began with Perugino, Botticelli and Giovanni Bellini. The latter, particularly, reveals the trend toward a new monumentalism that is to find its culmination in the High Renaissance. In the Virgin and Child with Saints, the grouping is significant of the change. Three saints on either side of the elevated Madonna produce a stable balance and the architectural niche provides a closed but ample space that limits the dramatic action, being like a stage-set that permits the eye to view only that which is important. The setting does not attract undue attention but merely acts as a sounding-board for the dominant melody. Everything in Giovanni Bellini's pictures contributes to the new grandeur of style which is manifest in a more monumental use of the architectural setting, and in increased order and rhythm in the treatment of forms and draperies.

Before the close of the 15th century Leonardo da Vinci summed up the accomplishments of the age, but his art was so radical and the style he inaugurated so influential upon the art of the new century that for our purpose it is better to consider him in the light of the High Renaissance, though he is the one figure who overlaps and links the two main periods of Italian Renaissance painting.

### B. The High Renaissance in Florence and Rome

The early years of the 16th century in Italy have been called the Golden Age; names of the masters of this period have rightfully become household words—Leonardo, Michelangelo, Raphael. Through these minds Italian art came under a discipline that gave it the status of classic authority. The local schools were dwarfed by the prestige of a cosmopolitan expression developed in Florence. Even today few laymen recognize the names of many of the greatest Italian masters belonging to the early years of the Renaissance. It would be a mistake to think of men like Piero della Francesca, Mantegna or Masaccio as minor stepping-stones to the achievements of the High Renaissance for these earlier men served their age in creating sublime concepts of their world. But they were the pioneers; those who followed refined and systematized what had to a very large degree been established. Leonardo, the most fertile and original mind of the High Renaissance, was tutored in the artistic lore of the 15th century by Verrocchio, a distinguished sculptor (cf. Figs. 321, 322), craftsman and teacher. In this sculptor's workshop the youth, beginning at thirteen, studied for ten years the most advanced art of the Early Renaissance and made himself master of all the lore accumulating in the studios. Like other 15th-century masters, Verrocchio was primarily concerned with translating the centuries-old religious themes into naturalistic terms. This translation was a process of imparting blood and fiber to the bare symbols of the Middle Ages, a method that is generally called humanism since it expressed abstractions of love, sacrifice and divinity in terms of humanity, concepts which for ages past had been formulated in a language of symbols. The gods, this time the Christian gods, came down to earth as they did in Hellenistic art. Instead of being symbolized in an abstract pattern, the Virgin was represented as a loving and compassionate mother. Thus was the message of St. Francis realized in the humanism of Renaissance thought. Man and his world is the theme of modern painting, and the human figure is the vehicle for the expression of everything pertaining to him.

When the Early Renaissance cult of naturalism had run its course, when it seemed that painting had reached the limits of representation and dramatization, Botticelli turned to his inner dreams. Had all his contemporaries followed his example, painting could hardly have lived;

but there appeared at the end of the 15th century a greater intelligence than had hitherto been known, to further the study of nature and at the same time to find in it new truths bearing upon life. Leonardo da Vinci (1452-1519) was the first of those giants of whom we always think when the Renaissance is mentioned. In our day, we are prone to consider him a scientist quite as much as an artist, because

Fig. 414.—LEONARDO DA VINCI. The Adoration of the Magi.
*Uffizi, Florence.*

his notebooks were filled with scientific observations, projects for the submarine, military tank and airplane, and anatomical, geological and astronomical studies of bewildering diversity. But because he lived in an age when art was the universal medium of expression, his greatest influence came through his activity in art.

His scientific mind was directed toward the problems of art and he early mastered all the learning of the 15th century, adding his own observations on perspective, movement and anatomy. He recognized the conflicts and limitations of the new naturalism. He witnessed the secularization of sacred themes and the effort to dramatize nature. The reconciliation of naturalistic art with spiritual expression was the problem of Leonardo's first and one of his most important paintings, *The Adoration of the Magi* (Fig. 414). He interprets the often-repeated legend in a new light, making of it a pilgrimage of the heart, the world paying homage to the Holy Child as a symbol of love.

Instead of confining the Virgin to a cramped throne or a narrow space before a window, Leonardo shows her seated graciously upon a bank in the open air. The throng which has gathered can only be guessed at from our small print, but there are some sixty figures represented. The earlier pictures also contained many figures (cf. Fig. 402), sometimes so many, indeed, that it was difficult to identify the principal persons. One of the outstanding tasks of the 16th-century masters was to restore to painting the clarity, monumentality and dignity appropriate to the sacred theme which had been lost in the exuberant and indiscriminate naturalism of the late 15th century. Through a development of *chiaroscuro* effects, Leonardo gives the illusion of deep space by atmospheric suggestion. Furthermore, by modeling in light and shade he accents the significant figures and subordinates the minor ones. In our picture, it is clear that the three or four main actors have been made dominant by their lightness against a dark background. Lesser pilgrims are also present, but one sees only the flash of a face or a hand; the body is obscured in shadow. The principal figures are welded into a firm pyramidal design rendered stable by the dark statuesque figures at the extreme right and left. In this carefully planned structure, Leonardo introduces the richest variety of human types. Far back in the space near the architectural ruins are tilting knights, a memory of the mediaeval past. In the foreground, the holy pair is encircled by young, passionate faces; old, ascetic, religious faces; men and women from the corners of the earth, all under the spell of love for the young Savior.

Leonardo left the Adoration unfinished in 1481, for it is essentially a drawing with the *chiaroscuro* developed in the monochrome underpainting. But for years he had worked on it, making many experimental drawings, turning over in his mind the complex problems of perspective; he weighed again and again the psychological significance of the whole and of the details. Where others had relied upon rule-of-thumb, he planned and tested, evolving a pictorial scheme so sound, so balanced and organically effective that this picture served a whole generation as a veritable reservoir of artistic lore. There are echoes of this painting in scores of Renaissance pictures, including the most majestic works of Raphael and Michelangelo.

To the consideration of human personality Leonardo gave the same intense study as he gave to relatively formalistic problems of space and design, not to mention his purely scientific problems. All his

FIG. 415.—LEONARDO DA VINCI. ST. ANNE AND THE VIRGIN. Cartoon. *Burlington House, London.*

paintings and notably his Mona Lisa reveal the fascination of the problem. Place the drawing called a cartoon, St. *Anne and the Virgin* (Fig. 415), beside Fra Filippo Lippi's Madonna (Fig. 405). Leonardo's figures appear suddenly to live as vivid active forms in tangible space, but also they live in a new psychological dimension. There is a psychic world of persons existing in the most highly articulated relation to each other. The wise old Anne contemplates the rapt devotion of the Madonna for the infant Christ who in turn blesses the enthralled St. John. The compact interlacing of bodies finds its psychological equivalent in the unspoken dialogue of earthly and heavenly love. The awkward theme of Mary seated in Anne's lap was dictated by tradition. Leonardo's solution of the problem through *chiaroscuro* and through accentuation of the psychological drama leaves one almost unaware of the physical incongruity. As in so many of the master's works, this massing of figures in a compact monumental pyramid served as a guide to almost all of his contemporaries, especially to Raphael, whose Madonnas and Holy Families almost always reflect some phase of Leonardo's work.

Many have seen in this drawing the epitome of his art and the individualism of his age. The personal character of this psychological study is not something that could be *learned* or *practiced* by others. The wordless dialogue, the inscrutable passion of Saint Anne, the loveliness of the Virgin, the mother lost in joyous tenderness for her babe—all this drama of love is the culmination, the classic statement, of what men had been striving to say for generations. Leonardo's statement is at once supremely human and supremely spiritual.

In one epochal work Leonardo gave a definitive exposition of the Renaissance science and art of painting. *The Last Supper* (Fig. 416) is a ruined masterwork, an unsuccessful experiment in painting on a dry wall. Aside from the grand scheme, its original beauty can be known only from some of the rare drawings, such as the *St. Philip* (Fig. 417), made as studies. How completely Leonardo revolutionized the casually discursive style of the late 15th century may be seen in comparing his Last Supper with Ghirlandaio's (Fig. 409). Where the latter is prolix in detail, Leonardo is brief and dramatic. In the 15th-century picture, the disciples sit placidly at the table, almost as if unaware of Christ's words. The incidentals are as interesting as the main subject; one's eye is caught by the cat waiting expectantly on the floor, the vase of flowers in the window, the birds sailing over the garden. Leonardo banishes all such trivialities. He directs our attention to what is happening as Christ says, "One among ye shall betray me." His disciples are electrified with sudden emotions of protestation, horror, despair. Each responds according to his nature in a torrent of released emotion. Pictorially a highly complex problem has been resolved *in the design*. Every gesture and accent is clearly defined and contributes to the total effect. The question may well arise how Leonardo, while preserving a closely coordinated and

Fig. 416.—LEONARDO DA VINCI. THE LAST SUPPER. S. Maria delle Grazie, Milan.

monumental design, still manages to tell so much about the thirteen characters and sustain the dramatic unity at the same time. The answer is found in an analysis of his design. A tapestry-hung room bare of all objects is the setting for the long table. The disciples with Christ in the exact center are grouped on one side of the table with Judas, who in previous pictures had been isolated in an awkward position on the other side. These thirteen figures are divided into five groups, the disciples being in units of three, while Christ occupies the middle space alone, isolated psychologically as well as physically from the others. To give further emphasis to Christ, His head is silhouetted against the sky in a kind of natural halo of light effected by means of a window in the end wall. If the lines of the architecture, the tapestry edges, the beams of the ceiling and the pavement lines are projected, they converge at Christ's head and make Him the point of optical concentration. The disciples through the system of grouping form integral units of the design, even those who are standing being related in the rhythmic horizontal movement toward Christ created by the gestures that also furnish a psychologically unifying element in articulating their emotion. Only Judas, his dark face in the shadow, recoils in hate and fear. As in the Adoration of the Magi, Leonardo has given a universal image of man. The disciples he represents are not

FIG. 417.—LEONARDO. ST. PHILIP. *Windsor Castle.*

literal renderings of chance models but typical men, abstractions condensed and generalized from thousands of studies of humanity made by the painter. Strictly speaking, this celebrated religious painting is not fundamentally religious in character. It represents the psychological observations of the profoundest scientist of his century arriving at a synthesis of his investigations through the medium of pictorial design.

In the Last Supper, Leonardo was faced with the problem of achieving unity of a psychological nature in his expressive treatment of the thirteen protagonists in the Christian drama, and this he did by placing them in a definite situation to which they responded as individuals, each in accordance with his personal temperament. The grip that the great painting has maintained on the imagination of those seeing it from the time of its creation down to the present is a consequence in no small degree of the directness with which such human

FIG. 418.—LEONARDO DA VINCI. MONA LISA. *Louvre, Paris.*

values are transformed into and expressed by the formal elements in the design. The same thing is true on what is if anything an even more abstract level in the no less famous *Mona Lisa* (Fig. 418), which Leonardo began to paint about 1505 and which he considered still unfinished when he died in 1519. Mona Lisa was the wife of a Florentine citizen, Francesco del Giocondo; we know little of her otherwise save that she was saddened by the loss of a loved one at the time Leonardo was painting her portrait and that music was played to distract her mind as she posed. These circumstances may account for the actual painting but they are of little importance in suggesting its character for there is no reason to think that Mona Lisa was more than a woman of average intelligence and personality, hardly likely to have been the self-sufficient and worldly-wise being Leonardo has painted under her name. The portrait is, in fact, an ideal one, like those another great Florentine was to carve in stone for the tombs of the Medici scions two decades later (cf. Fig. 327), and also like them, it tells us much more of the creator than of the relatively undistinguished person portrayed. The painting has been changed somewhat since Leonardo's time, for it was originally a little wider and columns were shown at the sides framing the figure with its landscape background. It has also darkened very considerably because Leonardo, always the scientific experimentalist, used pigments that were chemically unstable and that changed to the dark browns and greens that make it difficult to appreciate the praise of early writers for its bright and rosy colors. But even in the somber hues of the crackled pigment it is still possible to discern the amazingly minute modeling of the hands and face—the almost imperceptible planes by which the forms are built up and which are translated by the observer to the psychological account of the portrait, to result in the impression of vivid actuality that is responsible for the popular conception of the smile on the face though there is actually no such expression. The composition as a whole is unbelievably simple, with curving lines and the delicate *chiaroscuro* modeling establishing the solidly three-dimensional form of the torso, arms and head in pictorial space that develops into the indefinite reaches of the mountain landscape in the background.

Like the Last Supper, the Mona Lisa is an expression of psychological values in formally unified pictorial terms. She exists as a physical entity by virtue of the structural elements described above, and as a psychological one as well—calmly aware of herself, her surroundings, and the observer—and so completely is she the mistress of herself that she seems likewise the mistress of any situation that might arise. Herein lies the interpretive contrast between her portrait and the Last Supper, which is a group portrait of thirteen differing personalities in a single situation whereas she is a single personality in no specific psychological environment but capable of dominating any in which she might find herself; it has been well observed that under the spell of the portrait one feels that nothing can be thought which she has not thought before. It thus becomes a statement of all the worldly ideals of Renaissance thought, the adjustment of human personality to experience through feeling and intelligence. The mystery of the picture lies not in its expression but in the fact that the wife of a Florentine burgher could evoke such a symbol of rational understanding and perception from one of the greatest minds the world has known. For it is not La Gioconda who gazes with inscrutable mien from the canvas but Leonardo, and her self-sufficiency is that of the man who, more than any other of his time, had looked upon all that human eyes of his time could see and had understood it as profoundly as was possible for any mind of his generation.

It was through his continuous study of nature, which he viewed as the artist's only true guide, that Leonardo fertilized European art with profound spirituality. Everything he touched he endowed with grace and loveliness, dignity and grandeur. He is a living reminder that the artist with intelligence and sensitivity may shape the symbols of love and faith by which men live. More than any other man he closed the gap in men's minds that separates man from nature. Through comprehension and love he translated science into poetry and harmonized the two worlds of outer and inner experience.

Like Leonardo, Michelangelo (1475-1564) belongs among the Titans of the 16th century. As sculptor (cf. Figs. 323-328), architect (cf. Figs. 131, 133, 138), painter and poet he embraces all the arts. But it was as a sculptor that he revealed himself and his age even when he painted. As a youth he had learned the painter's craft with Ghirlandaio, but he soon devoted himself exclusively to sculpture until the pope demanded that he leave his chisel and marble to decorate the ceiling of the Sistine Chapel in Rome, upon which he worked from 1508 to 1514. Given a free hand, he conceived a tremendous decorative scheme, using the nude human figure as a basis for the huge fabric. Down the center of the ceiling in nine rectangular panels is recorded the epic of mankind from the Creation to the Deluge. In the *Fall of Man* (Fig. 419) the two heroic parents receive the forbidden fruit from the serpent. The Garden of Paradise is a desolate rocky spot in the wilderness, but Adam and Eve themselves are instinct with colossal powers. Eagerly they accept the fruit of knowledge and with bitter reluctance they take their leave of Paradise, thrust out into a world of pain and labor by an angel with flaming sword, Adam overwhelmed by an awful sense of guilt, Eve bitterly bewailing her un-

happy fate. As Leonardo interpreted the Biblical subjects with profound insight, so Michelangelo too passed beyond a conventional narration of an ancient legend. To him, the fall of man from his first
innocence was the beginning of his endless conflict with evil, a conflict
that forces him to labor with sweat and pain to attain peace that is
denied by an inexorable world, a strife which strains every nerve and
fiber of his intellectual and moral nature. All that Michelangelo says
is conveyed through the action of the figure. Impelled by the dramatic
force he sensed in the frescoes of Masaccio and Signorelli, and guided

FIG. 419.—MICHELANGELO. THE FALL OF MAN.
*Sistine Chapel, Vatican, Rome.*

by exhaustive knowledge of the body gained through intensive study of
cadavers, he made the human form more expressive than it had ever
been before.

The last panel painted in the Sistine Ceiling series represents *God
Separating Day from Night* (Fig. 420). How vain to attempt the
rendering of so colossal an idea in pictorial language! But Michelangelo overwhelms us by the thought he embodies here. From the outer
darkness of uncreated chaos a supernatural and cosmic being emerges,
so mighty that the imagination can hardly conceive it. With a powerful movement involving the whole body, the Almighty thrusts back
the clouds of darkness and performs the miracle that rendered the
universe intelligible. As if the painter realized that the imagination
must be deeply engaged to grasp the meaning of the idea portrayed,
the sharply defined sculpturesque figures employed elsewhere in the

series are renounced for a half-obscured image engulfed in the receding shadow of the heavens. The effects produced suggests the rhythm of
cosmic forces convulsed in creation.

FIG. 420.—MICHELANGELO. GOD SEPARATING DAY FROM NIGHT.
*Sistine Chapel, Vatican, Rome.*

The main panels of the Sistine Ceiling appear as if they were rectangular openings in the vault of the chapel, framed by painted mould-

ings. These mouldings are in turn supported by painted cornices with a heavy block at each corner of the panels, upon which are the seated figures of nude athletes (Fig. 421). Ostensibly their purpose is to support the heavy garlands and ribbons connecting the decorative medallions; actually they perform a kind of plastic dance to accompany the figures of the main panels. Varying spiritual moods are expressed in contortions which are impossible of human attainment in many cases yet are rendered plausible by the painter's utter command of

FIG. 421.—MICHELANGELO. ATHLETE. *Sistine Chapel, Vatican, Rome.*

design. Some of the youths are weighted down by their burden, their joints and muscles are compressed under the crushing weight. Others appear so light and volatile that they all but spring from their positions. Depression and exaltation, lassitude and vitality all appear in these figures as attributes of the human spirit and the human body which are not considered by Michelangelo as a duality but as one and the same. Similar psychological concepts appear in the heroic Prophets and Sibyls. The *Jeremiah* (Fig. 422), most melancholy of the prophets, is thought to be a portrait of Michelangelo himself since it is clothed in a sculptor's smock. Crouched on a low throne, the massive figure assumes an almost circular form. Heavy falling lines define the ponderous bulk of the body. The head inclining heavily upon the arm supported by the knee, the muscular inert left hand, bespeak a colossal power made impotent by frustration. For a parallel to such tragic brooding, one must look, other than to the master's sculpture (cf. Fig. 328), to the Book of Job or the Melencolia I (cf. Fig. 443) of Dürer, Michelangelo's great German contemporary. A contrasting mood is that of the *Delphic Sibyl* (Fig. 423). The seer, holding the script of her prophecy, is buoyantly elevated by a voice toward which she suddenly turns. The spirit and the flesh are made strong and free by under-

| Fig. 422.—MICHELANGELO. | Fig. 423.—MICHELANGELO. |
| Jeremiah. *Sistine Chapel, Vatican, Rome.* | The Delphic Sibyl. |
| | *Sistine Chapel, Vatican, Rome.* |

standing. The erect head, the strong serenity of the clear glance, the lifted arm and the triumphant sweep of the mantle all speak of a will to life that is denied to the Jeremiah.

In his frescoes Michelangelo expressed himself much as he did in sculpture. By eliminating or severely subordinating the incidentals of the setting, he concentrated attention upon the large monumental figures which he painted with the same clarity and Titanic vigor seen in his sculpture. Through bodily movements that are in themselves trivial or even unnatural, they communicate the life-giving impulse of the spirit that created them. Our own muscles and joints respond to the kinaesthetic sensations so powerfully suggested by statue or painted image. The language of the sculptor has been translated by

Michelangelo to the flat walls in symbols which are so deeply charged with meaning that in the ordinary sense they cannot be called beautiful. The sweet graciousness of Leonardo's lyric naturalism is denied them, for Michelangelo swept it aside in a thunderous language of plastic forms. Nor are the forms realistic in the sense of being representations of actual or even typical living men and women. Rather through abstractions of his models based upon an enormous knowl-

Fig. 424.—MICHELANGELO. The Resurrection. Drawing.
*British Museum, London.*

edge of the physical body, he constructs heroic and convincing symbols of humanity.

The mysteries of birth and death, of exaltation and suffering, lie tragically in the master's every artistic thought. With pen, crayon, chisel and brush he expounded those mysteries. The drawing *Resurrection* (Fig. 424) becomes, through its packed energized forms viewed in relation to the supple ripples of cloth and rigid plan of the tomb, an embodiment of man's will and spiritual fortitude. The factual statement of a Christ emerging from the grave is translated into a universal drama vaster than any religion of any time or place. We are presented with the unfathomable miracle of life. That it is couched in terms of Christianity is irrelevant.

Raphael (1483-1520), the third of the great High Renaissance painters, was the opposite of Michelangelo in temperament and personality. Taught in the studio of Perugino in Perugia, he came to Florence to discover that the serene and deliberate style he had faithfully absorbed from his master was now old-fashioned. Leonardo and Michelangelo were the popular gods in Florence, and Raphael was quick to perceive the validity of their unquestioned leadership. It was clear that the small delicate landscapes, the dreamy-eyed saints and the quiet rhythms of his compositions in Perugino's style would not suffice in a city that was becoming accustomed to the heady outpourings of Michelangelo's art. His first attempts in Florence to combine his natural lyric grace with the dramatic force of the current style were almost grotesque. But it was his peculiar genius to absorb the artistic gifts of those about him; with extraordinary intuition he was able to grasp the architectural concepts of Bramante, the sculptural impulses of Michelangelo and the pictorial subtleties of Leonardo, welding them with intelligence and tact into a style that was his own.

Like Michelangelo and many another, Raphael was called to Rome to the service of the pope, and it fell to his lot in 1508 and the following years to decorate the rooms of the Vatican palace. One of his large decorations is the *School of Athens* (Fig. 425), an allegory of philosophy. Under the spreading vaults of a fanciful temple are gathered all the celebrated scholars, scientists and philosophers of the ancient world. With the Last Supper of Leonardo in mind, Raphael composed a lucid and integrated mural decoration in a monumental scheme. In the center are the two great philosophers of ancient Greece, Aristotle and Plato. Lest they be lost in the throng, a compelling triple accent of soaring arches rises immediately above them. The actual shape of the wall is echoed in the painted architectural vaults, and through these spreading arches the multitude is unified in articulated space. The figures in the middle ground, flanking Aristotle and Plato, are arranged in a continuous horizontal band. In the foreground, right and left, the two smaller groups balanced one against the other further articulate the pictorial space. It is an almost perfect solution of the problem of mural decoration. Stated simply, this problem is to decorate a wall pictorially without destroying its space-defining function as part of the actual architecture. The effect Raphael produces is not that

FIG. 425.—RAPHAEL. THE SCHOOL OF ATHENS. *Camera della Segnatura, Vatican, Rome.*

of a hole broken through the wall and revealing depth, an effect produced inadvertently by too many over-zealous 15th-century masters. By organizing the individual figures of the coordinated groups into surface patterns horizontally oriented, he preserves the wall plane inviolate. Its surface is perfectly integrated with the abstract space representation. The inborn feeling for space organized by articulate rhythms that Raphael inherited from his Umbrian master Perugino is raised in the School of Athens to its highest capabilities of expression.

FIG. 426.—RAPHAEL. THE SIS-
TINE MADONNA. *Gallery, Dresden.*

For sheer intelligence combined with a sense for the harmonious and rational, it is one of the finest decorative murals ever conceived.

The most widely known works of Raphael are his various paintings of the Madonna and Child. Usually these consist of some variation of the scheme evolved by Leonardo, who with fine condensation arranged his figures in pyramidal groups, as in the Adoration of the Magi (Fig. 414) and the Cartoon of St. Anne (Fig. 415). Raphael brought forth his most sublime treatment of the theme in the *Sistine Madonna* (Fig. 426), painted about 1515. Characteristic of the High Renaissance style is the monumental treatment of the figures to which the background has been subordinated. The Virgin, silhouetted against a cloud of tiny cherub heads, is balanced symmetrically by the figures of Pope Sixtus and St. Barbara. The design has been unified largely through the flowing line rising in the garment folds of the Pope and continuing through the silhouette of the Virgin, attaining the apex of her head. From this point the line falls slowly and gracefully, descending through the curtain and the billowing mantle. The double accent of the wind-blown drapery arrests the downward movement, which comes to a full pause in Saint Barbara, only to continue through her lowered glance. The elfish cherubs on the lower frame halt the movement once more and then deflect it upward again to complete the wonderfully rhythmic and continuous flow of line and surface that gives movement to figures which in themselves are motionless. Through the melodious cadence of the forms, Raphael attains the grandiose dignity befitting his theme. While lacking the penetrat-

ing psychological and formal analysis of Leonardo and Michelangelo, he
has contrived a classic harmony of forms that recalls certain phases of
Greek and Roman art.

One of the finest of Raphael's earlier Madonnas, painted about
1510, is in the National Gallery at Washington, *The Alba Madonna*
(Fig. 427). In an expansive landscape Mary rests in somber con-

FIG. 427.—RAPHAEL. THE ALBA MADONNA.
*National Gallery, Washington, D. C.*

templation of the child Jesus and St. John, the notable plastic patterns
of the group both complementing and being emphasized by the circular shape. All that is individual, accidental or casual is suppressed for
what is noble and restrained. The ideal and aristocratic Madonna is a
far cry from the pretty snub-nosed girl Madonnas of the 15th century (cf. Fig. 405). In the High Renaissance there remains no place

for the fresh random aspects of nature; every form must be rendered in terms of a deliberate and gracious harmony.

The peculiar requirements of decorative frescoes and religious themes demanded abstraction and generalized treatment, but in his portraits Raphael explores profoundly the human heart and mind. The power and intelligence of many Renaissance personalities were unforgettably recorded by his brush in a series of celebrated portraits, among them that of *Tommaso Inghirami* (Fig. 428). The flowing outlines of the

Fig. 428.—RAPHAEL. Tommaso Inghirami. *Gardner Coll., Boston.*

bowed shoulders merge with the contours of the face and the cap, and create a movement that continues in the arms and contrasts the entire body with the static forms of the table and books. Nor has the characteristic physical appearance of the individual been sacrified to an abstraction of moral and intellectual qualities. The defect in the Cardinal's eye is clearly evident, but it has been properly subordinated to the basic personality of the man. In seeking clarity through order and consistency Raphael pursued a dominant principle of Italian art. In less sensitive and less intelligent men these principles led to empty phrases and shallow posturing, but the decorative ideal was for Raphael not so much an end in itself as a means to symbolize human need of order and continuity. It is his sense for world-embracing harmony that gives authority to his decorative schemes. The majesty and serenity of his Madonnas have made Raphael admired through the centuries. What for others was debased in sweetness and sentimentality he sublimates in a transcendent drama of energy and grace by his superb genius for organizing line, color and space in living symbols.

## C. The High Renaissance in Venice

Intellectual and spiritual leadership belonged to Florence in the Early Renaissance; Rome had by turns taken her art and deepened, urbanized or diluted it. In a very real sense it yet remained for Venice to endow the art of Italy with those attributes which were to enable it to become ultimately effective in the wider European world. Historically this implementing rôle was made possible by a number of factors which include her wealth and accessibility to the maritime world, especially the East, her background in Byzantine culture, and particularly her contacts with the mature art of Florence. It should be observed that the closest collaboration was realized between Venice and the mainland for generations. In the neighboring city of Padua Giotto and Donatello had left monumental works (cf. Figs. 316, 389, 392), and it was here that Mantegna gave his instruction to the brothers Bellini (cf. Figs. 400, 408, 413), founders of a great age of painting in Venice.

From the first the painters of Venice reflect the buoyant and worldly character of a city which was one of dazzling splendor. Her citizens must have been something like the Chinese or the French in their prudent worldly good sense. They were lovers of pleasure and good living. Proud of their independence and secure in their wealth, they were quick to respond to a natural craving for ornament and luxury. The color and light of the sea and canals may have bred a sensitivity to color which is the prime characteristic of their painting, but her painters' love of warmly sensuous colors is consistent with the pagan worldliness of the Venetian way of life.

The first illustrious name in Venice of the High Renaissance is Giorgione (1478-1510). Only a few out of scores of paintings attributed to his hand are actually his, but during his own life and for a long time thereafter his art was reflected in that of many Venetian masters, making exact attribution in some cases almost impossible. Under his brush the local forthright tones of his predecessors, the brothers Bellini and others, give way to colors of throbbing vitality organically related to each other. Line, light and color are so treated that their interrelation creates a consummation of the form. One is no longer aware of linear areas enriched with color, for Giorgione's form is an equilibrium of interacting or interweaving lines, mass, light and color. As Masaccio was the first painter to key his art to the habits of the eye with respect to mass in atmosphere and space (Fig. 395), so Giorgione is the first to apply the habits of the eye to color. An object like a human figure or a complex of drapery folds is, as far as our direct perceptions go, a mass of color and not a series of lines with color between the lines. This Giorgione never forgot and through this he contributed to one of the fundamental traditions valid for centuries of painting.

Occasionally we encounter a work of art so perfectly made that

Fig. 429.—GIORGIONE. Sleeping Venus. *Gallery, Dresden.*

nothing intervenes between the thing itself and our complete grasp of it. In other words, we do not think or feel anything except the miracle of the artist's experience which he passes on to us in its nascent state. The world which the artist lives in is completely ours, with no reservations in our mind as to time or place or means of accomplishment. Like the sudden harmony wrought from the melodies of a Bach chorale, or the perfect timing of a dancer's movement, the result is a completely satisfying resolution of all forces involved. The equation balances. With the recognition of the part color plays in our optical perceptions Giorgione at once closes the first great epoch of naturalistic art and opens the second leading to the phase dominated by Titian, Tintoretto, the Spaniards and the Dutch.

There had never been seen in all painting anything like the opulent splendor of his *Sleeping Venus* (Fig. 429). Only the Greek sculptors had envisioned this exalted loveliness, but that sphere of sensuous reality which sculpture could not reach Giorgione attains in color and the amplitude of the enveloping world of landscape. The Venus becomes identified with the landscape, her melting contours merge with the hills and the silver satin of her couch. The painting, begun about 1508, was left unfinished at the master's early death, the landscape being painted by Titian, who momentarily understood and shared Giorgione's transcendent poetry.

*Courtesy the Isabella Stewart Gardner Museum, Boston*

Fig. 430.—GIORGIONE. Christ. *Gardner Coll., Boston.*

The brief span of Giorgione's life—thirty-three years—was so fruitful that though we know but a few of his works these will always live as almost ultimate values of their kind in the painter's art. Uncounted masters in his time and since have felt the hushed passion of his paintings. One would like to know more about him than the few scraps legend gives us. He may have come under the spell of Leonardo, who was in Venice in 1500. As a youth he worked with Giovanni Bellini and later paid homage to him by painting the *Christ Bearing the Cross*

(Fig. 430) now in Boston, almost exactly following a painting of Bellini. Giorgione gives us a Christ which once seen can never be forgotten. Not even Leonardo ever created the features of the Savior at once so compassionate and tragic as this. Titian often attempted in his early

FIG. 431.—GIORGIONE. THE THREE PHILOSOPHERS. *Gallery, Vienna.*

work to recapture Giorgione's mood as in his Tribute Money, and El Greco a hundred years later essayed the mood, but in Giorgione's panel is encountered the enduring essence.

The great artist has a peculiar sixth sense for the genius of his medium. With Giorgione and Piero della Francesca this sense is an awareness of the mute, arrested world of painted forms which because of their fixed character must always vibrate with enigmatic overtones. Few masters have possessed the ability to seize upon this apparent limitation to translate it into sustained musical reality. In the painting called *The Three Philosophers* (Fig. 431) of about 1510, Giorgione does just this. Taking as he often does an obscure theme from myth or legend he submits it to his own interpretations, bringing forth a passionately felt drama of man and nature which requires no literary explanation or reference. Three ages of man, three temperaments, establish their identity in a mysterious and haunting landscape. It seems vain to probe for fugitive literal explanations in the presence of this completely realized world of imagination. The wisdom of the pagan world lives again in this appeal to our deepest feelings through sensuous perceptions, half-forgotten slumbering sensations stored ages ago in the memory of the individual and the race. The mute harmony of spirits called the Sacred Conversation of Giovanni Bellini (Fig. 413) is taken by his pupil Giorgione and enriched and broadened to encompass the Platonic concepts then flowing in Renaissance thought.

Yet it remained for another mind to bring Venetian art to its fulfillment. Titian (1477-1576), schooled under Gentile Bellini in his early years, is first known in a style like that of Giorgione, who was Titian's own age but far more precocious, and early works by him are scarcely to be distinguished from those of his contemporary, so closely are Giorgione's mood and technique emulated. Both masters quite naturally turned to the use of oil in contrast to the prevailing medium of fresco and tempera in Rome and Florence. Fresco with its dry cool surface was the ideal medium for an art that called for crisp linear definition of forms and restrained color appropriate to the decoration of large public buildings, but Venetian preferences were for other things. Under the aegis of Titian, painting was to pass beyond the old horizons, and even beyond the world of mood and colorful revery created by Giorgione. The total human experience of mind and body was his theme. Michelangelo had made the human figure more expressive than it had ever been. Titian was in effect to place man in the breathing world—a creature of feeling and passion, soil and cloud. In the almost legendary length of his ninety-nine years it was his destiny to interpret man as an integral creature of his environment as perhaps no painter has ever done before or since his time. It is no accident that he created one of the first modern landscapes (Fig. 432), giving a definite dramatic expression to what had been only suggested by earlier masters.

Here Titian projects himself into the landscape, intimately identifying himself with it. The massy bulk of trees, shrubs and herds is so sensitively built up that the eye gains free access stage by stage to the space lying before it. Earlier landscapes had been portrayed as static topography; now they come to life pulsing with the forces of wind and cloud and the vitality of growing things. When Rubens, Gainsborough, Delacroix and Renoir come upon the scene, each will be fortified by Titian's observation that man and nature are one. Titian brought into Italian art a refreshing pagan sensualism unknown to the austere art of central Italy.

To follow through the development of Titian's art is to examine the evolution not of one man's art but that of a whole epoch. It leads from

FIG. 432.—TITIAN. LANDSCAPE. *Buckingham Palace, London.*

his early enthusiasm for Giorgione's lyricism to the inventive and strenuous period of his middle years and finally to the full glory of his last conceptions. Between 1516 and 1518, about the time he emerged from Giorgione's spell, he painted *The Assumption of the Virgin* (Fig. 433). The poetry of Giorgione is modified by the dramatic gusto that characterizes so many of Titian's works. A profitable comparison may be made of this painting and Raphael's Sistine Madonna (Fig. 426), which had been painted in Rome only a couple of years earlier. Instead of the sublime tranquillity of Raphael's picture, there is a splendid pageant, the grandiose culmination of an opera. Superb movement, deeply human emotion, sustain the moment of Mary's greatest glory. This splendor of color and drama was what the Venetians loved, and Titian brings to the theme a supreme mastery of sensuous experience. The types are Venetian, full-bodied and vigorous. Renaissance worldliness

Fig. 433.—TITIAN. The Assumption of the Virgin.
*Church of the Frari, Venice.*

and ecclesiastical symbol are here reconciled so far as it was possible to make that reconciliation. Frequently in Venice the Christian themes are treated in a more frankly pagan manner; Titian's Fall of Man is an example.

In the entire history of painting there is nothing comparable to the phenomenon of Titian, strong and ever-creative even under the weight of three generations, yet exploring with matchless taste and incredible originality the fields of myth, legend, drama, sacred history, landscape, portraiture. Approaching eighty he painted, as he had earlier, one of the cosmic themes recurring in all art—the fruitfulness of love. The nymph *Danaë* receiving her lover Zeus in the guise of a golden shower (Fig. 434) is a dramatization of nature convulsed in creation no less noble than Michelangelo's more austere conception on the Sistine ceil-

Fig. 434.—TITIAN. Danaë. *Prado, Madrid.*

ing. Here is a case so often encountered in the history of art when a master using a subject of popular appeal transforms it into sheer symbolism. With imagination and passion the artist removes the theme from the realm of the decorative or the erotic into the sphere of allegory. There are, of course, earlier treatments of this theme by the master in which no such lofty vision prevails; sometimes, as in the Venus of Urbino, there is little more than a splendid transcription of physical beauty.

At the end of Titian's career, after his ninetieth year, were produced perhaps the profoundest creations of his mind. The *Madonna and Child* (Fig. 435) is of this time, having been painted between 1570 and 1576. Touching the elemental springs of man's being it belongs to no time or place; over three hundred years after its painting Renoir traveled a path close to Titian's (cf. Fig. 507). This and the great *Pietà* (Fig. 436) reveal a tragic conception of life shared by only the few greatest spirits. When the master was carried off by the plague, he was at work on the Pietà which was to mark his tomb. Among the greatest of all colorists, Titian here makes almost no use of color except as it shines through the silver and russet overpainting. Color seems too transitory and uncertain an experience to expound this drama of life and death —only silver across deep shadows—light and dark, figures falling into

FIG. 435.—TITIAN. MADONNA AND CHILD. *National Gallery, London.*

a compact classical frieze in space that dilates and murmurs. El Greco, Rembrandt, Rubens, Poussin and Renoir will be shaped by this man, who here portrays himself as Joseph of Arimathea on his knees seeking grace in the touch of Christ's hand.

A primary and peculiar place was given in Renaissance art to the treatment of space. In painting we may trace its development from the severely restricted space patterns of Giotto (Fig. 391), who was content with the skillful manipulation of the narrow span of a stage. Following him, Taddeo Gaddi (Fig. 393) made bold and disastrous experiments without adequate knowledge of the means to control and organize his spaces. In the 15th century, with Brunellesco and Masaccio (Fig. 395), the beginning of a rationally constructed space pattern appears which is brought to a climax in the scientifically con-

FIG. 436.—TITIAN. PIETÀ. *Accademia, Venice.*

trolled designs of Leonardo in the High Renaissance (Fig. 416). Thereafter painters plan space patterns with increased freedom but with due respect to pictorial clarity and to the architectural nature of their picture limits or the wall surface they were decorating.

Men of northern Italy, Mantegna (Fig. 400) and the Venetians (Fig. 439) had long shown a predilection for bolder and more experimental treatment of space. In Venice the employment of oil as a medium gave impetus to a more intricate space and in the provincial schools of Parma and Padua near Venice the traditions of art were more flexible. In Parma, Correggio (1489-1534) continued the earlier experiments of Mantegna. In decorating the inner dome of the Cathedral of Parma between 1526 and 1530 (Fig. 437), he wholly obliterated the ceiling surfaces to create a breath-taking expanse of unbounded space; the heavens open and Mary ascends. Compared to Raphael's School of Athens (Fig. 425) or Michelangelo's ceiling paintings, Correggio shows an unorthodoxy that links him with the baroque masters

FIG. 437.—CORREGGIO. THE ASSUMPTION OF THE VIRGIN.
*Dome, Cathedral, Parma.* (After Toschi's copy.)

of the next century rather than with his own generation. Unused to viewing decorative figures floating in clouds, some of his critics called his dome a frog pond, but Titian spoke high praise of it. A similar taste for the lyrical and exotic, fundamentally at variance with the sober Renaissance humanism of Florence and Rome, is apparent when Correggio undertakes with incredibly melting colors the interpretation of exotic types. An example is seen in the detail of an *Angel* (Fig. 438) from his Madonna with St. Jerome, which suggests the narrow line separating the morbid from the spiritual. Followers and admirers were to seize upon this note of exoticism or eroticism with sometimes brilliant results. While not properly a Venetian, Correggio shows close kinship with the men of that city and his painterly style links him to the development stemming from Venice.

A story is told about Titian which illuminates the last important phase of Venetian painting. One day the master entered his studio and chanced to see some drawings by one of his numerous pupils. He

FIG. 438.—CORREGGIO. AN ANGEL. Detail of the Madonna with St. Jerome. *Museum, Parma.*

asked who had made them and thereupon told his assistant to have the young apprentice expelled from the studio. The legend has been interpreted rather naïvely as a sign of Titian's jealousy of a gifted potential rival; if the tale is true, it is more likely that the master saw substantial evidence that the young Tintoretto (1518-1594), a youth more than a generation younger than his teacher, could learn nothing of value under his tutelage. Certain it is that Tintoretto's brilliant intuitive art was to violate the essential pattern that Titian had set.

The older man had thought of his canvas as a kind of stage. He drew a sharp line excluding spectator from the stage or spectacle— the Pietà (Fig. 436) is an example. The opposite is true of Tintoretto, who (to maintain the analogy) figuratively places a ramp from the stage to the audience so that the old barrier of footlights is removed. Flashing diagonals lead the eye directly into deep space, figures are always in action or poised for movement. He abolishes the basic conception of the figure set *against* a background, for with him there is no such thing as background. Walls, banks of trees, horizon lines are

FIG. 439.—TINTORETTO. The Last Supper.
*San Giorgio Maggiore, Venice.*

so handled as to make them as dramatically potent as the figures. He thus achieves an all-over pattern with broken lines, curved lines, light that bursts and dies. His *Last Supper* (Fig. 439) illustrates his method. Where Leonardo invented a clearly designed and neutral boxlike room for the setting of his drama (Fig. 416), Tintoretto made his whole canvas dramatic. Leonardo's treatment is illustrative and descriptive of psychological values, depending as it does upon facial expression and movement of hands and arms. The design in line, color, light and dark, and space are all used by Tintoretto to make the surface of his canvas surge and flow and thus to emphasize the drama of the scene. Even though we could not see a single face clearly, the force of his colors the crackling and splashing light, the daring of the designed space, would be adequate to arouse powerful emotion. Late in his life Titian, while not so bold, worked in much the same manner for his color and light became increasingly powerful as a means of expression, but the late years of Tintoretto's art found him even further advanced in the art of abstract and expressive design. The sketch of 1587 for *Paradise*, in the Ducal Palace in Venice (Fig. 440), shows how bold and inventive and "modern" he had become. El Greco and Rubens were to feel the impact of Tintoretto's dramatic language and adapt it to their painting, and the art of many moderns is based upon just such a conception of painting. The individual figures become part of the "landscape" in this view of heaven. They coalesce with clouds of light to form vast concentric swirls. Light, color, space merge in a tremendous cosmic drama

FIG. 440.—TINTORETTO. PARADISE. Sketch. *Louvre, Paris.*

to which individual figures as actors are subordinated. The closest analogy with other arts is found in music in which sheer sound becomes a vehicle for incalculable shades of emotion. The world is configured by the painter as it is by the musician in an untranslatable idiom of sensuous stuff. Tintoretto does not go as far as do Kandinsky and Picasso in the 20th century but there is ample evidence that he had a clear understanding of the revolutionary principles implied by his art.

In literature the use of devices such as figures of speech (irony, hyperbole, metaphor) is so common that we are almost unaware of it until they are pointed out and explained. Because most people are relatively unfamiliar with the language of the pictorial arts they are frequently puzzled when a painter employs similar devices. With men like Tintoretto it seems on the surface that they violate inherent rules of art when in reality they are using established principles of design in a new manner more appropriate and more effective for the generation to which they belong. For instance, he unconsciously accepted the freer and more casual arrangements of space and forms that had long prevailed in Venetian painting and developed his art further in that direction. The Venetian colorists had always composed a picture on the basis of color spotting as opposed to the linear designs of central Italy (Raphael, Michelangelo). Tintoretto carried this practice to what, for his time, was a daring conclusion, plunging the spectator into active imaginative participation in his dramas. This practice can be observed a hundred years earlier in the frescoes of Mantegna (cf. Fig. 400), but it was Correggio and particularly Tintoretto who gave currency to the idiom which was to prevail even into our own day.

While Veronese (1528-1588) maintained a high level of Venetian art in his sumptuous festivals and splendid decorations, he remained a local Venetian spirit, whereas Giorgione, Titian and Tintoretto belong to a larger world. And of these three it is Tintoretto who enkindled the imagination of later men. Actually he belongs not to the High Renaissance but to the baroque. The path which he takes leads specifically to El Greco, Rubens and Rembrandt and other masters of the 17th century.

# Chapter XXVII. Renaissance Painting in the North ~~~~~~~~~~~~~~~~~~~~~~~~~~~~~~~~~

*THE TRANSFORMATION OF ART AND LIFE IN ITALY* during the 15th century did not materially affect the contemporary art of northern countries beyond the Alps, for the Gothic pattern persisted there for a century or more after the basic sensuous and individualistic ideas of the Renaissance had permeated Italian art. The mediaeval painters in France, Flanders and Germany had before them models of a highly naturalistic art in the sculptures of the cathedrals. Had Renaissance art been simply a matter of imitation of nature, then one might say that the northern peoples were well in advance of the Italians; but the classical ideas that also shaped the cultural pattern of Renaissance Italy were relatively scattered in the north or came there only sporadically before the 16th century. Then, largely through the personality of Albrecht Dürer, classical art became integrated with the native Gothic art to effect a synthesis comparable to the new art of Italy.

At a time when Italy was producing the robust art of Filippo Lippi (cf. Fig. 405) and Pollaiuolo (cf. Fig. 406), German artists were still adhering to the Late Gothic style. Its essential features are found in the *Madonna in the Courtyard* (Fig. 441), an engraving of about 1480 by Martin Schongauer (1445-1491). The Madonna is no aristocratic or noble lady elevated to a queenly throne but a bourgeois woman adoring her child, an example of the folk character in German art which was a strong and healthy heritage of the Middle Ages. Schongauer illuminates the theme with delicacy of line and sensitivity to space patterns. His Madonna rests in a veritable sea of crisply breaking folds, one of those late mediaeval mannerisms of pattern that also appear in the sculpture and architecture of the time. Richness of decoration for its own sake had become an aesthetic burden which was to disappear with the influx of classical thought. There is, moreover, a conflict between the tortured drapery and the sensitively felt silhouette of the tree. The inconsistency between this sympathetic observation of the *nuances* of nature's forms and the deliberate artificial pattern of

the draperies is but one of the many manifestations of internal conflict to be found in this transitional art.

Schongauer lived in the century that saw the invention of printing
and he used an art form the development of which probably had a
good deal to do with this invention. From about 1400, Europeans began
to print designs on cloth and paper from blocks of wood, a practice
known to the Chinese in the 9th
century, and also from engraved copper plates. As printing gave widespread knowledge of the new ideas,
so the *printed picture* made for the
dissemination of knowledge. The
Flemish and Germans were quick to
adopt the practice of print-making.
Cultural ideas received the fullest
dissemination in local areas and over
an international field. With the exchange of prints from town to town
and country to country, local and provincial schools might come within the
orbit of larger and more cosmopolitan
thought. Something comparable has
occurred in our own day in the perfection of processes of color reproduction. The collotype perfected only a
few years ago makes it possible for a
painting reproduced in full color to

*Courtesy the Museum of Fine Arts, Boston*
FIG. 441.—SCHONGAUER.
THE MADONNA IN THE COURT-
YARD.

pass into the hands of millions where formerly the single painting
often passed into the almost total obscurity of a private collector's living room or storeroom.

In the Germany of the 16th century, Albrecht Dürer (1471-1528)
saw the great potentialities of the printed picture. While he was
also a painter, it was through the graphic arts—the woodcut, engraving, etching—that he made his greatest contribution to European
thought. In his hands the woodcut and the engraving on copper became
major vehicles of expression. Beginning in his youth in the tradition
of the mediaeval Schongauer, he lived to raise German art to world-
wide importance in that of the Renaissance.

An example of the early and still quite mediaeval phase of Dürer's
artistic career before he was thirty is the woodcut, from a series called
The Large Passion, of *Christ Bearing the Cross* (Fig. 442) which is
dated about 1498 and in which the forms are weighted with lavish
and nervously felt detail similar to the over-embellishment of Late

FIG. 442.—DÜRER. CHRIST BEARING THE CROSS.
Woodcut from *The Large Passion*.

Gothic architecture and sculpture. Crumpled folds of drapery break in cascades of movement as the surfaces are disturbed and restless. Dürer has sensitively gauged the aesthetic resources of the small print and the confines of a black and white pattern. The distribution of the dominant geometrical forms like the architecture, and the halberd carried by the soldier at the right is planned to yield maximum clarity to an extremely rich plastic pattern. It is this clarity of structure which makes possible the intense psychological drama involving the complacent brutality of the soldiers and the pathos of human suffering. Random symbols are welded into a schematic sustained drama more eloquent than anything seen in the graphic arts to this time.

At the time that the woodcuts of the Large Passion were made, Dürer had been in Italy once for a short time, and he was also familiar with the work of many Italian artists through the medium of prints like the Ten Nudes of Pollaiuolo (Fig. 406), but little influence of such things is perceptible in his work. He was much aware of the difference between his rather harshly angular figures and those of his Italian contemporaries, however, and for a period in the first ten years of the 16th century he strove conscientiously to grasp the principles of classic beauty by which they were guided, studying, for example, the theory of Leonardo da Vinci as set forth in that master's *Treatise on Painting* and other writings, and even inaugurating a theory of his own. A second visit to Italy in 1505-1507 found him less impressed than he had been by many things seen on his first journey, and also turned him momentarily from the graphic processes to painting. But with his return to Germany, he reverted to the art of the print in works which make it evident that he had realized the impossibility of translating his own northern concepts into the formal idioms of Renaissance Italy. His woodcuts, often issued in book form, were usually cut by especially trained craftsmen after his drawings, but the engravings are entirely by his own hand. Three of these, made in 1513 and 1514, are his most celebrated works—Knight, Death and the Devil; St. Jerome in his Cell; and the *Melencolia I* (Fig. 443)—and reveal the compromise which he had achieved between the fundamentally emotional values of his northern inheritance and the rational beauty of Renaissance thought. Technically these prints have never been surpassed in the craftsmanship by which lines laboriously incised in the copper plate are turned to the recording of such minute details as differences in texture between glass and polished metal. Expressively, the pattern of the woman seated in the repose of mental inertia rather than physical weariness, surrounded by the symbols of fruitless learning, is filled with a pessimism of almost Faustian profundity.

The clarity with which these ideas are set forth is the quality which

Dürer gained from his long study of Italian art, realizing the necessity for couching even the most subjective concepts in organized formal patterns if their nature is to be fully perceived. If the Melencolia I is comparable in content to Michelangelo's Jeremiah (Fig. 422), she is like-

FIG. 443.—DÜRER. MELENCOLIA I. Engraving.

wise a northern counterpart of Leonardo's Mona Lisa (Fig. 418) but incapable of escaping the northern heritage of spiritual experience that renders her frustrate when confronted by objective phenomena capable of being understood only in rational terms. The positive evaluation of such experience is seen in another of the great prints of 1513-1514 by Dürer, the St. Jerome in his Cell, and also in the somewhat later one of *St. Anthony before the Walls of Nuremburg* (Fig. 444), which was engraved in 1519. Here the forms of nature fall into lucid and orderly patterns, the buildings in the town mounting up in a pyramid that reinforces the form of the saint profoundly absorbed in his meditations in the foreground in a composition as forceful in its embodiment

FIG. 444.—DÜRER. ST. ANTHONY BEFORE THE WALLS OF NUREMBURG
Engraving.

of finally realized truths as the Melencolia I is of doubt and despair. Dürer thus remains true to his inheritance of significant spiritual experience, but embodies it in patterns that effectively represent the first creative fusion of northern content with the formal concepts of Renaissance Italy.

But however great the impact of Italy with its wealth of classic ideas upon the forms of Dürer's art, he remained wholly Germanic in feeling. The force of his line as an expressive instrument never failed. In the great body of his work, painting and graphic art, nothing can compare for sheer beauty with the drawings and water-color studies. In these he is seen to be one of the great naturalists, an artist like Leonardo, sensitive and responsive to the infinite riches of nature. Among the drawings done long after his Venetian visit is a charcoal study of his mother (Fig. 445) made in 1514, the year of her death. Here there is no hint of Italian formalism in the interweaving of eloquent expression-laden lines, but through this restless arabesque Dürer translates with energy and compassion the gaunt wisdom, the patience and fortitude of a woman who had brought to life nineteen children. It was with such capacity for feeling as is here revealed that Dürer, the friend of Luther and Erasmus, brought, with them, the light of the Renaissance to the northern world.

Fig. 445.—DÜRER. The Artist's Mother. Drawing.
*Print Cabinet, Berlin.*

There are three major voices in German painting—Dürer, Grüne-wald and Holbein. The brief span of fifty years, 1500-1550, saw the beginning and the end of their heroic effort. If Dürer is the supreme master of line, Matthias Grünewald (*ca.* 1468-*ca.* 1531) is his equal as a master of color. His greatest achievement is the Isenheim Altarpiece painted about 1510. It is a folding altarpiece like the one painted by the van Eycks in Ghent, with scenes of the Passion and the lives of saints. The *Crucifixion* (Fig. 446) is the central and climactic act in a series of epochal transformations. As the Gothic artists symbolized in the cathedral all heaven and the shadows of earth, and as Michel-angelo undertook in the Sistine Ceiling to create a mighty all-inclusive cosmos, so Grünewald's colossal imagination embraces pictorially the entirety of human experience. Like Bosch he explored the nether world of dreams in the Temptation of St. Anthony; the Nativity (Fig. 447) is a paean to creation. The Incarnation is the divine mystery set forth in the Annunciation. The Crucifixion is the climax followed by the pathos of Entombment and the fearful consuming light of the Resurrection. This awful pageant of man and salvation can be compared only with the supreme creations in art: it is like the *Divine*

FIG. 446.—GRÜNEWALD. THE CRUCIFIXION. The Isenheim Altarpiece. *Museum, Colmar.*

*Comedy* in scope and force, or the Greek tragedies; and as the masses of Palestrina and Bach unfold the drama of life step by step so does this altar with its successively unfolding panels.

In German art generally, color is subordinate to linear design, but Grünewald uses it with extraordinary force, less for its structural function, as in Venetian painting, than to effect a psychological impact. The Madonna is a beaming German girl radiantly maternal in the *Nativity* (Fig. 447), the Magdalene of the Crucifixion a study in morbidity. The model for the Christ crucified is the festering corpse of one pitifully racked with frightful disease. The altar was painted for the monastery of St. Anthony at which venereal diseases were treated, and the artist has taken such a broken and diseased body as might have been seen there to symbolize the agony of the Redemption.

If Grünewald is mediaeval in his utterly religious purpose and in the intensity of his psychology, he is modern in his persistent use of nature in homely intimacy and the grand scale of his drama. But in another

Fig. 447.—GRÜNEWALD. The Nativity. The Isenheim Altarpiece. *Museum, Colmar.*

sense he rises to expressive heights beyond any art tradition or local school. There has been no one else like him in the Germany of his day or since.

The third great German master, Hans Holbein (1497-1543), came a full generation after his illustrious compatriots. His father was a painter in the mediaeval tradition, but the son came into a cultural world that had experienced the impact of Renaissance humanism. The moral fervor and passionate convictions of Grünewald and Dürer were scarcely shared by Holbein, who was a man of the world both as an artist and as a personality. As a graphic artist, he executed a brilliant series of woodcuts called The Dance of Death, a theme commonly found in northern art of the times, but his religious paintings are relatively perfunctory and it is only natural that in an age of increasing secularism he should have found his principle work in portraiture. Seeking patronage, he found it in England where he became court painter to Henry VIII, and as a result, that monarch's court circle is probably the most thoroughly documented pictorially of any in history. Scores of portraits—among them Anne of Cleves, Sir Thomas More, Jane Seymour—come from him in oil and drawings. In every instance Holbein is a rationalist, cool and detached. His portrait of *Henry VIII* (Fig. 448), painted about 1539, is crafty and intelligent. Henry, bravely arrayed in the pompous trappings of his office, stands full-face in a frame which seems too small to contain his overbearing presence. The bull neck, beady eyes, tight sensuous mouth and small puffy hands are displayed against the elaborately detailed costume. The richness of fabric and jewels emphasizes the florid personality reveling in barbaric splendor. Though the portrait is extraordinarily analytical, the details are united in a lucid and coherent pattern. When Holbein painted the features of the humanist *Erasmus* (Fig. 449) the design varied from that of the other portrait, just as the personality of his subject was different. The figure is smaller, the room space more ample. The tightness and tension of the King's portrait have vanished. Here the scholar sits at ease in the quiet atmosphere of his study, his attention directed to his writing. The warm blended colors and the apparently casual composition of the forms characterize the mood and activity of a gentle contemplative spirit. Holbein, with an eye quick to contrive a flat decorative pattern with which to summarize the solid bulk of his subject, always achieved a design that was harmonious in itself, even if there is little in his portraits to recall the charged linear patterns of Dürer. Holbein was the last pictorial genius to emerge from Germany. The ravages of the Thirty Years' War, in which a great part of the population of Germanic countries was annihilated, brought to an end any further important development in the arts for a whole century.

Fig. 448.—HOLBEIN. Henry VIII. *Corsini Gallery, Rome.*

In Flanders, painting possessed a rich heritage in the van Eycks, Hugo van der Goes and others of the 15th century. In the 16th century, it attained fresh vitality at the hands of Peter Bruegel the Elder (1525-1569). As Leonardo and Michelangelo in the south had studied the human figure to make it a vehicle for the expression of thought, so Bruegel in Flanders expressed his profoundest convictions through landscape. Landscape painting had had its beginning in the

Fig. 449.—HOLBEIN. Erasmus. *Louvre, Paris.*

tiny miniatures of Late Gothic manuscripts and the 15th-century masters had continuously been occupied with its interpretation in the backgrounds of their paintings, but it remained for Bruegel to explore its deepest implications. In a series of paintings representing the four seasons executed about 1565, he gave an exhaustive account of the peasant's activity, the intimate experience of man in closest contact with the freezing air of winter, the harvest of summer and bronzed autumn. The picture representing *Summer* (Fig. 450) hangs in the Metropolitan Museum in New York. Here peasants heavy with fatigue and the lassitude of noonday heat sit eating or sprawl asleep beneath a tree in a harvest field. Bruegel sees everything; the peasants' greedy habits of feeding, the precise method of harvesting grain, the jug of water standing in the shade, the birds in the air, the village in the distance with children at play. For the first time in art, the anonymous and inarticulate aspects of man's communal activity and the familiar life of the landscape have been recorded on a monumental pictorial scale. Yet the hundreds of observations, the almost countless birds and people, the buildings that sprinkle the landscapes are so skillfully distributed and controlled in the large pattern of space that the landscape is seen as a unit, as logically constructed and lucidly articulated as a

FIG. 450.—BRUEGEL. SUMMER. *Metropolitan Museum, N. Y.*

figure composition by Leonardo. By means of a large pattern in which the details become integrated structurally and psychologically, the landscape is rendered expressive of its greatest spiritual implications. Man is conceived as an integral part of nature; the landscape results from his labors and has significance only in terms of the form that he gives it. This is the identical truth that Leonardo had expounded in Florence earlier in the century; it is the truth that gives such great authority to the art of Titian.

The Reformation sweeping the northern countries was implicitly expounded by Bruegel. When he painted the Crucifixion it became a veiled comment on the ravages of the Spanish Inquisition which at that time was crucifying Flanders. In a deep landscape containing hundreds of tiny figures the peasants come trooping out of the town toward a distant Calvary. A ring of curious sensation-seekers collects about the cross almost invisible in the distance. The implication is clear, since the setting is the Flemish countryside and the soldiers are obviously Spanish. By the same token, his Slaughter of the Innocents is portrayed as a savage searching party of the Inquisition brutally seizing its victims in a Flemish village. His love of the uncouth celebrations of the peasants recorded in weddings, dances and drinking bouts earned Bruegel the name of Droll Peter and Peasant Bruegel.

FIG. 451.—BRUEGEL. WEDDING DANCE. *Institute of Arts, Detroit.*

There are good reasons for considering him the first great modern master in the sense that his unself-conscious portrayal of common things—children at play, peasants dancing, farmers at work—indicates a mind that saw in the customary routine of humanity the meaning of life. Thus the landscape is no more only a picturesque sight, but a pattern of man's life activity. The *Wedding Dance*, now in Detroit (Fig. 451), becomes more than a quaint record of folk customs. One may see all manner of things in a Bruegel painting—the obvious narrative, the picturesque customs, the lively recorded anecdote. But beyond this is the clear statement of a man who recognized the underlying implications of a civilization. A peasant wedding dance is a drama of human forces no less than the Dionysiac revels of Greek times and as revealing of spiritual implications as the ceremony of an 18th-century minuet or a 20th-century jam session. The seasonal ritual —the celebration of the harvest, the planting time, the marriage—are focal points revealing the zest for life known to all peoples. No artist graphs these life impulses more explicitly and with greater assurance than Bruegel. His art is a deeply religious one though it does not always employ the symbolism of Christianity. It celebrates a drama older than Christianity itself, one that will be manifest in the art of Rembrandt, Goya and Daumier in ages to come.

As the tide of Gothic thought receded and humanism replaced it as the dominant way of life, the process that was in full tide in 15th-century Italy came to its height in the north, but not until the 16th century. While the new synthesis of thought was undoubtedly taking place spontaneously within Germany and Flanders, it was immeasurably accelerated by the continuous contact which the Northerners had with the more advanced thought of the Italians. Dürer, Bruegel, Holbein and perhaps Grünewald all visited Italy and their art was deeply influenced by that contact. And Italy in turn was impregnated with the vital energies of the Gothic spirit that lay behind the northern Renaissance. The following century was to see a complete fusion of European art and thought, but the vitality of Italy waned and the leadership was assumed by France, the Netherlands and Spain.

# Chapter XXVIII. *Painting in the Seventeenth Century*

IT IS DIFFICULT TO GENERALIZE ABOUT THE NEW painting of the 17th century, for art had a larger and more extended audience in that period than it had had in the 16th century in either Italy or the north. Painting was still to serve the Church by appealing to the emotions of the faithful; in other instances it served the more popular purpose of photographic naturalism. But to a large degree its function as symbol which had given direction and purpose through the Renaissance was relaxed. In the waning years of the 16th century in Italy the grand, formal and expressive discipline of the older masters was not renewed by their successors. There were those who paid homage to the earlier masters, to be sure, and confidently expected to acquire by easy imitation the energy and nobility they recognized in Raphael, Michelangelo and Titian; but the result, of course, was only facility, superficiality and eclecticism.

The basis of eclecticism was the emulation of the Renaissance masters including the exotic Correggio. Without recourse to the emotional and intellectual forces of an earlier day the Italian Eclectics sought to sustain the lofty style by learned imitation. Two cousins, Lodovico Carracci (1555-1619) and Annibale Carracci (1560-1609) of Bologna, were the leading exponents of the movement. Annibale's principal work is the painting of the great hall of the Farnese Palace in Rome (Fig. 125). Here he has followed the grand decorative scheme of Michelangelo's Sistine Ceiling, with the decorative borders dominant in the scheme. The enframed pictures are scarcely more than medallions about which revolve the decorative nudes.

The showmanship and sensationalism of the Eclectics were encouraged by the Church, which, following the schism resulting from the Reformation, had found itself in a perilously weakened position. To fortify itself, the Society of Jesus had been organized to compel allegiance and faith. Begun by Ignatius Loyola, the Society encouraged architects, sculptors and painters to dramatize Church doctrines to the point of sensationalism. The results may be found in masters who came

specifically within the orbit of the Catholic Church, notably Bernini
in sculpture (cf. Fig. 333) and architecture, Rubens and El Greco in
painting.

While the eclectic masters were exploiting movement and melodrama to persuade men of wavering faith, another assault upon the
sensibilities was being made by the Realists. The Eclectics were reaching out for a wider public and made practical efforts to sway its thinking through an emotional appeal. The Realists made their appeal
through the senses too. With Caravaggio (1573-1610) comes a change

Fig. 452.—CARAVAGGIO. Peter Denying the Lord.
*Vatican Museum, Rome.*

in European art that has been felt down to our own time. His subjects
are those having a lively appeal for the unlearned; they are as often as
not taken from everyday life, like the Card Players and Fortune Tellers.
His realism is simple and pragmatic, being based upon the look of
things rather than upon knowledge of construction or the organization
of forms into self-sustaining patterns. The Biblical illustration becomes
a straight bit of nature dressed up with dramatic lighting as in *Peter
Denying the Lord* (Fig. 452) of 1600, where Caravaggio presents as
skillful a handling of light as one could find in any expert Hollywood

movie. The shrill accusing voice of the woman is conveyed by the impetuous gesture. The shadow muffles the garbled response of the wavering Peter.

This ingenious descriptive literalness will not be confused with the profound psychological analysis of a Leonardo or a Correggio or the architectonic constructions of a Raphael. The practice of this vivid and arresting art made a great impression, none the less, on the German and Flemish artists living in Italy at the turn of the century, and by direct or indirect means the method reached Spanish, Dutch and Flemish masters, who found it consistent with the expanding democratic function of their art. Rubens will modify it with the power of Venetian color. Rembrandt will refine it into mystery of space, and Velasquez into the lucid rhythms of his extraordinary perception. For in this Italian world at the turn of the century were formed the styles of the northern artists who are the giants of the 17th century. El Greco had already gone to Spain after apprenticeship in Venice. But to Rome came the two Frenchmen, Claude Lorrain and Poussin, and from Flanders came Peter Paul Rubens, dissatisfied with the Italianate Mannerists he had known at home who seemed to understand neither Italian nor Flemish art. Educated in their feeble imitative Italianized ways in Flanders, Rubens (1577-1640) turned eagerly to a first-hand study of the work everyone seemed obsessed with copying. From 1600 to 1608 he was in Italy painting and intently observing everything, especially the great 16th-century masters. His Eclectic and Realist contemporaries were likewise given close attention and Rubens with energy and above all intelligence absorbed of these influences too what was useful to him, rejecting the artistic deadwood.

Almost everything he painted later tells of his contact with Michelangelo's heroic figures, the richness of Titian's structural color and the drama of Tintoretto. Movement and energy pervade all that he touches, the relatively stable plan of a Renaissance figure or design being rejected. His vast knowledge and the fluency of his energetic style make the work of the Italian Eclectics look dry and barren in comparison.

With deep and complex space patterns he deliberately constructs grandiose plans or stage sets for the enactment of miracles or the narration of the classic myths. One might say that Rubens interprets life in terms of dynamic contrasts—in the active thrust and athletic movements of heroic giants reminiscent of Michelangelo. Those who seek in art the ideal of a serene harmony will find little comfort in his swirling volcanoes of energy.

The style of the Counter-Reformation called for a crescendo of emotion. Rubens supplies it in plastic terms, finding richness of color, space and line to suit the psychological tempo. The often-told account of the mourning for the dead Christ usually treated with reserve and reticence (cf. Fig. 401) is for Rubens (Fig. 453) an occasion for almost unbelievable drama. Christ's body is that of a Michelangelesque athlete. The Virgin pathetically closes the dead eyes. The Savior's death induces uncontrollable anguish bordering on the pathological among the witnesses. This torrent of feeling is reminiscent of the excesses of the

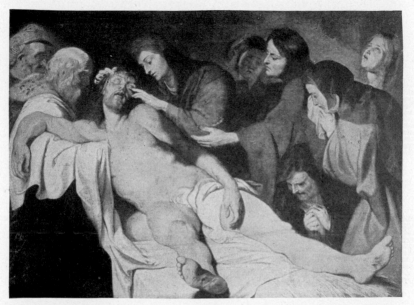

FIG. 453.—RUBENS.  THE LAMENTATION. *Liechtenstein Gallery. Vienna.*

later Middle Ages, but the heroic nude suggests more a pagan ritual of death than the ascetic resignation of Christianity.

As a classical scholar Rubens had a deep feeling for the pagan attitudes. The religious themes are not wholly congenial to his temper and he handles them always frankly, with an eye to their pathetic and emotional implications. The depiction of miracles frequently requested by the Church meets with his inherent taste for energy and drama. Love is a recurring theme in his art and appears in his pagan legends like the Three Graces, the Rescue of Andromeda, the Judgment of Paris. The selfless love of the Madonna for her Child is portrayed but not with the confidence of the lyrical outgoing splendor of the Venus, the Diana or Andromeda. For Rubens the Venus is a symbol of earth's fertility, as all his themes are unerringly seen in terms of their widest implication. The impulses of love are wild and orgiastic or restrained in bourgeois conventions, as the case may be. In the *Garden of Love* (Fig. 454) of 1632, he dwells upon the theme as manifested in his own society. Courtly folk decorously disport themselves in a courtyard before a baroque palace. The fountain figure is an opulent Venus with flowing breasts who presides over a court filled with winged loves. The master and his wife, Helena Fourment, are embracing at the left while an ardent Cupid busies himself with his task of persuasion. Rubens took

Fig. 454.—RUBENS. The Garden of Love. *Prado, Madrid.*

the opulent charms of Helena as the model for many if not most of his later feminine characters. The type is most unclassical and even repellent to many in our day. Whether it was a matter of personal idiosyncrasy or not, one may justly say that Rubens found in the type of buxom ripeness what he considered inherent characteristics of the Venus, the archetype of the mother of mankind, ample of hip and breast, a symbol of fertility.

More characteristic of the master's gift for interpreting the subject of love is the *Rape of the Daughters of Leucippus* (Fig. 455), an earlier work painted in 1614. The broken shimmering surfaces, the rich space pattern of the Garden of Love are not so highly developed here; more stable and simpler patterns prevail. The pagan theme gave ample opportunities to his enormous energies. No illusionism or naturalism is intended. The struggle is an elaborate theatrical display of feminine loveliness and masculine ardor. In a fine tableau like an episode in grand opera, the bronzed brothers, Castor and Pollux, eagerly but with noble discretion, seize their prize. The women, with appropriate rhetorical appeals to the gods, unreluctantly enact this ritual of love.

Like many of Rubens' works this painting was made with the aid of assistants. The artist maintained a veritable picture factory, he furnishing designs and his assistants doing much of the preliminary painting, the whole being supervised and the finishing colored glazes added by Rubens. Some of his men were specialists in one field or another like

Fig. 455.—RUBENS. The Rape of the Daughters of Leucippus. *Museum, Munich.*

still-life or animal figures. Van Dyck, his most gifted assistant and student, had a part in the last-mentioned work.

Rubens lived on a grand scale intellectually and socially. His art was enormously successful throughout Europe and he reaped a rich material reward for his incredible energy. To a very large degree he integrated the art traditions of the north with those of Italy. In his great Kermesse in the Louvre he proved how thoroughly he carried on the plastic and cultural concepts of that 16th-century giant Bruegel (Fig. 451), and in his late landscapes he continued a tradition extending back in Flemish art to the time of Pol de Limbourg and the days of Jan van Eyck and Bosch. As he enriched Flemish art with the forms of Michelangelo, with the lyric and structural colorism of Tintoretto and Veronese, he passed these on transformed to the 18th-century masters, notably Watteau, and to the 19th-century Romantics. His swirling decorative style became the stock-in-trade of lesser men who exploited his pictorial methods endlessly.

Rubens' disciple, Jordaens, popularized the method in superficial melodrama and Anthony van Dyck (1599-1641) is but an extension of the master's talent, selecting from Rubens the softer, more feminine aspects to exploit. It was as a portraitist that van Dyck had his chief vogue (Fig. 456). There is a certain aestheticism in his work as though he looked upon a painting as a decorative design not having specific relation to any serious interpretation of life. He is most congenially occupied in creating flattering and engaging portraits of aristocratic people. Many of these portraits are out-and-out commercial jobs with no expressive merit. At his best, however, he sometimes penetrates deeply, reaching and illuminating intimate and personal life more completely than Rubens. The influence of van Dyck was very great and perhaps out of proportion to his intrinsic merit. As court painter to the English King. Charles I, he followed in the path of Holbein a hundred years earlier. In his decorative brilliance he anticipates the style of the 18th century, especially in the English

FIG. 456.—VAN DYCK. JAMES STUART, DUKE OF LENNOX. *Metropolitan Museum, N. Y.*

school. The English found in his work exactly the model for their rococo portraits and landscapes, but it is significant that the French masters of the 18th century turned to Rubens rather than to the more superficial van Dyck.

It would be difficult to over-state the effect of Rubens' art in his own century and the following two centuries. His presence was felt wherever art flourished. Though he never attained the greatest heights of men like Giotto, Titian or Rembrandt, he was one of the most influential painters who ever lived.

The art of Italy, which fired Rubens with desire for the heroic and the grandiose and fed his appetite for all that was noble in the classic past, only indirectly affected neighboring Dutch artists. Flanders was Catholic, and Rubens shared the afflatus of the Counter-Reformation, which sought to revive the waning authority of the Church through the dazzling splendor of the spectacular and dramatic in architecture, sculpture and painting. Rubens was furthermore a gentleman of wealth and aristocratic culture. As an ambassador of kings and a scholar of note, he belonged to the social world of the aristocrat and the intellectual.

The painters who were his Dutch contemporaries present quite a different appearance. Holland was Protestant and wealthy, her citizens good industrious merchants. The Protestant faith had no use for showy altarpieces nor was there a demand for religious painting of any kind in Protestant churches. What the Dutch did demand was small realistic paintings for interior decoration. They were pleased with pictures of interiors, still-lifes of luscious fruit and vegetables, landscapes and genre studies of everyday scenes of the home and street, and especially they loved portraits, either singly or in groups. The Dutch painter did not try to express a subtle and abstract idea as the Italians had and as Rubens had under southern influence. Having won her centuries-long conflict, first with foreign powers and then against the encroaching sea, Holland set about enjoying her freedom and prosperity. Secure within herself, she asked of her painters only that they paint her likeness. There was nothing too trivial not to be of interest. Subjects unthought-of by Rubens and the Italians now became of first importance to her painters. Adrien Brouwer (1605-1638), a brawling tavern tippler, was fascinated by animated scenes like roisterers in a saloon. Typical is *The Surgeon* (Fig. 457), in which a determined barber dresses the wound of a boy who makes a wry face at the pain.

Brouwer with Adriaen van Ostade and Jan Steen are commonly known as the Little Masters of Holland. Together they explore from varying vantage points the life of the peasantry, the city and country slums, the middle-class manners, and folkways. Brouwer is almost obsessed with pain and violence and brute passion, though his studies are painted with exquisite sensitivity and high technical discipline. Jan Steen (1626-1679) is an inheritor of Bruegel's zest for folk drama, making it more intimate and descriptive. The Dutch masters painted with the frankest literalism the free, pleasure-loving, pub-crawling habits of their people. Their biographers have often made out the artists themselves to be abandoned, wife-beating drunkards, but these legends of dissipation are little substantiated by the frequent longevity of these

painters and above all by the vast quantity and consistently high quality of their craftsmanship, not to mention their artistry.

FIG. 457.—BROUWER. THE SURGEON.

That Jan Steen was a hearty liver, a robust, genial, witty and forthright spirit is indeed the only conclusion to be drawn from his painting
celebrating the festival of *Twelfth Night*. A detail (Fig. 458) reveals
a family feast, that of the painter's own household. Steen and his wife
appear across the table over the shoulder of the central figure. A beaming baby surprised and delighted at having been brought from his bed
to be crowned king of the feast commands our attention if not that of
the diners. Across at the left Steen's daughter is smug and unbending.
Beside her, bedeviled by a clown, is her husband, glum and Puritani-
cal amid the boisterous hubbub. Steen is not the profoundest mind
among the Dutch but he has the liveliest eye. Perhaps more than any
man of his generation he tells of the energy, the spirit and humor of a
violent and lusty society.

While the scientists were analyzing the physical world in order to reduce it to categories and systems in the fields of astronomy, physics and chemistry, the painters were likewise observing and making note of any and every bit of human experience. If some of this popular painting seems trivial, it must be remembered that from this self-observation, from this inquiry into the most intimate aspects of experience, was fashioned the greatest spirit of the age, Rembrandt. It must also be

FIG. 458.—JAN STEEN. TWELFTH NIGHT. Detail. *Private Coll.*

borne in mind that the Dutch were materialists with voracious appetites for hearty worldly pleasure, and as such they supported the painters who could best mirror themselves. Franz Hals (1584-1664) reflects them vividly in portraits of bubbling humor and contagious buoyancy such as the Gypsy Girl and the Laughing Cavalier, which are deservedly popular. In such works as these, Hals broke down for northern painters the formal barrier that remained in Rubens' art as a heritage of the Italian Renaissance, and showed the way to an art of profound human understanding based on sympathy for common mankind.

Protestant Holland was producing a culture in the 17th century which functioned outside the orbit of the Church. Her middle-class citizens had no understanding or taste for the gods of Olympus, being engrossed in military affairs, with commerce and industry. Where Flemish Rubens had found patronage in the Church and in the rich and powerful English lords and Italian dukes who bought his pictures, the Dutch painters found patronage within the middle class. Caravaggio in Italy had also reached this new market with a clever and sensational realism, but the realism of Hals is rather of a different character since it lies not so much in the exploitation of dramatic situations with

Fig. 459.—HALS. The Merry Lute Player. *Thompson Coll., Chicago.*

an arresting spotlight illumination as in building a painterly form through structurally realized passages of light and color. Like that of every painter, his work is uneven in quality. There are many works that have surface showmanship as to both technique and theatrical gestures, but even the obvious bravura of the *Merry Lute Player* (Fig. 459), painted about 1627, is carried off with provocative spirit and gayety. At times Hals was able to approach the heights attained by Rembrandt in his penetration to the very essence of his sitter's personality. Such a painting is the later *Lady Regents of the Hospital* (Fig. 460) of 1664, a group portrait in which the five personalities fuse into a natural harmonious pattern. Each individual is distinctly portrayed, yet each participates in the psychic interplay of personality that is the essence of a group. The dexterity and facility of his brushwork produced effects of refreshing spontaneity. A complex detail is rendered in its totality by a single broad stroke of his brush and the whole amplified in a few accents of color and light that reveal suddenly the whole character of the subject.

Dutch art of the 17th century flowered in profuse response to the needs of a rich and energetic middle-class Protestant society. With Rembrandt van Rijn (1606-1669) Dutch art was crowned with a tower-

FIG. 460.—HALS. THE LADY REGENTS OF THE HOSPITAL.
*Hals Museum, Haarlem.*

ing genius. His name belongs with the few very great: Giotto, Leonardo, Michelangelo, Raphael, Titian and El Greco. In his breadth of interest he spanned the century, revealing every phase of its spiritual and intellectual character; from the realism and materialism of its scientists, its Little Masters in painting, to the mysticism of its saints—everything can be found in the paintings and etchings of this master. No artist ever turned his heart and hand to so great a diversity of subject matter. With the sense of actuality that was born of the analytical and scientific spirit of his age, Rembrandt set about systematically to make himself master of reality in its smallest and most unobserved particles. Characteristically he took for analysis what was closest to him. With the aid of a mirror he sketched, painted and etched his own face repeatedly, not from vanity, for his features were coarse, but to reduce the texture of flesh and hair and the complex pattern of light and color to a schematic arrangement on paper or canvas. Very early he came to a realization of the fact that light was the binding medium that flowed over all visible things and united them as mortar holds together the bricks of a building. And he further observed that the light was something fluid; that it had a rhythm of movement and was endowed with a life of its own more real than that of the objects it casually illuminated. Where Raphael had found the common unifying element of art in the line and Michelangelo in the sculptured mass, Rembrandt, with the Venetians, found it in color and atmosphere.

Early in life, while yet intent upon capturing the exact appearance of things, fitting the details into the fabric of design, he was continually

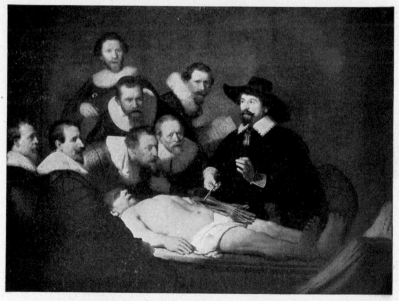

FIG. 461.—REMBRANDT. DR. TULP'S ANATOMY LESSON.
*Mauritshuis, The Hague.*

making essays in the rhythm and flow of light and color. The early landscapes are symphonies of luminous color, harmoniously orchestrated, Wagnerian in their sweeping emotional depths. At times he came close to the border-line of the abstract, to music, in the denial of the literal shape of trees and houses and streams, by abstracting from his subjects the flow and movement of light. This aspect of his development may be traced in a series of group portraits. Commissioned to paint a group of medical students of Dr. Tulp in 1632, he faithfully rendered in the *Anatomy Lesson* (Fig. 461) the scene of the dissection room, with each of the auditors distinctly portrayed as they listen to the argument of the demonstration. A strong light strikes full upon the cadaver and illuminates the face and hands of Dr. Tulp, who is appropriately set off from his students. But one has the feeling that the demands of a factual clear-cut delineation of each face have resulted in a certain artificiality and coldness. The picture represents a series of juxtaposed individuals rather than a lucidly unified group. Eight years later he painted another group portrait, the famous Night Watch in Amsterdam. By this time, Rembrandt had come to feel that the demands of a mere descriptive realism were in conflict with what was for him the greater function of his art: to produce a fully unified vision of light and color playing over the forms.

From a purely technical point of view the Anatomy Lesson must be considered inferior in invention to several group portraits already done by Hals. In the Night Watch of 1642, Rembrandt demonstrated that his genius belonged to an inestimably wider sphere. As a group portrait it was a compromise. The men are portrayed, to be sure, but individual identity is absorbed into the mysteriously poetic world of Rembrandt's invention—his golden *chiaroscuro*. The greatest artists have always transformed their subjects in one way or another. The local, the topical, the isolated character of things and persons is absorbed in a universal order imposed by a superior intuition. A portrait by Titian or Raphael, a landscape by Bruegel or Claude Lorrain bears the imprint less of the person represented or the scene represented than the spirit of the artist who takes purely sensate impressions and gives place and scale to them in the realm of values.

Considered as an example of pictorial style, the Night Watch is a development of the "dark manner" inherited by Rembrandt from Caravaggio's school but developed by him into a method. Earlier he had made many small paintings like the Philosopher with the Winding Stairs in which *chiaroscuro* renders space almost musically eloquent in terms of movement unified in cadence and mood. The Night Watch was an adaptation of this peculiar art language to the exacting requirements of realism in portraiture. The results are mixed. Some twenty years later, in 1662, he had the occasion to make another group portrait called *The Syndics of the Amsterdam Cloth Guild* (Fig. 462). Here five Dutch businessmen with their clerk are engaged in a routine meeting. The unpromising and prosaic material is enlivened and dramatized when Rembrandt invents a trivial episode: the conference is interrupted, the attention is shifted from the work in hand to an unseen visitor. The dark swirling *chiaroscuro* of the Night Watch finds no place here. The darks have become luminously transparent, the space echoes and vibrates with the light. Above all, the artist has become aware of the controlled patterns he had observed in Italian art. He draws the accents of the wainscoting, the horizontals and verticals of chair and table, even the tilt of a collar and hat into a design of the utmost lucidity. The sobriety of the Dutch merchants finds its plastic equivalent in the severity of the structural pattern. But over all is the

Fig. 462.—REMBRANDT. The Syndics of the Cloth Guild.
*Ryks Museum, Amsterdam.*

rich life-giving warmth of the *chiaroscuro* which glows in the smoldering spot of red on the near corner of the table covered with an Oriental rug and penetrates to the farthest reaches of the room. No individual represented is sacrificed to any formal or stylistic requirement. Each is a unique personality and acquires humanity by social relationship.

While Rembrandt's art is Dutch from beginning to end, it was profoundly shaped by his intimate study of the Italian masters. Unlike most baroque painters he had not visited Italy but he knew Italian paintings in Holland and collected them. His drawings, a rich mine for the Rembrandt student, show how he studied the designs of Leonardo's Last Supper to construct his own Sampson's Wedding Feast and the Supper at Emmaus. Frequently these drawings give a keener insight into the master's intentions than do the formal paintings. They are like kernels of thought reduced to a pithy phrase. Many of Rembrandt's drawings, like the *Study of a Nude* (Fig. 463), are perfect plastic organizations. It is like some great line of Shakespeare. The complete crystallization of a pictorial idea, the absolute economy and felicity are proofs of its authorship.

Pictorial reality came to mean to Rembrandt something more than the skillful organization of sense impressions one finds in the work of the Little Masters. More and more he grew to look upon objective real-

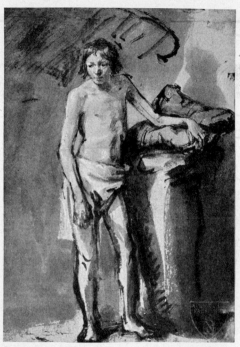

FIG. 463.—REMBRANDT. NUDE FIGURE. Wash Drawing. *Vienna.*

ity as something to be translated into intrinsically expressive rhythms. His later paintings, drawings and etchings offer less and less of illustration and sheer description as he organizes his compositions from within to create drama in space, mass and color; and as a result they possess a peculiarly timeless character. In the *Bathsheba* of 1654, a detail of which is represented (Fig. 464), the figure is no more specifically Dutch than Michelangelo's Jeremiah (Fig. 422) is Italian. In this woman of the Old Testament, Rembrandt suggests every impulse to which the image of woman has ever given expression—the Venus of olden times, the Eve, and the Virgin and Mother of the Middle Ages, the instrument through which from generation to generation the stream of life flows. In the sphere of religious painting Rembrandt produced hundreds of illustrations of the Biblical texts, pictures whose purpose and

FIG. 464.—REMBRANDT. BATHSHEBA. Detail. *Louvre, Paris.*

nature differ from all the devotional altarpieces and decorative murals of the past. In each theme, he presented with consummate understanding its human significance rather than its hieratic or symbolic implications. The story of the *Good Samaritan* (Fig. 465) is dramatized in concrete detail. The Samaritan is seen stopping at nightfall in the court of an inn. While the boys and servants attend to the wounded man, he

FIG. 465.—REMBRANDT: THE GOOD SAMARITAN. *Louvre, Paris.*

confers with the keeper about the care of the unfortunate traveler he has befriended. The story is told for the kernel of compassion that animates the simple Bible tale. Tenderness of the strong for the weak has never been so touchingly portrayed. A glance is sufficient to inform the observer of the whole complex movement. The head of the Samaritan turning to indicate his charge, the inquisitive peering of the boy toward him, the people looking out of the windows—all is so organized that the drama is more pathetically moving than it would be were we to behold the event with our own eyes. The well-head and the rope center attention upon the sick man; the very contours of the architecture assist in the articulation of the drama. It is the qualities of mercy and compassion that are the subject of the painting, abstractions implicit in the behavior of the characters. The greatest of Rembrandt lay in this capacity to reveal in terms of line and color the deepest human experience with authority and conviction.

As an etcher, Rembrandt is unrivaled, and his prints share an equal place with his painting. Etching was an almost unexplored medium when he began, but he made it into a subtle and flexible instrument of expression. He recognized the peculiar scope of the abstract black and white print and never confused its technique with that of painting. It is notable that in his drawings and etchings some of his most intimate observations and experiences are recorded. In well over three hundred plates, Rembrandt left a record not only of his artistic development but of his intimate life. Even more fully than his paintings, they give direct accounts of the artist's appearance, particularly in the early years. His wife Saskia is seen, radiantly happy in the years before her early death in 1642, an occurrence which marks the beginning of tragic years for Rembrandt.

While many of the etchings were produced for an art market, as were the majority of his fashionably finished oil portraits in the 1630's, to a large degree the prints are the artist's most personal works. Many of them have a primitive simplicity and directness in design, for Rembrandt used a kind of pictorial shorthand suggesting infinitely more than he represented. It is no wonder that in the full prime of his life there were few who understood his work, for Rembrandt had left that comfortable and familiar ground of objective description expected of every Dutch artist, to explore the mysteries of the mind. In our time this phase of his art is sometimes called *expressionistic* since the distortion of normal appearance aims at emotional expression beyond any material portrayed. Yet Rembrandt was at the same time a supreme realist with the keenest relish for living things, and delight in the grotesque and the infinite vagaries of nature. In this respect he was in closest kinship with the whole northern tradition. Though he learned much from the Italians, he was never lured, even in his early days, to

court their art modes which he must instinctively have felt were foreign
to his nature. The Italians, pursuing classical ideas, saw the human
figure as an object of all beauty and perfection. Rembrandt saw it as a
part of the larger world, one that included the border-lands of doubt,
tragedy and mystery.

An early etching of 1638, *The Fall of Man* (Fig. 466), suggests his
imaginative range in this medium. The picture sparkles with the con-

*Courtesy the Museum of Fine Arts, Boston*

FIG. 466.—REMBRANDT. THE FALL OF MAN. Etching.

trasts of every shade from black to white. The two innocents are seen
on a hill with a spacious view in which, of all the animals of Paradise,
only an elephant is visible. Enframed by the trees and rocks, the
human figures are the focal point of attention. The subject is one expounded by many masters since mediaeval times, yet Rembrandt gave
it a treatment differing from any of the traditional interpretations. He
saw the theme not so much as an episode in the Christian mythology
but as a study of primitive mentality. The primaeval parents of humanity are not god-like creatures, sole rulers of the world; they are simple and child-like in their ignorance, knowing only their native impulses and the one forbidden act that makes them human. The

psychological differences between man and woman suggested by the Italian masters are here accentuated, Eve all eagerness to devour the fruit and Adam restraining her. This drama of the Fall is reminiscent

Fig. 467.—REMBRANDT. Woman Seated Before a Stove. Etching. *Rosenwald Coll., Jenkintown.*

of Milton's version in *Paradise Lost* (written about the same time) in its deep understanding of human nature.

It is interesting to compare this thoroughly naturalistic treatment of the legend with one of the pre-Romanesque period (Fig. 293). Characteristically, the mediaeval sculptor at Hildesheim related the episode in a series of panels, all of which are required to tell the story fully. The modern artist, while he is no more graphic in representing typical action, is able to condense the episode into a single composition expressive of the complete drama. This condensation was made possible through the complexity of the realistically portrayed setting and the elaborate analysis of human behavior. One becomes aware imaginatively not only of the immediately presented acts but of those that preceded and those that inevitably followed them. This condensation of narrative is possible only when the eye has been disciplined to great subtlety of pictorial representation; it cannot appear in pre-naturalistic art such as the Greek or the Romanesque.

The Fall of Man was made in 1638 when the artist's mode was descriptive and explicit. An etching done twenty years later (1658), *Woman Seated before a Stove* (Fig. 467), reveals quite another side of Rembrandt's personality and of his graphic technique. Linear forms have become solid masses, space is represented by movements of light and dark. There is no narrative or anecdote. The nude is in no way beautiful, but the etching is supremely moving and mysterious. The velvet tones of *chiaroscuro* give some precious relevance to every object. Rembrandt, in the scale of tone between the white of paper and almost total black, has here achieved a drama of wonder and beauty unsurpassed even in his own painting. The mystic dream of a complete and sufficient world is realized in a Dutch interior. The blocking out of interlocking rectangles of light and shapes and the relating of the figure to these rectangles produce compactness, balance and ultimate serenity.

In the person of Jan Vermeer (1632-1675), Holland created a master who painted some of the most beautiful pictures of the century. In his whole career he produced only about forty pictures and these few are almost all alike in plan and subject matter; the *Young Woman with a Water Pitcher* (Fig. 468) of about 1665 is like many of them, a figure—usually a woman—performing some household task, reading or writing letters, or making lace. The figure is seen against a flat wall which is broken by a map or a picture frame and by silhouetted objects in the foreground. Certainly Vermeer was no seeker after novel or startling pictorial effects, but as no one else of his time and very few since, he gave the feel of a spacious room flooded with light. Where Rembrandt had invented his own golden light in his oils and a brooding shadowy world in his late etchings, Vermeer kept a clear palette to evoke the sparkling poetry of his light-flooded interiors.

His method is more linear than that of most baroque masters, but line interacts with color and light so harmoniously and structurally that one is unaware of color or line as such; they are wholly attributes of things. Like Giorgione he takes into account the normal process of seeing and presents in his paintings nothing that deviates from ordinary perception. The result is a high degree of reality. But this sense of realism is obtained by constructing his painting with an eye to the inner logic of light and space patterns, of color harmonies consistent with the space and the light. Vermeer anticipates the screening process of normal vision in subordinating details to the basic psychological theme. With structural handling of color the forms emerge logically and compellingly as having an inner life beyond the surface appear-

Fig. 468.—VERMEER. Young Woman with a Water Pitcher. *Metropolitan Museum, N. Y.*

ance. There is no peep-show illusionism involved, for Vermeer creates a heightened reality not only of light and color but of textures, the weight and density of porcelain, of oriental fabrics, of cool linen, glass and copper. Chardin in France a century later had the same unique gift in this respect though it is doubtful if he ever saw Vermeer's work.

While Vermeer is extraordinarily conscious of the quiet moods of women seen in their unself-conscious household acts he approaches the problem of portraying them through the construction of the enveloping space. Like other baroque painters he finds in *space* an element that may be molded and shaped as artists of another age shaped the dense masses of tangible marble and bronze or simulated those stable masses in their painting. The Renaissance artists seem scarcely aware of space in the sense in which Vermeer or Rembrandt understood it. In Italy only the Venetians, particularly Tintoretto, divined its incalculable possibilities in pictorial design. In the other arts, literature, music, architecture and sculpture—parallel developments occur.

Although the Dutch school of painting was relatively free from any direct influence of the Italian Renaissance, El Greco (1541-1614), the first of the great painters in Spain, was greatly influenced by Italian art. Born a Greek on the island of Crete, he worked in Venice as a young man, under the influence of Titian and Tintoretto, and his early works are quite Venetian in character, being especially linked with Tintoretto's style. In his adopted Spain where he went in 1576 to spend the rest of his life, his manner of painting underwent a radical change. The break-up of the High Renaissance style of Raphael and Titian with its sculpturesque forms, its poise and equilibrium, its static space compositions, appears in the art of Tintoretto; with El Greco, the transition to the baroque style is complete. As in Rubens and Rembrandt, the space patterns are infinitely complex and the dramatic play of light becomes a primary element in their composition. In the *Nativity* (Fig. 469), painted between 1606 and 1608, supernatural light emanating from the Holy Child flashes from object to object like quiet lightning. Its leaping movement is echoed in the ecstatic gestures of the shepherds, who rapturously express their wonder and adoration. Here there is nothing of the sober matter-of-factness of the Dutch, or the grandiose spectacle of Rubens. It is an imaginative translation of a miracle into the articulate language of color, space and movement. The Church, seeking through the Counter-Reformation to maintain its authority, found in El Greco and other baroque artists the means to declare the verities of the miracles that were being discredited by the humanists and the scientists. But a miracle that is merely described in language of color and design is a miracle explained in concrete and rationalized terms and therefore destroyed as an authentic manifestation of the supernatural. The significance of El Greco's art lies in his capacity to employ the rhythms of fluid light, the emotion-arousing color, the nervous tempo of moving bodies. These rhythms he combined in incredibly beautiful arabesques that are to the highest degree symbols of human emotional and spiritual experience.

Like all the baroque masters, El Greco was an acute observer of nature. The elongated forms and the distortions of his later art arose from a knowledge that things have in themselves no meaning until imagination plays upon them, until they are shaped into intelligible communicative patterns. Direct observation and analysis are seen in

FIG. 469.—EL GRECO. THE NATIVITY. *Metropolitan Museum, N. Y.*

the portrait he painted in 1600-1601 of *Cardinal Guevara* (Fig. 470), the prosecutor of the Spanish Inquisition. No master has ever excelled El Greco in the brilliant handling of the intricate lace against the rich luster of silk. But he goes beyond these casual objective facts to observe the nervous gestures of the Cardinal seated on the edge of his chair, the febrile hands that are studiedly idle, the alert erect head. The face is a study in arrested energy. The wide hard mouth is devoid of pity or compassion of any kind;

the cold eyes stare through thick lenses. Ruthless zeal and cruel fanaticism were never so pitilessly laid bare. More than a portrait of an individual, this is a portrait of the Inquisition. As an interpreter of the spiritual history of his time, El Greco is rivaled only by Rembrandt.

The portrait and the landscape are two forms of painting upon which the baroque masters lavished their greatest efforts. At a time when life was being reoriented toward a new naturalistic synthesis, the artist searchingly scanned the human face as though in recognition of the active rôle the individual was assuming in the shaping of his own destiny. In the Middle Ages the portrait was all but unknown, since the individual was looked upon as an insignificant unit of a hierarchy at whose head stood the Deity. In the

FIG. 470.—EL GRECO. CARDINAL GUEVARA.
*Metropolitan Museum, N. Y.*

Renaissance the portrait made its appearance as soon as the individual asserted himself as a creative agent in the moulding of his world. In landscape one finds an objectification of the portrait; that is to say, it becomes a portrait of the artist's personality. Though the minor Dutch masters gave a factual account of its physical features even as they rendered with simple directness the pots and pans of their kitchens, Rembrandt made it a vehicle for his waves of undulating color harmony. The fields and forests of Rubens are as sensuous and living as his female nudes. For each, the actual scene was transformed by the imagination according to what of his own consciousness the painter found reflected in it. Such a landscape is El Greco's *View of*

*Toledo* (Frontispiece) painted late in his life, about 1610. The flashing crest of buildings that follows the rolling hills is silver against deep green shot with black. The sky oppressed with ominous clouds seems bursting explosively with blinding light which transforms the world into nightmare. It is a scene pregnant with some awful foreboding. Actually Toledo is a city of dead gray stone lodged on the bare granite hills, so arid and drenched by the blazing sun that only a few olive trees relieve the stark monotony of its drabness. But through El Greco's eyes it becomes more than a dusty provincial hill town; it is the scene of mystery and passion, light and darkness, growth and decay.

In the older accounts of painting, the name of El Greco is barely mentioned and often omitted because his concept of what is real does not coincide with the usual one of painters. It has even been suggested that his strange visions resulted from defective eyesight. With the appearance of the Post-Impressionists late in the 19th century El Greco has been understood and appreciated for the mystic and seer that he was. Perhaps the failure of people for almost three hundred years to understand Greco's immensely stirring art is to be explained by the appearance in the same century of another Spanish master who, by recording with consummate genius all the intricacies of light and color playing over the forms of nature, was able to achieve to an amazing degree the pictorial naturalism which was for so long the implicit aim of painting in the popular sense. And even if he did little more than this, never has painter shown a greater mastery over the technical means of his art than Velasquez (1599-1660).

Where El Greco saw miracles, the triumph of the Cross, the spiritual agony of Hell and the ecstatic visions of Heaven, Velasquez' sober eye encompassed strolling musicians, beggars, peasants eating their noonday meal of cheese and wine. An aristocratic counterpart of the contemporary Dutch masters, he did not engage in moral, philosophical or religious contemplation. When he painted mythological subjects, such as Apollo appearing at the forge of Vulcan, the theme alone belonged to antiquity; Velasquez attempted only to paint realistically a semi-nude youth standing in a blacksmith's shop addressing a muscular blacksmith. He did not search in the literary past for an interpretation. His religious paintings are but nominally religious, for he was incapable of clothing sacred legends with the imagination of El Greco or the tender humanism of Rembrandt. As empirical as the scientists of his time, he could only paint the visible realities. But that is enough, for no painter ever had his sensibilities of vision, his capacity to see the *nuances* of color and light, and the fluid sequence of space that results from harmonious blending of the forms in atmosphere.

On a visit to Rome in 1650, Velasquez painted a portrait of *Inno-cent* X (Fig. 471). His approach to the subject was not like El Greco's, who set out to reveal the innermost soul of Cardinal Guevara (Fig. 470) through analysis and interpretation. It is as though Velasquez had walked into the presence of the Pope, painted impersonally the image before his eyes and stopped with that. One feels that no judgment has been made, no intervention of a conscious mind between

FIG. 471.—VELASQUEZ. INNOCENT X. *Doria Gallery, Rome.*

the subject and the canvas. One seems to be in the very physical presence of the shrewd and crafty Innocent X. The story that the Pope was displeased with so objective a scrutiny of his countenance may well be credited, for Velasquez recorded not the majesty of the head of Christendom, not the spiritual leader of the Church, but the lowering scowl on a face, and shimmering silk and lace. The texture of the moist skin, the vibrating whites and crimson of the silk, the hand casting a luminous shadow on the white fabric—these are the things that Velasquez painted. But it is apparent that he did not paint scrupulously minute details as the 15th-century Flemish masters did. Fully aware that the eye sees only salient accents, Velasquez painted these accents, leaving the details blurred and rendering them as tone masses. The treatment of the lace is a point in question. A collar or sleeve is represented as a spot of white blending with other spots to form the characteristic pattern made by the ensemble. In such an impressionistic view, all suggestion of the sculpturesque and statuesque is gone. Even the spacing within the frame differs from that em-

FIG. 472.—VELASQUEZ. THE MAIDS OF HONOR. *Prado, Madrid.*

ployed by artists of the previous century. The casual placing of the figure off center, the seemingly accidental exclusion of the lower part of the chair and the figure, give an amplitude to the space and an informal effect that characterizes baroque art wherever it is found. It is from such compositional factors that the freshness and reality of the subject are realized.

In Rome, Velasquez painted his first landscapes. They too are faithful records of sunlight filtering through trees, reducing architecture and figures to a spotty arabesque. For the first time direct observations of the effects of light and atmosphere were made and veraciously recorded in paint. One might easily mistake them for the studies of those specialists in painting sunlight, the Impressionists of 19th century France, but these were random and casual pictures, soon forgotten in the master's absorption in interiors. Realizing the inability of pigment to attain the absolute scale of outdoor light, Velasquez turned to the half and quarter lights, the fugitive tones and silvery shadows that exist in the indirect illumination of interiors. We have observed repeatedly the baroque painters' special predilection for the rendering of space, in Rembrandt, Vermeer, Rubens, El Greco. Velasquez sensed space as something that might be made dynamic and living through the blending of tonal values, i.e., the amount of light or dark in colors. In the *Maids of Honor* (Fig. 472), which was painted in 1656, space becomes deeply expressive. The subject of the painting is so involved as to require some explanation. The King and Queen, just visible in the mirror in the background, look into a room where Velasquez as the official court painter is standing before a huge easel whose straight accent sets the limit of the scene. In the foreground near the painter are various members of the court; a little princess in elaborate costume is attended by two maids from whom the title of the picture is oddly enough derived. Among several others is a dwarf, a pathetic creature kept like a pet animal to amuse and flatter the vanities of the royal household. The room itself is described with mathematical exactness, the rapidly foreshortened wall at the right converging with the rear wall and the ceiling. The pictures, the mirror and the door-frame break up the rear wall into a series of rectangles. The play of atmosphere, the uneven illumination and the variety of colors blended through air and distance exclude any feeling of rigidity or hardness from this cubic frame. The figure of Velasquez himself looks outward into undefined space where imaginatively the spectator stands. The observers (in this case the King and Queen) give reality to that space by being shown in the mirror, thus doubling the distance represented, a device used by Jan van Eyck (Fig. 374). Further elaboration results when the eye, making a sudden leap from the figures close at hand, observes through the open door a series of steps upon which a courtier stands looking back through the tangible space toward the court scene. The spontaneous movement of the figures within this fluid space gives it final verification. The interrelation of lines converging in depth and varying hues of surface make for a closely integrated pattern of the greatest subtlety.

If there is such a thing, Velasquez is the painter's painter. For him the meaning of painting lay in making his scene articulate through observation of continuous patterns of color and light and space. The identification of the object he painted seems almost a by-product of his observation of the continuity of a pattern that embraces all. In this respect he is close to Vermeer, at moments to Rembrandt and especially to Poussin. In certain canvases of these men, the created world is all-sufficient, a microcosm closed and complete, like little worlds in which the tension, the drama and tumult of the actual universe are resolved into the harmonious music of form and color. A conception of unity and harmony, such as that which Christianity had given the world spiritually in the 13th century, obsessed the minds of these baroque masters, who thought to realize a comprehensive unity through rationalistic and intellectual means. In spheres outside of art, it was sought in the moral and aesthetic Neo-Platonism of Shaftesbury in England, in the absolute monarchy of Louis XIV in France, in the philososphical systems of Leibnitz and Spinoza and in the absolutism of the Counter-Reformation and the Jesuit movement. If, indeed, all ages have directly or indirectly searched for the basic harmonies, the ultimate unity of the world, the images of this harmony evolved by the 17th century are peculiarly articulate and complete. No artists in the following centuries succeeded in evolving a synthesis approaching them in universality, except the musicians Bach (so close in spirit to the 17th century) and Beethoven.

All human activity is directed toward some satisfaction or other. A problem is stated in order that its conflicts may be resolved. A dramatist creates complex situations so that he may untangle them to the satisfaction of his audience. Classic art is based upon complete clarification and perfect satisfaction in the solution of moral and intellectual and emotional problems, whether in a Greek tragedy that explains the relation of the gods to men, or a Greek statue embodying the concept of the ideal man. From the time of antiquity on, this concept in art has been a powerful shaping force. In Renaissance Italy, for example, the classic ideal was dominant, particularly in the 16th century when many artists consciously strove to regenerate its expressive idioms.

In the 17th-century baroque period, the classic conception of self-sufficient clarity was largely displaced by ideals of drama, energy and mysticism and by romantic or sensational naturalism. But there is one notable exception in the French master Nicholas Poussin (1594-1665). Of the few truly great creative painters, he has been one of the least known and least understood. Until recent decades, there were hardly any paintings by him even to be seen in this country, yet today many recognize his art as the cornerstone in the structure of modern painting. For the French school he has been, and is, a guiding star, a criterion of integrity. It was not Poussin's weakness but his greatness that caused the Academicians to misinterpret his meaning and prompted them to degrade his principles to the dry rot of a school formula.

When Poussin went in 1624 to Rome, then the art capital of the world, he was thirty years old. Caravaggio was dead, but his style was enjoying an international vogue. Rubens was already a major artistic light. There were choices to be made for a young artist; there was the sensuous and turbulent drama of Rubens, the clever naturalism of Caravaggio and the classic severity of the Graeco-Renaissance style. It is an over-simplification to say that Poussin chose the latter immediately, for his early work is both sensuous and romantic, but it grows increasingly classic with the years. His acceptance of the classic view is made in its broadest terms and not in the easy adoption of formulas. He effected a translation of classic attitudes into the current idiom of baroque art, enriching the formal patterns of antiquity with the light, color and space characteristic of the painting of his century. The poised and serene system of Raphael undergoes revivification, and from the Venetians he learns how sculpturesque figures may be infused with vitality and warmth.

As the Greeks and Romans and High Renaissance masters had rejected everything that was topical, momentary and accidental, Poussin likewise came more and more to dwell upon the ideal, the beautiful, the harmonious. In his work the superficial qualities of the purely charming, picturesque, diverting or sensational were rigorously excluded at a time when these values were the stock-in-trade of most painters. In this respect Poussin was in complete agreement with the principles then being expounded in the French classic drama. Corneille inaugurated an epoch in the theatre with Le Cid (1637), in which the unities of time, place and action were strictly maintained. The force of his drama comes from the passionate assertion that a man is master of his own fate through the exercise of his intellect and the control of his emotions. Here he expressed a sentiment which is but an elaboration of the implication of Greek tragedy.

Undoubtedly Poussin took this moral view for himself and his art. As an artist he severely subjected his work to the judgment of his intellect, leaving nothing to chance. Impulse and emotion are under rigid control. His work never reflects a fleeting impression or a transitory feeling, for he felt that behind the casual surface appearance there was some larger order, some reality that must be divined more by the mind than by the first impulsive response of emotion. This rationalistic attitude is the exact opposite of impressionism, romanticism or realism. Poussin saw these principles carried out in the austere, orderly and unified art of the Renaissance. They are expressed in his *Holy Family* of *ca.* 1651 (Fig. 473). To a casual observer the painting looks not unlike a Raphael or the work of some other Renaissance master, but closer observation will bring to light a wholly different scheme of plastic organization of space and line in the off-center wall fragment

FIG. 473.—POUSSIN. THE HOLY FAMILY. *Sachs Coll., Cambridge.*

with the landscape that balances it. Above all, Poussin brings to bear a rich and organically integrated space pattern in the arrangement of figures and in the landscape. The group while organized internally in a left-to-right orientation (classic order) has also its regular space-in-depth movement (baroque order). The landscape has the measured cadence of the figures with a transparent film of air softening and enveloping its cubes and planes. Everything—to the remotest tower, the reflections in the water—has a specific and characteristic shape. Corot in the 19th century will paint similar landscapes and Cézanne will consciously undertake to give his paintings the structure and logic of Poussin.

For insight into the formation of Poussin's grand formal periods, one can look to his drawings. In these preparatory sketches are found realistic studies of emotion and drama reminiscent of Rembrandt or Daumier. But these animated drawings are only observations of nature, useful studies in preparation for the formal structure of the paintings in which the incisive, direct, psychological thrust is sublimated to the level of deliberate rhetoric. An analogy may be made between Poussin's mode of painting and the style of an actor's delivery. An actor does not buy a Pullman ticket with the same studied voice and gesture that he uses in speaking his lines on the stage. There he seeks to project himself and the content of his lines in a sustained *illusion* of reality that is not an imitation of actuality but a formal recreation of a situation. Poussin consciously raised everything he painted to the level of the characteristic, the typical, as Corneille and Racine did in the French theater. The landscape of *St. John on Patmos* (Fig. 474) is not *a* landscape but *the* landscape. Space and mass, the enduring and universal elements of *all* landscapes, are subjected to clarification in rhythmic patterns. All accidental, atypical or casual features of the scene are scrupulously removed from his design so that the central conception is sustained and heightened.

This classic concept of art is as valid as any other so long as it is infused with the fire and passion of a great spirit. Like all significant ideas it was seized upon by men incapable of understanding it. Charles le Brun institutionalized it in the establishment of the French Academy of Painting in 1648. Rules were set up governing subject matter and ways of painting; exact methods were taught on the assumption that a painter need only follow prescribed methods to make himself an artist. For a couple of hundred years, the academies dominated much of the art-thinking of Europe, particularly in France; and to hundreds of painters art was only a skill, a vehicle for pedantic display of learning, until the term *academic* became synonymous with sterility. At best the Academy produced a kind of pompous historical portrait and a grandiose scheme of decoration. But the history of art was to be made by the men who submitted to a discipline infinitely more exacting than the pedagogical rules of the classroom; the discipline of creation. Poussin was himself no academician even though the Academy deified him. The school saw only his outward conformity to the ideas of antiquity; they failed to observe that the master was one of the great colorists and landscapists. They shut their eyes to the original and creative side of his art and slavishly confined themselves to its least significant aspects—classicizing subjects of allegorical character, interpreting them in a linear and colorless style of the utmost monotony.

Poussin's friend and fellow expatriate in Rome was Claude Lorrain

(1600-1682); together they form the background of all French paint-ing since the 17th century. Of the two, Poussin was the scholar, the intellectual and philosopher. Claude Lorrain was none of these; rather he was the lyric poet of nature, with a rare gift for land-scape painting. The tiniest fragment of a Roman sculpture, a broken Corinthian capital, was of the most vital interest to Poussin, but the things that took the eye of Claude were the direct experiences of nature, the light from the river, the wan lemon hues of early dawn, and dissolving foliage against the light. Simple in taste, he was indiffer-ent to heroic striving for absolutes. While Poussin was engrossed in the art and literature of antiquity, Lorrain was cultivating the friend-ship of certain Dutch and German landscape painters living in Rome, for landscape was the only subject that interested him. In certain ex-ternals, his pictures are like Poussin's in their largeness of view in-volving grand vistas, picturesque ancient ruins, and, incidentally, figures of Biblical or classical derivation. Claude himself cared nothing for the figures, but tradition demanded some element of narration or edifying drama so he dutifully tucked into his compositions a few harmless shepherds or Biblical persons, calling this landscape a Flight into Egypt and that the Marriage of Isaac and Rebecca. He thought little of these incidentals and used to say, "I give my figures away but I sell my landscapes," and often enough he permitted a hack assistant to paint them into his finished scene. For Poussin, such a procedure would have utterly destroyed the underlying significance of his grand architectonic design. Yet Lorrain's landscapes have some-thing of the same balanced organization of Poussin's, with a formality that has given rise to the term *heroic landscape* to distinguish them from the intimate landscapes representing fragments of meadow or forest such as were painted by the Barbizon school in 19th-century France.

Claude builds up his scene usually according to an established for-mula consisting in a rather detailed foreground flanked at the sides by imposing masses of trees, through which one looks into deep luminous distance. The movement of the light emanating from the opaque sky, caressing the hills, gleaming from water and piercing the foliage of the trees is the life of these landscapes. Where Poussin's are static and classical, Lorrain's are more romantic with their appeal to the emotions by movement and warm colors. Lorrain adhered only nominally to the classic principles of order and balance, but to the extent that this discipline has been felt, it gives special point to the emotive elements of color and movement.

The theme he liked most to paint is found in a *Harbor Scene* (Fig. 475) painted *ca.* 1646. A simple bit of analysis will indicate how greatly

Lorrain was indebted to Poussin for the compositional elements of
his pictures. If lines are drawn from opposite corners of this painting,
it will be seen that the composition falls into four triangles. The triangles converge at a point far in the central distance, effecting a
pyramid of space, the apex of which is the source of illumination. The
rising sun acts as a magnet toward which the trees bend and the very
architecture inclines. If the lines of the cornice, the balustrade and

Fig. 475. CLAUDE LORRAIN. Harbor Scene. *Louvre, Paris.*

even the accents in the pavement be projected, they will terminate in
the golden light that flows back, tipping the crest of the ripples and
rounding the smooth columns of the temples. Lorrain had no philosophical understanding of the classic tradition but he used it with tact
and intelligence as an instrument to express a pantheistic naturalism.
Deriving his experience from a continuous contact with nature, he
reduced his impressions to patterns so lyrically expressive of its inner
life as to rival the subtlest design of the Chinese masters. His freest
and most spontaneous statements are found in his drawings (Fig. 476).
In these he felt no need to repress the fleeting experience of the moment. The dense mass of the foliage whitened by the sun, the movement of wind circulating through the plumed branches—such ob-

servations will be cherished in times to come by the romantic landscape painters of the 19th century. In his finished paintings, Lorrain suppressed this dramatic activity of the landscape, searching as Poussin

FIG. 476.—CLAUDE LORRAIN. LANDSCAPE. Wash Drawing.
*Louvre, Paris.*

did for the larger, more inclusive, architectonic pattern. As an intuitive poet of nature, he had no equal in European landscape painting of his time; his influence upon Watteau and Corot in France, upon Turner in England and nearly every subsequent landscapist is incalculable.

# Chapter XXIX. Painting in the Eighteenth Century.

*THE ESTABLISHMENT OF THE FRENCH ACADEMY IN* the 17th century was an authoritarian act of a monarchical system. The monopoly of art education established by the state and maintained by subsidy fostered an official style that was correct and accomplished but spiritually bankrupt. Those 18th-century masters operating outside the Academy or only on its borders are the ones who were ultimately recognized as the living spirits of the age, and a somewhat similar situation prevailed through the 19th century. For the Academy had promulgated a conception of the absolute validity of classic art, i.e., it had thought to find models in Greek, Roman and Italian Renaissance styles that could guide the modern artist, and in thus closing by precept the eyes and minds of its adherents to the vital springs of immediate experience, it condemned their work to polished sterility even before it was started.

But the first great French painter to emerge in the 18th century, Antoine Watteau (1683-1721), found the bases for his art in Rubens rather than the ancients or the Italian Renaissance masters or even in Poussin. He came from a Flemish province that was annexed by France shortly after his birth, and because he was the first great French painter in modern times to develop within the boundaries of his own country, he is called the founder of the French school. Deprived of the benefits of official recognition, he lived in poverty, conscious of the artificial world of play-acting in the time of Louis XV to which he did not belong. Polite society, constrained under the monarchy and regency to the ritual and routine of absolutism, based its pleasures, its fashions and manners on the artificial life established by the Court. The masked ball, the company of Italian players, the garden party, appear again and again in Watteau's canvases as with detached air he observes the gay company making love and music as though these were the end of all desire. A society isolated by a government that reduced human intercourse through its fixed mechanism to a game of intrigue and strategy found its expression in every form of graceful amorous play. Wealth and power, concentrated at the Court and spreading to the thin layer of the privileged few who lived through its favors, created a society founded on leisure and elegance. The divertissement of this aristocratic society Watteau took for his special subject.

The theme of festive love-making had engaged the imagination of northern artists from mediaeval times. It is found in early German woodcuts and engravings. Dürer had represented the lusty dance of the peasant; Bruegel had painted the wedding party (cf. Fig. 451), the Kermesse of village folk. Rubens particularly had often been absorbed by the wild orgy of the Dionysiac revel through which he expressed the passions of men and women drunk with wine and lust. Even Poussin had repeatedly painted the subject of the drunken feast of Bacchus with penetrating insight into its significance as a symbol of renewal. But Watteau, unlike the classicist Poussin, went to the Fleming

Fig. 477.—WATTEAU. Embarkation for the Island of Cythera. *Palace, Potsdam.*

Rubens, to his dynamic life rhythms, his inexpressibly living orchestrations of color. He made dozens of drawings from Rubens' pictures and learned from them not only the secret of their vital patterns of movement but also something of the great 17th-century master's marvelously decorative color. Watteau's greatest painting, the *Embarkation for the Island of Cythera* (Fig. 477), executed about 1718, was directly inspired by such paintings of Rubens as the Garden of Love (Fig. 454). The refinement of love in this treatment of the theme by Rubens appealed to the sensibilities of Watteau, as it more nearly approximated the languorous festivals of his age than the violent frenzy of the Bacchic dance usually portrayed by the Flemish painter. The robust types of Rubens were changed by Watteau to slight graceful French forms and the mood is more wistful, but the fanciful setting is similar, with the scented atmosphere of the park opening into the depths of a misty expanse. The winged loves and the garden sculpture of the Venus as the presiding deity of the festival appear in both. But Watteau refined the gleaming silks, made the passage from color to color more subtle, the movements more graceful and harmonious. His festival of love belongs wholly to the dream world of the imagination, whereas Rubens' touches actuality in the veracious portraits, the solid tangible baroque architecture and the substantiality of a hundred realistic details. The episode Watteau illustrated—the departure of the felicitous ones for the island of eternal love—is itself a fantasy, a dream. Lovers are fleeing from the constraints of the real world in a golden barque with gauzy sails into the pearly mists. The winged cherubs urge the reluctant or swing in flowery circles about the golden mast. All movement is from the shady grove where lovers sit, toward the gleaming promise of bliss. They move as in a dance through varying stages from reluctant hesitation in the seated figures to acquiescence in the rising ones, culminating in the languid anticipation of the pair moving down the path. Though lovers, barque and landscape are spun of the imagination, the mood of yearning that is evoked is none the less real.

No master in all 18th-century art painted with greater feeling for delicate *nuances* of color and line than Watteau. His drawings (Fig. 478) give clues to his introspective vision. The turn of a head, the resting arm or the tilt of a hat sets in motion other forms as the break of still water creates a shimmering surface in a quiet pool. Every stroke of brush or crayon brings to life the forms in liquid silver and light. Like Rubens before him he learns how every object implies movement. Most rococo art is far removed from the heroic mood of the 17th century, for where the baroque is epic, the rococo is lyric. A Poussin or a Rubens encompasses a vision of the vast world in which man is a heroic actor; Watteau constructs no such large drama but is content with a song, a melody at once witty, lovely and melancholy.

Although the French Academy admitted Watteau to its ranks only in a special and inferior category, his style was to dominate the century. The superb decorative element in his painting, more particularly his use of color, set a precedent that prevailed among his successors like

Fragonard and Boucher. J. H. Fragonard (1732-1806) was a creature of his age and of a particular social stratum of 18th-century France, but because he did not project himself beyond that era he is all the more valuable as a representative of it. His *Lover Crowned* (Fig. 479), of *ca.* 1773, has qualities which are found in most works of the 18th century such as costumes, architecture (cf. Figs. 167, 168), music and

FIG. 478.—WATTEAU. STUDY OF FIGURES. Drawing. *Louvre, Paris.*

literature. These qualities are grace, charm, delicacy and a sprightly energy which is at once disciplined and wayward.

One might assume that Fragonard represented a hedonistic society dedicated to pleasure, and so he does. The privileged few of a monarchical system (as in France) or a landed gentry (as in England) exercise their last perquisites before political and industrial revolutions. But in that interlude artists create exquisite things. Artificiality becomes a norm. The landscape of Fragonard's painting is the cultivated grounds of a palace with its ornamental sculptures and boxed orange trees, the light that glows among the trees is a theatrical glow of warm mixed colors, the air is perfumed. Even the drama of love is not real but play-acting: a tableau contrived ostensibly for the exquisitely costumed painter making a sketch. The swirling manner of Rubens and the color of Venice are transformed in gayety and brilliance. Such talent abounded in Europe of the 18th century in the early work of Goya in Spain, of Gainsborough and Hogarth in England and

Tiepolo and Canaletto in Italy. This tradition of decorative art in its flexibility, its lightness and drama was an extension and a variation of basic elements in baroque art. Its influence has been felt in all decorative arts calling for fantasy and sheer ornament and many modern painters, notably Renoir (Fig. 508), have found sources of enrichment in the tradition.

*Copyright, Frick Coll.*

Fig. 479.—FRAGONARD. The Lover Crowned. *Frick Coll.*, N. Y.

Watteau and Fragonard had derived their styles from Flanders and Venice by modifying and gallicizing Rubens. J. B. Chardin (1699-1779), the third important French master of the 18th century, drew similarly from 17th-century Dutch genre painters. His bourgeois life knew nothing of the cosmopolitan wit and sophistication of Fragonard. Following the example of the Dutch, he painted only the most familiar objects—bunches of vegetables on a table, intimate homely utensils of his own narrow kitchen. An honest craftsman, he painted slowly and with scrupulous application. For Chardin, realities were the things he could touch and taste and smell—a bun beside a sugar bowl, a bottle of wine—and to these he brought a feeling for their familiar qualities and a sensibility quick to appreciate the moist flaky crust of pastry, the hard glaze of the porcelain bowl, the bloom of the fruit. With sober and naïve eye, he saw the texture of common things, the slime of the newly caught fish, the transparent luster of a

*Courtesy the Art Institute, Chicago*

FIG. 480.—CHARDIN. STILL-LIFE. *Art Institute, Chicago.*

bowl of eggs ready for the beating ladle, the pearly gleam of onions (Fig. 480). The atmosphere that surrounds his inanimate objects vibrates with reflected light so that at a distance a single unified vision arises like the effect of a direct experience of the eye. Nor is there any trick of illusionism involved, since no literal representation how-ever skillful can make one feel the inner radiance, the essential qualities of objects as Chardin does.

With the same powers of observation for people, he caught the in-tense absorption of children spinning their tops or making a *House of Cards* (Fig. 481), the child saying grace with scarcely restrained haste while the mother watches with tolerant humor; all these he

painted with marvelous insight into the atmosphere of sentiment that
gives each scene its special flavor. A painter who found such a wealth
of intimate experience of people and things everywhere close at hand
had no need for posturing models. His subjects were the kitchen table
with pots and bottles, and his wife and children, and they were
enough because they were the known realities of his world of sense
and sentiment. The market woman stepping into the kitchen with

FIG. 481.—CHARDIN. THE HOUSE OF CARDS.
*National Gallery, Washington, D. C.*

her burden of fragrant newly baked bread with its powdery crust,
the sack of provisions containing a chicken for the Sunday dinner, was
a subject to produce from him a design of space and light that becomes
a coherent pattern of thought and feeling. Light enters into Chardin's
color in somewhat the same way it does in that of Velasquez and
Vermeer, giving buoyancy and even body to his forms. The organization of his pictures is so subtle in arrangement of balanced masses,
and in the integration of space and color in an harmonious design, that
one associates him with the greatest masters of pictorial art.

In a century characterized by the domination of the intellect over the total experience of mind and body, Chardin stands as one who integrated and oriented his life with sureness and finality. While philosophic and legalistic minds were desperately striving to attain a balanced and articulate conception of life through juggling philosophical abstractions of the religious life, the natural man, reason and law, Chardin was unobtrusively attaining a synthesis without recourse to top-heavy intellectualizations. Unconsciously he represents the spiritual forces of the submerged middle class that was soon to destroy the machinery of the monarchy which was proving inadequate to administer the affairs of the nation; its fall in 1789 was to have profound reverberations in the development of French art.

Watteau's art is the highest expression of an age which sees the formal pictorial ideas inherited from the 17th century employed with increasingly brilliant results for decorative purposes. In Spain, Italy, the Netherlands, wherever painting is found there emerges a style which is of notable charm and frequently of great beauty. In England the mode was that imported through the painting of van Dyck a century before. The English with no active native tradition in the plastic arts had from time to time given patronage to foreign painters like Holbein, Rubens and van Dyck, and from the latter Gainsborough and Reynolds developed in the 18th century. In this age English art becomes more and more the expression of a political and economic class, and Thomas Gainsborough (1727-1788) is shaped as a painter by the local considerations of the aristocracy. Protesting his chief interest in landscape, he nevertheless must be regarded primarily as a creator of portraits for the wealthy. In these he records with superb taste, if not with notable originality, the elegance and loveliness of the noble folk. The *Honorable Mrs. Graham* (Fig. 482), painted in 1775, is characteristic of Gainsborough's peculiar skill in setting forth the pride and charm of woman in a still semi-feudal society. This type of decorative painting is well represented in America by his Blue Boy, now in the Huntington Collection in California.

The costumes of the 18th century reflected the attitude of the period. The wig powdered and elaborately arranged, the voluminous folds of lace and rich stuffs indicate a love of decoration, a frank acceptance of an aesthetic of form. Nature was something to arrange in tasteful patterns. A studied artificiality is the ideal. The landscape of the Graham portrait is a bit of stage property as is the classic pedestal upon which rests her fragile arm. In painting, the piquant, the picturesque and poetic values are sought and, too often, the pretty and sentimental as well. Only William Hogarth (1697-1762) preserves

some more convincing contact with reality. He is the greatest of the
English painters of his time, and his art has something of the earthy
vigor of English literature. A comparison of his Mary Edwards, in the
Frick collection in New York, with a Gainsborough portrait will readily
show his greater mastery of structure, his deeper conception of human
values.

FIG. 482.—GAINSBOROUGH. MRS. GRAHAM.
*National Gallery of Scotland, Edinburgh.*

In England as in France a great deal of art was watered down to
the level of a luxury adornment for the rich, but the healthy vigor
of Chardin's and Hogarth's art is indicative of the new forces being
exerted in European society. The 18th-century English writer Richardson invented the novel as an art form in which to write sympathetically
about the lives of common people, thereby marking an epoch in the
history of English letters. In painting, Hogarth undertook a critical
comment on the life and manners of English society from the point
of view of the discreet common man. Where Gainsborough portrayed
only the exotically beautiful and the picturesque, Hogarth forthrightly

employs a humorous and didactic art to reveal the evils in the various social levels of English life. In *Marriage à la Mode*, a series of paintings that were reproduced in engraving and widely circulated, he tells a lively story of the degradation of marriage in the aristocracy. English life was split between the great landholding gentry and the degraded gin-drinking rabble, to the corruption of both classes. As a journalist, but one with immense talents, Hogarth reports the chaos in English society, using the

FIG. 483.—HOGARTH. THE COUNTESS' DRESSING ROOM.
*National Gallery, London.*

medium of the copper engraving to broadcast his moral dramas, such as A Rake's Progress and A Harlot's Progress. From *Marriage à la Mode*, which was executed about 1740, comes *The Countess' Dressing Room* (Fig. 483), describing the distractions by which a faithless wife seeks relief from boredom in a loveless union. The vacuous faces of the characters indulging in the fashionable amusements of the day are recorded with explicit realism. The character of Hogarth's moral fervor is revealed in his inclusion of two pictures by Italian mannerists on the walls, the implication being that such pictures were only further manifestation of debased morals. Art is now taking on the function of criticism and becoming an instrument of social reform. Like a dramatist, the painter realistically proclaims the message of reformer and moralist. His method

is frankly that of the theatre, to entertain with wit, satire and irony
while he preached. Bernard Shaw in our time does the same thing
in his plays.

Hogarth's lusty use of art was so original and unprecedented that
"right-thinking" people condemned him, but the English public took
him to their hearts. The cheap engravings of his work made for great
popularity, and in thus using the graphic processes he was reviving
the means to reach a large public as Dürer and Rembrandt had done
before him and as Goya and Daumier were to do later. Purists may
cavil at his mixture of drama, illustration and didacticism, but he proves
again that the house of art has many mansions and that no narrow
theory of art can long confine a vigorous spirit.

In France the sentimental philosophy of Rousseau found a powerful

Fig. 484.—GREUZE. The Village Bride. *Louvre, Paris.*

champion in the critic Diderot, who believed that painting should be
a kind of graphic literature illustrating moral issues. If the picture
was in addition beautiful, so much the better, but the chief value
lay in the moral that it contained. Diderot found his ideal painter
in Jean Baptiste Greuze (1725-1805), the painter of the "picture that
tells a story." With syrupy sentiment, he extolled the natural good-
ness of rustics in detailed dramatic pieces like *The Village Bride* (Fig.

484) of 1761. The fine sentiments of Chardin were broadened by Greuze to the most obvious banality. The domestic virtues of the villagers are laid on with conscious bathos. The overwhelming popularity of such mawkish, anecdotal painting can be understood only in view of the hunger of a public starved by the trivialities and insincerities of the fashionable painters who in their own way were just as far removed from reality as Greuze. He appeared to be a spokesman for the inarticulate mass of people that had never been reached by the suggestive and titillating art of Fragonard and Boucher. In the languorous, half-depraved pretty milkmaids and shepherdesses of Greuze, there was just enough of the voluptuousness of the old art to make them intelligible to all, together with a flattering and obvious morality that met the current demands of popular sentiment. With the Revolution of 1789, his false and ambiguous position was recognized and along with Fragonard and all the aristocratic artists of the century he was discredited.

When the French Revolution liquidated the whole class that had dominated the culture of the 18th century, the style of art changed as radically as the style of government. From the beginning of the century Watteau had developed the baroque language of Rubens, giving greater expression to atmosphere and evolving a freer arrangement with figures of decreased size to produce a more expansive pattern of light and space. Fragonard had gone even further in his decorative treatment of color and forms. Chardin, Boucher and Greuze had turned more and more toward the inspiration of the Dutch and Flemish masters of the 17th century. A vigorous tradition of landscape painting among minor painters had flourished during the century, deriving largely from the Netherlands.

Then just before the Revolution of 1789 there appeared a man fresh from the Roman Academy who ultimately became the art dictator of France. As a winner of a *Prix de Rome*, Jacques Louis David (1748-1825) had submitted to the classical training of the Academy. His style had been formed on the models of Poussin, Florentine painting of the High Renaissance and classical sculpture, for no influence of Chardin or Watteau was permitted to taint the minds of students isolated by the iron-bound routine of the Academy. David brought to Paris in 1784 one of those elaborate machines promoted by the Academy, a ponderous composition involving a classical subject with sculpturesque figures. Had the *Oath of the Horatii* (Fig. 485) been brought to light at any other time, it would have caused no particular stir, but coming as it did into a revolutionary atmosphere it was hailed as a symbol fraught with iconoclastic implications of stalwart republican virtues. The three sons of Horatius, in a triple accent of extended arms, swear to their father to come home with their shields or upon them. Here, it was felt, was a simple expressive style dealing with heroic social qualities and free from the gauzy fripperies of the hated aristocratic art. As the art of antiquity had been closely integrated with the state, so now it became a servant of the Revolution and, under the consulship of Napoleon, David became the official state painter.

FIG. 485.—DAVID. THE OATH OF THE HORATII. *Louvre, Paris.*

The ordinary processes of development in painting were brought to a sudden halt by the establishment of David's style as the dominant mode of expression. The Oath of the Horatii is cold to the point of frigidity, the dull colors are monotonous and inert, and the light serves only to round the rigid and lifeless contours. The arrangement of the figures against an architectural background, their planiform spacing in a monumental order are descriptively reminiscent of the Florentine and Roman painting of the High Renaissance and were taken intact from the severely unified stage-sets of the classical French theatre. So intent was the painstaking David upon rhetorical anecdote that he disregarded the lessons he might have learned from the baroque painters in the treatment of atmosphere of color and movement. He designates each stone in the pavement, every sandal strap, with exactitude. The garment folds seem literal transcriptions of sculptural forms. This very minuteness and clarity made his art more acceptable to a military caste that required a symbol of itself dignified by history and legend. Similarly in our own country classical forms were borrowed at this time for public buildings and sculpture (cf. Fig. 188) to give official dignity to a government that had not yet developed its own organic symbol. As a propagandizing agency, art is unquestionably of great value. It

Fig. 486.—DAVID. Mme. Hamelin.
*National Gallery, Washington, D. C.*

had been an instrument of the Church in early times and more recently of the Counter-Reformation, and now at the end of the eighteenth century and the beginning of the nineteenth it gave voice to the authority of the new French nation. Yet this use of art was at the expense of its larger function of interpreting life as a whole. Art in totalitarian Germany under Hitler has been somewhat similarly an authoritarian expression of a political party. The party has encouraged a revival of an outgrown style to advance national and political ideas.

The best work of David was done when he was unconstrained by the exacting requirements of his official duties of glorifying the exploits of Napoleon. In the sphere of portraiture, he produced many fine character studies, among them the portrait of *Madame Hamelin*, painted in 1800 and now in the Chester Dale collection in the National Gallery in Washington (Fig. 486). The harsh and urgent rhetoric of the historical paintings finds no place in this most harmonious study. With rarest discrimination David plays off the flowing lines of the figure and the drapery against the rectangular shapes of the picture frame and the furniture. The theme is regarded as a problem in ideal harmony to be achieved through the reconciliation of verticals and horizontals in an integrated structure. While the effect is one of complete naturalness, it is clear that the master has subjugated every detail to the creation of harmonious interaction of lines and forms. Even the color so often handled by David with scant regard is here sympathetically related to the cool and deliberate pattern. In such works David justifies his method and his leadership.

In his severe simplicity, in his adherence to the classical or Neo-classical ideals David is no isolated phenomenon. His age is that of the Greek Revival in architecture, the Neo-classic ideal in sculpture as seen in his Italian contemporary Canova (Fig. 339), whose marble portrait of Pauline Borghese is in style almost an exact counterpart of David's Madam Recamier. Europe and America respond to the same impulses as they seek once again to derive sustenance from the classic tradition. For the art of the new century, David broke with a single stroke the prestige of an art that had become soft and expressive only of a decadent society, replacing it with one which while anachronistic was pregnant with moral idealism.

# Chapter XXX. Painting in the Nineteenth Century

## A. The Neo-classic School

*DAVID'S CAREER PARALLELS THAT OF NAPOLEON FOR*
he rose with the Emperor and went into banishment when he did.
The school of art which he fostered produced no great masters except
Ingres, however, and the romantic impulse, finding its most universal
expression in Napoleon, generated new and revolutionary tendencies
among David's immediate pupils. One figure of great talent was
Prudhon, whose contact with Italian art was different from David's.
Under the influence of Correggio and Leonardo he exhibited none of
the hardness of the official school in paintings of subtle and vaporous
colorism blended with nervously sensitive drawing. A poet of rare
sentiment, he retained something of the lyrical beauty of the 18th
century masters who were eclipsed by the Revolution.

The real successor of David was his pupil Jean Auguste Dominique
Ingres (1780-1867). Though both adhered to the classic tradition of
noble sentiment and sculpturesque figure compositions, Ingres revealed
considerably more flexibility in his drawing. His enthusiasm for severe
Roman types was modified by a great sensitivity for the lucid rhythms
of Greek art, particularly those that appear in vase painting, and he
admired and studied as well the Italian primitives, the work of Giotto
and the 15th-century masters. In accordance with the academic conception of the classical tradition known as Neo-classicism he conceived of painting in terms of drawing and asserted that if a picture
was well drawn it was well enough painted. His remarkable drawings
are extremely sensitive and vigorous but his color is indifferent, being
often dry and lifeless. Like David, he conceived grand decorative compositions. A ceiling decoration in the Louvre is characteristic of his
more ambitious style which he modeled after Raphael. The Apotheosis
of Homer, one of his best-known works, is learned and cold with its
symbolism of the Parthenon, before which is enthroned an heroic
Homer accompanied by the great artists and writers of ancient and

modern times. With little talent for unifying large spaces, Ingres was still a master of single figures; and several details, namely, the allegorical Iliad and some of the portraits, are vigorously executed.

But in his more intimate portraits Ingres exhibits a great sensitivity for personality and a fine feeling for the pattern of line with which

Fig. 487.—INGRES. GRANET. *Museum, Aix-en-Provence.*

the figure is created. His portrait of M. Bertin in the Louvre is one of the finest of the century. In it he obtains not only an arresting likeness but one that is typical of the whole class to which the model belongs. The precision of the Neo-classic linear style is admirably adapted

FIG. 488.—INGRES. ODALISQUE. Metropolitan Museum, N. Y.

to the requirements of portraiture. With it the likeness may be made gratifyingly concrete; forms may be given definition and finish. However much Ingres relied upon the discipline of Raphael, the salient fact must be recognized that he was able to turn the method to creative ends of his own in interpreting the personality of his epoch. His portrait of *Granet* (Fig. 487), painted while in Rome in 1807, follows the scheme Raphael used in his portrait of Cardinal Inghirami (Fig. 428) in the firm and sensitive line, the geometric function of accessories: the

FIG. 489.—INGRES. THE STAMATY FAMILY. Drawing. *Louvre, Paris.*

book, the balustrade and the solidly constructed Roman buildings in the landscape. Though the Renaissance method is employed, the personality which emerges is that of the youthful hero. Here is a romantic interpretation characteristic of a basically romantic age.

There are moments when Ingres' theories betray him beyond his capacities and there are figure compositions like his celebrated *La Source* which suggest vanity in his attempt to rival the sublimities of Greek art. His constant endeavor to "correct nature" will at times lead him into a betrayal of nature. Thus *La Source* inclines to prettiness and suavity where nobility and drama of form are intended. In his best work, by which of course one must judge his talents, one finds the austerity of a noble mind. No over-sweetness or sentimentality mars the *Odalisque* of 1858 in the Metropolitan Museum, New York (Fig. 488). The exotic subject is realized in a tense and lyrical linear design which makes it one of the great modern studies of the nude. A discriminating musician, he raises the drama of his paintings to that level of tension called concert pitch. One senses in his work a musical strain in the flowing cadence of line.

To augment a dwindling income during his long residence in Italy, Ingres sometimes made rapid pencil portraits. Anyone but he might regard these casual commissions as boring commercial assignments to be got over as painlessly as possible; one of them, *The Stamaty Family* (Fig. 489), which is dated 1818, proves the integrity of his art. The deft silvery pattern with which he draws together the individual members of his family group indicates the art of a man who in his least tasks regards his work as a sacred calling. Perhaps it is this all-absorbing seriousness, this fanatical dedication of his life, which accounts for the high level of his work and too for the occasional lapses in judgment. His lapses are great ones but when they occur they are not the failings of faintness or compromise.

## B. THE ROMANTIC SCHOOL

No one who has experienced the art of Titian, Velasquez, Rembrandt and Rubens can imagine that the theory behind Neo-classicism could long be honored. Only the die-hards of the Academy, those entrenched in the advantages of wealth and position, long continued to take its dictates seriously. Ingres stood off the rising tide of individualism which he felt to be a destroyer of a true art. He lived to 1867, long enough to witness many strong and able men dedicated to a principle called Romanticism. No pat definition of the term entirely adapts itself to the ramifications of acknowledged Romantic art. In general Romanticism is a renewal of Renaissance individualism. The Neo-classic masters had from late in the 18th century held that the artist should subordinate his personal feelings to an ethical ideal expressed in classical forms, and when Ingres and David portrayed the Emperor Napoleon, their paintings expressed the supreme ideal for which in their eyes the Emperor stood. He was serene, noble, godlike—in short, a hero. Likewise in their portraits of less exalted persons their objective was the *type* rather than the individual. None of their portraits could be described as naturalistic studies of character. Much of their validity as painters lies in their power to express universal humanity in the types they present.

The Romantics in the arts of literature and music—Victor Hugo, Wordsworth, Byron, Beethoven, Berlioz, Wagner and, among painters, Delacroix, Corot, Constable—are men who found the old rules of art inadequate for their uses. How could Beethoven have conveyed his feeling expressed in the Eroica in the musical idiom of Mozart? No more could Wordsworth have expressed his understanding of nature and freedom in the classical couplets of Pope.

Freedom was the battle cry of the young spirits of the early 19th century—Liberty, Equality and Fraternity was the slogan of the French Revolution when the French middle class broke the antiquated political forms of the monarchy. In all phases of life European society was experiencing a demand for a fresh interpretation of man and nature, a new realization of itself. Neo-classicism was a belated attempt to apply reason and the authority of ancient art ideals to the modern scene. Jean-Jacques Rousseau in the 18th century had proclaimed the doctrine of nature, assuming, perhaps on faith, that man was good by birthright and corrupted only by institutions—the Church, the schools, the laws. In the 19th century this attitude toward Nature with a capital N became dominant; in art, men should be free to give voice to their feelings, their passion, fear, love and longing. They were to celebrate the *natural man*, to shake loose the restraints placed upon artists by the authority of an Academy or of a bygone day.

Specifically this attitude meant for painting that all kinds of experiences previously suppressed were to find their way into art. The landscape appears again as a favored theme in France and England and America. The mysteries of love and death were to be explored. Drama and sentiment replace the decorum and reticence of the Neo-classic masters. The atypical as opposed to the typical fascinated the romantic artist since it was part of the unfathomed mystery of an inscrutable world. Violence and arresting or shocking contrasts permeate much of the literature and art of the epoch.

The 19th century was a period which saw philosophical, political, social and scientific ideas formulated in earlier times come into the possession of society at large. The Industrial Revolution tended to make science something more than a cloistered disinterested study of scholars. The poverty of the industrial workers gave increased point to social theory. Extensive urban life made men more acutely conscious of the landscape.

All phases of intellectual activity were to a great extent dominated by the scientific attitude. Science itself is based upon empiricism, the evidence of the senses. The art of the 19th century closely follows science in being created from the empirical experience of the individual. In art what the painter *feels* about his subject became roughly equivalent to what the scientist *knows* about his material. Thus the manner in which an artist worked was conditioned by his imagination, his sensations and his feelings. There arose, therefore, a great variety of styles—Romantic, Realist, Impressionist and Post-Impression-

Fig. 490.—GOYA. Queen Maria Luisa. *Private Coll.*

ist. But in each the common denominator is nature: *Art is nature seen through a temperament* is the way one writer expressed it. Since there are as many temperaments as there are individuals one might suppose that such a theory would lead to undiscriminating chaos—a kind of artistic anarchy. Something much like anarchy did result when one takes into account the untold thousands of imitative and feeble pictures made in the past hundred years. Certainly no epoch in history has produced so much quantitatively both good and bad. The great variety of expression in the Romantic age made it extremely difficult for a confused public to distinguish the sheep from the goats. But out of this welter of painting there did emerge men of great stature who made an intelligible interpretation of their world.

Of the great individualists of the new epoch the Spanish master, Francisco Goya (1746-1828), must be given a foremost place. There is no one who so fully embodies in his art so much that we consider peculiarly modern. One can scarcely name a major pictorial development in the past two hundred years to which Goya did not contribute. His early works belong to the rococo decorative tradition and are not unlike the paintings of Watteau and Fragonard, as gay and spirited, as witty and delightful as any in the 18th century. Elevated to the post of court painter, Goya increasingly shows his admiration for Velasquez. His royal appointment did not hamper his artistic development since he was not wholly dependent upon court patronage, and in his considerable work for himself and members of the court and the wealthier middle class he was enabled, as he said, "to make observations for which commissioned works generally give no room, and in which fantasy and invention have no limit."

Fantasy and invention were so far developed by Goya along psychological and technical lines that one may say that single-handed he anticipated and often directed the art of many European masters for a century. The position of court painter naturally called for large numbers of portraits; his supreme gift is in giving reality and drama to his persons. Where Velasquez produced a profound vision of luminous but static figures, Goya's have a kind of smoldering vitality. His sense of design with light playing over the figures gives arresting psychological point. Queen Maria Luisa (Fig. 490) is given an unusual illumination not unlike the flat stage lighting used by Degas and Daumier later. By introducing a kind of false note in illumination Goya emphasizes the gross neck and the hard features, the coarse brutality of the arms. The glitter of jewels and the rich stuff of the costume are built up consciously to produce another off-note which is communicated to us as a caustic interpretation of a sluttish and depraved harridan. All his work is characterized by a highly personal vision. This is the weakness and the strength of Goya's art. Whatever he undertakes has the impact of his will and his judgment. He is a moral force in an age of incredible moral disintegration. Only the strongest, most ruthless, even brutal person could have survived with integrity the corruption of the Spanish scene at this time.

Late in life he witnessed the horrors of the French invasion, record-

FIG. 491.—GOYA. WHY? Etching and aquatint. Rosenwald Coll., Jenkintown.

ing the catastrophe in a series of prints made in 1810 called Disasters
of the War. With relentless and devastating literalness Goya describes
the bloody terror of a mass execution, the heaps of slaughtered women
and children being dumped into a pit. With scalding irony he names
one of them Charity. In others dismembered bodies are hung from
trees, Spanish men are mutilated, women raped. These prints call to

FIG. 492.—GOYA. BULL FIGHT AT BORDEAUX. Lithograph.
*Rosenwald Coll., Jenkintown.*

mind the incredible ghastliness of the rape of Nanking and Poland, so
immediate and overwhelming is their power. If the paintings prove
Goya a master of trenchant design, these prints reveal, if anything, an
even greater genius for compression and economy. In one to which he
has given the terse inscription *Why?* (Fig. 491) some measure of his
method is seen. The space of the print is broken by a single wedge-
shaped pattern containing the two figures of the hanged Spaniard and
the ironically quizzical French officer. A few vertical accents suggest
the unending tragedy of torture and slaughter. Nothing is described
exactly but everything is suggested. That is the power of Goya: to suggest in appealing to the imagination with what is omitted. It is the
method that is generally adopted in his painting and graphic art. His
graphic work is mainly dated from his last years when he was a virtual
refugee in Bordeaux. In France, removed from the constant dangers of

reprisals of the Church and state, he was free to speak candidly of the nightmare he had witnessed. Old, deaf and embittered, he continued to lift his voice against the clouding miasma of man's calculated bestiality.

In his exile at the age of seventy-three he mastered the newly invented process of lithography and in the *Bull Fight at Bordeaux* (Fig. 492) of 1825, he draws upon stone the drama of blood and courage of the bull ring. The same incisive pattern, the same suggestion of action are seen here. The French Romantic Delacroix met Goya and in his own illustrations in lithographs reflects Goya's methods. His influence was not to be felt in its full tide, however, until some decades later when Manet discovered and adopted his technical pictorial ideas.

Goya's death in France in 1828 came at a time when French art was experiencing many waves of the new feeling from within her borders and from abroad. Géricault and the young Delacroix were impressed by the English landscape painters—Turner, Bonington and most of all Constable. The exhibition of Constable's *Haywain* at the Salon of 1824 prompted Delacroix to repaint passages in his own *Massacre of Chios* in the same exhibition. The English have always had a predilection for landscape and country life. John Constable (1776-1837), growing out of a minor school of English landscapists, found those abiding charms in nature common to most Romantic artists. The rain-drenched fields, the elms stirred by the wind were emotional actualities to him. He saw the Dutch landscapes of the 17th century and found kinship in them. He discovered that their intimate mood had little in common with the heroic landscapes of Poussin and his followers. In his own paintings he seeks the infinite variety of nature, the random color and above all the mood. His landscapes are not conjured up in a studio but are based upon intimate knowledge of first-hand experience. Like Goya he discovered that there are no lines in nature, but only areas or masses of color, and with him lays the foundation for Impressionism. *Stoke-by-Nayland* (Fig. 493), painted in 1836, suggests how his light-swept landscape breathes and vibrates. His color is made fresh and alive in a mosaic of broken fragments. This method was not so much a device to increase brilliance, as it was to be for the Impressionists, but the result of simple observation of visual realities. There are few solid color areas in nature; objects like a tree or field are actually vast complexes of color spots though we may *think* of them as being brown or green. The older painters had represented foliage as muddy brown or at the most a subdued olive hue; Constable met an objection to his bright colors by placing a violin against the boughs of trees to demonstrate the fact that the foliage was not really brown.

In practice Constable anticipated the principles of French Impressionism by almost forty years. This distinction is sometimes given to Turner, whose vaporous atmosphere and spectacular splashing of color were an even more radical departure from the classical concept of painting. Turner too is an unqualified Romantic, and if his work is sometimes superficial and melodramatic in evoking moods of sun and storm and the mysteries of the sea, it was in his practice of painting light

*Courtesy the Art Institute, Chicago*

Fig. 493.—CONSTABLE. Stoke-by-Nayland. *Art Institute, Chicago.*

and atmosphere in broken patches of pure color that Monet was to find a clue to solving his problem of reconstructing sunlight on his canvases.

While Goya and the English masters were well advanced in Romantic expression in the first decade of the 19th century, the French because of the strong hold of Neo-classicism found their way more slowly. Even professed disciples and students of David found it difficult to reconcile their art to the rigid code of the school. Romanticism as an attitude toward life did not have any single source; it was in the air of the western world.

In France the first definite assertion of an articulate revolt from the French neo-classicist camp appears in the painting of a brilliant young artist named Théodore Géricault (1791-1824). A man of means, he was not dependent upon the good will of the official custodians of art, and he proceeded to Italy where he studied the frescoes of Michelangelo instead of the diluted formulas of the academic pedants. Too intelligent to copy Michelangelo literally, he did absorb his great plastic rhythms and the controlling designs into which they were cast. His studies in Italy, like the *Riderless Races at Rome* (Fig. 494) of 1819, indicate his profound understanding of the athletic forms of the Sistine Ceiling. His jockeys and horsemen are but modern transcriptions of the nude athletes of Michelangelo (Fig. 421). Where the athletes bend

FIG. 494.—GÉRICAULT. RIDERLESS RACES AT ROME.
*Walters Gallery, Baltimore.*

their enormous strength of sinew and mind to the task of supporting slender garlands in an abstract allegory of strife and conflict, the jockeys of Géricault exert their energy to restrain the impetuous horses about to enter a race. The contingencies of realistic action demanded less the concentration upon single figures than the weaving together of scores of figures in a coherent pattern of movement. The theme itself, a popular horse race along the Corso, a street in Rome, was utterly antagonistic to the accepted standards of what was considered legitimate subject matter for the artist of 1819. Horses might be painted, surely, but only as adjuncts to Greek or Roman heroes, and then they must be depicted as still and lifeless as cast-iron statues. From Rubens, Géricault obtained an idea of how the horse might be treated as a plunging, pawing embodiment of energy, and also a concept of the expressive value of color. His own passion for horsemanship led him to enlist as a cavalryman in the Napoleonic wars. All his life he was an enthusiastic horseman, and like a sensible person he saw no reason for not painting the dramatic colorful spectacle of the races. Visits to England where he came into contact with the popular sporting prints gave further impetus to the painting of horses.

In their training, the Academies had insisted upon the minute representation of detail in clear sharp lines with exact rendering of every buckle and strap and lock of the horses' manes. But Géricault knew that when he witnessed a race, his eye saw not these details but the race as a whole—the flashing curve of a neck, the spot of white on a horse's head, the sudden gesture of a jockey bringing down his whip. The excitement and movement of the scene could not be expressed in the severe lines of the classic style so he proceeded to adopt the broad manner of Rubens to animate his forms with surging violence. The masters of the 17th and 18th centuries had well understood this method of painting by suggestive spots, the color and light accents seen by the eye. The Neo-classicists had reverted to an archaic style, isolating each object through the decisive metallic line that bounded it. Géricault too realized that the complex action of a group must be unified and given clarity or else its pictorial effectiveness would be weakened. All the Renaissance masters taught him the necessity of simplification through order, and in the Riderless Races this simplification is achieved geometrically. The excited horses and the spectators are restrained by the rope and the pavilion. The diagonal accents which they form create a movement in space terminated by the rectangle of the palace in the background. Against the foil of straight lines and unbroken planes the dynamic action of the race itself holds one's undivided attention. The many spectators are portrayed by a single band of mottled light and shade in which no one person stands out. This method of subordinating details to the composition as a whole was not fully appreciated by Géricault's contemporaries and immediate followers. Not until later in the 19th century were painters fully to realize its significance as a means of attaining unity from diversity.

When Géricault returned to Paris in 1818 he painted a huge picture that was condemned by the Academicians and lauded by the Romanticists. A short time before, the newspapers had given an elaborate account of a disaster at sea when the ship *Medusa* had been wrecked and its survivors battered for three stormy weeks on its single life raft. In painting the Raft of the *Medusa*, Géricault expressed realistically the desperate agony of the survivors as they hail a ship seen on the horizon. Exhibited at the Salon of 1819, it at once set aflame the smoldering controversy between the Neo-classicists and Romanticists. It was termed the worst of daubs by one group and acclaimed as a great modern masterpiece by the other. The recognition won by Géricault as a result was so great that had he not died a few years later he would have become the undisputed leader of the Romantic movement in painting. He was its champion and his example profoundly influenced those who followed him. He established the precedent of painting the image of the world about him and proved the independence of the artist to choose for himself the means of color and form that were needed to express that vision.

In the intelligent and cultured Eugene Delacroix (1798-1863), the Romantic school found its leader on the untimely death of Géricault from an accident during a horse race. Lacking Géricault's native instinct for painting, Delacroix was nevertheless a man of great inventive genius and imagination. As a youth he had been swept off his feet by the expressive vitality revealed in Géricault's art, and his imagination had also been fired by the romantic poetry of Byron, Goethe and Shakespeare which he later illustrated in many lithographs and paintings. His illustrations, whether inspired by contemporary literature or the classics, are never a pale transcription of or addition to the literary text. With free imagination and insight he rendered the inner psychological intensity and the spirit of the theme with such force that they are independent of any text. Technically the results are not illustrations in the ordinary sense, because they are self-contained concepts developed from the themes suggested by literature. One does not have to be conversant with the tragic destiny of Euripides' heroine to appreciate the dramatic scene depicted in *Medea* (Fig. 495), a work of 1838, though some knowledge of the Greek tragedy gives additional point to the painting. In a desolate craggy landscape the betrayed wife of Jason crouches within a cavern, about to slay her two children. While the babes twist and cry pitifully beneath her resolute arms, Medea hesitates; the turning of the horror-stricken face indicates not a moment of indecision but the instant when the tumult in her breast reaches its greatest intensity. The tragic depths of the woman's soul are revealed in that moment when, hovering between the past and the future, she is overwhelmed by realization of the awfulness of her revenge. Only a spirit with the same human sympathy that inspired Euripides could have conceived so tremendous a symbol of pity and terror. The great poetic imagination of Delacroix leaped beyond the impediments of pseudo-classical forms to express the essence of the tragedy and, in doing so, is more truly Greek than those who slavishly imitated them. He might have said with Millet, "He is the most Greek who is most himself."

Color, which the Neo-classicists David and Ingres had relegated to the rôle of a descriptive adjunct to drawing, was for Delacroix the essence of painting. From the Venetians and Rubens he found how to

Fig. 495.—DELACROIX. Medea. *Louvre, Paris.*

give depth and brilliance. His forms are built up in rich color volumes as opposed to the traditional style of augmenting the drawing with color. In the Medea, the reverberating hollow of the cavern is felt in the depth of pulsating color, rather than described by a literal rendering of the scene. And in its ominous depths one finds the psychological equivalent of the conflict of Medea. Like a musician who builds up a mood through abstract tonal qualities, Delacroix finds the psychological equivalents of emotions in terms of color. With color and light, space dilates and condenses dramatically, shapes appear and dissolve as color solidifies into substance.

To Delacroix the world was a place of danger, glamour and exotic beauty. Like his literary counterparts he found material for his art in

Fig. 496.—DELACROIX. Christ on the Sea of Galilee.
*Walters Gallery, Baltimore.*

the remote in time and place. He traveled in Morocco and painted the picturesque and strange beauty of the tropics. His Lion Hunts are reminiscent of Rubens upon whom he constantly draws. Like the Romantic poets he is haunted by the sea, finding in it a kind of symbol of mortality. Death flits through many of his paintings as a heroic fulfillment or an inevitable conclusion of man's conflict with nature. The cloudy mysteries of life are pondered in his Bark of Don Juan and *Christ on the Sea of Galilee* (Fig. 496). While Christ sleeps, the storm rages with the fury of shrieking wind, the pounding of waves, the savagely snapping wind-ripped sail. In these symbols, man's place in the universe is described with passionate eloquence.

With Delacroix there enters into the body of French painting elements that had long been absent: baroque design, the color of the Venetians and Rubens, and pictorial drama. Though he uses these elements with force and conviction, his art is inclined to be circumscribed by literary concepts; often the mood of his paintings springs from romantic episodes in literature and history. He relies perhaps more than a painter should upon an experience at second hand. By 1863, the year of his death, his conflict with Neo-classicism had been won, but it was the men who gave their attention to specific contemplation of nature —the Barbizon masters, Courbet the Realist, and Daumier—who were to consummate the Romantic revolution.

One of the most characteristic and significant features of Romantic art is the return to the landscape as found in the poetry of Wordsworth and in the formal language of painting. Since the time of Poussin and Claude Lorrain, the subject had been treated only by a few minor masters. Watteau's garden scenes were the nearest he came to it. David and Ingres with their absorption in classical themes involving figures alone were scarcely conscious of its being. Constable early in the 19th century was the artist who opened the eyes of Delacroix to the emotional and pictorial possibilities of landscape painting, and he gave him a method of realizing its possibilities as well. Then, around the year 1830, a few painters living in Paris began to drift out to a small village near the city called Barbizon, where living was cheap and there were woods and fields to paint. Corot, Rousseau and Millet were among those who formed the Barbizon school.

As Chardin in the 18th century had painted still-lifes and interiors with an intimate feeling for the glowing warmth of fruit and vegetables and the atmosphere that surrounds them, the Barbizon painters endowed their landscapes with a sentiment that finds in each meadow and forest path its peculiar intimate beauty. Théodore Rousseau paints the solitary oak dominating a flat patch of pastureland. He sees the peculiar rugged character of the gnarled branches, the coarse density of the oak foliage, the tufts and clods of the turf with pools of standing water like glass reflecting the sky. The grand compositions of the heroic landscapes of Poussin are replaced by others that express the spontaneous and informal aspects of nature in the manner of the Dutch landscape painters. These nature lovers, Daubigny and Diaz among others, saw the landscape with fresh naïve eyes in its quiet moods. Seldom if ever did they bring to it the romantic passion of

Delacroix nor did they view it as a background for narrative; they loved it for its own peculiar charm and painted it for its intrinsic delight.

This group of painters would have been of rather local interest had not Camille Corot (1796-1875) attached himself to it. Corot is Chardin out-of-doors. Everything he sees is instinct with visible charms. He has something of the innocence of Claude Lorrain. Taking no account of the heated controversies between Romanticists and classicists, he de-

Fig. 497.—COROT. The Inn. *Wellesley College Museum, Wellesley, Mass.*

manded of life only paint and canvas and adequate leisure for their use. An indulgent father supplied him with a small income and he never felt the necessity of modifying his style to suit critic or patron. As a result, his art has an indescribable charm of ease and casual simplicity. Yet this very simplicity is disarming, for Corot had a sure sense for composition and balance in his pictures. His designs are so spontaneous and free from strain or artificiality that they seem like happy accidents. Like so many others he was drawn to Italy where he was enthralled by the mellow light and the melting hills of the Latin landscape. In the land of classic art he seems to have absorbed the principles of structural logic in painting.

While the popular works of Corot have been those semi-literary scenes of dancing nymphs in misty woodland glades, paintings reminiscent of haunting romantic music, the student of art will find greater satisfaction in the severe figure compositions and solidly designed landscapes. The stature of an artist must be measured by his resources and his insight more than by his exploitation of a passing mood or style. In pictures like *The Inn* (Fig. 497), dated 1831, Corot unconsciously explores the artistic theories underlying his own work for another forty years and that of other masters for a hundred years. Here the severe

FIG. 498.—COROT. AGOSTINA.
*Chester Dale Coll., National Gallery, Washington, D. C.*

structural pattern of converging planes in related masses integrated to form a monumental design indicates a thorough undertaking of the great plastic traditions of the Italian Renaissance and anticipates the moderns, Cézanne and Picasso. Aside from the feeling for light there is nothing that suggests the romantic painting of Corot's popular works. The picturesque and descriptive drama is subordinated to the grand harmony of a compelling structure of solid and coherent forms. It is a stripped art devoid of the embellishments so readily admired by the gallery visitor easily seduced by superficial prettiness or novelty. Corot many times in his painting of misty groves was to yield to the popular romantic demand for charming sentiment, but Courbet, Daumier and Cézanne later on were guided by his genius for the underlying structurally articulate design. In recent decades Corot's figure paintings have risen in esteem as his art has been reevaluated. The small nudes are among the finest of the century; they have none of the archaeological remoteness of the Neo-classic or the brutality of Courbet. The late

FIG. 499.—MILLET. HAYMAKING. *Louvre, Paris.*

figure painting *Agostina* (Fig. 498), while created in 1866 at a time when the popular misty landscapes were being painted, is so solid and monumental as to bear comparison with the best of Goya or Titian. The warmth of the blues and the depth of the dark tones yield in the design an indescribable aura of mystery. Housed in the National Gallery in Washington, the romantic Agostina makes a striking contrast with David's Neo-classic Madame Hamelin (Fig. 486).

None of the Barbizon school and perhaps no other Romantic painter reaches the stature of Corot, but J. F. Millet (1814-1875) marks an important redirection of social attitudes of the 19th century and an extension of Romantic thought. As the Romantic revolution gave rise to a fresh contemplation of the landscape, so also we find a new interpretation of humanity. Millet's thought and feeling are for the *creator* of the landscape, the peasant. In turning to figure composition he returns to the great tradition of Mediterranean culture—Graeco-Roman and Renaissance. He views the gleaners of the field, the sower of grain, as monumental symbols of man's essential morality. They are endowed with mute dignity eloquent of the anonymous ritual of toil wherever men have husbanded the gifts of nature. His deep moral purpose is not unlike David's, but where the latter saw meaning only in grandiose historical persons like Napoleon or Roman heroes, Millet found it in those who create a culture directly through the daily pattern of their lives. The worker, his relation to society, the sanctity of human life so eloquently implicit in Millet's pictures are dominant concepts in world thought, in art, in philosophy and in politics.

It is no accident that Millet is the one popularly known French master in America. The somber eloquence of his pictures is universally understandable especially to a people emerging from a pioneer life of hard work and little adornment. His pictures are strong and simple like the *Haymaking* (Fig. 499), with condensation of all elements in a few broad accents. The figures are disposed in a pattern unifying them with the contours of the field and the haystack so that they become an integral part of the landscape. In the spontaneous design lurks no self-conscious bid for the Salon, no musty reminiscence of the Academies. Worked from memory and without models, his compositions are planned along large and ample lines reminiscent of Poussin. A reader of the Psalms and of Greek pastoral poetry, Millet reflects their ageless humanity.

## C. THE REALISTS

No name like *Romantic* or *Realist* goes very far in describing the thought and feeling which an artist may express in his work. The terms are convenient labels but often not very accurate, for any survey of Millet or Corot will disclose representative works which bear strong classical features though we apply the term *Romantic* to them. Ingres likewise, even in his own day, was charged with having Gothic and Romantic tendencies. Never the less, up until about the middle of the 19th century one may say that modern painters were basically divided in attitude and technical procedure between the Neo-classic school of thought and the Romantic. The individualism of the Romantics grew to overwhelming authority as time went on, with only the academies of art staging a last-ditch fight for the studio practices, if nothing more, of the classic tradition.

It was Gustave Courbet (1819-1877) who added the term *Realism* to modern painting. Self-taught, arrogant and opinionated, he could not stomach what he felt were the affectations of both Romanticists and Classicists. The Romanticists had seen the world through a veil of poetry and sentiment; the Neo-classicists had scarcely seen it at all, preoccupied as they were with notions of Greek and Roman ideals. Courbet would demonstrate once and for all that painting was a matter of physical realities. Why should any painter compose lyrical rhapsodies in painting a landscape or torture figures into sculptured perfection when no one had even been able to paint the bare facts of actuality? Courbet would show them. And he did. His landscapes lack the mystery of the fusing light Corot's searching eye had deliberately sought. They are sober and harsh. Where Corot had seen the picturesque poetic aspects commonly found by a city-bred man who goes into the country, Courbet avoided them. When he painted a nude he was careful not to betray his theories by making the figure suggest a Venus, a nymph or a Danaë. His nude is a female model seated on the bank of a stream or resting on a studio couch. The detachment which he sought often led to a cold and repellent brutality. But the human body is not a slab of meat nor the landscape a parcel of rocks and sticks as Courbet well knew, and many of his paintings are deeply felt and expressive though sometimes his theories made for self-conscious gestures. While shunning the attitudes which dominated the pictorial art of his time, he had the courage to reexamine nature and to expand the resources of his medium. He studied the methods of the Spaniards and the Dutch to learn how colors and textures and planes might be handled to produce effects of great strength and sober realities. The weight and mass of rocks, the heaviness of snow upon the fields and roofs, the rolling surf are recorded with feeling and conviction. Though there are in his work curious passages of a kind of awkwardly expressed sentiment and sometimes of an over-explicit naturalism, his art is fresh and vigorous.

Some of his best works are in American collections, among them the *Preparation for the Wedding* (Fig. 500) at Smith College. With something of the skill of Velasquez, Courbet makes an arrangement of space-creating planes relating values of blue and gray to effect transitions from figure to figure and space to space. Purely illustrational details are subordinated to structural considerations. Being an unfinished canvas, it gives a better view of Courbet's talents than some of his works which are burdened with factual details of irrelevant surface treatment. His claim to the liberation of art from the faked sentiment of "noble" themes came at a time when the representational potentialities of photography were first being realized. In literature writers were following a similar path in a movement known as Naturalism. Balzac, Flaubert, Zola in the novel and Ibsen in the drama are kindred spirits.

While Courbet was shocking French sensibilities with his pictorial iconoclasm, Honoré Daumier (1808-1879) was making himself felt in the field of journalism as a political cartoonist. No one of his time sus-

pected that the man who made an almost daily illustration for the
press was one day to be reckoned a supreme master of modern painting. His cartoon illustrations were in the main routine tasks, political
editorials often weighted with enormous satire and irony. One of them
directed at the King sent Daumier to prison for a term of six months.
No major artist has ever reached so wide and varied a public as he in

Fig. 500.—COURBET. Preparation for the Wedding. Detail.
*Smith College Museum, Northampton, Mass.*

the thousands of published lithographs that made Parisians laugh at
their own foibles and vanities.

Like Dürer, Rembrandt and Goya, Daumier brought the graphic arts
to a new status. Goya had been the first major artist to use lithography
and Daumier was the first to use it extensively and fully to exploit its
expressive possibilities. The picture is drawn in reverse with crayon
on a prepared stone; copies are made in any quantity in the printed
text of a publication or in individual prints. In his drawings and lithographs, Daumier exhibits the humanity of Rembrandt and the satirical
fire of Goya with a profound interpretation of character peculiarly his
own. A staunch republican, he loves his Paris and all its people even
when he makes them the point of his humor or irony. Stupidity, vanity,

human frailties of all kinds are no more often represented in his work than courage, patience and tenderness. A great-hearted humanity pervades Daumier's art. He reserved his most scalding comments for injustice and callous brutality; for common human frailty he has an indulgent but salty humor. The lithograph of 1834 called *The Vile Body of the Legislature* (Fig. 501) is as devastating as any social comment of Goya. Although directed at a particular legislative assembly, it is in reality a passionate protest against all legal banditry. The theme

FIG. 501.—DAUMIER. THE VILE BODY OF THE LEGISLATURE. Lithograph. *Rosenwald Coll., Jenkintown.*

of entrenched rapacity, the mockery of justice is presented with equal force in his painting Christ Shown to the People. The tragi-comedy of the law courts calls forth a long series of drawings, lithographs and paintings dealing with lawyers and their peculiar comedy of manners. He explores their pomposity, their rhetorical behavior in court, their sly complacency, their thousand characteristic actions. They are, he observes, shrewd and calculating actors, opportunists performing before complacent judges, defenders of pretty blonde criminals, petty chiselers or bewildered citizens.

But Daumier's art is rich in human warmth as well as in scorn for sham and hypocrisy. Equally he scans the lives of all classes of men, with such capacity for seeing and understanding that he creates a kind of bourgeois mythology comparable in the world of formal art to the *Comédie Humaine* of his great contemporary, the writer Balzac. No

artist of any age has had his unique ability to compress in a few spare
lines the temper, the character, the nerve and the heartbeat of a society.
When he paints a game of chess he cuts through to the essence of the
game, seeing it as a life-and-death struggle. He draws a musician playing and the line trembles and vibrates with the sound. Infallibly the
inner laws operating to animate the theme find expression in a tense

FIG. 502.—DAUMIER. THE SIDE-SHOW. Water color.
*Esnault-Pelterie Coll., Paris.*

direct pattern. He paints or sketches the theatre and the circus, noting
the tension of the performer, the pathos, the specious gusto and thin
tinsel of showmanship. Whatever grotesque attitudes men take they
are always human beings to Daumier. In *The Side Show* (Fig. 502)
the weird trappings of the carnival of freaks meets the eye, but the
artist sees the face of the drummer darkened by some private sorrow.
In his own way Daumier was realizing the great ethical ideal of classic
art: to portray essential humanity stripped of accidents and irrelev-
ancies. Spontaneously his noble mind perceived what was noble in his
world and laughed and makes us laugh at what is pretense and vanity.

In his monumental paintings he speaks with the authority of the greatest masters. Like Giotto, Michelangelo and Rembrandt he expresses the deepest mysteries. His somber drama is seen in *The Washwoman* (Fig. 503), a mother helping her child up the last step. The

Fig. 503.—DAUMIER. The Washwoman. *Museum of Modern Art, N. Y.*

Madonna and Child has seldom been given more tenderness, or the human figure been shaped so trenchantly to convey the quality of mind and spirit. Daumier unconsciously illuminates whatever he touches. He is a modern mystic rendering intelligible what is chaotic, broken and obscure.

### D. Impressionism

The story of 19th-century painting is one of a democratic and bourgeois society incubating individualistic artists or groups of artists. At first the new men are rejected and then finally accepted often only after their death, a process that has continued into the middle of the

20th century. One explanation for this phenomenon lies partly in the romantic and individualistic foundations of 19th-century art and the appearance of a relatively large public for art. The founding of public galleries, with newspapers carrying stories of exhibitions, gave an artist a wider art-consuming public than is to be found in any previous period of history. Up to 1850, Daumier had reached a really vast public to be sure, but only through the broad humor and satire of his lithographs; his paintings remained unknown to any but the smallest circle of fellow artists. But among that small group his influence was very great.

The emergence of each new "school" brought forth indignant protests not only from an irresponsible public of gallery visitors but from fellow artists, from critics and from journalists. The Impressionists were attacked for being revolutionists, incompetents, anarchists and perversely immoral, i.e., on aesthetic, political, moral and social grounds. Perhaps a more valid reason for their rejection was a natural human reluctance to change established habits and opinions at a time of great cultural ferment. A man who brings a new idea to the court of public opinion invites the wrath of the complacent, the stupid and the ignorant along with the considered judgment of his peers. Many conflicts are bound to occur since every individual is inclined to invest himself with authority, especially in matters involving aesthetic judgment.

The Realists and to a large degree the Romantics had taken nature for a model. They outlawed a threadbare classicism and a faded romanticism that no longer had validity for a socially dynamic materialistic age. They took themes from the familiar world about them, scrupulously avoiding anything that suggested the grand manner, the lofty sentiments of patriotism or piety. Daumier and Courbet were profoundly moved by visual sensations and kept their work relatively free of a literary or sentimental consideration. For these visual experiences to have any significance as art, they of course needed to be organized into intelligently coherent and illuminating patterns. When the Realists achieved this, they did so by emphasizing direct visual experience and avoiding the stereotyped conventions of the academies in regard to composition and color treatment.

In the '60's there emerged a number of the younger painters who in general followed the practice of the Realists. They were, however, in a few years to evolve a radical art language which came to be known as Impressionism. Their early predilection for realism gave them a bad name with the officials of the government and the traditional academies and with the public. When protests at their exclusion from the Salon grew too strong, Napoleon III provided a special means of showing their work to the public in the famous Parisian *Salon des Refusés* in 1863. Here all the rejected pictures from the official Beaux Arts Salon were shown. On a visit with the Empress, Napoleon III was shocked at a painting by Édouard Manet (1832-1883) called Luncheon on the Grass. This painting shows two couples picknicking; the difficulty arose because one of the women was unclothed. Manet had intended a pastoral like Giorgione's Concert of Renaissance times, but it was to be modern in style and subject treatment, that is to say, realistic. A couple of years later he exhibited a nude called Olympia which again raised a storm of abuse. The episode is of no special significance to the development of painting except that it sheds light on the increasing gulf between the artist and a public with mixed and contradictory opinions about art. Manet was in the process of developing his art from sources antagonistic to the Academy, going to the Dutch and especially to the Spanish masters for ideas about handling light and color. He saw how, in contrast to everything he had been taught, they had worked with broad areas of color instead of tight line drawing. These spots of color were made rich with light, and the shadows were frequently subordinated so that the color might be kept fresh and lively. Playing down the shadows or representing them as deeper color instead of gray produced a flat design which appears in the early Olympia of 1863. Ten years later his pictures are spotty patterns of color as in *Washday* (Fig. 504), with an informal or unstudied arrangement. Objects converge in the atmosphere as Manet attains relationship through the binding light of day. The white wash is blue according to its juxtaposition with surrounding colors. Details are rendered broadly as the whole is taken in by a glance.

In Japanese prints the Impressionists found how Oriental artists had made wonderfully expressive patterns "in the flat" by ignoring or telescoping space intervals and arranging figures in striking unbalanced poses. Photography may likewise have been an influence in the designs of this period. Manet was a painter of urban and cosmopolitan background who was interested in good painting from an aesthetic standpoint. One will not be moved by his work as by that of Daumier. If it lacks passionate human warmth, it has other qualities no less valid —discrimination, sensitivity and intelligence.

Some of Manet's painter friends were a good deal more radical and original though they were not necessarily superior to him. Pissarro, Sisley, Monet and Renoir turned their eyes to the pragmatic task of finding the means to make their paintings more truly representative of visual reality. Landscape painting interested them particularly, not for the romantic moods and grand architecture which Corot had found but for its color and light. Like scientists they inquired *with their eyes* what a particular landscape looked like, and they painted only from the visual sensations. Physically any landscape is no more than a series of color sensations. These colors are not flat and local, isolated from others, but extremely complex, fusing in atmosphere. The better to observe and record this dancing and ever-changing kaleidoscope, these men went out-of-doors to paint. Monet made a dozen paintings of the same strawstack because he saw that at different times of day, the sunlight was of varying intensity and direction; the strawstack presented a wholly new

FIG. 504. MANET. WASHDAY. *Barnes Foundation, Merion.*

appearance each hour. He and others cultivated rapid brushing to capture in a few minutes this fleeting show. The sketchy unfinished effect of their pictures gave the name *Impressionist* to the school. Monet's *Fishermen* (Fig. 505) of 1882 is a study in flickering color in which a flat sheet of water is broken by several objects that happen to be men and boats. Nothing is allowed to obstruct the visual analysis made on the spot; there is no narration or illustration of "fishing." The method produced incredibly luminous and sparkling pictures of a character rarely found in the old masters. Where the latter had painted in the cool even light of the studio from notes and drawings made at another time and place, the Impressionists worked directly in the presence of the thing they were painting, for no memory could adequately retain the sunlight and the colors as they underwent continuous change with the passing hours.

Fig. 505.—MONET. Fishermen. *Museum, Vienna.*

The science of color and light was studied in the literature of physics. Practical methods were examined, such as the division of color. Green mixed on the palette produced only dead solid color, but a bright green could be made by spotting the canvas with pure yellow and pure blue. Short dabs of the color produced effects of movement and atmospheric vibration. Shadows were not darker tones but deeper purples or yellows. Most of these observations had been made by earlier masters, notably Titian, Watteau, Delacroix and Constable, but now they became the stock-in-trade of the school. Blacks and muddy browns disappeared from painting along with lines and small details.

Some have called Impressionism a kind of color photography, a type of painting in which all meaning is sacrificed to impersonal scientific observation. They argue that the fishermen of Monet are not men but areas of yellow and purple and therefore the painting is void of any significance. But this partial truth is modified by other considerations. While excluding illustrative narration and moral and intellectual values, all of which may be and are found in painting, the Impressionists discovered an exhilarating beauty in nature. What splendor they found is communicated to us. Their discovery of light in color may be called the last great achievement in an analysis of nature beginning in Giotto's time.

There have been tens of thousands of Impressionistic paintings made. There are belated souls still painting them after a formula which no longer calls forth any spiritual response, for the formula means little in itself without the informing spirit of its creators. The term Impressionist is a convenient one to designate a group of men who more or less were in agreement as to a method. Claude Monet most completely utilized the method. Manet became an Impressionist only in the latter and perhaps the lesser phase of his artistic career. Edgar Degas (1834-1917) scarcely qualifies for the name. His talent was for a disciplined draftsmanship and design at a time when most of his contemporaries in the Impressionist camp had their minds set on other matters. He found in Ingres, if not an ideal, a great master of linear construction to emulate. When Degas was asked why he didn't go outdoors to paint as the others were doing he replied, "Painting is not a sport." The remark is indicative of his pithy wit and revealing of his mode of working. While he accepted the high palette and the broken color of his friends and exhibited with them, he gave his attention to subjects calling the human figure into play. But his interest in the figure is limited. He brought to it nothing of Daumier's all-embracing humanity or Renoir's sympathetic intuition. He found in it material for a design of a peculiarly individual character. The nude figure is most often represented as a bather in a bathroom wholly unconscious of any spectator. The unself-conscious pose rendered in a firm and logically coherent design is his aim. Portraits, for which he had a special gift, are likewise of people not posing but caught at their accustomed tasks. One study of this character was made in New Orleans when he visited his brothers who operated a cotton exchange there.

Ballet dancers rehearsing in the studios or on the stage of the Opera (Fig. 506) called forth a great many paintings and pastels and lithographs. Not a profound colorist, he no less than the others of his group employs color with charm and spirit, especially in pastel. But fundamentally he is a draftsman and one of the best of the century. He is an example of an enormously talented man viewing his world in limited fragments. Certain personality traits deny him the possibility of

complete understanding of life and consequently the completest fulfillment as an artist. His biting and sardonic comments spring from the
circumscribed mind of an anti-Semite, a rabid nationalist and royalist,
and a bachelor. The deep and generous affirmations of Daumier, Renoir
and Cézanne are not to be found in his life or in his art.

But no artist can be evaluated by any means except his work. The
breadth of his spirit is measured only in the humanity of his art. The
impulses operative in artistic creation are obscure, and only the art

Copyright, Frick Coll.

FIG. 506.—DEGAS. THE REHEARSAL. *Frick Coll., N. Y.*

object offers any effective measure of those impulses. Some masters bring
to their art faltering and unsteady talent which appears at first of no
account; Rembrandt was one whose early work gave little or no indication of what was to come. Technical gifts are one thing and spiritual
energy and magnitude another. The latter will call out and expand
technical equipment. To a period which saw an astonishing outcrop-
ping of artistic talent came one man endowed with no supreme natural
gifts for painting. Auguste Renoir (1841-1919) even to his friends
seemed at first an unpromising painter. What they could not see were
the hidden energies and the capacity for spiritual growth; these were

the imponderables which made him one of the greatest single forces in a richly creative epoch.

To call Renoir an Impressionist is to name only one phase of his extraordinary career. His early work is in the dark firm manner of Courbet stemming from the tradition of Velasquez and Goya. With the use of pure pigments in broken patches, his great genius as a

Fig. 507.—RENOIR. Mother and Child. *Hunt Coll., N. Y.*

colorist emerges and Impressionism as a method blossoms into a style. He had a facility for invention in coloristic terms unprecedented in his century. Color assumed a primary rôle in the structure and form of his work and is handled with strength and sensuous warmth. His own natural buoyancy and charm seem miraculously to flow into his pictures; joy in life is an inherent gift which finds spontaneous expression in all his work. This joyous warmth is not something occasionally observed in things or people but is the constant outflowing of a measureless vitality.

For all the iridescence and flower-like delicacy of Renoir's pictures, they have in addition *reality*. Some artists are destined to have a very limited appeal because they speak from some peculiar experience to those who are able imaginatively to reconstruct that artist's experience. Other artists operate from a broader more universal base, reaching a correspondingly wider circle of humanity. The Venetian masters of the Renaissance by developing a highly sensuous colorism infinitely enriched and enlarged the appeal of European art. Modern painting does

*Courtesy the Museum of Art, Cleveland*

FIG. 508.—RENOIR. THREE BATHERS. *Museum of Art, Cleveland.*

not fully employ the communicative instrument of Venice, i.e., sensuous color, until Renoir's time. Drawing upon the Venetians, Rubens and Watteau, he becomes one of the few supreme colorists.

His common touch is like Daumier's and Rembrandt's. Searching always to expand the power and appeal of his work, he found the formula of Impressionism too restrictive though he had attained great artistic and material success through it. In common with other French masters he began to strengthen his designs and to compose figures with firmer linear accents. From this period of renewed concern for structural values comes his *Mother and Child* (Fig. 507), painted in 1886. Without sacrificing the sparkle and movement of color the figures are drawn into a crisp lozenge-shaped pattern and poised against the secure accents of the fence, the building and the tree trunk. Such compositions are also found in the work of Ingres, whose Stamaty Family (Fig. 489) is similarly designed.

Mother and Child is a study of Madame Renoir and their son Pierre, but it is only incidentally a portrait. In its extraordinarily compact pattern with all objects falling logically into interacting rectangles fusing with repeated egg-shaped forms, the "Mother and Child" theme emerges with the utmost freshness and reality, like a happy incident of observation. The strong underlying formal structure found in the art of Corot, Daumier and Renoir sets their art off from much work that is too largely illustrative and superficially descriptive. From this time on Renoir's art becomes increasingly classical. He gives more thought to weight and mass, to the solid forms of Renaissance and baroque painting. The line becomes an interweave of light and color of remarkable strength.

In the latter phases of his career his mastery of color and line and light is such that he creates supremely symbolic works. As Rembrandt, Poussin and Titian had reserved for their latest years their full intellectual achievements, so it is with Renoir. The *Three Bathers* (Fig. 508) of 1897 demonstrates the incandescence of his color, the solidity of his dynamic figures. A lover of women and children, he paints them as though they were exquisite flowers, the jewels of creation. Flesh is the color of mother-of-pearl with the firmness of Praxitelean marble. A bather's dress or hat on the sand glows with the mystery of a precious jewel. Without leaving the knowable world Renoir carries us with him into a realm of wonder and glory.

### E. The Post-Impressionists

Renoir's search for an artistic language beyond Impressionism should be considered in the light of other masters who came to be known as the Post-Impressionists. These men, Cézanne, Seurat, Gauguin and Van Gogh, were engaged through the '80's in the same quest. Each in his own way found a method that was essentially personal, but despite a high degree of individuality some general characteristics emerge. They all evolve from Impressionism and employ the full rich light and color of the school. They all on the other hand seek a solid structure and give a more systematic treatment in their painting, feeling that the Impressionists had relied too much on a rule-of-thumb practice. The greatest of the Post-Impressionists was Paul Cézanne (1839-1906). In his own words, he "wished to make of Impressionism something as solid and lurable as the old masters in the museums." He was thinking of the monumental art of the Italian Renaissance of Masaccio and Michelangelo, of Titian and of Poussin. In the older art he recognized qualities of solidity and continuity of rounded forms integrated in stable space rhythms. Cézanne particularly admired the work of Poussin, who had created harmonious and lucid patterns in mass and space. The problem Cézanne set for himself was to take the luminous atmospheric colorism of Impressionism and with it to construct images that would have the stability, the depth and solidity of the older pictures. He felt that the characteristic form of things had been dissolved into intangible and meaningless color spots by the painters of his day. He recognized the Impressionist achievement in restoring color to its place as a fundamental pictorial element, but he also saw that in the process they neglected considerations of contour and form limits, rendering the forms themselves vague and without substantial reality.

In his long labors to evolve a method that would render nature more comprehensively and at the same time more expressively than Impressionism had done, Cézanne made many false starts. All of his fumbling attempts met with the most caustic and cruel disparagement from nearly everyone who saw or even heard of his work. He was the ugly duckling of the Impressionists when he was working in their method. Apparently he had no gifts or talents. Nothing he did pleased anyone, least of all himself. Retiring from Paris to his birthplace, the provincial city of Aix-en-Provence, he isolated himself from all external influences to "remake Poussin after nature." No painter ever had so many failures or showed more courage to go on and on after a thousand abortive efforts. He worked largely with still-life because a bowl of apples on a table never moves and can be studied at leisure. He would investigate the architectonic relations of the round bowl and the spheres of the fruit, noting the movements in color and accent that established relationships between the essential shapes, coordinating them with the fold of a napkin and the table edge. He submitted the still-life to the same analysis that Raphael gave to a Holy Family, observing the formal relations that make for adhesion and unity. He would first view the subject as an abstract design, a pattern of shapes, in order to realize the dynamic relations of its component parts interacting. But his interest was not in a pleasing and unified design for its own sake. His concern with inner organization was solely to effect a complete realization of every aspect of his subject. In short, he aimed at the most realistic image of the apples and napkin that was possible.

When Cézanne worked he would take nothing for granted. He had no formula; each canvas was a new venture, a new problem calling for a solution that tested all of his resources to the limit. In this respect he

was like Rembrandt, constantly studying the means to greater condensation, a shorter, more direct path to the fuller expression in his medium. He found that problems presented in a still-life were the same as
those offered in the portrait and the landscape. There were the same
elements of space, of surface texture, of density and mass to be reckoned with. No two of his paintings are alike since his eye profoundly
tested the infinite variety of nature. To achieve the harmonious organ-

FIG. 509.—CÉZANNE. STILL-LIFE WITH FRUIT DISH.
*Lecompte Coll., Paris.*

ization of color and line in design prompted him to distort the physical
appearance of objects. In the *Still-life with a Fruit Dish* (Fig. 509) of
1877-1879, the variety in oval and circular forms calls for the distortion
of the top of the dish and wine glass. All painters have distorted the
shape of things to some degree or other; Cézanne's distortions were
only a little more obvious. The spherical shapes are played off against
three broad planes marked by the table edge, the table and the wall.
Within those areas there is an animated drama of shape, color and
space.

Cézanne's search for a means of expressing the depth of cubic form
led him to make an exhaustive study of the continuous planes that
make up a solid. Each plane he designated by a certain color intensity,

FIG. 510.—CÉZANNE. THE ARC VALLEY. *Metropolitan Museum, N. Y.*

and by careful gradations in the planes he effected a powerful illusion of three-dimensional forms. It is obvious that not all of the infinite planes that make up a solid can be differentiated by the painter. He must simplify, indicating enough of the consecutive planes to make the object appear on the canvas as it does in nature. In *The Arc Valley* (Fig. 510) of 1885-1887 with its view of the often painted Mont-Ste.-Victoire, there is a lack of picturesque subject matter, of the description of familiar things that ornament most landscapes. Cézanne like Poussin avoids the topical, which he considers irrelevant to his primary aim of organizing the space, the colors and the forms into an animated pattern.

One unacquainted with the elliptical nature of modern painting or seeking to "read" a painting for its report on lively anecdotal subject matter will find Cézanne's pictures difficult to understand. At first sight they may appear smudgy and barren as they did to nearly everyone in his own day. But with a little attentive study their inner logic, the cohesion of form to form, the rhythms of organically conceived patterns become apparent. A heightened sense of space is created as the landscape opens up plane by plane beyond the towering center tree and the closer forms.

Cézanne had many failures to every success, but even his failures are magnificent fragmentary revelations of experience. He recognized better than anyone when he had succeeded or failed to "realize his sensations" as he put it. He thought of himself as a primitive working in the method he had discovered. And there is indeed something of primitive directness and instinct for essentials in his pictures. The *Card-Players* (Fig. 511), one of his greatest figure pieces, brings complex plastic bodies into equilibrium with the fluid space of the room. Everything essential has been rendered convincingly—the texture of cloth, the flesh tones, the cards and the atmosphere—and all are translated into an arresting pictorial reality. The picture gives the subject an immediacy and directness similar to that of Jan van Eyck's Portrait (Fig. 374), together with the monumental stability of Giotto and Masaccio.

A Post-Impressionist of the utmost originality was Georges Seurat (1859-1891), who, like Cézanne, was conscious of the looseness of Impressionist design. He composed his color areas by tiny disks of pigment (pointillism), suggesting mass and receding space by variations of intensity. Where the Impressionists wished to show flickering light in restless motion, Seurat strove for a monumental tranquillity, a repose of solemn grandeur that uncannily suggests the most momentary and casual movement. His *Sunday Afternoon on the Grande-Jatte* in the Chicago Art Institute (Fig. 512) is his masterpiece, painted between 1884 and 1886. The forms are disposed upon the canvas with such exact understanding of their relation to each other, their position is so

FIG. 511.—CÉZANNE. THE CARD PLAYERS. *Louvre, Paris.*

justly established with respect to the total design that the strollers in the park seem crystallized in their most characteristic attitude as in timeless space. The most trivial forms—a plug hat, the silhouette of a bustle, the arc of an open parasol—are so subtly interwoven in the fabric of the design that they become permanent and signally revealing elements of a moment in time forever fixed. There is a kind of super-reality attained by his rigid adherence to rules of order and harmony that places Seurat's work in the grand classic tradition in French art. But it is classic in feeling, as Cézanne's and Renoir's works are, with no mustiness of archaeological formulas. Even today despite the curious fashions in costume, the world he portrayed has the pictorial authority of the old masters. Seurat finds deep psychological and social implications in the costume and behavior of his figures and makes his humane observations integral with his design.

While Cézanne and Seurat were finding the means to realize solid forms and classically lucid patterns of space, Vincent Van Gogh (1853-1890), a Dutch painter working in France, was evolving a style the exact antithesis of theirs. His art cannot be disassociated from the conditions of his intimate life, for no master has ever poured out his passionate being in his painting as did he. In his early years, Van Gogh had been a preacher in miserable mining towns. His passionate love for humanity and the excessive zeal with which his almost insane devotion manifested itself led him into all manner of tragic conflicts. People were revolted by his fanaticism and he was defeated at the very beginning of a career that absorbed him body and soul. He was a mature man when he turned to the study of painting and in a few years, whereas most artists take decades, he mastered the technique and developed a personal style. Following now Millet or Delacroix, now Daumier and now the Impressionsits, he finally evolved a method that was entirely his own. In painting of the most violent colorism he found symbols for the burning intensity of his visions. The sunflowers he paints writhe and twist, consumed by the heat of their own radiance. Forms take motion to correspond to the sensation of the painter who sees them as living embodiments of energy like himself. He paints cypress trees that bend to the wind, their foliage twisting in long darts like tongues of fire. Color excites him to a frenzy of activity, and he paints the sun-drenched wheat fields as if they were caldrons of molten gold.

Every subject he essays is a search for the inner life. For the externals he cares nothing except as they offer a clue to some unseen reality. With tense linear patterns, with nervous staccato stipple (Fig. 513) he constructs surfaces and masses into the unforgettable and haunting face of a peasant. He is attracted by Daumier's deep human-

Courtesy the Art Institute, Chicago

FIG. 512.—SEURAT. SUNDAY AFTERNOON ON THE GRANDE-JATTE. Art Institute, Chicago.

ity and follows his methods in giving powerful movement to planes and lines.

In his work is found the greatest variety of expression from the most lyrical beauty to studies in morbid psychology. The interior of a small *Café in Arles* (Fig. 514), painted in 1888, is not so much the portrayal of a place as it is the calculating analysis of a heightened emotional experience. He describes his picture in a letter to his brother Theo as representing a place of livid horror where one might go mad.

FIG. 513.—VAN GOGH. PEASANT. Drawing. *Private Coll.*

To most eyes the café might not look different from a hundred others, but Van Gogh's extreme sensibilities to color and mood find in it an inferno of suspended horrors. In fact, it is no less than a nightmare of dilating space; shapes of chairs and tables assume tortured patterns; light coagulates about the lamps. The colors are ghastly in their power to shock and disturb and are harmonious only in that they are all calculated to flay the nerves. They are decaying purples, poisonous greens and hard inflaming reds. Such lurid studies speak of the mind tortured by suffering of a man terribly aware of the spiritual conflicts in his own personal life and the life of his society. In his writing and his painting he speaks of a world transformed, and as we may see, it is a world seen through the enraptured eyes of a mystic. On another occasion he

FIG. 514.—VAN GOGH. CAFÉ IN ARLES. *Hanloser Coll., Winterthur.*

FIG. 515.—VAN GOGH. CYPRESSES IN THE MOONLIGHT. Drawing. *Bremen.*

writes that he is painting a landscape but fears that what he has done is after all *only* a landscape. The meaning is clear, that he endeavors to make his landscape convey some degree of the unfathomable mystery of life and creation.

As a colorist he introduces the boldest ideas into modern art. His contemporaries found his bright contrasting colors garish and unpleasant, but today they are seen to be deeply expressive of the intoxicating beauty he expounded. Equal to his color sense is his draftsmanship. In black and white drawings he simulates color values to an extraordinary degree. Swirling, twisting, gyrating linear patterns are used in the drawing of 1890, *Cypresses in the Moonlight* (Fig. 515), much as in

FIG. 516.—GAUGUIN. AREAREA. *Durand-Ruel, Paris.*

the paintings the heavily coiled rolls of pure pigment accentuate nervous movement. The slumbering village lies engulfed by the mysterious orgiastic convulsion of light and the throbbing earth.

Though many artists have felt Van Gogh's powerful influence, he was scarcely a master to attract the following that Cézanne has had. His art was too purely personal and intimate; his method was created specifically to carry the weight of his unique visions. No one else could profitably employ his peculiar artistic language. For some time Van

Gogh was associated with the painter Paul Gauguin (1848-1903), who in some respects is his French counterpart. Both were convinced of the corruption of their society and of modern culture generally. Van Gogh tried to reconcile himself to it by the fierce consuming mysticism of his art as Daumier before had through his moral and rational idealism. The gathering storm clouds culminating in the holocaust of the 20th century were manifest in many ways in the art of the late 19th century. Gauguin echoed something of the idealism of the Romantics in his dramatic flight from European civilization. Discovering the art forms of the East and the simple patterns of primitive art, he formulated a style of flat decorative design. In the South Sea Islands he looked for a utopia among the Polynesians, only to find that the idyllic life described by Herman Melville had long since vanished. The simple people had under the French colonial policy become demoralized and sickened by the sharp exploitation of the white men and by their diseases. Nevertheless, Gauguin remained and made a life for himself with the native population. Through his art he created the substance of his dreams. What might have been a foolish gesture became a noble assertion of human dignity in the scores of paintings centering on the mysteries of folk customs and the exotic tropical landscape. *Arearea* (Fig. 516) is representative of the way he combined broad flat areas of exotic color. The space pattern is consciously reduced in a tapestry-like surface that glows sensuously. The exotic people and animals are rendered in decorative shapes. He and other Post-Impressionists anticipate the originality and the bold individuality that characterize the diverse art activity of the 20th century.

# Chapter XXXI. Contemporary Painting

*PAINTING IN THE 20TH CENTURY AS IN THE 19TH HAS* been almost a French monopoly. That country has produced in the past century and a half a nearly unprecedented body of pictorial art of a very high character. Where men of other nationalities have risen to prominence like the Spaniard Picasso or the Dutchman Van Gogh, they are masters who have been shaped by the French tradition and have lived extensively in France.

The French masters of the 19th century including the Post-Impressionists developed their art in opposition to the hostility of the schools, the critics and the public. The conflict was between those who thought of art as a kind of high-toned luxurious adornment and those who thought of it as a means of realizing the deepest spiritual values in experience. The reactionary schools looked upon painting as the art of the graceful and learned embellishment of some subject appropriate to a cultured society. The emphasis had been upon representation and illustration. Cézanne and Van Gogh had demonstrated with great authority the value of an art which made free adaptations of physical appearances. Like El Greco they had distorted the shape of nature out of psychological or compositional considerations. They had abolished many traditional *clichés* of composition along with picture-book illustration. Their work seemed harsh and brutal and even savage to most people unaccustomed to their direct and powerful methods, but for the next generation of painters in the early 20th century they had unambiguously created a mode of expression that was authoritative.

Cézanne's unorthodox treatment led the younger painters to exercise the greatest freedom in their work. Because their distortion of subject matter outraged the common man's sense of propriety, the new painters were called *Fauves* or wild beasts. Among this group coming on to the scene from 1905 on were Rouault, Matisse and Braque—men who with others came to be known as the School of Paris. In method they followed the examples of Cézanne, Van Gogh and Gauguin. Their interpretation of Cézanne's ascetic formalized art led some to greater and still greater abstraction. Cubism as a method of painting developed from Cézanne, whose search for formal integration had led him to frequent distortions of his subject and the exclusion of descriptive illustration. His followers assumed that he was concerned only with orchestration of light and color in a self-sufficient design with no thought to interpretation of his theme. They began to think and to talk of painting "liberated from the tyranny of nature" that would be a "free" expressive art like music. A remark of Cézanne's was often quoted to the effect that

*Courtesy the Art Institute, Chicago*

FIG. 517.—PICASSO. GUITARIST. *Art Institute, Chicago.*

all things in nature tend to assume the shape of cones, spheres and cylinders. Georges Braque (b. 1881) and Pablo Picasso (b. 1881) began between 1908 and 1910 to experiment with compositions of abstract patterns in which natural shapes were reduced to a minimum or wholly disappeared. Kandinsky, a Russian, composed designs in color without constructing any stable pattern of recognizable forms.

No artist of our day has explored the formalistic resources of painting with the magnificent talent of the Spaniard Picasso. His energy and originality make him a living symbol for many painters of our day. He follows no regular course but changes radically from year to year. In 1903 he painted the somber *Guitarist* (Fig. 517), which in color, distortion and mood is reminiscent of El Greco; yet the regular geometric structure in the design suggests the Italian Renaissance. As one of the originators of Cubism he constructed patterns of planes, surfaces and

FIG. 518.—PICASSO. NEWSPAPER AND VIOLIN.
*Museum of Art, Philadelphia.*

textures woven into articulate design. These paintings are not pictures in any ordinary sense (Fig. 518). Here is a composition involving some recognizable shapes like a violin with its curves and keys taken out of their usual order in space and arranged in an arbitrary surface of contrasting shapes and colors. Areas of newsprint make interesting surface patterns against which to play unbroken colors and textures. A wine glass appears as it might be viewed from several points simultaneously.

Letters, mottled apples and pears of a nursery catalogue are used for design purposes. Familiar prosaic shapes take on new vitality when placed unexpectedly in new relationships.

Those who are inclined to look for hidden meaning or symbolism in such paintings could spare themselves because Picasso admittedly had no thought of such things. The painting is no more and no less than a pattern, rather flat like an Oriental rug, but a design that has great richness and complexity. Picasso's design elements are derived from a

FIG. 519.—PICASSO. LANDSCAPE. *Private Coll.*

bewildering variety of sources—from the Post-Impressionists, from Greek art, the Renaissance, particularly from Piero della Francesca, Negro sculptors, to name only a few. Classical and French influences are found in many paintings like the *Landscape* of 1921 (Fig. 519). In it one sees how his mastery of abstract design results in a lucid articulation of the planes of wall surfaces, the movement of tree forms in a picture that has a close resemblance to the landscapes of Cézanne and Poussin. While Picasso has been said to flout all tradition, the truth is that no artist has ever been more conscious of the past and more keen to enrich his own work with the living element in it.

Great minds sometimes reveal themselves most fully and most powerfully in salient and unique masterworks in which earlier ideas come to fruition. For Picasso this culmination of effort appeared in the 30's in *The Mirror* (Color Plate III) of 1932 and *Guernica* (Fig. 520) of 1937. Frank Lloyd Wright and other architects of the 20th century had been rethinking the whole question of space and had once and for all rejected the idea of boxed-off cubicles for rooms lying snugly within a master shell. As the architects designed continuous space to unify exterior and interior, the painter likewise telescopes figure and space in a dynamic unity. In The Mirror he rejects the method of hollowing out pictorial space as the basis for a painting along with the lifelike image. In doing so he aims at intensifying the idea (woman) clothing it in mystery and glamour. Here he works in harmony with the creators of the medieval church windows effecting in the diamond color shapes and other areas overwhelming radiance rivaling those great masters of color. In the interlocking ovals are echoed the feminine shapes that Raphael and Leonardo inherited from the classic sculptors. Picasso brings these design elements into modern perspective through their integration with contemporary concepts of synthesized time and space. The double view of the face in profile and full face repeated by the mirror are, with the vibrating color shapes, the means by which the concept is projected.

A great deal of Picasso's art has nothing directly to do with the moral and intellectual conflicts of his age. Much of it never seems to touch the life of ordinary men and probably never will. But any study of the great body of his work will reveal scores of paintings of great human warmth and passion. Another generation will likely find them richer in expression than has his own. But that Picasso does not lead a studio existence remote from the world was dramatically demonstrated when he painted *Guernica* in 1937 (Fig. 520). Most now recognize the Spanish Civil War (1936-1938) as the opening battle of the Second World War. During the Spanish conflict German bombers pulverized an unprotected Spanish town called Guernica, destroying thousands of the helpless citizens simply as a test of the German air force. Picasso had already made a series of symbolic etchings called Dreams and Lies of Franco in opposition to the Fascists, comparable in spirit to Goya's war etchings (Fig. 491). Then two days after hearing of the massacre he began a large mural in black and white—the Guernica. The symbolism is deep and involved. His theme is the holocaust of war, the calculating frightfulness that descended upon a Spanish town and upon the world. A woman falls from a burning building, another leans from a window holding a lamp and viewing the destruction, a dead warrior lies dismembered, a woman shrieks over her dead child. A horse pierced by a spear dies while a bull symbolic of death witnesses this triumph

PL. III. PICASSO. THE MIRROR

of death. It is doubtful if any man but a spiritual descendant of El Greco and Goya could have conceived so appalling a symbol of human fury. No man without Picasso's vast resources in concentration and abstraction could have shaped so incisive and universal a picture of the world's agony.

In the Guernica Picasso's work is close to the method called Expressionism. German artists like Franz Marc (1880-1916) had expressed in their painting violent emotion through form distortion. In the general group of Expressionists are Van Gogh, Munch and Kandinsky. One may include the French painter Georges Rouault (b. 1871), who creates hauntingly tragic pictures deeply tinged with Christian mysticism. There is something prophetic about Rouault's somber and tragic studies of dancers, prostitutes, clowns, judges and religious figures (Fig. 521). He views them with the compassion of Rembrandt and Daumier. One may find clues to his expression in the mediaeval windows and sculptures. He furnished designs for modern stained-glass windows and in his painting separates color with broad lines not unlike the lead settings of stained glass. His color is deeply clouded or glowing with great inner radiance and is always used with passionate force. There have been few mystics in modern art and perhaps none who so surely reach into the verities of life as he.

A phase of modern painting far different from the Expressionistic is found in the work of Henri Matisse (b. 1859), who with Picasso has been a leading figure in the 20th century. He exemplifies the decorative tradition always very strong in French art. In the light of Cézanne, Van Gogh and Gauguin he continues the decorative tradition in painting which dominated the 18th century. Matisse marks the termination of a curious development in the French school. The 19th-century masters had repeated in effect earlier trends. Ingres had investigated phases of the Renaissance, the Romantics and Realists had discovered the baroque, and Matisse recreates something of the joyous lightness of rococo painting.

Like most of the moderns he accepts the distortion and formalism of Cézanne, combining with them the striking color patterns of Van Gogh. But he develops these features to his own purpose in an original and personal way. Where Cézanne had developed forms that were massive and weighted, space elements that were strong and deep, Matisse telescopes space and works three-dimensional forms into flat patterns (Fig. 522) like Gauguin's. The striking colors that Van Gogh had evolved for arresting psychological ends Matisse modifies for decorative enrichment. Like Picasso he freely adapts his subject matter to his design; it is distorted and sometimes cannot even be identified. He has never become a Cubist but often approximates its methods.

FIG. 520.—PICASSO. GUERNICA. *Artist's Coll.*

In the 20th century art becomes peculiarly international as artist after artist finds and uses the structural, expressive or decorative modes of art in all times and places. This internationalism in artistic spheres corresponds to the political and cultural international trends in thought of the century. Matisse like Picasso draws heavily from the Oriental arts, Japanese prints and Persian miniatures, from Negro

FIG. 521.—ROUAULT. THE OLD KING. *Carnegie Museum, Pittsburgh.*

sculpture and the simple patterns of primitives, as well as from the body of western art generally. Most people have been impressed by the child-like naïveté of his pictures. Before children become conscious of sophisticated art they often show in their pictures an uncanny genius for elemental, flat, bright color and surface patterns. Matisse, sensitive to all authentic elements in design, makes ample use of these, lifting them to an artistic level by intensification and consistent elaboration. Unlike the Expressionists he ponders none of the conflicts of his time and culture. His themes are dancers, still-lifes, landscapes or portraits, figures in a room; these are transformed and given reality by the magic of his inventiveness. Matisse offers a feast for the eye and while he does not venture into the wider sphere of interpretation he brings to his art a great talent, sensitivity and intelligence. ·

FIG. 522.—MATISSE. THE GAME OF CHECKERS.
*Paul Rosenberg Coll., Paris.*

Many modern artists, notably the Germans, have undertaken to ex-pound the mysteries of the unstable contemporary world in a cryptic language of abstract symbols, but like so many others who have eschewed naturalistic representation, their interpretations have largely remained cloudy and inarticulate. Otto Dix and George Grosz while avoiding complete abstraction have produced powerful symbols of the social disintegration and reconstruction in Germany following the First World War. In their mordant realism or pointed symbolism they are the antithesis of the Cubists and Abstractionists. The confusion of aims and methods witnessed in the art of the past fifty years is a symbol of a social and intellectual reorientation of society occurring in the world revolution of our day. The hundreds of movements, schools and cliques into which artists formed under the leadership of now one, now another idea or personality, indicate efforts to find a solid ground upon which to build.

FIG. 523.—OROZCO. CHRIST CUTTING DOWN THE CROSS.
*Baker Library, Dartmouth College, Hanover, N. H.*

In the social-political philosophy of Communism the world has seen the most dynamic effort toward reorganization. Under the spur of enthusiasm for a new social philosophy Diego Rivera and José Orozco, two Mexican artists, have revived the technique of mural painting in fresco in order to promulgate their faith in a socialistic state. They founded a painters' syndicate in Mexico City in 1922 which identified the artist with the worker. In their art and writing they declared that art was the language of the people and should be employed to express the truths by which they live. With magnificent courage and imagination they have painted and are painting upon great walls the social and cultural history of the New World. Their concern with large themes—the epic of America, the history of labor, the machine—reflects minds that offer a realistic pictorial interpretation of modern life in contrast with the French school which seems bent upon aesthetic and intellectual refinement.

There is something of the old masters in the craftsmanship and the large purpose of these Mexicans. Turning to elemental issues of the

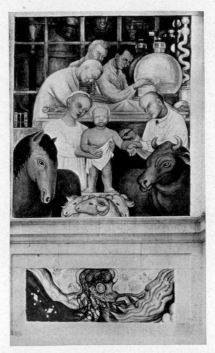

Fig. 524.—RIVERA. Vaccination. *Institute of Arts, Detroit.*

20th century, Orozco (b. 1883) interpreted the spiritual values of the American culture. The comment on present-day abuse of Christianity is mordantly eloquent in his *Christ* (Fig. 523), a detail from the epic mural painted at Dartmouth College in 1932-1934. No eye can escape the stark drama of this angry Lord striking down the symbol that has been desecrated by a rapacious and materialistic age. Of the two leaders in Mexico, Orozco is the more profound and passionate in the pictorial expression of his ideas. Rivera (b. 1886) aims at a more readily grasped symbolism. He finds it implicit in the common activity of the soldier, the peon, in the assembly line of factories. In Detroit he painted the history of the city in terms of automobiles and airplane factories, laboratories and foundries. His symbol of the pharmaceutical

*Courtesy the San Francisco Museum of Art*

FIG. 525.—RIVERA. THE FLOWER VENDOR. *Museum of Art, San Francisco.*

industry, represented by *Vaccination* (Fig. 524), created a furor because of some analogy between his painting and the traditional Holy Family theme. A colossal mural he painted in Radio City was torn from the walls because it contained a small portrait of Lenin which was supposedly distressing to the tenants of the building. Many easel paintings and water colors are free of any special ideological content. These, like the *Flower Vendor* (Fig. 525), are compact and flat in design, the dominant earth colors heightened with sensuous passages. The painting of acres of wall space in Mexico and in the United States has resulted in a style that is ample and sure and above all decorative.

While Rivera uses his art to specific social and political ends, his style was shaped by the school of Paris. In Paris he studied Cézanne's art and for a time was intimately associated with Picasso and the Abstractionists. In his murals in Mexico, Detroit, New York and San Francisco he has brought to the New World much that was valid in French art. Orozco has decorated walls for Dartmouth College, Pomona College in California and the New School for Social Research in New York. Among the younger generation of Mexicans is David Alfaro Siqueiros (b. 1894), a mural painter of great talent.

Of all the cults and *isms* of modern art, Super-realism or Surrealism has probably attracted the widest public attention. Art has always made itself felt in the realm of the unconscious. No historian or psychologist or philosopher is able to explain or ultimately to evaluate art. Long before Sigmund Freud (1856-1938) presented to the world his monumental studies in the psychology of the *unconscious*, artists had explored the world of fantasy and dreams. In painting, Bosch, Grünewald, Goya and Redon are examples. The best-known illustration of Surrealist art is *Alice in Wonderland* in which reality and fantasy, logic and illogic are mingled in a narrative that crosses and recrosses the boundaries of conscious and unconscious. Freud told how dreams are but a continuation, usually in concealed symbols, of our waking thoughts. Writers like James Joyce in stream-of-consciousness technique record the unspoken or unexpressed thoughts of their characters, and painters produce works that propose to follow a similar method in order to exploit a rich vein of experience. The pictorial dream has of course immense possibilities for all manner of curious and strikingly effective devices. Many of the paintings of the Surrealists have been of a highly realistic nature; others have combined the designs of the Abstractionists with realism. The Spaniard Salvador Dali (b. 1904) is the best-known exemplar of the movement. His inventiveness seems limitless as he reconstructs fragments of memory from his childhood or the ambiguous experiences of dreams in compositions of objects and persons and their symbols juxtaposed with disturbingly convincing incongruity. His ingenious titles give some indication of their fantastic and enigmatic character: The weaving of furniture—nutrition, Debris of an automobile giving birth to a blind horse biting a telephone. His exact rendering of nature in many works is a departure from the abstraction of most modern painting and leads to literary interpretation. Frequently his art touches that of Expressionism when some idea is recorded with unusual force as in *Soft construction with boiled beans; premonition of civil war* (Fig. 526), which is dated, significantly, 1936. Horror and loathing, the playful and the obscene mingle in a convulsive agony of writhing shapes. Death motives as in dreams have poignant significance in a time of universal slaughter.

Surrealism, while it cannot be considered a major stage of modern art is one of the manifestations of an era of war and catastrophic de-

FIG. 526.—DALI. SOFT CONSTRUCTION WITH BOILED BEANS; PREMONITION OF CIVIL WAR. 1936. *Arensberg Coll., Hollywood.*

struction with the suppression and annihilation of almost all humane values. At such times men like Bosch and Goya dream and in their dreams they live the nightmare of a waking reality.

What another age will think of our art and our culture is anyone's guess. But this we do know: it will find symbols both of death and of life. Within the compost of decay are strong viable seeds that grow through to the light. More often than not, the most vigorous art of our time has been categorically assigned to perdition by barbarians here and abroad in the name of sanity, fake racial theories or chauvinistic patriotism. Sincere people have inquired narrowly for a reassuring serene art expressive of some transcendent spiritual tranquillity. But the artist creates as variously as nature and his work is no response to wishful thought: where there is no tranquillity in thought, there can be none in art. For art emerges from the total experience of the human race, from life impulses of past times as well as from our own insistent present. In art we may see, if we have eyes for it, the large design of human history.

# Chapter XXXII. *Painting in the United States*

*A PROFOUNDLY EXPRESSIVE ART TRADITION TAKES* centuries to develop. There are no mushroom growths in any effort of men to give form and meaning to experience. Whether we think of art as the shaping process men give to the raw materials of nature, or as the formation of rules by which a society is governed, i.e., in practical terms of the way houses are built or a city managed, it is clear that a very long history is involved. A carpenter making a cabinet uses methods and instruments that had their origin perhaps thousands of years ago. Cézanne in painting a canvas is guided by principles expressed in art hundreds of years before Christ. Into his work goes something that is more than the impulse of a day or a year; it was a living part of an ancient culture and continues its life in our time.

When a culture—that is to say, a pattern of life—persists for a long time, it inevitably produces symbols of itself in music or architecture and in all the arts. Whatever art symbols have been forged in the United States must be considered in the light of the centuries-old culture of which ours is an integral part.

When the American colonies seceded from England in the 18th century a new political unit was established, but it is obvious that a political organization is not the same thing as a cultural tradition, it being but one manifestation of a larger whole. The latter is involved and complex, requiring many generations to acquire its peculiar characteristics. An integrated culture comes only after an organic way of life has been established a long time. Even now, after nearly one hundred and seventy years, our nation is still in a formative state. With a novel political organization, with widely disparate types of culture occupying a territory almost the size of all continental Europe, the integration of our national life had, and still has, many obstacles to surmount. At first, only in New England was there a fairly stable society, based upon handicraft and agriculture. With the coming of the Industrial Revolution, that social unit was largely disrupted. Before the Civil War the South, having a highly profitable plantation system,

*829*

attained perhaps the most urbane and promising culture the country has ever known. It was at this time, when the nation was in a position to realize its potentialities, that the Civil War inflicted a devastating blow to national morale, and the decades that followed were the dreariest and most sordid that we have endured. Yet paradoxically it was these very post-war years that witnessed the appearance of the painters who most deeply express the spirit of our national life. Painting was slower than literature to appear as an articulate and original expression for the simple reason that whereas books circulate freely and written language is almost universally comprehensible, works of plastic art were very scarce in our early days and their formal language was difficult to understand even under the best of circumstances. Removed by thousands of miles from the painting of Europe, the early Americans knew next to nothing of the technical practices of European art. The pressing consideration of making the wilderness a habitable place was a self-evident deterrent to the creation and the patronage of the arts in the Colonial period of our history.

In the early years of the colonies and before the Revolution the portrait had flourished, not so much as a work of symbolic art, but as part of the cultural furniture of great and wealthy families. The makers of portraits traveled from house to house, from city to city, with ample supplies of canvases representative of various types of people and completely prepainted except for the faces. They were called "limners" and "face-painters," and their pictures were known appropriately enough as effigies. Among them were many skilled craftsmen who had come by their art through painting signs. Created with unguided skill and patience, these truly primitive portraits are often of great homely charm in their dogged fidelity, representing the literal facts of lace and bows and texture of surfaces. Recently they have come into a belated popularity for their very genuine picturesque and decorative qualities.

The best of them are labors of love wholly foreign to the more or less facile commercial products. Sometime around 1675 an unknown person painted the portrait, *Mrs. Freake and her Baby Mary* (Fig. 527), a work of extraordinary charm. It is the type of picture that is made by one wholly unlearned in technical resources of any school or tradition but with an instinctive sense for design in line and color and a solid craftsman's feeling for the medium of paint. Such untrained artists appear from time to time in our history and leave memorials of their spirit.

It was only natural that the portrait should first engross the attention of our early painters. Face paintings were in demand, and people were willing to reward the skillful artisan who could produce a valuable family record. To have a good likeness of its more distinguished members was almost a family duty in 18th-century America. In the 17th century when Holland emerged from political and military conflict her first demand of her artists was portraits; in much the same matter-of-fact spirit, the Americans asked to have their own images painted when they became conscious of their cultural and political attain-

FIG. 527.—MRS. FREAKE AND HER BABY MARY.
*Coll., Mrs. W. B. Scofield & Mr. A. W. Segourney. Museum of Art,
Worcester.*

ments. More specifically the popularity of the portrait in America was a direct heritage from the English, if one can speak of a "heritage" at a time when the colonies were simply an arm of the English nation. The English have always been patrons of portrait painting, as can be seen in the 18th-century activities of Hogarth, Reynolds and Gainsborough (Fig. 482).

The outstanding portraitist of our Colonial days was John Singleton Copley (1737-1815), a painter who gained fame not only in America but also in England. Trained under his stepfather and other teachers, he came by the methods that prevailed in the English school.

There is something of the wooden character of the primitives in his earliest pictures, but he rapidly gained considerable mastery over his technique. He brought no innovations to the methods of his contemporaries, but with a remarkably conscientious and searching eye he translated the spirit of his people into the paint of his canvas. His temper of sobriety and reserve fits well the austere Puritans whom he portrays, but his reserve never manifests itself in dryness or dullness. It is somewhat relaxed in the lively portrait of *Mrs. Seymour Fort* (Fig.

FIG. 528.—COPLEY. MRS. SEYMOUR FORT.
*Wadsworth Athenaeum, Hartford.*

528), which he probably painted between 1772 and 1776. The redoubtable Mrs. Fort appears to us in the full vigor of her moral and physical being. With characterful strength and humor she seems a witty and gentle mistress of the sphere she dominates. It is rare to find in either English or American portraits of the 18th century so honest and forthright a treatment of character. Copley never makes his subjects more noble or beautiful than they are, but he had the happy faculty of eliciting from them their most essential character. Being a Loyalist, he withdrew to England on the eve of the Revolution in his middle thirties, ending his Colonial career. There he found patronage and honor, but his closer relation to the English tradition of art did not improve his style.

In the late 18th century Europe offered every strong inducement to the American artist. There the schools and the patronage and the art could be found that are so important to the student and the mature master. Benjamin West (1738-1820) spent the whole of his career in London, the first American painter to gain European prestige. Though a member of the English school, as friend and teacher he assisted all his fellow countrymen who went to England to study. Among his American friends was Gilbert Stuart (1754-1828), probably the ablest painter of faces of the time. Everyone is familiar with his portrait of Washington in the Boston Museum of Fine Arts, if only from its use on our postage stamps. The stoic nobility of that portrait has been accepted as the most characteristic feature of our first President. But the Washington in the Vaughn portrait is a far more subtly realized conception of the intimate character of the gallant and venerable country gentleman. Neither one is a great portrait of high interpretive merit, but both are admirable memorials to a great spirit. As historical documents, the portraits of our early period are of inestimable value, far overshadowing their artistic significance. Mather has pointed out Stuart's excellence as a painter of women. The portrait of *Mrs. Perez Morton* (Fig. 529) of *ca.* 1802 in the Worcester, Massachusetts, Gallery is his masterpiece. Of all other masters living at the time, only Goya could have made so penetrating an analysis of character interpreted in the most imaginative manner. For a brilliant illumi-

FIG. 529.—STUART. MRS. PEREZ MORTON. *Museum of Art, Worcester.*

nation of the most intimate depths of the Anglo-American type of woman, it has yet to be surpassed.

There was little if anything peculiarly American about the early face-painters. Their manner and method, if any origin can be discerned, were derived almost wholly from the English, but as time went on painters appeared who had come under the influence of the French. The professional and highly disciplined style of David was communicated to Rembrandt Peale and S. F. B. Morse (1791-1872), both artists of great talent. The weight of David's style was highly beneficial as a corrective to the superficial and easy decorative effects of the English. S. F. B. Morse could have had a splendid career as a painter had he not been discouraged from it by lack of interest in his paintings and a corresponding popular enthusiasm that resulted from his invention of the telegraph. His portrait of Lafayette hanging in the City Hall, New York, is a grand full-length picture of surprising depth and power.

The Romantic movement which had seen the elevation of landscape painting to first importance in Europe through Constable, the Barbizon painters and others, was profoundly felt in America. The New England landscape was celebrated in the verse of Whittier as early as 1831. The nature poetry of Wordsworth was as fully appreciated in America as in England. As portraiture began to decline in the period before the Civil War, the landscape came more and more to occupy the talents of our painters. Thomas Cole (1801-1848), taught by an itinerant face-painter on the frontier of Ohio, was deeply impressed by the wild and romantic aspect of the untamed mountains and forests. Working in the Catskills and along the Hudson River he with others formed the first group of landscape painters in America. The Hudson River school found little in the landscape save sentiment and the random beauty of the picturesque. Where Bruegel (Fig. 450), Millet or Corot (Fig. 497) saw the land as an abode of men who had shaped it by fields, walls, canals and bridges, American painters too often divorced it from any social or human values. We have considered the land as *scenery* or as an object of exploitation and plunder for quick profits. Vast areas have been reduced to desert wastes. More recently, of necessity, a scheme of conservation has been followed by states and agencies of the federal government that should restore the landscape as a practical and aesthetic symbol of our national culture. That we have not had landscapists of the highest order is accounted for by the fact that we have yet to attain the integrated and humanized culture that produces the landscape in actuality. But the deep feeling of American painters for nature in the widest sense of the term has made landscape painting our most distinctively native art. Ryder, Homer, Inness and a score of others have treated the American scene with great insight and power, ranging in expression from the heroic mood of the 17th-century Claude Lorrain and Poussin and the tender sentiment of the romantic passion, to abstractions in recent times like John Marin's.

The development of American landscape painting owes much to Winslow Homer (1836-1910), who brought to his subject a singularly sensitive and intelligent talent. At a time when most American painters were absorbed by showy sentiment and patriotic bombast or almost wholly enthralled by the mellowness of Old World masterpieces, Homer was an outspoken realist. With pragmatic directness he studied the lakes and rivers, the fisherfolk and the northern trappers. There is an almost impersonal deliberation in his dispassionate record of out-of-door life. Largely without reference to the knowledge and practice of centuries of painting, he contrived honest studies of immediate experience, finding for his pictures the colors that described veraciously the actual ones appearing in nature. At the time Manet was shocking Paris with his original use of color, Homer, without any self-consciousness, was exercising the greatest freedom in its use. If he lacks

FIG. 530.—HOMER. ADIRONDACKS.
*Fogg Museum, Harvard University, Cambridge, Mass.*

the great mastery of his European contemporaries he is at the same time disencumbered of their aesthetic theories. As an illustrator and some-time journalist he developed extraordinary sensitivity to pictorial values and integrated them with the formal structure (Fig. 530). He had a forceful and virile style which expressed what he had to say without hesitation or gropings. His experiences of nature were so deeply felt and his integrity so great that there is no false note of half-realized sentiment or idea to mar his pictures. Lewis Mumford notes that the significance of Homer lies not so much in the quality of his pictures as in the fact that he accepted the life about him and made what he could of the seacoast with its weather-bronzed faces reflecting the struggle and the homely decencies of heroism and defeat. He established the familiar native scene in all its aspects as the subject with which the artist should rightly concern himself. To Americans of this time, accustomed as they were to look to the European past for their models, this was no small contribution to a new culture.

In Albert Pinkham Ryder (1847-1917), American painting finds its profoundest spirit. He shares with Whitman and Melville the almost undisputed primacy in our artistic tradition. Furthermore, with his two literary contemporaries Ryder assumes a place of rank not confined to the sphere of his own country but in relation to the art of the western world. Seen in this perspective, he belongs unquestionably with the Romantic school.

In nearly every respect Ryder's art differs from Winslow Homer's. Where the latter gives specific particulars of character to place and events, Ryder gives expression to his inner experiences. Of all his landscapes and marines, only three have definite reference to a specific place. He realized more fully than any other American painter that the sphere of the artist is the mind, which transforms the raw

Fig. 531.—RYDER. Toilers of the Sea. *Addison Gallery, Andover.*

stuff of the external world into articulate meaning. Surface appearance means nothing to him except as it evokes some feeling beyond the realm of mere sensation. His groping efforts to attain comprehensible expression of that thought are reflected in his painfully laborious methods of painting. Months and even years after a canvas had been almost complete he would still revise it; he often called in those that had been sold to make final additions and amendments. In explanation of his desultory methods he said, "Have you ever seen an inchworm crawling up a leaf or twig, and there clinging to the very end, feeling for something, to reach something? That is like me. I am trying to find something out there beyond the place on which I have a footing." These are words very like Van Gogh's. By concretion and concentration, he packs into his art infinitely more than is seen or heard by the senses. Something of the resounding poetry and music of Chaucer, Shakespeare and Wagner, whom he loved, emerges from the ghostly pale lights of his marine nocturnes. He gave poetic titles to his pictures, like Toilers of the Sea and the Waste of Waters is their Home, and even wrote verses to accompany them. Though many of his canvases are inspired by literature, they are never mere illustrations any more than were those of Delacroix.

In all of his paintings one feels the presence of the mysterious forces that lie in the unfathomed depths of nature, forces that Melville symbolized in the Great White Whale. For Ryder as for Melville, the sea had a peculiar fascination as a symbol of the incalculable destroyer and preserver. During his boyhood in New Bedford, the whaling port where since the 17th century men had wrested a living from the treacherous sea, he must have been moved by the tragic beauty of the ocean. Its austere mystery is felt in his Toilers of the Sea (Fig. 531). With the simple design of a smudgy fishing vessel outlined against the moonlit sky swept by long slow clouds, he gives utterance to the solitude of the soul of man. The illimitable plane of the sea, the inscrutable breadth of the sky, are conveyed by the coruscated light emerging from the enameled depths of the canvas.

Ryder profoundly spiritualizes his themes, whether they are derived from literature, legend or the homely commonplace of daily existence. Hearing of a waiter in his brother's hotel who had committed suicide upon losing all his savings on a race horse, Ryder painted the picture called The Race Track, or Death on a Pale Horse (Fig. 532). The skeletal rider, scythe in hand, circles interminably a desolate race track on his ghostly horse. Ryder was out of touch with the art of Europe, but he found in his plodding experimental methods the means to express the part of experience that eludes direct statement, that must be approached through parables. Though he was a mystic and poet, his art touches with directness and sureness the commonplace and elemental experiences of humanity.

Somewhere between the romantic naturalism of Winslow Homer
and the mysticism of Ryder, the realism of Thomas Eakins (1844-
1916) finds its place. Unlike the other two, Eakins had founded his
technique on the tradition of European painting through study in one
of the celebrated academic studios in Paris. He had a surprising intelligence in regard to his training, recognizing that what he had to

Fig. 532.—RYDER. Death on a Pale Horse. *Museum of Art, Cleveland.*

learn was simply the technique of painting, how to prepare a canvas
and mix pigment and the craft of picture-making. It must have been
obvious to him, even in his youth, that his highly competent masters
had little or nothing to teach him as to what he should paint or how
his subjects should be interpreted. This independence, admirable because it showed that he could not be impressed by the studio small
talk of ambitious simpletons, was at the same time a limitation. When
French art was beginning to reform along the line taken by Manet,
Renoir, Cézanne and Van Gogh, Thomas Eakins was unaware of
any such movement. Had his residence in Paris not been from 1866-
1869 but a few years later, the course of his art might have been
very different.

When he returned to this country he set about soberly and sensibly to paint the scenes about him that he knew intimately: portraits of his friends, boat races, prize fights, the interiors of his fellow artists' studios and the demonstration clinics of the hospitals. There is something in Eakins of the old masters, both in the learned technical methods he followed and in the self-assurance of his approach to his work. The searching realism of his painting and his friendship with the celebrated scientists of his native Philadelphia attest to his intense interest in scientific thought. "All the sciences," he said, "are done in a simple way; in mathematics, the complicated things are reduced to the simple things. So it is in painting. You reduce the whole thing to simple factors; you establish these and work out from them, pushing them toward one another. This will make strong work. The Old Masters worked this way." Walt Whitman, in whose *Democratic Vistas* is recorded the same acceptance of the American scene that characterizes Eakins' art, said, "I never knew of but one artist and that's Tom Eakins who could resist the temptation to see what they think they ought to see rather than what is." Certainly no painter was ever freer from pose and affectation than he. The popular American taste has always been more than tinged with the English concept of art as a decorative embellishment of life. For Eakins, it was no such matter any more than for Ryder. He saw in it an instrument of almost scientific precision to formulate enduring monuments of his experience.

Everything Eakins painted has the authority of one who never questioned the validity of his conscious power to *see* and to understand. In the solid masses of his forms are the same rightness and factualness, the direct contact of mind with things, that are found in Cézanne's pictures. Indeed the portrait of *Arthur B. Frost* (Fig. 533) in the collection of the Pennsylvania Museum of Art in Philadelphia, painted in a wholly different technical idiom from the Frenchman's, might almost have been done by Cézanne, so powerfully does the personality emerge from the planes delineating the solid masses of the head. His portraits are sober and factual, unrelieved by the bravura of showmanship. They were too faithful and too probing for his clients, who rather hoped for something more flattering and showy.

Like Whitman, Eakins had the widest interest in all the life about him. His pictures of the prize ring are as intensely studied as his monumental paintings of the Gross Clinic and Dr. Agnew's Clinic. Perhaps his most dramatic work, in both subject and treatment is called The Salute. A prize fighter, nude except for shoes and loin-cloth, turns with lifted arm and face to receive the roar of adulation from the crowd. The exact moment is recorded when the lithe and muscular athlete, trained to an edge, holds the attention of the frantic mob.

Calm and tense, he seems to be arrested for an instant by the torrent of applause that rushes upon him. Somewhat less intrinsically dramatic, *Between the Rounds* (Fig. 534), painted a year later in 1899, is broader and more monumental in design. The extensive background of the action is simplified by the accents of the horizontals and the subdued illumination of the scene. The white flesh of the boxer resting

FIG. 533.—EAKINS. ARTHUR B. FROST. *Museum of Art, Philadelphia.*

in his corner glows warmly in the murky atmosphere. The arrangement of the telegraphic reporter attentive at his key, the seconds busy with their fighter, is spontaneous and yet compact. Eakins never makes his figures more colorful than they are, or his drama more intense than the actuality. There is a sober poetry about his staid realism that escaped the men of his own time who found his art too severe as the French found that of Courbet and Daumier lacking in elegance and charm. The great integrity of these men has been recognized in our own time for what it is—the highest gift of the artist.

Eakins exercised great influence upon his followers and his presence is felt more and more with the years. The Philadelphia group including

Luks, Glackens, Henri and Sloan came under his spell. And George
Bellows (1882-1925) more recently has reflected his gusto and boldness,

Fig. 534.—EAKINS. Between Rounds. *Museum of Art, Philadelphia.*

notably in his painting and lithographs of prize fighters. His several
versions of the climax of the *Dempsey-Firpo Fight* of 1924 (Fig. 535)
showing Dempsey being hurled through the ropes are slashing reminiscences of the robust days of the prize ring.

In his own day, Eakins was eclipsed by a popular painter of talent
who had also studied in the Paris schools but a few years after Eakins
and with quite different ultimate results. John Singer Sargent was
everything that Eakins was not. A cultured cosmopolite in background,
he was taught in the *atelier* of a sophisticated portrait painter of eclectic

FIG. 535.—BELLOWS. DEMPSEY AND FIRPO. Lithograph.
*Goodyear Coll., N.Y.*

derivation whose style Sargent mastered and exploited with facility
and a certain dehumanized brilliance, impressing his clients with his
unerring eye for the obvious and commonplace. He created a type of
society-portrait that is somewhat more sinister than the transparent
counterfeit of straight commercial work.

From the outwardly uncongenial atmosphere of American life following the Civil War, so admirably characterized by Lewis Mumford
as the Brown Decades, an ever-increasing group of artists found haven
in the capitals of Europe. Lack of patronage and prestige sent many to
seek recognition and guidance in countries with long-established traditions in the arts. Leaving her native Philadelphia, Mary Cassatt (1845-
1926) developed under French Impressionism a fluent and delicate

style inspired largely by Degas. Her portraits of women and children are especially fine, but she must be considered a French painter since there is almost nothing in her manner of working or her expression to suggest any but French influences.

By far the most celebrated American painter is James McNeill Whistler (1834-1903) (another expatriate), though by no means the greatest. Receiving his early training in Paris, he exhibited with the moderns of the time who were in revolt against the stultified archaisms of the Academy. He maintained that art was its own justification and should not concern itself with narration, description or morality. He professed the theory of art for art's sake, projecting his aesthetic beliefs in witty and provocative paradoxes. His view was that art had nothing to do with the mechanical finish so much prized by the Academicians or the elaborate literary and historical subject matter they employed. Here he was of the same mind as the progressive French contemporaries with whom he associated, though in his works he falls considerably short of their accomplishments. His paintings are basically decorative arrangements often similar to the flat patterns generally adopted by the French masters. Space and mass are subordinated to a fan-like surface spread of related color areas. The titles of his paintings—Nocturne Symphony, Arrangement—are such as to suggest that his pictures were not studies of specific scenes but free organizations of color and tone. In his "arrangements" he only partly follows the general trend of modern art. There is nothing of the vigorous and sensuous color of Impressionism or the form-searching of Cézanne. Silver and gray heightened with warmer color notes making a screen effect is his usual formula. Like Corot he liked the half-light where specific accents are softened and silhouettes converge.

It was in etching that Whistler made his chief contribution, participating in the notable revival of the graphic arts in the 19th century. Here his talent for refinement in pattern and tone found an ideal medium. Etching is an intimate art in which subtleties of values and line play an all-important rôle, adapting it well to a temperament as sensitive to formal *nuance* as Whistler's, as can be seen in *The Traghetto* (Fig. 536), a Venetian scene etched in 1879-1880. In the technique of preparing the plates and in printing them, in the refinements of the art, he was surpassed only by the great Rembrandt. But in all of his work there remains something attenuated and a little arty. He skillfully adapted Oriental design, particularly that of the Japanese woodcuts. With sensitivity and taste he borrowed the rare tonalities of Velasquez' art for his own, but with a certain self-conscious aestheticism.

The development of Impressionism in France was inevitably felt by the painters on this side of the ocean. Twachtman, Hassam, Sargent, Glackens, Sloan and a score of other able painters were profoundly affected by French luminism. The work of these men has not been invested, however, with the great imagination and penetrating realism of their predecessors Ryder and Eakins. The powerfully constructed art of Cézanne and Seurat was first appreciated in America by Maurice

FIG. 536.—WHISTLER. THE TRAGHETTO. *Rosenwald Coll., Jenkintown.*

Prendergast (1859-1924). Perhaps the same intelligence that gave the latter a ready understanding of Post-Impressionism led him to evolve a style quite different from Cézanne's but founded in the same desire as his to stabilize pictorial design. He became a highly imaginative and decorative figure painter, constructing his forms by broad touches of pure colors to create a glowing mosaic of great charm and depth of feeling (Fig. 537).

The spectacular and bewildering work of the modern School of Paris was introduced to America in the famous New York Armory Show in 1913. Here for the first time the paintings of the *Fauves* or wild beasts, as they were called—Matisse, Picasso, Braque—became known to the American public. Art dealers and enthusiasts widely publicized the theory of free expression that lay back of the abstract treatment of the modern School of Paris. While the often grotesque effort to imitate the French produced a good many faddish and fatuous paintings, the trend attained the dignity of a movement in the intelligent and sensitive work of men like Demuth, Marsden Hartley and Dove. It is reflected in the brilliant abstract and symbolic painting of Georgia O'Keeffe.

Fig. 537.—PRENDERGAST. Central Park.
*Collection of Whitney Museum of American Art, N. Y.*

On a popular level have appeared painters like Grant Wood and Thomas Benton who through the '30's exploited native subjects with novel and at times arresting ingenuity. The journalists have found them good copy and they have enjoyed a popular success. Though both have very limited pictorial resources, Benton has made the most of his talents as a mural decorator. There has been a real need for muralists to adorn the walls of public buildings. The need has been met in part by borrowing the Mexican masters Rivera and Orozco. The federal art projects have provided the means for a vast amount of mural painting during the depression years in the United States, and there have been some works painted on private commission as well. An example is Henry Varnum Poor's *Land Grant* fresco (Fig. 538) at Pennsylvania State College, painted in 1940. It is executed with a fine sense of the not always reconciled individualities of both architectural setting and pictorial composition, in sober yet well-harmonized colors, and deals in a forthright way with a theme of immediate import.

In general, American painting of the 20th century has not crystallized in any school. There have been and are relatively local groups centering about some gifted teacher or art school, but these associations have never been very permanent. Never before have we had so many gifted painters, men of unusual ability and sound craftsmanship; but these men have at their best been able to project in their work little but their personal experience and points of view. Charles Burchfield, with a great talent for water color, paints with deep feeling

FIG. 538.—POOR. THE LAND GRANT.
*Old Main Hall, Pennsylvania State College, State College, Pa.*

the fragments of our landscape that are redolent of the past. The curiously tortured houses which our grandfathers found beautiful, the old decaying "Gothic" farmhouse, these are painted with tenderness and insight. In *Lace Gables* (Fig. 539) the artist presents a drama of the disintegration of something precious and human. The abandoned yard, the unused doors and windows shaped for human needs now invite the rank growth of weeds and flowers. Here is a philosophical and spiritual context unclouded by shallow sentiment or quaintness. Burchfield makes trenchant and revealing comments on our native scene where the professional regionalists too often concoct only picturesque over-simplifications.

For all these virtues, Burchfield's art remains in a minor plane. Like the body of American work in recent decades it is without any great power or authority. Only a few of our painters have attained the pictorial mastery, the learning and assurance that make for a larger spiritual communion. The great prestige of Max Weber (Fig.

Fig. 539.—BURCHFIELD. Lace Gables. *Root Coll., Clinton, N. Y.*

Fig. 540.—WEBER. Winter Twilight. *Associated American Artists, N. Y.*

540) among painters testifies to the rarity of this mastery in America. His paintings cannot be called "projections of an interesting personality" for the very reason that he has the depth and resources of learning and intelligence to embody a spiritual world in a canvas. There are no rare passages in his paintings, the whole canvas is one. Cohesion of his forms and color interprets a positive clearly articulated concept.

In the sphere of abstract painting Walter Houmère uses design to graph the unseen forces of energy operative in psychic and physical phenomena (Fig. 541). His art has the authority of an articulate mind

Fig. 541.—HOUMÈRE. Lute, Flute and Dance. *Artist's Coll.*

working with insight and capacity to encompass abstract concepts where others find only isolated sensations. This ability to create an imaginatively valid cosmos is a salient attribute of John Marin. His water color *Lower Manhattan* (Fig. 542) seeks the indwelling pulse beat of the cityscape. The bolting streak of a suspended bridge, the thrusting point of a tower, the running or crawling movement of color are organized in a design which wakens one to the reality of a drama only vaguely felt before. Such shorthand and cryptic translations of material objects into intuitive symbols are likely to become commonplace in western art. Only recently have we come to understand more fully these same methods when employed by El Greco and Van Gogh. Those artists who comprehend the exacting art language they inherit and use it for deliberate symbolic interpretation are few in any age, including our own.

The power to translate sensate experience into some larger frame of reference, i.e., to render sensations meaningful, is the supreme function of art. The painter with line and color and simulated space creates pictorial drama on a sheet of paper, canvas or a wall. Whatever his method—realistic or non-realistic—whatever his nationality or race,

Fig. 542.—MARIN. Lower Manhattan. *Goodwin Coll., N. Y.*

this line and color must function as living actors in the drama he creates. The American artist uses the same means as the German or the Chinese. With these means the artist in the United States must seek the same imaginative truth as any other thinker, whether he be a chemist or a physician. His interpretation of his world must have validity effective beyond the limits of time or oceans, the validity of a spiritual force made articulate.

# THE MINOR ARTS

# Chapter XXXIII. General Considerations—Pre-Classic, Classic and Mediaeval

*IN ALL PERIODS OF WORLD HISTORY, THE VISUAL ARTS* have included other forms than those of architecture, sculpture and painting—forms which are termed variously the minor arts, the useful arts, the decorative arts or the functional arts. Whatever the name applied to them, it is employed to distinguish them in purpose at least from the fine arts, for they are in general represented by objects that have a measure of utilitarian as well as aesthetic value. Indeed, it is usually the utilitarian function of the object that is the major factor in accounting for its existence in contrast to the non-utilitarian purpose of the fine arts such as sculpture and painting. It is to architecture that the minor arts can be most directly compared in this sense of the utilitarian as an element of equal importance with the aesthetic or the expressive—in which usefulness is as vital a consideration as appearance but differing chiefly in the matter of scale. For it is the furniture and the dishes, the metal work and the picture frames, the rugs and carpets and the vases that are the minor arts which contribute by the fitness of their design alike to utilitarian purpose and to pleasure in the balance of form, flow of surface, rhythm of line or contrast of texture that makes them as much a work of art as they are effective tools for their intended use.

The historical continuity of medium that characterizes the fine arts of architecture, sculpture and painting is not found in the minor arts to anything like the same degree. This is largely a consequence of the different ways of living that prevail in different times and places and that exercise a more direct influence upon the functioning forms of the minor arts than upon the less utilitarian ones in the major categories. Thus, for all the important contrasts between the form of a Greek temple and that of a modern office building, they none the less have more in common than do the crater in which the Greek mixed the wines that accompanied his banquets and the cocktail shaker that performs the same duty for his modern counterpart, and a mediaeval chalice is hardly to be compared with either one save in the most general way. If, therefore, it seems difficult or even impossible to discern a common quality or way of thinking in the varied categories of the minor arts that can be compared with the sculptor's concern with plastic form or the architect's interest in patterns of space or the painter's interpretation of three-dimensional experience in two-dimensional design, no matter what the period in which they worked, this is no more than logical in view of the variety of specific purposes which the forms themselves are intended to meet.

If continuity and uniformity of purpose and form are lacking in the minor arts to an extent comparable to that which prevails in the major arts, it is none the less to be noted that within a given period they have much in common with the major arts. This will be immediately evident in the more detailed discussion to follow, but it is to be noted here that the quality of an example of the minor arts may be said to reside in the extent to which it reflects the most characteristic formal and expressive values of its age. Thus, the organization of the mass and ornament of a Greek vase is as basically geometrical as it is in a contemporary statue or building. The casket that enshrined the holy relics in a mediaeval church is built up in an architectonic pattern that creates in it a microcosm of the church itself. An 18th-century chair has the same delicacy of scale and gracefulness of form as a painting by Watteau or Fragonard, and the crystalline severity of plane and texture that characterizes a modern building or painting is directly paralleled in the contemporary forms of furniture and china. The term "minor arts" when applied to forms possessing such characteristics should therefore not be considered as one of derogation; it is not so intended, but rather as a generally accepted convention by which their utilitarian purpose as a primary factor is implied.

Two additional considerations of a general nature regarding the minor arts remain to be noted. The first has been touched upon in other connections in this book, namely, their importance in supplementing the major arts in certain periods. Thus the visual evidence of the art of painting as practiced by the Greeks before the fourth century B.C. is limited almost entirely to the ornament of vases and jars and the like, although it is known from literary sources that monumental wall painting was executed at least as early as the middle of the fifth century B.C. Small clay or terra-cotta models that were used for religious cult purposes tell much of otherwise unrepresented phases of the early architecture of Greece and the Etruscans. The sculptural tradition of one of the great branches of early mediaeval art, that of the Byzantine East, would be much less well known were it not for the carved ivory plaques that decorate the covers of manuscript books or are combined to form altarpieces and reliquary caskets. In such

instances as these, it is the minor arts that make possible the comprehensive knowledge of a period and its way of thinking that is one
of the fundamentals for the interpretation and understanding of human
thought and experience.

It is in this same sense of the work of art as a human experience
that the second general consideration concerning the
minor arts is advanced. If the ancient Egyptian seems
closer to us in the delightfully intimate figure of the
little girl who is the handle of a perfume spoon than
in the hieratic form of the Pharaoh, it is because its
everyday purpose is more readily paralleled in our
own experience than is the mystical concept of deity
on earth that underlies the monumental statue. The
chest in which the Florentine bride treasured her
wedding finery may arouse a homely emotion that is
more immediate and moving than the wistful nostalgia of the classic gods and goddesses in the paintings that hung on the walls of her palace. Such reactions as these are admittedly more in the realm of
sentiment than of form—they are anecdotal and literary in quality rather than aesthetic—but to the
extent that they lead to an understanding of a work
of art as a consequence of human feeling and emotion, they may contribute to the broadened experience that is the true end of knowledge.

### A. Pre-classic Minor Arts

From earliest times man has sought to make the
implements of his daily life and activity something
more than tools—works of art as well as being useful.
Among the first such objects known is a *Reindeer-
horn Dart-thrower* (Fig. 543) that dates from the
Palaeolithic Age of prehistory which came to an end
about 10,000 B.C. With this device, the hunter was
able to hurl darts farther and with greater power than
was possible with the arm alone, it serving as a sort of
extension of the arm. This mechanical function of
the thrower could have been performed quite as well
by a straight stick with a notch at one end, so it is obvious that more
than this was involved in both the choice of material and the way it
was handled. The material was supplied by one of the animals upon
which Palaeolithic man depended for his food, and the form in which

Fig. 543. —
Dart Thrower.
Reindeer horn.
*Museum, Saint-
Germain.*

it is carved is that of another—the antelope. His motive in so transforming an inanimate substance into a work of art—for the accomplished adaptation of the beast's head and forequarters to the cylindrical form of the piece of bone reveals a high degree of skill in selecting the memorable aspects of the animal to record its appearance—can only be surmised, but two ideas have been suggested as possibilities. One is that the natural form of the object suggested the animal and the prehistoric artist simply heightened this suggestion by carving a few lines as a sort of diversion or because of some subconscious and intuitive urge to render its form into an organized visual pattern. The second is that by manipulation of the material in accordance with the impulses of the artist and controlled by him, his power in the hunt would be increased and he would have magic influence over his prey through the medium of the pictorial representation thereof. The first of these suggestions, that the artist was motivated by aesthetic impulses, seems to be borne out by further examples of prehistoric art like many pottery vessels on which linear patterns of purely decorative character can be seen. On the other hand, the organization of the groups of painted animals in one of the prehistoric caves at Altamira in Spain (Fig. 355), also of the Palaeolithic period, complies in only the most elemental degree with generally accepted principles of composition and arrangement such as symmetry, accenting or dramatic continuity. This leads to the conclusion that if the motivating impulse were only of an aesthetic nature, the primitive artist was able to see an order which is not clear today; while if the motive were one of magic from a superstitious belief in the power held over the animals themselves by the artist able thus to represent them, its lack of larger compositional principles involved in the relationship of multiple forms is not a major consideration. In the relatively late period of prehistory when the dart-thrower was carved, it is possible that both aesthetic and magic factors were involved, the former counting for more than it does in the case of the wall paintings because of the less complex nature of the form and motive. In either case, it remains an outstanding early example of the minor arts in its combination of pleasing appearance with utility of form.

In the more developed pre-classic cultures of Egypt, Mesopotamia and the Mediterranean and Aegean cities of Crete and Greece, the minor arts figure very prominently. The discovery of metals and minerals and the evolution of processes by which they could be manipulated made available many of the materials that have remained in use for such purposes down to the present time—gold and silver, glass and enamel, precious and semi-precious stones—and which figure in the creation of utilitarian and decorative forms, along with the more prosaic mediums of stone and wood and pottery. Many objects of this character,

FIG. 544.—FALCON HEAD. Gold. *Museum, Cairo.*

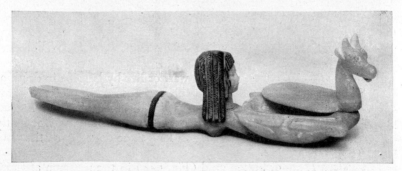

FIG. 545.—PERFUME SPOON. Alabaster and slate.
*Metropolitan Museum, N. Y.*

in fact the majority of them, have been preserved in consequence of the unvarying belief of all these cultures in the necessity of preserving in burial the body and possessions of the human being after death. Thus the Pharaoh of Egypt wears in his sarcophagus the jeweled necklace and breast ornament that symbolized with such opulence his semi-divine position in life, and his daughter's cosmetic container accompanies her in her tomb as it did on the dressing table in her palace.

FIG. 546—MIRROR. Bronze. *Metropolitan Museum, N. Y.*

The golden cup of an ancient Greek warrior lies by his side in death as it stood on his table in Vaphio, and the bull-headed harp of the Babylonian princess stood by her sarcophagus as it did by her throne. Thanks to this practice and the objects thus preserved, as much is frequently known of the way of living practiced in long-since ended dynasties as of much contemporary life.

The *Falcon Head* of beaten gold (Fig. 544) in the museum at Cairo was excavated from the ruins of an ancient temple at Kôm-el-ahmar in Egypt. The date of its execution was about 2500 B.C. and it was originally part of a group symbolizing the protection of the king by

Horus, who was represented in Egyptian art with a falcon's head. This part of the figure was riveted to a bronze body after being beaten into shape, probably over a wooden form, and the eyes of red jasper were inlaid. To be noted is the fine sense of the craftsman for his material—the flexible gold being rounded over to secure the maximum brilliance of surface—and also for the wild and savage spirit of the bird. In this latter respect the artisan shows himself one with his sculptor colleagues whose lively and spirited portrayals of animals so often stand in striking contrast to the rigid and stylized monumental figures of humans (cf. Fig. 233) which they executed under the immutable

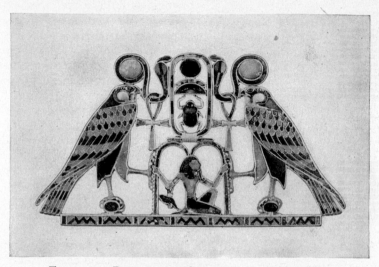

Fig. 547.—Pectoral of Senusert II. Gold, inlaid.
*Metropolitan Museum, N. Y.*

laws controlling such forms. This is not invariably true of the human form in Egyptian art, however, for the salve or *Beauty-cream Container* (Fig. 545), in the form of a nude girl swimming behind a wild duck whose open back holds the salve, shows a figure that is natural in proportion and easy in movement. It is of alabaster and slate and dates from about 1400 B.C. in the general period of Egyptian history called that of the New Kingdom. It is not at all uncommon for the human form to be introduced in the decoration of such utilitarian objects, another instance being the girl holding a silvered bronze disk (Fig. 546) and thus figuring as a slave supporting a mirror. It too is of the New Kingdom period and has in common with the salve container a conception of the figure that is in stylized terms to the extent that it is necessary to serve as a handle to the object but otherwise is surprisingly free and convincing in appearance. The object between the girl's head and the mirror disk is in the form of a papyrus capital; the parallel to the practice of builders of the period who often employed human heads for capital decoration is to be noted. Both objects are distinguished by the same craftsman's sense of the material that characterized the gold falcon's head—the texture of the stone being an element in the design of one and the rhythmic flow of smooth metallic line that unifies the human with the geometrical form in the other.

FIG. 548.—THRONE OF TUTANKH-
AMEN. Cedar and Gold.
*Museum, Cairo.*

Among the most spectacular examples of the minor arts in Egypt are the *Pectorals* or breast ornaments that were a part of the state costume of the ruler in his life and lay on his mummy after death. An example of about 1900 B.C. in the Middle Kingdom period (Fig. 547) bears the name of Senusert II in the hieroglyphic cartouche flanked by two snakes in the upper portion. Below, kneeling, is a figure that is presumably the monarch himself, with a falcon heraldically posed on either side. The material is gold with carnelian, lapis lazuli and feldspar inlay. As a design, unity is attained through the symmetry of the arrangement, with the smoothly flowing curves of the various forms merging easily with one another. Very effective too is the brilliant color pattern of the whole, which consists of a series of repeated accents in an abstract allover pattern. Nor should the symbolism of the various details be overlooked—the *crux ansata* or cross of life that hangs from the snakes which are themselves a symbol of royal power, and the falcons representing the god Horus, protector of the Pharaoh. Such forms as these reveal the opulent and hieratic form of the minor arts in the official world of Egypt as the salve container and mirror represent more intimate and personal aspects.

A *Ceremonial Throne* from the tomb of Tutankhamen (Fig. 548) is a further example of the minor arts in an official capacity in Egypt. Of wood, it was one of the many objects found in the subterranean burial place of this New Kingdom ruler who was not one of the great figures in Egyptian history but whose name is outstanding in the annals of archaeology by virtue of the fact that his tomb was virtually intact when discovered by Howard Carter in 1923 and provided an unprecedentedly rich treasure of the burial paraphernalia of a Pharaoh. The body of the throne is cedar, and the carved ornament, consisting of symbolic figures of the king and the gods and hieroglyphic inscriptions, is covered in some places with gold leaf. The employment of animals' claws for the feet is a conception similar to that of the human figures serving as handles for the salve spoon and the mirror (Figs. 545-546), while the architectural details in the frame and the openwork of the back are comparable in effect to the pectoral. The close-grained wood has resulted in a different effect of surface texture and scale, however, and the design as a whole is conditioned by the practical necessity of comfort in sitting that produces the gentle curving lines of the seat.

The stone-worker and the potter are represented in the minor arts of Egypt along with the woodcarver and the goldsmith. Alabaster jars and other types of vessel, sometimes decorated with inscriptions but as often left plain (Fig. 549), are a characteristic product of the former in which the simple curved outlines and the intrinsic texture of the material itself appeal more strongly to the modern eye, perhaps, than do the more striking works of the goldsmith.

FIG. 549.—JAR. Alabaster. *Metropolitan Museum, N. Y.*

The Middle Kingdom *Terra-cotta Hippopotamus* (Fig. 550) covered with a blue glaze over black papyrus buds and blossoms is an amusing example of Egyptian ceramic art that is at the same time a well-composed form (observe the appropriateness in the design of the floral motives to the part of the animal where they are found, opened blossoms on the rotund body and the vertical accent of the buds on the shoulder and haunch) and a further indication of the Egyptian artist's simple pleasure in identifying the forms of nature that do not fall within the rigid laws of hierarchic monumental art. Here again is evidence of a strong instinct for stylization such as is found in the monumental stone figures, yet the appeal to a modern temperament is much greater in the terra-cotta animal for it seems to have been controlled by an aesthetic sense much more closely allied in kind to that of the contemporary world than the symbolic stylism of the statues, and the impression created by it and the similarly conceived forms discussed above is far more one of human beings capable of human emotions as the creators rather than the strictly curbed and rigidly ruled artists whose formulas in the larger figures are contrived to convey as directly as possible the sense of beings partaking alike of human and divine attributes.

The second and most Oriental of the pre-classic cultures that developed in the Mediterranean world, that in the Near East or Mesopotamia, was also rich in the minor arts. Many small cult objects such as seals and rings might be mentioned as illustrations, but the character of Mesopotamian art in this field is so well summed up by one object

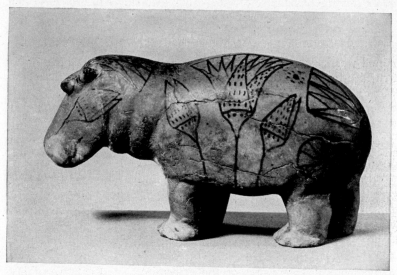

FIG. 550.—HIPPOPOTAMUS. Terra-cotta. *Metropolitan Museum, N. Y.*

that it will serve as the basis of discussion—the *Harp of shell, lapis lazuli and gold* found in a tomb near Ur in Chaldaea by a joint expedition from the British Museum in London and the University of Pennsylvania Museum in Philadelphia (Figs. 551-552). It is among the most ancient of historical objects from the region, dating between 3500 and 3200 B.C. The harp is of wood overlaid with carved shell and gold, with accenting details of blue lapis lazuli, the rich color effect standing for all that is exotic and Oriental in the popular mind. The bull's-head terminal has the same vigor of feeling noted in the animal sculptures of the Mesopotamian style, combined with a fine decorative effect from the contrasting colors of the gold and the lapis lazuli details of the eyes, horn tips and beard, the contrasting textures of the stone and metal, and the adjustment of the whole to its place on the front of the harp. Immediately below the head are four small scenes with grotesque figures—illustrations of songs which were sung to harp accompaniment and having to do with beings in Mesopotamian religion and mythology. The figures are cut from pieces of shell and are set in a dark background; although quite small in size, they have the same sense of vitality and life that characterizes some of the stone

FIG. 551.—THE HARP OF QUEEN SHUB' AD. Gold, lapis lazuli and shell.
*University Museum, Philadelphia.*

sculpture on a much larger scale of a later period in Mesopotamian art (cf. Fig. 246), and the decorative scheme of color and texture of the harp is further enriched by these characteristics in the small reliefs. The sumptuous exoticism of the combination of qualities described accords well with the semi-barbaric Oriental character of Mesopotamian culture as it is otherwise indicated in art and literature.

It is in the fields of pottery and metal work that the minor arts are most completely represented in the culture of the Aegean world that is the third of the pre-classic traditions to develop in the Mediterranean area. On the island of Crete, the sites of the great palaces built by the Minoan kings at Knossos and Phaistos and many less extensive ones have provided through excavation a considerable number of vases and jars in whose ornament a high degree of decorative skill is often apparent. Abstract geometrical designs are frequently used, but the motives derived from nature—flower and plant forms and the creatures of the sea that islanders would naturally be particularly interested in—are those to which the greatest interest attaches, such as the *Lily Vase* (Fig. 553). The period in which the Cretan or Minoan potter achieved what now appear to be his finest results was that called Middle Minoan, from about 2100 to 1580 B.C., and it is from the latter part of this epoch that the lily vase comes. Of great technical perfection as an example of ceramic method, the background is of a light color while the bell and stem of the lilies are painted in darker tones. The pattern of blossoms is admirably adapted to the shape of the vessel, the long stalks rising from the base through the almost straight sides and flowering in a spreading design that fills the curved top in an effect that is satisfying both as representation and in adaptation to the form of the vase. Other *Vases* of about the same period (Fig. 554) are decorated with abstract geometrical patterns—rosettes, spirals, rectangles and the like. In the shape of these vases there is a suggestion of work executed in metal rather than pottery, as in the handles, for example, which look like curved strips riveted to the body of the vessel; and it seems likely that such were the models which the ceramicist attempted to copy.

FIG. 552.—MYTHO-LOGICAL SCENES. Detail of Fig. 551.

A little later than the Middle Minoan examples just considered is the *Octopus Vase* found at Gournia in Crete (Fig. 555), which comes from the first part of the Late Minoan period, probably about 1500 B.C. The color harmony is one of browns, dark in the figure of the octopus and in the seaweed, light buff for the background. The theme of sea life is characteristic of this later period which preferred such motives to the geometrical and flower forms used earlier; in this respect it is interesting to note that the Aegean vase painter avoided the human figure almost entirely in contrast with the practice of contemporary mural decorators (cf. Fig. 359). As in the lily vase, the primary concern of the painter has been exactness of appearance stylized to achieve the maximum decorative effect. The octopus seems to float in the sea

*From a reproduction*

FIG. 553.—THE LILY VASE. *Museum, Candia.*

surrounded by the seaweed, urchins and anemones, the writhing tentacles floating out to fill the bulbous contours of the jar with rhythmic linear patterns that are unified by the repeats of dots and circles. If the effect is somewhat less restrained than the static simplicity of the lilies on the earlier vase, it none the less is well in accord with the sumptuous sophistication of life in the palace culture of the Late Minoan period.

The same freedom of design is found in two examples of metal work of Aegean origin—a *Ceremonial Dagger* (Fig. 556) with a scene of cats hunting birds found in a grave at Mycenae, and a pair of *Gold Cups* discovered at *Vaphio* (Fig. 557), both cities on the mainland of Greece. The blade of the dagger is of bronze and the figures are inlaid in gold and silver set off by a hard black paste-like substance. This method of working metal is called damascening and is particularly effective for the contrasting colors, sheen and textures that can be attained. Here it is used to represent the dashing cats seizing the fluttering birds in a scene of great animation that is given continuity by the long flowing line of the river with fish swimming in it and bordered

FIG. 554.—VASES FROM KNOSSOS. *Museum, Candia.*

with papyrus plants. The formal pattern is well adjusted to the long tapering shape of the blade and the repeated accents of the papyrus blossoms tie the whole together. An interesting point is the choice of motive, for the hunting cats, the river scene and the papyrus plants are not native in the Greek mainland as the flowers and octopus of the Cretan vases were on the island, but are distinctly Egyptian in character. The possibility of its having been created in Egypt cannot be overlooked, but it is more probable that relations between Egypt and Mycenae were such that the motive had been transmitted from its place of origin to the other land.

The theme of the Vaphio cups, on the other hand, is associated completely with Aegean culture. The bull figures prominently in the portrayal of religious rites and practices both in Crete (cf. Fig. 359) and on the mainland, probably as a symbol of fecundity in the semi-primitive worship of natural forms and principles that prevailed there, and it is doubtless with some such background as this that the incidents on these cups must be understood. On the one to the left, a bull tied by one hind leg bellows to a wild companion who is seen being decoyed by a cow on the other side. The second cup shows the wild bull dashing off in alarm on one side and hopelessly snared in a net on the

*From a reproduction*

Fig. 555.—The Octopus Vase. *Museum, Candia.*

other. These cups are executed in a technique called *repoussé*; the walls are hollow with the inner one left plain, the design being executed on the outer one by beating the malleable gold over a form of wood or terra cotta on which it was first carved or modeled. There is perhaps less concern apparent in these cups with the problem of adapting the pictorial theme to the basic form than in the dagger or the vases; the head of the tethered bull is obscured by the handle, for instance, and the inconsistency between the stylized trees and the naturalistically rendered animals cannot be overlooked. But the vigorous plunge of the fleeing bull and his desperate efforts to free himself from the net are well caught on the one cup, and his fatuous response to the lure of the decoy cow on the other is a masterpiece of animal characterization.

The pre-classic phase of western culture in which originated the examples of the minor arts thus far considered is characterized by an attitude primarily utilitarian and symbolic toward the forms created. The idea of a vase or a piece of furniture as something that needs only aesthetic justification is characteristically modern; to the man of the ancient world, the desirability of an object lay in its usefulness or the excellence of its craftsmanship or its power as a symbol. A relief in an Egyptian tomb shows two stone workers carving vases; their conversation, indicated by hieroglyphics, has been translated as follows: "This is a beautiful vase that I am making," "Indeed it is," which would

*From a reproduction*

Fig. 556.—Dagger from Mycenae. Bronze, damascened.
*National Museum, Athens.*

seem to contradict the preceding statement. But the symbol translated as "beautiful" is used also to mean "good" or "fine" in Egyptian writing, and the connotation is as often as not such as to permit the interpretation of these terms as "useful" or "well-made." At the most, it was only a pleasure in fine craftsmanship that could have been experienced in the presence of these objects by their makers, an emotion quite different in character from an aesthetic response. As has been pointed out, this is true as well of the concept of the major arts that prevailed at the same time, a convincing demonstration of the honesty of purpose and sincerity of meaning that is one of the most fundamental distinctions between the arts of ancient times and those of today, wherein for the most part abstract aestheticism is considered the sole necessary justification for the existence of a work of art. It is this quality, too, that makes a jewel or vase or chair of ancient times as characteristic in its way of the mode of thinking that produced it as the temples or monumental stone figures with which it is contemporary.

## B. The Minor Arts of Greece and Rome

The rich treasure of the minor arts in the pre-classic Mediterranean cultures is one of the historical consequences of the developed burial cults that existed in Egypt, Mesopotamia and the Aegean phases of life in the Greek mainland and islands. For reasons pointed out elsewhere, such a cult did not exist in anything like the same degree in the classic world and the relative absence of certain categories in the

*From reproductions*

FIG. 557.—THE VAPHIO CUPS. Gold. *National Museum, Athens.*

minor arts of Greece and Rome may be traced directly to this fact. The gold, silver and jewels which once no doubt existed have long since been transformed into other objects; the wooden utensils and furniture that the dry air of a sealed Egyptian tomb preserved for centuries have disintegrated with time or been destroyed in the hearth fire of an insensitive owner; even bronze figurines and ornaments have crumpled with erosion or been melted to supply metal for other purposes. For the most part, it is only those objects which are of a material at once durable and incontrovertible that have been preserved to illustrate today the classic genius in the minor arts, although indirect sources may shed some light on the nature of its products. Thus in the scene of an old man being served with wine, painted on the inside of a drinking cup that dates from early in the fifth century (Fig. 558), there is an illustration of a bench or stool with legs that terminate in a pair of opposed scrolls like those of an Ionic capital (cf. Fig. 32). More developed is the form of the chair on which Hegeso is seated on the stele carved in her memory (Fig. 267); without superfluous ornament and consisting of legs fastened with pins to the horizontal slab of the seat and the upright of the back, it is rendered beautifully decorative by the opposed yet complementary curves that are as subtle in line as the echinus of a Doric capital. Like the architectural forms with

FIG. 558.—INTERIOR OF A KYLIX. Red-figured. *Museum, Corneto.*

which it is contemporary, its design is simple yet very effective by virtue of its refinement of functional form and its clear statement in visual terms of the nature of the material, which was wood in this case.

The largest single category of the Greek minor arts that has been preserved is that of the vases—pottery jars, storage vessels, drinking cups and the like which were useful implements in the Greek world. Their preservation is a consequence of the humble material of which they are made which is at the same time lasting and without great intrinsic value, but their importance as art objects far transcends this, for, as has already been pointed out, the decoration of which they were often made the object provides a knowledge that would otherwise be far from as complete as it is of the process by which the incomparable concept of visual form developed which is one of the great inheritances of later generations from the Greek world.

The *Forms of Greek Vases* are many and varied, determined by the use to which they were put. The illustration (Fig. 559) shows a number of the more characteristic ones with the names that indicate their

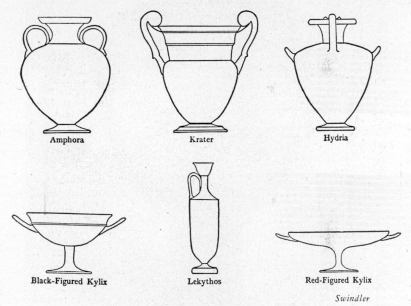

*Swindler*

Fɪɢ. 559.—Gʀᴇᴇᴋ Vᴀsᴇ Sʜᴀᴘᴇs.

usage. The amphora is a rather wide-mouthed jar that was used to store wine and oil; the somewhat similar hydria has a flattened lip and three handles that assist in its function of carrying and pouring water. The crater is a large open bowl in which water and wine were mixed at the banquet table, and the kylix is a flat cup from which the mixture was drunk. An oenochoë is a wine pitcher and a lekythos is a small flask-like container that could be easily corked and which was used to hold the oils employed in ceremonial rituals. It should be noted that the form in each case is well adapted to its use; the wine is poured from its container not directly into the cup but into the crater with its generous opening that even the most bibulous could reach into with his kylix, and the narrow neck of the lekythos permits the preservation of the last drop of precious perfumed oil.

The manufacture of the Greek vase involved the use of a rotating table or wheel on which a mass of moist clay was placed, the form being modeled by the potter who in all probability depended largely upon his instinct for determining the proper curvature of line and proportion of mass, guided only by an inherited feeling for the most ap-

Fig. 560.—Dipylon Crater. *Metropolitan Museum, N. Y.*

propriate form. When the fabric of the vase was thus completed, it was placed in an oven and baked hard, after which it was usually of a characteristic red-brown color. Vessels intended for ordinary use might have been left in this state, but it was more usual to paint the vessel on the outside and sometimes within as well. This was done with a liquid preparation called a slip; following its application, the vase was fired once more in the course of which the slip was hardened to a black glaze of highly enameled and lustrous texture and appearance.

In the inside of the vessel this glaze served to render the porous clay impermeable to liquids; on the outside it was sometimes used simply to cover the body of the vase with an even coat but more often it was so applied as to form a definite design. It is with cases in the latter category that the ensuing discussion will be concerned, involving as they do problems of composition and design and the rendering of forms and figures that make the vases thus decorated one of the most considerable and important classes of Greek art.

The history of Greek vase painting goes back to the earliest times in which the ideals of the classic tradition are suggested—the dim and darkened years of the ninth and eighth centuries B.C. when the fusion of Aegean culture with that of the invading barbarians from the lands north of Greece was still in process of taking place. Of this period is a great crater-like *Dipylon Vase* in the Metropolitan Museum in New York (Fig. 560), which stands over four feet in height and was used as the container of ashes from a cremated body, a funereal function that is common to nearly all the known examples of this type of vase and which determines the decorative themes as well. These, in so far as they involve figures, represent the deceased on his bier in the upper level, accompanied by his household and a procession of mourners, while below are the funeral games celebrated in his honor, consisting of chariot races and armed combats as described in the twenty-third book of the *Iliad*. The figures are painted on the vase in a black glaze that is similar technically to Minoan practice in the Aegean period, but the style of figures and decoration alike is different, consisting as it does of strictly geometrical forms for the latter and a reduction of the former to equally stylized geometrical elements—bodies and limbs consisting of triangles and the heads in profile. The armed warriors in the lower level are thought of as standing behind their shields, which are in the shape of a double-headed axe. Equally primitive is the filling of the background of each figured panel with rosettes, dots and zigzags. But the organization of the decorative scheme in horizontal zones with the main subject occupying a large panel in the center of the upper figured level is more advanced than anything of its type in the Aegean period and reveals the sense of formal relationship between form and ornament that develops and prevails in all subsequent periods of Greek art.

This same decorative scheme—simplified, clarified and yet more complexly organized—recurs in the *François Vase*, a crater discovered in an Etruscan tomb in Italy but of Grecian origin (Fig. 561). It bears inscriptions that identify the subjects represented, dealing chiefly with the stories of Peleus and his son Achilles and thus including episodes from the story of the Trojan War. It is also identified by inscriptions as the work of the potter Ergotimos and the painter Klitias, a type of signature that often occurs in the later Greek vases and which reveals the equal esteem in which craftsman and painter alike were held. The François Vase was made in all probability about 560 B.C. and is a fine example of the "black-figured" type of Greek vase painting that was

Fig. 561.—KLITIAS AND ERGOTIMOS. THE FRANÇOIS VASE. Black-figured Crater. *Museo Archeologico, Florence.*

developed from the process described above, although actually other colors are used as well—red and purple and some white. The subjects being primarily narrative, the composition of each frieze is more or less continuous and is somewhat lacking in accent; but taken as a whole, the design builds up from the stylized ornament of the base through an animated frieze of grotesques into a figured frieze of some action in the main band, that on the level of the greatest diameter of the vase, which is painted with a procession of figures that move in slow and stately accents. The upper two friezes are not so wide, and

the decorative rhythm is speeded up once more. It is thus clear that
the decorator was as much if not more concerned with the effect of
his figures as elements in an abstract visual pattern controlled by the
basic design of the vase than with simply representing them or telling
a story. The figures are, withal, much more realistic in general appearance and detail than in the earlier funereal vase.

The black-figured technique of the François Vase also appears in the

FIG. 562.—EXEKIAS. DIONYSOS. Black-figured Kylix. *Museum, Munich.*

decoration of a kylix painted by Exekias, one of the great masters of
the style, probably about 530 B.C. The kylix being a drinking cup, its
decoration deals appropriately with the Greek god of wine, *Dionysos*
(Fig. 562), of whom legend told that, having been kidnaped by pirates
who sought to carry him off in a ship to Egypt, he caused the mast to
be transformed into a grapevine and the ship to stand still, whereupon
the terrified pirates leaped into the sea and were changed into dolphins.
With the exception of the sail, the forms are dark against the lighter
body of the cup, having been painted in silhouette; the details of the
dolphins, the features of Dionysos' face, the outlines of the grapes

and the like are then incised in the black glaze so that after firing the light background of the cup shows through the lines. It is in this exacting and inflexible technique that Exekias has produced one of the masterpieces of decoration in the Greek minor arts; in a prevailingly symmetrical composition whose axis is established by the ship's mast, there is a fine balance between the pattern of grapes above and the

Fig. 563.—EXEKIAS. Ajax and Achilles Playing Draughts. Black-figured Amphora. *Vatican Museum, Rome.*

dolphins below, while the opposition and repetition of curving lines in the sail, the hull, the shapes of the dolphins in relationship to the circle of the cup bottom result in an effective sense of rhythmic movement. Equally fine as a decorative composition is the scene of *Achilles and Ajax Playing Draughts* that Exekias painted on the side of an amphora which dates from about 540 b.c. (Fig. 563). The necessity for covering the entire outside with decoration of some kind that the painter of the funereal vase (Fig. 560) seemed to feel is no longer sensed and even the less crowded compositional canon of the François Vase has been changed. Other than the main pictorial panel, which is placed on the broadest level of the vase, only a band of stylized rays appears, the greater part of the outside being covered with a lustrous black glaze of great beauty in tone and texture. In the central panel the Greek heroes bend intently over their game in such fashion that the curved lines of their backs repeat the profile of the vase, and their spears are held at such an angle as to continue the line of movement created by the curved top of the handles at the joining to the body of the vase. The decoration thus reinforces the structural lines of the vase itself, yet it is also of independent interest, for the figures are symmetrically placed yet varied in detail to result in a well-composed scene; they form a triangle with the apex supplied by Achilles' helmet.

Considered only as a medium of decoration, the black-figured style is an eminently satisfactory process; the physical difficulties of the medium limit the pictorial devices to silhouette and incision, both of which lead to forms that are basically two-dimensional and which thus lie well on the surface to be decorated. The result when the human figure is portrayed is similar in quality to the schematic forms of archaic Greek sculpture with which they are contemporary (cf. Figs. 249-251). At about the same time that the sculptors began to strive for a figure style that more closely approximated the canon of nature, the vase painters too began to explore the possibilities of forms that would be what might be termed pictorially rather than decoratively functional. To achieve these results, a more flexible medium had to be evolved and this—the red-figured style—made its appearance about 525 B.C. (Fig. 558). Like the Dionysos painting by Exekias, this is on the bottom of a kylix or drinking cup, a vase type that became increasingly popular during the fifth century B.C. when it was painted, probably between 500 and 480. Here it will be seen that the background is now dark and the figures light, while the lines that represent details and modeling are dark. Technically, this painting is the reverse of the earlier example; the clay of the vase itself appears in the figures which are reserved, as this effect is described, in the background which is now painted, and the lines are put on with a fine-pointed brush instead of being incised in the painted black slip. The greater freedom which this technique permits the painter is immediately obvious in the multiplication of details, the variety of linear effects and even some attempts to distinguish textures in the garments and to foreshorten the forms in depth.

The success with which the more flexible red-figured technique was used to achieve effects of greater pictorial complexity than the older method made possible is illustrated by a work of the artist called the

*Kleophrades Painter*, who was active around 500 B.C. (Fig. 564). The subject is one of the labors of Heracles, his battle with the Nemean Lion, and the vase is a stamnos or wine jar. In the foreground, the heavily muscled giant is locked in a duel to the death with the lion; at the left is Heracles' club and his bow is hanging from a limb of the tree in the background. The ease with which it is possible to distinguish

FIG. 564.—THE KLEOPHRADES PAINTER. HERAKLES AND THE NEMEAN LION. Red-figured Stamnos. *University Museum, Philadelphia.*

these spatial relationships indicates the differing purpose of the Kleophrades Painter as compared with Exekias; the master of the red-figured style is interested primarily in suggesting the effect of three-dimensional forms in depth, whereas the older artist is concerned almost solely with achieving a pattern in a flat plane whose chief function is its relationship to the form of the object to be decorated. As representation, the Kleophrades Painter's picture is very effective. The anatomical structure of the struggling giant is stylized but accurate, the chief trace of archaism being in the head; the legs and torso are shown in profile positions and the artist has even dared to cover some parts of the body with others, for the plasticity with which the observed portions are represented allows the concealed ones to be inferred even if they are not seen, an idea for which the black-figured reduction of the form to descriptive planes could not provide.

The vase painters of the middle and later fifth century continued to

Fig. 565.—THE MEIDIAS PAINTER, attr. Thamyris and the Muses. Red-figured Hydria. *Metropolitan Museum, N. Y.*

develop the representational resources of the red-figured style and were increasingly less sensitive to the structurally decorative function which the black-figured masters so ably demonstrate. The painting of Odysseus and the ghost of Elpenor on a vase in the Museum of Fine Arts at Boston (Fig. 361) was executed about 440 B.C. The figures move freely and with ease, anatomically accurate and appearing in well-observed foreshortened poses. The drawing is simple and linear in character, with but little modeling by shadow. The forms are composed in one plane that lies parallel to the background but in such a way as to suggest very decidedly the depth of the landscape setting in which the episode occurs. From this it is only a step to considering the dark picture field as space itself (Fig. 565); the relationship of the figures in this scene of *Thamyris and the Muses* on an amphora of 420-400 B.C. attributed to the *Meidias Painter* can be understood only if the background is thought of as a pictorial symbol of three-dimensional depth in which the plastically modeled forms can move freely. Such effects as these were suggested in all probability by the paintings of the famous wall-decorators of the Golden Age in Greece, of whom

FIG. 566.—THE ACHILLES PAINTER. Toilet Scene: Farewell. White-ground Lekythoi. *Metropolitan Museum, N. Y.*

Polygnotos was the most famous. These mural works are known only from descriptions, but the history of contemporary vase painting indicates that their influence on the less monumental art was increasingly more apparent as the century wore on. The result, as is evident in the Meidias vase was an almost complete abandonment of decorative for representational values. Intriguing though many of these later red-figured vases may be for their often quite striking technical ingenuity, as examples of design integrated with form they cannot be ranked with the masterpieces of the late sixth century.

A third technical category of Greek vase painting in addition to that of the black- and red-figured types is the white-ground style. In this technique, which was practiced as early as the seventh century B.C. and continued in use from that time on, the clay ground of the vase was covered with a light-toned slip and the designs were applied in dark outline. Various types of vase in this technique are known, in-

FIG. 567.—MIRROR. Bronze. *Metropolitan Museum, N. Y.*

cluding some fine drinking cups, but the most important and extensive use to which it was put was in the funereal lekythoi. Such is the example of the mid-fifth century attributed to the Achilles Painter which is illustrated (Fig. 566)—a slender vase in which ceremonial oil could be brought as a gift to the tomb, a subject which often figures in their decoration. Otherwise—and this too is illustrated by the present example—the theme is allied in subject and interpretation to those of the sculptured funereal stele (cf. Fig. 267) and may be no more than a scene in the life of the deceased or the saying of farewells. Reticent alike in sentiment and in the beautifully simple draftsmanship, these are among the most appealing examples of the Greek vase painter's art.

Great value was placed upon the works of the leading potters and vase painters by the Greeks. One evidence of this is the practice of signing the vases that has been pointed out above in the case of the François Vase—a practice which has the value of making it possible for the historian to associate with signed examples the stylistic relatives that permit the reconstruction of the artist's productive career. It also permits the further affirmation of the value placed on the works themselves, for although many of them were made as containers for wine and oil and other things to be shipped from one place to another, the presence of the François Vase which was made in Athens and found in a tomb in distant Etruria cannot be thus explained. A cup signed by the same Klitias who painted the François Vase has also been found in Phrygia, far to the east of Greece; and in other similar instances too numerous to mention, the esteem in which the works of the great ce-

Courtesy Museum of Fine Arts, Boston

FIG. 568.—DECADRACHM OF SYRACUSE. Silver. Obverse and reverse.

ramicists was held is indicated. It is a question, however, whether the value attached to them was on aesthetic grounds or for other reasons. In some cases it was certainly for associative or sentimental considerations, for many of the drinking cups bear dedications to handsome youths much admired in their times who were doubtless boon companions in many a symposium. In other cases the value of the name was probably that of a trade-mark as Wedgwood and Lenox are today. Any inference therefrom that the vase was used only as an object of visual admiration would probably be no better founded than in the case of the proud housewife of today.

The same instinct that the Greek reveals for decorative utilitarian forms in his painted vases is apparent also in a variety of metal objects that have been spared by chance from the fate in the melting pot that must have befallen innumerable further examples. For instance, a *Mirror* (Fig. 567) consisted originally of a polished or silvered bronze disk supported by the figure of a girl with two sphinxes; the basic idea is not unlike that of the Egyptian mirror (Fig. 546), but the function of transition in the design from the handle to the disk that is performed by an architectural capital in the Egyptian example is performed less artificially here. Coins, too, give an excellent indication of the same attitude; symbols of place names like the owl of Athene on the coins of Athens figure prominently in the decorative themes, combined sometimes with inscriptions. The *Ten-drachma Piece* from *Syracuse* in Sicily (Fig. 568), struck about 480 B.C., is beautifully composed. Around the profile head representing the nymph Arethusa who was especially honored in Syracuse play four dolphins, a symbolic reference alike to the legend of the nymph and the nautical interests of the city; a literal inscription further identifies the origin of the piece. All these elements are wrought into a circular pattern that lies well on the form of the coin. The irregular shape of Greek coins is a consequence of the way they were made. A relatively thick piece of metal was placed between the dies on which the face and reverse were cut in intaglio and a heavy blow was struck on the upper one; the edge of the metal disk was thus raised as it was squeezed out, forming a ridge that protects in some degree the relief pattern of the coin.

FIG. 569.—COIN OF NERO. Gold. *University Museum, Philadelphia.*

In turning from the minor arts of the Greeks to those of the Romans, a significant change in attitude is apparent, a change that is indicated on a small scale but no less clearly for that, if the Syracusan coin be compared with one struck during the reign of Nero (A.D. 37-68) in Rome (Fig. 569). Possibly the most immediate observation is the naturalism of the head; it is a profile portrait which in a sense renders unnecessary the stolidly executed inscription surrounding it. Of composition and arrangement there is but little; there is an awkward space in front of the face and neck while the inscription is crowded behind between the head and the dotted rim of the coin. It is obvious that where the designer of the Greek coin was concerned in considerable measure with producing a combination of forms that would be pleasing to the eye as well as indicating the character of the object, the Roman had no intention beyond evolving a symbol of the Emperor's promise to pay for value received. It is not inappropriate that a symbol of the ruler should replace that of the city or country, a practice that has continued from late classic to modern times.

The difference between the Greek attitude of decorative functionalism in the minor arts and the Roman one is further illustrated by the example of a *Silver Dish* on which there is a bust in high relief representing Africa in symbolic form (Fig. 570); it was found in excavations at Boscoreale, a village not far from Pompeii which suffered the same fate as the city in the eruption of Vesuvius in 79 A.D. As a demonstration of the handling of material to secure a striking effect, the dish is very fine; details like the serpent and the wild beasts—symbols along with

FIG. 570.—DISH WITH BUST OF AFRICA. Silver. *Louvre, Paris.*

the plant forms and the horn of plenty of the produce of the continent —are executed with great naturalism. In fact, naturalism is the keynote of the entire decorative scheme, for the bust and all its accessories look as if they had simply been applied to the bottom of the dish, a procedure which effectively prevents it from any practical use; compare the effect of drinking from this cup with that of using the Exekias kylix (Fig. 562)! It should be added that such a useful purpose was probably not intended—the plate is entirely ornamental in function— but the contrast with Greek practice is none the less illuminating; the Greek made his utilitarian object decorative as well, while the Roman makes it striking at the cost of both decorative consistency and utility.

This plate was never intended as anything other than a "museum piece," treasured for the factual and naturalistic quality of its ornament and for the intrinsic value of the material. Once it is realized that the collectors' attitude is the primary motivation of much in the Roman minor arts, the value of the object being determined by its cost, rarity or curiosity, the contrast in principle and result with the Greek forms can be easily understood.

Fig. 571.—Bowl. Arretine Ware. *Metropolitan Museum, N. Y.*

The conception of ornament as something to be applied to the basic form of the object that has been pointed out in the silver dish from Boscoreale is also found in the ceramic art of the Romans. A vase with figures representing the four seasons is an example of *Arretine Ware*, so called because much of it was made in or near Arezzo (Fig. 571); the characteristic red color is in the base clay and also the glaze which hardens to a glossy coral color on being fired. The body of the vase was formed on a wheel, but the decorative figures were executed with the aid of moulds of baked terra cotta in which the ornament was incised in sunken relief; it was thus possible to make innumerable examples of a given design, an instance of the mass-production methods followed by the Romans in many of their artistic pursuits. The general shape of the vessel is not unlike a Greek crater (Fig. 561), but the omission of handles is a characteristic indication of the purely decorative and non-utilitarian function of the Roman object.

Roman taste for the striking and extraordinary is shown by the popularity of cameos and related glass techniques among the minor arts.

Fig. 572.—The Deified Augustus. Cameo. *Cabinet des Médailles, Paris.*

The former are cut from pieces of semi-precious stone like sardonyx which have alternate layers of different colors, brown and white in this case (Fig. 572), through which the artisan cut to produce the contrasting effects characteristic of the medium. The cameo of the *Deified Augustus and His Family* in the Cabinet des Médailles in Paris was executed in 17 A.D. and is one of the largest examples of the technique known, measuring about ten by twelve inches. The subject is the protection by the deified Augustus of his successor Tiberius, Augustus appearing in the upper level accompanied by deities of the Roman Pantheon while below are the members of his family with figures of allegorical character similar in import to those which have been noted in the historical relief sculptures of the Ara Pacis and the Arch of Titus (Figs. 285, 286) with which they are roughly contemporary. In the execution of the cameo, a high degree of technical skill is apparent, the figures being cut in no less than five planes to produce the contrasting color effects that play so important a part in the illusion of real figures which constitutes its major stylistic quality. In this latter respect as well as the glorification of the Emperor that is the ultimate purpose

Fig. 573.—The Portland Vase. Glass. *British Museum, London.*

of the work, further parallels with contemporary sculpture are noted. Cameo portrait medallions were also popular with the Romans, the varied color layers permitting such effects as white for the flesh and brown for the beard, hair and eyebrows.

The relative costliness of the semi-precious stone used for cameos and the limited size of available slabs were restrictions to its general popularity that found compensation in the development during the 1st century A.D. of new processes in the handling of glass. Although it had previously been moulded like the clay or terra cotta of a vase, the discovery of the blowpipe method of forming the vessel opened up the possibility of such effects as can be seen in the *Portland Vase* in the British Museum (Fig. 573). By dipping the mass of molten blue glass that forms the background into opaque white, the vase when blown out was actually made in two layers of which the outer one was cut away to form the desired design. The subject is mythological—probably the wooing of Thetis by Peleus; the effect, aided by the semi-translucence of the material, is much like that of a painting, with its minutely dif-

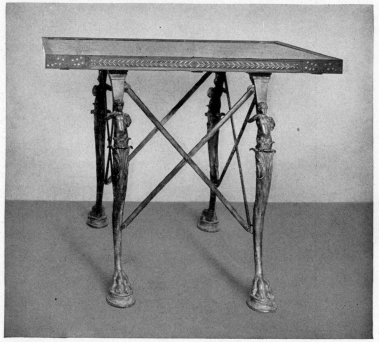

*From a reproduction*

Fig. 574.—Table from Pompeii. Bronze. *Museum, Naples.*

ferentiated planes and the resultant sense of depth in the third dimension; as decoration for the curved walls of the vase, it is open to the same criticism that has been suggested in the case of the silver plate (Fig. 570). Another use of glass developed by the Romans is seen in the mosaic-ware or millefiori vases; these are made by fusing innumerable threads or strands of colored glass in a mould to produce an effect when held to the light that the Italian name—literally thousands of flowers—aptly indicates. They are generally in forms resembling vases carved in stone, a fact which suggests the probability that they were intended to simulate the effect of vessels cut from the veined and colored marbles that abound in Italy but with less effort involved in their creation.

The fondness of the Roman for elaborate decorative effects is illustrated by examples of furniture as well as the objects already discussed. A *Bronze Table* from Pompeii (Fig. 574) is characterized in general by the lightness of proportion and delicacy of detail that are so apparent in the architecture and painting of that city, but a comparison of its carefully calculated forms with those of the Greek chair in the Hegeso Stele (Fig. 267) is illuminating. The legs are successively the feet of animals, leaves composed to form cups and the torsos and heads of cherubs, designed in a curve that is graceful and pleasing enough in itself but which lacks the sense of elastic support that the simpler lines of the Greek chair convey. One longs in the atmosphere of display and opulent richness of the Roman house and its furnishings for the straightforwardness and matter-of-fact appearance of their strictly utilitarian forms such as the aqueducts which supplied them with water (Fig. 61).

In the minor arts of Rome, the conception of an art form of aesthetic rather than primarily utilitarian worth is apparent. This attitude is entirely consistent with Roman practice in other categories—an attitude which cannot be more completely characterized than by calling it that of the collector. The intrinsic or rarity value of many Greek objects was the chief stimulus in the formation of the great collections of sculpture that were accumulated in Rome after the conquest of Greece, and such were the values for which the Roman asked in the objects made at his command. Deficient for the most part in the acute sensitiveness to formal quality that characterized the Greek temperament to a degree hardly conceivable today, the Roman desired ostentation and display more than anything else. Richness is likewise a quality to be found in the minor arts of the Middle Ages, but motivated, as will be seen, by quite different ideals.

# Chapter XXXIV. The Minor Arts of the Middle Ages and the Renaissance

## A. The Mediaeval Period

*THE MINOR ARTS OF THE MIDDLE AGES CONSTITUTE* one of the most varied and extensive categories of the art of that period with which the historian may deal; by comparison with the preceding classic and pre-classic periods this is particularly the case. Whether or not the need for objects of utilitarian or symbolic value was greater then than before it is impossible to say, but it is certain that the employment of such objects by the Church was the reason for the creation of many of them and it is even more sure that had it not been for the agency of the Church in preserving them, there would be an even smaller number in existence today than is the case. From literary sources it is known that many such objects of great intrinsic value and highly venerated for their religious associations have been destroyed or melted down for the sake of the precious metals used in making them; the number still in existence is very great from which it is possible to infer an almost incredible production during the mediaeval period as a whole. Without taking into account for the moment the needs of the laity for the implements and furniture of the household, the place in the Church for objects in the category of the minor arts was large. Altars were frequently covered or enclosed with decorated panels of gold and silver. The relics of saints were treasured in shrines of the same materials or ivory or enamel. The books used for the service or in the libraries of cathedrals and monasteries were bound in elaborate covers decorated with ivory plaques, filigree work of gold or silver, and precious stones. The vestments of priest and bishop were richly embroidered, and tapestries of amazing complexity of form and color might cover the walls of the church itself. Every church that was the seat of a bishop or archbishop possessed an impressive throne of wood, stone or metal in which he sat while taking part in the ceremony of the Mass. It is from these among the many and varied categories of the mediaeval minor arts that a few examples will be selected for discussion.

The dependence of the Church in both a physical and an intellectual sense upon the classic culture that it almost entirely displaced in time has been pointed out before; the same principle is basic in much of the minor art of the Middle Ages. An objective illustration of this point is supplied by a *Chalice* (Fig. 575), now in the Widener Collection in Elkins Park, Pa., which was commissioned by the famous Abbot Suger of the great abbey church of Saint-Denis in the outskirts of Paris. It consists of a sardonyx cup of antique origin, provided with handles, rim and base of gold filigree set with precious stones

Fig. 575.—The Chalice of Suger. Sardonyx, gold and jewels.
*National Gallery, Washington, D. C.*

that were executed during the primacy of Suger (1122-1151) which are fine examples of the goldsmiths' work of the period; around the base is a series of medallions with figures in low relief of Christ and other Biblical characters, a symbolic device that establishes the Christian function of the object. A parallel case of mediaeval adaptation of antique relics is the so-called *Dagobert Throne* in the Bibliothèque Nationale in Paris (Fig. 576). Of bronze, the lower part, including the legs in the form of stylized lions' paws and heads, is of classic origin, while the back of circular medallions in an openwork frame and the sides were added to it in all probability in the 11th or 12th centuries. The folding type of chair represented by the Dagobert throne was used quite extensively during the Middle Ages.

Throughout the entire mediaeval period the carving of ivory was practiced and the examples of this art provide a valuable continuity of medium in what is otherwise a field of such variety that clear-cut impressions thereof are not easy to form. At the outset of the Christian

FIG. 576.—THE DAGOBERT THRONE. Bronze. *Bibliothèque Nationale, Paris.*

era, the style of ivory carving was strongly influenced, as can easily be imagined, by the methods and conceptions of the late classical artists. An example is *The Diptych of Anastasius*, executed in 517 A.D. (Fig. 577). A diptych is formed by hinging two slabs of ivory on the long sides, the outer faces being decorated and the inner ones hollowed out to be filled with soft wax. The diptych under discussion was made to celebrate the taking of office of Anastasius as pronconsul of one of the Roman provinces, an event signalized by his formal opening of the gladiatorial games and combats in his capital city when these diptychs were given to guests of the proconsul as a sort of souvenir score-card, the tallies being marked in the wax by a sharp stylus. The outsides of the ivory plaques show the consul giving the signal to begin the games; at the top is an inscription with his name and office and immediately beneath are medallion portraits of the rulers he represents. The consul is seated under a canopy upon an elaborate throne with legs in the form of lions' forequarters, his scepter of office

Fig. 577.—Diptych of Anastasius. Ivory. *Bibliothèque Nationale, Paris.*

in one hand and the handkerchief whose fall is the starting signal raised in the other; at the bottom are the games, with acrobats and wild beasts in the arena which opens out through doors at the sides. This decorative scheme with its combination of realistic and symbolic elements is executed in the characteristic Latin or western version of late classic style; the official figures above are shown in rigid frontal poses and the more animated arena group below is seen as if from above, the inability of the artist to suggest accurate relationships in the third dimension forcing him to a purely descriptive attitude in which the distant forms are merely placed above those supposedly

Fig. 578.—An Angel. Ivory. *British Museum, London.*

nearer. If the results are without decorative rhythm or grace, their flatness is at least somewhat in accord with the planar character of the form of the ivory slab.

The antique sense of decorative form that the Latin artists of the Early Christian period had lost in their descriptive stylized figures was retained by their contemporaries in the eastern or Byzantine kingdom

Fig. 579.—The Throne of Maximianus. Ivory. *Cathedral, Ravenna.*

with its capital at Constantinople or Istanbul. The beautiful *Angel* on a leaf from an ivory diptych of the 5th or 6th century in the British Museum (Fig. 578) reveals its eastern origin in Greek inscription as well as in the functional distribution of the drapery forms, in the solid if rather ill-articulated figure, and above all in the rhythm of line and surface which is so lacking in the Anastasius diptych. If the relationship of the figure to its arcade setting is somewhat ambiguous—the feet cover three steps at the bottom and appear to be at the back of the niche while the left arm and the right hand are in front of the columns that enclose it—it is mentioned only to emphasize the artist's sensitiveness to the decorative organization of what was doubtless a classic original and his relative lack of interest in its naturalistic qualities. The imposing *Throne of Maximianus*, who was bishop of Ravenna from 546 to 556, was probably executed some time earlier than the incumbency of the man whose name is associated with it, about 500 A.D. (Fig. 579). Of wood covered with elaborately carved

FIG. 580.—THE HARBAVILLE TRIPTYCH. Ivory. *Louvre, Paris.*

ivory panels, it was the work of Byzantine craftsmen who were working in Alexandria in Egypt, or of artists trained there rather than in Constantinople. On the front are five panels with representations of John the Baptist and the four Evangelists framed by bands of elaborately carved foliage one of which encloses the monogram of Maximianus; the sides and back of the throne are further decorated with foliate strips and with a considerable number of smaller slabs on which are the story of Joseph from the Old Testament and the Miracles of Christ from the New. The carving of the figures and foliage is very deep, creating patterns in pronounced contrasts of light and shade

which are at the same time rather naturalistic representations of form
and elements in an abstract decorative pattern, for the varied scales of
the figures and depths of the cutting are controlled by the location of
the various panels on the throne. In these two works which are roughly
contemporary, the evidence of a creative adaptation by the Byzantine
artists of the classic formal tradition to the needs of Christian expression is seen in contrast with the dull and spiritless forms used by
the western or Latin craftsmen.

Fig. 581.—Casket. Ivory. *Metropolitan Museum, N. Y.*

The historical importance of the Byzantine ivories in supplying an
indication of this continuity of tradition has been mentioned before;
there is relatively little stone sculpture on a large scale from the East
Christian world (cf. Figs. 289, 290). This was a consequence in part
at least of the sentiment which led to the Iconoclastic movement under
Leo the Isaurian in 726 whereby the creation of images was forbidden and many already in existence were destroyed. The iconoclastic
edicts did not hold, however, for the small figures to which the ivory
worker was limited by the scale of his material, and the manufacture
of such masterpieces of decorative religious art as the *Harbaville
Triptych* (Fig. 580)—a triptych because it has three panels instead of

the two that would make it a diptych—was never entirely discontinued. The ivory worker was even permitted the representation of secular or pagan themes. One of the most attractive categories of the Byzantine minor arts is the series of fifty or more *Caskets*, dating from the end of the 9th or early 10th centuries, with representations of warriors, hunters, dancers and the like (Fig. 581). Ancient myths often supply

FIG. 582.—THE CRUCIFIXION. Ivory. Cover of Ms. cim. 57. *Staatsbibliothek, Munich.*

the subject matter; the delicacy of carving, the unerring sense of scale that adapts the forms so well to the size of the object, and the rhythmic interplay of line and shadow and the color with which the forms were often further accented make them singularly well adapted to their purpose as jewel containers.

It was from the fusion and compromise between the Latin and Byzantine styles, to which may be added the barbaric vigor of the

Teutonic northern tribes which is illustrated by an example in the category of jeweled metal work (Fig. 588), that the attempt made by Charlemagne (742-814) to regenerate his kingdom intellectually and spiritually as well as politically is illustrated in the minor arts. The *Crucifixion* panel in the cover of a manuscript book in the State Library in Munich (Fig. 582) was executed about 870 and is thus a little later than the time of Charlemagne himself, but the combination of stylistic elements corresponds to the process indicated. The classic element is strongest in the decoration of the margins, in the architectural details and in the use of figures as personifications of natural principles, like the two in the lower corners which represent Earth and Ocean and are taken directly from the kind of figure by which classic artists symbolized rivers and the like. Byzantine is the allover pattern of light and shade and, originally, of color in which it resembles the Harbaville Triptych in principle though not in the sense of movement which is the Teutonic element in the style of the relief. The artist who carved this panel in all probability had before him a manuscript book with illustrations like those of the Utrecht Psalter (Fig. 368); the animation of the composition produced by the waving lines of the ground level, the energetic movement of the individual figures and the pattern of light and shade already mentioned are evidence of this. To these formal qualities should be added the Christian symbolism of the forms themselves. The subject is the Crucifixion with symbols of the sun and moon in the sky and personifications of the Church and Synagogue—the Old and New Dispensations—in the groups at the base of the cross. Below this level is the scene of the Three Holy Women at the Tomb and at the bottom, with the personifications of Earth and Ocean and the seated figure which is the city of Rome, is the Resurrection. As an embodiment of this subject, the book cover is more narrative or descriptive than formally interpretative in visual terms; the effect, especially when taken into account with the rich border of gold work and jewels, is none the less very striking and impressive.

Other elements than those cited above enter into the formation of developed mediaeval style. The ivory panel of an *Apostle* (Fig. 583) was carved in 1059 as part of the decoration of the casket in which the relics of Saints John and Pelagius were kept in the church of San Isidoro at León in Spain, and in its decoration there is found a contribution from the Moslem arts in the frame of the arch in which the figure stands. This, it will be observed, is more than a semicircle at the top—the so-called horseshoe arch—which is very common in Moorish architecture and was brought by the Moslems to Spain when they conquered that country in the 8th century. After the Christian reconquest in the 11th century, many Moslems abjured their own faith and became Christians, but at all times Moorish workmen were employed in various capacities in the service of the Church. The work they did is called Mozarabic and it is often characterized by the mingling of western and Oriental qualities that appears here, for the style of the figure is to be related to that of the Byzantine tradition and classic elements are also evident. The importance of the ivories

Fig. 583. — An Apostle. Ivory. Casket of SS. John & Pelagius. *San Isidoro, León.*

Fig. 584.—Christ on the Road to Emmaus, and Appearing to Mary Magdalene. Ivory. *Metropolitan Museum, N. Y.*

executed in León—for this is but one of a number—is more than in these qualities, however, for it seems probable that the craftsmen who carved them were also called upon to do the stone carving in the church of San Isidoro itself which was built in part in 1063 and is one of the earliest monuments in which the full-fledged Romanesque style is to be seen.

During the Romanesque period of the 12th century, ivory carving continued to be practiced as one of the decorative arts producing forms used as a rule to decorate larger objects such as book covers, caskets and shrines. An example is the fine large relief of Christ and two apostles on the *Road to Emmaus* (Fig. 584) now in the Metropolitan Museum of New York; in the lower part is the Appearance of Christ to Mary

FIG. 585.—SCENES FROM THE PASSION. Ivory.
*So. Kensington Museum, London.*

Magdalene. It was probably carved about the middle of the 12th century and comes from southwestern France or Spain. The fusion of earlier formal traditions that has been seen taking place in the Carolingian and 11th-century ivóries is now completed and the style is very characteristically that of the monumental stone sculpture with which the portals of cathedrals and churches were being decorated (cf. Fig. 297) in the proportions of the figures, the animated gestures and the swirling folds and lines of draperies. Although subject matter and dogmatic values are still paramount, the admirable spacing of the figure groups in their framing mouldings is notable as well as the manner in which the heavier figures in the lower compartment create the visual effect of a base for the more slender ones above.

In the later Middle Ages or the Gothic period, the art of the ivory carver is illustrated by forms of varied character and purpose which are for the most part self-sufficient rather than intended for use in conjunction with a larger object. An example is an ivory diptych carved with *Scenes from the Passion* (Fig. 585) which was once in the treasure of Soissons Cathedral in France and is now in the South Kensington Museum in London; it dates from the closing years of the 13th century. The purpose for which it was originally meant is characteristic of the Late Gothic period when it was executed—as the central object on the altar of a small chapel or private shrine rather than in a great cathedral. Beginning in the lower left compartment is the Betrayal with the Trial and Flagellation across on the right; the sequence then moves up with the Crucifixion on the right side and back to the left with the Entombment and Resurrection, and it is concluded in the upper row with the Holy Women at the Tomb, the appearances to the Magdalene and the apostles at Emmaus, and Pentecost, again reading from left to right. The two panels of the diptych are thus seen to be complementary, unfolding to reveal for the aid of private meditation the pathetic story of the last days of Christ on earth. Other than this, the setting and the style of the figures are typical of the time. It is a platitude to remark the focusing of all mediaeval thought upon the Church and its ways of thinking, yet this is clearly the case here in which the figures in each of the three levels on both panels are placed under pointed arches framed with crocketed gables and pinnacles like those of the cathedral itself. The figures with their curving bodies, broad draperies and bushy-haired heads are of the same style as the stone sculptures of the cathedral portals like the Vierge Dorée at Amiens (Fig. 303) or the Virgin of Notre-Dame at Paris (Fig. 304).

The pathos that characterizes the telling of the gospel story in the diptych is even more apparent in the contemporary group of ivory figures representing the *Deposition*, or the taking of Christ's body from the cross, which is in the Louvre in Paris (Fig. 586). It is also like the diptych in being an object for personal and private meditation rather than public symbolism and the emphasis upon sorrow and suffering is characteristic of the expressive aims of Late Gothic art. Around the edges of the robes it is still possible to discern traces of the colored decoration that once covered the ivory figures and made of them some-

FIG. 586.—THE DEPOSITION. IVORY. *Louvre, Paris.*

thing even more jewel-like than the semi-precious quality of the ivory itself would suggest.

At the same time that the religious art of the Late Gothic period was emphasizing the human emotive element in the Bible stories, an art of secular subjects was also developing. Two *Ivory Reliefs* in the Louvre (Fig. 587) came originally from a decorated writing tablet and are carved with scenes representing characteristic sports of the later 14th century, one being the familiar blindfold game known today as "hot-hand." Jewel caskets and mirror cases are other purposes to which ivory carving was put at this time, decorated with scenes of

FIG. 587.—MEDIAEVAL SPORT. Ivory. *Louvre, Paris.*

love, sport, jugglery and other secular pursuits of the time. It is interesting to observe, however, that in spite of the character of the scenes portrayed, the setting is almost invariably one made up of the pointed and gabled arches that derive ultimately from the church architecture of the time; the basic decorative principle is that of the cathedral— multiplicity and variety of detail organized and related by the fundamentally abstract order of the architectonic relationships of pointed arch and gable.

The importance of color as an element in the art of the Middle Ages has been mentioned in other connections, particularly in the discussion of the stained-glass windows in the churches. Color was also used to accent the sculptured figures in the portals and to lend further beauty to the interior, as many isolated fragments of painted ornament reveal even today. It is hard, however, on the weather-beaten exteriors of mediaeval buildings to recreate the effect of this ornament; save

Fig. 588.—The Crucifixion. Gold and jewels. Cover of Ms. 1. *Morgan Library, N. Y.*

for one or two interiors, the overwhelming impression of the myriad hues of the windows is no longer to be seen. What the mediaeval artist was striving for can be sensed none the less in the minor arts; the use of color in the ivories has already been indicated, but it is in those categories that involve directly the use of colored materials that the effect can be seen at its richest—work in gold, silver and precious jewels, and the various enamel techniques.

The jeweled golden book cover of a manuscript of the Four Gospels in the Morgan Library in New York (Fig. 588) is one of the finest examples of Carolingian work in this category that has been preserved. In the center is the Crucifixion, executed in repouseé—that is, by being pounded out from the back—in a sheet of gold; above the inscription are symbolic figures of sun and moon; in the four angles of the cross are clusters of gems in settings with figures above and below them which represent four angels in the upper angles while those below are the Virgin and John the Beloved Disciple with two of the Marys who came to Christ's tomb. The cross is outlined with jewels and others are used to form a wide border around the entire cover. It was made in the workshop of the great abbey at Saint-Denis at some time while that institution was under the patronage of Charles the Bald (823-877). Comparison with the contemporary ivory cover (Fig. 582) shows the relative lack of interest in narrative in the gold cover and more stress upon decorative effect. Symbolism is present as always, a particularly interesting detail being the representation of the moon facing in one direction and the sun in the opposite one to portray the darkening of the earth from the ninth to the twelfth hours while Christ hung on the cross. But the figures in the reentrant angles of the cross are placed decoratively rather than descriptively or symbolically and the symmetrical pattern resulting therefrom is a major factor in the impressive effect created by this masterpiece of the goldsmith's art.

A later example of precious metal in the minor arts of the Middle Ages is the silver *Madonna of Jeanne d'Evreux* (Fig. 589), which was executed in 1336 and is now in the Louvre. It is almost exactly contemporary with the stone Virgin of Paris in Notre-Dame (Fig. 304) and is closely related to it in style. The base is treated in what will by now be easily recognized as a characteristic Gothic fashion—with the sides divided into panels by buttress-like forms with canopies and statues in the contemporary architectural manner. In this as in the innumerable shrines and reliquaries and other objects of gold and silver executed in the Middle Ages, the richness of the material is an important factor in the decorative effect and also in what might be termed one aspect of the usefulness of the objects themselves; for if such costly material can be used as the container for an object, it must surely be of superlative value whether it be the written words of the Scripture, the relics of a holy saint or the wafer used in the ceremony of the Eucharist which is the body of Christ on earth. It is not then merely to delight the eye or to achieve display that the mediaeval artist used his gold and silver and gems so lavishly but to symbolize the even greater preciousness of the objects treasured within the containers that he made.

On the side panels of the base of the silver Madonna will be seen somewhat dimly a series of pictures; these are in an enamel technique, the minor art of the Middle Ages which along with stained glass and the illumination of manuscripts is most striking and brilliant in terms of color. Two enamel methods were extensively employed in the mediaeval period—cloisonné and champlevé. The former was the first to be developed and was practiced most generally in the Byzantine east, an example being a medallion representing *The Virgin Mary* in the Metropolitan Museum in New York (Fig. 590). The illustration is the same size as the original and reveals the technique quite well. On a plate of gold a design was formed by soldering narrow strips or cloisons which were also of gold; the areas thus defined were then filled with a paste made of vitreous powder colored with various kinds of metallic oxides which when fired is transformed into a hard, translucent substance; the surface was then polished, producing a brilliant pattern of gleaming colors defined and separated by the gold cloisons and ren-

FIG. 589.—THE MADONNA OF JEANNE D' EVREUX. Silver and enamel. *Louvre, Paris.*

dered almost luminous by the gold background shining through the glass-like enamel. The gold cloisonné enamels of Byzantium were usually on a rather small scale because of the costliness of the material and this, combined with the somewhat restrictive nature of the technique itself, led to the employment of forms strongly stylized in pattern although it is clear that this quality was in no sense considered undesirable by the artists. The example illustrated is of the end of the 10th or early 11th centuries, but the technique had been practiced long before then; it was one of a series of medallions used to decorate the frame of an icon or holy picture to which is was fastened by nails driven through the holes that can be seen in the margin of the enamel.

The gold cloisonné enamels of Byzantium were treasured both for their intrinsic value and for their religious associations and many of them found their way to western Europe. An Anglo-Saxon craftsman was possibly inspired by one in creating the scepter ornament called the *Jewel of Alfred the Great* now in the Ashmolean Museum at Oxford (Fig. 591). The technique is the same as that of the Byzantine

FIG. 590.—THE VIRGIN. Cloisonné enamel. *Metropolitan Museum, N. Y.*

example except that there is no backing and the effect of light through the translucent enamel is as if it were in fact the precious stone that the name implies. Otherwise, the flat and linear pattern of the forms and their schematic stylization make this a characteristically northern interpretation of the human figure with its large head, long and pointed in shape (cf. Fig. 292). A Celtic inscription reading "Alfred had me made" supplies the name of the object and allows the period of its creation to be deduced—between 871 and 901.

The second enamel technique—champlevé—is represented most extensively by western examples in mediaeval art. It differs from cloisonné work in using copper as the background instead of gold and in the fact that the cells to be filled with paste are formed by gouging out this backing to leave ridges between the enameled areas instead of by fastening cloisons to it; the application of the enamel and its subsequent treatment are the same as in cloisonné. The greater economy of this method allowed it to be applied on an appreciably larger scale than was the case with the gold Byzantine enamels, and from the time of its first use in the 11th century it is not uncommon to find shrines and altar frontals of considerable size decorated throughout in this way. The earliest examples known are Spanish or French in origin; its most extensive development occurred at Limoges in France—to such an extent, indeed, that the term "Limoges enamel" is almost a synonym for champlevé, which means literally "excavated field" after the process of execution. A *Casket* in the Metropolitan Museum (Fig. 592) is a characteristic example of the late 12th or early 13th centuries; on the side panel is the Crucifixion and Christ sits in judgment on the slanting top, while figures in arcades fill out the ends of each section. The fabric of the casket is bronze and the heads of the figures have been modeled separately and applied to it. The backgrounds have been decorated with vines executed in a technique of light incisions called chasing; the robes of the figures and the half-rosettes

FIG. 591.—JEWEL OF ALFRED THE GREAT.
*Ashmolean Museum, Oxford.*

of the margins are enameled. The colors are not numerous, blue and green predominating with some accents of yellow and red, and there is no gradation or shading of their intensity, but the effect, combined with the gilt applied to the bronze of the background, is one of great richness and splendor. With the arts of stained glass and manuscript illumination, enamel work is one of the most characteristically mediaeval of the minor arts; its practice was continued in some places in the Renaissance period but the aims of later enamelers were influenced by those of painters rather than being controlled by the nature of the medium itself. It is worthy of note in passing, however, that the art of enamel work was indirectly responsible for the development of one of the most character-istic Renaissance developments—the graphic arts; according to legend, it was the practice of a metal worker in Florence of transferring the de-signs of his metal plates to paper by inking the ridges and pressing them on it that suggested the idea of consciously making pictures in that way.

Any consideration of the minor arts in the Middle Ages must take the textile arts into account. Examples from relatively early periods have been preserved in spite of their inherent fragility, a fact which in itself is indicative of the value placed upon them, an example being the

FIG. 592.—CASKET. Champlevé enamel. *Metropolitan Museum,* N. Y.

silk fragment with woven representations of the *Annunciation* (Fig. 593) and the Nativity in the treasury of the Sancta Sanctorum in the Vatican at Rome. It was made in the 6th century in Alexandria in Egypt, its eastern origin being characteristic of the majority of early textiles of the Christian period since the only available source of silk at that time was in the Orient. Eastern too is the style of the decora-tion in its symmetry and flatness of form as well as the stylized foliate motives—all of which render the design more appropriate as decoration of the flat surface of the textile itself. The effect is one of subdued color, there being no less than five tints employed but very soft and harmonious in character. The preservation of such early examples of the textile arts as this was a consequence of the value placed upon them and the use to which they were put. Holy relics were wrapped in pieces of costly cloth to be placed in the no less sumptuous caskets in which they were kept, and this practice has kept many of them in a surprisingly good state of preservation. They were also easily transported and many were exported from the Near East to western Europe.

FIG. 593.—THE ANNUNCIATION. Silk.
*Capella Sancta Sanctorum, Vatican, Rome.*

In western mediaeval Europe, the textile arts made more extensive use of wool and linen than of silk, the culture of which did not exist outside of China before the 6th century and was of great cost at all times. Such an enterprise as the *Bayeux Embroidery* (Fig. 594) would have been impossible of achievement in the more rare material. Of linen, embroidered with blue, green, red and yellow worsted, it is now 230 feet in length and nineteen inches in width; there is some evidence to the effect that it has been shortened somewhat. The subject portrayed is the invasion of England by William the Conqueror. According to popular tradition it was executed by William's queen Matilda and her maids-in-waiting but there is no direct evidence for this; the circumstance of its having been used since time immemorial

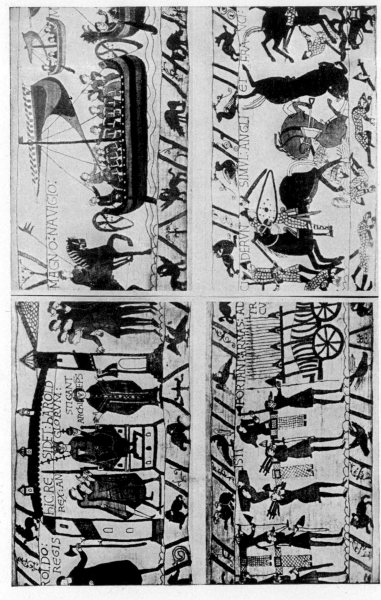

FIG. 594.—The Norman Invasion of England. The Bayeux Embroidery. *Museum, Bayeux.*

as an ornament for the nave of Bayeux Cathedral in Normandy makes it not improbable that it was commissioned by Odo, William's bishop, who had his episcopal seat there. In any event, the probable date of origin is in the latter part of the 11th century, a time that is suggested as well by the style of the figures which is similar to that of Anglo-Norman manuscript illuminations of the period. The portions of the embroidery illustrated show Harold of England seated in the palace after taking the crown left by Edward, an act considered as disloyal by William to whom Harold had sworn fealty; the Normans stock their ships with armor and food in the next part and the third shows them crossing the English Channel; in the fourth is the Battle of Hastings with which this frieze-like embroidery comes to an end in the flight of the English after Harold's death. The lively and animated movement of the figures is one quality of the original that appears in the reproductions, but the equally gay effect of the varicolored worsteds on the creamy linen background can only be guessed. The grotesque animals and birds in the upper and lower margins of the greater part of the work are in the manuscript tradition of the time; only at the end—as in the third and fourth examples illustrated—does the main action spread into these parts where the sails of the ships rise to the top and the soldiers killed in battle are shown below the battle itself. Apart from its technical and decorative interest, the Bayeux Embroidery is of outstanding importance in being one of the first extensive instances of secular subject matter in mediaeval art— and this in spite of its intended purpose as the decoration of a church.

Of all the textile arts practiced in the Middle Ages, that of tapestry is the most familiar and the most extensively represented. In tapestry, the design is woven into the fabric itself by a process of winding the weft or woof, the name given the horizontal threads, around the warp or vertical ones, the work all being executed by hand and the stitches pressed tightly against each other so that the warp is entirely covered by the woof. Tapestry weaving of this type appears to have been practiced in Europe since the 9th century at least, but it was in the 14th century that the famous manufactory at Arras in Flanders was established and the tapestries that made the name of that city synonymous with the art began to be executed. However, the whole area of the Low Countries and northern France is represented in the most ancient known examples of mediaeval tapestry, of which the outstanding single work is undoubtedly the one representing the *Apocalypse,* now in the cathedral of Angers in France (Fig. 595). In its entirety this tapestry was originally nearly 500 feet in length and contained ninety scenes from the story of the end of the world related in the Book of Revelations in the New Testament; the various episodes were designed by a painter named Jean Bondol of Bruges on the basis of illuminations in an ancient manuscript book that is still preserved, and the execution took place in the workshop of Nicolas Bataille, a tapestry maker in Paris. It was done between 1364 and 1380 for the Duke of Anjou, who ordered it for the decoration of his private chapel in the château at Angers and left it to the cathedral of the city after his death. In spite of mutilation that has reduced its length to 328 feet and the total number of scenes to seventy-eight, it is still one of the most impressive examples of mediaeval tapestry extant when it is on display over the nave arches of the cathedral. The illus-

Fig. 595.—The Apocalypse; the Vials of the Wrath of God. Tapestry. *Cathedral, Angers.*

tration is of the passage in the first verse of the sixteenth chapter of Revelations—"And I heard a great voice out of the temple saying to the seven angels, Go your ways, and pour out the vials of the wrath of God upon the earth." The figure at the left represents John, who sees this as a vision while the angels are in the center; at the right are figures symbolizing the people of the earth upon whom the wrath of God is to fall. The style of the drawing is similar to that of contemporary manuscript illumination in the way the figures are represented and in the flower pattern of the background. Although the dyes used in coloring the wool of which the tapestry is woven have faded somewhat, the effect is still one of great richness; the flatness of the design combines with the texture of the material which is quite coarse at close view but is eminently fitted to make it count for the most as a decorative adjunct to an architectural interior. The tapestries are hung so that two rows of scenes are formed, the upper ones having blue backgrounds and red being seen in those below, a device by which an abstract unity is contrived in the ensemble.

FIG. 596.—HUNTING THE UNICORN: THE UNICORN DEFENDS HIMSELF. Tapestry. *Metropolitan Museum, N. Y.*

The growing secular interests of the late Gothic period are reflected in the tapestries of the 15th and early 16th centuries made in the Low Countries, which continued to be the center of this activity. More then than before was their purpose utilitarian, moreover, for the wall hangings of many a great hall served to relieve the dark cold of stone and to render the damp rooms of palace or castle somewhat more comfortable. If the patronage was more secular, symbolism and

allegory remained in the choice of subject, however, as a series of six
tapestries now in the Cloisters of the Metropolitan Museum clearly
reveals (Fig. 596). The subject of the series is *Hunting the Unicorn,*

FIG. 597.—EPISCOPAL CHAIR. Stone. *S. Niccola, Bari.*

the example illustrated being the fourth, in which the unicorn defends
himself from the hunters and their dogs. This was a popular allegory
of the time, the unicorn being a symbol of purity and his capture
being interpreted as the Incarnation of Christ since this could be

effected only with the help of a virgin. But the religious significance of the theme is not emphasized; it is rather the picturesque panoply of an aristocratic hunting party that is stressed in the realistically portrayed costumes of the protagonists and the flowers and trees and birds and castles that provide a background for the several episodes of the hunt. These, though more naturalistic in detail than the background in the Angers Apocalypse, are woven into a fine decorative pattern that still lies flat in the picture plane and makes it an effective ornamental device. The color, too, is used with great skill in composition; the foliage is green, while reds, yellows, blues and oranges are employed in the details of the figures, all serving to make the white of the unicorn stand out as the decorative and dramatic center of each panel. The popularity of the subject is indicated by its use in one of the best-known of late mediaeval tapestries, the famous Lady and the Unicorn in the Cluny Museum in Paris which is contemporary with the Metropolitan example; its general similarity in idea to the literary allegories like the famous *Roman de la Rose* so widely read at the same time is obvious.

If a general subdivision of the minor arts as a whole were to be made, it would be possible to distinguish the decorative arts on the one hand and the useful arts on the other. In the former category would come the majority of the mediaeval examples considered up to this point, for while there is a definite reason for the existence of all of them, the decorative function, as symbol or ornament, is still the primary one. In the second class would come such things as furniture, in which the useful purpose is the major consideration and decorative effect is secondary. The Dagobert Throne (Fig. 576) is one example of mediaeval furniture that has already been considered. Another is the *Episcopal Chair* in the church of San Niccola in Bari in southern Italy (Fig. 597), which was made for the bishop Elias about 1100. Like the Dagobert Throne it represents the continuation of a classic tradition in the use of human figures called caryatids as supports (cf. Fig. 43); in this instance, these figures are among the earliest in the Romanesque style, being contemporary with those carved by Guglielmus on the façade of Modena Cathedral (Fig. 298) and having little in common expressively with the rigid maidens of the Erechtheum. Further to be noted is the decoration of the seat and arm supports which are carved in low relief with rosettes and grotesque animals; the backgrounds were originally filled in with a black paste that made the figures reserved in the stone stand out quite prominently; both technique and decorative detail are of Byzantine origin, a fact which is not surprising in view of the close relationships always maintained between southern Italy and the Near East. As an example of Roman-

esque furniture, the Bari Throne is undoubtedly exceptional; it should
not be imagined that all chairs of the time were like it, but it is characteristic of its period none the less in the character of its ornament as
well as the solid and massive proportions so appropriate to the stone of
which it is formed.

FIG. 598.—ROOM OF THE 15th CENTURY. *Museum of Art, Philadelphia.*

The Gothic period was one in which wood was quite extensively
used for furniture of both secular and religious function. The view of
a *Room of the 15th Century* (Fig. 598) in the Philadelphia Museum of Art shows a characteristic late Gothic interior ensemble. The
walls are wainscoted or paneled with wood; this paneling is carved with
the motives employed in the stone buildings of the time—tracery and
pinnacles and "linen-fold" motives, and is so distributed as to accent
the openings of doors and windows. The tapestry of the Coronation of
the Virgin over the windows is in a technique similar to that of the
Unicorn Hunt. Much of the furniture of a Gothic room was built in,
another illustration of the fundamentally architectonic character of
mediaeval art; in the Philadelphia Museum Room, the cabinet seen
at the extreme left is so treated. To be noted otherwise are the heavy
chest at the right with its similar decoration and some typical metal

work in the wrought-iron hinges and handles, and the 15th-century walnut chair with its elaborately carved back standing between the windows. Decorative motives similar to those seen in the 15th-century room are found in a *Gothic Chair* of the same period (Fig. 599), which is also in the Philadelphia Museum; the high back is typical, and it performs a dual function in being a chest as well as a seat, a common practice in mediaeval times that allowed relatively complete furnishing of a room with a minimum of separate pieces, it being not unusual, for instance, for a chest to serve as table and bed in addition.

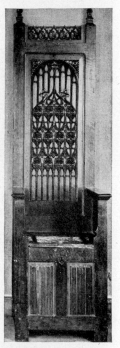

Prominent in the furniture of the church were the *Choir Stalls* (Fig. 600) where the members of the clergy participating in the Mass took their places during the service. The seats are in an unbroken row, with high backs that are elaborately carved with pointed arched canopies, pinnacles, cusps and the further architectural detail that makes them such appropriate elements in the Gothic church interior. The backs serve at the same time as a screen to isolate the sanctuary from the ambulatory and as a field for sculpture. Carving is also found very often on the under side of the tipping seats; the motives on these misericords, as they are called, are usually of secular or genre subjects and are sometimes obscene, supplying the same contrast with the religious subjects elsewhere in the interior ornament of the church that the grotesques and gargoyles do on the outside. Oak and walnut were the woods most frequently employed in the furniture of the Gothic period and the quality of design and effect in the greater part of it is a consequence of the nature of the material. The proportions are heavy; the impression is one of the massiveness in the bulk enlivened by carving with the sharp lines and crisp planes that the close-fibered tough wood makes possible.

Fig. 599. — GOTHIC CHAIR. Oak. *Museum of Art, Philadelphia.*

There is probably no period in the history of art in which distinction between the so-called major and minor arts on the basis of expressive quality is more arbitrary and artificial than in the Middle Ages. Certain categories of mediaeval art often considered as minor ones include some of the most lofty and elevated embodiments of mediaeval faith that have been created, notably manuscript illumination and the art of stained glass. And even in the most humble chest or casket, there is the sense of oneness with the great cathedrals—apparent in form as well as purpose—that reveals the consistency of thought of the period. In wood or gold, in enamel or wool, the mediaeval craftsman was working for the greater glory of the Church and of God in the same way that his architectural and sculptural colleagues were realizing their monumental symbols in stone of a reality transcending that of earthly experience in ultimate significance. The moment of this perfect

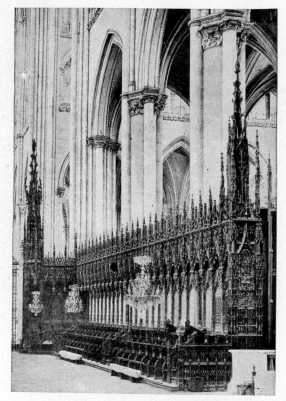

Fig. 600.—Choir Stalls. Oak. *Cathedral, Amiens.*

idealism was short. The infusion of more worldly values that has been noted already in one or two instances was to become more and more persistent and the Renaissance period was to bring once more a differing concept of the minor arts than that which prevailed in the preceding epoch.

## B. The Minor Arts of the Renaissance

The long-established historical convention of a sharp line of de-marcation between the Middle Ages and the Renaissance is primarily one of convenience. In a broadly simplified study, it is possible only to see such obvious and significant contrasts as those that exist be-tween characteristic examples of the respective periods (cf. Figs. 100 and 130) without being able to follow the frequently well-nigh im-

Fig. 601.—The Annunciation and Nativity. Enamel.
*Museum of Art, Philadelphia.*

perceptible changes that lead from one form to another. So while it is particularly illuminating to observe the differences between the products of the mediaeval point of view and that of the Renaissance in forms that invite comparison by being in the same medium and involving similar technical procedures, it is even more important that the special aptness of different mediums to different periods be noted.

An example of a technical procedure that reached its highest point of expressive development in the Middle Ages and was continued in the Renaissance is enamel. The Renaissance example illustrated, a *Triptych of the Annunciation and Nativity* (Fig. 601), was made in Limoges in France as was the earlier Gothic one already discussed (Fig. 592), and dates from about 1500. Technically, it reveals a considerably greater dexterity in the handling of the physical substance of the medium which continues to be vitreous paste fired on a bronze plate though the earlier dividing cloisons or reserved ridges are no longer found, the enamel having been spread with a brush or spatula; none the less, the careful shading and hatching by which forms are modeled and the perspective devices to suggest three-dimensional depth would have

FIG. 602.—RAPHAEL. THE MIRACULOUS DRAFT OF FISHES. Tapestry.
*Sistine Chapel, Vatican, Rome.*

been impossible without extraordinary manual skill. As a work of art, however, in which inherent quality of material is a factor in creating expressive values, the Renaissance enamel is not as satisfactory as the mediaeval one, for the man who designed it was thinking not as an enameler but as a painter (cf. Fig. 377). If these panels were used as the decoration of a casket, the solid forms would seem to make bumps on its surface and the depth in which they exist would be a denial of the flat plane which has the functional duty of closing in the side of the box. On the other hand, if they are to be thought of as a free decoration, hanging on the wall like a painting, the technical-limitations which are still present in spite of the craftsman's considerable success in surmounting them are such that it is at once apparent that a painter working in oils on panel or canvas could have secured even more impressive effects.

Tapestry is another medium that was continued from mediaeval times into the Renaissance but at the cost of losing many of its inherent qualities to more pictorial conceptions. The outstanding example by reason of the designer's fame, and greatly influential because of it, is the series representing the Acts of the Apostles designed by Raphael to decorate the Sistine Chapel in Rome. There were eight in all—the example illustrated (Fig. 602) being the *Miraculous Draft of Fishes* as related in Luke v, 1-11. By a happy circumstance, the cartoons or full-scale working models used by the weavers for this series have been preserved and are now in the South Kensington Museum in London; comparison with the finished tapestries reveals the faithfulness with which the Flemish craftsmen followed the designs, the weaving having been done in Brussels, which was then the most important center of such activity, between 1515 and 1518. Their character as works of art is indicated among other things by the freedom with which cartoons and tapestries alike have been cited by critics and historians of art as examples of Raphael's developed style as a painter. The most casual observation will reveal the lack of tapestry quality; the flatness of pattern, simplicity and strength of drawing in two dimensions and above all the texture of the material that are fundamental to the medium are forsworn for magnificent pictorialism in the main subject and for an astonishingly accurate transcription of the effect of a carved stone relief in the lower border. The extraordinary skill of the weavers in reproducing with unfailing accuracy the slightest *nuances* of tone and color in the cartoon commands the greatest admiration, but the result is a "woven picture" instead of a tapestry in the expressive and decorative sense as well as technically. The side borders with cherubs and foliage mingling in a type of decoration called *grotteschi* which Raphael had used otherwise in his decorations of the Vatican Loggie have much more of the tapestry quality than do the main subjects.

Motives of this type are used extensively in one of the most ingratiating of Italian Renaissance decorative arts—the ceramic ware called *Majolica* (Fig. 603), which has an earthen base covered with an enameled glaze containing a high percentage of tin. In the earlier examples of the 15th and early 16th centuries, these arabesque motives are used with naïve enjoyment of their supposedly classic elements but to very fine decorative effect; later on, the majolica ware too succumbs to the pervasive practice of imitating pictorial models and loses its originally attractive decorative character. It is to be noted in passing that the ceramic technique involving the use of glazes containing tin was employed for substantive or independent sculpture as well as plates like this; in this respect it is indissolubly associated with the name of the della Robbia family, whose products still ornament with great charm the walls of many Florentine buildings of the Renaissance period.

There is no better illustration of the principle that every age must develop for itself the forms in which its characteristic ideals are set

FIG. 603.—ORAZIO FONTANA. ADAM AND EVE LABORING. Majolica. *Metropolitan Museum, N. Y.*

forth than is supplied by the history of the book. It has been pointed out elsewhere that in the Middle Ages the written word had transcendent value, being not merely the record of mortal thought but the Word of God made manifest in literal symbol. This idea is basic to the whole concept of the illuminated manuscript, for the blaze of color and gold with which the mediaeval artisan decorated his pages was justified by the preciousness of the words inscribed thereon and the essential fitness of the handwritten word and the hand-illuminated picture to the page of the book makes their abstract identity clear to the beholder. But once this ideal concept of the value of the word was questioned, as it was in the declining Middle Ages, a new value was

developed to take its place, as is evident in any example of late mediaeval illumination (Fig. 372); the reality of the word has been lessened
and the reality of the picture has been increased, for the spiritual
experience that gave a communal transcendental significance to the
word no longer exists and it is only in the objective evidence of the
senses that a counterpart for it can be found. As an adjunct to the
written word, then, the picture as conceived by manuscript illuminators had lost its expressive validity just as the designs of the enamelers
and tapestry makers had done.

The illuminated and handwritten book died in the late Middle
Ages; its place was taken by the printed book illustrated by mechanical processes (Fig. 604). The development of printing from movable
type as applied to the making of books was without doubt the most
significant single factor in the evolution of the Renaissance and
modern conceptions of life. The whole idea of the handwritten book
was based on the assumption of a limited privileged class—the clergy
in the early Middle Ages, the feudal aristocracy in the later part—
for each example was unique and could be reproduced only by a
method as long and arduous as that by which the original was created.
The individualism of the Renaissance could not tolerate such a concept;
once the validity of individualism for all is established, it follows as a
natural consequence that equal privileges must be enjoyed by all, and
as far as the book as a symbol of this is concerned, it too must be
available to all. Only by a mechanical reproducing means could this
be carried out and the development of the printing press supplied that
means. It has often been remarked that the printing press killed the
Middle Ages; it is rather that the printing press is a symbol of that
life that sprang up from the dust of an outworn and dying way of
thinking for only by such means could it find the expression that it
demanded.

The example of Renaissance illustrated printing that is reproduced
here is from a book published in Venice in 1499 by Aldus Manutius,
one of the first to appreciate the humanistic value of the process.
His avowed purpose of making the great literary classics available in
the most perfect typographic form that was possible is indication of
his more than mercenary motives; the result here is a striking instance
of the development of a form in accordance with its inherent characteristics, for this is clearly a printed page and not a printed imitation
of a handwritten one like so many of the earliest incunabula as the first
printed books are sometimes called. The subject of the book was a
long and involved semi-religious allegory called The Strife of Love in
a Dream—*Hypnerotomachia Poliphili* in the Latin of the original title—
which is hopelessly dull to modern readers. The illustration at the top

POLIPHILO QVIVI NARRA, CHE GLI PARVE AN-
CORA DI DORMIRE, ET ALTRONDE IN SOMNO
RITROVARSE IN VNA CONVALLE, LA QVALE NEL
FINE ERA SERATA DE VNA MIRABILE CLAVSVRA
CVM VNA PORTENTOSA PYRAMIDE, DE ADMI-
RATIONE DIGNA, ET VNO EXCELSO OBELISCO DE
SOPRA. LA QVALE CVM DILIGENTIA ET PIACERE
SVBTILMENTE LA CONSIDEROE.

LA SPAVENTEVOLE SILVA, ET CONSTI-
pato Nemore euafo, & gli primi altri lochi per el dolce
somno che fe hauea per le fesse & proſternate mébre dif-
fuso relicti, me ritrouai di nouo in uno piu delectabile
sito assai piu che el præcedente. Elquale non era de mon
ti horridi, & crepidinose rupe intorniato, ne falcato di
strumofi iugi. Ma compositamente de grate montagniole di non tro-
po altecia. Siluose di giouani quercioli, di roburi, fraxini & Carpi-
ni, & di frondoſi Esculi, & Ilice, & di teneri Coryli, & di Alni, & di Ti-
lie, & di Opio, & de infructuoſi Oleastri, disposti secondo laspecto de
gli arboriferi Colli. Et giu al piano erano grate filuule di altri filuatici

FIG. 604.—POLIPHILUS DREAMING. From the *Hypnerotomachia Poliphili.*
Woodcut and metal type. *Rosenwald Coll., Jenkintown.*

of the page is a woodcut—the type of illustration first evolved for use in conjunction with mechanical printing—and the beauty of the page lies in the completely satisfactory visual effect of the linear effect of picture and type face, an identity of aesthetic character that is the same in the mechanical processes involved as is that of the handwritten and hand-painted pages of the earlier manuscript books. Proportion and balance, variety and contrast are as carefully studied here as in any

Fig. 605.—Lantern. Wrought iron. *Florence, Strozzi Palace.*

painting—as comprehensive an example as can be found of the great Renaissance contribution to the minor arts, the art of typography. It is possible to make out a good case for painting as the artistic medium most completely adapted to giving expression to the Renaissance ideal in its broadest aspect; if this be true, the development of an illustrative style such as this can hardly be denied as the most fruitful application of pictorial values to the decorative and complementary purposes that are an intrinsic quality of the minor arts.

Decorative forms in wrought iron are among the most attractive and individual contributions of the Renaissance to the minor arts (Fig. 605). The utilitarian and ornamental function of such a form as this— a *Lantern* on the Strozzi Palace in Florence— is a direct expression of the secular culture of the time in which a growing emphasis upon the wealth and social position of the owner is to be noted in the tendency toward more elaborate treatment of the palace exterior. The lantern holder is placed on the angle of the building, carried out from the wall on an ornamental bracket, the source of light being inside the small enclosure formed by miniature pointed Gothic windows; the spreading spikes projecting above enhance the scale of the holder itself and tie it into the architectural design of the building. The basic design is a rather simple one because the necessity of working quickly in the red-hot metal that the iron forger handles does not permit over-detailed effects. These are achieved in the subsequent finishing and chasing of the form, but thanks to the effectiveness of the large design

FIG. 606.—PISANELLO. MEDAL OF JOHN PALAEOLOGOS. Bronze.

they do not overshadow it. The combination of Gothic and Renaissance forms is to be noted; the latter is dominant, in the console brackets and the base and the cornice, but the little windows of the lamp-house are Gothic as already noticed. At the date when this was executed in 1489, the Renaissance style in architecture was well established in Italy (cf. Figs. 119, 121, 122); the occurrence of Gothic elements in the design is an illustration of the general conservatism of artisans and craftsmen who as a rule remain faithful to the principles of outmoded styles after the architects, sculptors and painters have adopted new ways.

Another characteristic type of Renaissance metal work is seen in the bronze medals and plaques of the period. These were generally of a commemorative nature and the artistic problem they presented was one of an effective decorative relationship of the portrait bust of the person in question, the inscription identifying him or supplying the reason for the execution of the medal, and the circular field of the medallion. Usually on a rather small scale—the greater number are no more than three or four inches in diameter—the sculptural problem of the relief planes is also an important one. The most famous of Italian *médailleurs* was Antonio Pisano, usually called Pisanello (*ca.* 1395-1455), who is also well known as one of the most important painters of the early 15th century in northern Italy. The medal that is illustrated was made by him in honor of *John Palaeologos* (Fig. 606), a dignitary of the court at Constantinople; it is a fine example of skill in composition in relating the elements mentioned as well as Pisanello's ability as a draftsman in reducing the profile head to a series of beautifully drawn lines that suggest in a few planes the structure of the head and the character of the subject. It is in this essentially Renaissance contribution to the minor arts that a practice was begun that has continued down to modern times—the creation of commemorative medals and plaques.

Still another aspect of the minor arts in metal that was developed to an extraordinary degree in the Renaissance is seen in gold and silver work. Again the vast amount that is in existence permits little but mention, but it must be noted that Florence was a recognized center of goldsmith work in the 15th and 16th centuries and that training in the ateliers of workers in precious metals was the lot of nearly every sculptor and many of the painters who were foremost at that time, particularly in the earlier period. Their products were intended for both ecclesiastic and secular purposes—caskets and shrines for the former and jewelry for the latter being the most numerous classes. An example of the latter is a *Pendant* in the form of a mermaid (Fig. 607) in the collection of the Metropolitan Museum, which dates from the 16th century. It is somewhat larger than a similar object would be today because its effect in the sumptuous costumes of the period had of necessity to be a striking one. Gems are usually employed as elements of equal importance with the metal work and are cut much more simply than modern taste requires, being rounded over for the most part and cut in few facets when treated in this way. Pearls predominate in the example illustrated, one of irregular shape—called "baroque"—being used to suggest the body of the mermaid. Further examples of this branch of goldsmith work will be seen in many of the painted portraits of the time, especially in those of the 16th century.

A name in the history of Renaissance goldsmith work that is known to many for reasons not particularly related to the visual arts is that of Benvenuto Cellini (1500-1571). His popular fame rests upon his *Autobiography,* in which the egotism that was his outstanding personal characteristic is the motivation for the telling of many picturesque incidents and the basis of much derogatory criticism of others. His achievement as a sculptor is considered elsewhere in this book and is there characterized as reflecting his training and activity as a goldsmith. Of the many examples of goldsmith work that are attributed to him, including a jasper cup in a jeweled and enameled setting in the Metropolitan Museum, the only one that can certainly be considered his is the *Gold and Enamel Saltcellar* in the Kunsthistorisches Museum in Vienna (Fig. 608) which he made for Francis I of France in 1543. As an example of decoration, it is characterized by the same bravado that appears in the *Autobiography.* Technically it is the work of an accomplished manipulator of materials; incredibly fine detail is seen in the bowls that hold the salt and pepper and their setting of waves, sea beings and the like that accompany the nude figures of Neptune and a nereid on the top; similarly accomplished is the decorative gold work of figures and marine motives on the ebony base. But the forms are not original with Cellini, having been adapted without change except in scale from the powerful stone fig-

Fig. 607.—Jeweled Pendant. *Metropolitan Museum, N. Y.*

ures on Michelangelo's Medici Tombs (Figs. 138 and 327); particularly flagrant is one whose head is left unfinished in the gold work just as it is on the tomb. This and the obvious disparity between the monumentally conceived figures and the relatively commonplace function of the object are matters for criticism that can hardly be favorable. They are the result of bringing into the decorative arts a canon developed in a monumental medium, just as is the case with the Renaissance enamel and tapestry discussed above (Figs. 601, 607), and they reveal a fundamental misunderstanding of the essential character of both the forms that are copied and the one on which they are used.

In no field of the minor arts is the character of the Renaissance more clearly indicated than in that of furniture. The process of secularization that began in the Late Gothic period and was responsible for a perceptible increase in the utilitarian forms of everyday living at that time was carried on and amplified in the 15th and 16th centuries and produced some of its most distinguished and characterful results in Italy.

Fig. 608.—CELLINI. Salt Cellar of Francis I. Gold and enamel.
*Kunsthistorisches Museum, Vienna.*

The habit of an architectonic form having been established in mediaeval furniture, it is not surprising to find it continued but with change in the character of the detail (Fig. 609). The combination *Table and Chest* of Isotta da Rimini, the friend of Sigismondo Malatesta of Rimini who was the humanist patron of Alberti in designing the church of San Francesco (Fig. 119), combines Gothic and Renaissance motives in a way typical of its period in the mid-15th century. The treatment of the base as a pedestal rather than with feet is characteristic, and its mouldings are essentially those of architectural

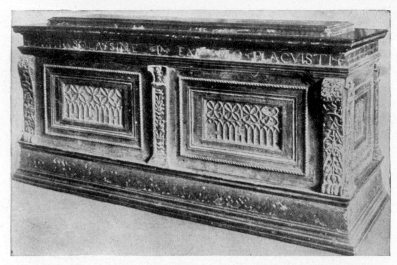

Fig. 609.—Table and Chest of Isotta da Rimini. Oak.
*Figdor Coll., Vienna.*

Fig. 610.—Cassone from the Strozzi Palace. Wood, Painted.
*Metropolitan Museum, N. Y.*

design as is also the case with the cornice-like top; arabesqued pilasters and consoles divide the side into panels which are filled with Gothic tracery. The chest or *Cassone* of *ca.* 1475 from the Strozzi Palace in Florence (Fig. 610) that is in the Metropolitan Museum in New York is similarly organized in architecturally structural terms with its elaborate mouldings and heavy consoles, but the side panels are painted instead of being carved. This was a common practice in the 15th century when the most famous painters did not consider it beneath

Fig. 611.—The Davanzati Palace. Bedroom. *Florence.*

them to execute such decorations; Botticelli, to mention but one, is known to have painted the panels on a number of these *cassoni*, the subjects being chosen as a rule from the myths of ancient Greece and Rome.

The somewhat sparse furniture of the Gothic room was increased in the Renaissance period and although such an interior as that of the *Davanzati Palace* in Florence (Fig. 611) might still be considered somewhat bare by modern standards, it represents the ideal of luxurious equipment of its time. The palace itself was built in the late 14th century, but the excellent restoration has brought into a harmonious relationship the products of later periods in the Renaissance. The heavy piece on the left wall in the illustration is called a *cassapanca*, from the Italian words *cassone* and *panca* which mean respectively chest and bench; it is a characteristic Florentine form and the example here illustrated, with its baroque figures in the cresting of the back, is of the 17th century. The bed is of the 16th century and is typical in its massive proportions and the reduction of the ornament to a series of panels framed by mouldings; this is the more usual practice in the High Renaissance, taking the place of the painted or applied gesso (a kind of plaster or stucco) decoration that characterized the earlier furniture like the Strozzi *cassone*. These two pieces establish the character of the room and although in different styles are quite in harmony. This is a consequence of two factors—the material of which they are made and their scale. The material is walnut which was used almost exclusively in Florence in the Renaissance, a wood whose close grain and texture permitted the most delicate of carving and which has a very attractive color when waxed or oiled as these pieces are. As for the scale, it is rather large, but this again is a direct consequence of the size of the room and of its relatively scanty furnishings; pieces of small size or delicate scale would not be particularly effective in such a setting. The chairs are of two types—a backed stool called a *sgabello* and the developed Renaissance form of the mediaeval folding type which is called a Dante chair; in both the seat is of wood with at best a thin pad of fabric or leather. Not until the late 16th century are chairs upholstered in leather or textile found in any great number (Fig. 612), when the throne type previously limited to the use of royalty or other persons of rank came into more extensive use.

FIG. 612.—CHAIR. Wood and Leather. *Museum of Art, Philadelphia.*

Italian Renaissance furniture is distinguished by local styles in the same way that contemporary painting and architecture are. In northern Italy, for example, the practice of inlaying the object with other kinds and colors of wood was quite extensive in the regions of Lombardy and Venice. A striking example of this method of woodworking, called *certosina* or *intarsia*, is provided by the decoration of an entire *Room from Urbino* in the Metropolitan Museum in New York (Fig. 613), which dates in all probability from the last third of the 15th century. The planned effect of the ornament is in accordance with the

FIG. 613.—ROOM FROM URBINO. Intarsia. *Metropolitan Museum, N. Y.*

FIG. 614.—VENETIAN GLASSES. *Metropolitan Museum, N. Y.*

passionate interest of the period in perspective and foreshortening; the skill of the craftsmen in creating such effects as those of open cupboards or bookshelves, and the impression of vast extension of the actual floor area by the converging lines of the patterns in the lower walls are evidence of a remarkable facility in the medium. These tricks are not in themselves any indication of good decorative sense, but con-

FIG. 615.—HIGH-BACKED CHAIR. Oak. *Museum of Art, Philadelphia.*

tinued study of the room soon puts them in a relatively subordinate place for the fine feeling for the quality of the material itself is a much more lasting value. Contrasting textures and colors and the dull gleam of carefully treated surfaces are the outstanding elements in the effect of the room, which is one of the decorative masterpieces of the woodworker's art. The architectural membering by means of pilasters and panels and mouldings is in the current classicizing tradition of the period.

One of the high points in the art of the glass blower was reached in Venice in the 16th century where work in this medium, which the Early Renaissance had tended to use in an enamel technique (cf. Fig. 603), takes on a more independent character (Fig. 614). From the earliest period of the existence of the city, it had been a center for the glass industry in the making of colored cubes or *tesserae* for use in mosaics, inheriting from its Byzantine antecedents a taste for the deep and refulgent color that characterizes that process. In the later Renaissance, as these examples illustrate, Venetian glassware tends toward the development of forms of independent interest, depending upon qualities of brilliance, transparency and color for effects in types of vessels that are essentially glass-like in shape and proportion. The crystalline bowls of the containers in these drinking glasses and the delicately curved stems are possible only from a craftsman with an infallible sense of his material; each being intended for a specific purpose that dictates its form. Later in the 16th and 17th centuries, Venetian glass is often more elaborate in form and decoration and reveals extraordinary dexterity in handling the material, but it cannot vie with such examples as these in decorative quality.

Outside of Italy, the history of the minor arts in the Renaissance is a repetition of that which can be followed in the major forms—the imposition of Italianate decorative detail upon forms still structurally Gothic. A *High-backed Oak Chair* of the 16th century in France (Fig. 615) is structurally very much like the earlier Gothic example (Fig. 599). The ornament, however, is inspired by north Italian Renaissance models—cornice-like mouldings on the back and arms, and panels filled with arabesques of foliage, cherubs and classic heads that are direct adaptations of the style of ornament current in the late 15th and early 16th centuries in Italy (cf. Figs. 122, 603). It was in

FIG. 616.—CAQUETOIRE. Walnut. *Museum of Art, Philadelphia.*

France, however, that the practical conception of the chair as an object for easy and comfortable use began to develop and that the widest variety of this form is found in the 16th and 17th centuries. But one illustration can be given, the light and easily portable form called *Caquetoire* or gossip chair—a name which illustrates alike the French genius for concise and illuminating terminology and the social conditions leading to its development (Fig. 616); one has only to imagine the effect of an informally arranged group of the earlier stall chairs to perceive the greater effectiveness in both use and appearance of the *caquetoire* under such circumstances.

In the Renaissance period of the 15th and 16th centuries, the distinction between the decorative and useful categories in the minor arts is one that determines, by and large, the character of the results as a work of art. In the former classification would be placed such things as the enamels, tapestries and much of the gold work; in the latter are iron work, glassware and furniture. To sum up the discussion of these various examples, it will be seen that in the decorative category there is a pronounced tendency to achieve effects imitating those of other arts, notably painting and sculpture, while in the useful arts it is the function of the object and the nature of its material that control the design for the greater part. In the next chapter, the influence of new circumstances, differing uses and possibly more than ever the availability of new materials play their part in the ever-changing forms considered under the general heading of the minor arts.

# Chapter XXXV. The Minor Arts of the Post-Renaissance and Modern Periods

TO DRAW A HARD AND FAST LINE BETWEEN THE Renaissance and Post-Renaissance periods in history is possibly an even more arbitrary procedure than establishing a distinction between the Middle Ages and the Renaissance, nor is it essential for reasons other than expediency to define the exact chronological span of the modern age. But since some such structure is necessary in the interests of clarity, the Post-Renaissance period will be here considered as embracing the 17th and 18th centuries and the modern era will commence with the year 1800. For this separation there is some justification; the 17th century saw for the first time a comprehensive political focus in the principle of absolutism that made France a world power whose essential character as a political entity was not modified in principle until the closing years of the 18th; this modification was itself a manifestation of the changing philosophies of a world that was shortly to produce the Industrial Revolution that stamps the 19th century with an unmistakable character that is only now being resolved into its basic and essential elements.

The preeminence of France in the culture of the 17th century in Europe is one of the fundamental facts in the history of the Post-Renaissance period, and in the selection of the majority of the examples of the period from French work, this is recognized. It is also to be observed that furniture supplies the most consistently evolving forms, running parallel in character with the architectural designs that provide a setting for them. Thus in the Louis XIII period of the early 17th century, a characteristic example is a *Cabinet of ebony, ivory and gilt bronze* (Fig. 617) in the Metropolitan Museum. This is true not only of the form which was quite extensively employed at that time in various types but also of the decoration; the use of legs and ornamental details that have been turned on a lathe now begins to be general; the elaborate carved panels are similar in general design to much contemporary work in Flanders which supplies a direct comparison with the architecture of the period (cf. Fig. 147). The general effect of rich ornamentation combined with heavy and massive proportions is the touchstone of the style.

The Louis XIV period of the later 17th century contributes to the minor arts a style that is well in accord with the proud and opulent spirit of *Le Roi Soleil.* A *Cabinet* in the Louvre (Fig. 618) is the work of one of the leading designers of the period, *A. C. Boulle,* who is famous for the method of marquetry that his name is associated

Fig. 617.—Cabinet. Ebony, ivory and gilt bronze.
*Metropolitan Museum, N. Y.*

with. This consists of inlaying wooden panels, usually of ebony, which was thought to have an effect of magnificence lacking in the now outmoded oak or walnut, with a design formed by inset pieces of other woods or, preferably, of ivory, mother-of-pearl, bone, brass, tortoise shell and the like; brass or bronze appliqué work completes the effect of great ostentation. Elaborate though the decoration is, the structural form of the cabinet is relatively simple, with straight lines predominating and vigorous moulded profiles accenting top and base. In the closing years of the 17th century this rectangular simplicity of form is modified as the *Writing Desk* (Fig. 619) made by Boulle for Max Emanuel, Elector of Bavaria, reveals; the double curve in the legs produces a form called cabriole which became very popular in the 18th century. The chair is also an important form in the Louis XIV period; when strict protocol governed order of seating at the grand court functions, it is easy to see how essential it was that the social

Fig. 618.—A. C. BOULLE. Cabinet. Ebony, inlaid. *Louvre, Paris.*

position of the occupant should be appropriately indicated by the form and proportions of his chair. The throne of Louis XIV himself, for example, was of solid silver draped with crimson velvet, the back standing eight feet high; even this was enhanced in effect by the golden embroideries draped over it which were carried by caryatides who topped it by seven feet more. Less overwhelming in effect is a *Chair* of the period (Fig. 620) in the Metropolitan Museum in New York; to be noted are the curving diagonal stretchers bracing the console legs, and the elaborate carving of the wooden portions of the chair.

Tapestry, needlepoint, brocade or velvet supply the material for the upholstery; leather is but seldom used.

One of the high points in the history of the decorative arts is reached in France in the 18th century in the reign of Louis XV and Louis XVI. The ideal of pompous austerity that prevailed in the preceding century was considerably relaxed and the keynote of social usage

Fig. 619.—A. C. BOULLE. Desk. Ebony, inlay and enamel.
*Montague House, London.*

was rather one of intimacy and refinement. The forms of furniture and the accessories of the period are seen in a *Room in French Eighteenth-century Style* in the Philadelphia Museum (Fig. 621) which presents on a quite comprehensive scale the varying aspects of both earlier and later periods. Dominating the whole is the series of tapestries on the walls representing the story of Cupid and Psyche, designed by one of the most popular painters of the period, François Boucher (1703-1770), and executed between 1741 and 1770 in the famous Beauvais tapestry factory in northern France. Like the Raphael tapestry discussed elsewhere (Fig. 602), the style of the Boucher examples is primarily pictorial, but as decoration they are none the less extremely fine since the pictorial ideal they represent is basically decorative in character. Particularly notable is the color scheme which is in rich but subdued tones well calculated to appear to advantage in the light cast from the crystal chandeliers.

Two styles and various materials are represented in the furniture of the room. The chairs with the delicately curved cabriole legs are in the Louis XV manner, upholstered in tapestry of flowers on a rose ground; the complex curvature of backs and arms in these Louis XV

FIG. 620.—CHAIR. Walnut and tapestry. *Metropolitan Museum, N. Y.*

examples is in the so-called rococo manner, a word derived from *rocaille* and *coquille* which mean respectively rock and shell and in this combination refers to the irregularity of contour and surface that makes such furniture so effective a complement of the rococo interior (cf. Fig. 167). The Louis XVI style is seen in the tables and commodes of more simple lines in which rectangular and circular forms predominate and with legs that are straight though still quite richly carved. This tendency toward less complicated structural forms that characterizes the Louis XVI style in furniture in contrast to the earlier Louis XV manner is one of the consequences of an increased interest in and knowledge of ancient classic art that has been mentioned elsewhere; it will be noted in English forms that are contemporary with these and is developed into the Empire style of the early 19th century.

The tables and commodes of the 18th-century room also illustrate a decorative technique that was developed by the cabinetmakers of the time in the applied ornament which is called ormolu from the French *or-moulu*, meaning literally moulded gold. The object was first cast in

Fig. 621.—Philadelphia Museum of Art. The Rice Room.

bronze and after being chiseled to the desired finish was covered with an amalgam of mercury and gold. The piece was then heated which caused the mercury to vaporize and the gold to be deposited on the surface of the bronze. This technique produced results much more lasting than simply applying liquid gold to the object; the usually fatal consequence to the workmen of the mercury vapor freed in the process was apparently not considered a matter of much importance if the widespread employment of decorative motives so created be considered. In the objects illustrated ormolu is used for the mounts on the tables and chests —rosettes, medallions and the like—but it was also employed for larger free forms like the candle sconces flanking the fireplace and for clocks (cf. Fig. 619); on the furniture, its color and surface texture make it an admirable foil for the dark polished ebony which continued a favored material for the 18th-century cabinetmaker.

Other forms entering into the 18th-century decorative ensemble are the sculptured busts and the terra-cotta figurines that can be seen on the chests in the room; Clodion was especially admired in the 18th century for his taste in the creation of such forms as these (cf. Fig. 337). Also to be noted are the various objects in porcelain that appear—chiefly vases and urns but also furniture mounts in the form of plaques. This is mostly Sèvres ware, created at the factory established at Vincennes in 1740 and granted royal patronage in 1745; here processes leading to effects of extraordinary charm of color and surface were developed during the 18th century. In their refinement and delicacy of form, these porcelain objects take their place in an ensemble which reveals throughout the sense of elegance, gracefulness and unerring taste that is characteristic of the "boudoir art" of the 18th century in France and that for sheer decorative effectiveness in the terms indicated can be equaled only with difficulty and certainly is unsurpassed in any other time or country.

England developed a furniture style in the 18th century that is no less distinguished in character than that of France under Louis XV and XVI, although that character is quite as individually English as the examples just considered are French. Previous to that time, English furniture was more likely than not to be a variant or combination of the continental styles, with Italian, Flemish or French influences predominant according to the prevailing political tendencies of the period. This is reflected in the names given the various modes—Tudor, Jacobean, William and Mary, Queen Anne and the like—corresponding to the different monarchs and embodying the preferences resulting from their relationships to continental countries. One form deserves special notice, however, for its importance and popularity in the New World— the gate-leg table (cf. Fig. 180) which was evolved during the 17th century. The most characteristic examples are from the time of Cromwell, *ca.* 1650, and show in their massiveness a continuation of the 16th-century types but with less decoration than appears earlier, the ornament being limited for the most part to the turned legs. Oak was the material most used in the Elizabethan and early Jacobean periods in the late 16th and early 17th centuries, with walnut tending to replace it in the latter part of the 17th century in the William and Mary and Queen Anne styles.

The early 18th century of the Georgian period finds a continued assimilation of continental elements of style in English furniture— cabriole legs, ball-and-claw or hoof feet, masks, rock-and-shell motives —that are derived from the baroque-rococo decorative repertory. A new material also makes its appearance at this time—mahogany; imported for the most part from the New World, it was not until it became plentifully available in England after the originally heavy import tax was modified in 1733 that it was used by cabinetmakers on any scale. Once introduced, its strength, ease of workmanship and the attractive finish it was capable of receiving led to its supplanting native woods almost entirely during the mid-period of the 18th-century, and it is the material most completely identified with the first of the famous 18th century English furniture designers, Thomas Chippendale (1718-1779).

Fig. 622.—CHIPPENDALE. Full-front Desk with Cabinet Top. Mahogany. *Metropolitan Museum, N. Y.*

In this connection, it should be stressed that other cabinetmakers than those whose names are most frequently encountered in histories of furniture were active and produced designs of quite as great distinction. It was, in fact, by virtue of the general sense of material combined with adaptation to purpose—the functionalism of their designs as against the chiefly decorative aims of the 18th-century French—that English furniture of the period as a whole achieved its undebatable success. It is this quality combined with the now thoroughly assimilated stylistic elements

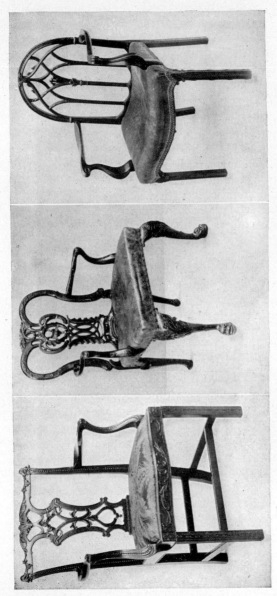

FIG. 623.—CHIPPENDALE. CHAIRS. Mahogany. *Metropolitan Museum, N. Y.*

of continental design that establishes the character of English furniture of this period.

The preeminence of Chippendale in the mid-18th century can be attributed to various factors. His designs reveal him to have been a consummate master of his material; they are couched in terms that evolve naturally from pieces of wood joined to realize to the utmost both structural and decorative consistency. His influence was widespread through the medium of his publication in 1754 of *The Gentleman and Cabinet-Makers' Director* in which he included designs of inexhaustible variety—French, Gothic, Rococo, Chinese—but all conceived against a background essentially structural in terms of wood that made them a fertile source of inspiration for the craftsmen and joiners of wood in England, Ireland and the Colonies. In this respect, the Chippendale style in the larger sense is similar in character to the Georgian architectural style with which it is contemporary; it is rendered consistent and unified in spite of regional variations or even provincial awkwardness by the common quality of being eminently in terms of the material employed.

As an example of work in the basic manner of Chippendale, a mahogany *Full-front Desk with Cabinet Top* (Fig. 622) reveals a fundamental simplicity of form enlivened by treatment of surface and well-chosen decorative details. These are never so prominent as to obscure the main structural lines, however, and the impression of something solid and well made that can stand use is always foremost in a well-designed Chippendale piece. The fact that many of his designs were executed in collaboration with architects may have had something to do with this, but his ability to create forms that look both solid and graceful at the same time and are easy and comfortable to use as well is his own particular and personal contribution. Innumerable are the varieties of his chair designs, for example (Fig. 623)—ribbon-back, Gothic, Chinese—whatever the taste of the client dictated but all with an unfailing quality that is his own. Observe, for example, that whatever the pattern of the splat in the open back of the chair it is always firmly fixed at the top and the bottom; whether the legs are basically straight rectangular pieces or subtly curved and with elaborate carving, they are so designed that they seem to grow out of the seat and rest solidly on the floor. In the more elaborately carved forms, the close texture of the mahogany makes possible a refinement of motive and a minuteness of scale that are essentially rococo in spirit, whatever the specific character of the ornament may be.

One of the most novel features of European 18th-century style in the decorative arts is the employment of Oriental themes and forms.

This was a direct outcome of the opening up of commercial relationships with the Far East in the late years of the 17th century and the exploitation thereof in the following century that was systematized in the formation of the East India Company in 1708. This in itself might not have been sufficient to stimulate the *chinoiseries* and *singeries*—decorative patterns of pagodas, bamboo trees, people in Chinese costumes, and monkeys—that appear with such frequency in French interiors of the time, nor would it account for the construction of a Chi-

Fig. 624.—CHIPPENDALE. "Chinese" Bed. Lacquer.
*So. Kensington Museum, London.*

nese pagoda in Kew Gardens in London by Sir William Chambers, had there not existed a pronounced taste for the strange and exotic that was by way of being a reaction against the solemn and pompous dignity of the 17th-century manner. It is thus as another aspect of the refined frivolity of the rococo that Chippendale's Chinese designs must be considered; in the chairs the Oriental quality is not prominent for the outstanding characteristic is nothing more than a latticework of more or less complexity. A Chinese bed by Chippendale (Fig. 624) is much more consciously derivative, however, with its characteristically curved canopy lines ending in flying dragons, the lattice back and an elaborate decorative scheme executed in lacquer on the posts and top. If this is more of a curiosity than anything else, it none the less embodies quite completely one aspect of the taste of the time.

Taste as a factor in the evolution of style accounts for the popularity in the later 18th century in England of the forms created by the Adam Brothers (Robert, 1728-1792; James, 1730-1794), who were among the most prominent figures in the field of English architecture of their time. Robert, the elder of the two, returning to England in 1758 after four years of travel and study in Italy, brought with him so great an

Fig. 625.—ROBERT ADAM. Chairs and Screen. Painted wood and tapestry. *Museum of Art, Philadelphia.*

enthusiasm for the arts of ancient Rome as newly revealed in the excavation of Herculaneum that the delicate classicizing style he developed in architecture and the decorative arts soon replaced in popularity the Chippendale of the earlier 18th century in the decorative arts and the baroque-rococo manner in architecture. A similar development for similar reasons has already been noted in the change from the Louis XV to the Louis XVI style in France. In England the difference is possibly even more pronounced, however, since it involved a new canon of proportion and new materials as well as different formal qualities. The circumstance that the Adams were architects and decorators first of all rather than cabinetmakers results in a conception of the interior as a consciously composed ensemble in which the design of furniture, lamps, hangings, carpets, wall decorations is controlled by a single idea which is classic and Pompeiian in the majority of their designs. The unity of effect that is achieved cannot be denied even though it is of a different character than that of an interior like the French 18th century one already discussed (Fig. 621), in which what might be termed the inherent and traditional stylistic sense of a number of craftsmen has produced a formal harmony, whereas the English ensemble is the consequence of a consciously contrived, not to say academic uniformity of detail.

Comparison of the Adam style in furniture (Fig. 625) with the earlier Chippendale reveals at once the presence of a different stylistic sense. The irregularity of detail and elaboration of form that remain

Fig. 626.—Wedgwood Ware. *Metropolitan Museum, N. Y.*

as a rococo element in the earlier work have given way to simplicity of basic form and regularity of individual motives in the later work. Tapestry backs, for example, replace the open splats, and the decorative motives are often of classic mythological subjects. Mahogany has been discarded for satinwood or harewood and painted decoration is often employed, the colors being soft pastel shades that are repeated in the walls of the room itself and in the accessory objects of ceramic ware that are a characteristic detail in the Adam interior (Fig. 626). These were often after designs by leading artists of the time in the Neoclassic vein and were executed at the Wedgwood factory which came into existence primarily to supply objects of this type in England as the Sèvres plant did in France at the same time. Jars and vases and plaques to be set into the walls or mantelpieces are among the most characteristic products of this firm, the decoration being based for the most part upon the refined and delicate classic style which the excavations of Pompeii and Herculaneum were then revealing and which enjoyed an extraordinary popularity.

The Adam interpretation of classic style is the basis of the two most generally accepted modes in late 18th-century furniture in England— Hepplewhite and Sheraton. The names are those of cabinetmakers who, like Chippendale, published books of furniture designs that were widely disseminated and correspondingly influential. George Hepplewhite collaborated with the Adam brothers in executing many of their designs and the type of work with which his own name is associated represents

Fig. 627.—HEPPLEWHITE. Chair. Satinwood.
*Metropolitan Museum, N. Y.*

an individual modification of their taste (Fig. 627). Although he designed all types of furniture, chairs are most numerous in his published designs and the example illustrated is characteristic of his manner. The legs are rather sturdy as a rule, straight or with very slight curvature and fluted or inlaid. The backs, however, are quite fragile in effect, with sweeping curves predominating in heart or shield shapes unsupported at the base, a specific point of contrast with Chippendale's style, for example, that indicates a differing conception of design that is not without some significance. Chippendale is still the craftsman working with functional consideration as a primary basis and making decorative effect subordinate to it, whereas Hepplewhite has taken an attitude that when carried to its logical conclusion reduces the chair to a decorative accessory, for the fragility of his designs is actual as well as seeming. Thomas Sheraton (1750-1806) also reflects the classic taste of the Adams in his designs but by emphasizing straight lines and rectangular forms achieves somewhat more substantial effects than are found in Hepplewhite's work; his *Chairs* (Fig. 628), for example, have open splat backs in which vases and lyres are prominent as motives, but a bottom rail renders them more sturdy than Hepplewhite's. A *Commode*, a type of

FIG. 628.—SHERATON. CHAIRS. Mahogany. *Metropolitan Museum, N. Y.*

cabinet evolved in England in the 18th century (Fig. 629), is illustrative of his style in its simple lines, the curving front and the inlay work of contrasting woods in panels of harewood. More than either the Adams or Hepplewhite does he approach in general character the Louis XVI manner in France and like that style too his work immediately foreshadows the completely classicizing tendencies of the Empire period.

In the English colonies in the New World, the familiar pattern of adaptation and modification of the basic types of the mother country is to be observed in the minor arts as it is in architecture and painting. In discussing the architecture of the Colonies it was pointed out that inasmuch as the first settlers in New England were from the lower middle classes of English society, their architectural forms were not the elaborate classicizing ones of Inigo Jones' Palladian palaces or Christopher Wren's baroque churches but were rather in the vernacular idiom of frame and fill construction, using wood and sparing of ornament. The furniture of the early Colonial period in the 17th century is of similar character. The interior of the Capen House at Tops-

FIG. 629.—SHERATON. COMMODE. Harewood, inlaid.
*Metropolitan Museum, N. Y.*

field, Mass. (Fig. 180) has been restored with furnishings of its period, it having been built in 1683. Although in many respects it was rather more elaborate in construction than many houses of the time, its furnishing is probably no more so than many others. Prominent is the gate-leg table which is of the type with turned legs evolved in the mid-17th century in England mentioned above. In the background is a low heavy chest with turned feet and simple paneling on the front and ends; if less elaborate in decoration than English chests of the late 16th century, the proportions are none the less very similar to them. The chairs are of the so-called ladder-back type in which horizontal slats replace the splats noted in the English 18th-century chairs; in these examples, the slats are flat instead of being turned or carved as some earlier examples are. The form as it appears here is still in part the product of turning, the posts and stretchers having been so made, but comfort is a major consideration, and the attitude is the craftsman's rather than the decorator's. Turning on a lathe as the principal technical method is also characteristic of the Windsor type of chair (Fig. 630) which is distinguished by legs pegged into the wood or rush seat and a back of turned spindles enclosed in a carved or bent-wood frame. This type of chair appears to have been used first in the vicinity of Windsor Castle in England (whence the name) about 1720 and the earliest American examples are from after 1725. It is basically a woodworker's form rather than a cabinet-maker's and probably for this reason was considerably developed in the Colonies where its ease of manufacture, lightness, comfort and the variety of forms in which it could be used made it very popular. Being easily available, pine, maple and birch are among the materials most extensively employed in American furniture in the 17th century, as well as the traditional English oak. Of whatever character, the wood was often left unfinished after being smoothed, to acquire polish and color in the normal processes of use.

Fig. 630.—Windsor Chair. Pine. *Metropolitan Museum, N. Y.*

American furniture in the 18th century is the product of native craftsmen of highly developed manual skill working in the same formal tradition as their English contemporaries and often with the aid of the same books and designs. It is not surprising to find an identical sequence of styles under these circumstances and it is possible to speak of Chippendale and Sheraton styles in American furniture as it is in England, for the general characteristics are much the same. There is even a general parallel in the taking up of different materials at various times, for mahogany tends to replace oak and walnut in Colonial furniture in the 18th century as it did in the products of the mother country. There are differences, however, in the American tradition that should be noted. The Chippendale style, for example, enjoys a longer period of popularity here and the 18th-century classicizing tendencies are not so pronounced. Certain types, moreover, continue in general use in the Colonies after disappearing in England itself, a case in point being the high chest which English taste had not found appealing after the first quarter of the 18th century, the lower commode (Fig. 629) being preferred. The chest appears in a considerable variety of forms in Colonial furniture, of which the most notable are the high-boy in which the supports are cabriole legs of such height as to re-

Fig. 631.—Chest-on-Chest. Cherry. *Metropolitan Museum, N. Y.*

semble a stand on which the chest seems to be placed, and the *Chest-on-chest* (Fig. 631) whose form is well described by the name. Though both these forms have English precedents, the types developed in the Colonies are uniquely American. The chest-on-chest that is illustrated shows in addition a regional distinction in the block front, the term applied to the alternate recessed and protruding paneling of the lower part. The block front was a product of Rhode Island and was not made in other parts of the Colonies, a detail which suggests that in furniture as in architecture the 18th century was one of local schools and styles within the larger framework of the period style as a whole; this was the case.

Among the local styles in American furniture of the 18th century, that which developed in Philadelphia was one of the most distinguished. Various circumstances contributed to this—a large and prosperous merchant population with aspirations to establish a definite social position being one of the most important. A strong sense of local pride was another factor responsible for the prevalent currency of the term "Philadelphia Chippendale" as a definite style in furniture which

FIG. 632.—Philadelphia. MOUNT PLEASANT. Bedroom.

likewise provides a clue to its formal quality. Upward of two dozen cabinetmakers are known who labeled their products as made in Philadelphia. A *Bedroom* in the fine Georgian house called *Mount Pleasant* built on the bank of the Schuylkill River in what is now Fairmount Park in Philadelphia by Captain John MacPherson in 1761 (Fig. 632) contains a number of pieces by such craftsmen. The chest-on-chest in the background is believed to be by Jonathan Gostelowe (1744/5-1795); its cabriole feet, scroll pediment with latticework and flowered urn and the elaborate brass mounts are typical Philadelphia details of the Chippendale idiom. It is of mahogany while the chest of drawers with the bowed front in the foreground is of walnut but in the same style; it bears a label indicating it to have been the work of Gostelowe. The two chairs in the room are also Philadelphia Chippendale in style—the one by the bed with a simplified "Gothic" back, the

FIG. 633.—PAUL REVERE. URN-SHAPED SILVER.
*Metropolitan Museum, N. Y.*

other having a very elaborate lyre motive for the splat. The four-poster bed with its needle-work hangings and spread and the small three-legged table are consistent with the pieces described. Also in the Philadelphia style is the furnishing of the room from the Powel House in the Metropolitan Museum (Fig. 182), characterized by the elaborate carving on the cabriole legs of the chairs and tables. Less ornate is the sofa, but its general lines and the massive proportions are in the best Colonial Chippendale tradition. Even the wall paper in this room reflects the interests that attach to Chippendale's style, for the Chinese motives are the result of the same decorative taste that figures in some of his furniture designs though not in any of the examples here illustrated.

Further details in the Powel room are of interest in representing the minor arts of 18th-century America. The elaborate carving of the mantelpiece and the frame on the chimney breast with its broken pediment are executed with the same nicety of detail and vigor of line that characterize the decoration of the furniture. The crystal chandelier or luster and the little pottery figures on the mantel were probably im-

Fig. 634.—STIEGEL. Glassware. *Metropolitan Museum, N. Y.*

ported from Europe but reveal a taste that parallels that of contemporary France and England. The silverware, on the other hand, is of Colonial origin and serves as a reminder that a flourishing trade in the manufacture and sale of such objects was carried on in the New World in the 18th century. It is a matter of historical as well as artistic interest that Paul Revere was a silversmith of great renown; pieces by him (Fig. 633) are in demand as much for their formal quality as for their associations. They are less ornate as a rule than contemporary European work but reveal to an extraordinary degree the unerring instinct of a master in his chosen field—the craftsman's sense of his material. Of similar character is another of the famed products of the 18th century in the American minor arts—the *Glassware* produced by *Heinrich Wilhelm Stiegel* at Mannheim in Pennsylvania (Fig. 634). The brilliant colors and occasional etched or painted designs of these pieces are effective complements to the shapes and forms of the vessels which so clearly reveal the character of the substance of which they are made.

The inherent craftsman's sense of material has been spoken of before in discussing the quality of Chippendale's furniture designs—the feeling for wood and its intrinsic properties that underlies the best of his formal ideas. It is this quality that makes the Colonial adaptations of his work as distinguished as the original work itself, executed as they were by men of the same temperament who responded to the qualities described with intuitive perception of their character since they themselves were equipped by training and experience to achieve similar effects. It is this as well as the normal lag in following the current tastes always apparent in comparisons between the cultural phenomena of mother country and colony that accounts for the belated appearance of the refined classicism of the Adams, of Hepplewhite and Sheraton, in the minor arts of the New World—in which a conscious aesthetic is co-equal with the craftsman's feeling that was dominant in the earlier Chippendale period in both England and the Colonies. A *Secretary-bookcase* of mahogany and inlaid satinwood of Philadelphia origin, made about 1790 (Fig. 635), reveals both Hepplewhite and Sheraton characteristics, a mixture not uncommon in furniture of the late 18th century in America since the handbooks of the various English styles of the time were used indiscriminately. In this piece, the general rectangularity of form and the pattern of the leaded glass in the bookcase doors are Hepplewhite in character,

FIG. 635.—SECRETARY-BOOKCASE.
Mahogany, inlaid.
*Museum of Art, Philadelphia.*

whereas the inlaid ornament of the lower part is more in the Sheraton manner although as a general rule it was the practice to inlay chests and case pieces of this period instead of carving them as had been done earlier.

The post-Revolutionary development in American furniture represented by the Philadelphia secretary-bookcase is one in which the outstanding characteristic is gracefulness of line and surface combined with delicacy of proportion and a pleasing sense of the decorative quality of materials. The cabinetmaker's craft was still pursued on a high

FIG. 636.—ROOM WITH FURNITURE BY DUNCAN PHYFE. *Metropolitan Museum, N.Y.*

level of taste and the names of some of America's outstanding designers come from its practitioners—notably Samuel McIntire, "the woodcarver of Salem," Charles Bulfinch and Robert Wellford. Works by men of the caliber of these are of as great distinction as the best English furniture of the same period. At the hands of Duncan Phyfe (1768-1854) an adaptation of the classicizing Sheraton manner was developed which is one of the most distinguished furniture styles of the period in either Europe or America (Fig. 636). His shop was established in New York in the later years of the 18th century and his

FIG. 637.—LEMARCHAND. CABINET. Mahogany and Ormolu.
*Musée des arts décoratifs, Paris*

most effective designs date from that period and the first years of the 19th century. A *Room in the style of ca. 1800* in the American Wing of the Metropolitan Museum in New York has been furnished with pieces from this period; the table is of the pedestal type which Phyfe frequently employed and the surrounding side-chairs have the lyre backs which he did much to popularize while others have latticework and curved patterns of Sheraton inspiration but given individual quality by him. In all of these pieces, the beauty of the wood, whether solid or veneered, is an important factor in the design, accented by carving or reeding of delicate scale appropriate to the

lightness of the forms, and with legs of subtle curvature well calculated to achieve the sense of elastic support desired in a form of this
type. The upholstery textiles are soft in color as befits the impression
of refinement and good taste created throughout.

To the cabinetmakers who created the styles of the later 18th century, the classic was a source of inspiration; to the men who followed
them in the early 19th century, the classic was a style to be copied.
No more than a glance at the cabinet designed by Geoffroy Lemarchand in the Musée des Arts décoratifs in Paris (Fig. 637) is needed
to see how the entire concept of form has changed from one in
which a feeling for material is combined with a taste for classic decorative motives to one that seeks to reproduce an effect that was first
achieved in quite other ways than those seen here. For the massiveness
of Lemarchand's Empire piece is the result of trying to reproduce in
wood the heaviness of sculptured stone forms, by contrast with Chippendale massiveness which is intrinsic in the methods of joining and
construction that he used. Other than this the use of supposedly classic
motives—lions' heads, busts, cherubs, nude goddesses and various foliate
forms, in gilded appliqué—shows how completely the furniture designer's inspiration is controlled by the archaeologist's vision rather than by
functional requirement or decorative fitness of form to material. Occasionally the former grace of line and form appears—an illustration being
the chaise longue in David's portrait of Madame Recamier—but uninspired heaviness and archaeological literalness are the order of the day
for the most part. Even Duncan Phyfe's later work shows him yielding
to the general trend of the times in pieces of graceless heaviness that
were popularly known as "Butcher's furniture." Biedermeier is a name
often used in a broad way to mean early 19th-century furniture of
this type; it is more specifically applied to the Empire style in Germany which was distinguished chiefly by its simplification of the carved
ornament of French models, the name being that of a fictitious character in a German comic weekly who was the personification of bourgeois
tastelessness. If this general characterization does not do justice to an
occasional piece in which sturdy simplicity is a source of some aesthetic
pleasure, it is none the less applicable to the greater part of the furniture of the period.

In discussing the furniture of the 18th century, the examples thus
far considered have been creations of the master designers working in cosmopolitan centers for aristocratic patrons. In the provinces
—the outlying or rural districts—the magnificence and ostentation of
such forms as these were known but seldom; moreover the cost of furniture by the famous cabinetmakers was too great for the average man.
Yet it is often from such circumstances as these that many attractive

pieces have come. French provincial furniture of the 17th and 18th centuries has a character all its own resulting from the assimilation and modification of the more sophisticated ideas of Parisian cabinet-makers to local and regional tastes; the work of many an anonymous artisan is infused with the craftsman's sense of material and intuitive feeling for distinguished design that are the keynote of all effective forms in the minor arts. Among the best-known examples of such work in the American Colonies are the *Painted Chests* of the

Fig. 638.—Painted Chest. Pine. *Philadelphia Museum of Art.*

settlers in eastern Pennsylvania in the 18th century (Fig. 638). The wood is usually that immediately available—pine in this case—and the methods of working it are of the simplest, the panels here being dovetailed at the angles. Carved decoration of a simple type is not unknown, but the most general practice was painting; the motives are quite varied with flowers, people, animals and the like, but are always treated with a naïve simplicity that seldom ventures beyond symmetry as the basic organization. The colors are quite simple too, and the result has a charm that is immediately sensed; it is the consequence in no small degree of the flat stylization of the forms that make such patterns as these so fitting as decorative adjuncts of the objects as a whole.

The minor arts of the 18th century are products of the last great period of hand craftsmanship, in which the artisan is guided as much by a feeling for his medium as anything else. Even without invalidating this general statement, it must, however, be pointed out that in the last years of the period there had appeared an ideal of judgment that was not essentially an artistic one but was rather aesthetic

in a dogmatic way, stressing associative values and symbolic implications rather than line and mass and texture and color. This shift
in the basis of taste is one of the significant factors in the background
of the minor arts of the 19th century. Another was the development
of mechanical processes as aids to carving, weaving, painted decoration and the like, the first beginnings of the mass production that
was the great contribution of the Industrial Age to modern culture.
Similarly a manifestation of the Industrial Age was the appearance

FIG. 639.—THE "DAY DREAMER." Papier-mâché. *Great Exposition of 1851.*

of a type of patronage that was unknown or at the most of very
small influence in preceding periods—the middle-class industrial worker
who was provided, even at the low wages paid, with sufficient income
to enable him to purchase for his needs rather than make for himself.
There thus appear as the fundamental factors in determining 19th-
century style in furniture, chinaware, decorative objects and the like,
the general decline in taste, the existence of a demand for such things
on a scale so large that it could not possibly be met by traditional

handicraft processes, and the development of mechanical methods of manufacture to meet this need.

The mid-19th century ideal in the minor arts found its most comprehensive statement in the displays forming the Great Exhibition in the Crystal Palace in London (Fig. 195) in 1851. This was one of the first of the expositions that were held at frequent intervals from the middle of the 19th century to present times; they are another characteristic manifestation of the increasingly industrialized culture of the west, seeking to emphasize the greatness of past achievement and pointing the way to still further conquests. Albert, Prince Regent of England, who was primarily responsible for the idea of the Crystal Palace, stated as its purpose to give "a living picture of the point of development at which mankind had arrived, and a new starting point from which all nations will be able to direct their future exertions"; that this starting point was to be the machine was quickly apparent for the crowds that thronged the Exhibition from its opening day soon showed a marked preference for the mechanical displays over all the others and the objects which attracted the most attention otherwise were those created by mechanized processes. Such was a chair in papier-mâché called the *Day Dreamer* (Fig. 639), which was described as follows in the official catalogue: "The chair is decorated at the top with two winged thoughts—the one with bird-like pinions and crowned with roses representing happy and joyous dreams, the other with leathern bat-like wings, unpleasant and troublesome ones. Behind is displayed Hope under the figure of the rising sun. . . ." The popular appeal of such an object as this was twofold. Its symbolism delighted an age that took pleasure in sentimentality, and the material of which it was moulded, being synthetic rather than natural, represented a triumph of mechanical ingenuity which also permitted unlimited reproduction. Such formal qualities as it has are exaggerations of the classicizing ornament of the 18th century; a leaf is not merely a decorative adjunct to the leg as it would be in Chippendale's design, it has actually become the leg.

Textile designs were an important feature in the Exhibition since they represented one of the key industries of 19th-century industrial England. A velvet pile tapestry carpeting (Fig. 640) was one of the many widely acclaimed achievements in this field and illustrates, like the chair, the dependence of its designers in a formal sense upon the craftsmen of the 18th century. For with all the available mechanical aids at their disposal, the inspiration of the creators of this design was limited to attempting to reproduce the patterns of early similar objects, possibly one like that seen in the French 18th-century room discussed earlier (Fig. 621). The difference in effect is unmistakable, however; the leaf patterns that lie flat in the plane of the carpet in the French room and make it an admirable floor covering and ornament are treated by the 19th-century designer in a way so naturalistic, what with modeling shadows and perspective foreshortening, that the illusion of treading on actual stems and blossoms is created. The 18th century patterns are also realistic, but in creating them on the loom the crafts-

FIG. 640.—TAPESTRY CARPET. Velvet Pile.

man's sense of style and the minutely individual variations in each recurrent example of the motive result in something that is both decorative and vigorous, whereas the mechanically identical forms of the 19th-century carpet are stereotyped and dead. Neither the nature of the material nor the purpose of the object has been a factor in the design— both absolutely fundamental considerations in any creative approach to the forms of the minor arts.

Prevalent as were the ideals implicit in the papier-mâché chair and the carpet during the 19th century when they are associated with

Victorian style, there were certain more reassuring developments too. The designs of John H. Belter, an American cabinetmaker in New York around 1850, have the over-ornate and naturalistic decoration that connotes Victorian taste, but the craftsmanship of his pieces is excellent and his use of wood quite distinguished. Sir Charles Eastlake attempted to establish a foundation for popular taste in his book called *Hints on Household Taste* published in England in 1870 and reprinted widely in the United States; his hope was to adapt the mediaeval forms then widely popular to machine production by simplifying them. However praiseworthy his intentions, they were so considerably distorted in the realization that his name is practically synonymous with the most completely debased taste of the Victorian epoch. But it was such attitudes as his in attempting to substitute the machine for the craftsman simply as an aid to increased production of traditional forms that were primarily responsible for a phenomenon in the minor arts of the 19th century which was more or less isolated and had little immediate influence but is none the less of great importance—the Arts and Crafts Movement sponsored by William Morris (1834-1896).

The Arts and Crafts Movement was the outcome of an attitude which could have existed only in 19th-century England. There was first of all a sense of aesthetic disgust for the cheap, shoddily made objects produced by mechanical means that revealed lack of taste and absence of a genuine craft tradition. Secondly, there was a moral objection to these same qualities as symbols of a brutal and debased philosophy that was a direct consequence of the industrialization of western culture by the machine, with a consequent emphasis upon purely mercenary and materialistic values. Thirdly, there was the by now strongly ingrained habit of historical criticism that led men to turn for inspiration to other times when a more desirable way of thinking produced more beautiful forms. It was because of these various considerations that William Morris found it impossible to expect his bride to live in the "immoral" atmosphere of a house built and furnished in the prevailing taste of the time, and turned to the art of the Middle Ages as the sort of thing produced by men inspired by lofty and elevated ideals and for that reason, according to him, beautiful. With a group of associates and sympathizers of similar ideals known as the Pre-Raphaelite Brotherhood, he attempted to bring about a return to the mediaeval tradition of fine handicraft motivated by considerations of taste that played no part in the industrial output of the time. An example of the products of this attitude is the *Wall-paper pattern*, one of many that he designed (Fig. 641). Morris had learned the lesson of mediaeval tapestries (Fig. 595) and made his pattern lie flat on the wall; it is stylized rather than naturalistic in detail, clear and soft in color, light and delicate in drawing and tone. Inspired as to motive by the foliate decoration of mediaeval illuminated manuscripts, the execution was by hand blocking and tinting. The reforms attempted by Morris are found in other fields as well; the chair which he designed and gave his name to is a piece of simple joinery forming

FIG. 641.—WILLIAM MORRIS. THE "DAISY" WALLPAPER.

a frame that supports loose cushions for seat and back; it is intended for comfort rather than display and is characterized otherwise by its solid construction. Typography too attracted his attention and the hand-set pages of books printed at the Kelmscott Press have much the same brilliance of tone and effective relationship of type-face and illustration that are found in the 15th-century incunabula (Fig. 604) that were his models.

Basic to Morris' conception of the arts was the principle that only hand craft could have aesthetic character; his opposition to the machine amounted to a phobia—a feeling that was no doubt amply justified by the machine products of his age but which his attitude concerned itself with only in a superficial way since he condemned the tool rather than the inspiration that guided it. As the voice of one crying in the wilderness of tastelessness and mercenary values, his example was invaluable for he kept alive the principle of formal values of line and mass and color as essential and primary in the applied arts. But it was of value primarily historically, for his blind opposition to the new creative possibilities of the machine and his attempt to revive the

FIG. 642.—VAN DE VELDE. ART NOUVEAU INTERIOR.

moribund tradition of handicraft were in effect nothing more than a refusal to live in his own time and an effort to turn back the hands of the clock to an age forever gone.

Acceptance of the machine and designs in terms that are appropriate to its productive capabilities are the basis of the applied arts in modern times. Perception of this fact is evident in various trends that developed toward the close of the 19th century in which a new conception of ornament is apparent. It was only natural that attempts to reform the aesthetic abuses of mid-19th-century unrestrained industrialism should be first directed toward this end, for it was in the stereotyped machine versions of traditional decorative forms that the limitations of mechanical processes were most obvious. So in the style called *Art*

*Nouveau,* which is represented in this interior (Fig. 642) designed by Henry van de Velde (1863-1939), there is no reference to traditional ornamental motives of acanthus leaves, ball and claw feet, pediments and scrolls and the like. Instead, the prevailing characteristic is the curved contour line of complex and subtle geometric character that is the earmark of the style. This grows out of van de Velde's study and analysis of the functional nature of the form itself which he attempts to visualize in the character of the curves in the design— slight and easy in members that support, for example, and more vigorous and pronounced in those that provide a transition from one structural member to another. This is combined with a feeling for decorative color relationships in other elements in the room that derives from van de Velde's early training as a painter. The aesthetic unity of an interior by him is obvious, but it is also clear that this consideration is often of too great importance; to live constantly in a work of art is as artificial as existence in surroundings without any formal character is degrading, and over-emphasis on aesthetic value is scant compensation for lack of comfort. In the hands of others, moreover, and particularly when the matter of industrial production of *Art Nouveau* forms was raised, the subjective character of the style became apparent, for as long as the basis of a style is a decorative ideal it follows that there can be but little of fundamental structural foundation on which to work. The excesses to which *Art Nouveau* was carried in commercial exploitation cannot obscure the vital character of van de Velde's original work, but they also make clear the reason underlying its short-lived existence and ultimate discrediting.

The example set by William Morris in the Arts and Crafts Movement was one of van de Velde's inspirations toward the development of a new style; and if he was unable by force of historical circumstance to make the machine an element in it, he none the less was able to appreciate the weakness of Morris' theory and to open the way for still further achievements on the part of others. By publicizing that theory on the continent of Europe, for example, an interest in the applied arts and a revival of handicraft were stimulated that were destined to make significant contributions in the early 20th century. The *Deutsche Werkbund* was a craft organization founded in 1907 with the avowed purpose "to ennoble industrial labor through the cooperation of art, industry and handicraft"; and by virtue of the sincere idealism combined with intelligence that its members exemplified, it soon came to exercise great influence in industrial design in Germany. From the beginning, however, the machine and its potentialities were recognized as basic factors, an attitude summed up in a statement by one of its members as follows: "There is no fixed boundary line between tool and machine. Work of a high standard can be created with tools or with machines, as soon as man has mastered the machine and made it a tool. It is not the machines in themselves that make work inferior, but our inability to use them properly." Even more succinctly is this idea summed up in the title of a paper by Frank Lloyd Wright in 1903—"The Art and Craft of the Machine"—then and for many years to come a lone figure preaching the gospel of integrity in the artistic wilderness that was the United States in the early 20th century.

Fig. 643.—MARTHA ERPS. Knotted Tapestry. Smyrna Wool.

The most casual survey of the minor arts in contemporary times will make the observer aware of the infinite variety to be found in this category of formal creation—greater, possibly, than at any other time in the history of western culture. It is variety that is qualitative as well as quantitative, ranging from objects of superlatively fine design to others of the dullest and most stereotyped monotony. This is because of the circumstances controlling the creation of furniture and glassware and jewelry and hangings and all the myriad types that might be considered—the extraordinary demands of an ever-increasing bourgeois class in society and the meeting of them by objects produced in mass for commercial profit for the most part but with increasingly a realization of the possibility and necessity for developing even under such conditions things of character and distinction from a formal point of view. Even a limited and hurried general examination of contemporary minor art is beyond the possibility of this discussion, but note can be taken of what has been without doubt the most vital influence in shaping the significant trends to be seen therein in the years since the First World War—the principles and practices of the Bauhaus.

The Bauhaus idea stemmed originally from the *Deutsche Werkbund* attempt at synthesis of "machine style" with the "arts and crafts" concept and was developed first at the Academy of Arts and Crafts in Weimar in Germany when the direction of that school was taken over by Walter Gropius in 1919 with the intention of making it a "consulting art center for industry and the trades." The name of the school was then changed to Bauhaus, which means literally the "house of building," and its aims and principles were defined. These were at base to provide designs for the objects needed in a modern way of living, instruction in their creation being given by teachers who would be ideally both artists and craftsmen, that is, have a sense for both formal character and the nature of the materials to be employed. It was to this end that many of the foremost artists of the time—architects, sculptors and painters—as well as leading practitioners of the practical arts were on the Bauhaus staff in the early 1920's, making it a focal point of the progressive trends in the creative formal thought of the period. In 1925 the Bauhaus was moved from Weimar to Dessau where it was housed in buildings especially designed for the purpose by Gropius, including the famous workshop (Fig. 214), an outstanding example of the International Style of the period following the First World War, in which the designs created by the students of the school were submitted to the ultimate test of determining their adaptability to mechanical mass production.

Stated briefly, the method of the Bauhaus involved instruction in crafts and in form carried on concurrently to the end that at the same time that the material characteristics of a substance were being determined, the formal qualities in which those physical properties could best be utilized were also being perceived. Thus one preliminary to creation of a *Knotted Wool Tapestry* (Fig. 643) was handling and manipulating the yarn until the designer was thoroughly, almost instinctively, conversant with its tensile strength, texture, etc. In similar fashion, the designer of the *Tea and Coffee Pots* (Fig. 644) worked with metal to acquire a feeling for its nature as material, and also with the various processes by which it is formed and shaped. Along with this went studies of a more theoretical nature concerning the use to which the objects were to be put, the form by which that use

could best be served, and the abstract qualities of design by which
that form could be given its maximum character as a work of art.
The similarity of the tapestry to a painting of the type represented by
Picasso's Newspaper and Violin (Fig. 518) is considerable, a similarity
that illustrates the basic theory of the Bauhaus that formal character
is an immutable quality regardless of the immediate nature of the
medium and in accordance with which the instruction in the design
of such forms is as much a matter for the painter as for the craftsman in textile. There is likewise more than the use of comparable
materials common to the Tea and Coffee Pots and the metal-framed
building of the Bauhaus itself, for the primary concern in each case
was one of structural appropriateness.

FIG. 644.—BRANDT. COFFEE AND TEAPOTS. Metal.

The influence of Bauhaus ideas and products since the middle of the
1920's has been widespread. It is recognizable in many fields—household objects and accessories, textile design, ceramics, to mention some
in which the original character of Bauhaus ideas has often been obscured in products aping the superficial character of the originals without perceiving the motivation. But in other fields, notably typography
which in a certain sense may be said to date its modern phase from
the developments in the Bauhaus, and in the field of furniture design,
later developments have been unequivocally directed along lines clearly
defined by Bauhaus concepts. It was an instructor at the Bauhaus,
Marcel Breuer, who designed the first *Tubular Metal Chair* (Fig.
645) in 1925, using the material not as a substitute for traditional
substances, but studying through the entire problem of the object,
the use to which it was to be put, the materials and the form in which

all these would be most clearly and effectively incorporated, in accordance with the best Bauhaus theory. Today this chair may have a rather primitive look about it, in the same way that a 1925 automobile or airplane would; the vitality of the Bauhaus concept is shown by nothing more clearly than the fact that during the short life of the school (it was closed in 1933 with the incidence of the Nazi régime in Germany) the members of its staff were the first to make improvements upon their own ideas. Miës van der Rohe, who took over the

FIG. 645.—BREUER. CHAIR. Tubular steel and fabric.

direction of the school in 1930, was another pioneer in developing furniture forms in accordance with the inherent properties of metal and in being the first to utilize the spring quality of bent steel legs (cf. Fig. 216). Le Corbusier was also in the forefront of architects, realizing the appropriateness of such forms as these to the International Style interior.

Possibly the most significant contribution of the Bauhaus to the problem of effective design has been the demonstration of untold possibilities among the materials provided by modern industrial developments when used intelligently and imaginatively. Along this same line has been the work of Alvar Aalto, a Finnish designer, who in

Fig. 646.—AALTO. Chairs. Plywood and upholstery. *Museum of Modern Art, N.Y.*

1932 produced a chair of bent plywood and tubular metal, following this a short time later with a series of *Chairs in bent plywood and upholstery* (Fig. 646). The nature of this material, made of thin veneers of wood glued together with the grain at right angles in alternate layers, is such that it can be manipulated and formed in an almost unlimited variety of curved shapes and planes, as the different designs in the illustration clearly show. Aalto's furniture is admirably suited to the contemporary interior by virtue of its fine proportion and dependence upon inherent quality for decorative effect, and is moreover characterized by pleasant texture and color in a way that the metal furniture cannot always equal.

It is not possible to do more than mention in conclusion many categories of the minor arts of modern times not touched upon in the discussion—lighting fixtures, glassware and china among others—and the developments in other fields such as the designing of stage sets, of automobiles and airplanes, of refrigerators and radios, in which the realization is growing that fine design is not incompatible with production in the 20th-century manner. It is in these categories, in fact, that the modern concept of the decorative arts as something involving materials developed by science and tooled by machines touches most closely the general life, for the as yet somewhat limited field for the pioneering forms such as those discussed has a direct bearing on their still considerable cost. There are still many people, moreover, who prefer the machine-made replica of a Chippendale chair to the machine-made original after the designs of a Breuer or Aalto. Yet withal, the recognition of the inherent distinction of forms such as the latter is growing and will doubtless continue to do so, with increasing perception of the direct relationship between them and the cultural environment out of which they have grown and which they symbolize in every line and plane.

# Selected Critical Bibliography

## THEORY OF ART AND AESTHETICS

Bell, Clive. *Art*. N. Y. Stokes. 1913.

One of the earliest attempts to establish an aesthetic of modern character.

Croce, Benedetto. *Aesthetic as a Science of Expression and General Linguistic*. N. Y. Macmillan. 1909.

————. *Essence of Aesthetic*. London. Heinemann. 1921.

Basic studies by one of the foremost contemporary philosophers.

Focillon, Henri. *The Life of Forms in Art*. (Tr. C. Beecher Hogan and George Kubler.) New Haven. Yale University Press. 1942.

A concise but comprehensive theory of formal expression.

Greene, Theodore M. *The Arts and the Art of Criticism*. Princeton. Princeton University Press. 1940.

A carefully reasoned and sound attempt to determine the basis of formal expression in the arts from the observer's point of view; well illustrated.

Neuhaus, Eugen. *Appreciation of Art*. Boston. Ginn. 1924.

Ogden, C. K., Richards, I. A., Wood, James. *The Foundations of Aesthetics*. N. Y. International Publishers. 1931.

One of the most significant and influential works in the field.

Phillips, Duncan. *The Artist Sees Differently*. 2 vols. N. Y. Weyhe. 1931.

Sensitive essays on the nature of artistic experience.

Phillips, Lisle March. *Art and Environment*. N. Y. Holt. 1911.

————. *Form and Color*. London. Duckworth. 1925.

Read, Herbert. *Art and Society*. N. Y. Macmillan. 1937.

Interpretive studies by one of the foremost contemporary English critics.

## GENERAL BIBLIOGRAPHY

Cheney, Sheldon. *A World History of Art*. N. Y. Viking. 1939.

Traditional in its strictly chronological arrangement and in attempting to present all phases of the visual arts from a formalistic point of view.

Faure, Elie. *History of Art*. 5 vols. (Tr. Walter Pach.) N. Y. Harper. 1921-1933.

A monumental study, inspirational in purpose and stimulating for the advanced student, but likely to be misleading to the beginner.

Gardner, Helen. *Art Through the Ages*. N. Y. Harcourt. 1936.

Encyclopaedic and factual with emphasis on formal analysis; traditional in organization.

Michel, André. *Histoire de l'art depuis les premiers temps chrétiens jusqu'à nos jours*. 8 vols. in 17. Paris. Colin. 1905-1929.

A collaborative work, still useful for general statements.

Pijoan, Joseph. *History of Art.* 3 vols. (Tr. R. L. Roys.) N. Y. Harper, 1927.
Useful for its many illustrations.

Reinach, Salomon. *Apollo.* N. Y. Scribner. 1924.

Stites, Raymond. *The Arts and Man.* N. Y. McGraw-Hill. 1940.
An ambitious attempt to present and synthesize the history of all human artistic expression.

## GENERAL BIBLIOGRAPHY OF AMERICAN ART

Cahill, Holger, and Barr, Alfred H., Jr. *Art in America: A Complete Survey.*
N. Y. Reynal and Hitchcock. 1935.
A well-illustrated handbook.

LaFollette, Suzanne. *Art in America.* N. Y. Norton. 1929.
The arts of America studied as a social phenomenon.

Mumford, Lewis. *The Brown Decades.* N. Y. Harcourt. 1931.
American art of the late 19th century viewed by one of the most perceptive critics of modern society.

Richardson, Edgar P. *The Way of Western Art.* Cambridge. Harvard University Press. 1939.
One of the first interpretations of American art in relationship to European movements.

## ILLUSTRATIONS

*Propyläen Kunstgeschichte.* 16 vols. Berlin. Propyläen-Verlag. 1927-1934.
Each volume is a treatise on some large phase of art history; copiously illustrated.

Roos, Frank J., Jr. *An Illustrated Handbook of Art History.* N. Y. Macmillan. 1937.
A collection of pictures to illustrate the principal monuments of European art.

*University Prints.* Newton, Mass.
Inexpensive reproductions in half-tone of a wide selection of subjects from all periods and styles.

Individual monographs on periods, styles or artists in the series published by *Editions Tel,* Paris; the *Phaidon Press,* Vienna, London, and New York; and the *Hyperion Press,* Paris and New York, contain well-reproduced illustrations, often with useful details.

## ARCHITECTURE

### GENERAL BIBLIOGRAPHY

Fletcher, Sir Banister. *A History of Architecture on the Comparative Method.*
N. Y. Scribner. 1938.
A convenient reference work, valuable chiefly for numerous plans and drawings.

Hamlin, Talbot. *Architecture Through the Ages.* N. Y. Putnam. 1940.
Well written and readable, though somewhat lacking in factual matter; primarily an interpretive work.
————. *The Enjoyment of Architecture.* N. Y. Scribner. 1921.
Kimball, Fiske, and Edgell, George H. *A History of Architecture.* N. Y. Harper. 1918.
Sound analyses of styles from a formal point of view, tracing the development of the elements of architectural form.
Lescaze, William. *On Being an Architect.* N. Y. Putnam. 1942.
The problems of the modern builder, by a recognized leader in progressive architectural thinking.
Mumford, Lewis. *The Culture of Cities.* N. Y. Harcourt. 1938.
————. *Technics and Civilizations.* N. Y. Harcourt. 1934.
Brilliantly effective propaganda for better order and broader vision in planning the life of the modern community.
Scott, Geoffrey. *The Architecture of Humanism.* Boston, Houghton. 1914.
Still the most perceptive and creative architectural theory of modern times.
Simpson, F. M. *A History of Architectural Development.* N. Y. Longmans. 1921-1922.
Towndrow, Frederic. *Architecture in the Balance.* N. Y. Stokes. 1936.
A plea for more objective thinking in solution of modern architectural problems.
Whitaker, C. H. *Rameses to Rockefeller.* N. Y. Random House. 1934.
A practicing architect records the excitement of creative building.

PRE-CLASSICAL ARCHITECTURE

Bell, Edward. *The Architecture of Ancient Egypt.* London. Bell. 1915.
————. *Prehellenic Architecture in the Aegean.* London. Bell. 1926.
Evans, Sir Arthur J. *The Palace of Minos at Knossos.* 4 vols. in 6. London, Macmillan. 1921-1935.
A monumental publication by one of the leading archaeologists of the 20th century of one of the greatest monuments of pre-classic civilization.
Handcock, P. S. P. *Mesopotamian Archaeology.* N. Y. Putnam. 1912.
Osborn. H. E. *Men of the Old Stone Age; Their Environment, Life and Art.* N. Y. Scribner. 1921.
Smith, E. Baldwin. *Egyptian Architecture as Cultural Expression.* N. Y. Appleton-Century. 1938.
The only satisfactory discussion in English of the forms of Egyptian architecture, their development and their meaning.
Warren, H. L. *The Foundations of Classic Architecture.* N. Y. Macmillan. 1919.

### GREEK ARCHITECTURE

Anderson, W. J., Spiers, R. P., and Dinsmoor, W. B. *The Architecture of Ancient Greece.* London. Batsford. 1927.
> One of the standard general works on the subject.

Bieber, Margaret. *The History of the Greek and Roman Theatre.* Princeton. Princeton University Press. 1939.
> A thorough and sound discussion of this difficult and controversial problem.

Carpenter, Rhys. *The Esthetic Basis of Greek Art.* N. Y. Longmans. 1921.
> A stimulating and successful attempt to interpret the forms of Greek art.

Collignon, Maxime. *Le Parthénon.* (Revised by G. Fougéres.) Paris. Hachette. 1926.
> Detailed description, accompanied by exhaustive pictorial documentation.

D'Ooge, M. L. *The Acropolis of Athens.* N. Y. Macmillan. 1908.
> A careful and accurate description of the sites and monuments of the Acropolis, useful even though outdated in some respects by recent discoveries.

Marquand, Allan. *Greek Architecture.* N. Y. Macmillan. 1909.
> The standard archaeological reference work.

Robertson, D. S. *A Handbook of Greek and Roman Architecture.* Cambridge. Cambridge University Press. 1929.
> The most comprehensive general discussion in English, with exhaustive bibliography up to the date of publication.

Rodenwalt, G., and Hege, W. *Olympia.* N. Y. Westermann. 1936.
————. *The Acropolis.* N. Y. Westermann. 1930.
> Of value for the beautiful illustrations in which the character of the monuments is well suggested.

### ROMAN ARCHITECTURE

Anderson, W. J., Spiers, R. P., and Ashby, T. *The Architecture of Ancient Rome.* London, Batsford. 1927.
> A standard work, dealing with methods of construction and design.

Choisy, Auguste. *L'Art de Batir chez les Romains.* Paris. Ducher. 1873.
> The basic discussion of Roman ways of building.

Hülsen, Christian. *The Roman Forum.* (Tr. J. B. Carter.) N. Y. Stechert. 1909.
> A useful guidebook in studying this characteristic expression of the Roman architectural temperament.

Rivoira, G. T. *Roman Architecture.* (Tr. G. McN. Rushforth.) Oxford. Clarendon Press. 1925.

Walters, H. B. *The Art of the Romans.* N. Y. Macmillan. 1921.

General interpretive discussion of the principal monuments of Roman art.

### Early Christian and Byzantine Architecture

Butler, H. C. *Architecture and Other Arts.* N. Y. Appleton-Century. 1903.

Cummings, C. A. *A History of Architecture in Italy.* Boston. Houghton. 1901.

Outdated in many respects but still useful for the early Christian buildings outside Rome.

Frothingham, A. L. *Monuments of Christian Rome.* N. Y. Macmillan. 1908.

A convenient general handbook.

Hamilton, J. A. *Byzantine Architecture and Decoration.* N. Y. Scribner. 1934.

A general discussion in which the major monuments are taken up.

Jackson, T. G. *Byzantine and Romanesque Architecture.* 2 vols. Cambridge. Cambridge University Press. 1920.

Informally written and treating most of the important examples; illustrated chiefly by drawings.

Strzygowski, Josef. *Origin of Christian Church Art.* (Tr. Dalton and Baumholtz.) Oxford. Clarendon Press. 1923.

A condensation of this author's highly influential theories concerning the beginning of Christian art.

Swift, Emerson H. *Hagia Sophia.* N. Y. Columbia University Press. 1940.

A discussion of the outstanding monument of Byzantine architecture in the light of recent discoveries.

### Pre-Romanesque and Romanesque Architecture

Baum, Julius. *Romanesque Architecture in France.* London. Heinemann. 1912.

A convenient collection of illustrations with brief discussion.

Clapham, A. W. *English Romanesque Architecture Before the Conquest.* 1930.

—————. *English Romanesque Architecture After the Conquest.* 1934.

Informative presentation of basic material concerning a school whose importance is becoming more clearly realized.

—————. *Romanesque Architecture in Western Europe.* Oxford. Clarendon Press. 1936.

The best treatment in English of Romanesque architecture and decoration.

Lasteyrie, Robert de. *L'architecture réligieuse à l'époque romane.* Paris. Picard. 1929.

The standard work on French Romanesque architecture.

Porter, A. K. *Lombard Architecture.* 4 vols. New Haven. Yale University Press. 1917.
A landmark in the archaeology of Romanesque architecture.
Puig y Cadafalch, J. *Le premier art roman.* Paris. Laurens. 1928.
One of the first successful attempts to discern the significant trends in European architecture in the period before the Romanesque.
Ricci, Corrado. *Romanesque Architecture in Italy.* Stuttgart. Hoffmann. 1925.
Illustrations and brief factual discussion of the principal examples.
Whitehill, W. M. *Spanish Romanesque Architecture.* London. Oxford University Press. 1941.
The definitive statement of the facts concerning an important school of Romanesque building.

## GOTHIC ARCHITECTURE

Gardner, S. *A Guide to English Gothic Architecture.* Cambridge. Cambridge University Press. 1922.
Jackson, T. G. *Gothic Architecture in France, England and Italy.* 2 vols. Cambridge. Cambridge University Press. 1915.
A popular treatment of the principal schools of Gothic building.
Lasteyrie, Robert de. *L'architecture réligieuse en France à l'époque gothique.* Paris. Picard. 1926-1927.
The standard archaeological treatment of French Gothic architecture.
Parkhurst, Helen Huss. *Cathedral: A Gothic Pilgrimage.* Boston. Houghton Mifflin. 1936.
Porter, A. K. *Medieval Architecture.* 2 vols. New Haven. Yale University Press. 1912.
Important for its development of the organic character of mediaeval vaulted construction.
Prentice, Sartell. *The Heritage of the Cathedral.* N. Y. Morrow. 1936.
————. *The Voices of the Cathedral.* N. Y. Morrow. 1938.
These volumes, primarily interpretive in purpose, are characterized by many passages of most subtle perception.
Ward, Clarence. *Medieval Church Vaulting.* Princeton. Princeton University Press. 1915.
The definitive work on this abstruse and difficult subject.

## RENAISSANCE ARCHITECTURE

Anderson, W. J., and Stratton, A. *Architecture of the Renaissance in Italy.* London. Batsford. 1927.
The most satisfactory general discussion.
Blomfield, Reginald. *History of Renaissance Architecture in England.* Abridged edition. London. Bell. 1900.

Gromort, Georges. *Italian Renaissance Architecture.* (Tr. Waters.) Paris. Vincent. 1922.
> A convenient handbook, though somewhat spotty in treatment of later periods.

Jackson, T. G. *The Renaissance of Roman Architecture: Italy, England, France.* 3 vols. Chicago. University of Chicago Press. 1922.

Ricci, Corrado. *High and Late Renaissance Architecture.* N. Y. Brentano. 1923.
> Illustrations and brief factual discussions of the most important examples of Italian Renaissance architecture.

Stokes, Adrian. *Stones of Rimini.* N. Y. Putnam. 1935.
> A stimulating attempt to define the expressive character of Renaissance formal idioms.

Ward, W. H. *Architecture of the Renaissance in France.* 2 vols. London. Batsford. 1926.
> A carefully detailed discussion of French Renaissance building from the late 15th century to the early 19th; the basic work.

### Post-Renaissance Architecture

Briggs, Martin S. *Baroque Architecture.* N. Y. McBride. 1914.

Clark, Kenneth. *The Gothic Revival.* N. Y. Scribner. 1929.
> Invaluable for its penetrating analysis of the motives leading to the revival of mediaeval forms in English 18th- and 19th-century building.

Fokker, T. H. *Roman Baroque Art.* 2 vols. London. Oxford. 1938.
> The only work in English dealing with baroque style in a comprehensive way; many controversial points are ineffectively handled, but the illustrations are numerous and good.

Hobhouse, Christopher. *1851 and the Crystal Palace.* N. Y. Dutton. 1937.
> An amusing but informative presentation of the genesis and history of this significant structure.

Pevsner, Nikolaus. *Pioneers of the Modern Movement.* London. Faber. 1936.
> Occasionally superficial but the clearest statement of the outstanding developments in 19th-century art and architecture.

Ricci, Corrado. *Baroque Architecture and Sculpture in Italy.* London. Heinemann. 1922.

Sitwell, Sacheverell. *German Baroque Art.* N. Y. Doran. 1928.

————. *Southern Baroque Art.* London. Duckworth. 1931.

————. *Spanish Baroque Art.* London. Duckworth. 1931.
> Primarily literary studies of 17th-century culture but with illuminating critical and interpretive passages.

### Modern Architecture

Barr, Alfred H., Jr., ed. *Modern Architecture; Catalogue of the International Exhibition.* N. Y. Museum of Modern Art. 1932.

Well-illustrated discussion of the outstanding developments in architecture from the close of the First World War to 1932.

Behrendt, Walter C. *Modern Building.* N. Y. Harcourt. 1937.
The soundest and most important critical discussion of architecture in the 19th and 20th centuries.

Cheney, Sheldon. *The New World Architecture.* N. Y. Longmans. 1930.
Elementary but still useful for its insight into attitudes.

Giedion, Siegfried. *Space, Time and Architecture.* Cambridge. Harvard University Press. 1941.
A bold attempt to interpret the modern temperament through its architectural expression, frequently involved and ambiguous but thought-provoking.

Gropius, Walter. *The New Architecture and the Bauhaus.* London. Faber. 1935.
The theory of the "International Style" by one of its outstanding representatives.

Hitchcock, H.-R. *Modern Architecture.* N. Y. Payson. 1929.
The basic English presentation of the historical data of western architecture from 1800 to 1929.

————, and Johnson, Philip. *The International Style; Architecture Since 1922.* N. Y. Norton. 1932.
A selection of pictures illustrating this trend in modern building.

Le Corbusier (Charles-Edouard Jeanneret). *The City of Tomorrow.* (Tr. Frederick Etchells.) N. Y. Payson. 1929.

————. *Towards a New Architecture.* (Tr. Frederick Etchells.) N. Y. Payson. 1927.
Manifestoes in the cause of modern architectural style by a leading figure in contemporary building.

Platz, Gustave. *Die Baukunst der neuesten Zeit.* Berlin. Propyläen-Verlag. 1931.

————. *Die Wohnraum der Gegenwart.* Berlin. Propyläen-Verlag. 1933.
Comprehensive collections of pictures illustrating modern architectural style in both exterior and interior designs.

Richards, J. M. *An Introduction to Modern Architecture.* N. Y. Penguin. 1940.
A concise and intelligent discussion of the premises of contemporary architectural theory, constituting an excellent introduction, and published at very low cost.

Wright, Frank Lloyd. *Modern Architecture: The Kahn Lectures for 1930.* Princeton. Princeton University Press. 1931.
Authoritative and significant development of the building theories of the leading architect in the United States.

Yorke, F. R. S. *The Modern House.* London. Architectural Press. 1934.
A survey of a significant aspect of contemporary design.

### Architecture in the United States

Eberlein, H. D. *Architecture of Colonial America*. Boston. Little, Brown. 1915.

Embury, Aymar. *Early American Churches*. N. Y. Doubleday. 1914.

Gutheim, Frederick, Jr. *Frank Lloyd Wright on Architecture; Selected Papers. 1894-1940*. N. Y. Duell, Sloan and Pearce. 1941.

Hamlin, Talbot. *The American Spirit in Architecture*. The Pageant of America Series, Vol. XIII. New Haven. Yale University Press. 1926.

Abundantly illustrated and extensive discussion of American building from its beginnings.

Hitchcock, H.-R. *The Architecture of H. H. Richardson and His Times*. N. Y. Museum of Modern Art. 1936.

A detailed and factual study of the buildings designed by one of the leading architects of the late 19th century in the United States.

————. *In the Nature of Materials: The Buildings of Frank Lloyd Wright. 1887-1941*. N. Y. Duell, Sloan and Pearce. 1942.

A critical survey, with complete data and illustration.

Kimball, Fiske. *Domestic Architecture of the American Colonies and the Early Republic*. N. Y. Scribner. 1922.

The basic work in the archaeology and criticism of American domestic architectural style in the early period.

Major, Howard. *Domestic Architecture of the Early American Republic: The Greek Revival*. Philadelphia. Lippincott. 1926.

Morrison, Hugh. *Louis Sullivan, Prophet of Modern Architecture*. N. Y. Norton. 1935.

Fundamental to any understanding of this significant figure in late 19th-century architecture.

Mumford, Lewis. *Sticks and Stones*. N. Y. Boni. 1924.

A pioneering work in the social criticism of architecture, and still to be read profitably for its acute observations.

Sullivan, Louis. *The Autobiography of an Idea*. N. Y. American Institute of Architects. 1924.

Difficult but instructive writing by an architectural pioneer.

Tallmadge, T. E. *The Story of Architecture in America*. N. Y. Norton. 1936.

The most satisfactory available general history of American building.

Upjohn, Everard M. *Richard Upjohn, Architect and Churchman*. N. Y. Columbia University Press. 1939.

A sympathetic study of a leading figure in mid-19th-century American architecture.

Wright, Frank Lloyd. *An Autobiography*. London. Longmans. 1932.

### Housing

Thinking in this critical field is in a state of constant change, affected by political, social and economic as much as by architectural factors. The most up-to-date bibliography will be found in periodical literature, but the following may be consulted with profit.

Bauer, Catherine. *Modern Housing*. Boston. Houghton. 1934.
An effective statement of the necessity for more than individual contributions to effective housing.

Geddes, Patrick. *Cities in Evolution*. London. Williams and Norgate. 1915.
One of the classic works by one of the first modern authorities in the field.

Haverfield, F. *Ancient Town-Planning*. Oxford. Clarendon Press. 1913.
The authoritative work on the history of city-planning.

Le Corbusier. *The City of Tomorrow*. N. Y. Payson. 1927.

Mumford, Lewis. *The Culture of Cities*. N. Y. Harcourt. 1938.
A challenging discussion, using material from past and present, of the necessity for planned communities.

## SCULPTURE

### GENERAL BIBLIOGRAPHY

Chase, G. H., and Post, C. R. *A History of Sculpture*. N. Y. Harper. 1925.
The standard reference work for the general history of sculpture.

Gill, Eric. *Beauty Looks After Herself*. N. Y. Sheed and Ward. 1934.
A plea for expressive content in sculpture by a distinguished English practitioner of the art.

Hoffman, Malvina. *Sculpture Inside and Out*. N. Y. Norton. 1936.
The methods, practice and purpose of sculpture. Particularly useful for its illustrations.

Parkes, Kineton. *The Art of Carved Sculpture*. 2 vols. London. Chapman. 1931.
A general discussion, with numerous illustrations of rather limited selection.

Post, C. R. *A History of European and American Sculpture from the Early Christian Period to the Present Day*. Cambridge. Harvard University Press. 1921.
Comprehensive in its coverage but limited in critical conclusions and handicapped by sparseness of illustration.

### PRE-CLASSIC SCULPTURE

Murray, Margaret. *Egyptian Sculpture*. London. Duckworth. 1930.
All inclusive, but indifferently illustrated and subjective in criticism.

Petrie, Sir Flinders. *The Arts and Crafts of Ancient Egypt*. London. Foulis. 1923.
A handbook by one of the foremost Egyptologists, particularly useful for its description of the methods of Egyptian artists.

Ranke, Hermann. *The Art of Ancient Egypt*. Vienna. Phaidon. 1936.
   Vivid illustrations, well reproduced, of Egyptian art through its history.
Spearing, Herbert G. *The Childhood of Art*. 2 vols. London. Benn. 1930.
   The best general discussion of prehistoric painting and sculpture.
Zervos, Christian. *L'art de la Mesopotamie*. Paris. Cahiers d'Art. 1935.
   A collection of illustrations, many of them details, spectacular in scale
   and frequently illuminating as to style and expressive character.

### CLASSIC SCULPTURE

Beazley, J. D., and Ashmole, Bernard. *Greek Sculpture and Painting*. N. Y.
   Macmillan, 1932.
   A condensed but highly illuminating discussion of Greek art from the
   archaic to Hellenistic periods, apt in characterization and well illus-
   trated.
Casson, Stanley. *The Technique of Early Greek Sculpture*. London. Oxford
   University Press. 1932.
   A study of the methods of Greek sculpture as they affect style.
Dickins, Guy. *Hellenistic Sculpture*. Oxford. Clarendon Press. 1920.
   Though little more than an outline, this is a thoroughly satisfactory
   critical discussion of the most involved period in the history of classic
   art.
Gardner, E. A. *A Handbook of Greek Sculpture*. London. Macmillan. 1920.
   A convenient reference book, written from a conservative point of view.
Hekler, Anton. *Greek and Roman Portraits*. London. Heinemann. 1912.
Lawrence, A. W. *Classical Sculpture*. London. Cape. 1929.
————. *Later Greek Sculpture*. N. Y. Harcourt. 1927.
   Controversial works, written to discount traditional critical conclusions
   but not always justifiably.
Richter, Gisela M. A. *Sculpture and Sculptors of the Greeks*. New Haven.
   Yale University Press. 1930.
   The definitive critical work in English, indispensable to any study of
   the subject; well illustrated.
Strong, Eugénie. *Roman Sculpture*. N. Y. Scribner. 1907.
   Though outdated with respect to recent discoveries, this remains the
   best book in English on the subject.

### MEDIAEVAL SCULPTURE

Aubert, Marcel. *La sculpture française au début de l'époque gothique: 1140-
   1225*. Florence. Pantheon Press. 1929.
   Excellent illustrations of the outstanding examples of French Gothic
   sculpture.
Brown, G. Baldwin. *The Arts in Early England*. London. Murray. 1931.
Gardner, Arthur. *Medieval Sculpture in France*. N. Y. Macmillan. 1931.
   A general survey, sometimes insufficiently critical of its sources.

Hinks, Roger P. *Carolingian Art: Painting and Sculpture in Western Europe. A.D. 800-900.* London. Sidgwick and Jackson. 1935.
The only book in English on this important period; interpretive rather than archaeological.

Hubert, Jean. *L'art pré-roman.* Paris. Editions d'art et d'histoire. 1938.
A pioneering effort at archaeological synthesis of the arts of the Dark Ages.

Mâle, Émile. *L'art religieux du XII⁰ siècle en France.* Parsi. Colin. 1923.
————. *Religious Art in France, XIII Century.* N. Y. Dutton. 1913.
————. *L'art religieux à la fin du moyen âge en France.* Paris. Colin. 1925.
The standard and definitive discussions of mediaeval iconography.

Morey, C. R. *Christian Art.* N. Y. Longmans. 1935.
General interpretation of Christian art in the Middle Ages and the Renaissance by the foremost scholar of mediaeval art in the United States.
————. *Early Christian Art.* Princeton. Princeton University Press. 1942.
A profoundly scholarly discussion of sculpture and painting in Europe from antiquity to the 8th century; definitive and indispensable.
————. *Mediaeval Art.* N. Y. Norton. 1942.
The only satisfactory discussion of mediaeval art from the points of view of inconography, style and content.

Porter, A. K. *Romanesque Sculpture of the Pilgrimage Roads.* Boston. Marshall Jones. 1923.
A highly controversial discussion, but basic to the study of the material and invaluable for illustrations.

### RENAISSANCE AND POST-RENAISSANCE SCULPTURE

Lord Balcarres. *The Evolution of Italian Sculpture.* N. Y. Dutton. 1910.

Cellini, Benvenuto. *Autobiography.* (Tr. Symonds.) N. Y. Modern Library. 1928.

Fokker, T. H. *Roman Baroque Art.* 2 vols. London. Oxford University Press. 1938.

Fraschetti, S. *Il Bernini.* Milan. Hoepli. 1900.
Biography and criticism, amply documented and illustrated.

Goldscheider, Ludwig. *Donatello.* N. Y. Oxford University Press (Phaidon). 1941.
Primarily useful for the illustrations, some of which are over-dramatized, but in general are quite illuminating.
————. *Michelangelo.* N. Y. Oxford University Press (Phaidon). 1940.
A collection of illustrations of the sculptures.

Lemonnier, H. *L'art français au temps du Richelieu et de Mazarin.* Paris. Hachette. 1893.

Lemonnier, H. *L'art français au temps du Louis XIV*. Paris. Hachette. 1911.
Urbane and polished studies in a field that has not attracted much critical attention.

Maclagan, Eric. *Italian Sculpture of the Renaissance*. Cambridge. Harvard University Press. 1935.
General in character, emphasizing the humanistic element in Renaissance art.

Panofsky, Erwin. *Studies in Iconology*. N. Y. Oxford University Press. 1939.
Penetrating analyses of content and subject matter in a number of Italian Renaissance works of art, including sculptures by Michelangelo.

Ricci, Corrado. *Baroque Architecture and Sculpture in Italy*. London. Heinemann. 1922.

Wölfflin, Heinrich. *The Art of the Italian Renaissance*. N. Y. Putnam. 1913.
————. *Principles of Art History*. N. Y. Holt. 1932.
Basic studies in the analysis of Renaissance and baroque style.

### MODERN SCULPTURE

Casson, Stanley. *Sculpture of Today*. London. Studio. 1939.
Copiously illustrated survey, with brief discussion, of the field of contemporary sculpture.
————. *Some Modern Sculptors*. London. Oxford University Press. 1928.
————. *XXth Century Sculptors*. London. Oxford University Press. 1930.
Two volumes of essays on leading sculptors and trends in sculpture in the late 19th and 20th centuries.

Fierens, Paul. *Sculpteurs d'aujourd'hui*. Paris. Editions des chroniques du jour. 1933.

Hudnut, Joseph. *Modern Sculpture*. N. Y. Norton. 1929.
A brief but perceptive discussion of the expressive aims and formal character of contemporary sculpture.

Marceau, Henri. *William Rush*. Philadelphia. Museum of Art. 1937.
A discussion of the work of one of America's first sculptors.

Morey, C. R. *American Sculpture,* in *The American Spirit in Art*. The Pageant of America Series, Vol. XII. New Haven. Yale University Press. 1927.
Generously illustrated, and with brief but excellent critical discussion.

Rewald, John. *Maillol*. N. Y. Hyperion. 1939.
A comprehensive selection of illustrations of the artist's work.

Rogers, Meyric. *Carl Milles; an Interpretation of his Work*. New Haven. Yale University Press. 1940.
Biographical and critical observations, with many illustrations.

Story, Somerville. *Auguste Rodin*. N. Y. Oxford University Press (Phaidon). 1939.

Taft, Lorado. *History of American Sculpture.* N. Y. Macmillan. 1930.
Useful for biographical material.

Wilenski, R. H. *The Meaning of Modern Sculpture.* London. Faber. 1932.
A criticism of traditional concepts in the interpretation and evaluation of sculpture.

## PAINTING

### GENERAL BIBLIOGRAPHY

Abell, Walter. *Representation and Form.* N. Y. Scribner. 1936.
Of special interest to students of modern painting since it deals with the question of abstraction.

Barnes, A. C. *Art in Painting.* N. Y. Harcourt. 1937.
Bold and discerning analysis of painting as an art-language.

Fry, Roger. *Last Lectures.* N. Y. Macmillan. 1939.
Fry's writings are lucid and readable. He deals largely with art from a critical aesthetic point of view.

―――――. *Vision and Design.* N. Y. Brentano. 1920.

―――――. *Transformations.* N. Y. Brentano. 1926.

Hagen, Oskar. *Art Epochs and Their Leaders.* N. Y. Scribner. 1927.

Holmes, Sir C. J. *Notes on the Science of Picture Making.* London. Chatto. 1927.

Mather, F. J. *Estimates in Art.* Series 1. N. Y. Holt. 1922.

Moreau-Vauthier, Charles. *Technique of Painting.* N. Y. Putnam. 1928.
Excellent work on a difficult theme.

Stein, Leo. *A.B.C. of Aesthetics.* N. Y. Boni and Liveright. 1927.
A study in simple language of some basic problems in art interpretation, useful for both painters and students of art history as it bears upon modern art.

Wölfflin, Heinrich. *Principles of Art History.* N. Y. Holt. 1932.
Heavy but rewarding reading on some basic problems of art history.

There is a growing list of books consisting of excellent plates with the paintings of the old and modern masters. The Phaidon series, Oxford University Press, and the Hyperion series, Hyperion Press, N. Y., have published titles covering many fields in the history of painting.

### ANCIENT AND MEDIAEVAL PAINTING

Beazeley, J. D., and Ashmole, Bernard. See under *Classic Sculpture.*

Connick, C. J. *Adventures in Light and Color.* N. Y. Random. 1937.
An effective exposition and interpretation of the art of stained glass by a leading modern master of the medium.

Focillon, Henri. *Peintures romanes des églises de France.* Paris. Laurens. 1938.

Well-reproduced illustrations and fine criticism of an aspect of mediaeval painting insufficiently well known previously.

Herbert, J. A. *Illuminated Manuscripts*. N. Y. Putnam. 1911.
The only general work in English on the subject.

Mâle, Émile. See under *Mediaeval Sculpture*.

Morey, C. R. See under *Mediaeval Sculpture*.

Morey, C. R., and Greene, Belle da Costa. *The Pierpont Morgan Library Exhibition of Illuminated Manuscripts Held at the New York Public Library*. N. Y. Private. 1934.

Pfuhl, Ernst. *Masterpieces of Greek Drawing and Painting*. N. Y. Macmillan. 1926.
A selection of characteristic examples, well illustrated.

Swindler, Mary Hamilton. *Ancient Painting*. New Haven. Yale University Press. 1929.
Comprehensive in scope and excellent in treatment; indispensable.

Thompson, Daniel V. *The Materials of Medieval Painting*. New Haven. Yale University Press. 1936.

### ITALIAN PAINTING

Brown, Alice van Vechten, and Rankin, William. *A Short History of Italian Painting*. N. Y. Dutton. 1914.

Crowe, J. A., and Cavalcaselle, G. B. *A New History of Painting in Italy*. Ed. Edward Hutton. 3 vols. N. Y. Dutton. 1908-1909.

————. *History of Painting in Northern Italy*. Ed. Tancred Borenius. 3 vols. N. Y. Scribner. 1912.

Mather, Frank J. *A History of Italian Painting*. N. Y. Holt. 1923.
The standard systematic treatment of Italian painting.

————. *Venetian Painters*. N. Y. Holt. 1936.
A full treatment of a most important phase of Italian painting.

Panofsky, Erwin. See under *Renaissance and Post-Renaissance Sculpture*.

Siren, Oswald. *Giotto*. 2 vols. Cambridge. Harvard University Press. 1917.
The best presentation of Giotto. Excellent illustrations.

————. *Leonardo da Vinci*. New Haven. Yale University Press. 1916.

Thys, J. P. *Leonardo da Vinci*. London. Jenkins. 1913.

Van Marle, R. *The Italian Schools of Painting*. 15 vols. The Hague. Martinus Nyhoff. 1923-1934.

Wölfflin, Heinrich. See under *Renaissance and Post-Renaissance Sculpture*.

### PAINTING IN THE NETHERLANDS

Barker, Virgil. *Pieter Bruegel the Elder; a Study of His Paintings*. N. Y. New York Arts Publishing Corporation. 1926.
A brief survey of one of the supreme masters.

von Bode, Wilhelm. *Great Masters of Dutch and Flemish Painting*. N. Y. Scribner. 1909.

Caffin, C. H. *The Story of Dutch Painting.* N. Y. Century. 1911.

Cartellieri, Otto. *The Court of Burgundy.* N. Y. Knopf. 1926.
>    An historical study of the culture from which came the early Franco-Flemish masters.

Conway, Sir W. M. *The Van Eycks and their Followers.* N. Y. Dutton. 1921.

Fromentin, Eugene. *Masters of Past Time.* N. Y. Dutton. 1913.

————. *Old Masters of Belgium and Holland.* Boston. Osgood. 1882.

Hind, A. M. *History of Engraving and Etching.* Boston. Houghton. 1923.

————. *Rembrandt's Etchings.* London. Methuen. 1924.

Holmes, Sir C. J. *Notes on the Art of Rembrandt.* N. Y. Stokes. 1911.

Huizinga, J. *The Waning of the Middle Ages.* London. Arnold. 1924.
>    The chapters on the art as expressive of the cultural background especially recommended.

Mather, Frank J. *Western European Painting of the Renaissance.* N. Y. Holt. 1939.
>    A very valuable reference for Netherlands painting wholly readable. Many illustrations.

Michel, Émile. *Rembrandt.* N. Y. Scribner. 1903.

Rooses, Max. *Rubens.* 2 vols. London. Duckworth. 1904.
>    A monumental treatment, not casual reading.

Valentiner, W. R. *Art of the Low Countries.* Garden City, N. Y. Doubleday. 1914.

Weale, W. H. J., and Brockwell, M. W. *The Van Eycks and Their Art.* London. Lane. 1912.

Wilenski, R. H. *An Introduction to Dutch Art.* N. Y. Stokes. 1924.

## ENGLISH PAINTING

Armstrong, Sir Walter. *Art in Great Britain and Ireland.* N. Y. Scribner. 1913.

————. *Gainsborough and His Place in English Art.* N. Y. Scribner. 1913.

Dobson, Austin. *William Hogarth.* N. Y. Dodd. 1902.
>    Excellent book on the greatest English painter.

Holmes, Sir C. J. *Constable.* N. Y. Longmans. 1901.

Ruskin, John. *Modern Painters.* 5 vols. N. Y. Dutton. 1906.
>    Not casual reading.

Wilenski, R. H. *Masters of English Painting.* Boston. Hale, Cushman and Flint. 1933.

## FRENCH PAINTING

Barnes, A. C., and De Mazia, V. *The Art of Renoir.* N. Y. Minton, Balch. 1935.
>    A searching study of the anatomy of Renoir's work.

Bell, Clive. *Landmarks in Nineteenth Century Painting*. N. Y. Harcourt. 1927.

Caffin, C. H. *Story of French Painting*. N. Y. Appleton-Century. 1915.

Cheney, Sheldon. *Story of Modern Art*. N. Y. Viking. 1941.
> A popular book filled with information and illustrations covering all phases of painting from 1800 on.

Duret, Theodore. *Manet and the French Impressionists*. Philadelphia. Lippincott. 1910.

Fry, Roger. *Characteristics of French Painting*. N. Y. Brentano. 1933.
> An excellent essay on the genius of French painting.

Hourticq, Louis. *Art in France*. N. Y. Scribner. 1917.

Mack, Gerstle. *Cézanne*. London. Cape. 1935.
> This is an excellent biography. The literature on Cézanne is extensive and in general very good. Other writers are Fry, Barnes and Vollard.

Mather, Frank J. *Western European Painting of the Renaissance*. N. Y. Holt. 1939.
> Important chapters on Gothic background of French painting and on the 17th-century masters.

Mauclair, Camille. *French Impressionists*. N. Y. Dutton. 1903.

Meier-Graefe, Julius. *Vincent Van Gogh*. N. Y. Harcourt. 1933.
> Biography. The literature on Van Gogh is rather extensive and includes the celebrated letters of the painter. Irving Stone's *Lust for Life* is a popular fictionized life.

Sutro, Ester. *Nicholas Poussin*. Boston. Medici Society. 1923.
> No adequate treatment of this major figure is available in English.

Underwood, Erie. *A Short History of French Painting*. London. Oxford University Press. 1931.
> Useful as a handbook; critical material poor.

Wilenski, R. H. *French Painting*. Boston. Hale. 1931.

————. *Modern French Painters*. N. Y. Reynal and Hitchcock. 1940.
> An ingenious account of the goings and comings of the French masters from about 1860 to 1940 and what events took place in French life during the period. Not elementary reading.

Wright, W. H. *Modern Painting*. N. Y. Dodd. 1922.

### GERMAN PAINTING

Burkhard, Arthur. *Matthias Grünewald*. Cambridge. Harvard University Press. 1935.
> The first scholarly treatment in English. Good illustrations.

Conway, Sir W. M. *Literary Remains of Albrecht Dürer*. Cambridge. Cambridge University Press. 1889.

Dickinson, Helen A. *German Masters of Art*. N. Y. Stokes. 1924.
> A survey. Good illustrations.

Moore, T. Sturge. *Albert Dürer*. N. Y. Scribner. 1911.
Panofsky, Erwin. *Albrecht Dürer*. 2 vols. Princeton. Princeton University Press. 1942.
 A monumental study. One volume of illustrations.

## SPANISH PAINTING

Caffin, C. H. *Story of Spanish Painting*. N. Y. Appleton-Century. 1917.
Calvert, Albert. *Goya*. London. Lane. 1908.
 Goya's paintings and prints illustrated lavishly.
————, and Gallichan, C. G. H. *El Greco*. London. Lane. 1909.
 A popular treatment.
Harris, E. *Spanish Painting*. Paris. N. Y. Hyperion. 1937.
 Brief notes with many illustrations. The Phaidon Series *El Greco* has the best plates, some in color.
Mather, Frank J. *Western European Painting of the Renaissance*. N. Y. Holt. 1939.
 For chapters on mediaeval Spanish, the 16th and 17th centuries.
Mayer, August L. *Francisco de Goya*. London. Dent. 1924.
Meier-Graefe, Julius. *The Spanish Journey*. N. Y. Harcourt. 1926.
Poore, Charles. *Goya*. N. Y. Scribner. 1939.
 A popular treatment.
Post, C. R. *History of Spanish Painting*. Cambridge. Harvard University. Press. 1930—in progress.
 This is a monumental work. For the specialist.
Rutter, Frank. *El Greco*. London. Methuen. 1930.
Stevenson, R. A. M. *Velasquez*. London. Bell. 1912.
 An analysis of Velasquez' style.

## AMERICAN PAINTING

Benson, E. M. *John Marin*. Washington. American Federation of Arts. 1935.
Burroughs, Alan. *Limners and Likenesses; Three Centuries of American Painting*. Cambridge. Harvard University Press. 1936.
 The best general discussion of American painting.
Cahill, Holger. *Max Weber*. N. Y. Downtown Gallery. 1930.
————. *Art in America*. N. Y. Reynal. 1935.
 A profusely illustrated and informative survey.
Downes, W. H. *Life and Works of Winslow Homer*. Boston. Houghton. 1911.
Goodrich, Lloyd. *Thomas Eakins*. N. Y. Whitney Museum. 1934.
LaFollette. S. *Art in America*. N. Y. Norton. 1939.
Mather, Frank J. *American Painting*, in *The Spirit of America in Art*. The

Pageant of America Series, Vol. XII. New Haven. Yale University Press. 1927.

Mumford, Lewis. *The Brown Decades*. N. Y. Harcourt. 1931.
    Reflective study of the pattern of American art and life following the Civil War.

Sherman, Frederic Fairchild. *Albert Pinkham Ryder*. N. Y. Private. 1920.

Various books in the series of publications by the Whitney Museum of American Art and the Museum of Modern Art, both in New York.

### CONTEMPORARY PAINTING

Cheney, Sheldon. *Primer of Modern Art*. N. Y. Boni. 1924.

Gordon, Jan. *Modern French Painters*. London. Lane. 1923.

Helm, MacKinley. *Modern Mexican Painters*. N. Y. Harper. 1941.
    The best book on the Mexican masters.

Terrasse, Charles. *French Painting in the XXth Century*. N. Y. Hyperion Press. 1939.
    An essay with many excellent plates.

Wilenski, R. H. *The Modern Movement in Art*. N. Y. Stokes. 1926.

Wolfe, Bertram D. *Diego Rivera. His Life and Times*. N. Y. Knopf. 1939.
    A readable biography.

See also Roger Fry in the general bibliography on painting. See French painting list for Cheney, Barnes, Fry, Wilenski.

The publications of the Museum of Modern Art in New York deal extensively with modern painting. Among notable issues are *Picasso, Forty Years of His Art; Salvador Dali* (James Soby); *Joan Miro* (James Sweeney); *Cubism,* and *Fantastic Art, Dada, Surrealism.*

### GRAPHIC ARTS

Craven, Thomas. *A Treasury of American Prints*. N. Y. Simon and Schuster. 1939.
    Well-mounted illustrations of contemporary graphic work.

*First Century of Printmaking, 1400-1500.* Chicago. Art Institute. 1941.
    A catalogue with illustrations and introduction.

Furst, Herbert. *The Modern Woodcut*. London. Lane. 1924.
    Readable and lavishly illustrated.

Hind, Arthur M. *History of Engraving and Etching*. Boston. Houghton. 1923.
    An authoritative handbook.

————. *Rembrandt's Etchings*. London. Methuen. 1924.

Leipnik, F. L. *History of French Etching*. N. Y. Dodd, Mead. 1924.

Panofsky, Erwin. *Albrecht Dürer*. 2 vols. Princeton. Princeton University Press. 1942.

A monumental study of Dürer and his unique rôle in the sphere of graphic arts.

Pennell, Joseph. *Etchers and Etching.* N. Y. Macmillan. 1924.
Informal essays on the history and technique. Good illustrations.

Rich, Daniel Catton, Ed. *Art of Goya.* Chicago. Art Institute. 1941.
All types of the graphic work illustrated.

Schild, Constance. *The Complete Etchings of Rembrandt.* N. Y. Crown. 1937.

Zigrosser, Carl. *Six Centuries of Fine Prints.* N. Y. Covici-Friede. 1937.
The best general discussion of the entire field.

## THE MINOR ARTS

Ackerman, Phyllis. *Tapestry, the Mirror of Civilization.* N. Y. Oxford University Press. 1933.
A general discussion, primarily interpretive, but with illuminating descriptions of methods and useful historical data.

Aloi, Roberto. *Arredamento moderno.* Milan. Hoepli. 1934.
A comprehensive and well-rounded selection of illustrations of modern furniture.

Aronson, Joseph. *The Encyclopedia of Furniture.* N. Y. Crown. 1940.
Definitions, descriptions and brief historical discussions of nearly all the important styles in furniture; generously illustrated.

Faulkner, R., Ziegfeld, E., and Hill, G. *Art Today.* N. Y. Holt. 1941.
Suggestions concerning the place of art in contemporary environment and the part it can play in helping to create it.

Friend, Leon, and Heffer, Joseph. *Graphic Design.* N. Y. McGraw-Hill. 1936.
A convenient manual of printing and related illustrative processes.

Gropius, W., Bayer, H., and Gropius, I. *Bauhaus: 1919-1928.* N. Y. Museum of Modern Art. 1938.
The history of the Bauhaus and an exposition of its ideals during the time of its greatest creative originality.

Halsey, R. T. H., and Tower, Elizabeth. *The Homes of Our Ancestors.* N. Y. Doubleday. 1934.
Entertaining and informative discussion of houses and their furnishings in the American colonies, based on the material in the American Wing of the Metropolitan Museum in New York.

Lewis, Ethel. *The Romance of Textiles.* N. Y. Macmillan, 1937.

Maskell, Alfred. *Ivories.* London. Methuen. 1905.
The only book in English effectively covering the field.

Miller, E. G. *American Antique Furniture.* 2 vols. Baltimore. The Lord Baltimore Press. 1937.
A handbook for collectors; comprehensively illustrated.

Mongan, Elizabeth, and Wolf, Edwin, 2nd. *The First Printers and Their Books*. Philadelphia. The Free Library. 1940.
    The catalogue of an exhibition, with very useful historical data and beautifully reproduced illustrations.

Noyes, Eliot F. *Organic Design*. N. Y. Museum of Modern Art. 1941.
    The background of, and notes on, a competition for designs of modern furniture.

Peddie, R. A. Ed. *Printing—A Short History*. London. Grafton. 1927.

Percival, MacIver. *Old English Furniture and Its Surroundings*. N. Y. Scribner. 1920.

Pevsner, Nikolaus. *An Enquiry into Industrial Art in England*. Cambridge. Cambridge University Press. 1937.
    An attempt to determine the commercial importance of good design.

Read, Herbert. *Art and Industry*. N. Y. Harcourt. 1938.
    One of the most penetrating analyses and forceful presentations of the need for greater perception in industry of the place of art in modern life.

Richter, Gisela M. A. *Ancient Furniture*. Oxford. Clarendon Press. 1926.

Schottmüller, Frida. *Furniture and Interior Decoration of the Italian Renaissance*. Stuttgart. Hoffmann. 1928.

## HISTORICAL BACKGROUND

Adams, Henry. *Mont-Saint-Michel and Chartres*. Boston. Houghton. 1913.
    One of the finest attempts in English literature to define the spiritual character of mediaeval culture.

Ady, Julia. *The Perfect Courtier*. London. Murray. 1908.
    A study of life in Renaissance Italy.

Burckhardt, Jakob. *The Civilization of the Renaissance in Italy*. (Tr. Middlemore.) Vienna. Phaidon. 1937.
    A well-illustrated edition of a classic work on the subject.

Burton, Robert. *The Anatomy of Melancholy*. Ed. A. R. Shilleto. London. Bell. 1893.

Castiglione, Baldassare. *The Book of the Courtier*. (Tr. Opdycke.) N. Y. Scribner. 1903.
    The High Renaissance ideal expounded by one of its chief representatives.

Clark, G. N. *The Seventeenth Century*. Oxford. Clarendon Press. 1929.

Coulton, G. G. *Art and the Reformation*. Oxford. Blackwell. 1928.

————. *Medieval Panorama*. Cambridge. Cambridge University Press. 1938.
    Thought-provoking discussions of mediaeval and Renaissance culture from the point of view of the 20th century.

Croce, Benedetto. *History of Europe in the 19th Century.* (Tr. Furst.) N. Y. Harcourt. 1933.

Dickinson, G. L. *The Greek View of Life.* N. Y. Garden City. 1927.

Dopsch, A. *The Economic and Social Foundations of European Civilization.* London. Paul, Trench and Trubner. 1937.

> The heritage of Rome in mediaeval culture.

Durant, W. J. *The Life of Greece.* N. Y. Simon & Schuster. 1939.

> A vivid and lively discussion of a subject usually treated with too great reserve.

Frazer, J. G. *Pausanias' Description of Ancient Greece.* 6 vols. London. Macmillan. 1913.

> The most valuable contemporary source of information concerning the monuments of the ancient Mediterranean world.

Friedell, Egon. *A Cultural History of the Modern Age.* (Tr. Atkinson.) 3 vols. N. Y. Knopf. 1930-1932.

> A stimulating and thought-provoking attempt to define the funda-mental pattern of European culture from the Renaissance to the First World War.

Jones, Rufus M. *Studies in Mystical Religion.* London. Macmillan. 1909.
————. *Spiritual Reformers in the 16th and 17th Centuries.* London. Macmillan. 1914.

Kane, Elisha. *Gongorism and the Golden Age.* Chapel Hill. University of North Carolina Press. 1928.

> A study of mannerism in art, music and literature.

Maspero, G. *The Dawn of Civilization. Egypt and Chaldaea.* (Tr. McClure.) London. Society for Promoting Christian Knowledge. 1922.

Petrie, Sir W. M. F. *Social Life in Ancient Egypt.* London. Constable. 1923.

Pirenne, Henri. *Mediaeval Cities.* (Tr. Halsey.) Princeton. Princeton University Press. 1925.

> Excellent reconstruction of life in the Middle Ages.

Robinson, J. H. *The Mind in the Making.* N. Y. Harper. 1921.

> One of the classic interpretations of life and thought in the ancient world.

Spengler, Oswald. *The Decline of the West.* (Tr. Atkinson.) N. Y. Knopf. 1934.

> Monumental in scope, in attempting to interpret the whole of human endeavor, this is one of the most influential of modern books.

Symonds, J. A. *The Renaissance in Italy.* 10 vols. N. Y. Scribner. 1907-1910.

> Still authoritative, and the most comprehensive discussion in English.

Taylor, Henry Osborn. *The Mediaeval Mind.* 2 vols. N. Y. Macmillan. 1927.

This is in many ways the best-balanced interpretation of mediaeval thought in recent times.

——————. *Thought and Expression in the 16th Century*. N. Y. Macmillan. 1920.

Toynbee, A. J. *A Study of History*. 6 vols. London. Oxford University Press. 1934-1939.

# Glossary

The references to figures are not exhaustive.

*Abacus.* A slab forming the crowning member of a capital. Figs. 31, 32.

*Absidioles.* Small apse-like projections from the ambulatory and transepts of a church. Figs. 75, 98.

*Acanthus.* A plant whose leaves are reproduced in stylized form on the Corinthian capital. Fig. 34.

*Aerial perspective.* The indication in pictorial art of the effect of light and atmosphere upon distant objects, giving thereby an impression of depth in the picture or relief. Fig. 395.

*Akroterion.* Ornament on the peak or corners of a classic temple pediment. Figs. 29, 251.

*Ambulatory.* Passageway around the apse of a church. Figs. 75, 98.

*Amphora.* Greek vase in the form of a jar, usually fairly large, with two handles connecting the wide mouth or the neck with the body. Used for provisions. Figs. 559, 563.

*Applied order.* Column and entablature attached to a wall or pier; decorative rather than structural in function. Figs. 49, 50, 52, 118, 126.

*Apse.* Semicircular or polygonal recess, covered with a half-dome or other vault; more particularly, the semicircular termination of the choir of a church. Figs. 63, 65, 71, 75, 98.

*Aqueduct.* A channel or conduit to conduct water, often supported on masonry arches. Fig. 61.

*Arabesque.* Florid design involving foliate scrolls and forms of animals and humans, extensively used in Renaissance decoration. Figs. 122, 319, 399, 602, 603.

*Arcade.* A series of arches resting on piers or columns. Figs. 65, 76.

*Arch.* A structural device, semicircular or pointed in shape, formed of separate truncated wedge-shaped blocks to span an opening. Fig. 2.

*Architrave.* The horizontal beam or lintel that is the lowest member of the entablature in the classic orders; more generally, a horizontal member spanning the distance between two vertical ones: a lintel. Figs. 31, 32.

*Arris.* The sharp ridge between two flutes of a Doric shaft. Fig. 31.

*Art Nouveau.* A short-lived style of architecture and its accessories characterized by predominantly curvil[illegible] patterns that enjoyed some popularity in the last decade of the 19th and first of the 20th centuries. Fig. 642.

*Atrium.* The open outer court of a Roman house, usually surrounded by a roofed gallery, Fig. 59; the open court before the narthex of a Christian basilica or church. Figs. 62, 87.

*Baldacchino.* A canopy over a tomb or altar. Fig. 132.

*Balustrade.* A handrail, usually supported by small pillars. Figs. 133, 135, 181.

*Baroque.* Literally, irregular or fantastic; applied to the art of the 17th and early 18th centuries; a style in which an artistic medium is arbitrarily handled to produce striking effects. Figs. 140, 141, 334, 335.

*Barrel vault.* A vault that is semicircular in section. Fig. 53A.

*Basilica.* In Roman architecture, a rectangular building with nave and aisles used for business and judicial purposes, Figs. 51, 54, 55; in Christian architecture, a church of similar form, the longitudinal axis being the most important. Figs. 62-64.

*Bay.* An opening between two columns or piers, Fig. 31; more generally, a principal compartment or unit which is repeated to form an architectural design. See discussion of the *Church at Vignory*.

*Beam.* A horizontal piece of wood, stone or metal, used in the frame of a building: a lintel. Fig. 1.

*Black-figured.* The dominant style in Greek vase painting before the late sixth century B.C., in which the forms are black with incised details against a lighter background. Figs. 561-563.

*Broken pediment.* A pediment in which one or both of the cornices are not continuous: much used in baroque architecture. Figs. 140, 141.

*Buttress.* A mass of masonry employed to counteract the lateral thrust of an arch or vault. Fig. 2.

*Cabriole.* Double-curved furniture leg, extensively employed from the late 17th century on. Figs. 619, 622, 623 .

*Campanile.* Italian word for bell tower; usually free-standing. Figs. 71, 78, 87, 113.

*Cantilever.* A horizontal member attached only at one end to a vertical support, its stability depending upon the tensile strength of the material. A structural principle employed chiefly since the advent of steel as a constructive medium. Fig. 3.

*Capital.* The part of a column or pilaster that rests on the shaft, acting as a transition from it to the architrave or arch, and usually decorated. Figs. 31, 32, 48.

*Caquetoire,* also *caqueteuse.* A relatively light wooden chair with high back and curved arms, originating in France in the 16th century. Fig. 616.

*Cartoon.* A full-size preliminary sketch for a painting. Figs. 414, 415.

*Cartouche.* An ornament, irregular or fantastic in shape, on which armorial bearings or symbols are sometimes carved; frequently found in baroque architecture. Figs. 140, 335.

*Caryatid.* A support in the form of a female figure, taking the place of a column. Fig. 43.

*Cassapanca.* A settee formed by adding arms and a back to a chest. Italian. Cf. Fig. 611.

*Cassone.* Italian, meaning a large chest. One of the most characteristic forms of Italian furniture. Figs. 609, 610.

*Cella.* The principal chamber of a classic temple in which the cult statue stood: sometimes used with reference to the entire walled portion of the building surrounded by the peristyle. Fig. 40.

*Centering.* The timber framework supporting an arch or vault in the process of construction and removed after the insertion of the keystone which makes it self-supporting.

*Champlevé enamel.* A type of enamel in which the base, usually copper or bronze, is dug out leaving a design of ridges between shallow depressions which are filled with a vitreous paste that hardens after firing. Fig. 592.

*Chevet.* French, meaning literally pillow; term applied to the apsidal end of a French church, and including the semicircular or polygonal vault over the end of the choir, the ambulatory and the absidioles. Fig. 98.

*Chiaroscuro.* Italian, meaning literally light-dark; applied to contrasts of light and shade by means of which various elements in a painting, statue or architectural design are distinguished from one another.

*Choir.* Specifically, the part of a church where the singers are accommodated; in general, the arm of the cross between the transepts and the apse. Sometimes referred to as the chancel. Figs. 75, 98.

*Ciborium.* See *Baldacchino.*

*Cire perdue.* French, meaning literally lost wax. A method of casting statues in bronze or other metal, the original figure being modeled in wax over a core, the wax flowing out of the space between the core and the mould when melted by the hot metal which takes its place.

*Clapboard.* A flat piece of wood applied to the exterior of a building in such a way that its lower edge laps over a similar piece immediately below it to make a weather-proof joint. Fig. 179.

*Clearstory.* The part of the elevation of a church that rises above the aisle and ambulatory roofs and is pierced with windows to illuminate the interior. Figs. 62, 64, 89, 101.

*Cloisonné enamel.* A process in which small strips or *cloisons*, often of gold, are soldered to a metal plate to form a design of cells which are filled with a vitreous paste, the whole being fired and hardened and then polished. Fig. 590.

*Codex.* Latin term used for the first books made of pages fastened together on one side as distinguished from a *rotulus*. Figs. 367-370.

*Collage.* French, literally pasting. Employed to describe the practice of some 20th-century artists in introducing paper or other non-pigmented material in a painting. Fig. 518.

*Colonnade.* A series of columns connected by lintels, as contrasted with an arcade.

*Colonnette.* A diminutive column.

*Column.* A vertical support, usually circular in section, with a base, shaft and capital; distinguished from a pillar by the fact that there is a calculated ratio between its height and diameter. Figs. 31, 32.

*Compound pier.* A pier which is built up of various members, such as pilasters, shafts, colonnettes, etc., applied to a masonry core, the applied members acting as supports for the arches and ribs of a vault. Figs. 86, 101.

*Console.* A bracket; a projecting member to support a weight, usually formed of scrolls or volutes in an S-shape; also known as a corbel. Fig. 48.

*Corbel.* A block of stone projecting from a wall, often carved, and serving to support cross beams, etc.

*Corbel table.* A projecting course of masonry resting on corbels which are often connected by small arches. Figs. 86, 87.

*Cornice.* A horizontal projecting member crowning an entablature or wall; also any crowning moulded projection. Figs. 31, 32, 116, 199.

*Courses.* The horizontal layers of stone or brick in masonry construction.

*Crater,* also *krater.* A vessel with wide mouth and broad body, used by the Greeks for mixing wine and water. Figs. 559, 561.

*Crocket.* A carved projection from the edge of a gable, pinnacle, flying buttress, etc., in a Gothic building; usually in the form of a leaf. Fig. 100.

*Crossing.* The space formed by the intersection of nave and transepts in a church of cruciform plan. Figs. 75, 98.

*Crown.* The highest point in an arch or vault; the keystone. Fig. 2.

*Crux ansata.* The cross of life, an ideograph made up of forms embodying the male and female principles, used as a symbol of deity in Egyptian art. Figs. 239, 547, 548.

*Cuneiform.* Term used in referring to the wedge-shaped marks that served the Mesopotamians as writing. Fig. 245.

*Cupola.* A dome or hemispherical covering; also applied colloquially to any small structure above the roof of a house. Figs. 58, 68, 131.

**Damascene.** The inlaying of metal with other metal or substance in a decorative design. Fig. 556.

**Dentils.** Small, projecting blocks, suggesting somewhat a row of teeth, that appear in Ionic and Corinthian cornices. Fig. 48, D, E, F.

**Diaphragm walls.** Walls whose primary purpose is to stiffen construction that is liable to destruction by intrinsic weakness or strain. See discussion of *Sant' Ambrogio at Milan.*

**Dipylon vase.** A type of crater used in Greece in archaic times to store the ashes of cremated bodies and deriving its name from the finding of many examples in the cemetery near the Dipylon Gate of Athens. Fig. 560.

**Dome.** A hemispherical or polygonal vault. See also *Cupola.* Figs. 58, 68.

**Drum.** In a column, the circular disks that make up the shaft; Fig. 48, A, B. Also used with reference to the circular or polygonal wall on which a dome is placed.

**Eave.** The lower part of a roof projecting beyond the wall underneath.

**Echinus.** From a Greek word meaning sea urchin. The convex member of a capital that supports the abacus, usually parabolic or hyperbolic in profile. Fig. 31.

**Egg-and-dart.** A row of alternate ovoid and pointed members, usually carved and used as a decorative moulding. Figs. 32, 296.

**Elevation.** The vertical arrangement of the elements in an architectural design.

**Engaged column.** A member somewhat like a column but projecting from a wall, of which it is usually a part, instead of free-standing. Also known as an applied column. See *Applied order.* Figs. 49, 50, 52.

**Engraving.** The process of cutting a design with a sharp instrument on a copper plate from which impressions are made on paper after being inked. Also applied to such an impression. Figs. 441, 443, 444.

**Entablature.** The part of a building of lintel construction above the columns, extending to the roof or to a story above. Figs. 31, 32.

**Entasis.** A slight, almost imperceptible swelling in the profile of a column shaft. See discussion of the *Doric order.*

**Etching.** To engrave a metal plate by the corrosive action of an acid; also by direct application of a sharp instrument, when it is known as dry-point; also applied to the impression made on paper by a plate so prepared after being inked. Figs. 466, 467, 536.

**Extrados.** The outer face of an arch or vault. Fig. 2.

**Façade.** One of the faces of a building, usually that containing the main entrance. Figs. 93, 99, 100, 114.

**Faïence.** See *Majolica.*

**"False door."** The simulated openings in the external and internal walls of a mastaba, for the use of the "ka" or spirit. Figs. 7, 9.

*Fillet.* A narrow flat surface separating two mouldings; the surface between two flutes of an Ionic shaft. Fig. 32.

*Finial.* The decorative foliate termination of a Gothic gable or buttress. Fig. 100.

*Flutes.* The vertical grooves in the shaft of a column, usually semicircular in section or in the form of a segment of a circle. Figs. 31, 32, 48.

*Flying buttress.* A bar of masonry, supported by an arch or arches, at right angles to the longitudinal axes of the interior spaces of a Gothic church whose vaults it supports by carrying their lateral thrusts over the side-aisle or ambulatory roofs to vertical piers rising from the outer walls. Figs. 96, 97.

*Formal.* Of or pertaining to form as an element of artistic style.

*Fractional point of view.* The concept evident in many early or primitive art forms in which an object is visually described as a combination of different parts rather than represented as an organic unity. Figs. 230, 233, 356.

*Free-standing.* A term applied to a column or carved figure which is not part of a wall or background.

*Fresco.* Italian, meaning literally fresh. A method of painting upon wet plaster with colors of pigment mixed with water which sink into the plaster and dry with it; also used with reference to a painting executed in the foregoing manner.

*Frieze.* An extended horizontal band, often decorated with carved figures and mouldings; the portion of an entablature lying between the architrave and the cornice. Figs. 31, 32.

*Gable.* The triangle formed by the end of a ridged roof and the similarly shaped wall enclosed by the horizontal and raking cornices; called a pediment in classic architecture. Figs. 28, 31, 179, 256.

*Gesso.* The mixture of plaster with water or other liquid with which wooden panels are coated as a preliminary to painting.

*Girder.* A horizontal beam that supports a vertical load and bears vertically upon its supports.

*Gothic.* Term first applied to mediaeval art during the Renaissance in a derogatory sense. Now used to designate the art of the later Middle Ages, after the Romanesque.

*Grille.* A grating or screen, usually of iron or a perforated stone slab, but sometimes of wood.

*Groined vault.* A vault formed by the intersection of two barrel vaults of equal span, either semicircular or pointed, the diagonal lines of the intersecting under surfaces being the groins. Figs. 53, 84, 95.

*Guttae.* From the Latin *gutta,* or drop. The small cylinders or truncated cones pendenc from the mutules and regulae of the Doric entablature. Fig. 31.

*Half-timber.* A type of construction in which the spaces formed by the wooden beams of a building are filled with brick or clay, the beams being left exposed. Figs. 154, 156.

*Haunch.* The part of an arch or vault where the lateral thrusts are strongest about midway between springing and crown. Fig. 2.

*Hieroglyphs.* The ideographs or picture-words that served the Egyptians as writing. Figs. 234, 239, 356.

*Hipped roof.* A roof with inclined sides and ends, the diagonal lines formed by the intersecting planes being known as hips. Fig. 181.

*Historiated capital.* A capital with figures generally illustrating a specific subject. Most frequently employed in Romanesque times. Fig. 294.

*Hue.* The name of a color—i.e., red, blue, yellow, green, etc.—for which the term color is more generally used alone.

*Iconography.* The traditional manner of representing a subject in art, governed by more or less fixed rules.

*Illuminated manuscript.* A book in which the text is written by hand and illustrated with drawings or small paintings. Illumination was practiced extensively during the Middle Ages and declined after the growth of easel painting in the Renaissance.

*Impasto.* Italian, literally paste. Used with reference to the physical body of the pigment of a painting, i.e., light or heavy.

*Impost.* The horizontal member from which an arch springs. Fig. 2.

*Incunabula.* Name applied to the earliest books printed from movable type. Fig. 604.

*Intarsia.* A type of wood inlay in wood much practiced in Renaissance Italy. Fig. 613.

*Intensity of hue or color.* Strength as compared with a standard gray; a coefficient of saturation.

*Intrados.* The inner face of an arch or vault; also known as the *soffit.* Fig. 2.

*Isocephalism.* A convention by which all the heads in a row of figures are placed arbitrarily at the same height. Figs. 265, 295.

*Joist.* A horizontal timber in a floor or roof.

*Keystone.* The central voussoir of an arch which renders it stable when put in place. Fig. 2.

*Kylix,* also *cylix.* A shallow bowl, usually on a high stem and with two handles, used for drinking. Figs. 559, 562.

*Law of frontality.* A convention observed in archaic art in which a straight vertical line bisects the figure from the front, there being no movement to either side. Figs. 232, 236, 248, 250.

*Leading.* The strips of lead by which the pieces of a stained-glass window are held together. Fig. 371.

*Lean-to.* A supplementary structure added to a building, usually covered by a roof in a single slanting plane. Fig. 179.

*Lekythos.* A jug, usually rather slender, with a single handle, used for oil and perfume and as a funereal offering. Figs. 559, 566.

*Linear perspective.* The art and science of suggesting depth in space in pictorial art, based on observation of the fact that receding parallel lines seem to converge on the horizon line. One of the first systems of linear perspective was evolved by Brunellesco.

*Lintel.* The horizontal beam in the post and lintel system, Fig. 1; also used with reference to an architrave.

*Lithography.* A reproducing graphic process invented by Alois Senefelder in 1796-1798, based on the chemical affinity of ink for grease. Originally using stone blocks, whence the name, but utilizing prepared metal plates in recent times. Figs. 492, 501, 535.

*Majolica.* A type of earthenware enameled with tin-base glazes, much used in Renaissance Italy. Also known as *faïence ware*. Fig. 603.

*Mastaba.* From the Arabian for bench. Used for the low masonry superstructure of the characteristic tomb type of the Old Kingdom in Egypt. Figs. 7, 11.

*Meander.* A motive employed for classic mouldings, consisting of patterns formed by the intersection of straight lines. Also called *Fret* and *Greek Key*.

*Medium.* In general, the vehicle in which an artist gives form to his ideas. Specifically in painting, the substance with which the painter mixes his pigments, i.e., water, oil, egg white, etc.

*Memory picture.* The portrayal of the most characteristic aspects of forms as seen in primitive and early art; an element in the *fractional concept*. Figs. 230, 238, 243, 354, 360.

*Metope.* The panel between two triglyphs in a Doric frieze, Fig. 31; originally an opening between two roof joists; sometimes carved. Figs. 252, 259, 264.

*Miniature.* A small drawing or painting in an illuminated manuscript. Figs. 366-370, 372.

*Modillion.* A console or bracket used to support a cornice. Fig. 48.

*Monolith.* Literally a single stone. Used to distinguish a column shaft cut from a single block of stone from one built up in drums.

*Mosaic.* A method of wall decoration in which designs are formed by cubes of colored glass or marble, set in wet plaster which holds them firmly in place on hardening. Figs. 362, 365.

*Moulding.* A projecting or depressed surface, either plain or decorated, employed to ornament a wall surface, cornice, capital, etc. Figs. 42, 116.

*Mullion.* A vertical member dividing a window into separate lights, Fig. 118; also used to support the glass in a stained-glass window.

*Mural.* Of or pertaining to a wall; fresco paintings are sometimes called murals. Fig. 396.

*Mutules.* Projecting inclined blocks on the lower face of a Doric cornice from which guttae hang. Fig. 31.

*Narthex.* The entrance porch of a Christian basilica or church, usually colonnaded and originally opening directly into the atrium, Fig. 62; sometimes in two stories, Fig. 87.

*Nave.* The chief interior division of a church in Latin cross form, corresponding to the long arm but separated from the side aisles, Figs. 63-65, 89, 98, 105; also applied to the corresponding portion of a Roman basilica. Figs. 51, 55.

*Nave arcade.* The series of arches and columns separating the nave of a church of Latin cross form from the side aisles. Figs. 64, 97.

*Necking.* The band between the shaft and echinus of a classic column. Figs. 31, 32.

*Niche.* A recess in a wall, as a rule either circular or rectangular with a circular head, in which statuary may be placed. Figs. 58, 138.

*Nimbus.* Sometimes called a halo. The disk of light behind the head of Christ, the Virgin, saints, etc. Figs. 289, 295, 371, 382, 386, 389.

*Obelisk.* A tapering shaft of stone, generally rectangular in plan and with a pyramidal peak; much used by the Egyptians as memorials. Figs. 57, 130.

*Order.* A system governing the design of column and entablature in classic architecture. There are two main orders, the Doric and Ionic, and one subordinate one, the Corinthian, in Greek architecture. To these, the Roman added the Tuscan, somewhat resembling the Doric, and the Composite, a combination of Ionic and Corinthian. Figs. 31, 32, 48.

*"Organic architecture."* An architecture involving the use of vaults, supported by piers, buttresses and ribs, the form and arrangement of which are dictated by the part they play in maintaining the stability of the vaults.

*Ormolu.* Gilt bronze ornament much used in France in the 18th and early 19th centuries as a decorative accessory to furniture, etc. Figs. 171, 619, 621.

*Palmette.* A certain type of stylized foliate form employed in classic mouldings; also known as *Anthemion.* Fig. 42.

*Pastel.* A picture made with a crayon of pigment mixed with some heavy binding medium such as gum; often classed with painting.

*Pediment.* A triangular space framed by a horizontal and raking cornices; in classic architecture, the space over the peristyle at the end of a temple, Fig. 29; in Renaissance architecture, used as a repetitive motive for window decoration. Fig. 125.

*Peristyle.* A continuous range of columns, bearing architraves or arches, surrounding the exterior of a building or the interior of a court. Figs. 29, 35, 117.

*Perspective.* The means by which three-dimensional pictorial effects can be suggested on a two-dimensional plane. See also *Aerial perspective* and *Linear perspective.*

*Pier.* A vertical support of masonry, built up in courses, distinguished from a column by greater massiveness and by a shape other than circular. Figs. 76, 86, 89, 101.

*Pietà.* Italian, meaning literally pity or compassion. A representation of the Virgin holding the body of the dead Christ. Figs. 382, 436.

*Pilaster.* A flat rectangular member, projecting slightly from a wall or pier of which it forms a part, and furnished with a capital, base, etc., in the manner of an applied column, from which it differs chiefly in its rectangular section. Figs. 52, 115, 118.

*Pillar.* A vertical, isolated mass of masonry used as a support that is not strictly speaking a column or a pier; generally employed to designate any vertical support, usually incorrectly; also applied to memorial shafts.

*Pinnacle.* A small decorative turret, surmounting a buttress, tower, etc. Figs. 100, 110.

*Plan.* A diagram indicating by conventional means the general distribution on the ground or some specified level of the various parts of a building. Figs. 30, 63, 85, 90, 98, 134, 153.

*Podium.* A continuous base or pedestal for a monument or building. Figs. 44, 50.

*Pointing.* A mechanical process employed by sculptors to reproduce a clay or plaster model in stone, points on the model being indicated in the stone block by holes drilled in it to the proper depth.

*Portico.* An open vestibule or porch, its roof supported by a colonnade or an arcade on one side. Figs. 57, 114.

*Post and lintel.* A structural system or unit of construction in which vertical supports bear the load of horizontal beams. Fig. 1.

*Primary hue or color.* The red, yellow and blue components of the spectrum.

*Pulvin.* The inverted truncated pyramid that appears between a Byzantine capital and the arch it supports. Also known as a *Stilt-block.* Figs. 70, 72, 365.

*Putto.* Italian, plural *putti*, meaning boy. Applied to the cherubs that appear in Italian Renaissance painting and sculpture. Figs. 314, 316, 405.

*Pylon.* The monumental gateway to an Egyptian temple; also the massive walls separating one court of an Egyptian temple from another; by extension, any gateway of classic design. Figs. 16, 18, 38.

*Quoins.* Stones or blocks, slightly projecting at the angle of a building. Sometimes spelled *coigns.* Fig. 125.

*Raking cornice.* The sloping mouldings of a pediment. Fig. 31.

*Red-figured.* The dominant style in Greek vase painting after the late sixth century B.C., in which the forms are reserved in the base color of the vase fabric, and the details and background are painted on. Figs. 361, 558, 564, 565.

*Regula.* The block under each triglyph, beneath the taenia of the Doric entablature, from which guttae are pendent. Fig. 31.

*Relief sculpture.* Figures carved or cast in such a way that they are attached to a background. Figs. 252, 265, 286, 318.

*Repoussé.* French, meaning literally pushed back. Used to describe designs executed by hammering a sheet of metal over a form or mould. Figs. 557, 588.

*Rib.* An arch of masonry, usually moulded, forming part of the framework on which a vault rests and usually projecting slightly from its under surface. Figs. 83, 86, 89, 94, 106.

*Ribbed vault.* A masonry vault with a relatively thin web supported by ribs. Fig. 86, 89, 94, 95, 101.

*Rinceau.* French, meaning foliage. A band of carved foliate ornament used as a frieze or moulding. Figs. 50, 293, 296.

*Romanesque.* Term applied to the period from approximately 1000 to 1200 in European history and to the art then produced by virtue of its embodiment of some of the principles of Roman art without being actually like it.

*Rotulus.* Latin, meaning a scroll. Used with reference to the earliest form of book consisting of a long strip of papyrus, parchment or paper, the reading of which involved rolling the strip from one spindle to another. Fig. 366.

*Rustication.* A method of treating masonry walls in which the joints between the stones are recessed while the outer surfaces are left rough or project beyond the joints. Figs. 111, 116, 143.

*Salient buttress.* A strip of masonry applied to the outer face of a wall at a point where the thrusts of a vault are concentrated. Fig. 87.

*Secondary hue or color.* The orange, green and violet components of the spectrum.

*Segmental pediment.* A pediment whose upper profile is a section of a circle instead of a gable. Figs. 125, 133, 161.

*Set-back.*    A step in the elevation of a skyscraper. Fig. 212.

*Sexpartite vault.*    A groined vault, usually with ribs, in which a transverse
rib to the crown divides the under surface into six parts or cells. Figs.
89, 91.

*Sgabello.*    A backed, three-legged chair of Italian origin. Fig. 611.

*Shaft.*    The vertical cylindrical or conoid section of a column between the
base and the capital, usually rather slender. Figs. 31, 32.

*Sizing.*    The preparation of a surface for the application of paint.

*Soffit.*    The under side of an architectural member such as an arch, cornice, architrave, etc.

*Spandrel.*    The triangular space formed by the curve of one-half of an
arch and lines drawn vertically from its springing and horizontally
from its crown, Fig. 2; also applied to the horizontal strips between
the windows of a skyscraper. Fig. 213.

*Spectrum.*    The pattern of hues or colors constituting white light as
shown by analysis with a prism or spectroscope, ranging from red
to violet.

*Spherical pendentive.*    Mathematically, a triangular section of a hemisphere. In architecture, the inverted concave triangle of masonry
placed upon a pier to sustain part of the weight of a dome. Figs.
66, 68.

*Sphinx.*    Combination of a lion's body with the head of a human or another animal. Figs. 11, 234.

*Spire.*    An elongated rectangular or octagonal pyramid that serves as the
termination of a tower. Figs. 99, 184.

*Splaying.*    Cutting the sides of an opening in a wall diagonally in such
a way that the inner opening is larger than the outer, or conversely.
Fig. 80.

*Springing.*    The point where an arch begins to curve over. Fig. 2.

*Squinch.*    A beam or arch across the angle of a square or polygon, employed to make such a shape more nearly round to serve as the base of
a dome. Fig. 86.

*Stamnos.*    A Greek vase in the form of a jar with high shoulder and short
neck and two horizontal handles; used for wine. Fig. 564.

*Stele.*    A slab of stone or a pillar erected as a memorial. Fig. 267.

*Stilt-block.*    See *Pulvin.*

*Stilted arch.*    An arch in which the springing is some distance above the
impost. Fig. 82.

*String course.*    Projecting horizontal course of masonry, often moulded,
that marks off one part of an architectural elevation from another.
Figs. 116, 125.

*Stud.*    Angle beam connecting the vertical and horizontal members of a
wooden house frame. Fig. 156.

*Stylobate.* Strictly, the outer part of the top step of a classic temple base; by extension, the topmost of the steps in its entirety. Figs. 31, 32.

*Swag.* A heavy garland of carved foliage used for architectural ornament. Figs. 126, 138, 161.

*Taenia.* The projecting band or fillet that crowns the Doric architrave. Fig. 31.

*Tapestry.* A textile in which a pattern or image has been woven. Figs. 595, 596, 602.

*Tempera.* A process of painting on a prepared panel with colored pigment mixed with egg.

*Terra-cotta.* Italian meaning baked earth. A form of pottery, baked in moulds and used for architectural ornament; also as a protective sheath for the steel framework of modern buildings; also employed as a sculptural medium.

*Thrust.* The force exerted horizontally outward by an arch or vault, created by the pressure of the wedge-shaped voussoirs against each other. Fig. 2.

*Tie-rod.* A rod, usually of iron, embedded in the masonry of an arch or vault at the springing and connecting its sides to counteract the lateral thrusts. Figs. 86, 115.

*Tracery.* Ornamental pattern of stone work in the windows of a mediaeval buildings. Figs. 100, 101, 107.

*Transept.* The large division of a cruciform plan church at right angles to the axis of the nave; the cross arm. Figs. 63, 75, 98.

*Transverse arches.* The arches across the nave or side aisles of a mediaeval church, connecting corresponding piers or pilasters with each other. Figs. 81, 82, 86, 101.

*Triforium.* The space between the sloping exterior roof over the side aisle of a church and the vault covering it on the inside; more generally, the story of an interior elevation immediately above the nave arcade. Figs. 76, 77, 80, 92, 101.

*Triglyphs.* The projecting blocks with vertical channels that alternate with the metopes in a Doric frieze. Fig. 31.

*Trumeau.* French, meaning pier. The member that divides a Gothic portal, often decorated with sculpture. Figs. 300, 303.

*Truss.* A framework of wood or metal beams, stiffened by cross braces; used for roofs, bridges, etc.

*Tympanum.* The space bounded by the horizontal and raking cornices of a pediment or enclosed by the lintel and arch of a doorway. Figs. 29, 300.

*Uraeus.* The serpent symbol of Egyptian royalty, often used as a head ornament but sometimes separately. Figs. 239, 548.

*Value.* The proportion of light or dark in a hue or color; a high value has more light, a low one more dark.

*Vault.* A roof of masonry, constructed on the arch principle. See *Barrel* and *Groined vaults.* Figs. 53, 84, 95.

*Vault web.* The relatively thin fabric of stone or masonry that constitutes the expanse of a ribbed vault, supported by the ribs.

*Volutes.* The scrolls of an Ionic capital; also found in Corinthian and Composite capitals. Figs. 32, 34, 48, 117.

*Voussoirs.* The truncated wedge-shaped blocks of stone used in an arch or vault. Fig. 2.

*Wainscot.* The wooden sheathing of an interior wall, usually paneled. Figs. 180, 598.

*Wedgwood.* A type of ceramic ware developed in England in the 18th century, when it was characterized by use of various colors and by "classical" style and subject matter. Fig. 626.

*White-ground.* A type of Greek vase in which the background is a creamy white and the figures usually appear in outline. Fig. 566.

*Windsor chair.* A type of chair made of wood employing turned spindles for the back and sides instead of carved members, originating in England in the early 18th century and much used in the American Colonies. Fig. 630.

*Woodcut.* A picture made by pressing on paper an inked block of wood that has been carved in such a way that a design stands out slightly from its surface in the manner of ordinary printing type. Fig. 442.

*Ziggurat.* Stepped, pyramidal masonry mass with ramps for ascent and descent, developed in Mesopotamia. Figs. 20. 21.

# CHRONOLOGICAL TABLE

The majority of the monuments discussed appear in this table, the numbers following the titles being those of the illustrations.

| Date | Architecture | Sculpture | Painting | Minor Arts |
|---|---|---|---|---|
| Aurignacian | | Menton fig. 229 | | |
| Magdalenian | | | Bison cow. 354 | |
| 3200–3000 | | Narmer Palette. 230 | | |
| 4th Mill. | Ziggurat, Ur. 20 | | | |
| ca. 3000 | | Sumerian Noble. 242 | | Gold Harp. 551 |
| ca. 2800 | | Naram-Sin Stele. 243 | | |
| ca. 2750 | Step Pyramid. 10 | | | |
| 2700–2600 | Pyramids, Gizeh. 11 | | | |
| ca. 2600 | Mastaba, Ptahotep. 9 | Menkaura. 231 | | |
| | | Hunting Hippo. 233 | | |
| | | Sheikh el-Beled. 232 | | |
| ca. 2550 | | | | Falcon Head. 544 |
| ca. 2500 | | | | |
| ca. 2400 | | Gudea. 244 | | |
| 2000–1600 | Knossos. 24 | | | |
| ca. 1900 | | | | Senusert Pectoral. 547 |
| ca. 1800 | Beni-Hasan. 14, 356 | Amenemhet III. 234 | | Hippo. 550 |
| | | | | Knossos Vases. 554 |
| | | | | Octopus Vase. 555 |
| 1600–1500 | | | | |
| ca. 1500 | Stonehenge. 6 | Snake Goddess. 248 | Toreador. 359 | |
| | Deir el-Bahari. 15 | Thutmose III. 236 | | |
| ca. 1450 | Luxor. 17 | | | |
| ca. 1400 | Mycenae. 26, 27 | | Nobleman Hunting. 357 | Throne, Tutankhamen. 548 |

## CHRONOLOGICAL TABLE—Continued

| Date | Architecture | Sculpture | Painting | Minor Arts |
|---|---|---|---|---|
| ca. 1400 | Tiryns. 28 | | | Bronze Mirror. 546 |
| 1400–1300 | | | | Dagger, Mycenae. 556 |
| ca. 1350 | | Negro Captives. 238 | | Vaphio Cups. 557 |
| ca. 1300 | Abu Simbel. 19 | Seti I Offering. 239 | | |
| 1257 | | | | |
| ca. 1250 | | Rameses II. 240 | | |
| ca. 1180 | Khons Temple. 16 | | | |
| ca. 1100 | | | Girl Acrobat. 358 | |
| 1100–700 | | | | Dipylon Crater. 560 |
| ca. 900 | | Assurnasirpal II. 245 | | |
| ca. 875 | | Winged Man-lion. 247 | | |
| 722 | Khorsabad. 21 | | | |
| ca. 650 | | Wounded Lioness. 246 | | |
| | | Saïtic Head. 241 | | |
| ca. 600 | | Apollo. 250 | | |
| 6th cent. | Ishtar Gate. 23 | | | Mirror. 567 |
| ca. 570 | | Victory of Delos. 251 | | |
| ca. 560 | Paestum. 35 | Hera of Samos. 249 | | François Vase. 561 |
| ca. 550 | | Perseus and Medusa. 252 | | |
| ca. 540 | | Striding Warrior. 282 | | Exekias. Dionysos. 562 |
| ca. 500 | | | | Kleophrades Vase. 564 |
| ca. 480 | | Aegina Sculpture. 254 | | |

| | Architecture | Sculpture | Painting | |
|---|---|---|---|---|
| 480–75 | | Euthydikos Fig. 253 | | Coin, Syracuse. 568 |
| ca. 480 | | Delphi Charioteer. 255 | | |
| ca. 475 | | Olympia Sculpture. 256–9 | | White Lekythoi. 566 |
| ca. 460 | | | | |
| ca. 450 | | Doryphoros. 260 | | |
| 450–40 | Parthenon. 39, 40 | Athena Lemnia. 263 | | |
| 447–32 | | Parthenon Metope. 264 | Odysseus-Elpenor. 361 | |
| 447–43 | | Parthenon Frieze. 265 | | |
| 442–38 | | Pericles. 266 | | |
| 440–30 | | Parthenon Pediment. 261–2 | | |
| 438–33 | | | | |
| 437–32 | Propylaea. 38 | Paionios Victory. 268 | | Meidias Vase. 565 |
| ca. 425 | | | | |
| 421–06 | Erechtheum. 41–3 | | | |
| ca. 420 | | Nike Balustrade. 269 | | |
| ca. 410 | | Hegeso Stele. 267 | | |
| ca. 400 | | Praxiteles. Hermes. 270–1 | | |
| ca. 350 | | Head from Tegea. 272 | | |
| 334 | Lysikrates Monument. 44 | | | |
| ca. 330 | Theatre, Epidauros. 45 | | | |
| ca. 325 | Priene. 46 | Apoxyomenos. 274 | | |
| 325–300 | | | Alexander Mosaic. 362 (original) | |
| ca. 310 | | | | |
| ca. 300 | | Nike of Samothrace. 275 | | |
| 300–250 | | Aphrodite of Melos. 276 | | |

CHRONOLOGICAL TABLE—Continued

| Date | Architecture | Sculpture | Painting | Minor Arts |
|---|---|---|---|---|
| ca. 241 | | Dying Gaul. 277 | | |
| 237–12 | Edfu. 18 | | | |
| 180–60 | | Pergamon Altar. 278 | | |
| ca. 50 | | Laocoön. 280 | | Silver Dish. 570 |
| | | Terme Boxer. 281 | | |
| 27 B.C.–A.D. 14 | | Julius Caesar. 283 | | |
| 20 B.C.–A.D. 50 | Maison Carrée. 50 | | | |
| 16 | | Augustus, Prima Porta. 284 | | |
| ca. 15 | | Ara Pacis. 285 | | |
| 9 B.C. | | | | |
| A.D. 20 | | | | Deified Augustus. 572 |
| 1st cent. | | | Theseus. 363 | Portland Vase. 573 |
| ca. 50 | Pont du Gard. 61 | Peasant and Cow. 279 | | |
| 50–79 | Colosseum. 52 | | Paris on Mt. Ida. 364 | Table, Pompeii, 574 |
| 75–82 | House of Vettii. 60 | | | |
| 79 | Arch of Titus. 49 | Titus Reliefs. 286 | | |
| ca. 82 | Trajan Forum. 51 | | | |
| Early 2nd | Pantheon. 57–8 | | | |
| 120 | Caracalla Baths. 56 | | | |
| 211–17 | Basilica of Maxentius. 54–55 | | | |
| 310–20 | | | | |

| | Architecture | Sculpture | Painting | Minor Arts |
|---|---|---|---|---|
| 315 | | Arch of Constantine. *287* | | |
| 326 | Old St. Peter's. *63* | | | |
| ca. 400 | | Berlin Sarcophagus. *289* | | |
| 5th cent. | | Two Brothers Sarc. *288* | | |
| 425 | Sta. Sabina. *65* | | | |
| ca. 500 | | | | Ivory Angel. *578* <br> Maximianus Throne. *579* <br> Annunciation Textile. *593* |
| Early 6th | | | Abraham Mosaic. *365* | |
| 517 | | | | Anastasius Diptych. *577* |
| 526–47 | San Vitale. *70* | | | |
| 532–62 | Hagia Sophia. *67–9* | | | |
| 534–49 | S. Apollinare in Classe. *71–2* | | | |
| 6th cent. | | Theodorus Sarc. *290* | Joshua Rotulus. *366* | |
| ca. 700 | | Sigwald Relief. *292* | | |
| 762–76 | S. M. in Cosmedin. *73* | | | |
| 772–95 | | | | |
| 790–804 | Chapel, Aachen. *74* | | | |
| 9th cent. | | | | |
| ca. 800 | | | Book of Kells. *367* | Crucifixion, gold. *588* |
| ca. 830 | | | Utrecht Psalter. *368* | |
| ca. 870 | | | | Crucifixion, ivory. *582* |
| 871–901 | | | | Alfred Jewel. *591* |
| 9th–10th | | | | Byz. Casket. *581* |
| 10th–11th | | | | Triptych, ivory. *580* |
| 11th cent. | | | | Madonna, cloisonné. *590* |
| ca. 1000 | | Madonna Orans. *291* | Otto III Gospels. *369* | |
| 1007–15 | | Hildesheim Doors. *293* | | |
| ca. 1050 | Church, Vignory. *76* | | | |

## CHRONOLOGICAL TABLE—Continued

| Date | Architecture | Sculpture | Painting | Minor Arts |
|---|---|---|---|---|
| 1059 | Pisa Cathedral. 77 | | | Apostle, León. 583 |
| 1063–1121 | S. Ambrogio. 85–7 | | | |
| 1077–ca. 1150 | | | | Bayeux Embroidery. 594 |
| Late 11th | Caen, S. Etienne, façade. 93 | | | |
| 1077 | | | | |
| ca. 1080 | Morienval. 82 | | | |
| ca. 1100 | N.D.-du-Port. 79, 80 | Bari. S. Niccola. 296 | | Bari Throne. 597 |
| Early 11th | | Modena Sculpture. 298 | | |
| ca. 1106 | | Vézelay Capitals. 294 | | |
| ca. 1110 | S. Sernin. 81 | | | Emmaus Ivory. 584 |
| 12th cent. | N. D. la Grande. 88 | | | Suger Chalice. 575 |
| ca. 1135 | S. Etienne vaults. 89 | Isaiah, Souillac. 297 | | |
| ca. 1140 | Trinité vaults. 91–2 | | | |
| ca. 1145 | Chartres façade. 99 | Chartres, W. portal. 299 | | |
| ca. 1160 | S. Germain-des-Prés, buttresses. 96 | | | |
| 1180–90 | | S. Trophime, façade. 295 | | Champlevé Casket. 592 |
| ca. 1200 | | | | |
| 1220–88 | Amiens Cath. 97–8 | Amiens portal. 300–2 | | |
| ca. 1225 | Salisbury Cath. 103–4 | Pisa Pulpit. 308 | | |
| 1260 | | | | |

| | | | | |
|---|---|---|---|---|
| 1270–90 | | Vierge Dorée. *303* | | |
| *ca.* 1280 | | | | Deposition, ivory. *586* |
| Late 13th | | | de Lisle Psalter. *370* | Passion Scenes. *585* |
| *ca.* 1285 | | | Cimabue. Madonna. *387* | |
| 1298–1301 | Pal. Vecchio. *111* | Pistoia Pulpit. *309* | | |
| 13th–14th | Carcassonne. *108* | | | |
| Early 14th | Exeter Cath. *106* | | | |
| 14th cent. | Pont Valentré. *109* | | | |
| 1304 | | | Giotto. Madonna. *388* | |
| 1305 | | | Giotto. Arena Chapel. *389–90, 392* | |
| *ca.* 1319 | | | Duccio. Gethsemane. *384* | |
| *ca.* 1320 | | | Giotto. Francis' Death. *391* | |
| *ca.* 1330 | | Virgin of Paris. *304* | | Silver Madonna. *589* |
| 1339 | | | Gaddi. Presentation. *393* | |
| *ca.* 1340 | | | | |
| 1342 | | | Lorenzetti. Birth of the Virgin. *385* | |
| 1351–1412 | Gloucester. Cloister vaults. *107* | | | |
| 1376–81 | | | | Angers Apoc. *595* |
| 1395–1403 | | Sluter. Moses. *305* | | |
| Late 14th | | | | Sports, ivory. *587* |
| 1416 | | Donatello. Zuccone. *313* | Limbourg Hours. *372* | |
| 1420–37 | Florence, Cathedral, Dome. *113* | | | |
| 1420–29 | Pazzi Chapel. *114–5* | | | |
| 1423 | | | Fabriano. Magi. *402* | |
| 1425–47 | | Ghiberti. Gates of Paradise. *310–1* | | |

## CHRONOLOGICAL TABLE—Continued

| Date | Architecture | Sculpture | Painting | Minor Arts |
|------|-------------|-----------|----------|------------|
| 1425–38 | | Quercia. Fall. *312* | | |
| 1426–33 | | Donatello. Annunciation. *314* | | |
| 1427 | | | Masaccio. Carmine. Frescoes. *394–5* | |
| *ca.* 1430 | | Donatello. David. *315* | | |
| 1432 | | | Van Eyck. Ghent Altarpiece. *373, 375* | |
| *ca.* 1432 | | | Rogier. Descent. *376* | |
| 1434 | | | Van Eyck. Arnolfini. *374* | |
| *ca.* 1435 | | | Uccello. Battle. *404* | |
| 1438 | | | | Pisanello. Medal. *606* |
| *ca.* 1440 | | | Fra Angelico. Lamentation. *403* | |
| | | | Lippi. Madonna. *405* | |
| 1443 | Jacques Cœur's House. *110* | Donatello. Gattamelata. *316* | | |
| 1444–59 | Medici-Riccardi Palace. *116–7* | | | |
| *ca.* 1445 | | | Castagno. Crucifixion. *396* | |
| 1446–55 | Rucellai Pal. *118* | | | |
| 1450–68 | S. Francesco, Rimini. *119* | | | |

| | | | | |
|---|---|---|---|---|
| *ca.* 1450 | | | Dom. Veneziano. Madonna. *397*  Fouquet. Charles VII. *381*  Lochner. Magi. *383* | |
| 1454 | | Tonnerre Entombment. *306* | | |
| *ca.* 1460 | | Pollaiuolo. Hercules. *320* | Mantegna. Circumcision. *399* | |
| 1464 | | | Piero della Francesca. Resurrection. *398*  Avignon Pietà. *382* | |
| 1465 | | Verrocchio. David. *321* | | |
| *ca.* 1465 | | | Gozzoli. Magi. *407* | |
| 1468 | | Rossellino. Palmieri. *317* | Memling. Madonna. *378* | |
| *ca.* 1469 | | | Pollaiuolo. Nudes. *406* | |
| *ca.* 1470 | | | Mantegna. Ceiling. *400* | |
| *ca.* 1471 | | Laurana. Beatrice. *319* | Van der Goes. Nativity. *377* | |
| 1474 | | | | |
| 1476 | | | Botticelli. Venus. *412* | |
| *ca.* 1478 | S. Satiro. *121* | | Ghirlandaio. Last Supper. *409* | |
| 1480–88 | | | Leonardo. Philip. *417* | |
| *ca.* 1480 | Vendramini Pal. *120* | | Schongauer. Virgin. *441*  Leonardo. Adoration. *414* | |
| 1481 | | Verrocchio. Colleoni. *322* | | |
| 1481–88 | | | | |
| 15th cent. | | | | Room from Urbino. *613*  Cassoni. *609–10*  Strozzi Lantern. *605* |
| Late 15th | | | | |

CHRONOLOGICAL TABLE—Continued.

| Date | Architecture | Sculpture | Painting | Minor Arts |
|---|---|---|---|---|
| Late 15th | | | | Unicorn Tapestry. *596* Amiens Stalls. *600* |
| *ca.* 1485 | | | | |
| 1493–1508 | Rouen. Palais de Justice. *112* | | | |
| *ca.* 1496 | | | Perugino. Pietà. *401* | |
| 1498 | | | Gentile Bellini. True Cross. *408* Leonardo. Last Supper. *416* Dürer. Way to Calvary. *442* | |
| 1499 | | | | Hypnerotomachia Poliphili. *604* Enamel Triptych. *601* |
| *ca.* 1500 | | | Signorelli. Damned. *410* Bosch. Christ before Pilate. *379* | |
| 1502 | | | | |
| 1502 | S. Pietro in Montorio. *123* | | | |
| 1504 | | Michelangelo. David. *323* | Leonardo. St. Anne. *415* | |
| 1505 | | Michelangelo. Madonna. *324* | Leonardo. Mona Lisa. *418* Giorgione. Christ. *430* | |
| 1506–92 | St. Peter's. *129* | | | |

| | | |
|---|---|---|
| 1508–14 | | Michelangelo. Sistine Ceiling. *419–24* |
| 1508–14 | | Raphael. Alba Madonna. *427* |
| ca. 1508 | | Giorgione. Sleeping Venus. *429* |
| 1509–11 | | Raphael. School of Athens. *425* |
| ca. 1509 | | Giorgione. Three Philosophers. *431* |
| ca. 1510 | Rouen Cath. Façade. *102* | Grünewald. Isenheim Altarpiece. *446* |
| ca. 1510 | | Massys. Deposition. *380* |
| 1511 | | |
| 1511–34 | Medici Chapel. *138* | Raphael. Sistine Madonna. *426* |
| 1512–14 | | |
| ca. 1513 | Michelangelo. Slave. *325* | Dürer. Artist's Mother. *445* |
| 1514 | | Dürer. Melencolia I. *443* |
| 1514 | | Raphael. Tommaso Inghirami. *428* |
| ca. 1515 | | Titian. Assumption of the Virgin. *433* |
| 1516–18 | | |
| 1517–46 | Farnese Palace. *124–6* | |
| 1518–24 | Azay-le-Rideau. *144* | |
| ca. 1520 | Princeton Saint. *307* | |
| 1523 | | Holbein. Erasmus. *449* |

CHRONOLOGICAL TABLE—Continued

| Date | Architecture | Sculpture | Painting | Minor Arts |
|---|---|---|---|---|
| 1525–33 | | Michelangelo. Medici Tombs. *327–28* | | |
| ca. 1525 | | | Correggio. Angel. *438* | Pendant. *607* |
| 16th cent. | | | | |
| ca. 1520 | Compton Winyates. *154–5* | | | |
| 1526–30 | | | Correggio. Assumption. *437* | |
| | | | Titian. Landscape. *432* | |
| ca. 1530 | | | | |
| 1535 | Massimi Palace. *127–8* | | Holbein. Henry VIII. *448* | |
| ca. 1539 | Louvre. Court. *145* | | | |
| 1541–48 | | | | Cellini. Salt-cellar. *608* |
| 1543 | Campidoglio. *134* | | | |
| 1546 | | Cellini. Perseus. *329* | | |
| 1548 | | Goujon. Innocents. *331* | | |
| 1549 | Vicenza. Basilica. *135* | | | |
| 1549 | Vicenza. Villa Rotonda. *137* | | | |
| 1552–91 | Ecouen. *146* | | | |
| 1552–64 | Valmarana Pal. *136* | | Titian. Danäe. *434* | |
| 1554 | | | | |
| 1556–66 | | | Bruegel. Wedding Dance. *451* | |
| ca. 1560 | | | Bruegel. Summer. *450* | |
| ca. 1565 | | | | |

| Date | Architecture | Sculpture | Painting | Objects |
|---|---|---|---|---|
| 1567–79 | Longleat. 157 | | | |
| 1568–83 | The Gesù. 139 | | | |
| 1570–76 | Warwick. Lord Leycester's Hospital. 156 | | | |
| 1571 | | | Titian. Madonna. 435 | |
| 1573–76 | | | Titian. Pietà. 436 | |
| ca. 1578 | | | Tintoretto. Last Supper. 439 | |
| 1580–88 | Wollaton Hall. 158-9 | | | |
| 1583 | | Giov. da Bologna. Rape of Sabine Woman. 330 | | |
| 1584 | | Pilon. René Birague. 332 | | Wood Chair. 612 |
| Late 16th | | | | Walnut Chair. 615 |
| 1587 | | | Tintoretto. Paradise. 440 | |
| ca. 1600 | | | Caravaggio. Peter Denying. 452 | |
| ca. 1600 | | | El Greco. Cardinal Guevara. 470 | |
| 1606–08 | S. Peter's. Façade. 130 | | El Greco. Nativity. 469 | |
| 1606 | | | | |
| Early 17th | | | El Greco. Toledo. *Frontis.* | Ebony Cabinet. 617 |
| 1610 | | | | |
| ca. 1610 | Hatfield House. 160 | | | |
| 1614 | | | Rubens. Lamentation. 453 | |
| 1615–24 | Luxembourg Pal. 147 | | | |
| ca. 1618 | | | Rubens. Leucippus. 455 | |
| ca. 1619 | Banqueting Hall. 161 | | | |
| 1624–1712 | Versailles. 150 | | | |

CHRONOLOGICAL TABLE—Continued

| Date | Architecture | Sculpture | Painting | Minor Arts |
|---|---|---|---|---|
| 1624–33 | S. Peter's Baldacchino. *132* | | | |
| ca. 1625 | | Bernini. Costanza Buonarelli. *334* | | |
| ca. 1627 | | | Hals. Lute Player. *459* | |
| 1632 | | | Rubens. Garden of Love. *454* | |
| 1632 | | | Rembrandt. Anatomy Lesson. *461* | |
| ca. 1634 | | | Brouwer. The Surgeon. *457* | |
| ca. 1635 | | | Van Dyck, James Stuart. *456* | |
| 1635–40 | Blois. Orléans wing. *148* | | | |
| ca. 1636 | | | Poussin. John on Patmos. *474* | |
| 1638 | | Bernini. Theresa. *333* | Rembrandt. Fall. *466* | |
| 1646 | | | Lorrain. Harbor Scene. *475* | |
| 1647 | | Four Rivers Fountain. *335* | | |
| 1648 | | | Rembrandt. Samaritan. *465* | |
| ca. 1650 | | | Rembrandt. Nude. *463* | |

| Date | Architecture & Sculpture | Painting & Decorative Art |
|---|---|---|
| 1650 | | Velasquez. Innocent. 471 |
| ca. 1651 | | Poussin. Holy Family. 473 |
| 1654 | | Rembrandt. Bathsheba. 464 |
| 1656 | S. M. della Pace. 140 | Velasquez. Maids of Honor. 472 |
| 1658 | | Rembrandt. Woman. 467 |
| 1662 | | Rembrandt. Syndics. 462 |
| | | Steen. Twelfth Night. 458 |
| 1662–67 | San Carlo. 141 | |
| 1662–82 | Versailles, Gardens. 153 | |
| 1664 | | Hals. Lady Regents. 460 |
| ca. 1665 | | Vermeer. Girl with Pitcher. 468 |
| 1667–74 | Louvre, Colonnade. 149 | Girardon. Nymphs. 336 |
| ca. 1669 | Whipple House. 179 | |
| ca. 1670 | S. Mary-le-Bow. 163 | |
| 1671–80 | | Mrs. Freake. 527 |
| ca. 1675 | St. Paul's. 162 | |
| 1675–1710 | Villa Torlonia, Gardens. 143 | |
| Late 17th | Versailles. Galerie des Glaces. 152 | |
| 1680–84 | | Boulle Cabinet. 618 |
| 1683 | Capen House. 180 | |
| ca. 1700 | Piazza di Spagna. 142 | |
| 1711 | Swan House. 165 | |
| ca. 1715 | | |
| 1718 | | Watteau. Cythera. 477 |
| 1724 | Blenheim. 164 | Watteau. Drawing. 478 |

CHRONOLOGICAL TABLE—Continued

| Date | Architecture | Sculpture | Painting | Minor Arts |
|---|---|---|---|---|
| 1728 | Hôtel de Biron. *166* | | | |
| 1736 | | | Chardin. House of Cards. *481* | |
| *ca.* 1740 | Hôtel de Soubise. *167* | | Hogarth. Countess' Dressing Room. *483* | |
| Mid-18th | | | | Windsor Chair. *630* |
| | | | | Chippendale Chest. *622* |
| 1752–55 | Nancy. Hemicycle. *168* | | | |
| 1753–63 | Paris. Place de la Concorde. *169* | | | Chippendale Bed. *624* |
| *ca.* 1755 | | | | |
| 1755 | Christ Church. *184* | | | |
| 1758–88 | Mount Vernon. *183* | | | |
| 1759 | Longfellow House. *181* | | | |
| 1760 | 15 St. James' Sq. *173* | | | |
| 1761 | | | Greuze. Village Bride. *484* | Mt. Pleasant. *632* |
| 1762–68 | Petit Trianon. *170–1* | | | |
| 1764–90 | Paris, Panthéon. *172* | | Chardin. Still-life. *480* | |
| *ca.* 1764 | | | | Adam Furniture. *625* |
| 1767 | Powel Room. *182* | | Fragonard. Lover Crowned. *479* | |
| 1768 | | | | |
| *ca.* 1773 | | | | |

| Year | Architecture | Sculpture | Painting | Minor Arts |
|---|---|---|---|---|
| 1775 | | | Gainsborough. Mrs. Graham. 482 | |
| 1778 | | Houdon. Voltaire. 338 | | |
| 1784 | | | David. Horatii. 485 | Revere Silver. 633 |
| Late 18th | | | | Hepplewhite Chair. 627 |
| 1785–90 | Va. Capitol. 185 | | Copley. Mrs. Fort. 528 | |
| 1788–91 | Brandenburg Gate. 174 | | David. Mme. Hamelin. 486 | |
| ca. 1800 | | | Goya. Maria Luisa. 490 | Sheraton Commode. 629 |
| 1800 | | | Stuart. Mrs. Morton. 529 | |
| ca. 1802 | | Canova. Pauline Borghese. 339 | | |
| 1805 | | | | |
| 1807 | Bank of U. S. 186 | | Ingres. Granet. 487 | |
| 1819–24 | Spencer House. 187 | | Géricault. Races. 494 | |
| ca. 1825 | | | | |
| Early 19th | | | | Phyfe Furniture. 636 Lemarchand. Cabinet. 637 |
| 1825 | | | Goya. Bull Fight. 492 | |
| 1831 | | | Corot. The Inn. 497 | |
| 1834 | | | Daumier. Legislature. 501 | |
| 1835 | | | Constable. Stoke-by-Nayland. 493 | |
| 1836 | | Rude. Marseillaise. 341 | | |
| ca. 1837 | | | Delacroix. Galilee. 496 | |
| 1838 | | | Delacroix. Medea. 495 | |
| 1840–60 | Parliament. 175 | | | |
| 1843 | | Powers. Greek Slave. 340 | | |

## CHRONOLOGICAL TABLE—Continued

| Date | Architecture | Sculpture | Painting | Minor Arts |
|---|---|---|---|---|
| 1843–50 | Bibl. Ste. Geneviève. 176–7 | | | |
| ca. 1845 | St. Patrick's. 190 | | | |
| 1850–79 | Crystal Palace. 195 | | | |
| 1851–4 | | | | |
| Mid-19th | Wedding-Cake House. 189 | | Daumier. Side Show. 502 | |
| ca. 1850 | U. S. Capitol. 188 | | | Day Dreamer. 639 |
| | | | | Carpet. 640 |
| 1851–65 | | | Courbet. Preparation. 500 | |
| 1856–70 | | | Ingres. Odalisque. 488 | |
| 1858 | | | Millet. Haymaking. 499 | |
| ca. 1860 | | | Daumier. Washwoman. 503 | |
| 1861 | | | | |
| 1863–68 | | Carpeaux. Flora. 342 | | |
| 1866 | | | Corot. Agostina. 498 | |
| 1871–83 | Brooklyn Bridge. 196 | | | |
| 1872–77 | Boston, Trinity. 192 | | Manet. Washday. 504 | |
| 1874 | Paris Opera. 178 | | | |
| Late 19th | | | Cézanne. Still-life. 509 | Morris. "Daisy." 641 |
| 1877–79 | | | Whistler. Traghetto. 536 | |
| 1879 | | | Degas. Rehearsal. 506 | |
| | | | Monet. Fishermen. 505 | |
| 1882 | Stoughton House. 193 | | | |

| | Architecture | Sculpture | Painting | |
|---|---|---|---|---|
| 1884–86 | Marshall Field Bldg. *194* | | Seurat. Grande-Jatte. *512* | |
| 1885–87 | | | Cézanne. Arc Valley. *510* | |
| 1886 | | | Renoir. Mother and Child. *507* | |
| 1887 | | St. Gaudens. Adams Memorial. *344* | | |
| 1888 | Eiffel Tower. *197* | | Van Gogh. Café. *514* | |
| 1889 | Wainwright Bldg. *199* | | Van Gogh. Cypresses. *515* | |
| ca. 1890 | | | | |
| 1891 | | | Gauguin. Arearea. *516* | |
| 1892 | | | Cézanne. Cardplayers. *511* | |
| ca. 1892 | | | Homer. Woodsmen. *530* Renoir. Bathers. *508* | |
| 1897 | | | | |
| 1898 | | Rodin. Kiss. *343* | | |
| 1899–1904 | Schlesinger-Mayer Bldg. *200* | | Eakins. Between Rounds. *534* | |
| ca. 1900 | | | Ryder. Toilers of the Sea. *531* | |
| 1901 | | | Prendergast. Central Park. *537* | |
| 1902 | | Maillol. Mediterranean. *345* | | |
| 1903 | Wertheim Store. *207* | | | |
| 1904 | Unity Temple. *206* | | Picasso. Guitarist. *517* | |
| 1905–06 | | | | Van de Velde. Room. *642* |
| ca. 1905 | | | Eakins. A. B. Frost. *533* | |
| 1905 | Metropolitan Life Bldg. *202* | | | |

CHRONOLOGICAL TABLE—Continued

| Date | Architecture | Sculpture | Painting | Minor Arts |
|---|---|---|---|---|
| 1909 | Robie House. *204–5*<br>AEG Factory. *208* | Barlach. Sorrowing Woman. *351* | | |
| 1910–13<br>*ca.* 1910 | Woolworth Bldg. *203* | Brancusi. Mlle Pogany. *346* | | |
| 1912 | | | Picasso. Newspaper and Violin. *518* | |
| 1913–27<br>1920 | Stuttgart Station. *209* | | Marin. Lower Manhattan. *542*<br>Picasso. Landscape. *519* | |
| 1921 | Millard House. *221* | | | |
| 1922 | | | Matisse. Checkers. *522* | |
| 1923 | Chgo. Tribune Bldg. *210* | | | |
| 1924 | | | Bellows. Dempsey-Firpo. *535* | Knotted Rug. *643* |
| 1924–27<br>1925<br>1926 | Worker's Houses. *217*<br>Nebr. Capitol. *201*<br>Bauhaus. *214*<br>N. Y. Telephone Co. Bldg. *212* | Meštrović. Lady. *350*<br>Lipchitz. Figure. *347* | | Tubular Steel Chair. *645*<br><br>Coffee and Teapots. *644* |
| 1929–30<br>1930 | Savoye House. *215* | Dobson. Figure. *348* | | |
| 1931<br>1931–39 | Tugendhat House. *216*<br>Rockefeller Center. *225* | | | |

| | Architecture | Sculpture | Painting | |
|---|---|---|---|---|
| 1932–34 | P. S. F. S. Bldg. *213* | | Orozco. Christ. *523* <br> Rivera. Vaccination. *524* | Aalto Chairs. *646* |
| 1933 | Penguin Pool. *218* | | | |
| 1934 | | Manship. Prometheus. *349* | | |
| 1935 | Mackley Houses. *226* | | Rivera. Flower Vendor. *525* | |
| 1936–39 | Johnson Bldg. *222* | Milles. Orpheus. *352-3* | Dali. Soft Construction. *526* <br> Burchfield. Lace Gables. *539* <br> Rouault. Old King. *521* <br> Picasso. Guernica. *520* <br> Houmère. Lute, Flute and Dance. *541* | |
| *ca.* 1937 | W'msburg Houses. *227* | | | |
| 1937 | Greenbelt. *228* <br> Day House. *220* <br> Goetsch-Winckler House. *223-4* | | | |
| 1939 | Welwyn House. *219* | | | |
| 1940 | | | Poor. Land Grant. *538* <br> Weber. Winter Twilight. *540* | |

# Index